T0215380

Delivering Applications with VMware App Volumes 4

Delivering Application Layers to Virtual Desktops Using VMware

Peter von Oven

Apress®

Delivering Applications with VMware App Volumes 4

Peter von Oven
Wiltshire, UK

ISBN-13 (pbk): 978-1-4842-6688-5 ISBN-13 (electronic): 978-1-4842-6689-2
https://doi.org/10.1007/978-1-4842-6689-2

Managing Director, Apress Media LLC: Welmoed Spahr
Acquisitions Editor: Celestin Suresh John
Development Editor: Matthew Moodie
Coordinating Editor: Aditee Mirashi

Cover designed by eStudioCalamar

Cover image designed by Freepik (www.freepik.com)

Distributed to the book trade worldwide by Springer Science+Business Media New York, 1 New York Plaza, Suite 4600, New York, NY 10004-1562, USA. Phone 1-800-SPRINGER, fax (201) 348-4505, e-mail orders-ny@springer-sbm.com, or visit www.springeronline.com. Apress Media, LLC is a California LLC and the sole member (owner) is Springer Science + Business Media Finance Inc (SSBM Finance Inc). SSBM Finance Inc is a **Delaware** corporation.

For information on translations, please e-mail booktranslations@springernature.com; for reprint, paperback, or audio rights, please e-mail bookpermissions@springernature.com.

Apress titles may be purchased in bulk for academic, corporate, or promotional use. eBook versions and licenses are also available for most titles. For more information, reference our Print and eBook Bulk Sales web page at http://www.apress.com/bulk-sales.

Any source code or other supplementary material referenced by the author in this book is available to readers on GitHub via the book's product page, located at www.apress.com/978-1-4842-6688-5. For more detailed information, please visit http://www.apress.com/source-code.

Printed on acid-free paper

To my family, for their continued support and for believing in me.

Table of Contents

About the Author xiii

About the Technical Reviewer xv

Acknowledgments xvii

Introduction xix

Chapter 1: Introduction to App Layering and VMware App Volumes 1

Application layering use cases 2

Helping desktop administrators 2

Enhanced end user experience 3

In this chapter 3

How does application layering work? 4

Creating application layers 4

Delivering application layers 6

VMware App Volumes 8

How does App Volumes work? 8

Application 9

Package 10

Program 10

Managing a single application 10

Managing a group of applications 12

Writable Volumes 14

Why deploy App Volumes? 15

App Volumes, ThinApp, and Horizon Apps 16

ThinApp 17

Horizon Apps 17

Just-in-Time Management Platform 18

How to license App Volumes ... 18
Using this book ... 19
AD requirements ... 20
App Volumes architecture and features ... 20
Terminology ... 20
App Volumes architecture ... 24
The end user's view ... 24
The IT administrators' view ... 25
Network ports ... 27
Chapter summary ... 28
Chapter 2: Installing VMware App Volumes ... 31
In this chapter ... 31
Before you start the installation ... 32
How to download the App Volumes software ... 34
Downloading a 60-day trial ... 34
App Volumes Manager installation ... 36
Hardware requirements ... 36
Software requirements ... 37
Accessing the App Volumes Manager ... 37
Database requirements ... 37
Installing the App Volumes Manager software ... 38
App Volumes Agent installation ... 50
Hardware requirements ... 50
Software requirements ... 50
Installing the App Volumes Agent software ... 51
Chapter summary ... 58
Chapter 3: Completing the Initial Configuration ... 59
Accessing the App Volumes Manager console ... 59
Supported browsers ... 60
Launching the management console for the first time ... 60

Completing the initial configuration tasks 62
License Information 62
AD Domains 66
Admin Roles 70
Machine Managers 78
Storage 83
Settings 92
Chapter summary 98

Chapter 4: Getting Started with the Management Console 99

Logging in for the first time 99
The Inventory menu 101
Applications tab 102
Packages tab 103
Programs tab 105
Assignments tab 107
Attachments tab 108
Writables tab 109
The Volumes (2.x) menu 112
AppStacks tab 112
Writables tab 113
Attachments tab 114
Assignments tab 114
Programs tab 115
The Directory menu 116
Online tab 116
Users tab 117
Computers tab 119
Groups 120
OUs 120
The Infrastructure menu 121
Machines tab 121

Storages tab 122
Storage Groups tab 123
The Activity menu 124
Pending Actions tab 124
Jobs tab 125
Activity Log tab 126
System Messages tab 127
Server Log tab 128
Troubleshooting tab 129
The Configuration menu 132
The Dashboard screens 132
Chapter summary 135
Chapter 5: Applications, Packages, and Programs 137
Building a packaging machine 137
Logging in to the management console 139
Creating an Application 141
Creating a Package 145
Installing an application into the package 152
Assigning applications 165
Testing the newly created package 173
Managing existing packages 174
Updating an existing package 174
Setting the CURRENT status of a package 186
Editing an existing Package 189
Deleting a Package 191
Moving a Package 192
Managing existing applications 194
Editing an existing Application 194
Deleting an existing Application 197
Chapter summary 199

Chapter 6: Writable Volumes 201
Creating a Writable Volume 202
Testing the Writable Volume 210
Managing existing Writable Volumes 212
Editing an existing Writable Volume 213
Disabling an existing Writable Volume 217
Expanding an existing Writable Volume 220
Moving an existing Writable Volume 221
Back up an existing Writable Volume 224
Restoring a Writable Volume 227
Deleting a Writable Volume 229
Importing a Writable Volume 230
Updating an existing Writable Volume 232
Rescanning the datastore for Writable Volumes 235
Writable Volumes and VMware DEM 236
Chapter summary 238
Chapter 7: Advanced Configuration 239
Creating custom templates for packages 239
Creating a new virtual hard disk 240
Creating custom Writable Volumes templates 264
Storage groups 265
Advanced App Volumes Agent config 270
Batch script options 271
The snapvol.cfg file 272
Configuration options for application packages 275
Writable Volumes 277
Chapter summary 278

Chapter 8: Just-in-Time Management Platform 279
The architecture 279
How it works 280
JMP orchestration components 281
Installing the JMP Server 282
Prerequisites 282
JMP Server installation process 284
Configuring the JMP Server 294
Time synchronization 294
Adding the JMP orchestration components 296
Chapter summary 307
Chapter 9: RDSH and App Volumes 309
The architecture 310
Capturing applications for RDSH 311
Installing and configuring the RDSH role 311
Installing the App Volumes Agent 325
Capturing an App Volumes application 334
Completing the Application capture process 344
Assigning and delivering applications with RDSH 359
Assigning the application to the RDSH server 360
Configuring the app package for RDSH 363
Launching and testing the application 370
Chapter summary 373
Chapter 10: Horizon Apps and App Volumes 375
The architecture 375
Installing App Volumes with VMware Horizon 376
Installing the Horizon Agent 378
Configuring a Horizon App farm 389
Configuring Application Pool 398

Testing the application 405

Chapter summary 409

Chapter 11: Horizon View and App Volumes 411

The architecture 411

Installing App Volumes with Horizon View 412

Installing the Horizon Agent 414

Installing the App Volumes Agent 423

Configuring the Horizon Console 432

Configuring a Desktop Pool for App Volumes desktops 433

Entitling end users to the Desktop Pool 446

Testing the solution 449

Chapter summary 453

Chapter 12: VMware ThinApp and App Volumes 455

Capturing a ThinApp application 456

Creating a ThinApp-based application package 480

Creating a ThinApp application in App Volumes 480

Creating the App Volumes package for ThinApp apps 481

Installing the ThinApp package 483

Chapter summary 487

Chapter 13: App Volumes and VHD Virtual Hard Disks 489

Installing the App Volumes Manager software 489

Launching the management console for the first time 503

Completing the initial configuration tasks 504

License Information 504

AD Domains 508

Admin Roles 512

Machine Managers 520

Storage configuration 520

Settings configuration 528

Chapter summary 533

Chapter 14: Upgrading App Volumes 535

Upgrading the App Volumes Manager 535

Upgrading from 2.x versions to 4.x 535

Upgrading to App Volumes version 2006 (4.1.0) 536

Upgrading the templates 544

Upgrading the App Volumes Agent 546

Migrating AppStacks to Application Packages 547

Chapter summary 548

Index 549

About the Author

Peter von Oven is an experienced technical consultant and has spent the past 25 years of his IT career working with customers and partners in designing technology solutions aimed at delivering true business value as well as authoring 14 books on VMware EUC technology solutions. During his career, Peter has been involved in numerous large-scale enterprise projects and deployments and has presented at key IT events, such as VMworld, IP EXPO, and various VMUG and CCUG events across the United Kingdom.

He has also worked in senior presales roles and presales management roles for some of the giants of IT, such as Fujitsu, HP, Citrix, and VMware, and has been awarded VMware vExpert for the last 6 years. More recently, he has become part of the VMware EUC vExpert program. Outside of work, Peter volunteers his spare time as a STEM Ambassador, helping, coaching, and mentoring young people in taking up careers in technology.

About the Technical Reviewer

Darren Hirons is a Senior End User Computing Solutions Engineer with VMware, specializing in Horizon and Workspace ONE technologies.

Prior to joining VMware, Darren has held a variety of IT roles in the public and financial sectors and has 25 years of operational experience.

Acknowledgments

This is, amazingly, the fourteenth book that I have written, and I would like to say thank you to Apress for giving me the opportunity to write with them. Even after having written several books, the whole process of planning and writing a book still presents a huge challenge. Given the current situation we all find ourselves in at this time of writing, authoring this book has come as a welcome distraction.

I would also like to acknowledge and thank the people who have helped with preparing this book. Thanks to Aditee at Apress for making sure I kept on track and answering questions about the process, and a really big thank you to Darren Hirons at VMware for not only providing his technical editing skills but for also helping with some of the questions and support issues I had along the way.

Finally, I would like to acknowledge you, the reader. Without you, this whole project would not be worthwhile, so again, thank you. I would also love to hear from you any suggestions or questions regarding this book or any other end user computing solutions book for that matter. You can find me on Twitter at @pvo71.

Introduction

"Deliver apps to virtual desktop environments in seconds, and at scale with the click of a button."

App Volumes delivers applications in real time to virtual desktop machines enabling VDI deployments to return even greater flexibility, agility, and cost reduction. Enterprises can now fully utilize the nonpersistent, floating desktop model in all VDI use cases, and before, where users such as developers required a persistent virtual desktop of their own, they can now take advantage of the lower-cost nonpersistent delivery model.

This book will focus on how to get started with VMware App Volumes and how to deliver applications to virtual desktop machines and RDSH-based application publishing solutions. In this book, we will not only look at VMware's own virtual desktop and app delivery solutions with Horizon View and Horizon Apps but also Microsoft RemoteApp and RDSH.

Throughout this book, we will work through the solution to enable you to design, install, configure, and manage an App Volumes deployment, using step-by-step instructions with real-life screenshots as you follow the test lab that is used throughout the book to demonstrate each key feature.

Starting with an in-depth overview of where the solution fits within the market, and its key features, we will then move on to explaining the architecture and components and then look at how to design an optimized solution. The next phase of the title is to start installing and configuring App Volumes for the different use cases such as VMware Horizon View, Horizon Apps, VMware ThinApp, and Microsoft RDSH.

Throughout the chapters, you will be given hints and tips, along with best practice, all seen from the eyes of somebody who works with this technology day in, day out, and in many different types of environments and scenarios.

By the end of this book, you will have acquired the skills to build an App Volumes environment for a proof of concept, a pilot, or in a live production environment.

What we will cover in this book:

- Learn how the VMware App Volumes solution can enhance the management and delivery of applications in your desktop environment
- Design a real-life App Volumes solution, using best practice and following the recommended sizing guides
- Install, configure, and deploy App Volumes ready to start delivering applications
- Create and prepare applications ready for delivering to end users
- Learn how App Volumes can enhance other desktop solutions by looking at how it integrates with VMware Horizon View, VMware ThinApp, and RDSH
- Learn how to configure the advanced options within App Volumes

Finally, I would like to say thank you for picking up this book. I hope that you enjoy reading the chapters and that they help you learn all about VMware App Volumes and how to deploy and manage the solution.

CHAPTER 1

Introduction to App Layering and VMware App Volumes

Application layering is a software-based technology solution that delivers applications to endpoint devices. It does this by capturing or containerizing just the application, including the application files and settings, and storing that on a virtual hard disk – hence the use of the word container. The virtual hard disk is often referred to as the container or in some cases the application package or application layer. This means you have abstracted the applications from the underlying operating system, and they are in a format whereby you can deliver them to your endpoints.

To deliver an application using application layering, the virtual hard disk containing all the application runtimes, settings, and files gets attached, over the network, to the endpoint device. Once attached, the application layering software will have an agent running on that endpoint that makes the application appear as if it were natively installed. Basically, this means that it will insert or layer, hence the name app layering, any settings such as registry settings and other pointers into the OS on the endpoint device that ensure any calls made to the application get redirected to the virtual hard disk containing the application. The agent also has the job of ensuring the correct files are called, especially where DLL files are concerned.

The virtual hard disks containing the application layers are stored on a file server or some form of network share and then attached to endpoint devices when required, and on demand, as the end user logs in or the endpoint machine boots.

P. von Oven, *Delivering Applications with VMware App Volumes 4*,
https://doi.org/10.1007/978-1-4842-6689-2_1

Application layering use cases

Having started the chapter with a high-level overview of what application layering is, let us now move our attention to why and where it would be used.

Helping desktop administrators

Application layering came about to try and solve the issue of delivering applications to fully stateless or nonpersistent virtual desktops. Before the advent of application layering solutions, desktop administrators had to manage multiple virtual desktop images to accommodate all the different applications required by their end users. One of the reasons they moved to a virtual desktop environment in the first place was to reduce management overheads and cut down on the number of images that they had to manage. But here we are back to managing multiple images all over again, albeit virtual images this time.

Multiple images also typically meant that a stateful or persistent virtual desktop model would be adopted, meaning every user had their own virtual desktop. Again, not very effective, and this certainly will not deliver the full benefits that virtual desktop infrastructures offer.

But the question is why have multiple images and persistent virtual desktops? The answer is simple: so that the apps can be delivered to the end user. In a stateless virtual desktop model, when the end users log out, either the virtual desktop gets deleted completely, or it gets reset back to a base level. Either way, the apps could or will be lost, and also the end users' personal documents and data. You could of course just install every app into the image, but that means you will have one big old image to manage, and also you will need to license every app within the image regardless of whether the end user uses it or not. That is not very cost-effective.

With application layering, applications are abstracted away from the underlying OS of the machine and can therefore be managed independently. That immediately takes away the need to have multiple OS images for different applications, as they can now be delivered independently of the OS image. So straightaway, savings can be achieved by deploying the more cost-effective stateless desktop model and only needing to have virtual desktops available when required – not just cost savings but management time in building and maintaining multiple images, as well as lower infrastructure costs as you do not need to deploy as many virtual desktop machines up front.

About management time and overheads, where else can savings be made? The first one is when updating applications. No longer is there the need to build a whole new OS image just because an app has gone from v1.2 to v1.3. Instead, the app layer can be created away from the OS, tested, and then easily delivered out. If by any chance something goes wrong, as long as the old virtual hard disk with the previous version of the app layer has been kept, then it's a simple case of detaching the nonworking app and going back to the known working one and allowing the end user to carry on while the problem app is remediated.

Enhanced end user experience

For an end user, they will have access to their applications much quicker than they would before, especially if it was an application they did not already have. No longer would they need to wait for the desktop admin team to come and install the app or give them a new virtual desktop OS image.

Instead, the desktop admins would simply click a mouse and allow that user to have access to the apps they need. Or if the end user changes role, the desktop administrator can simply change their AD group membership, and the user will automatically inherit the apps assigned to that AD group. The apps will simply appear on their desktop.

In this chapter

In the introduction to this chapter, I have given you an overview of what application layering is all about. A high-level overview of what it is, and then the use cases for an end user and a desktop administrator.

In the next sections, we are going to start diving deeper into the solution, and how it works, first from a general app layering perspective and then at a VMware App Volumes level.

This book will cover the theory of App Volumes, its components, how it works, and where you should use it, but then also covers the more practical elements and how to deploy and manage the solution as well as how to deliver the end user experience. Following these practical examples will allow you to build, configure, and deploy your own App Volumes environment.

Let us start by delving a bit deeper into how application layering works.

How does application layering work?

As we have already discussed in the introduction to this first chapter, application layering provides a solution that enables desktop administrator to abstract applications from the underlying operating system, so that those applications can be managed and delivered independently. But that was at a high level, so now we are going to dig deeper and see how it does it.

The concept of application layering is not too dissimilar to what we already do with other virtualization solutions, whether that's desktop or server based. The keyword here is abstraction.

With any virtualization solution, you are abstracting different components. In traditional virtualization technology, you are abstracting the server OS or the desktop OS in the case of VDI away from the physical hardware. Application layering performs its level of abstraction at the next level up, between the OS and the applications. In fact, it goes a bit deeper than just the applications as by deploying fully stateless virtual desktops, you also need to consider any user-authored data and other user-specific settings or end user personalization – the bits that make it personal to that particular end user. Basically, all the things that come together to build a full desktop experience for the end user.

I refer to this as the composite desktop model. The end user desktop experience comprises all those elements that come together to form a complete end user desktop experience and are abstracted, managed, and delivered independently. Elements such as the operating system, applications, user profiles, and user-authored data are all extracted from the operating system, centrally managed, and then delivered back independently in order to "reassemble" the complete desktop environment on demand. In this instance, with application layering, we are talking about the application element of this process.

Prior to this way of building the desktop experience on demand, all the desktop components would have been tightly integrated into the device operating system and therefore managed as a single entity.

Now for the technical bit, starting with how to create an application layer.

Creating application layers

Application layering can be described as a two-step process:

- **Step 1**: Creating and capturing the application layer
- **Step 2**: Delivering the application layer to the end users

In this section, we are going to look at the starting point for application layering, the create and capture process. This can be summarized using the diagram in Figure 1-1.

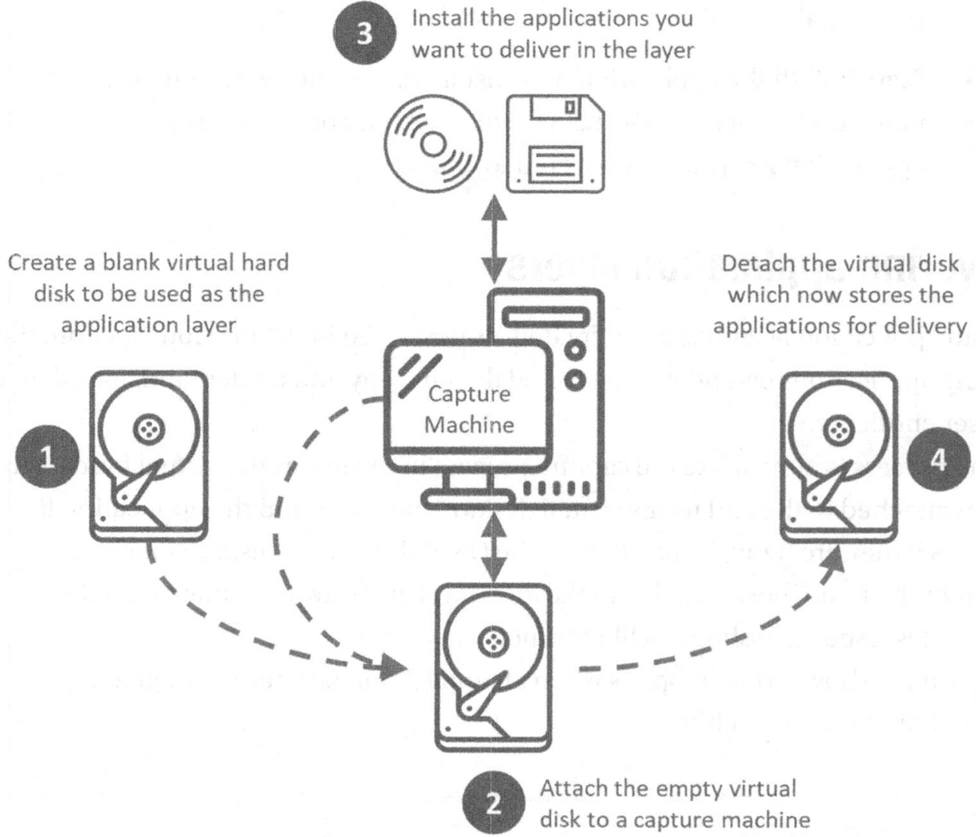

***Figure 1-1.** Creating and capturing application layers*

To look at the steps in more detail:

- **Step 1**: The first part of the process is to create the virtual hard disk that will be used as the application layer. This virtual hard disk is where the applications will be installed to create the layer.
- **Step 2**: The next step is to attach the virtual hard disk to a vanilla virtual desktop machine. By vanilla I mean a brand-new virtual desktop with a patched and up-to-date OS and no other apps or software installed other than the app layering software that is required.

- **Step 3**: You can now install your apps by switching your app layering software into "record" mode and then running the application installer. As the installation files are installed, they are redirected to the virtual hard disk.
- **Step 4**: With the application now installed, you can switch off record mode and detach the virtual hard disk, which now contains your application ready to be delivered to end users.

Delivering application layers

Once an application layer has been created, as described in the previous section, the resulting applications can now be delivered dynamically and on demand, based on the end user entitlement.

The process is almost like the capture process in reverse as the virtual hard disk is again attached to the end user's virtual desktop machine, and the application files appear as if they are natively installed on the OS of the virtual desktop machine.

Under the hood, however, the application layering software is managing the access to these files, especially should a file conflict occur.

Figure 1-2 shows what happens when an application layer is attached to an end user's virtual desktop machine.

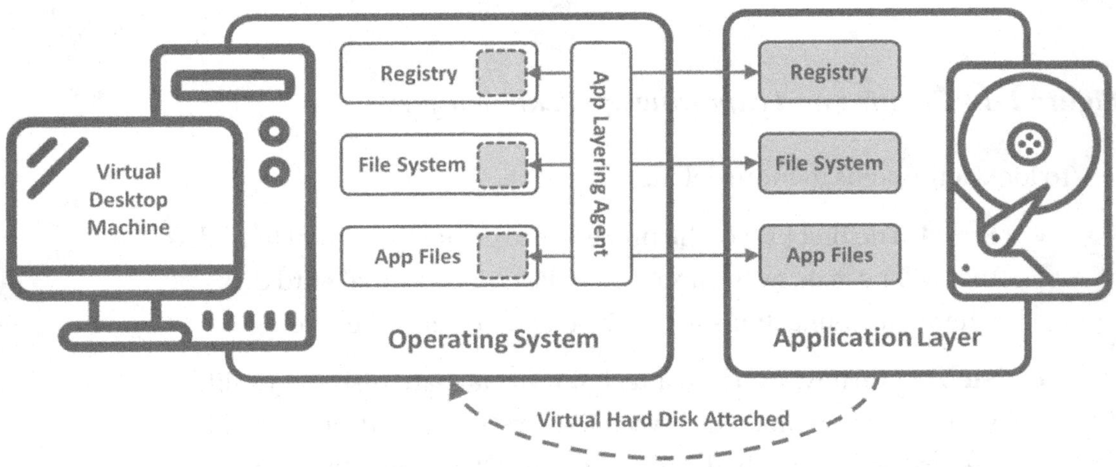

Figure 1-2. *Architecture of delivering an application layer*

When the end user logs in to their virtual desktop machine, the virtual hard disk or app layer that they have been entitled to is mounted to the operating system of the virtual desktop machine.

The application layering software on that virtual desktop machine, typically known as a filter driver or agent, temporarily inserts or layers all the files and settings that the application needs into the operating system of the virtual desktop machine. As far as the operating system is concerned, these application files and settings are installed and available locally. This is also true for the end user experience, with the icon for the layered application appearing on the desktop of the virtual desktop machine. They simply click it to launch it in the same way as they would for any other applications. As far as the end user and the virtual desktop operating system are concerned, the app is actually installed locally in the virtual desktop machine.

You can see this by opening and editing the registry of the virtual desktop machine. If you did this, then you would see the layered application registry settings present in the registry, even though in reality it has not been installed on that virtual desktop machine. The same is true for the application files. If you open Windows Explorer, for example, and navigate to something like C:\Program Files, there you would find all the application files, its executables, its DLL files, and so on. You would see everything that references the application, and to make it run, however, these files and settings reside on the virtual hard disk or layer that is mounted on the virtual desktop machine and not on the virtual desktop machine itself.

So, the end user is now running their layered applications. What happens when they log out of their virtual desktop machine?

When the end user logs out or shuts down their virtual desktop machine, the currently mounted layer, or virtual hard disk, is unmounted which means that the settings and the application files for the layered app no longer appear within the operating system of the virtual desktop machine. Essentially, it is as if the application has been uninstalled. The registry will have no mention of the application and neither will you find any other reference to the application, its files, or its settings. It is like it was never even there!

If the end user had shut down the machine rather than logging out, and that virtual desktop machine was a nonpersistent or stateless virtual desktop machine, then it would revert back to a clean state in preparation for the next user to log in.

When that next end user logs in, they may have a completely different set of applications that get layered into the operating system.

Having now covered the essentials to what application layering is, why you would need it, and how it works, in the next section, we are going to focus on the VMware implementation of application layering and look at VMware App Volumes.

VMware App Volumes

App Volumes came about when VMware acquired CloudVolumes in August 2014. CloudVolumes enabled the real-time delivery of applications to virtual and physical desktops. Then, in December 2014, after the acquisition, VMware rebranded CloudVolumes and changed the name to App Volumes and in doing so added an application layering solution to the VMware Horizon solution stack.

As an application layering solution, App Volumes works in the same way in which we have described application layering in the previous section. It is designed to enable the real-time delivery of applications within a virtual desktop environment.

Application layers are captured and stored on virtual hard disks within your virtual infrastructure environment. Then, when an end user logs in to their virtual desktop machine and is entitled to use a particular application, then the virtual hard disk containing that application is mounted, and the applications layered into the operating system ready to be launched. The end user will see just the application icon.

When the end user logs out, the layer is removed from the OS of the virtual desktop machine, and the virtual hard disk is unmounted.

How does App Volumes work?

We have already discussed the general mechanics around how application layering works, so now we are going to take those principles and look specifically at the VMware implementation of those with App Volumes.

As with any other application layering solution, App Volumes sets out to address the issue of how to deliver tightly integrated applications that are essentially part of the operating system image and take away that operating system dependency so that the applications can be delivered on demand and allow VMware customers to take advantage of the full Horizon virtual desktop solution and deploy a fully stateless virtual desktop.

App Volumes provides the layer of abstraction between the operating system and the applications, allowing the applications to be delivered to the end user's virtual desktop machine on demand and based on policy. The applications are effectively containerized within a virtual hard disk file (either VMDK based for VMware environments or VHD based for other virtual infrastructures). These virtual hard disk containers or layers were called AppStacks in previous versions of App Volumes, but this has now been replaced with a more application lifecycle management–based approach referred to as simplified application management (SAM).

SAM comprises the application, package, and program that go to make up the application layer as shown in Figure 1-3.

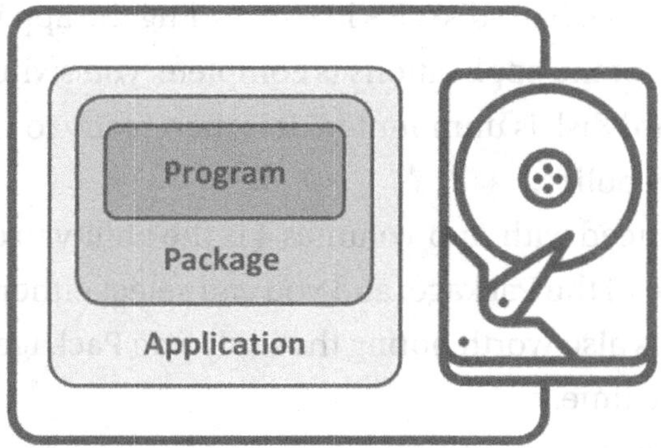

Figure 1-3. *Simplified application management (SAM)*

So that is at a high level. How does SAM look under the covers?

Application

The first part of creating a layer is to create an Application. In App Volumes 4, an application allows you to create a logical construct for an individual application or a group of applications. It is the application that is assigned to your end users.

As part of the application lifecycle management process, an application could be made up of multiple different packages and programs, so one thing to bear in mind is not to give the application a version number as it could well be made up from multiple different versions.

The next part to look at is the Package.

Package

The Package stage is more like the AppStack creation process of the previous version. Using a template virtual hard disk file from which to create the layer, a packaging virtual machine is used to capture the installation process of the application or applications you want to include in the Application construct, with the files and settings captured during install, redirected to a virtual hard disk that is temporarily attached to the package machine during app installation.

When the capture process starts, a copy of the template virtual hard disk file is mounted on the packaging machine. Once mounted, you can install the individual applications as you would do on any other machine with the application files and settings being redirected to the virtual hard disk. It's like recording the app installation process.

Once the installation of the applications is complete, you switch out of that record mode, and the virtual hard disk is unmounted. It is then ready to be assigned to end users based on AD group policy.

A new feature introduced with App Volumes 4 is the ability to choose the package stage. This is the lifecycle of the Package, and you can select either New, Tested, Published, or Retired. It is also worth noting that only one Package inside an Application can be current at any one time.

Finally, there is Program.

Program

The Program elements are automatically generated based on the applications you install during the Package stage. It is made up of the actual application executables and files that were captured during the Package phase.

So now that we have covered the three stages of creating an application layer, how does that translate when creating actual layers? First, let us look at the theory of how to manage an individual application.

Managing a single application

Taking the SAM approach with Application, Package, and Program, what would that look like in a real-life application lifecycle scenario?

So first you create the Application itself, so in this example, maybe that is for a PDF reader. This is the element that gets assigned to the end users. Once the application has been created, the next step is to capture the PDF reader application by installing it on the packaging machine. The files and settings for the PDF reader are then automatically created in Programs. Our PDF reader example would look something like Figure 1-4.

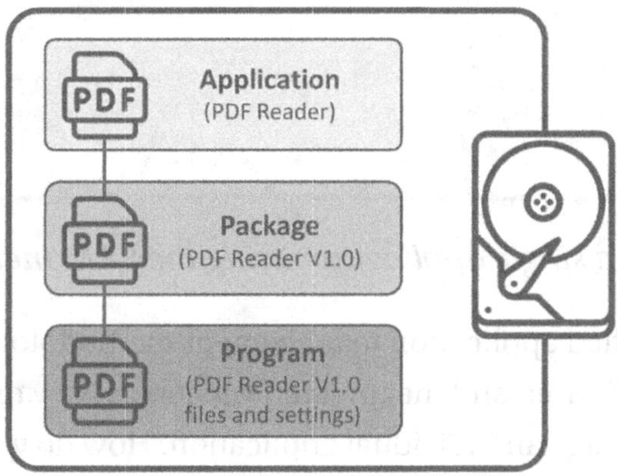

Figure 1-4. *Creating a single application using the SAM methodology*

The preceding example shows the process for a single application and a single version, but as we all know, applications do not stay on the same version for very long. So, what happens when the PDF reader updates to a new version?

Unlike when you create the application as we described previously, you do not need to create a new application. We already have an application for the PDF reader in place. Instead, you go straight to the Package process and capture the new version of the PDF reader using the packaging machine, which in turn creates the Program elements automatically. Once completed, you will have updated the Application with the new version of the PDF reader, which will look something like Figure 1-5.

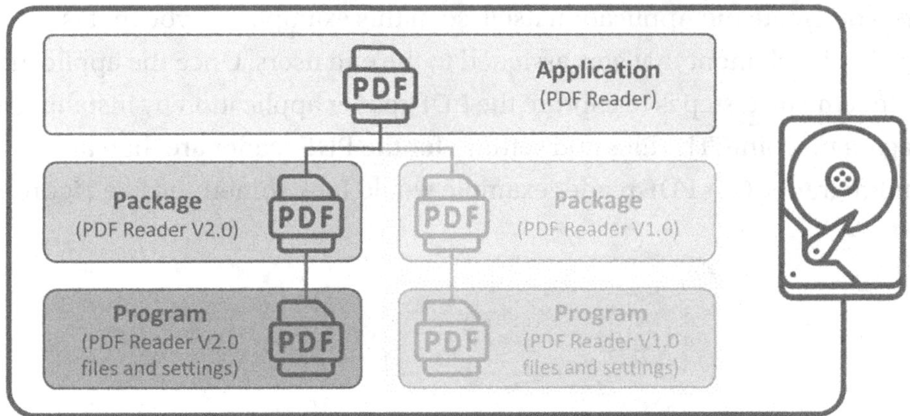

Figure 1-5. *Updating a single application using the SAM methodology*

As part of the simplified application management methodology, you could now mark the old version as Retired and the updated version as New or Published.

So that is how to manage an individual application. How do you manage a group of applications?

Managing a group of applications

Groups of applications are typically used to deploy multiple applications based on departmental use. So, for example, the finance department will have a set of specific finance-based apps, and the sales department will have a set of sales-based apps, and so on. In this example, we are going to create an Application for the finance department which contains a PDF reader and a spreadsheet application as shown in Figure 1-6.

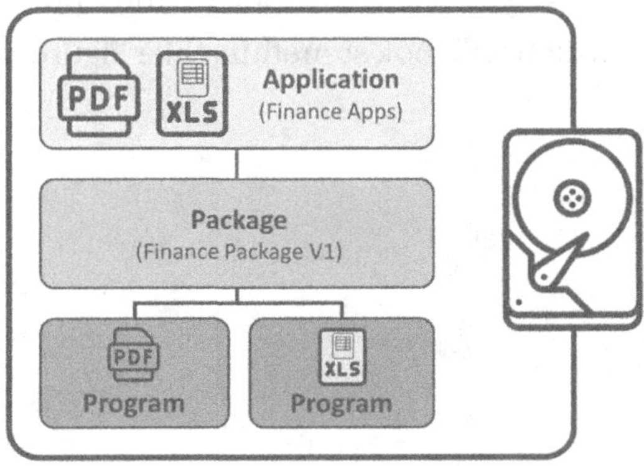

Figure 1-6. *Managing a group of applications using the SAM methodology*

So, let's run through a similar scenario as we did for single applications. First, you create the Application itself, so in this example, we are going to call it something department related rather than app specific, as this Application is going to contain more than one individual application. We have chosen the finance department for this example.

Again, the Application is the element that gets assigned to the end users, but in this case, it means more than one application. It is a set of applications. Once the Application has been created, the next step is to capture the applications by installing them on the packaging machine. The files and settings for each individual application are then automatically created in Programs. In this example, we have created a Package that contains Programs for the PDF reader and the spreadsheet app.

The next question is how do you update the Application should there be an update to one or more of the Programs? It is the same story as we covered with updating a single app.

You do not need to create a new application as that is already in place. Instead, you go straight to the Package process and capture the new version of the application you want to update, using the packaging machine, which in turn will update the Program elements automatically. This means you could update each application independently. For example, if the PDF reader updated and the spreadsheet app did not, then you simply just update the PDF reader, capturing that update using the packaging machine.

The new package will contain the updated app, as will the Programs. Once completed, you will have updated the Application with the new version of the PDF reader and spreadsheet app, which will look something like Figure 1-7.

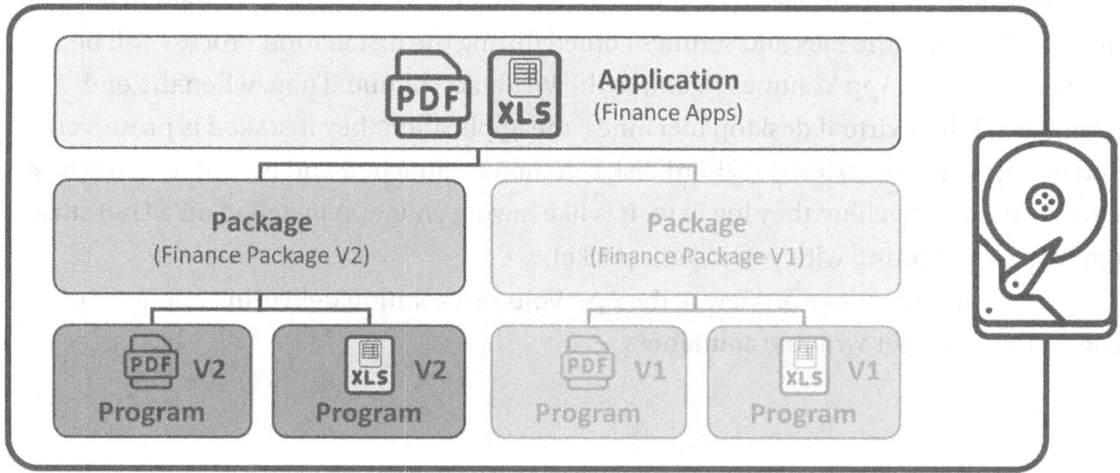

Figure 1-7. *Updating a group of applications using the SAM methodology*

So far in this chapter, we have discussed how to deliver applications to end users, in pursuit of delivering a fully stateless virtual desktop environment. However, when it comes to end users, there is one other thing that they may require on their desktop, and that is the ability to install their own apps or to save their personal data. This was typically another stumbling block for deploying stateless desktops, as anything an end user installed was removed, then they logged out, and the virtual desktop machine was refreshed.

The only answer for enabling end users to install their own apps was to provide the end user with a persistent or stateful virtual desktop machine. But VMware App Volumes has a solution for enabling end users to install their own apps with the Writable Volume feature.

Writable Volumes

The App Volumes Writable Volume feature enables end users to have their own dedicated virtual hard disk. This virtual hard disk is mounted to their virtual desktop machine when they log in and is used to capture anything that they install on their desktop machine. The Writable Volume is an application layer and works in the same way as we have discussed previously with the attaching of already installed applications. However, it differs from that approach as it starts off as an empty disk file, save for the App Volumes components already present on the Writable Volumes disk template that are required for mounting.

If an end user has access to their own Writable Volume, when they install their own applications, the files and settings copied during the installation process will be redirected, by the App Volumes Agent, to the Writable Volume. Then, when the end user logs off their virtual desktop machines, the application they installed is preserved and being available on a virtual hard disk can then be attached and mounted to the next virtual desktop machine they log in to. It is like having your app installed on a USB stick that you carry around with you in your pocket.

Figure 1-8 shows an overview of the App Volumes solution delivering application containers and user writable containers.

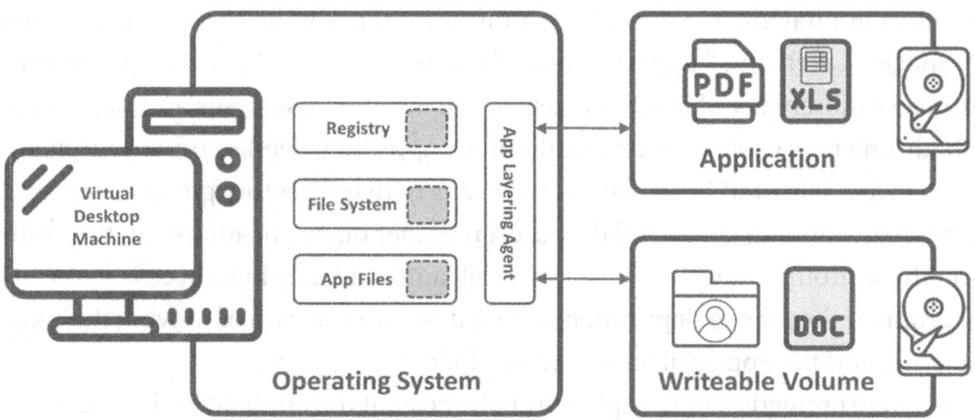

Figure 1-8. *App Volumes with Writable Volumes and Application Packages*

The other use case for Writable Volumes is for user profiles, the other component of a desktop machine that is personal to an end user. The Windows profile delivers the end user customization such as backdrops and other settings that are personal to the end user. With a stateless virtual desktop machine, these personalizations are deleted at the time of log off, and so by deploying a Writable Volume, the user profile can be stored as a layer, essentially making it portable. This feature complements user environment management solutions such as VMware Dynamic Environment Manager.

Having now discussed the how part of App Volumes, in the next section, we are going to discuss the why deploy App Volumes question.

Why deploy App Volumes?

App Volumes provides a solution that enables an organization to take full advantage of deploying a fully stateless virtual desktop environment. Decoupling the apps from the underlying operating system allows IT admins to deliver applications on demand, as and when the end user requires them. With the new simplified application management methodology introduced in App Volumes 4, this also provides added benefits when it comes to updating and deploying new versions of applications all with the added bonus of not disrupting the end users.

The ability to manage applications independently makes it far easier for patching and updating and all without having to touch the operating system. It also means that IT can respond much quicker should security patches need to be applied quickly.

It also means not having to worry about building and maintaining multiple copies of gold images. Often an IT department had multiple copies of gold images, each containing a different set of apps to cater for the different use cases and departments.

Onboarding new users, and getting them the apps they need, is much simpler too. Applications are delivered based on an end user's Active Directory group membership or which Organizational Unit (OU) they are a member of. Applications can be entitled based on those groups, and therefore a user will automatically have access to the apps via that group. If they move departments, then it is a simple case of moving their group membership, and the apps will automatically follow.

If the end user needs a new application, they can, if the application has been built and configured, have that application added on the fly. That means that they do not need to wait for somebody to come and install it; once entitled, it will simply appear on their desktop.

So far in this chapter, we have focused purely on the delivery of applications, but due to the dynamic nature of App Volumes, these applications can just as easily be removed. As we have discussed, when an end user logs from their virtual desktop machine, the virtual hard disk containing the applications gets unmounted, and the applications appear as though they are no longer installed. If you do not want a specific end user to have access to the applications, then you simply remove them from the group.

App Volumes, ThinApp, and Horizon Apps

VMware also have other solutions for delivering applications that often means customers asking what the difference is and when should I use one vs. the other. We are talking about VMware ThinApp and Horizon Apps.

The question is why do VMware have three different ways to deliver applications? The answer to this question is quite simple. These solutions may all deliver applications, but how they do it is completely different, and the reason why they are all different is that each one solves a different use case. It is also worth mentioning that they are not all solutions that run in isolation. All three could be combined to deliver an end-to-end solution that covers all use cases. In the next sections, we are going to briefly touch on each solution and how it integrates into the overall application delivery strategy and message.

ThinApp

VMware ThinApp is an application virtualization technology that takes an application and packages it into its own isolated bubble, complete with file system, registry, and virtualized components of the operating system that are required for the app to run.

This virtual package is delivered as a single executable file that is made up of all those captured parts and is used when you need to isolate the application from the operating system because the app is not compatible with the OS version on the device. For example, you might need to deploy an older version of a browser that does not run on your current OS. You could create a packaged instance of that browser using ThinApp, turning it into a single .EXE file.

In comparison to App Volumes, App Volumes does not isolate applications, so the applications you deliver to the host OS must be supported and able to run on that OS. App Volumes also does not present the apps as a single file; instead, it uses a virtual hard disk that contains multiple files (the files used by the app) and then integrates those files as layers into the virtual desktop operating system. ThinApp has an added advantage that it can run locally.

You could of course combine both App Volumes and ThinApp to create a virtualized, isolated application, capture that as an application layer, and then deliver it back on demand. The use case for doing this would be to deliver applications that do not run on the version of the operating system being used for your stateless virtual desktop machines. In this scenario, we have ThinApp packaged apps being delivered to the virtual desktop machine as an application layer.

One point to highlight is that ThinApp is included with the App Volumes Advanced Edition; however, it is called AppIsolation.

Horizon Apps

Horizon Apps is predominantly based on Microsoft RDSH technology and is more commonly known as application publishing. However, with the availability of Horizon 8, you can now publish apps from Linux servers using multisession mode or also from Windows 10 desktops. So how does this fit within the App Volumes world?

Basically, it delivers the same benefits as it does when delivering apps to end users, but in this case, there is a step before the end user. That step is the RDSH server which the apps are attached to.

In an app publishing environment, all of which are pretty much based on Microsoft RDSH server technology, applications are installed onto a multiuser server OS before being made available, or published, to the end users. As the apps would normally be installed on each server, it makes this a very static model and hard to manage apps and scale up. So, deploying App Volumes means that you abstract the apps from the OS – in this instance, a server OS. The apps are then attached to the servers as and when required and can be easily updated without having to rebuild the entire server or, worse, an entire server farm. The key difference here is that the application layers are entitled by machine or server rather than an individual user or user group.

Horizon Apps in this solution plays the part of the broker and is what allows apps to be entitled to end users. However, being based on a server OS and RDSH also means that App Volumes can be used to deliver apps to Citrix Virtual Apps and Desktops, as well as Microsoft RemoteApp environments.

The other difference from the desktop delivery model is that when capturing the package, the capture machine must be running the same OS as the machine you plan to deliver the layers to. So, in this case, the packaging machine would need to be running a Microsoft server OS.

In the previous sections, we've talked in detail about different solutions that all provide a different aspect of solving the overall use case of delivering applications in the most efficient way for IT and also of delivering the best end user experience possible. But VMware have gone a step further in automating the whole stateless desktop environment. It is called the Just-in-Time Management Platform, or JMP for short.

Just-in-Time Management Platform

JMP combines the Instant Clones feature of vSphere to build stateless virtual desktops on demand, App Volumes to deliver the applications, and VMware DEM to deliver the end user personalization.

We will cover the JMP, its architecture, the role App Volumes plays, and how to install and configure JMP in Chapter 8 of this book.

How to license App Volumes

Buying App Volumes is very straightforward, with two editions available depending on the features you require.

The first option is to purchase a stand-alone version of App Volumes which means you get just App Volumes in one of the two editions:

- **App Volumes Standard**: Supports real-time app delivery, user profile, and policy management and provides a platform for cloud-based solutions. Works with Horizon, Citrix Virtual Apps and Desktops, and Microsoft RemoteApp.
- **App Volumes Advanced**: Builds on standard and adds AppIsolation (ThinApp).

The second option is to purchase VMware Horizon Enterprise Edition. App Volumes is included as part of this license, and therefore you will get all the features including the components required for the JMP solution.

The other licensing consideration is which model to purchase. You can choose from the following:

- **Per Named User**: For virtual environments with users that need dedicated access to a virtual desktop machine throughout the day
- **Per Concurrent Connection**: For virtual environments with a high number of shift workers where machines are shared between workers throughout the day

Using this book

As well as discussing the theory behind the App Volumes solution, this book also provides you the opportunity to follow a more practical stream with a test lab environment that will be built along the way to demonstrate how to build the solutions and then how to configure particular elements.

This test lab will show you step by step how to complete these more practical exercises and use real screenshots from the solution along the way.

To build the test lab, and indeed to deploy the App Volumes solution, there are several prerequisites that need to be in place. These will be covered in each of the sections when we cover the installation and configuration, but before that there are some higher-level components needed, such as Active Directory.

AD requirements

You will need an administrator account and several Organizational Unit (OU) groups and end user accounts for entitling applications to for test purposes.

For administration, you should create a dedicated App Volumes administrators' group, but for this book, we will just use the standard administrator account. Depending on your environment, you could create other administrator accounts and groups should you wish to do so.

You will also need several Active Directory groups to reflect different departments and, in each group, make sure you have a few end user accounts that can be used to test that applications are available and can be launched.

App Volumes architecture and features

So far, we have looked at how application layering and App Volumes works. In this section, we are going to take a deeper dive into the App Volumes solution and focus on the core components that make up App Volumes and the overall architecture.

We are going to start with the terminology so that you are familiar with the naming conventions of the components and what part they play in the solution.

Terminology

In this section, we are going to name the component parts of the solution along with a description of that component it is responsible for.

App Volumes Manager

The App Volumes Manager is the central component in the App Volumes solution. Its job is to provide a management platform for IT admins to configure and manage the distribution and entitlement of applications to end users.

The console itself runs as an application that is installed on a Windows Server. From this server, or connecting remotely, you will use a web-based management console from which IT administrators can easily manage the delivery and entitlement of applications and Writable Volumes, plus the ability to create and manage application lifecycles. We will cover the installation process in the next chapter, along with a guided tour of the management console and how to drive it.

The App Volumes Manager also provides the communication to the external components such as your ESXi host servers that host the virtual machines, the storage, and datastores where your application layer virtual hard disk files and Writable Volumes live, as well as connecting to Active Directory for entitlements, and vCenter Server to manage the virtual infrastructure when it comes to creating new virtual hard disks and attaching them to virtual desktop machines.

It is not just the virtual hard disk files or layers that the App Volumes Manager manages. It is also responsible for managing any machines that have the App Volumes Agent installed. When a virtual desktop machine has the App Volumes Agent installed on it, the virtual desktop machine registers itself within the inventory of the App Volumes Manager which in turn allows you to configure your entitlements to the machine.

In summary, the App Volumes Manager delivers the following:

- Manage assignments of application layers and Writable Volumes to end users, groups, and computers
- Collect Application Packages and Writable Volumes usage information
- Maintain a history of administrative actions
- Automate assignment of applications and Writable Volumes for agents during desktop startup and user login

Next, we are going to look at the SQL database.

SQL database

The Microsoft SQL database or SQL Server Express database (ships with the App Volumes installation files) is used to store the configuration information for all the application packages and Writable Volumes that are created along with the end user and machine assignments.

App Volumes Agent

The App Volumes Agent is installed onto every virtual desktop machine onto which you want to deliver application packages and Writable Volumes. It also is installed onto the RDSH servers if you are using them to deliver published versions of the applications. The endpoint onto which the App Volumes Agent is installed is sometimes referred to as the target.

Application

An Application, in App Volumes terminology, refers to a collection of packaged versions of an application or applications that users, groups, computers, or OUs (Organizational Units) can then be entitled to receive a current Package or be assigned to a specific Package.

Package

A Package stores one or more Programs. Programs in the context of App Volumes mean the actual individual app, such as Microsoft Word, required for an Application to run. A single Package can be delivered to multiple computers and one or many users.

Program

A Program in App Volumes terms refers to the actual component parts of an application, for example, the .exe, .dll, and all the other settings and files an app needs to be able to run.

Packaging desktop

The packaging desktop (or server depending on whether you are packaging for RDSH) is a clean install of the OS, optimized for App Volumes, and with the App Volumes Agent installed. During the packaging process, this machine will be selected, and a new virtual hard disk will be attached to the machine. You then start the app installation on the packaging machine, with all the files and settings being redirected and captured onto this virtual hard disk. Once completed, the virtual hard disk will be unmounted from the packaging machine and will be available for end user entitlement.

Writable Volume

The Writable Volumes feature enables storage for end user-specific data such as application profile settings, documents, and user installed applications. The mode of storage is determined by the template that is selected during the Writable Volume creation process.

Storage Groups

Storage Groups are not a specific component of the App Volumes architecture and provide more of a feature. With Storage Groups, IT admins can configure replication for their AppStacks as well as the ability to distribute Writable Volumes across multiple datastores.

Defining storage groups allows IT admins to configure a group of datastores across which the same application packages will automatically be replicated. This enables you to provide disaster recovery for your application packages so that they are still available in the unlikely event of a storage failure. Without this, and if there was a storage failure, then your end users would potentially have no access to their application packages. This would mean that the IT admins would have to repackage the application packages all over again.

When it comes to storage groups for Writable Volumes, only some of the storage group settings are applicable, with the key things being template location and the distribution strategy.

What is the distribution strategy? The distribution strategy, as the name suggests, defines how Writable Volumes are distributed across the storage group. The configuration of the distribution strategy consists of the two options:

- **Spread**: Distributes files evenly across all the storage locations. When a file is created, the storage with the most available space is used.
- **Round-Robin**: Distributes the Writable Volume files sequentially, starting with the oldest location first.

So now you will have a good understanding of what the different App Volumes components are and what part they play in the overall solution.

We are now going to take that information and put it together and start to build out the entire App Volumes architecture, using architecture diagrams. This will help you design your own App Volumes environment. As part of this, we will also look at the overall VMware solution for delivering apps and desktops as part of their digital workspace initiative.

App Volumes architecture

In this section, we are going to look at the App Volumes architecture. First, we are going to look from the outside in and give an end user's perspective of that they would see from their virtual desktop machine. Then we will turn it around and look from the inside out, from the IT admins' perspective.

The end user's view

We are going to start by looking at the front end of the App Volumes architecture and how it would look to an end user once they have logged in to their virtual desktop machine. This example starts with the virtual desktop machine with the apps available as they would on any other desktop machine. However, from the architecture, you will see that in actual fact the apps are being delivered by application packages in App Volumes.

Figure 1-9 outlines the architecture as seen from the end user, although in reality they would have no idea that their apps are not actually installed onto their desktop.

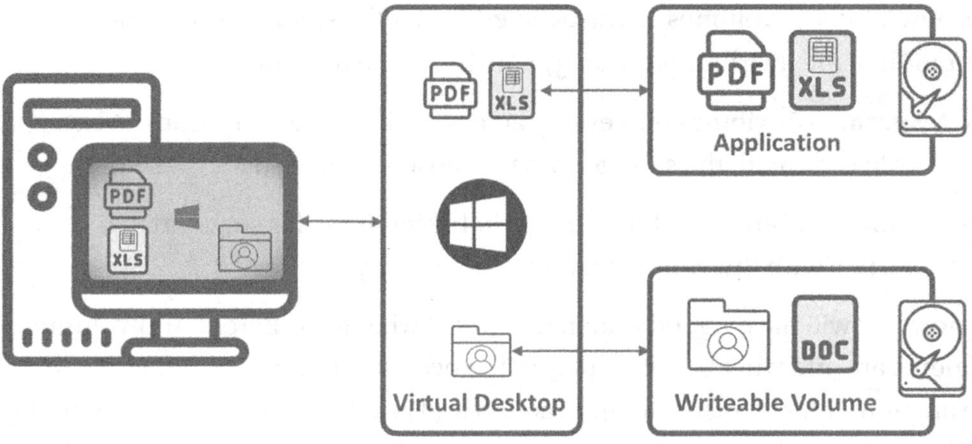

Figure 1-9. *App Volumes end user view*

In this example, the end user starts by logging in to their virtual desktop machine. As well as containing the base layer apps, that is, the apps that don't need to be delivered dynamically and so are left as part of the operating system, the virtual desktop machine is also running the App Volumes Agent which in turn registers the virtual desktop machine with the App Volumes Manager.

It is worth noting that any apps that are left in the base OS cannot be dynamically managed and updated with App Volumes. Instead, you would need to update the OS image with the new and updated apps and then roll that out to the end users.

You could of course choose to manage all applications with App Volumes; however, keep in mind that there are certain limitations for the number of application packages that can be attached to a virtual desktop machine at any one time. There may also be instances where the application does not capture during the packaging process due to some reason in the way it works. We will cover this later in the book.

With the end users now logged in to their virtual desktop machine, they will see the application packages that they have been entitled to appear on their desktop. As this is likely to be a stateless virtual desktop machine, it would have been built on demand and delivered as a clean install of the OS, with the apps now delivered separately. As a stateless machine, there would have been no end user personalization performed either; however, if the end user has a Writable Volume assigned to them for user profiles (also combined with VMware DEM), then this will ensure that the end user's personal settings and data will also be present when they log in.

From an end user's perspective, nothing changes. It's the behind the scenes that is different, and we will cover that in the next section.

The IT administrators' view

In this section, we are going to focus on the infrastructure side of App Volumes and look at the architecture of how the components fit together. As part of this, we will also include the other Horizon components and the network ports for enabling the connections.

Figure 1-10 illustrates the back-end infrastructure for an App Volumes deployment.

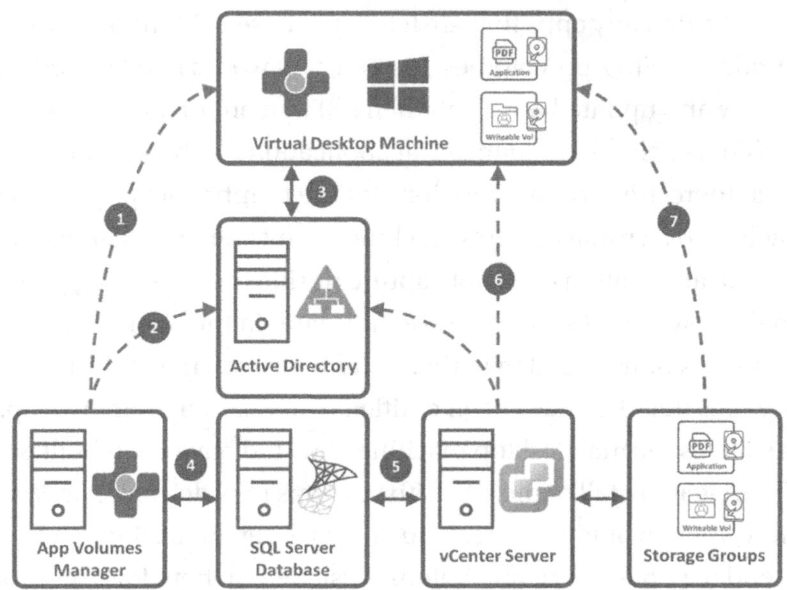

Figure 1-10. *App Volumes architecture for IT admins*

Figure 1-10 shows the complete App Volumes architecture and the process of what happens in the back end when an end user logs in.

It all starts when the end user logs in to their virtual desktop machine. This virtual desktop machine is running the App Volumes Agent which performs two key roles. First and foremost, it provides the role of the filter driver. The filter driver is responsible for ensuring the application package components are delivered to the correct place within the virtual desktop OS. So, this means ensuring the application files or programs, and registry settings are correctly delivered to enable the app to run. This is the layering part of application layering.

Its other role is to communicate with the App Volumes Manager (1). This allows the agent to read the user assignment information to see which users, groups, and machines have access to which application packages and Writable Volumes, and in turn the App Volumes Manager retrieves its information from Active Directory (2). This allows it to assign application packages and Writable Volumes based on users, groups, OUs, and machines.

In this example, the virtual desktop machine is domain joined and authenticates user logins using Active Directory (3) which also provides the application entitlements.

Configuration information regarding the assignment of application packages and Writable Volumes is in a Microsoft SQL database (4). As with any other VMware environment, a SQL database is also required for the vCenter Server (5) as well as the Horizon components if you are deploying the full VMware suite. As you are likely to be deploying stateless virtual desktop machines with Instant Clones, then this will also require a database connection. In this example diagram, the building of the stateless desktops is shown (6). The vCenter Server can also be responsible for mounting your App Volumes layers, although this can also be offloaded to the ESXi host server.

Once end users are logged in to their virtual desktop machine and the application package and Writable Volumes assignments have been read, the relevant virtual hard disk files can be attached to the virtual desktop machine (7).

The end users can now launch apps and use their virtual desktop machine.

In this section, we talked about the various components of the solution communicating with each other. The question that then arises is what network ports are used for the communication. We will cover this in the next section.

Network ports

In this section, we are going to show the network ports that are needed for the different App Volumes components to communicate with each other. This also includes components such as vCenter and Active Directory. To make sure App Volumes works seamlessly, you will need to ensure that these ports are open and are not blocked by any firewalls.

Figure 1-11 shows the network ports between each component that will need to be open.

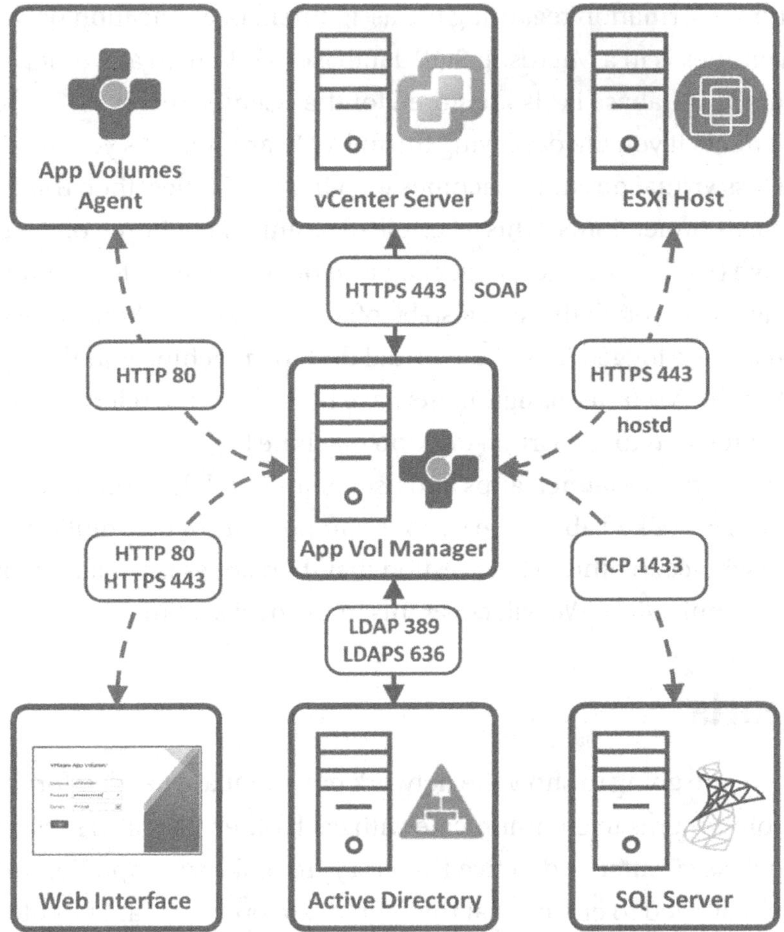

Figure 1-11. *App Volumes network port diagram*

The communication between the App Volumes Manager and the SQL Server, vCenter Server, and the App Volumes Agent can be secured using SSL certificates for a more secure connection.

Chapter summary

In this first chapter of the book, we have given you a comprehensive introduction to application layering and the VMware App Volumes solution.

We started the chapter by discussing the theory around what application layering is and how it works from a general technology perspective. Now understanding what application layering is all about, what it delivers, and how it works, we then focused on the App Volumes solution and its use cases.

In the next sections, we looked at some of the other VMware technology solutions for delivering applications and how they compare and integrate with App Volumes. As part of this discussion, we looked at the benefits and features of App Volumes.

Having now built a picture of how app layering and App Volumes works, we then looked at how to license and purchase the product, before we started our deeper dive look at the individual elements of App Volumes describing what they are and what part they play in the overall solution.

The chapter finished with an architectural overview of how the components connect and communicate.

In the next chapter, we are going to install App Volumes.

CHAPTER 2

Installing VMware App Volumes

In the beginning chapter of this book, we introduced you first to application layering as a technology and then the VMware version of application layering with App Volumes.

Now that you have a thorough understanding of the App Volumes solution, how it works, and each of the individual components that make up the solution, we can now move on to the first practical phase of this book and install the App Volumes software using a test lab environment.

In this chapter

In this second chapter, we are going to install the App Volumes software from an infrastructure perspective and the components that need to be installed on the end user side of the solution. Before we get started with the practical, we are going to cover the prerequisites and what you will need to already have in place for the installation.

To summarize, in this chapter, we are going to cover the following:

- Installation prerequisites (hardware and software) for installing
- App Volumes Manager
- App Volumes Agent
- SQL Server
- Active Directory requirements
- vSphere configuration and requirements
- ESXi host servers

P. von Oven, *Delivering Applications with VMware App Volumes 4*,
https://doi.org/10.1007/978-1-4842-6689-2_2

- vCenter Server
- Downloading the App Volumes software
- Installing VMware App Volumes Manager
- Installing VMware App Volumes Agent

As previously mentioned, to demonstrate the installation of App Volumes, we are going to work through the setup and installation using a test lab environment. This allows us to easily demonstrate each task step by step, using the actual screenshots from the product.

Taking this approach will enable you to first understand the theory of a particular aspect of the solution and then demonstrate what you have learned by putting that theory into practical practice, resulting in you building out your own test environment. This can then be used to work through a proof of concept or a pilot or even to help you build the solution for a production environment.

Before you start the installation

There are several prerequisites you need to have in place before you start to install any of the software. It is recommended to have these first as some of the details of these other components will be needed to complete the install. These are as follows:

- An AD service account that, as a minimum, has read access to the base DN. This is to allow the App Volumes Manager to query AD users, groups, and machines.
- An AD admin group for logging in to the App Volumes Manager.
- A vCenter service account that has administration privileges. This account will also need permission to browse the datastore so that App Volumes can add or remove files and folders, as well as the permissions set out in Figure 2-1.

- Datastore
  - Allocate space
  - Browse datastore
  - Low level file operations
  - Remove file
  - Update virtual machine files
- Folder
  - Create folder
  - Delete folder
- Global
  - Cancel task
- Host
  - Local operations
    - Reconfigure virtual machine
- Sessions
  - View and stop sessions
- Tasks
  - Create task
- Virtual machine
  - Configuration
    - Add existing disk
    - Add new disk
    - Add or remove device
    - Change resource
    - Query unowned files
    - Remove disk
    - Settings
    - Advanced
  - Inventory
    - Create new
    - Move
    - Register
    - Remove
    - Unregister
  - Provisioning
    - Promote disks

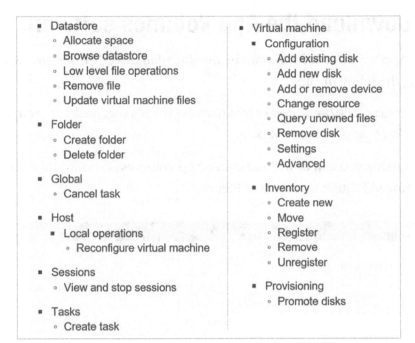

Figure 2-1. *vCenter Server account permissions*

- Admin privileges to the ESXi host servers if you are configuring App Volumes to mount directly to ESXi host servers.
- In the case that a firewall is used between system components, ports TCP 80 for HTTP, TCP 443 for HTTPS, 5985 for PowerShell web service, and 1433 for SQL communication should be opened.
- SQL Server database for storing configuration and assignment information for end users and application packages. (In this example, we are going to use the integrated SQL Express database that ships with the installation media.)
- For multiple App Volumes Managers, you will need to deploy a load balancer to distribute the traffic between the managers as App Volumes does not have this feature.

You will also need the VMware App Volumes installation media and license file. We will download these in the next section.

How to download the App Volumes software

The VMware App Volumes software can be downloaded directly from the VMware website, using the following link:

`https://my.vmware.com/web/vmware/downloads/info/slug/desktop_end_user_computing/vmware_app_volumes/4_x`

You will see that you can download either App Volumes Standard Edition or App Volumes Advanced Edition as shown in Figure 2-2.

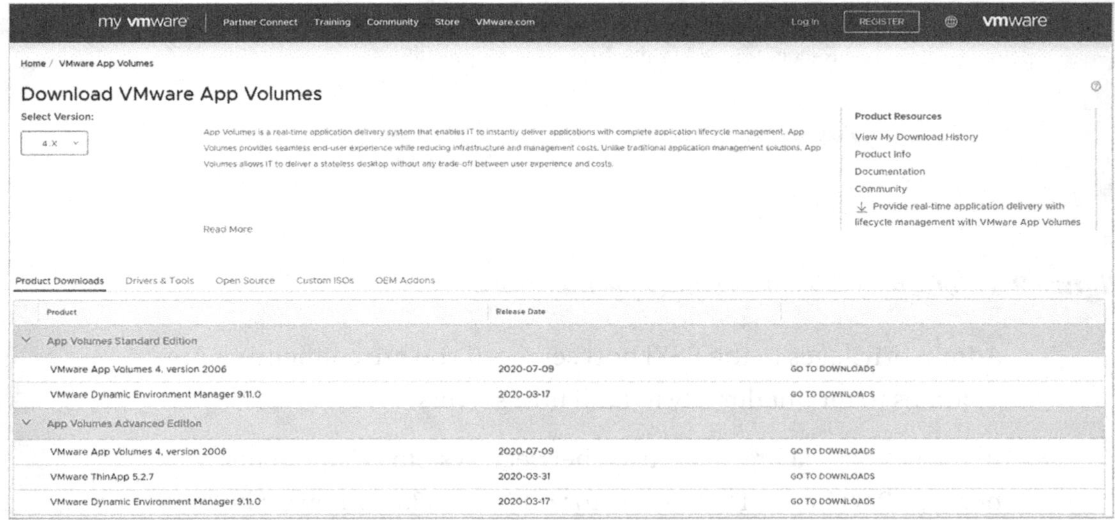

Figure 2-2. *VMware App Volumes download page*

To download the software, select the version you want from the Select Version box in the top left of the screen. You can then click GO TO DOWNLOADS to download the software. You will need to log in using an existing My VMware account, or you can easily register for a new account.

Downloading a 60-day trial

If you do not have access to the software, then you can register for a 60-day evaluation license by going to the following link:

`https://vmware.com/go/try-app-volumes`

You will see the VMware App Volumes Product Evaluation Center as shown in Figure 2-3.

***Figure 2-3.** VMware App Volumes Product Evaluation Center*

Registering or logging in with an existing My VMware account will allow you to download a trial version of the software for a 60-day period.

Once you have logged in and registered for the trial, you will now see the Download Packages as shown in Figure 2-4.

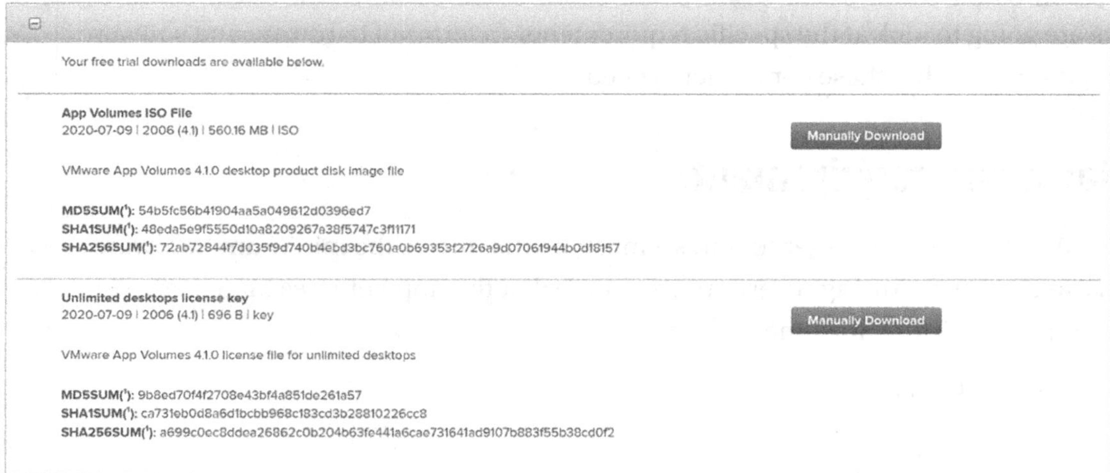

***Figure 2-4.** VMware App Volumes Download Packages page*

Download both the App Volumes ISO File and the Unlimited desktops license key. Once downloaded, you will see something like Figure 2-5.

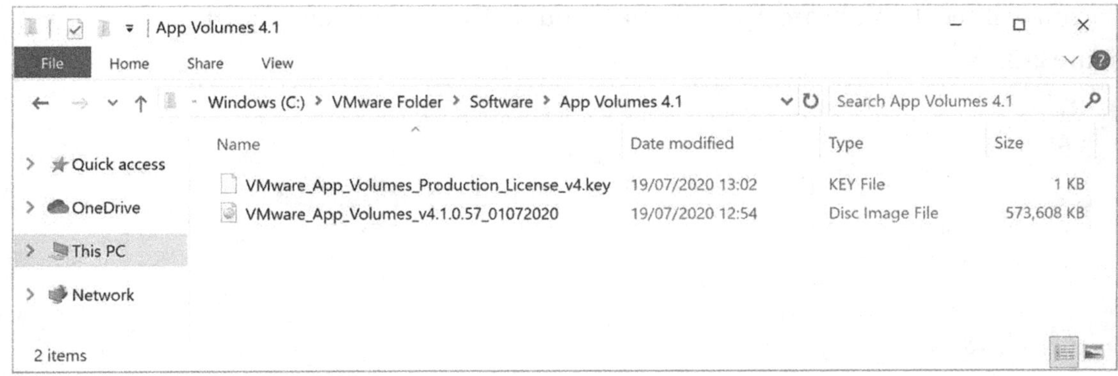

Figure 2-5. *VMware App Volumes software downloaded*

With the software now downloaded, we can start the installation, and the first component we are going to install is the App Volumes Manager.

App Volumes Manager installation

Back in Chapter 1, we outlined the different components of the App Volumes solution at a high level. In this section, and before we start the actual software installation, we are going to look at the specific requirements, in terms of hardware and software requirements, that these components need.

Hardware requirements

The App Volumes Manager requires a machine that meets the minimum hardware spec as listed in the following. These specs assume that the App Volumes Manager will be running as a virtual machine.

- 4 vCPUs
- 4 GB RAM
- 1 GB disk space

Next, we are going to look at the software requirements and the supported operating systems.

Software requirements

To run the App Volumes Manager, the server will need to be running one of the following operating systems:

- Microsoft Windows Server 2019 Datacenter and Standard
- Microsoft Windows Server 2016 Datacenter and Standard

Accessing the App Volumes Manager

The App Volumes Manager console is web based, and so to access it, you will need to do so using a browser, either directly on the server itself or using an admin desktop. Either way, you will need to use one of the following browsers:

- Internet Explorer 9 or later
- Mozilla Firefox 28 or later
- Safari 7 or later
- Google Chrome 21 or later

Next, we are going to look at the database requirements and the supported versions.

Database requirements

As we have previously discussed, the App Volumes Manager requires a database in which it can store information about users, application packages, and assignments. You will need to be running one of the following supported databases:

- SQL Server 2019
- SQL Server 2017
- SQL Server 2016 SP2
- SQL Server 2014 SP1 and SP2
- Support for SQL Server 2014 Enterprise SP3 64-bit

For high availability, App Volumes supports the following database features:

- SQL Server Clustered Instances (for high availability)
- SQL Server Mirroring (for high availability)

In the test lab for this book, we are going to use Microsoft SQL Express 2014 which ships with the App Volumes installation media. As part of the installation, SQL Server will automatically be installed and the database created.

This approach is perfect for a proof of concept or pilot deployment but is not recommended for production environments.

With the prerequisites now in place, it is time to start the installation.

Installing the App Volumes Manager software

For this book, we are going to use a test lab environment to install the software and deploy App Volumes. This will enable you to see firsthand how to complete the installation tasks.

To this end, we have already built a Windows Server 2016 virtual machine, with the hostname of **Appvol-4**, ready to install the App Volumes Manager onto.

To install the software, follow the steps described:

1. Open a console to the virtual server named Appvol-4.
2. Navigate to the location where you downloaded the App Volumes software to. In the test lab, this was saved in a folder called App Volumes 4.1 as shown in Figure 2-6.

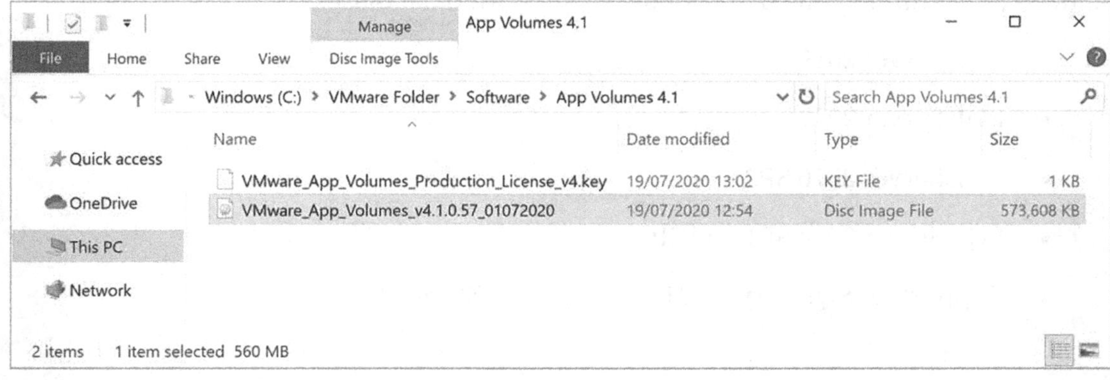

Figure 2-6. *VMware App Volumes software folder*

3. Double-click the **VMware_App_Volumes_v4.1.0.57_01072020.iso** file to mount the iso image. You will see the screenshot in Figure 2-7.

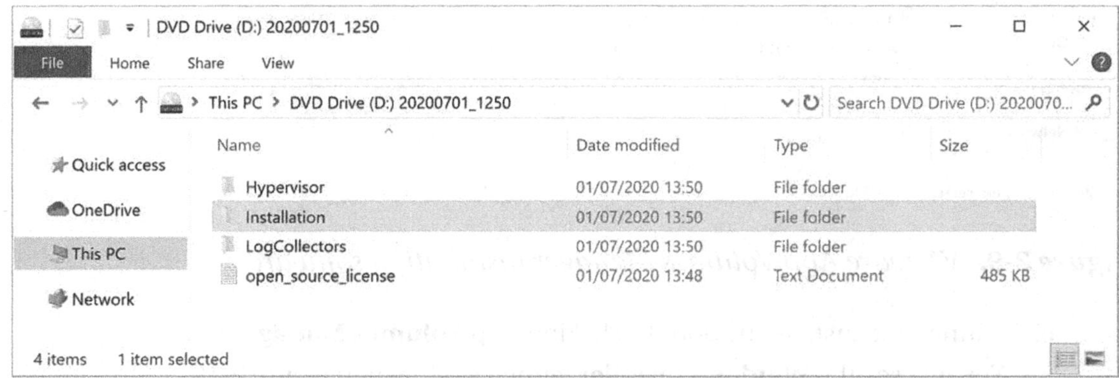

Figure 2-7. *VMware App Volumes software iso image mounted*

4. Double-click to open the **Installation** folder. You will see the folders in Figure 2-8.

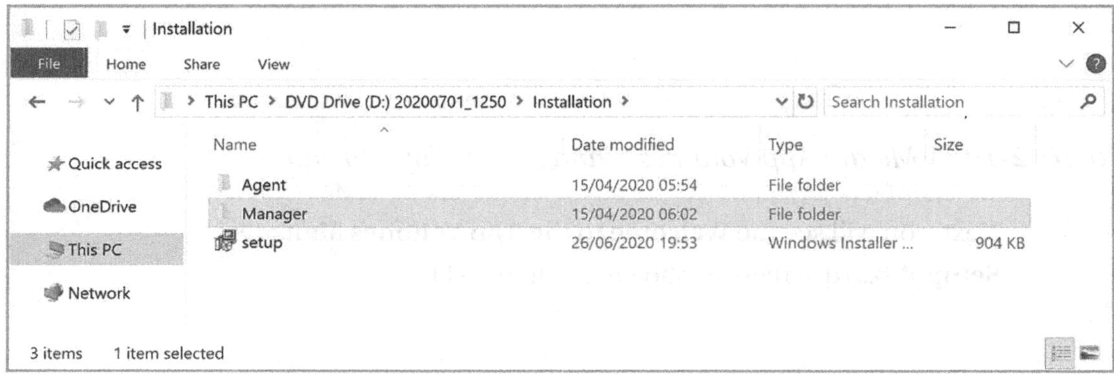

Figure 2-8. *VMware App Volumes software – installation folder*

5. Double-click the **Manager** folder. You will now see the contents of the folder containing all the installation components, including SQL Server (Figure 2-9).

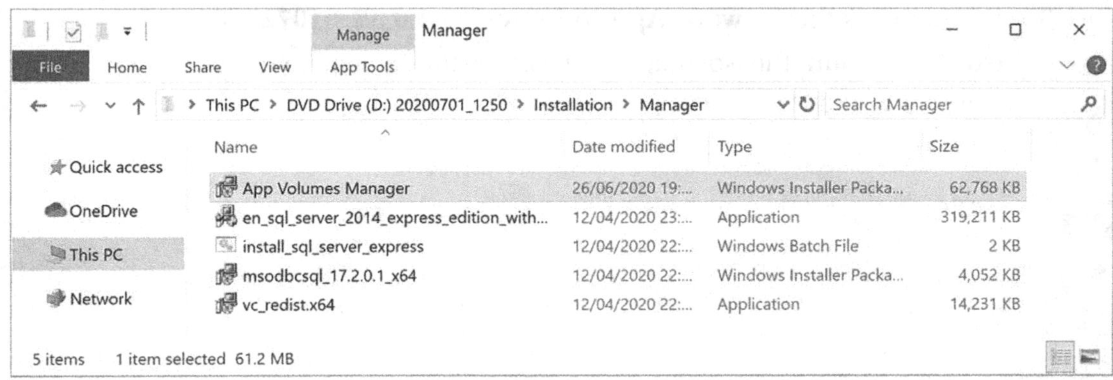

Figure 2-9. *VMware App Volumes Manager installation software*

6. Launch the installer by double-clicking **App Volumes Manager**. You will see the **Windows Installer** launch as shown in Figure 2-10.

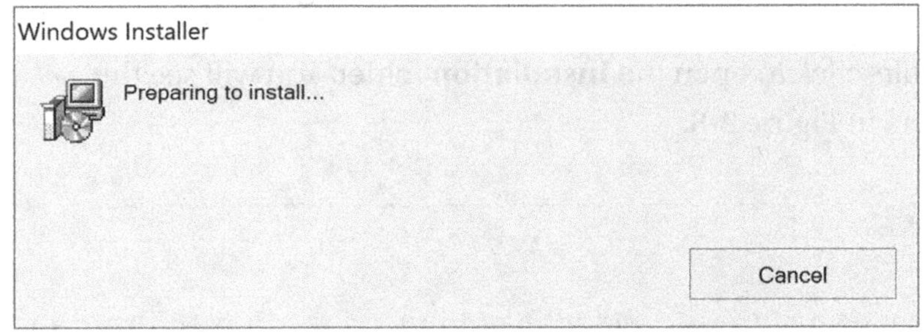

Figure 2-10. *VMware App Volumes Manager Windows Installer*

7. Next, you will see the **Welcome to the App Volumes Manager Setup Wizard** screen, as shown in Figure 2-11.

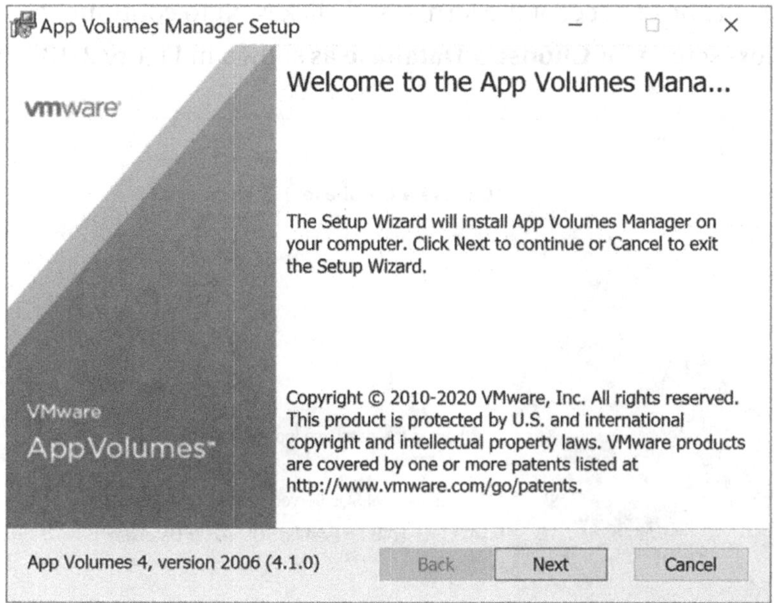

***Figure 2-11.** Welcome to the App Volumes Manager Setup Wizard screen*

8. Click **Next** to continue to the next screen. The next screen is for the **End-User License Agreement** as shown in Figure 2-12.

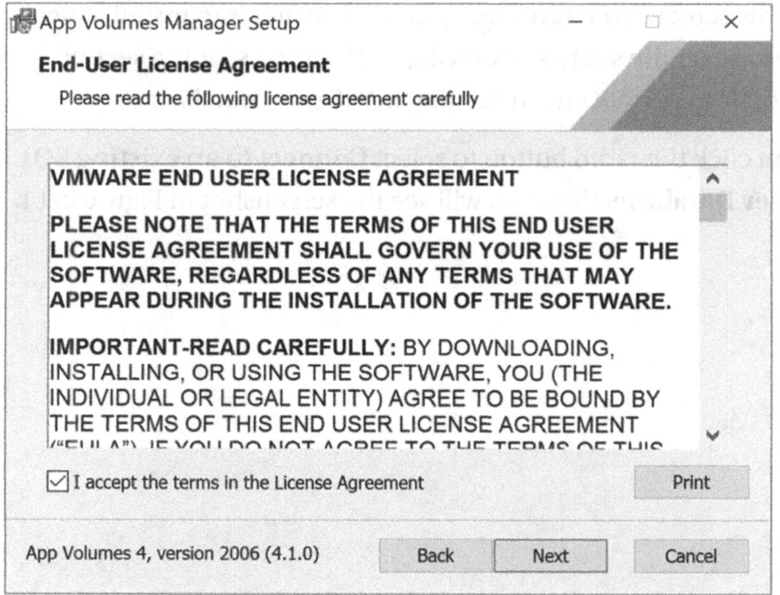

***Figure 2-12.** End-User License Agreement screen*

9. Check the box to accept the terms, and click **Next** to continue to the next screen for **Choose a Database** as shown in Figure 2-13.

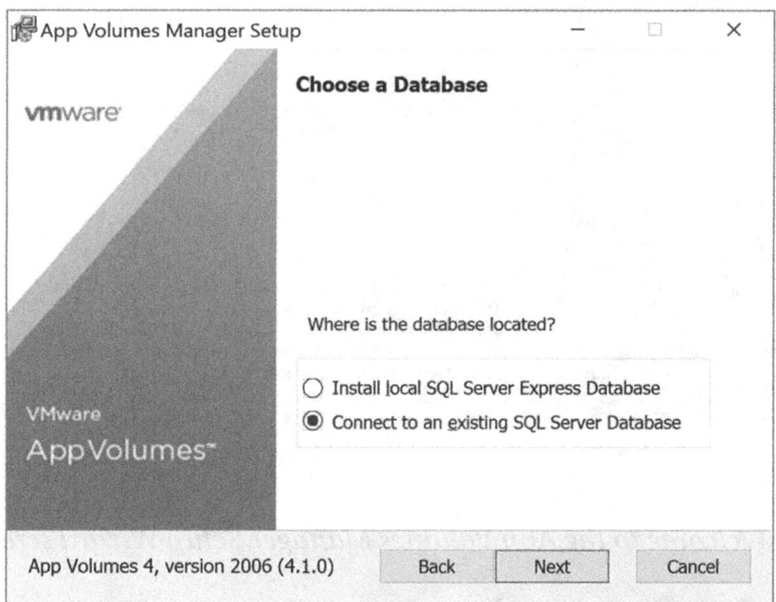

Figure 2-13. *Choose a Database screen*

10. On this screen, you have two options. The first is to install a local database on the same server using SQL Express, or the second option is to connect to an existing SQL Server database.

11. If you click the radio button to select **Connect to an existing SQL Server Database,** then you will see the screenshot in Figure 2-14.

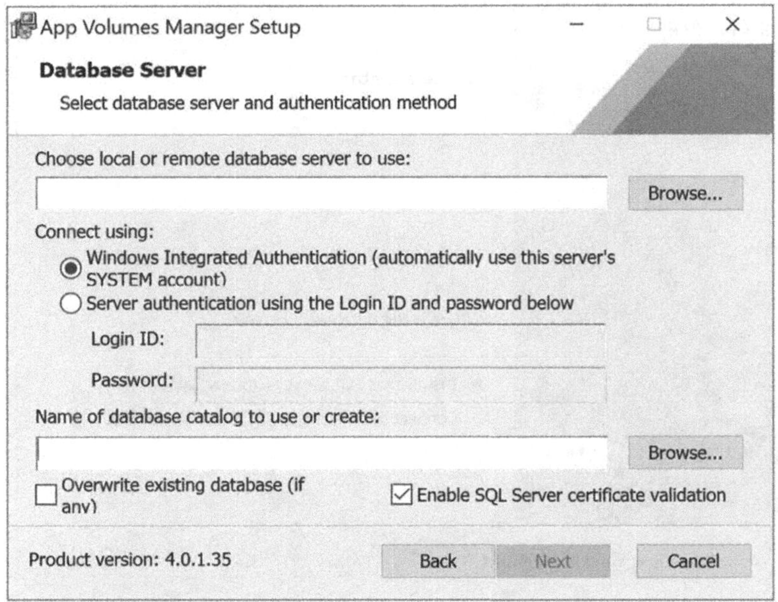

***Figure 2-14.** Configuring an existing SQL Server database*

12. On this screen, you can enter the details of the existing SQL Server database. You would use this option if you had created a new database for App Volumes on an existing SQL Server deployment, or if you uninstalled the App Volumes Manager software either due to upgrading your current version or you were adding additional App Volumes Manager servers.

13. In this example, we are building a test lab, so we are going to use the integrated SQL Server Express Database; so from the **Choose a Database** screen as shown previously, click the radio button to select **Install local SQL Server Express Database**.

14. This is shown in Figure 2-15.

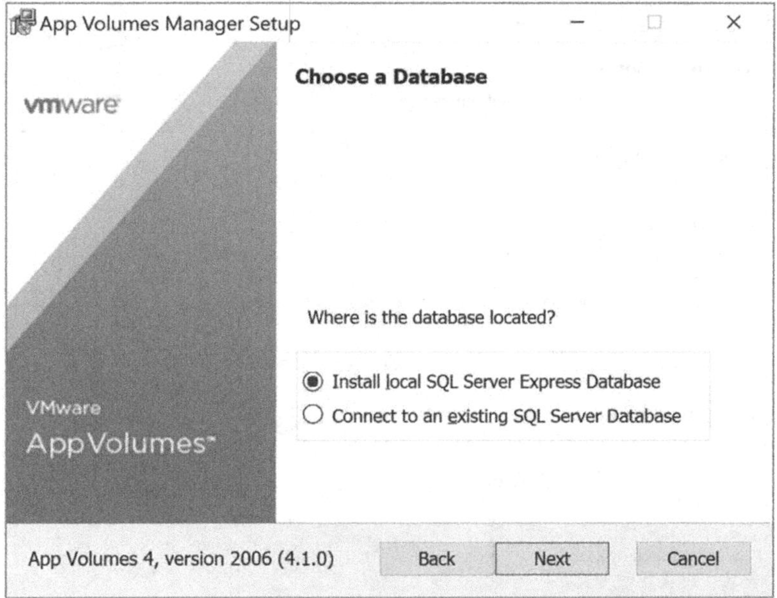

Figure 2-15. *Selecting the local SQL Server Express option*

15. Click the **Next** button to continue.

16. The installation of SQL Server Express will now start; however, be aware that you will not see the progress of this installation as there are no progress bars. Instead, you will see the standard Windows spinning wheel until SQL Server Express has completed and the next App Volumes installation screen is displayed.

17. When the installation has completed, you will see the screenshot in Figure 2-16.

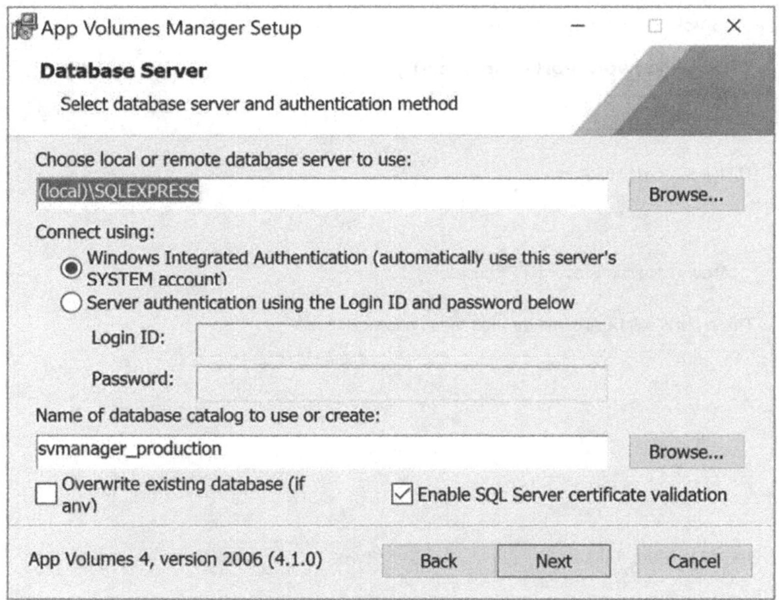

Figure 2-16. *SQL Server Express Database successfully installed*

18. On this screen, you also have a check box for Overwrite existing database. Be careful of this option if you are upgrading or installing an additional App Volumes Manager server as checking the box will delete the existing database and stop your App Volumes solution from working.

19. You are also able to Enable SQL Server certificate validation. This option is enabled by default as an additional level of security between the App Volumes Manager and the SQL Server database.

20. Click the **Next** button to continue the installation.

21. You will see the Choose Network Ports and Security options screen as shown in Figure 2-17.

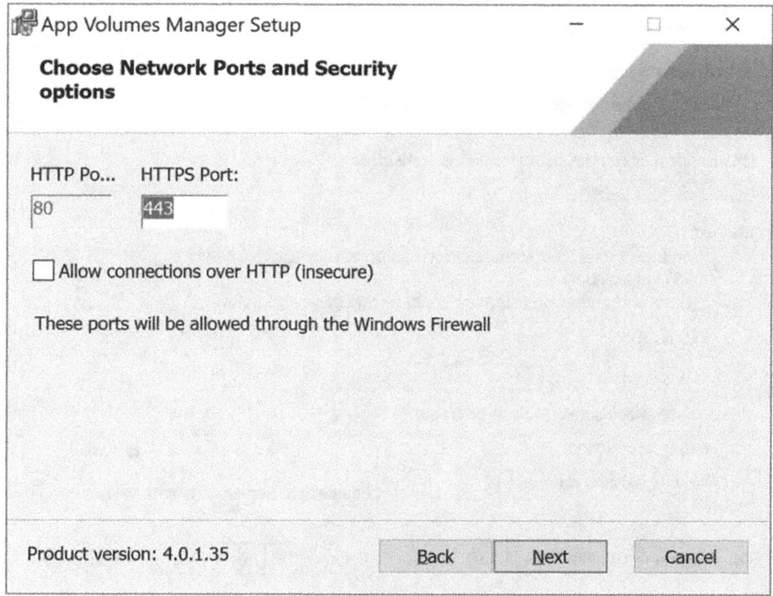

Figure 2-17. *Network ports and security configuration screen*

22. It is recommended to leave the HTTP and HTTPS ports as the default settings unless you really need to change them in your environment. If you change them, then make a note of what ports you are using as the App Volumes Agent will need to have the same port settings to enable communication between the two.
23. You also have the option to allow insecure connections over HTTP. These ports will automatically be configured to be allowed through your firewall.
24. Click the **Next** button to continue the installation.
25. The next screen you will see is the **Custom Setup** screen, as shown in Figure 2-18.

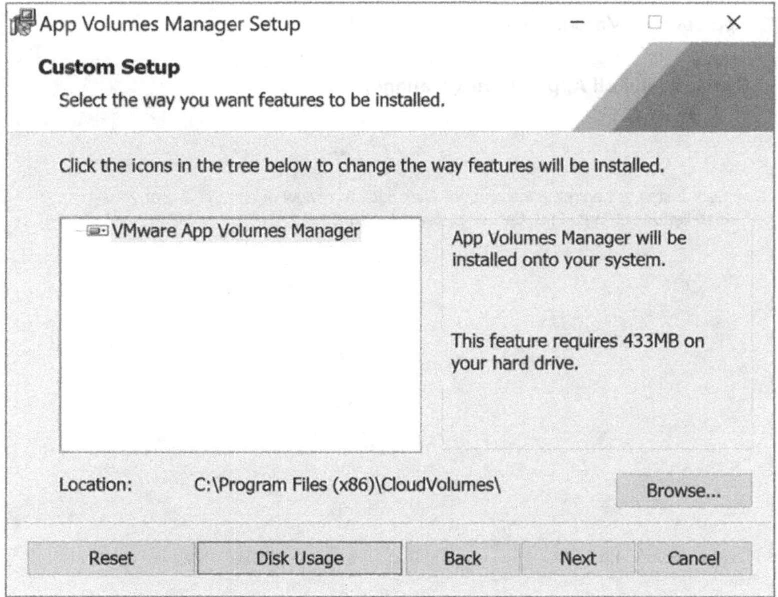

***Figure 2-18.** Custom Setup configuration screen*

26. On this configuration screen, you can choose which components to install. In this case, it is the App Volumes Manager. You can optionally change the installation location and check the disk usage.

27. Click **Next** to continue the installation.

28. You will see the **Ready to install App Volumes Manager** screen as shown in Figure 2-19.

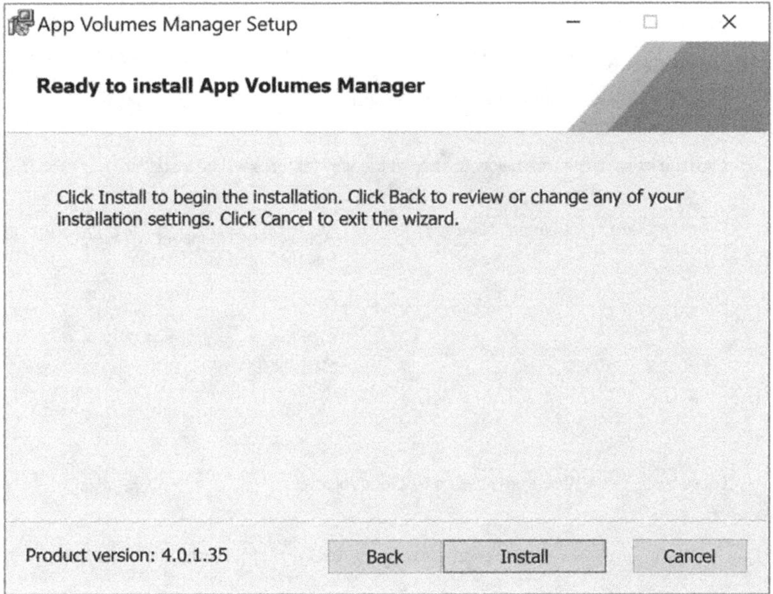

Figure 2-19. *Ready to install screen*

29. Click the **Install** button to start the installation. You will see the screen shown in Figure 2-20.

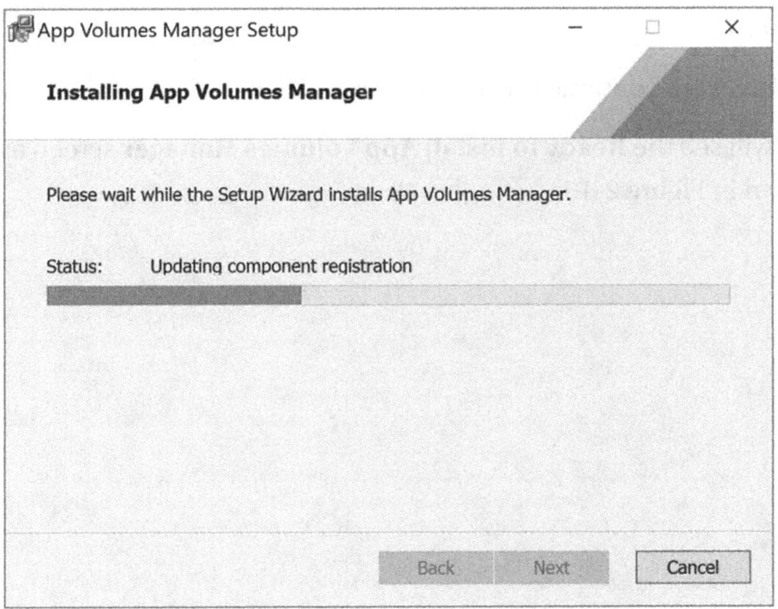

Figure 2-20. *Installing the App Volumes Manager*

Once the installation has successfully completed you will see the following screen shown in Figure 2-21.

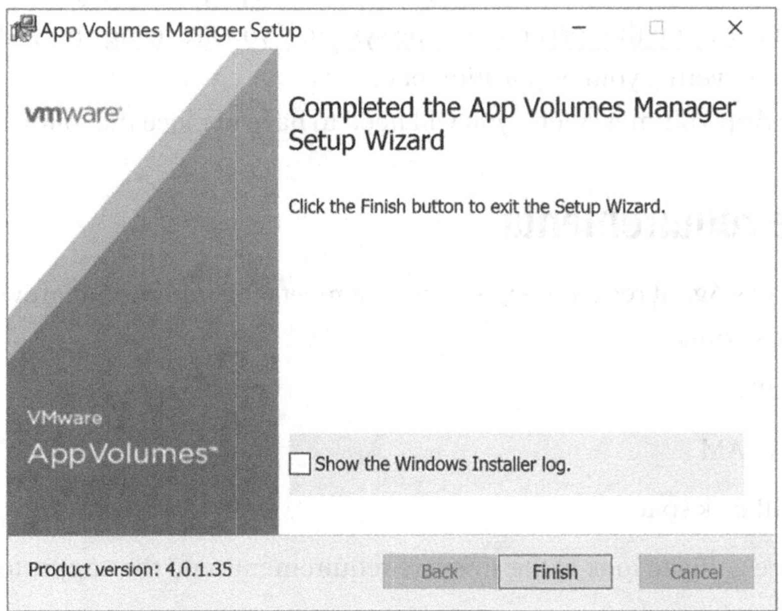

Figure 2-21. *Setup completed*

You will also see a desktop icon has been added as shown in Figure 2-22.

Figure 2-22. *App Volumes Manager desktop icon*

You have now successfully installed the App Volumes Manager software. The next stage of the installation process is to complete the initial configuration where you will configure the App Volumes Manager with details of your vSphere infrastructure and AD, to name a few options. We will complete this in the next chapter, Chapter 3.

Next, we are going to install the App Volumes Agent.

App Volumes Agent installation

The App Volumes Agent is installed on the virtual desktop operating system for delivery direct to end users or on the server operating system if you are using application publishing for delivering your application packages.

To run the App Volumes Agent, you will need to have in place the following.

Hardware requirements

The App Volumes Agent requires a machine that meets the minimum hardware spec as listed in the following.

- 1 vCPU
- 1 GB RAM
- 16 GB disk space

Next, we are going to look at the software requirements and the supported operating systems.

Software requirements

To run the App Volumes Agent, the virtual desktop machine or virtual server will need to be running one of the following operating systems.

Desktop operating system

- Microsoft Windows 10, version 2004 Enterprise and Pro
- Microsoft Windows 10 version 1909 Enterprise and Pro
- Microsoft Windows 10 version 1903 Enterprise and Pro
- Microsoft Windows 10 version 1809 Enterprise and Pro
- Microsoft Windows 10 version 1803 Enterprise and Pro
- Microsoft Windows 10 Enterprise LTSC 2019
- Microsoft Windows 7 SP1 Professional and Enterprise editions (Microsoft KB 3033929)

Server operating system

- Microsoft Windows Server 2019 Datacenter and Standard
- Microsoft Windows Server 2016 Datacenter and Standard
- 64-bit versions of OS are supported

With the prerequisites now in place, it is time to start the installation.

Installing the App Volumes Agent software

As with the installation of the App Volumes Manager, we are going to use a test lab environment to install the software and deploy App Volumes. This will enable you to see firsthand how to complete the installation tasks.

To this end, we have already built a Windows 10 virtual desktop machine, with the hostname of **WIN10-VDI**, ready to install the App Volumes Agent onto.

To install the software, follow the steps described:

1. Open a console to the virtual server named Appvol-4.
2. Navigate to the location where you downloaded the App Volumes software to. In the test lab, this was saved in a folder called App Volumes 4.1 as shown in Figure 2-23.

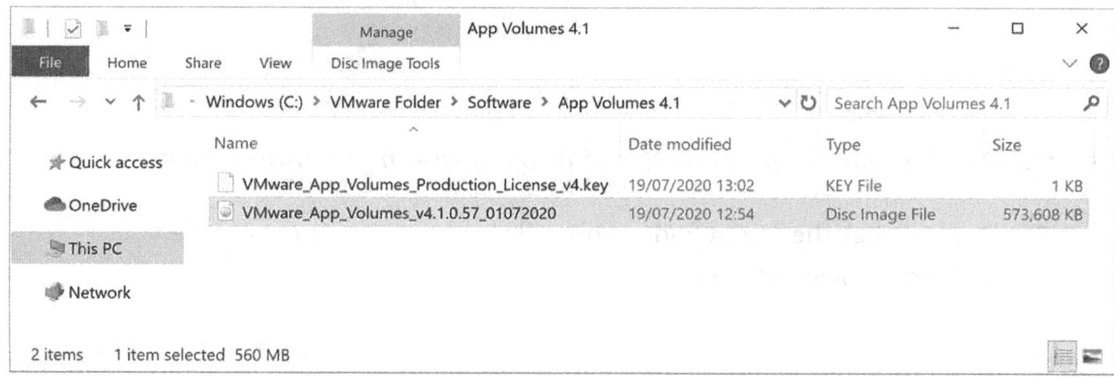

Figure 2-23. *VMware App Volumes software folder*

3. Double-click the **VMware_App_Volumes_v4.1.0.57_01072020.iso** file to mount the iso image. You will see the screenshot in Figure 2-24.

***Figure 2-24.** VMware App Volumes software iso image mounted*

4. Double-click to open the **Installation** folder. You will see the folders in Figure 2-25.

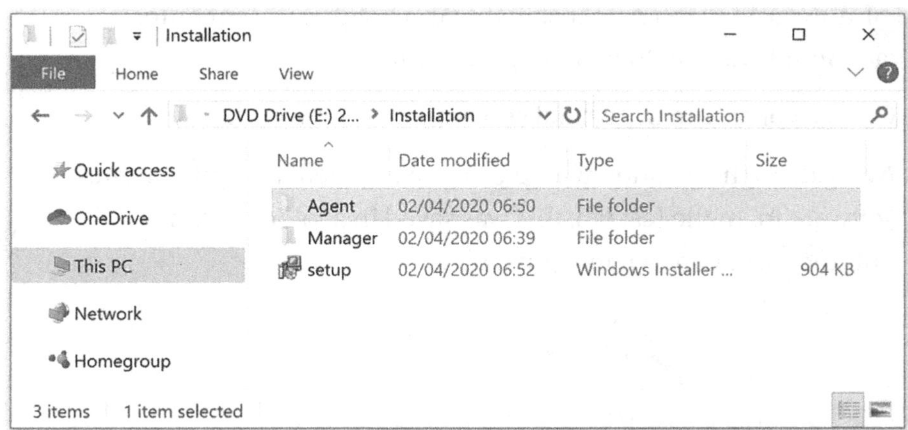

***Figure 2-25.** VMware App Volumes Agent software – installation folder*

5. Double-click the **Agent** folder. You will now see the contents of the folder as shown in Figure 2-26.

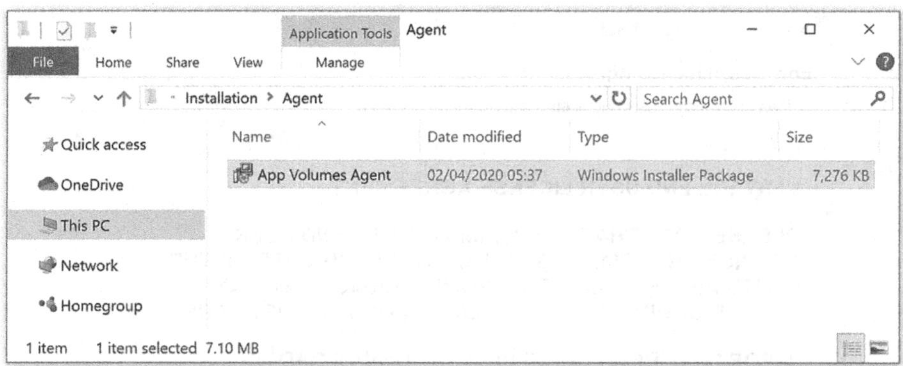

***Figure 2-26.** VMware App Volumes Agent installer*

6. Double-click **App Volumes Agent** to launch the installer. You will see the screenshot in Figure 2-27.

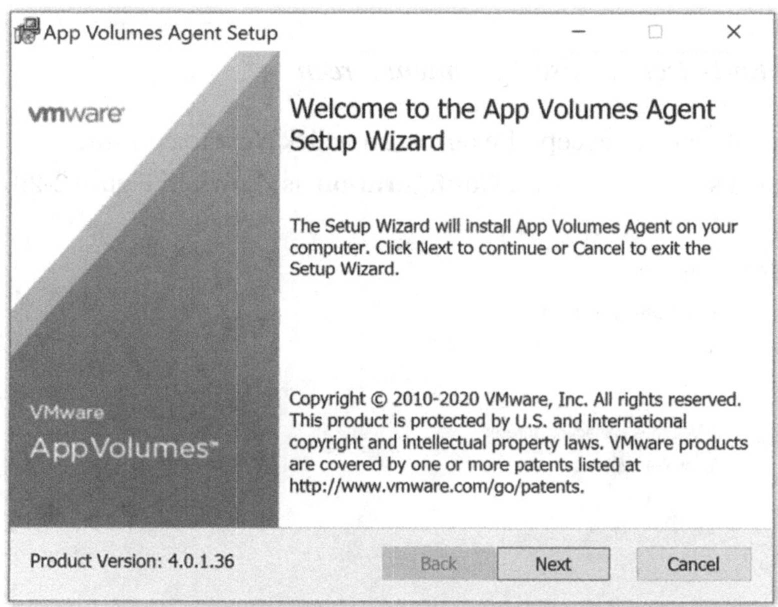

***Figure 2-27.** Welcome to the App Volumes Agent Setup Wizard*

7. Click the **Next** button to continue.

8. You will see the **End-User License Agreement** screen as shown in Figure 2-28.

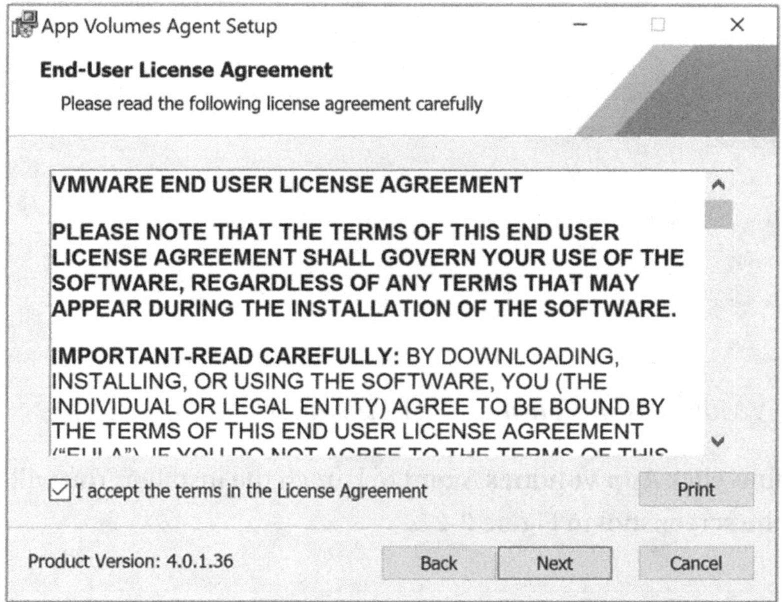

Figure 2-28. *End-User License Agreement screen*

9. Check the box to accept the terms, and click **Next** to continue to the next screen for **Server Configuration** as shown in Figure 2-29.

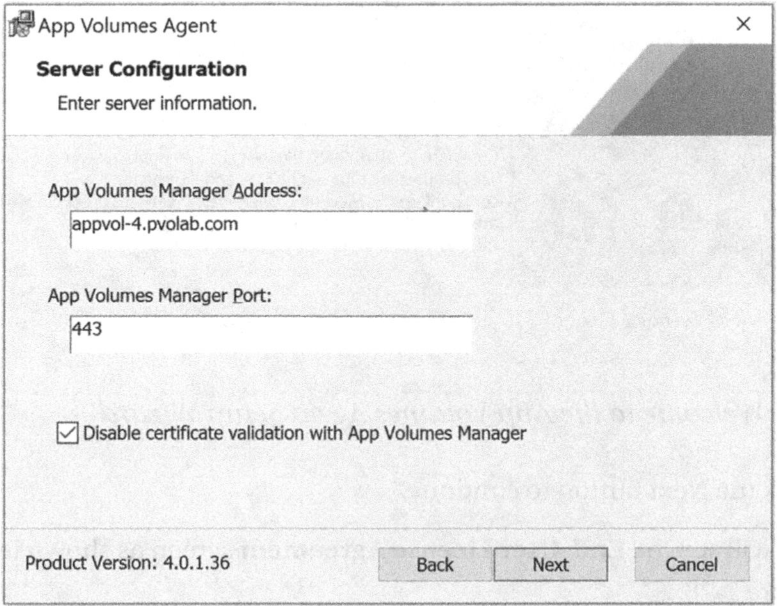

Figure 2-29. *End-User License Agreement screen*

10. In the **App Volumes Manager Address** box, enter the address to the App Volumes Manager. In the test lab, the address of the App Volumes Manager is **appvol-4.pvolab.com**. You could also use the IP address.

11. Leave the **App Volumes Manager Port** as **443** but ensure that this matches the port number you configured the App Volumes Manager with. If you changed the port number, then you will need to change the port number here too.

12. The final option on this screen is the check box to **Disable Certificate Validation with App Volumes Manager**. Check this box if you want to disable certificate checking. This is not recommended in a production environment, but is acceptable for a proof of concept or pilot.

13. Click the **Next** button to continue the installation. The next screen is the **Ready to install App Volumes Agent** as shown in Figure 2-30.

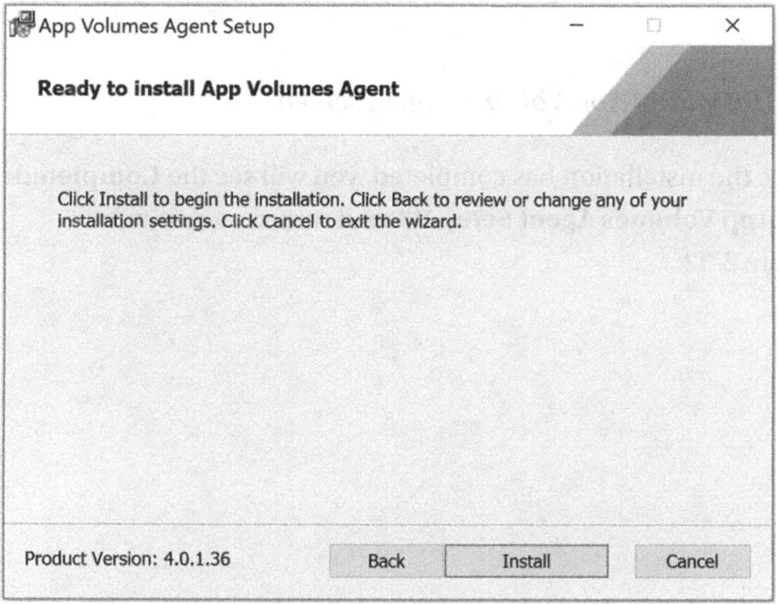

***Figure 2-30.** Ready to install App Volumes Agent screen*

14. Click the **Install** button to start the installation process.
15. You will now see the **Installing App Volumes Agent** screen showing the progress and the status of the installation (Figure 2-31).

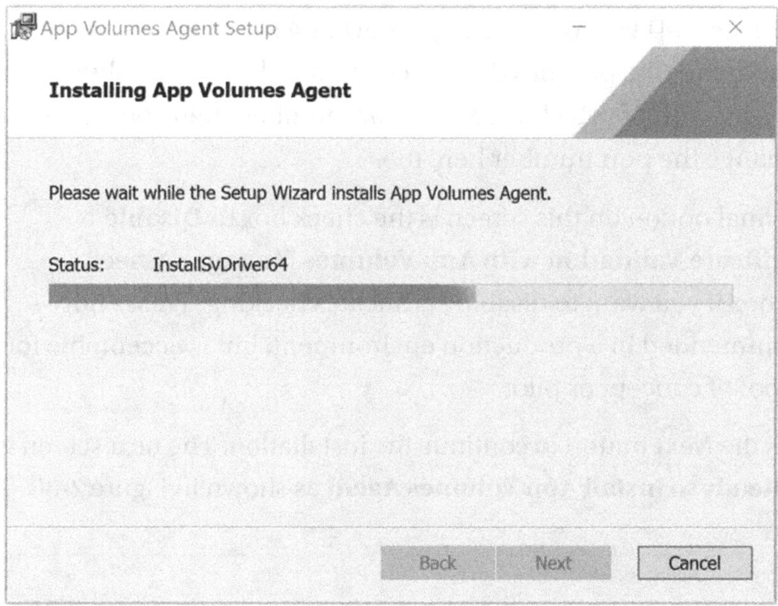

***Figure 2-31.** Installing App Volumes Agent screen*

16. Once the installation has completed, you will see the **Completed the App Volumes Agent Setup Wizard** screen as shown in Figure 2-32.

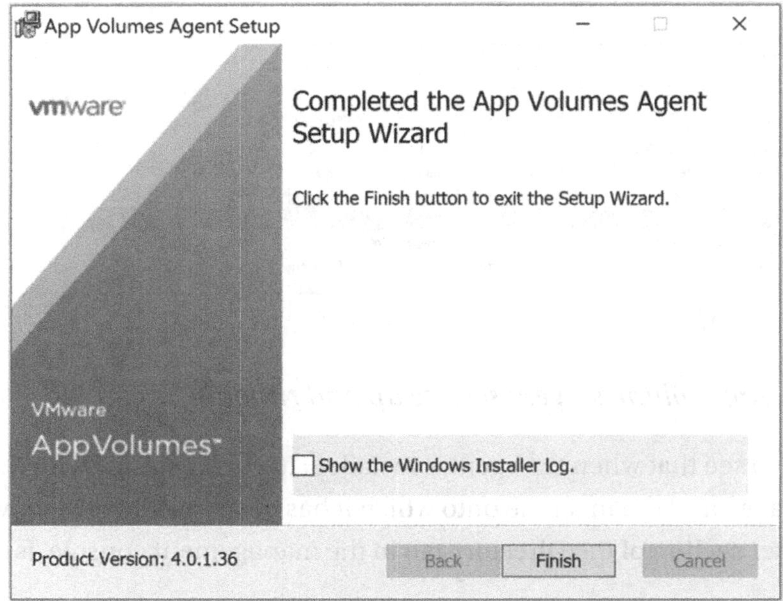

***Figure 2-32.** Completed the App Volumes Agent Setup Wizard screen*

17. Click the **Finish** button to complete the installation.
18. You will now be prompted to restart the system as shown in Figure 2-33.

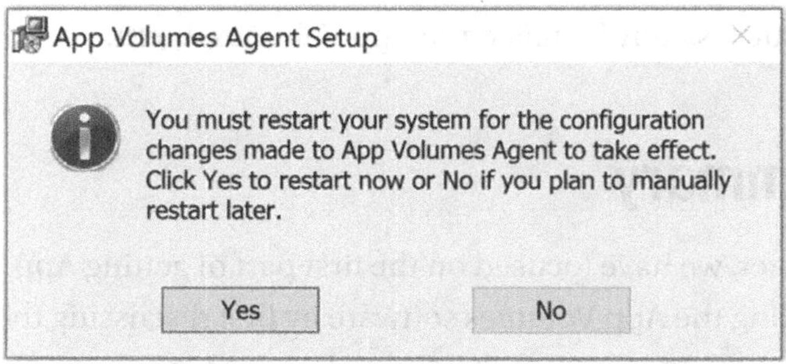

***Figure 2-33.** Restarting the App Volumes Agent*

19. Click **Yes** to restart.
20. Once the machine has restarted, as this is just the App Volumes Agent, then there is no desktop icon. To check whether the agent has installed and is running, you will need to look in the Windows Service console as shown in Figure 2-34.

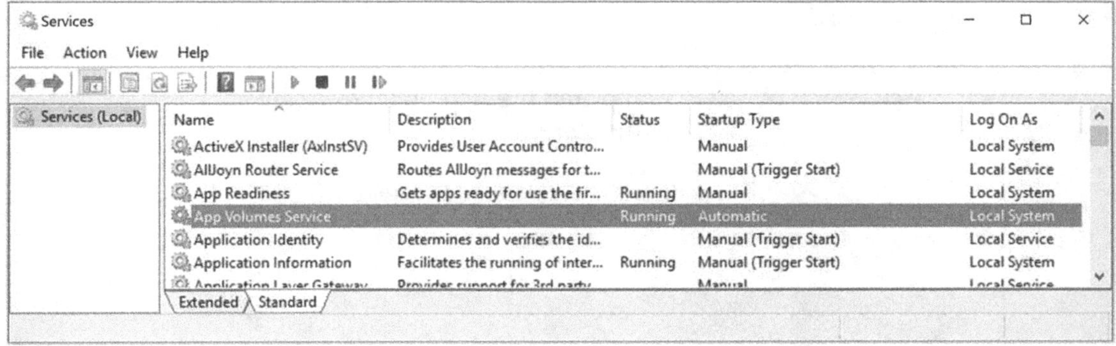

***Figure 2-34.** App Volumes Agent service up and running*

You will also see that when the agent is installed, it will "check in" with the App Volumes Manager, and the machine onto which it has been installed will now appear in the Computer section of the Directory tab in the management console as shown in Figure 2-35.

Computer	Agent	OS	🖫	🔗	⇄	⏻	Last Boot	Status
PVOLAB\WIN10-VDI$	4.0.1.35R	Desktop	0	0	0	5	Jul 13 2020 01:57PM	Enabled

Showing 1 to 1 of 1 computers — First Previous 1 Next Last

***Figure 2-35.** App Volumes Agent registered with the App Volumes Manager*

You have now successfully installed the App Volumes Agent.

Chapter summary

In this second chapter, we have focused on the first part of getting App Volumes deployed, by installing the App Volumes software by first discussing the prerequisites and requirements and then installing the App Volumes Manager and the App Volumes Agent components.

The installation was demonstrated by using step-by-step screenshots as we worked through the process using the test lab.

In the next chapter, we are going to look at the second part of the installation process by working through the initial configuration tasks followed by a guided tour of the App Volumes management console.

CHAPTER 3

Completing the Initial Configuration

In the previous chapter of this book, Chapter 2, we focused on installing the component parts of the App Volumes solution, namely, the App Volumes Agent and the App Volumes Manager.

Although we completed the installation of the App Volumes Manager, there are a few more things to complete before you can start to deploy your application packages. You need to configure the App Volumes Manager with things such as licensing, Active Directory connection, and virtual infrastructure.

In this chapter, we are going to complete those initial configuration tasks and then give you a brief walk around the console to familiarize yourself with the menus and where to find things.

We will start by looking at how to access the management console and what you need to do that.

Accessing the App Volumes Manager console

The App Volumes Manager management console is a web-based console. You can launch it from the desktop of the App Volumes Manager by double-clicking the App Volumes Manager icon. This will launch a browser and the console.

You can also do this from a remote desktop PC, such as an administrator's desktop. To do this, you would open a browser and enter the address of the App Volumes Manager server. For example, `https://appvol-4/` would be the address of the App Volumes Manager in the test lab.

P. von Oven, *Delivering Applications with VMware App Volumes 4*,
https://doi.org/10.1007/978-1-4842-6689-2_3

Supported browsers

The following browsers support running the App Volumes Manager console:

- Internet Explorer 9 or later
- Mozilla Firefox 28 or later
- Safari 7 or later
- Google Chrome 21 or later

Launching the management console for the first time

You can now launch the management console for the first time. In the test lab, we are going to do this directly from the App Volumes Manager itself, by double-clicking the desktop icon.

As this is the first time you have logged in, and the initial configuration has not been completed, you will be prompted for a username and password to access the management console.

You will see the **Welcome to App Volumes Manager** screen as shown in Figure 3-1.

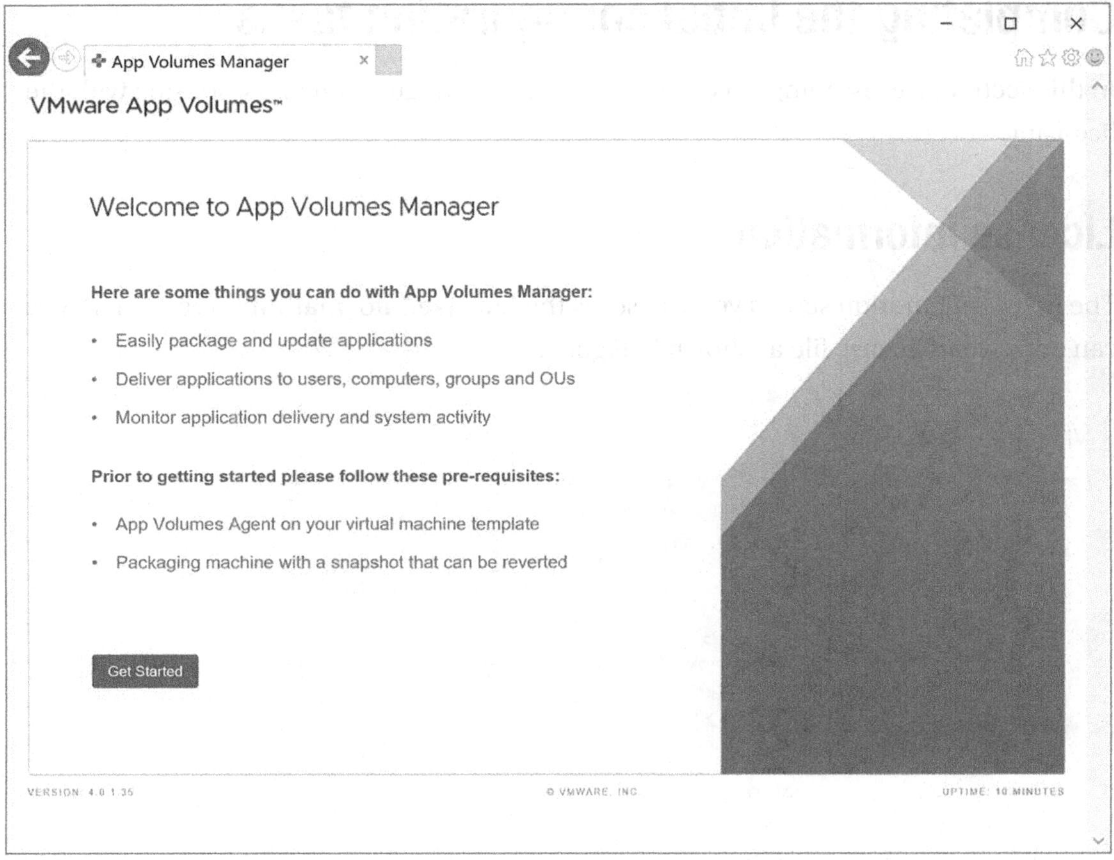

Figure 3-1. *Welcome to App Volumes Manager screen*

On the welcome screen, you will see that it lists some of the solution highlights as well as a couple of prerequisites. These are to have the App Volumes Agent installed on your virtual desktop machine template, which we will cover later in this book. It also mentions the need for a packaging machine which is to be used to create your application packages.

To start the initial configuration, click the **Get Started** button. We are now going to work through the initial configuration tasks.

Completing the initial configuration tasks

In this section, we are going to complete the initial configuration tasks, starting with the licensing.

License Information

The first configuration screen you will see is the **License Information** screen where you can add a valid license file as shown in Figure 3-2.

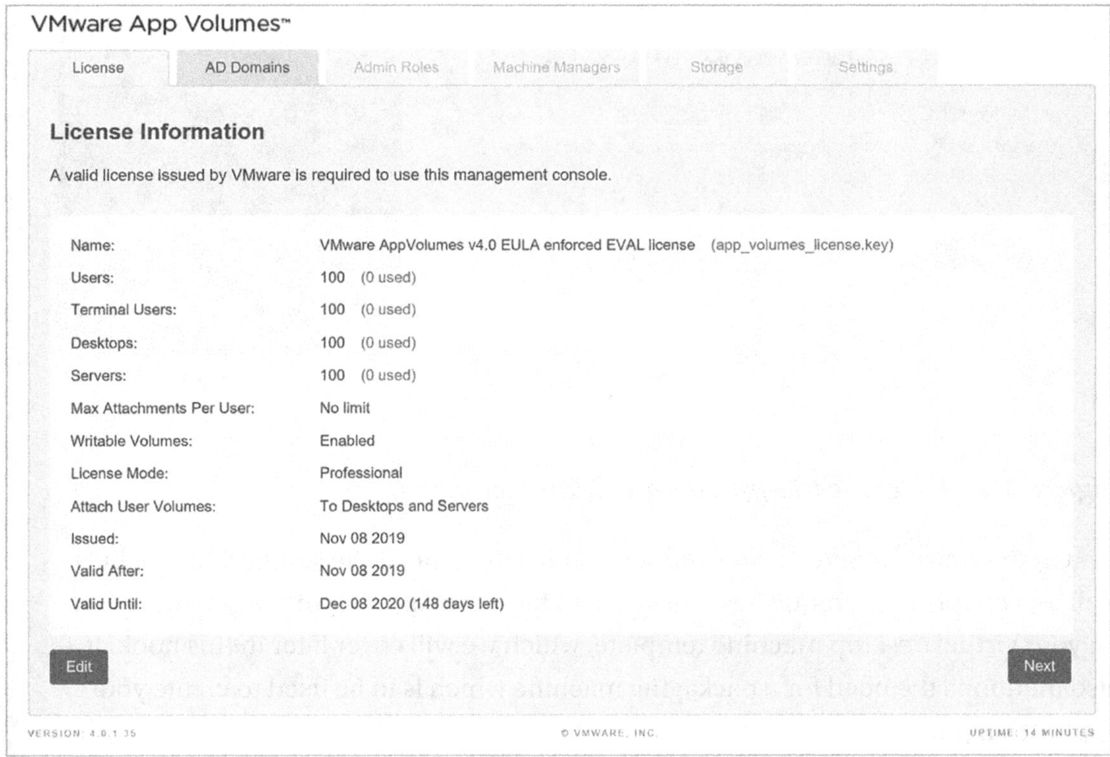

***Figure 3-2.** License Information screen*

As you can see from the screenshot, App Volumes ships with an evaluation license already, for 100 users. However, we are going to look at how to add your own license. To do this, follow the steps described:

1. Click the **Edit** button on the License Information screen.
2. You will see the screen in Figure 3-3.

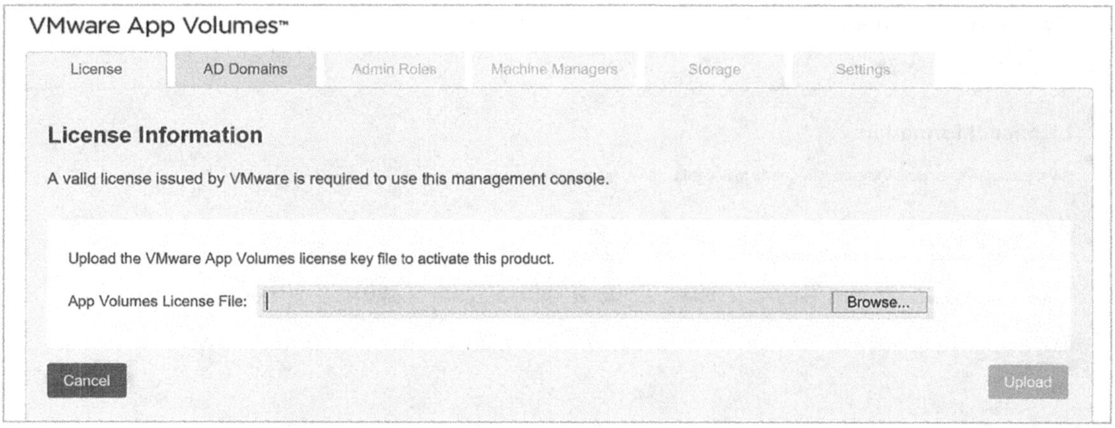

***Figure 3-3.** Uploading a new license key*

3. If you know the path of the license file you want to add, then you can type that directly into the **App Volumes License File** box. If not, then click the **Browse...** button to search for it as in this example in Figure 3-4.

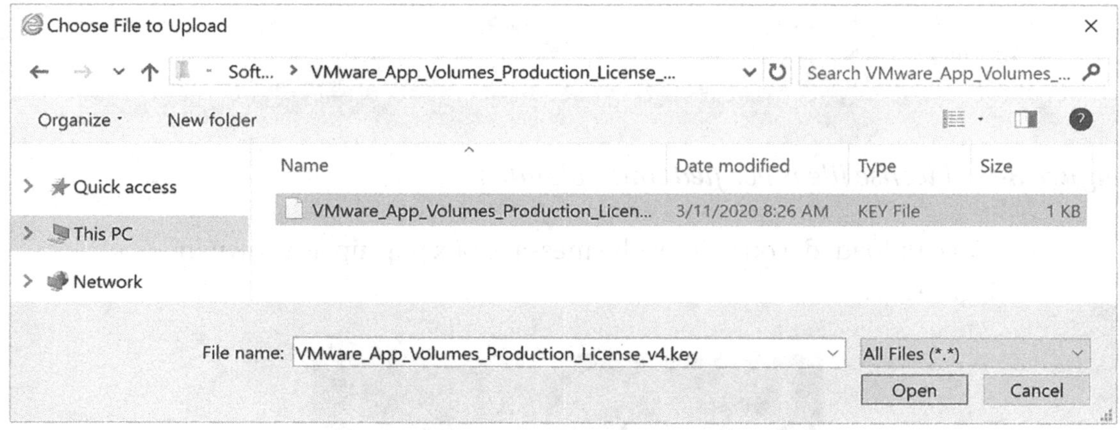

***Figure 3-4.** Choosing a new license key*

4. Click and select the license file you want to use and then click the **Open** button.

5. You will now see that the license file you selected has been added to the **App Volumes License File** box as shown in Figure 3-5.

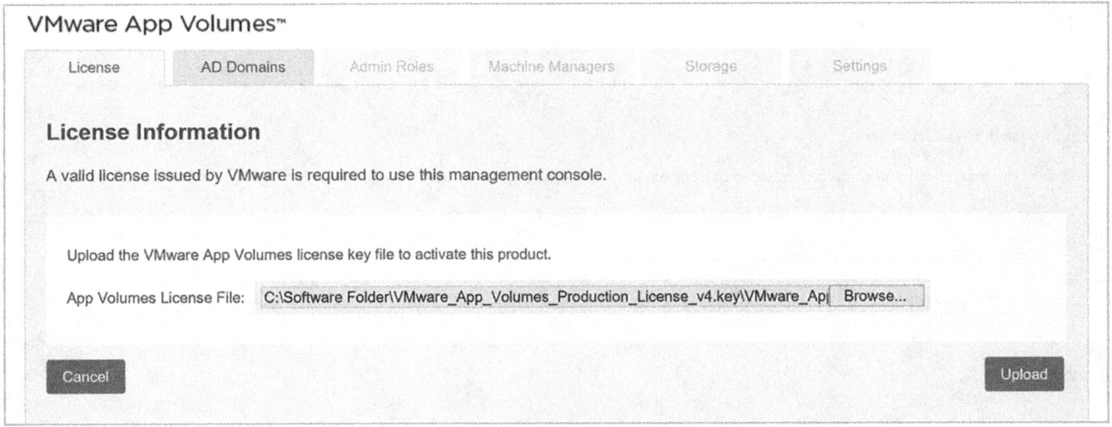

***Figure 3-5.** New license file selected*

6. Click the **Upload** button to upload the license file to your App Volumes Manager.
7. You will see the **Verifying License...** progress bar as shown in Figure 3-6.

***Figure 3-6.** License file is verified and uploaded*

8. Once uploaded, you will see the message box pop-up as shown in Figure 3-7.

***Figure 3-7.** License file successfully applied*

9. You will also return to the main **License Information** screen as shown in Figure 3-8.

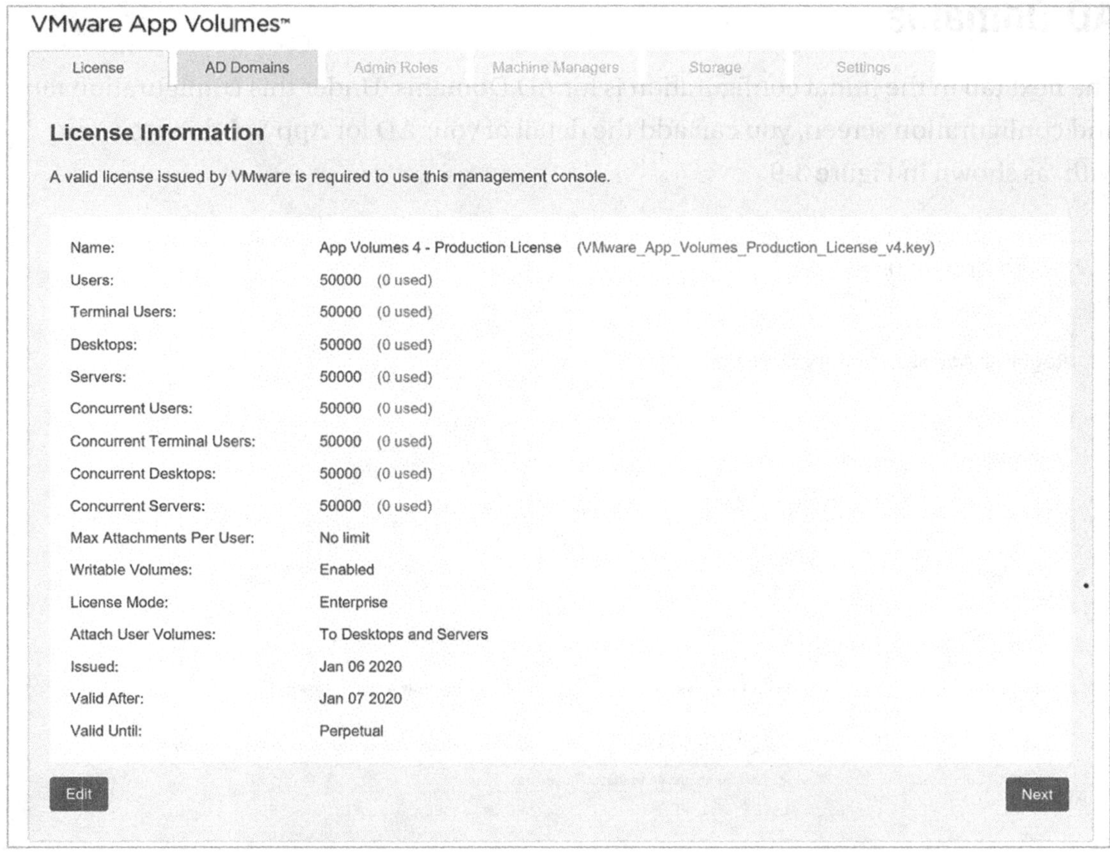

Figure 3-8. *License Information screen showing new license*

10. You will see from the license file that you have licenses for 50,000 users for attaching application packages to desktops, servers (RDSH), and terminal users. You can also see that the number of attachments per user has no limit and that Writable Volumes are also available.

11. Once you have uploaded your license, click the **Next** button to continue.

With the licensing configured, the next task is to configure the App Volumes Manager to work with your Active Directory.

AD Domains

The next tab in the initial configuration is for AD Domains. Under this configuration tab and configuration screen, you can add the detail of your AD for App Volumes to work with, as shown in Figure 3-9.

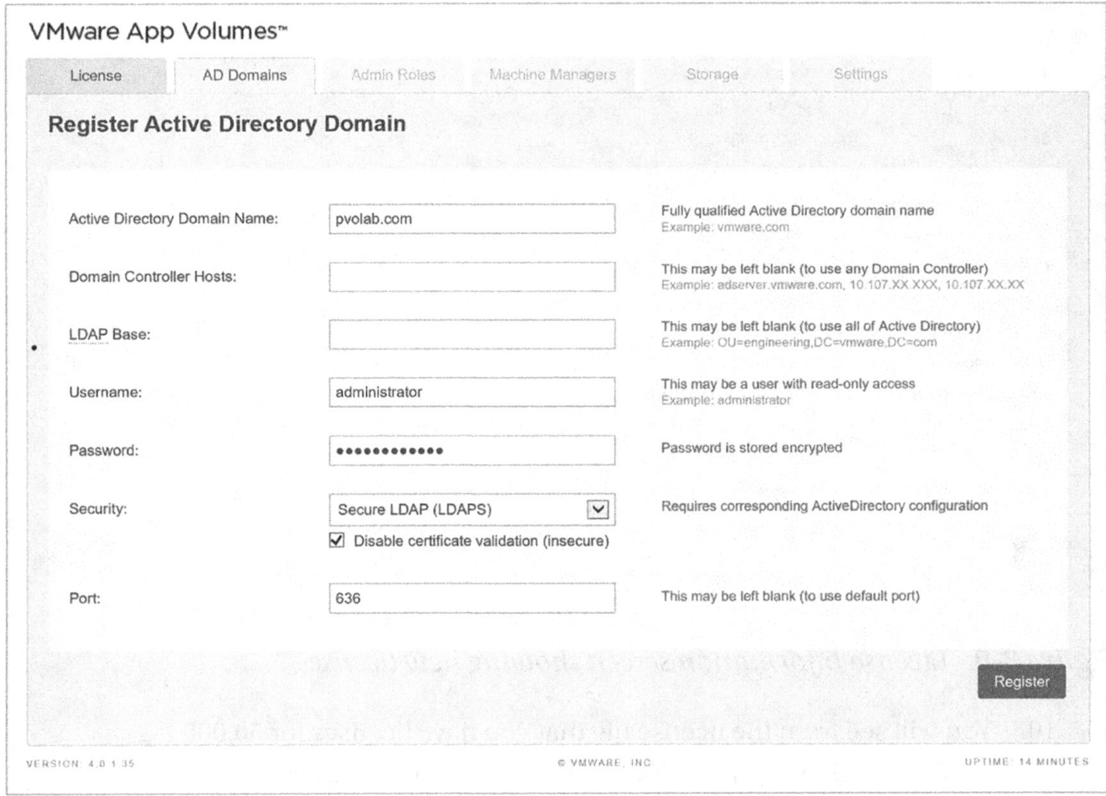

***Figure 3-9.** Register Active Directory Domain screen*

We are going to configure this screen using the following information:

12. In the **Active Directory Domain Name** box, type in the fully qualified name of your domain. This is the domain that contains all your user and computer accounts that will be used in your App Volumes environment. In our example, the domain is called pvolab.com. Don't forget that you will need to enter this as a fully qualified domain name.

13. Next, in the **Domain Controller Hosts** box, you can enter the details of any domain controllers you want to use. If you want to use all available Domain Controllers in your environment, then leave this field blank. If you want to only use a specific Domain Controller, then enter the details of that Domain Controller in the box. Again, if using the server name, then remember to use the fully qualified domain. Alternatively, you can use the IP address of the domain controller instead. In the test lab, we will leave this field blank so we can use any domain controllers.

14. Configuring the **LDAP Base** is the next configuration option. This allows you to configure a specific Organizational Unit (OU) for reading user, group, and machine information from Active Directory. For example, if you had a separate OU for the finance department, and only wanted to use AD objects within that OU, you could add something like the following: **OU=finance,DC=pvolab,DC=com**. This would mean that only those users, groups, and machines within the finance OU and downward would be available to use. Leaving this field blank means that the whole of AD would be used, so all OUs, and if you have a large number of OUs, this couple take an extended amount of time to complete the search.

15. The **Username** box is for you to enter the name of a user that has access to Active Directory so that App Volumes can read the information required. In the test lab, we have used the administrator account, but you can set up your own account for this. If you do, then it is worth remembering that this account only requires read access to Active Directory. It does not need write permissions. It is also worth using an account that does not have its password updated on a regular basis as doing so will mean that you must update your App Volumes configuration each time the password changes.

16. In the following **Password** box, enter the password for the account name you used for the Active Directory username. So, in our test lab example, we would use the administrator password. For the security-conscious organizations, this password is encrypted when stored in the App Volumes Manager.

17. In the penultimate box, you can configure the **Security** level. You will see that there is a drop-down box with three different options to choose from. These options are as follows:

    a. **Secure LDAP (LDAPS)**: Allows you to connect to Active Directory over SSL.

    b. **LDAP over TLS**: Allows you to connect to Active Directory over LDAP using TLS. To use this method, you will need to install a trusted certificate from a certificate authority (CA).

    c. **LDAP (Insecure)**: Allows an insecure connection to Active Directory.

18. When selecting the security option, you need to ensure that this corresponds with your Active Directory configuration. You will also see under the drop-down box that there is a tick box for **Disable certificate validation (insecure)**. Check this box if you want to turn off certificate validation, but remember this means the connection to Active Directory will be insecure.

19. The final option is to configure the **Port** setting through which the App Volumes Manager communicates with your Active Directory and domain controllers. The default port of 636 is added automatically, but if you have configured a different port, then change this accordingly so that it matches.

20. When you have added all the information on this screen, then click the **Register** button to register your App Volumes Manager with Active Directory. As the registration process completes, you will see the progress bar appear (Figure 3-10).

***Figure 3-10.** Registering Domain progress screen*

21. On completion, you will see the **Active Directory Domains** page as shown in Figure 3-11.

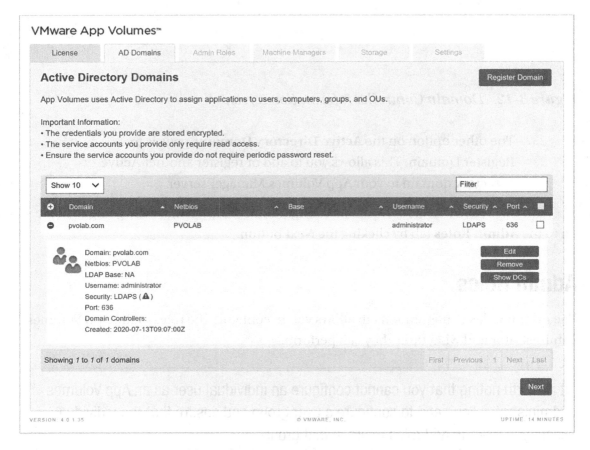

***Figure 3-11.** Configured Active Directory Domain information*

22. As well as displaying the information that you configured, you also have a few additional options. You can edit the current configuration, remove the currently configured domain information, or show DCs as you will see in the screenshot in Figure 3-12.

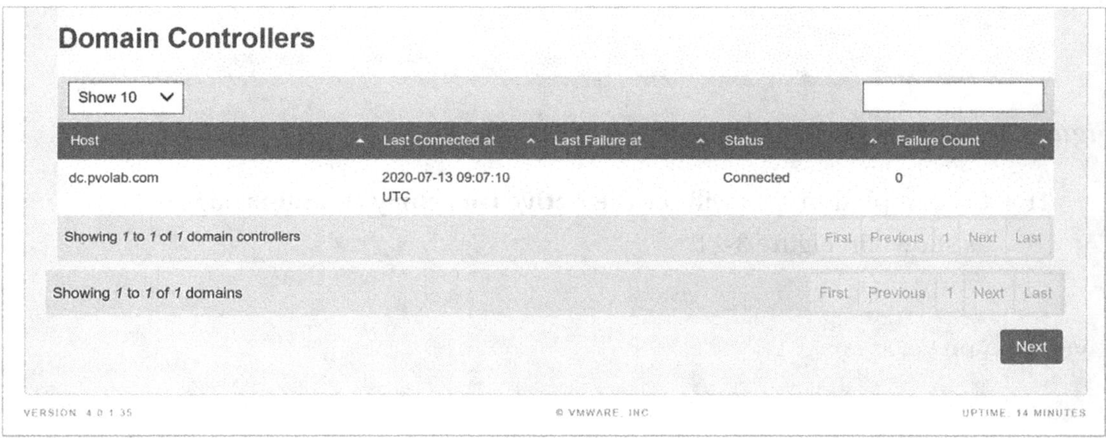

Figure 3-12. *Domain Controller information screen*

23. The other option on the **Active Directory Domains** page is to Register Domain. This allows you to add or register another Active Directory domain to your App Volumes Manager server.

With the Active Directory Domains configuration completed, we are going to move on to the **Admin Roles** tab by clicking the **Next** button.

Admin Roles

The Admin Roles configuration tab allows you to configure the roles of the App Volumes administrator and what tasks they can perform.

It is worth noting that you cannot configure an individual user as an App Volumes administrator. You need to configure a user group and ensure that the individual users you want to add roles to are in that group.

To configure administrator roles, complete the following steps:

1. From the **Roles** drop-down box, select the **Administrators** role from the list of options. You can choose from the listed roles in Figure 3-13.

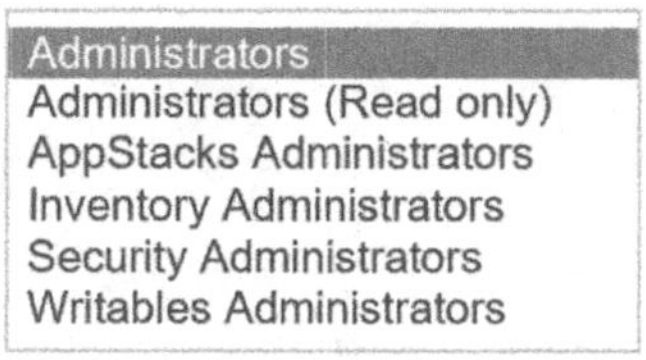

Administrators
Administrators (Read only)
AppStacks Administrators
Inventory Administrators
Security Administrators
Writables Administrators

Figure 3-13. *App Volumes Administrator roles*

2. Next, in the **Search Domain** drop-down menu, select the domain in which you want to search. In the test lab example, we have selected the option for **All**. This means that all the domains that are currently registered with the App Volumes Manager will be searched. Alternatively, if you know which particular domain you want to search, and it is registered with the App Volumes Manager, you can select the domain directly from the drop-down menu.

3. Next is the **Search Groups** box. This box is a filter to help you find the groups you want to assign the role to. Type in just the first few characters of the name of the group you want to search for. Then, from the drop-down menu next to where you have typed the group name, you can select an additional filter for the search. The filtered search options are **Contains**, **Begins**, **Ends**, or **Equals** the name you entered. In the test lab, we are going to type **admi** to search for the administrators' group in Active Directory, and we are going to select the **Contains** option from the additional filter drop-down menu. You also have the option to search all domains in the forest by checking the **Search all domains in the Active Directory Forest** box.

4. Now click the **Search** button.

5. The results will appear in the **Choose Group** box. If you click the drop-down menu, then the results of your search are displayed. You can then choose the correct group. In the test lab, you will see the option for **PVOLAB\Administrators** is listed.

6. Once you have selected the correct group you want to use, you will see the screenshot in Figure 3-14.

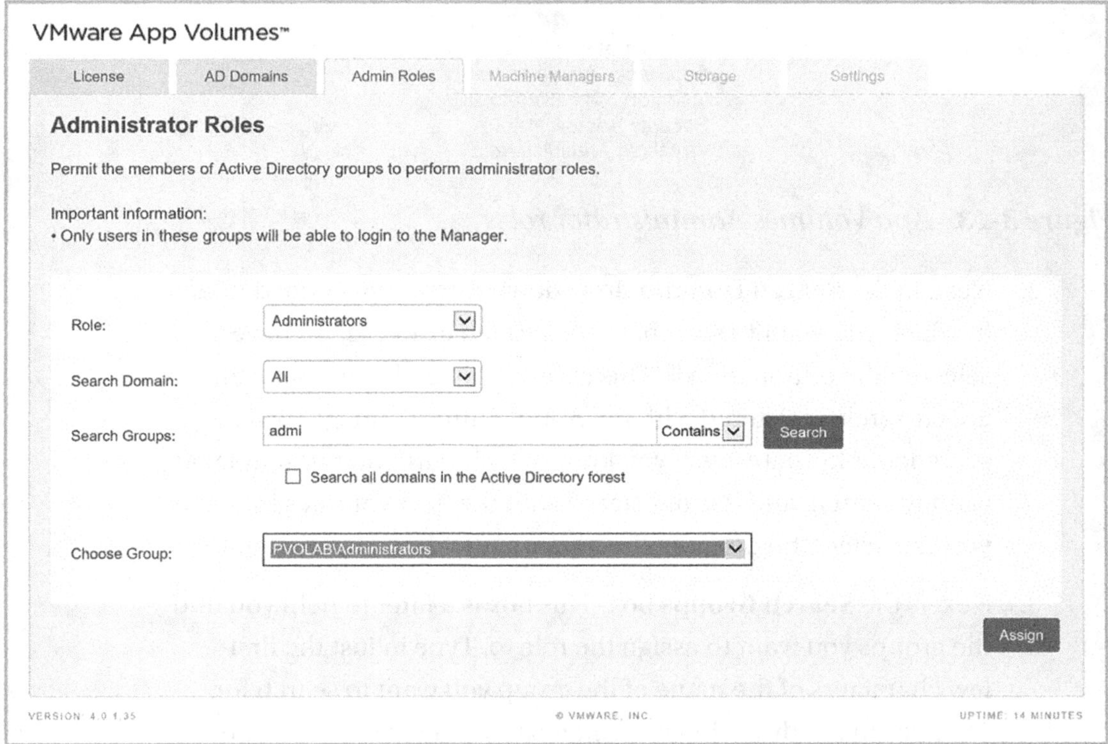

***Figure 3-14.** Configuring the administrator roles*

7. Click the **Assign** button.
8. You will see the **Assigning Administrators Role** progress bar as shown in Figure 3-15.

***Figure 3-15.** Administrator roles being assigned*

9. Once successfully assigned, you will see the message pop-up as shown in Figure 3-16.

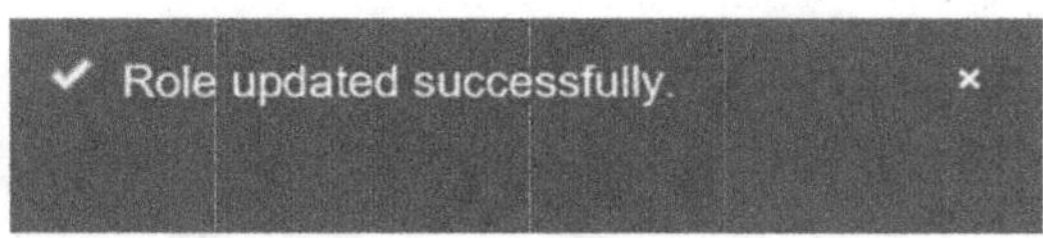

Figure 3-16. Administrator roles successfully assigned

10. Having added the administrator's role successfully, you will see the screenshot in Figure 3-17.

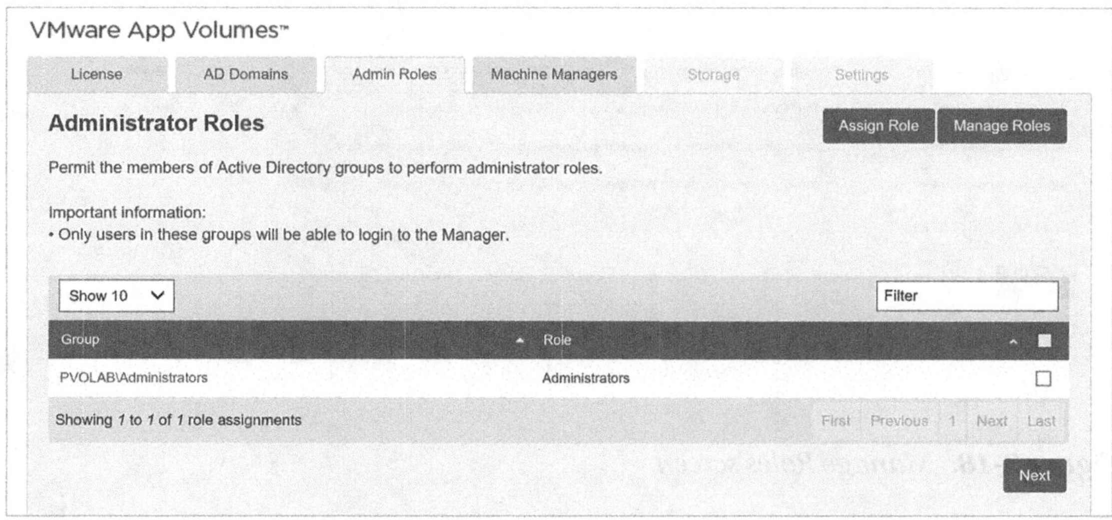

Figure 3-17. Administrator Roles summary screen

Figure 3-17 shows which group has been added and the role that group has been assigned. In the test lab example, you can see from the screenshot that the administrator's group in Active Directory has been assigned the administrators role.

Also, on this screen, you have two other configuration options. You can click the **Assign Role** button which will take you back to the previous configuration screen where you can then add another role, or by clicking the **Manage Role** button, you can customize the roles as shown in Figure 3-18.

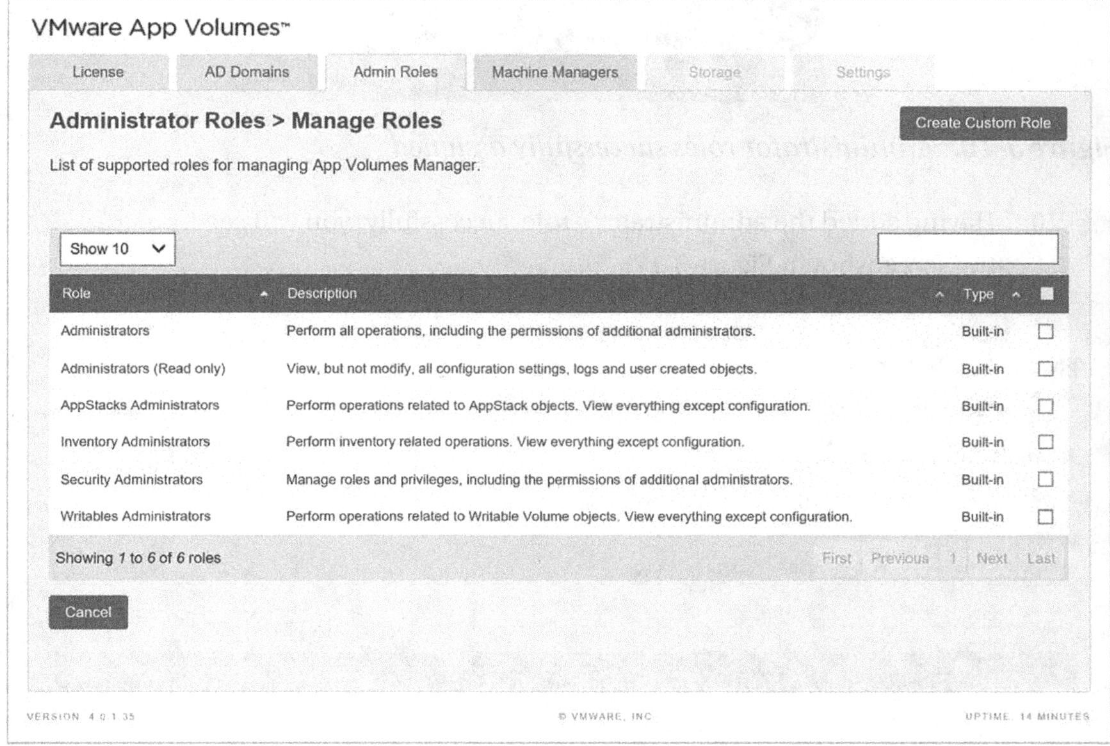

Figure 3-18. *Manage Roles screen*

To create your own custom role, complete the following steps:

1. Click the **Create Custom Role** button.
2. In the **Name** box, give the role a name. In this example, we have just called the new role **Test**.
3. Next is the **Description** box. In this box, you can enter a description for this new role. In this example, we have just called it **Test role**. Although optional, it's worth adding a good description, so you know exactly what this role is for.
4. The last thing to configure on this screen is the **Privileges** you want to assign to your new role. In the test lab, we have added the **Directory** privileges to the Test role as shown in Figure 3-19.

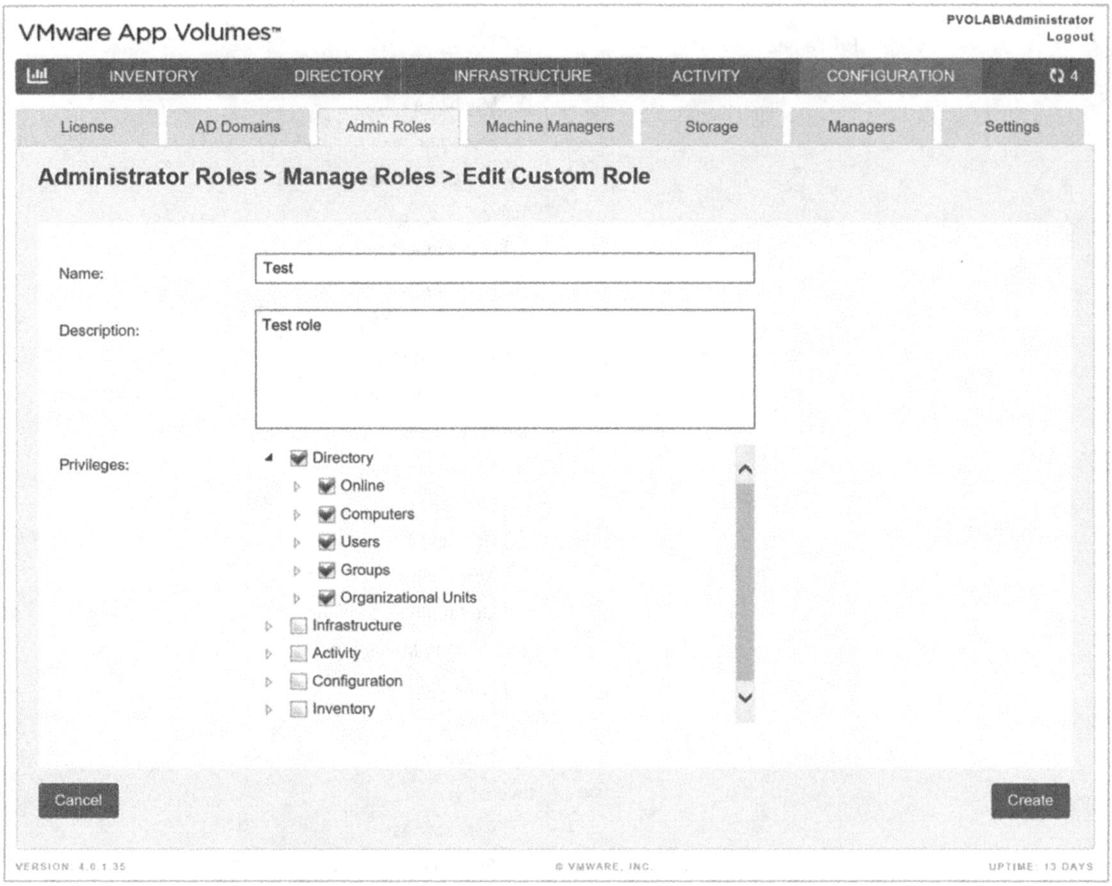

Figure 3-19. Edit Custom Role screen

5. If you expand each heading by clicking the arrow next to each privilege listed, you will see all the available options. In Figure 3-19, we have expanded the **Directory** option to show the options for this set of privileges.

6. Scroll through all the options adding the privileges you want to include in this role. Figure 3-20 shows all the available options.

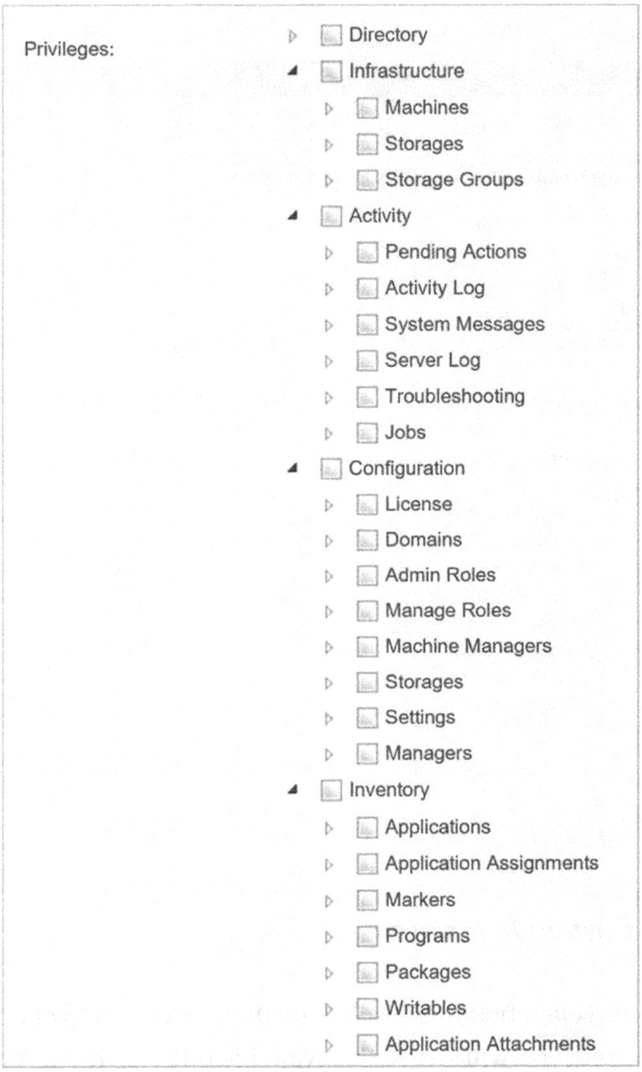

Privileges:

- Directory
- Infrastructure
  - Machines
  - Storages
  - Storage Groups
- Activity
  - Pending Actions
  - Activity Log
  - System Messages
  - Server Log
  - Troubleshooting
  - Jobs
- Configuration
  - License
  - Domains
  - Admin Roles
  - Manage Roles
  - Machine Managers
  - Storages
  - Settings
  - Managers
- Inventory
  - Applications
  - Application Assignments
  - Markers
  - Programs
  - Packages
  - Writables
  - Application Attachments

Figure 3-20. *Configurable privileges for the custom role*

7. When you have finished adding the privileges to your new custom role, click the **Create** button.

8. You will now see the **Adding new role** progress bar as shown in Figure 3-21.

Adding new Role - Test

Figure 3-21. *Adding the new custom role*

9. With the new custom role created and the **Admin Roles** section successfully configured, you will see the screenshot in Figure 3-22.

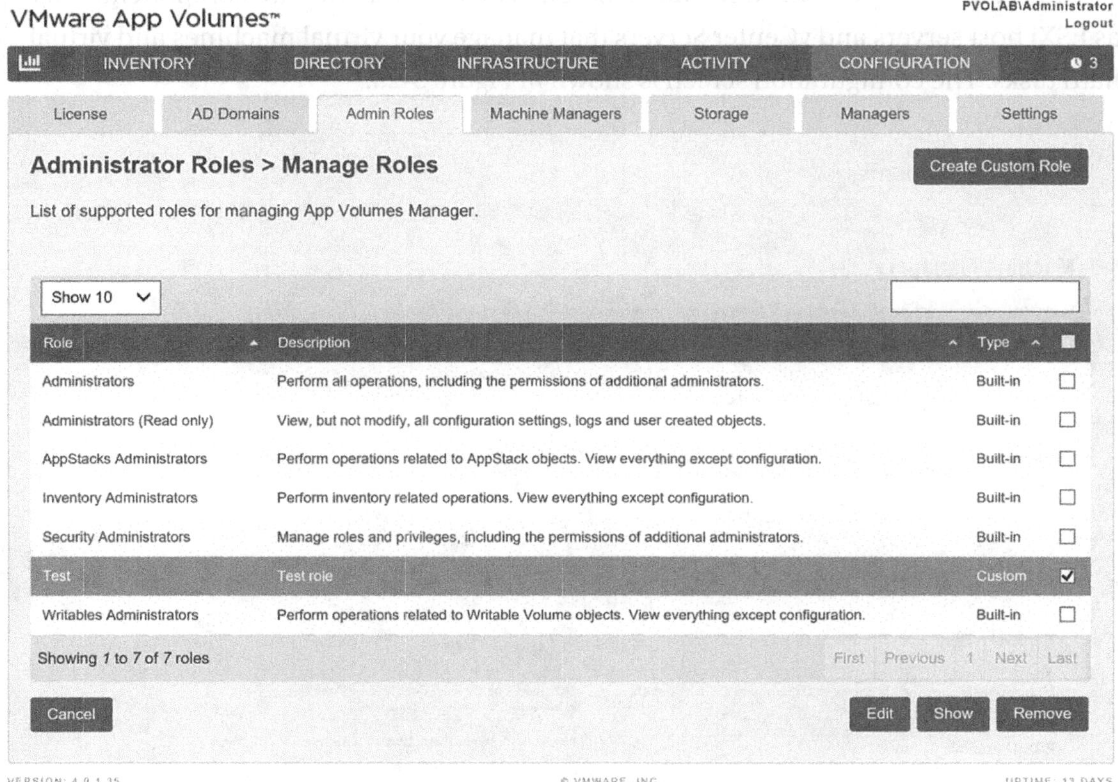

Figure 3-22. *Successful addition of a custom role*

10. If you check the box next to the role, you will see that you have several options available. You can **Edit**, **Show**, or **Remove** the selected role. You can also click the **Create Custom** Role button to create more custom roles.

You have now successfully added a new custom administrator role in the App Volumes management console.

The next configuration tab is for **Machine Managers**.

Machine Managers

The next configuration tab is for the Machine Managers configuration screen. In App Volumes terminology, a Machine Manager refers to the infrastructure components such as ESXi host servers and vCenter Servers that manage your virtual machines and virtual hard disks. The configuration screen is shown in Figure 3-23.

VMware App Volumes™

License	AD Domains	Admin Roles	Machine Managers	Storage	Settings

Machine Managers

Register and configure in-guest services or leverage the performance of VMware vCenter Servers to deliver volumes.

Type:	vCenter Server	
Hostname:	vcsa.pvolab.com	vCenter Hostname Example: server.your-domain.local
Username:	administrator@vsphere.local	vCenter Service Account Username Example: YOURDOMAIN\administrator
Password:	●●●●●●●●●●●●	vCenter Service Account Password Note: Password is stored encrypted
VMware Cloud:	☐ vCenter on VMware Cloud on AWS	vCenter is configured for VMware Cloud on Amazon Web Services
Mount ESXi:	☑ Issue mount operations to ESXi servers	When mounting, connect directly to ESXi servers Decreases vCenter server utilization
ESXi Username:	root	Must be the same on every ESXi host server Example: cvmanager
ESXi Password:	●●●●●●●●●●●●	Must be the same on every ESXi host server Note: Password is stored encrypted
Mount Local:	☐ Use local copies of volumes	Prioritize volumes available on locally attached storage when possible Increases IO performance by distributing utilization (unnecessary on VSAN)
Mount Queue:	☑ Use queues for mount operations	Use shared queues to store and process mount requests Decreases the number of active connections to vCenter and ESXi servers
Mount Async:	☑ Use asynchronous mount operations	Wait for the mount request completion in the background Increases Manager server throughput (requires queues)
Mount Throttle:	☑ Throttle concurrent mount operations	Limits the number of actively processing mount requests Decreases load on vCenter/ESXi servers (requires queues)
	5	Maximum number of concurrent mount operations per queue Each vCenter/ESXi server uses a queue per Manager process

Save

Figure 3-23. *Machine Managers configuration screen*

To configure Machine Managers, complete the following steps:

1. In the **Type** box, click the drop-down menu and select one of the available machine managers from the list shown. There are three options to choose from:

    a. vCenter Server

    b. ESXi Host Server

    c. VHD In-Guest Servers (for non-VMDK/VMware-based application packages

2. Once you have selected your Machine Manager type, you cannot change it. You can add additional Machine Managers of the same type, so, for example, you can add another vCenter Server, but not add a different type. If you want to deploy application packages using the VHD virtual hard disk format, then you will need to install a different instance of the App Volumes Manager to manage your VHD-based application packages. In the test lab, we have selected vCenter Server as the Machine Manager type.

3. In the **Hostname** box, type in the name of the machine that you selected in the Machine Type box in the previous step. So, in the test lab example, this is **vcsa.pvolab.com** which is the name of the vCenter Server.

4. Now, in the **Username** box, type in the account name that has the appropriate privileges to the vCenter Server. In the test lab, we are going to use **administrator@vsphere.local** as the username.

5. In the **Password** box, type in the password for the username that you entered in the previous step.

6. App Volumes supports VMware Cloud running on AWS, and so the next option, **VMware Cloud**, can be enabled by checking the box.

7. The **Mount ESXi** option allows you to select your ESXi host server to issue the mount commands for attaching your application packages to the virtual desktop machines and servers. By enabling this option, the vCenter Server utilization will be lower as it no longer performs the mounting process the ESXi host server does.
8. If you enable the **Mount ESXi** option, then the next box, **ESXi Username**, will need to be configured with the username that has the rights and privileges to be able to mount virtual hard disks.
9. Next, in the **ESXi Password** box, type in the password used by the username account you entered for the ESXi host server.

The username and password that you register with the App Volumes Manager must be the same across all the ESXi host servers that are registered within your App Volumes environment.

---

10. The next option is for **Mount Local**. You would enable this feature, by checking the box, if you want to prioritize volumes that are stored on local storage. This would increase the IO performance of the storage and potentially decrease the mount time of the application packages.
11. Next is the check box for **Mount Queue**. Enabling this option allows you to use a shared queue for storing and processing mount requests. This decreases the number of connections to your vCenter Server and ESXi host servers by allowing them to be queued.
12. The penultimate option is for **Mount Async**. Enabling this option means that the App Volumes Manager waits for the mount request to complete in the background. This allows for an increased throughput on the App Volumes Manager. To use this feature, you will need to enable the **Mount Queue** feature.
13. Finally, there is the **Mount Throttle** option. Enabling this option allows you to limit the number of mount requests that are issued. In the box underneath, type in the number of maximum mount

requests you want to configure. This feature helps to decrease the load on your vCenter Server and ESXi host servers and, like the **Mount Async** feature, will also need you to enable the **Mount Queue** option.

14. Scrolling to the bottom of Machine Managers screen will show you the list of vCenter Server permissions that the App Volumes Manager requires. These were covered in Chapter 2, but as a reminder they are shown in Figure 3-24.

- Datastore
  - Allocate space
  - Browse datastore
  - Low level file operations
  - Remove file
  - Update virtual machine files
- Folder
  - Create folder
  - Delete folder
- Global
  - Cancel task
- Host
  - Local operations
    - Reconfigure virtual machine
- Sessions
  - View and stop sessions
- Tasks
  - Create task
- Virtual machine
  - Configuration
    - Add existing disk
    - Add new disk
    - Add or remove device
    - Change resource
    - Query unowned files
    - Remove disk
    - Settings
    - Advanced
  - Inventory
    - Create new
    - Move
    - Register
    - Remove
    - Unregister
  - Provisioning
    - Promote disks

Figure 3-24. *vCenter Server permissions required for App Volumes*

15. With the configuration options selected, click the **Save** button to continue.

16. Depending on your configuration, you may see an **Untrusted Certificate** warning box pop-up as shown in Figure 3-25.

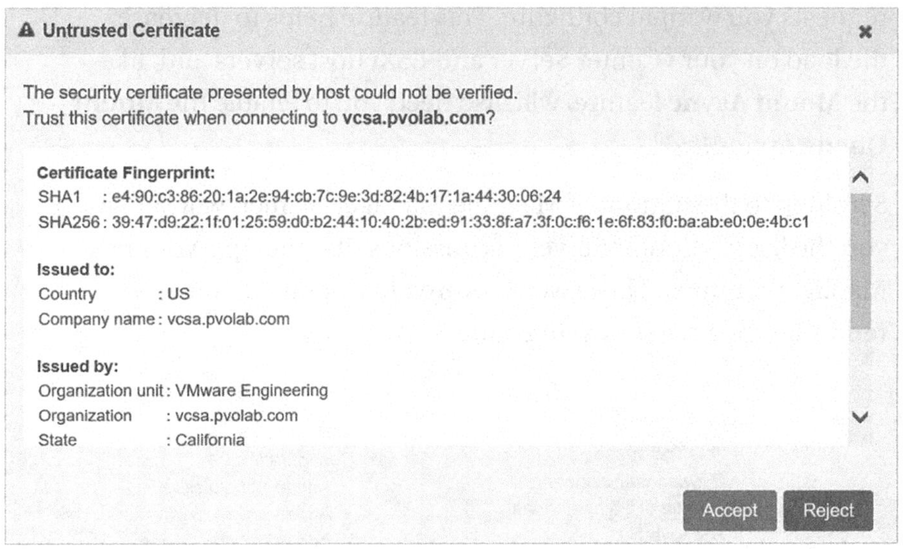

***Figure 3-25.** Untrusted certificate warning*

17. This is the certificate between the App Volumes Manager and your vCenter Server. In the test lab, we have not configured or installed certificates on each server, so we will click the **Accept** button to continue.

18. You will see the progress bar in Figure 3-26 as the certificate is added and the vCenter configuration information is saved.

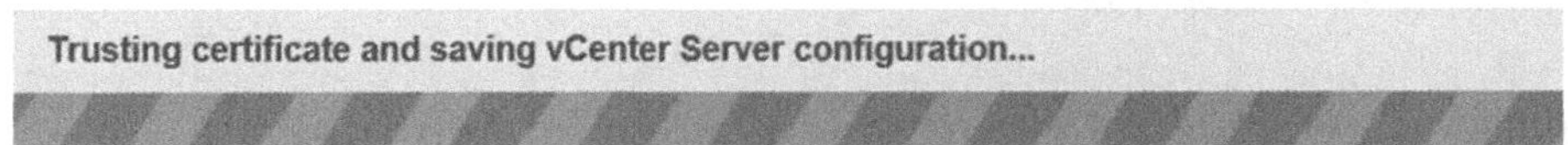

***Figure 3-26.** Trusting certificate and saving vCenter Server config*

19. You will now see the Machine Managers screen with the configured information as shown in Figure 3-27.

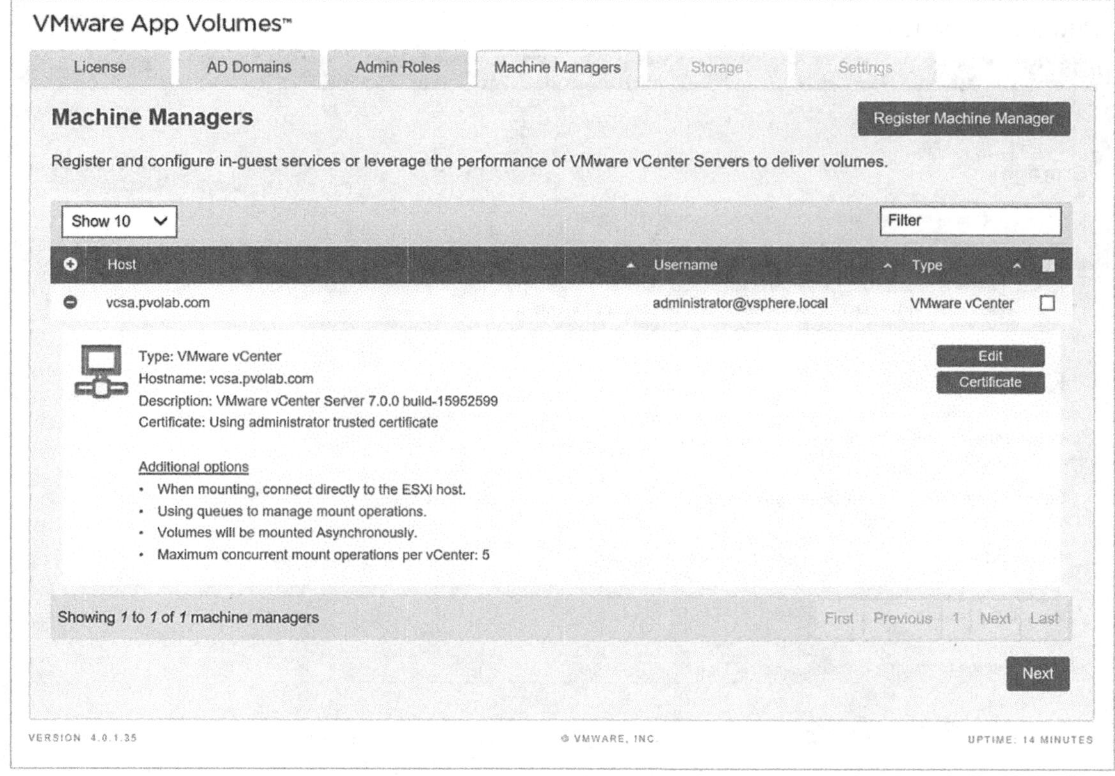

Figure 3-27. *Completed Machine Managers configuration*

20. You will see on this screen that there are several other options. You can click the **Edit** button to change or update the configuration, or by clicking the **View** button, you can view the certificate. The final button is the **Register Machine Manager** which allows to add another manager.

21. When you have completed the configuration, click the **Next** button to continue.

Now that you have successfully configured your Machine Managers, the next configuration tab is for storage.

Storage

The next element to configure is storage. This is where you are going to store your application packages and Writable Volumes. You will see something like Figure 3-28.

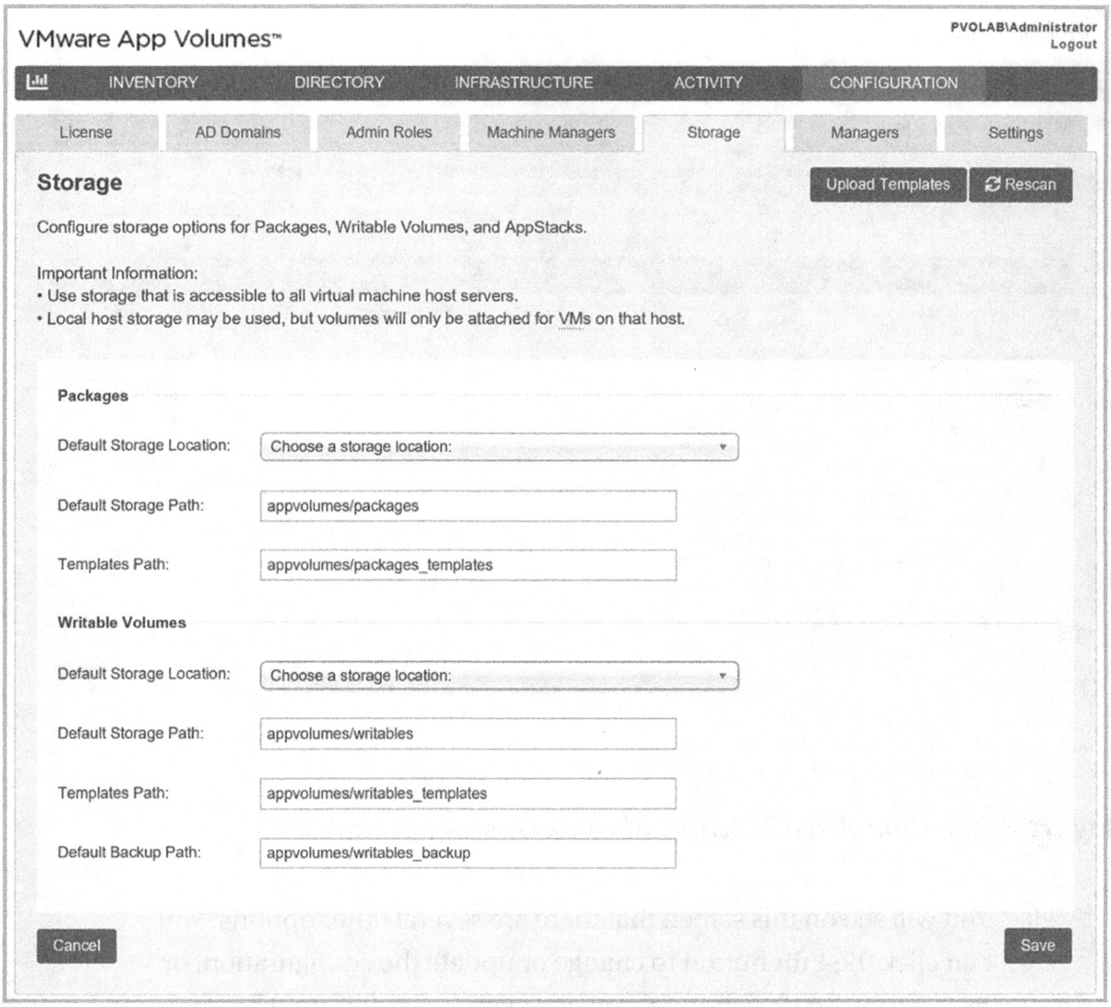

Figure 3-28. *Storage configuration screen*

To configure your storage, follow the steps described:

1. The first thing to configure is the location of your application packages in the **Packages** section of the configuration screen.

2. In the **Default Storage Location**, click the drop-down arrow on the **Choose a storage location** box as shown in Figure 3-29.

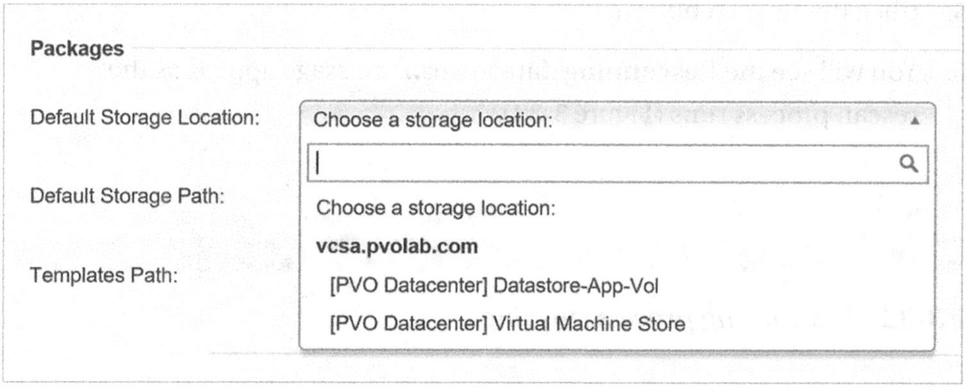

Packages
Default Storage Location:
Default Storage Path:
Templates Path:
Choose a storage location:
Choose a storage location:
vcsa.pvolab.com
[PVO Datacenter] Datastore-App-Vol
[PVO Datacenter] Virtual Machine Store

Figure 3-29. *Configuring the storage for Packages*

3. If you do not see any of your datastores listed, even after successfully adding your Machine Managers, then click the **Rescan** button in the top right-hand corner of the screen as shown in Figure 3-30.

PVOLAB\Administrator
Logout
ACTIVITY
CONFIGURATION
Storage
Managers
Settings
Upload Templates
Rescan

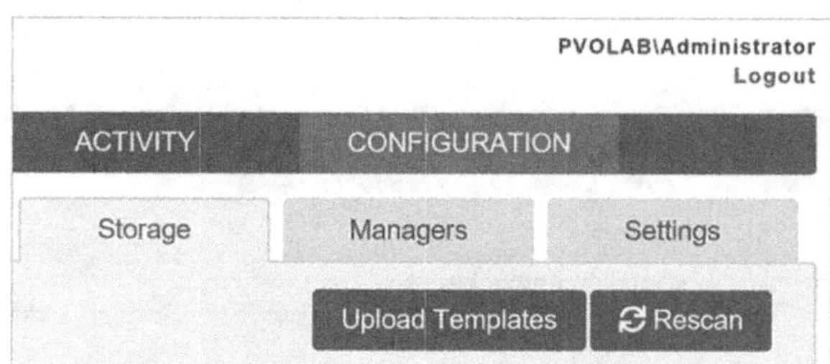

Figure 3-30. *Rescanning the datastores*

4. You will see the **Confirm Rescan** box pop-up as shown in Figure 3-31.

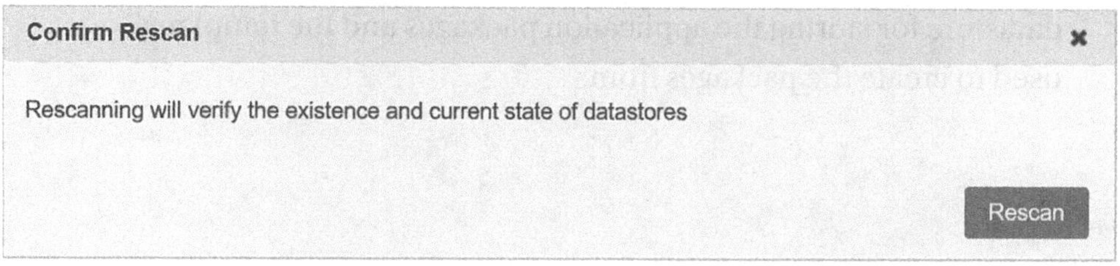

Confirm Rescan
Rescanning will verify the existence and current state of datastores
Rescan

Figure 3-31. *Confirm the rescan*

5. Click the **Rescan** button.

6. You will see the **Rescanning datastores...** message appear as the rescan process runs (Figure 3-32).

Figure 3-32. *Rescanning process running*

7. You will now return to the configuration screen.

8. With your datastores appearing in the drop-down list, select the datastore you want to use for storing your application packages. In the test lab, we have selected the **Datastore-App-Vol** datastore as shown in Figure 3-33.

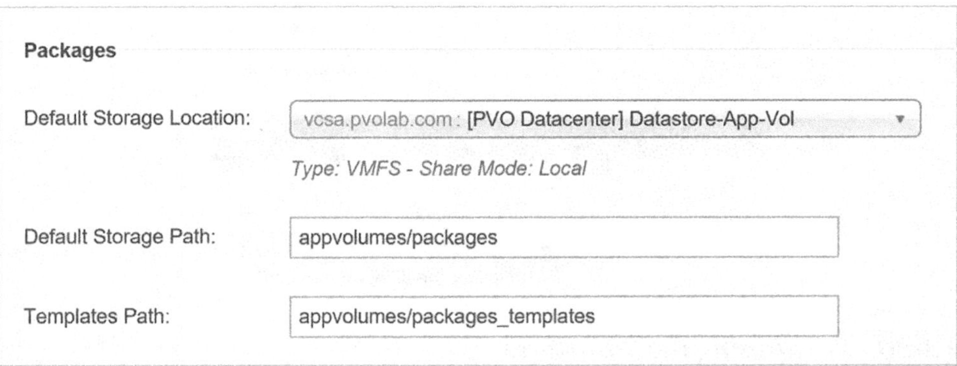

Figure 3-33. *Packages datastore configured*

9. Leave the **Default Storage Path** and the **Templates Path** as the default configuration. This creates a folder structure on the datastore for storing the application packages and the templates used to create the packages from.

Next, we are going to configure the storage for storing Writable Volumes, following the steps described:

10. Under the **Writable Volumes** section, in the **Default Storage Location**, click the drop-down arrow on the **Choose a storage location** box, and select the Datastore-AppVol datastore as shown in Figure 3-34.

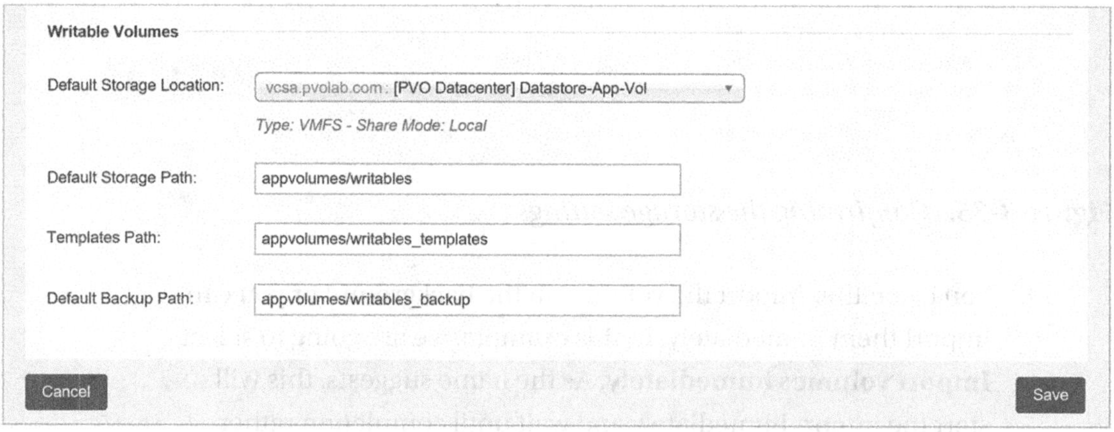

Figure 3-34. *Configuring storage for Writable Volumes*

11. Leave the **Default Storage Path**, **Templates Path**, and the **Default Backup Path** as the default configuration. This creates a folder structure on the datastore for storing Writable Volumes and the templates used to create them from, as well as the backup location.

12. Click the **Save** button to save the configuration.

13. You will see the **Confirm Storage Settings** box pop-up as shown in Figure 3-35.

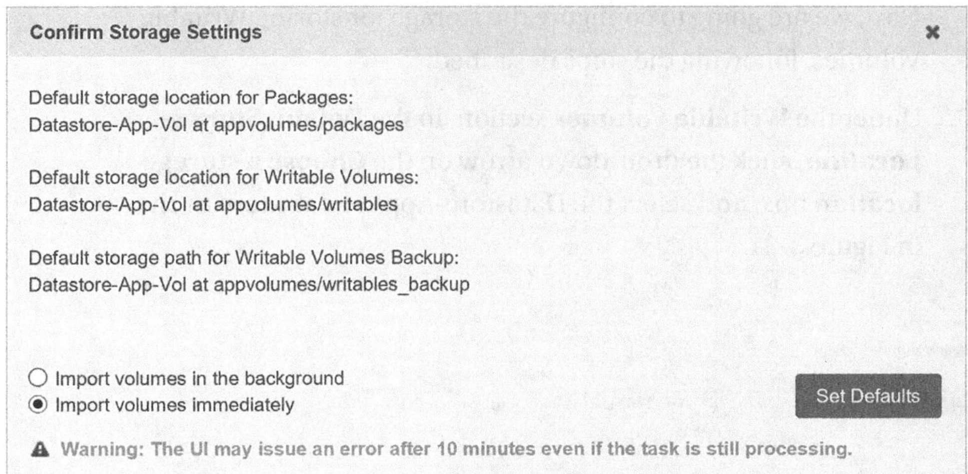

***Figure 3-35.** Confirming the storage settings*

14. You can either import the volumes in the background or you can import them immediately. In this example, we are going to select **Import volumes immediately**. As the name suggests, this will start the import immediately and wait until completion rather than run it in the background.
15. Click the **Set Defaults** button.
16. You will see the Setting Default Storage Locations message appear as the storage locations are saved, as shown in Figure 3-36.

***Figure 3-36.** Setting the default storage locations*

17. Once completed, you will also see the **Saved datastores** message as shown in Figure 3-37.

***Figure 3-37.** Datastores successfully saved*

It is worth noting that storage used for application packages and Writable Volumes must be accessible by all ESXi host servers and vCenter Servers that you configured as machine managers. The best practice is to use a shared storage platform such as a SAN or VSAN. Local storage is supported; however, be aware that volumes to be mounted can only be mounted and attached to virtual machines that are on the same host as the local storage.

18. Next, you will see the **Upload Templates** screen as shown in Figure 3-38.

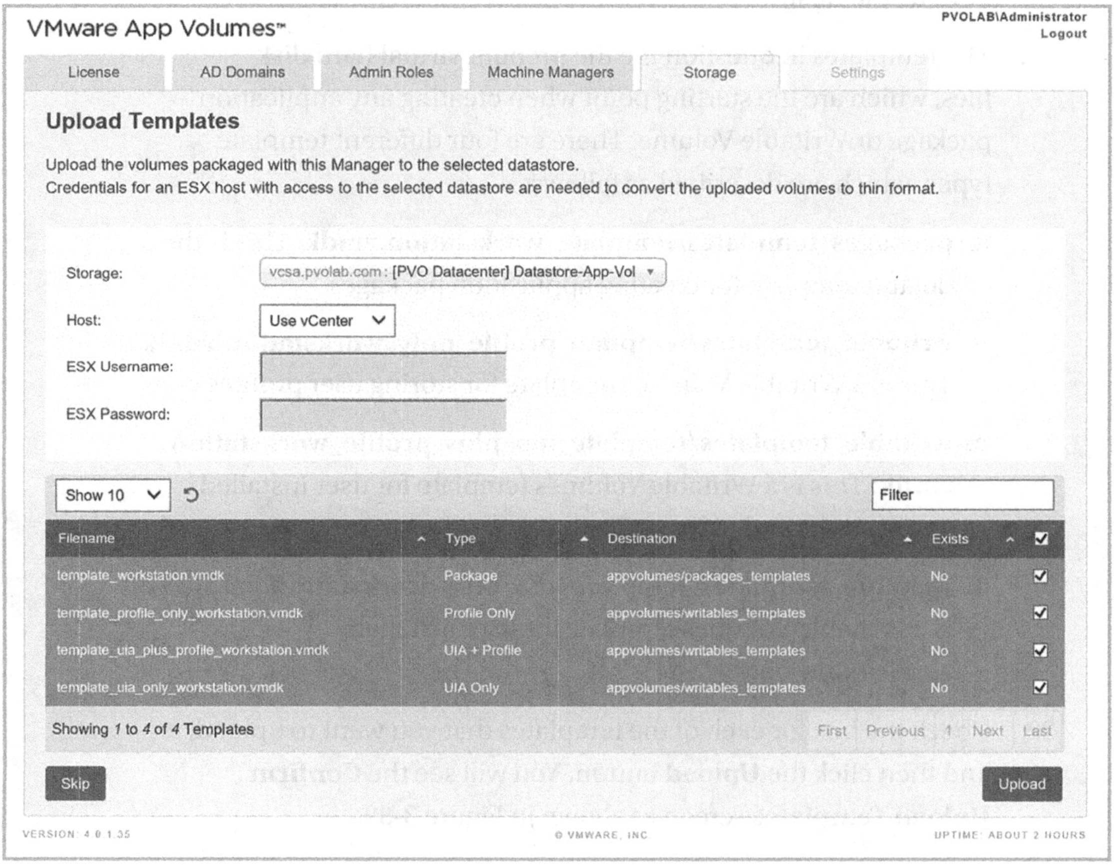

VMware App Volumes™

PVOLAB\Administrator
Logout

License | AD Domains | Admin Roles | Machine Managers | Storage | Settings

Upload Templates

Upload the volumes packaged with this Manager to the selected datastore.
Credentials for an ESX host with access to the selected datastore are needed to convert the uploaded volumes to thin format.

Storage: vcsa.pvolab.com: [PVO Datacenter] Datastore-App-Vol

Host: Use vCenter

ESX Username:

ESX Password:

Show 10 | Filter

Filename	Type	Destination	Exists	☑
template_workstation.vmdk	Package	appvolumes/packages_templates	No	☑
template_profile_only_workstation.vmdk	Profile Only	appvolumes/writables_templates	No	☑
template_uia_plus_profile_workstation.vmdk	UIA + Profile	appvolumes/writables_templates	No	☑
template_uia_only_workstation.vmdk	UIA Only	appvolumes/writables_templates	No	☑

Showing *1* to *4* of *4* Templates — First | Previous | 1 | Next | Last

Skip | Upload

VERSION: 4.0.1.35 © VMWARE, INC. UPTIME: ABOUT 2 HOURS

Figure 3-38. *Upload Templates screen*

19. In the **Storage** box, from the drop-down menu options, select the datastore you want to upload the templates to. In the test lab, this is the **Datastore-App-Vol** datastore.

20. In the **Host** box, you can choose whether these templates are uploaded to your vCenter Server or to your ESXi host server. In the test lab example, we are going to use vCenter. Selecting ESXi from the **Host** list would then mean you would need to enter user details for that ESXi host server. These would be entered in the **ESX Username** box followed by the password for that username in the **ESX Password** box. If you want to upload the templates in a thin provisioned format, then you will need to use ESXi as the host.

21. The templates in question are the prebuilt virtual hard disk files, which are the starting point when creating any application package or Writable Volume. There are four different template types, which are described as follows:

    a. **packages_templates/template_workstation.vmdk**: This is the default template for creating application packages.

    b. **writable_templates/template_profile_only_workstation.vmdk**: This is a Writable Volumes template for storing user profiles only.

    c. **writable_templates/template_uia_plus_profile_workstation.vmdk**: This is a Writable Volumes template for user installed applications and user profiles.

    d. **writable_templates/template_uia_only_workstation.vmdk**: This is a Writable Volumes template for user installed applications only.

22. Check the box for each of the templates that you want to upload, and then click the **Upload** button. You will see the **Confirm Upload Templates** screen as shown in Figure 3-39.

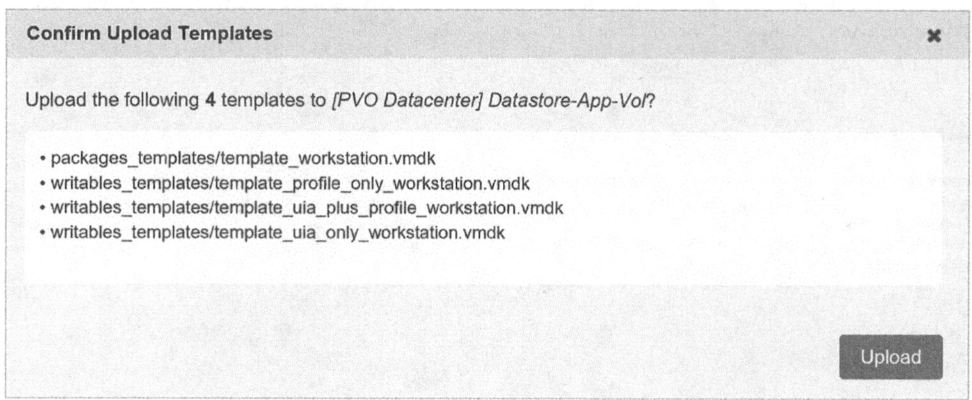

Figure 3-39. *Confirm templates to be uploaded*

23. Click the **Upload** button.

24. You will see the pop-up box in Figure 3-40.

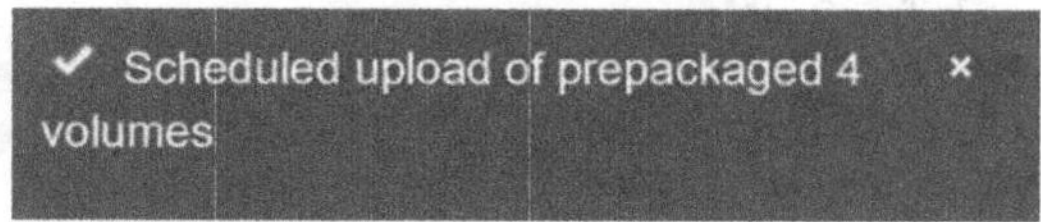

Figure 3-40. *Scheduled upload of the prebuilt VMDK templates*

25. You can easily check the upload by logging in to your vCenter Server and browsing the datastore that you selected to upload to. An example of this is shown in Figure 3-41.

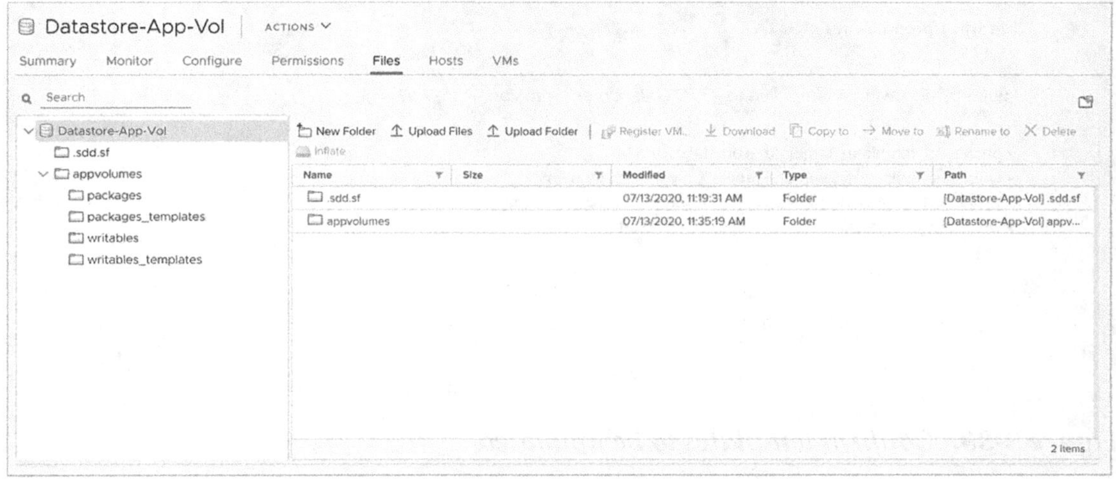

Figure 3-41. *Templates successfully uploaded to the datastore*

You have now successfully configured your App Volumes storage. Next, we will look at the final configuration tab for **Settings**.

Settings

This final set of configuration options, grouped under the **Settings** tab, contains the following categories of setting:

- General
- Volume Mounting
- Writable Volumes
- Active Directory
- Writable Volumes Backups
- Advanced Settings

As there are several settings, we are going to break these down into three sections starting with the settings for **General**, **Volume Mounting**, and **Writable Volumes**.

These are shown in Figure 3-42.

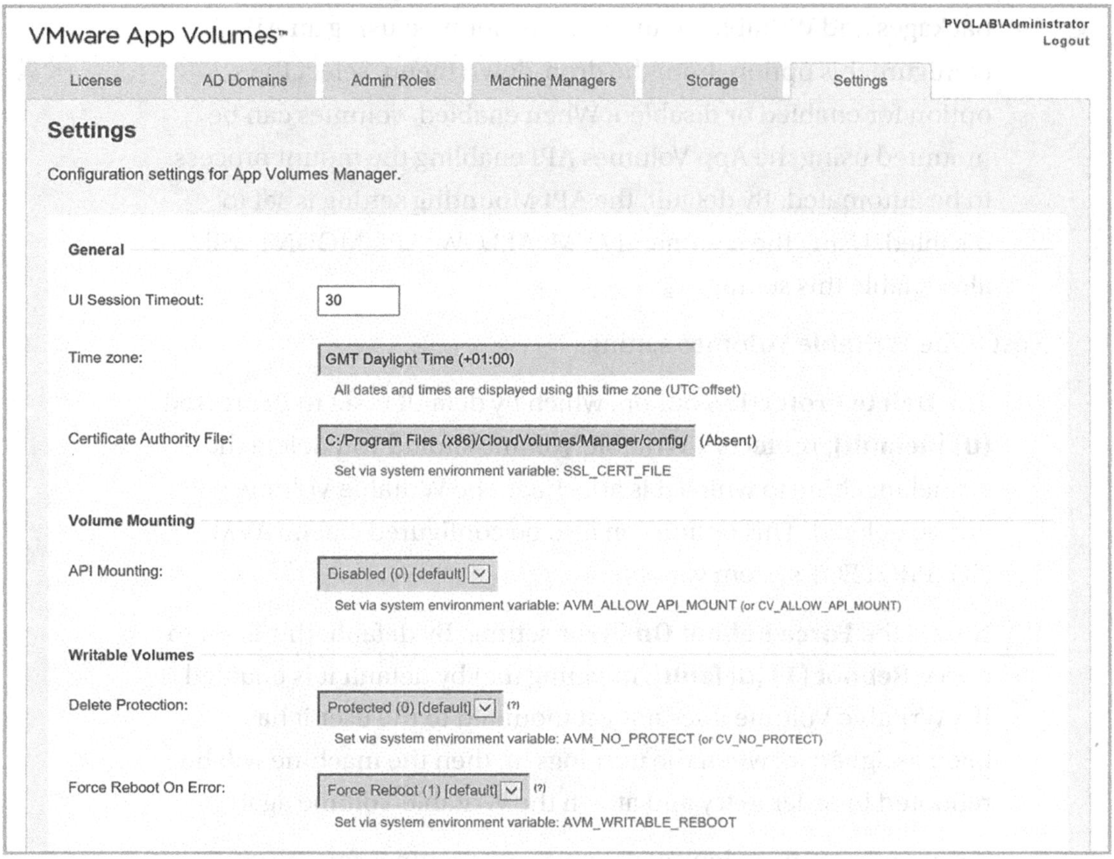

Figure 3-42. *Settings tab (1)*

We will start with the **General** settings.

1. The first setting is for **UI Session Timeout.** Here, you can enter an amount of time for when the management console times out and logs the user out. That means the amount of time that has passed with no activity. The default setting is 30 minutes, after which time with no activity will log the user out of the management console.

2. The **Time zone** box will show the currently set time zone.

3. In the **Certificate Authority File** box, you will see the path to the certificate file. This is set using the system variable SSL_CERT_FILE.

Next is the **Volume Mounting** setting.

4. With the **API Mounting** option, you can allow application packages and Writable Volumes to be mounted using an API. To configure this option, from the drop-down menu, select the option for enabled or disabled. When enabled, volumes can be mounted using the App Volumes API enabling the mount process to be automated. By default, the API Mounting setting is set to disabled. Using the command AVM_ALLOW_API_MOUNT will also enable this setting.

Next is the **Writable Volumes** setting.

5. The **Delete Protection** option, which by default is set to **Protected (0) [default]**, protects a Writable Volume should you delete the virtual machine to which it is attached. The Writable Volume will not be deleted. This option can also be configured via the AVM_NO_PROTECT system variable.

6. Next is the **Force Reboot On Error** setting. By default, this is set to **Force Reboot (1) [default]**, meaning that by default it is enabled. If a Writable Volume does not get mounted to the user it has been assigned to, when the user logs in, then the machine will be rebooted in order to try and attach the Writable Volume again.

   We are now going to look at the next set of settings for **Active Directory** and **Writable Volume Backups** as shown in Figure 3-43.

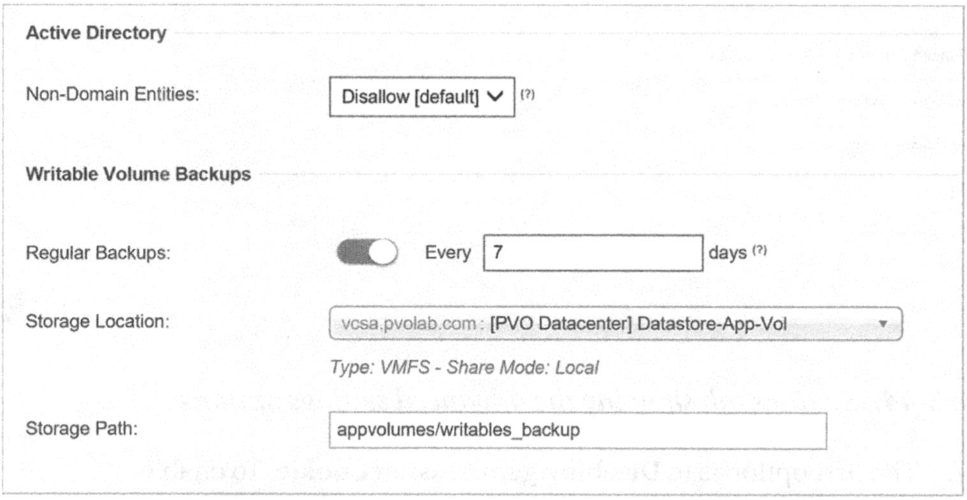

Active Directory
Non-Domain Entities: Disallow [default] (?)
Writable Volume Backups
Regular Backups: Every 7 days (?)
Storage Location: vcsa.pvolab.com : [PVO Datacenter] Datastore-App-Vol
Type: VMFS - Share Mode: Local
Storage Path: appvolumes/writables_backup

Figure 3-43. *Settings tab (2)*

7. Under the **Active Directory** section, you will see the option for **Non-Domain Entities**. From the drop-down menu, you can set this to **Allow** which means that any nondomain joined machine can have volumes attached to it. The default setting is **Disallow** so that no machines can have volumes mounted if they are not joined to your domain.

   Then we have the **Writable Volume Backups** settings.

8. First, you have the **Regular Backups** option. If you want to enable this, then first click the switch to turn the backup feature on. Next to it, you have a box into which you can enter the frequency of the backups. In the example lab, this is set to **Every 7 days**.

9. In the **Storage Location** box, from the drop-down menu, select the datastore you want to use for the backups. In the example lab, we have selected the Datastore-App-Vol datastore.

10. Finally, there is the **Storage Path** option. This is the folder that will be created on the datastore where the backups will be kept. This is created automatically.

    The final part of the settings screen is the **Advanced Settings** as shown in Figure 3-44.

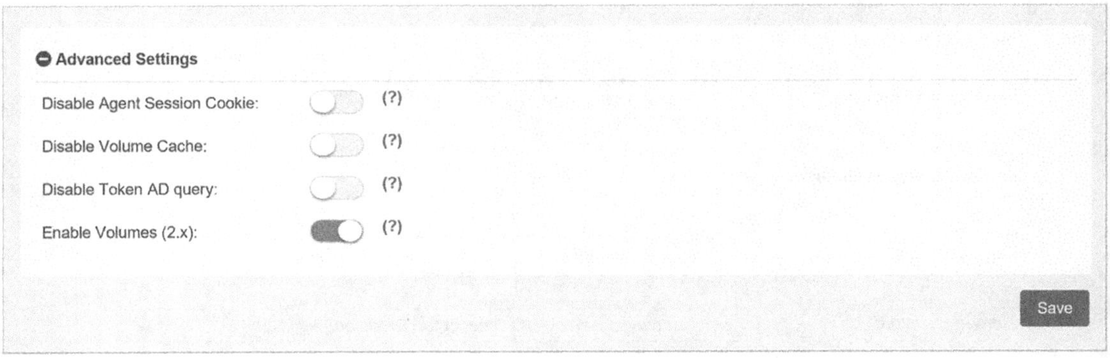

Advanced Settings

Disable Agent Session Cookie:		(?)
Disable Volume Cache:		(?)
Disable Token AD query:		(?)
Enable Volumes (2.x):		(?)

Save

***Figure 3-44.** Settings tab showing the advanced settings options*

11. The first option is to **Disable Agent Session Cookie**. To enable this setting, click the switch to turn it on. A session cookie is used to optimize communications between the App Volumes Manager and the App Volumes Agent. As part of troubleshooting, if you experience App Volumes Agent session issues, then you could try disabling the session cookies to see if that fixes the problem.

12. Next is the **Disable Volume Cache** option. App Volumes caches objects to improve performance. When troubleshooting and seeing increased memory usage, to fix this you could switch this setting on to disable the volume caching.

13. The **Disable Token AD Query** setting is next. App Volumes queries for AD group membership by using cached object SIDs. In previous versions of App Volumes, this query was performed by using group membership queries against Active Directory domains directly and recursively. You can revert to that way of querying AD by switching this feature on.

14. Finally, you have the **Enable Volumes (2.x)** setting. Switching this feature on allows you to manage App Volumes 2.x packages (AppStacks) and Writable Volumes. It also supports using the 2.x version of the App Volumes Agent. When this feature is enabled, you will see an additional menu option, **VOLUMES (2.x)**. Once you have migrated your AppStacks to application packages, you can disable this feature. In the test lab, we have switched this on so we can demonstrate the interoperability with App Volumes 2.x.

15. Once you have configured your advanced settings, click the **Save** button.

16. You will see the **Saving Settings...** progress bar as the settings are saved, as shown in Figure 3-45.

Figure 3-45. *Saving Settings in progress*

17. Once the settings have been saved, you will now see the INVENTORY screen as shown in Figure 3-46.

VMware App Volumes™

PVOLAB\Administrator
Logout

INVENTORY VOLUMES (2.X) DIRECTORY INFRASTRUCTURE ACTIVITY CONFIGURATION

Applications Packages Programs Assignments Attachments Writables

Applications

Create Import Rescan

Each application represents a collection of packaged versions of that application. Users, Groups, Computers or Organizational Units can be entitled to receive a current package or to be assigned a specific package.

Show 10 Filter

Name	Status	Packages		Created	
Test App	Active	1	0	Jul 13 2020	☐

Showing 1 to 1 of 1 Applications

First Previous 1 Next Last

VERSION 4.0.1.35 © VMWARE, INC. UPTIME: 14 DAYS

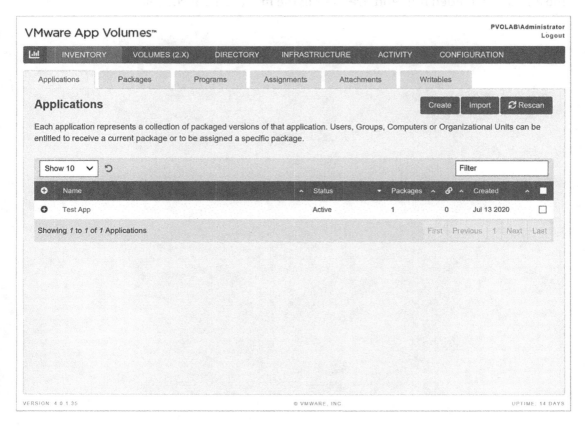

Figure 3-46. *The Inventory screen on completion of the initial setup*

You have now successfully completed the initial setup of the App Volumes Manager which is now ready to start creating and managing your application packages and Writable Volumes.

Chapter summary

In this third chapter, we have completed all the initial tasks in configuring the App Volumes Manager ready for use. We connected the App Volumes Manager to our virtual infrastructure for managing the virtual hard disks that will become our application packages and Writable Volumes and also connected to Active Directory so that the newly created volumes can be delivered to our end users.

In the next chapter, we are going to log in to the App Volumes Manager for the first time and take a guided tour and overview of the management console.

CHAPTER 4

Getting Started with the Management Console

Having completed the first three chapters of this book, you will now understand how App Volumes works from a theory perspective and will now have installed the software. In the previous chapter, you had your first taste of working with the App Volumes Manager console when you completed the initial configuration, post installation.

In this chapter, we are going to take a tour of the management console, so you can familiarize yourself with the menu options and where to find the various tasks required to manage your App Volumes environment.

Logging in for the first time

As we discussed in Chapter 3, the App Volumes Manager management console is a web-based console that can be accessed using a web browser (supported browsers are listed in Chapter 3) from the IT admin's desktop or directly from the App Volumes Manager server.

In the test lab, we are going to launch the management console from the App Volumes Manager by double-clicking the App Volumes icon.

1. In the login screen which will now be shown, in the **Username** box, type in the username for your App Volumes administrator. In the test lab, we are using the **Administrator** account that was added during the initial configuration tasks.

2. In the **Password** box, type in the password for the username you used earlier. So, in our example, this is the administrator password.

P. von Oven, *Delivering Applications with VMware App Volumes 4*,
https://doi.org/10.1007/978-1-4842-6689-2_4

3. Finally, in the **Domain** box, click the drop-down menu option; from the list shown, select the domain for the account you are using to log in with. In the test lab, this is the **PVOLAB** domain as shown in Figure 4-1.

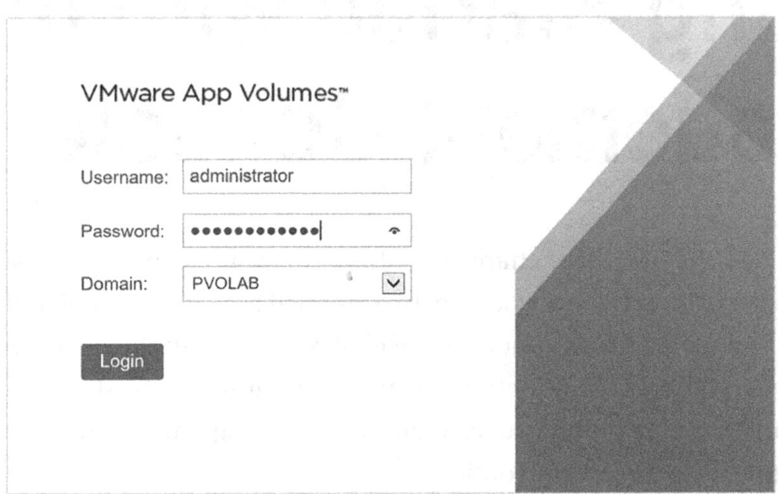

***Figure 4-1.** App Volumes Manager login screen*

4. Click the **Login** button. On successful login, you will see the **INVENTORY** screen as shown in Figure 4-2.

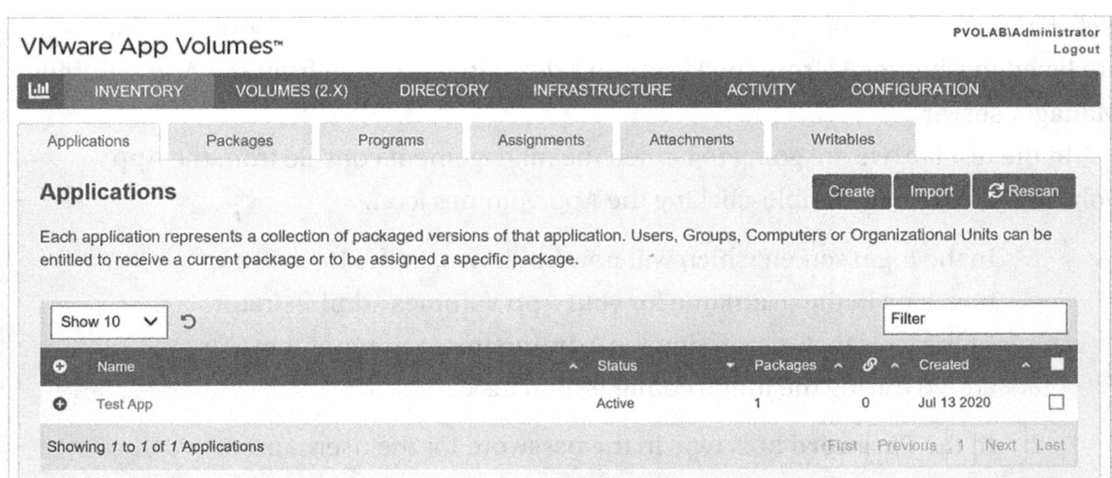

***Figure 4-2.** App Volumes Manager INVENTORY screen*

In the next section, we are going to look at what the **INVENTORY** menu is used for and the configuration options within it.

The Inventory menu

The **INVENTORY** menu is the first menu you see after logging in. As the name suggests, under this menu you will find the configuration information about creating your volumes, both for applications and Writable Volumes, as shown in Figure 4-3.

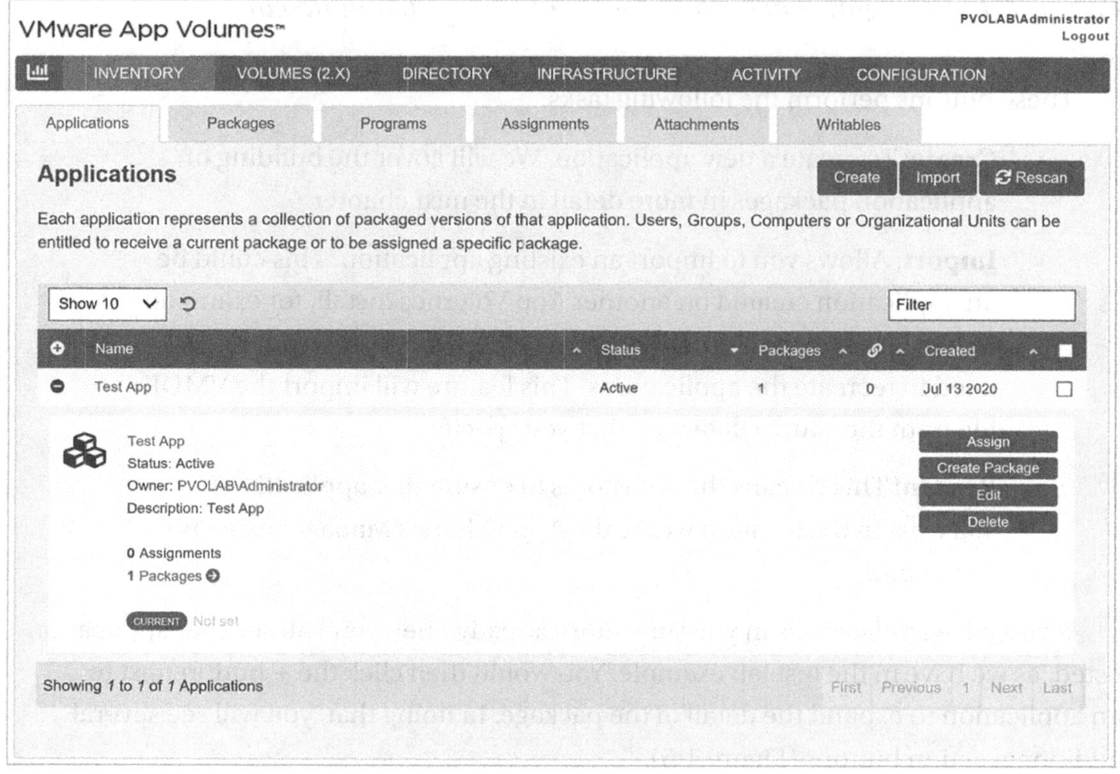

Figure 4-3. *App Volumes Manager INVENTORY screen and the Applications tab*

Within the **INVENTORY** menu, there are several different tabs for each of the elements that go to make up the App Volumes solution. In the following sections, we are going to briefly cover what each of these is used for.

Applications tab

The **Applications** screen is where you create your applications before they get packaged. There are several different options available, and we will look at these in more detail. First, at the top right-hand side of the screen, you will see the three buttons for the tasks or actions shown in Figure 4-4.

Figure 4-4. *Configuration buttons for Create, Import, and Rescan*

These buttons perform the following tasks:

- **Create**: To create a new application. We will cover the building of application packages in more detail in the next chapter.
- **Import**: Allows you to import an existing application. This could be an application created on another App Volumes install, for example, moving from a pilot into production where you do not want to or need to recreate the applications. This feature will import the VMDK file from the source datastore that you specify.
- **Rescan**: This rescans the datastores to ensure that applications still exist in the location where the App Volumes Manager expects to find them.

If you have applications in your inventory already, then you will see that application listed, as we have in the test lab example. You would then click the + button next to an application to expand the detail of the package. In doing that, you will see several additional action buttons (Figure 4-5).

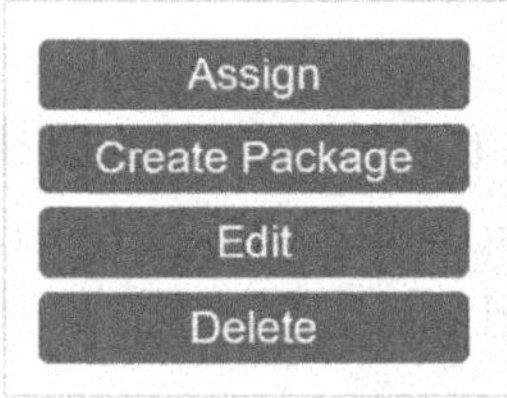

Figure 4-5. *Additional configuration buttons for existing applications*

These buttons are used for the following:

- **Assign**: Enables you to assign the application to users, groups, or computers
- **Create Package**: Will take you to the next tab for packages and enable you to configure and start the packaging process
- **Edit**: Allows you to edit the configuration of an existing application
- **Delete**: Will remove the application from the inventory

Next, we are going to look at the **Packages** tab.

Packages tab

In the Packages screen, you can create, configure, and edit your application packages as shown in Figure 4-6.

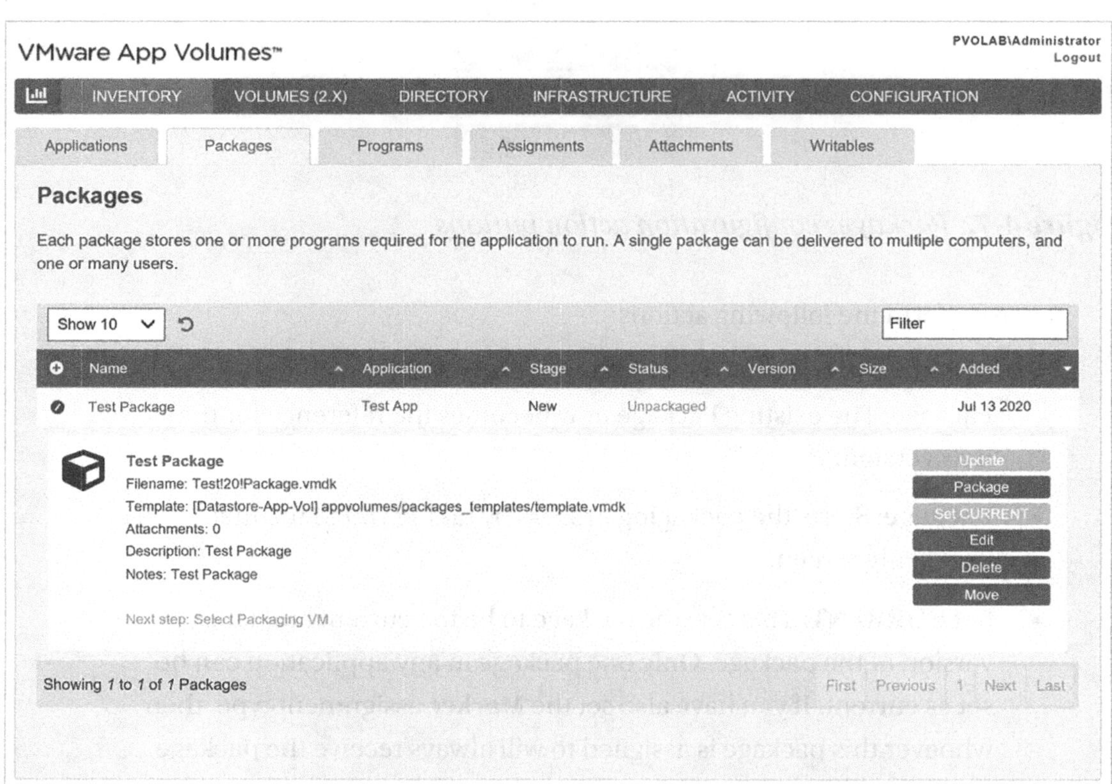

***Figure 4-6.** Packages configuration tab*

In this example screenshot, you can see that there is a package called **Test Package** listed. You will also see that this package is part of the Test App application, that it is at the New stage in terms of the app lifecycle, and that currently it has not been packaged. If it had been packaged, then you would see the version and size of the package.

Clicking the + button next to the package name will expand the package entry, showing you more detailed information about the package, such as the filename, the template used to create the package, how many attachments there are, and the description and notes you created during the configuration.

You will also see here, in orange text, that the next step is to create the package and to select the packaging VM on which to do this.

Also, by selecting the package, you will see several action buttons on the right-hand side as shown in Figure 4-7.

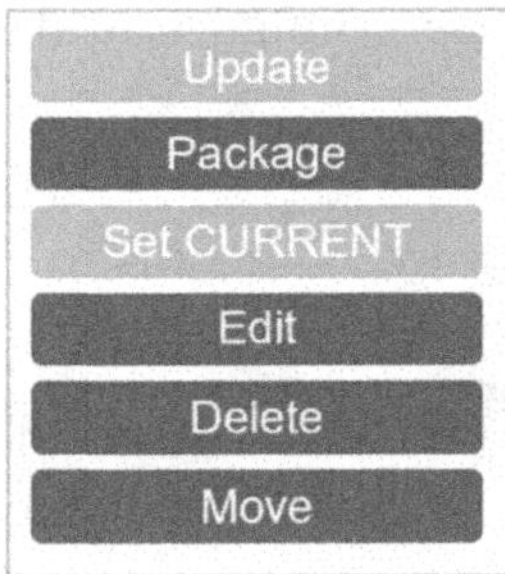

Figure 4-7. *Packages configuration action buttons*

These perform the following actions:

- **Update**: Allows you to create a new version of an already existing Package. The existing Package now becomes the reference for the new version.
- **Package**: Starts the packaging process by taking you to the first packaging screen.
- **Set CURRENT**: This sets the package to be the current and latest version of the package. Only one package in any application can be set as current. If you have also set the **Marker** assignment type, then whoever this package is assigned to will always receive the package that is set as current.

- **Edit**: Allows you to edit the current package information.
- **Delete**: Deletes the package.
- **Move**: Allows you to move the package to a different application.

The next tab we are going to look at is the **Programs** tab.

Programs tab

The Programs tab is purely informational and shows you the currently installed programs. It shows the name, version, publisher, and which package the program belongs to as shown in Figure 4-8.

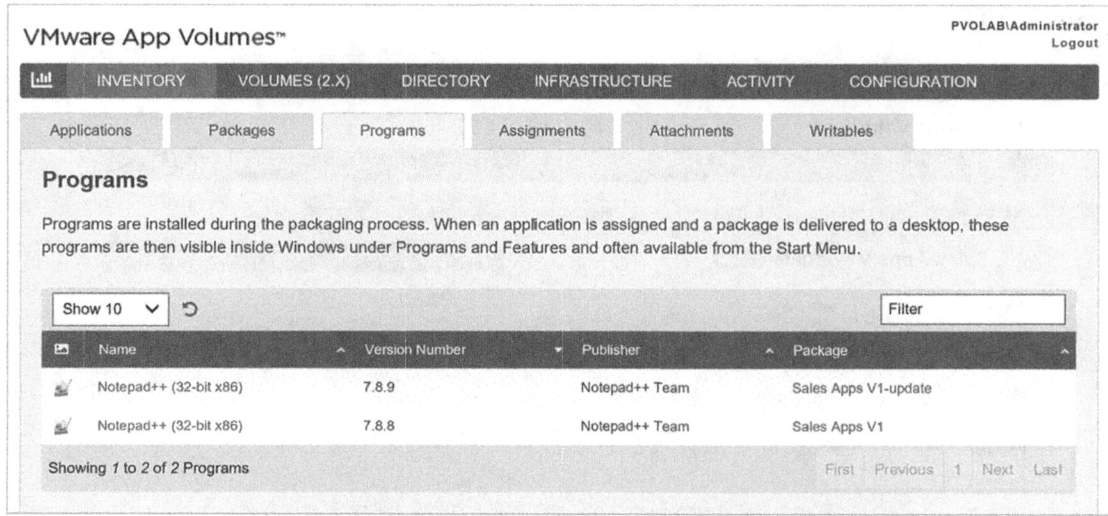

***Figure 4-8.** Programs tab showing installed programs*

In this example, you can see that there are two programs, for two different versions of Notepad++. The name of the program and the package details are shown as links, which take you to another screen that shows more details of each of these components. If you click the **Notepad++ (32-bit x86) 7.8.9** link, you will see the screenshot in Figure 4-9.

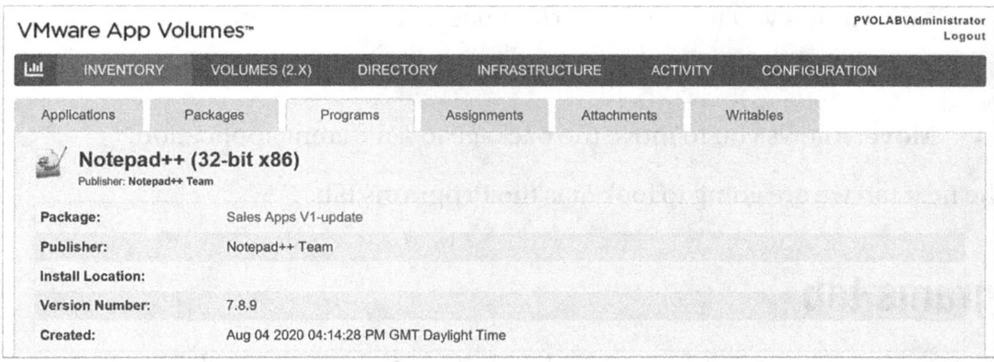

Figure 4-9. *Program details*

If you click the **Sales Apps V1-update** package link, you will see the screenshot in Figure 4-10.

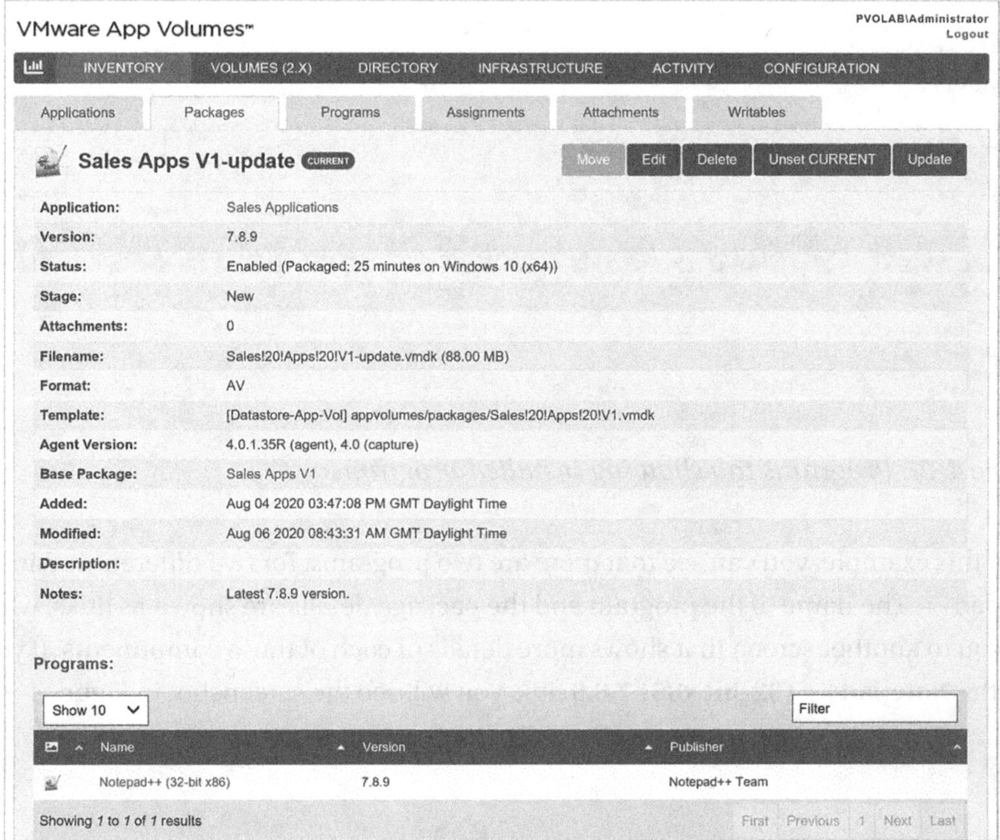

Figure 4-10. *Package details*

As you can see, you get taken back to the **Packages** tab where you can also edit the package if you need to.

Next is the **Assignments** tab.

Assignments tab

Under the Assignments tab, you will see a list of your entities, which in App Volumes terms means your end users, groups, computers, and OUs that have applications assigned to them. This is shown in Figure 4-11.

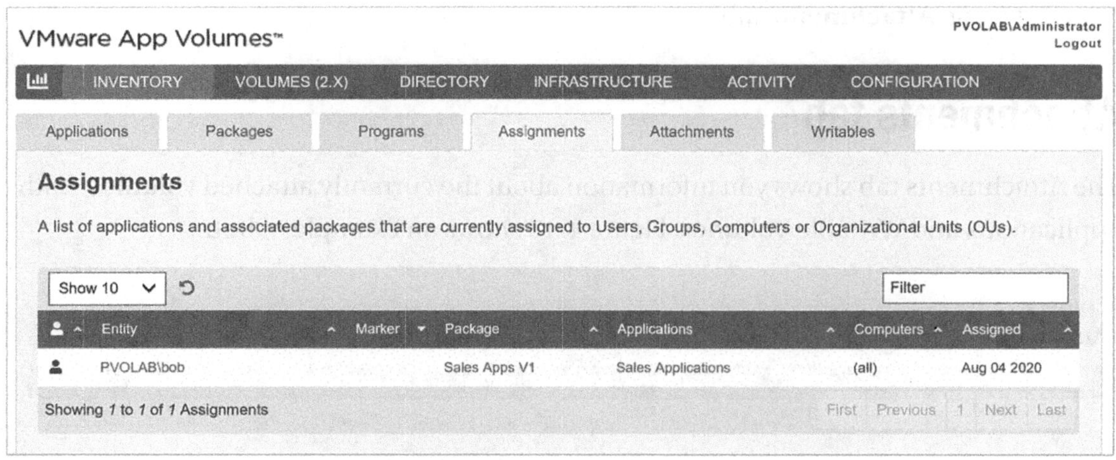

Figure 4-11. *Assignments tab*

In the preceding example, you can see the end user called **Bob** has been assigned the **Sales Application** application and the **Sales Apps V1** package. The assignment was created on **Aug 04, 2020**, and the applications will work on all computers that the end user logs in to.

The entity heading also shows an icon as to the type of assignment. The key to these icons is shown in Figure 4-12.

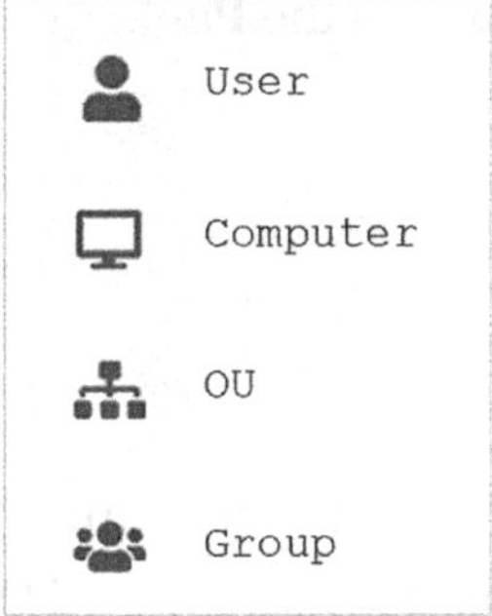

***Figure 4-12.** Key to the Assignments icons*

Next is the **Attachments** tab.

Attachments tab

The Attachments tab shows you information about the currently attached volumes, both applications and Writable Volumes. Figure 4-13 shows an example of both.

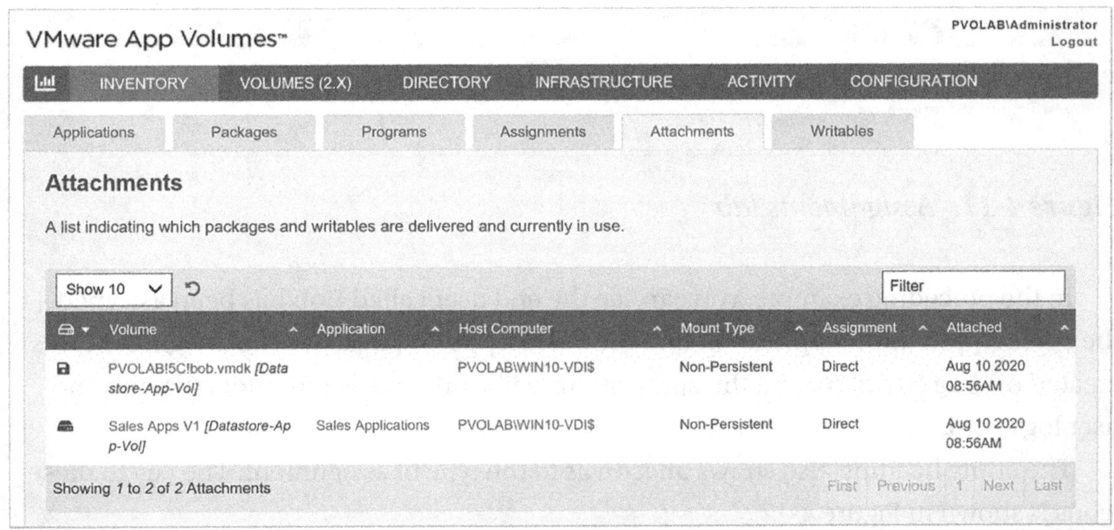

***Figure 4-13.** Attachments tab*

The information displayed shows the volume name, the applications, the host computer it is currently attached to, the type of assignment, and the date and time of when it was attached.

You will also see the attachment identified by the icons in Figure 4-14.

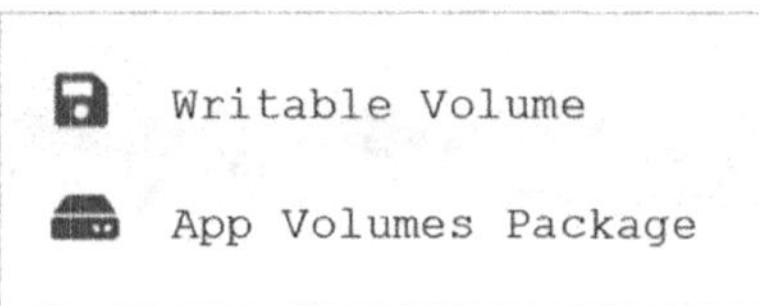

Figure 4-14. *Key to the Attachments icons*

Writables tab

The Writables tab is where you create and manage Writable Volumes. These are the volumes that are used for user installed apps and for storing end user profiles. An example is shown in Figure 4-15.

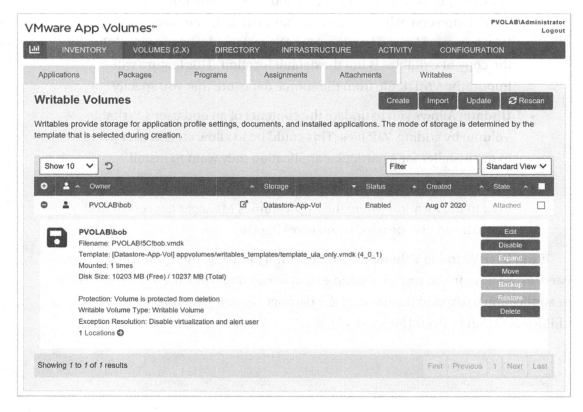

Figure 4-15. *Writable Volumes*

There are two sets of action buttons on the Writable Volumes screen. Let us look at the buttons across the top of the screen first (Figure 4-16).

Figure 4-16. *Writable Volumes task action buttons*

These buttons perform the following tasks:

- **Create**: Creates a new Writable Volume. We will cover the building and managing of Writable Volumes in more detail in Chapter 6.
- **Import**: Allows you to import an existing Writable Volume. This could be a volume created on another App Volumes environment. For example, when moving from a pilot into production, where you want to preserve what an end user has installed, or to keep their Windows profile, or when invoking DR and the datastore containing the copy of writables is not the default location. This feature will import the VMDK file from the source datastore that you specify.
- **Update**: Allows you to update the contents of an end user's Writable Volume by adding .ZIP files. This could be to allow an end user access to the installer for a particular application they want to install.
- **Rescan**: This rescans the datastores to ensure that applications still exist in the location where the App Volumes Manager expects to find them. It can also be used when invoking DR.

If you have Writable Volumes in your inventory already, then you will see them listed, as we have in the test lab example. You would then click the + button next to an application to expand the detail of the package. In doing that, you will see several additional action buttons (Figure 4-17).

***Figure 4-17.** Writable Volumes additional task action buttons*

These buttons allow you to perform the following tasks:

- **Edit**: Allows you to edit some of the settings of the Writable Volume, such as what to do if the volume is not available, or to specify specific computers that can have the volume attached.
- **Disable**: If an end user already has a Writable Volume attached, then it can be switched off using the disable button. This means it will not be attached the next time they log in.
- **Expand**: Allows you to increase the size of the virtual hard disk file used by the Writable Volume.
- **Move**: Allows you to move the Writable Volume from one storage location to another.
- **Backup**: Creates a backup of the Writable Volume.
- **Restore**: Allows you to restore a Writable Volume from another location.
- **Delete**: Deletes the Writable Volume virtual hard disk file from the datastore.

The next menu we are going to look at is for managing the previous version of App Volumes.

The Volumes (2.x) menu

In this section, we are going to look at the options for managing version 2.x deployments of App Volumes that you may still have within your organization that you are yet to migrate to App Volumes 4.2006 or 2009. We are not going to cover this in any detail in this book but will run through the options from within the management console. This menu option only appears when you configure App Volumes 2.x support in the settings and configuration or if you upgrade from version 2.x. We will start with AppStacks.

AppStacks tab

AppStacks is the App Volumes 2.x name given to Application packages in version 4.0. There was no concept of lifecycle management in previous versions. An AppStack is the virtual hard disk file that contains your programs that get attached to the end user's virtual desktop machine. The following screenshot shown in Figure 4-18 shows the AppStacks screen for App Volumes 2.x.

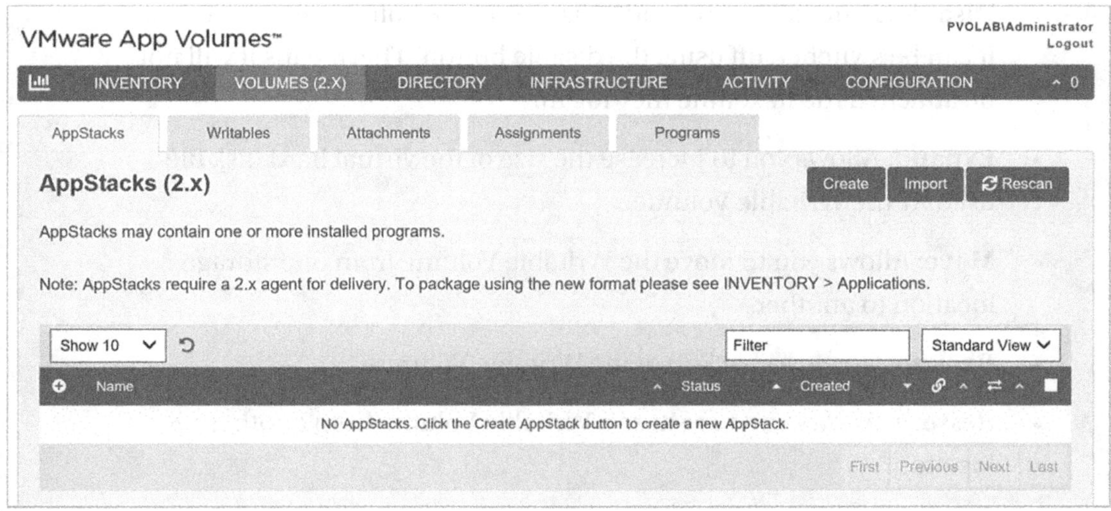

Figure 4-18. *App Volumes 2.x AppStacks screen*

As with the Inventory menu, on this screen, you can create, import, and rescan AppStacks. Any AppStacks within your environment would also be displayed on this screen, enabling you to manage them.

It is recommended to upgrade your existing AppStacks to the new App Volumes 4 format to take advantage of the new features, functionality, and performance benefits. This might also present an opportunity to review your application landscape.

Next is the **Writables** tab.

Writables tab

The Writables tab is where you create and manage Writable Volumes that were created in App Volumes 2.x. These are the volumes that are used for user installed apps and for storing end user profiles. An example is shown in Figure 4-19.

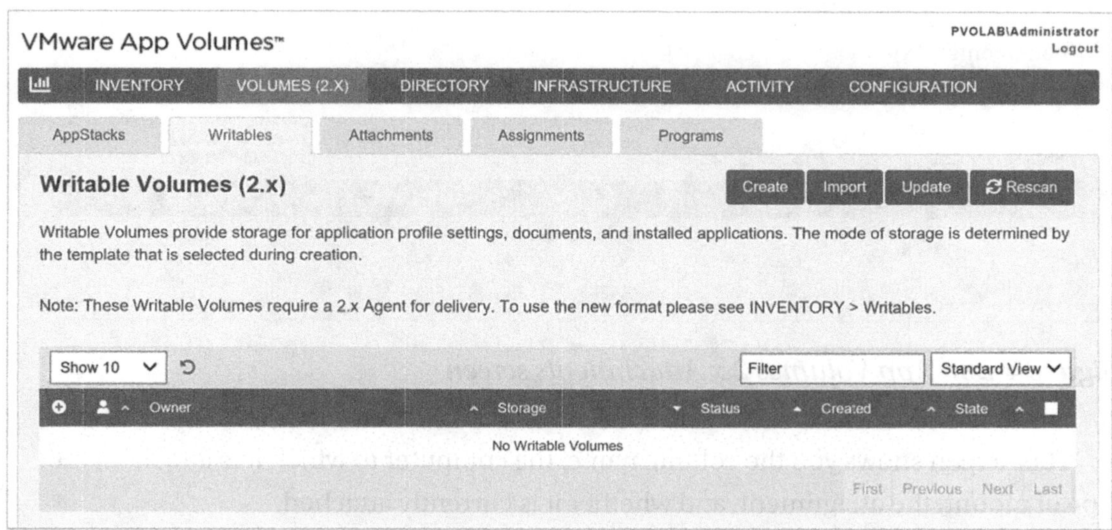

Figure 4-19. *App Volumes 2.x Writables screen*

The Writable Volumes screen for 2.x allows you to create, import, update, and rescan Writable Volumes, as well as perform the various management tasks that will be available if you have any 2.x Writable Volumes within your infrastructure.

As with AppStacks, it is recommended to upgrade your existing Writable Volumes to the new App Volumes 4.x format.

Next is the **Attachments** tab.

Attachments tab

The Attachments screen shows you any currently attached 2.x volumes, as shown in Figure 4-20.

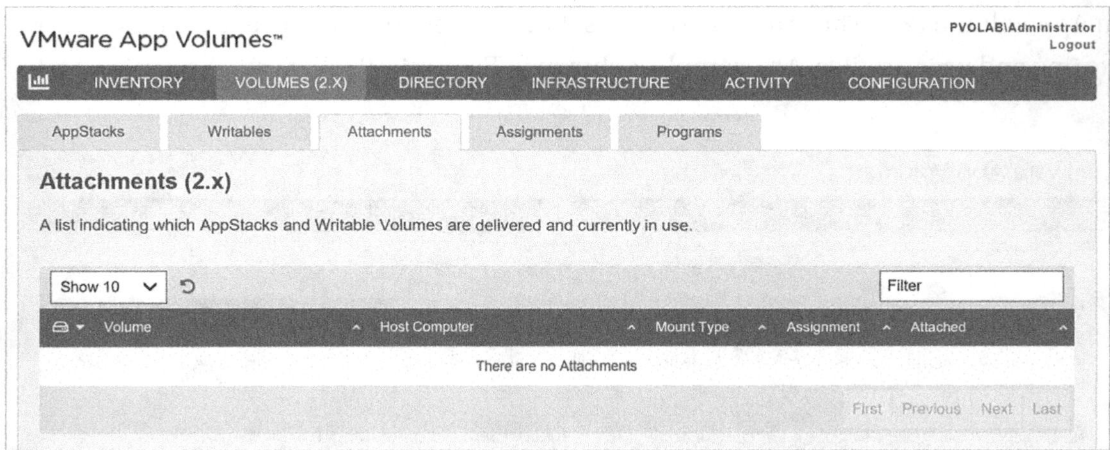

__Figure 4-20.__ App Volumes 2.x Attachments screen

This screen shows you the volume name, the computer to which it is attached, the type of mount, the assignment, and whether it is currently attached.

The penultimate tab is for **Assignments**.

Assignments tab

On the **Assignments** screen, you will see which of the entities within your environment currently have a volume assigned to them, as shown in Figure 4-21.

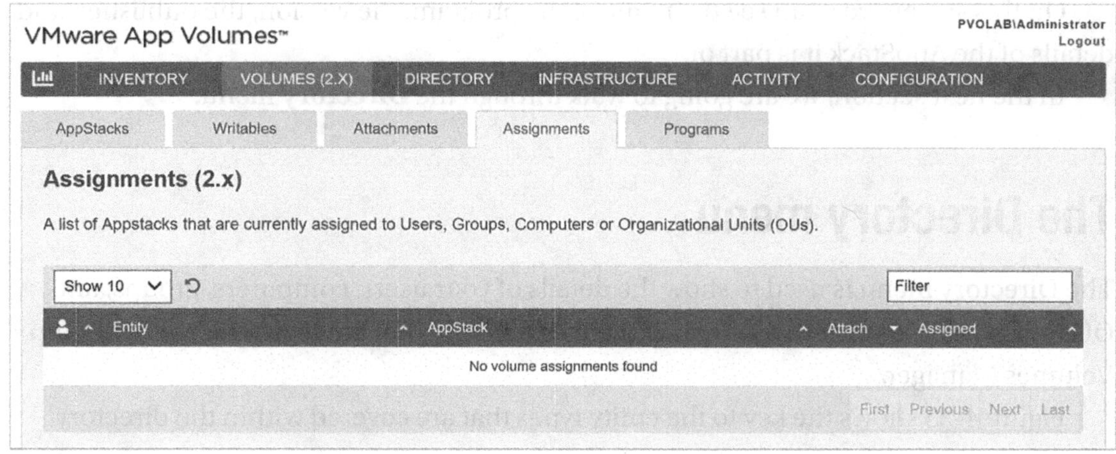

Figure 4-21. *App Volumes 2.x Assignments screen*

This shows you the name of the entity and whether it is a user, group, OU, or machine, the name of the volume, whether it is attached, and to whom it is assigned to.

The final tab is for **Programs**.

Programs tab

On the Programs screen, you will see a list of the programs that are installed within the AppStacks, as shown in Figure 4-22.

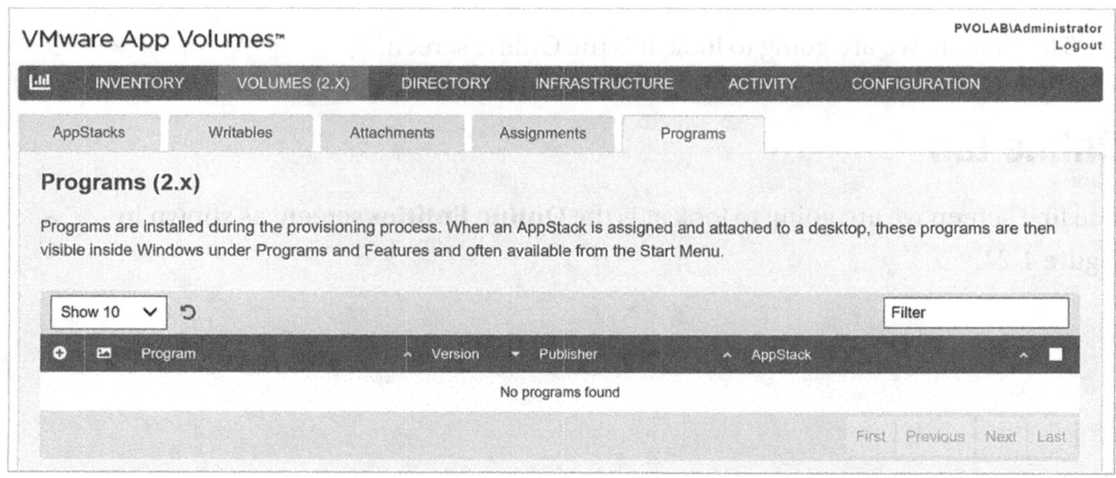

Figure 4-22. *App Volumes 2.x Programs screen*

On this screen, you can see the name of the program, the version, the publisher, and details of the AppStack it is part of.

In the next section, we are going to walk through the **Directory** menu.

The Directory menu

The Directory menu is used to show the details of your users, computers, groups, and OUs - basically, all the components in Active Directory that are registered with the App Volumes Manager.

Figure 4-23 shows the key to the entity types that are covered within the directory menu.

Figure 4-23. *Key to the icons used to show entities*

The first tab we are going to look at is the Online screen.

Online tab

The first screen we are going to look at is the **Online Entities** screen, as shown in Figure 4-24.

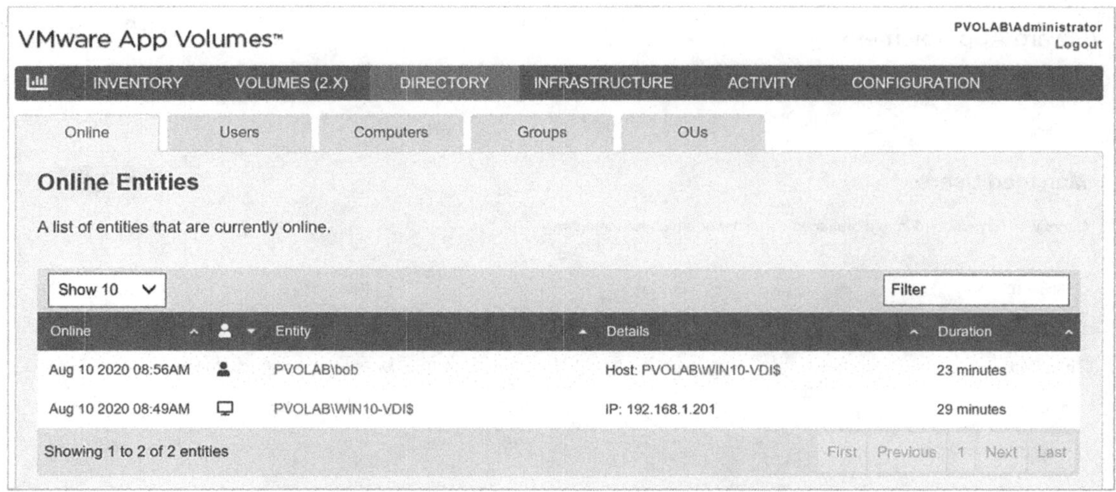

Figure 4-24. *Directory - Online Entities screen*

This screen displays the time the entity went online (when the user logged in and the volume attached), the type of entity as depicted by the icon, the name of the entity, the details of the host machine being used, and the length of time the entity has been online.

Next is the **Users** tab.

Users tab

The **Managed Users** screen shows you the end users that have logged in to an App Volumes managed machine - in other words, a machine that is running the App Volumes Agent and has registered with the App Volumes Manager.

If there appear to be users that are not listed that should be, then click the Sync button to refresh the screen and synchronize the data again.

The screen then shows you an overview of current users and their assignments, as shown in Figure 4-25.

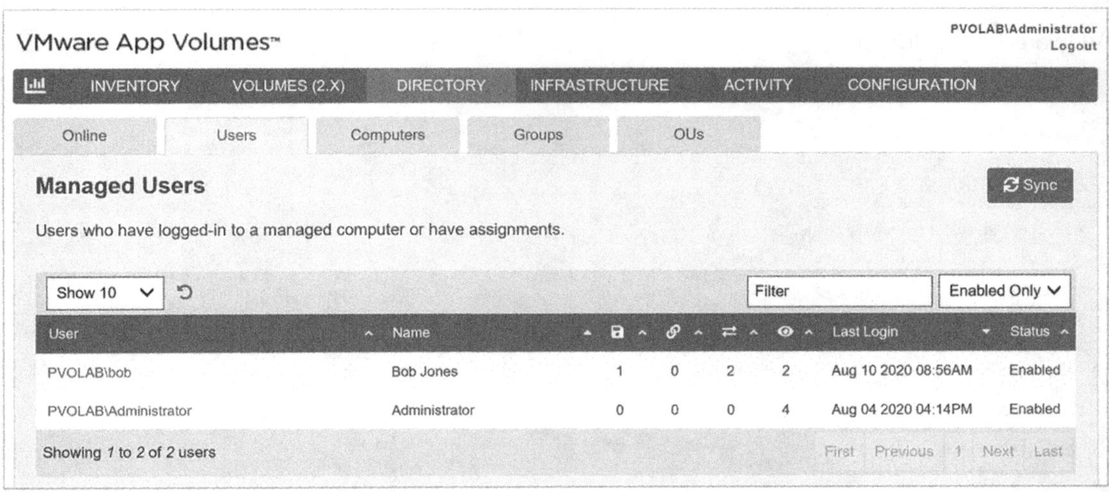

Figure 4-25. *Directory – Users screen*

As you can see in this example, the screen shows the user, the name of the user, the last time the end user logged in, and whether they are enabled.

You will also see a table of numbers with icons above. The key to these icons is shown in Figure 4-26.

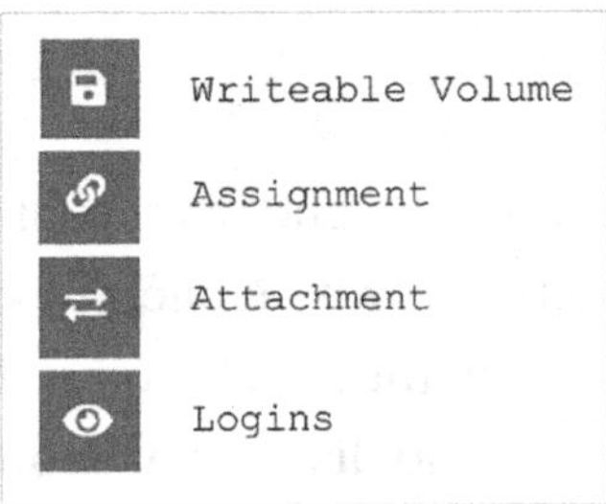

Figure 4-26. *Key to managed user icons*

So, in the example shown, the end user **Bob** has a Writable Volume, no assignments, two attachments, and has logged in twice. In addition, you can filter on the status of the end user, selecting to show all end users or just those that are enabled.

Next is the **Computers** tab.

Computers tab

The Managed Computers screen shows you the computers that have been registered with the App Volumes Manager, that is, those machines that are running the App Volumes Agent, or have volumes assigned to them rather than user assignments.

This screen is shown in Figure 4-27.

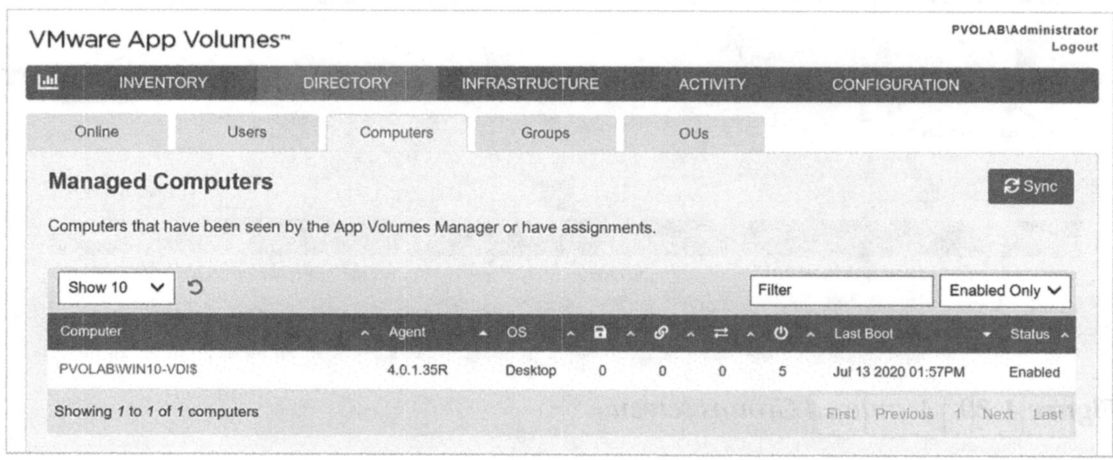

***Figure 4-27.** Managed Computers screen*

On this screen, you will see the name of the computer, the version of the App Volumes Agent it is running, the type of OS, either desktop or server, and then the icons for Writables, assignments, and attachments. You will also see another icon as shown in Figure 4-28.

***Figure 4-28.** Icon for machine boots*

The Boots icon indicates the number of times that a particular machine has booted. The final information shows the time and date of the last boot and whether the machine is enabled.

The penultimate tab is for Groups.

Groups

On the **Managed Groups** screen, you can see which groups have been assigned a volume as shown in Figure 4-29.

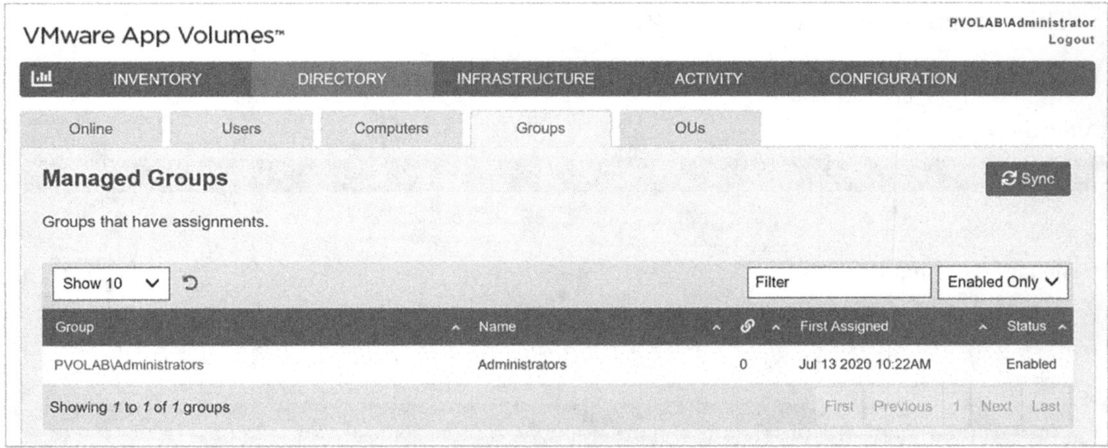

Figure 4-29. *Managed Groups screen*

You can see the AD group, the name of the group in App Volumes, the number of assignments, the time and date the volume was first assigned, and then the status.

As with previous screens under the directory menu, if there is information that seems to be missing, you can click the **Sync** button so that it resynchronizes with AD.

The final tab is for **OUs**.

OUs

On the final tab under the directory menu, you will find the **Managed Organizational Units** screen as shown in Figure 4-30.

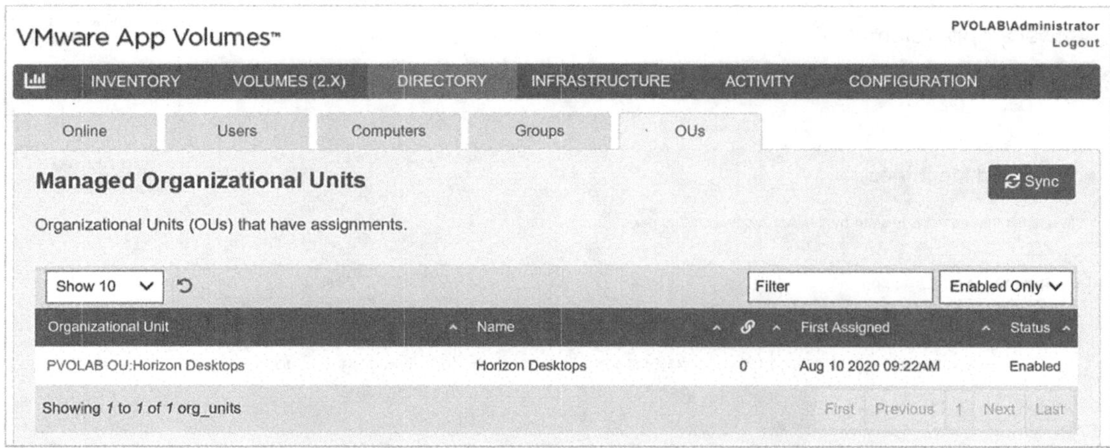

Figure 4-30. *Managed Organizational Units screen*

In this screen, you can see the OU, the name of the OU, how many assignments it has, the time and date of the first assignment, and finally the status.

The next menu item we are going to look at is the **Infrastructure** menu.

The Infrastructure menu

The Infrastructure menu is where you will find all the details about the machine registered with the App Volumes Manager and the storage used to store your volumes.

We will start with the Machines tab.

Machines tab

The Managed Machines screen, as the name suggests, shows you the details of all the machines that are running the App Volumes Agent and that have registered themselves with the App Volumes Manager.

An example of this is shown in Figure 4-31.

Figure 4-31. *Managed Machines screen*

On this screen, you will see the name of the machine and the host machine it sits on. In this example, you will see the IP address of the ESXi server in the test lab, the unique identifier of the machine, the source of the information, and in this case the App Volumes Agent and when the machine was created. Finally, you will see the status of the machine, in this example, existing.

You can also filter the results by showing just those machines that are active or show all machines.

Next is the **Storages** tab.

Storages tab

The Managed Storage Locations screen shows you the details about your datastores that are used to store your volumes.

On this screen, you will see the name of the datastore, the machine managing that is hosting the datastore, the current amount of storage used, the total size of the datastore, and the number of volumes being stored (AppStacks and Writable Volumes – Packages are shown on the left-hand side, if you expand the detail by clicking the + button).

You will also see whether the datastore allows attachments and its status.

Figure 4-32 shows an example of this.

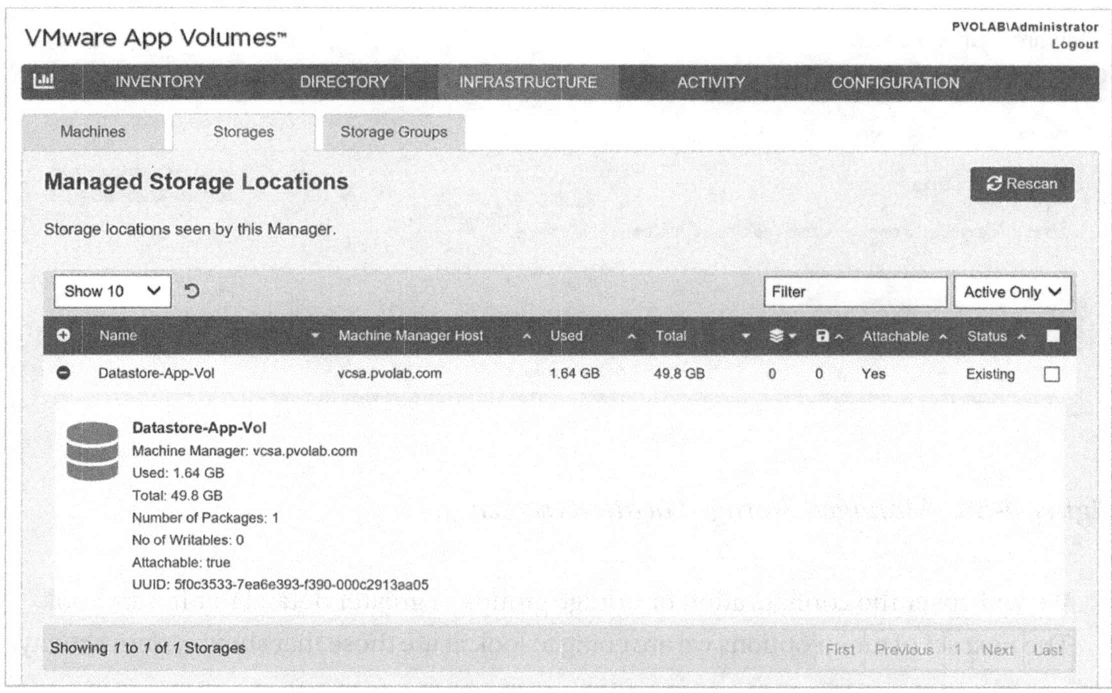

***Figure 4-32.** Managed Storage Locations screen*

The next tab is for **Storage Groups**.

Storage Groups tab

On the **Storage Groups** screen, you can configure a storage group. A storage group allows you to define a group of individual storage locations, so that they function as a single entity.

The Storage Groups screen is shown in Figure 4-33.

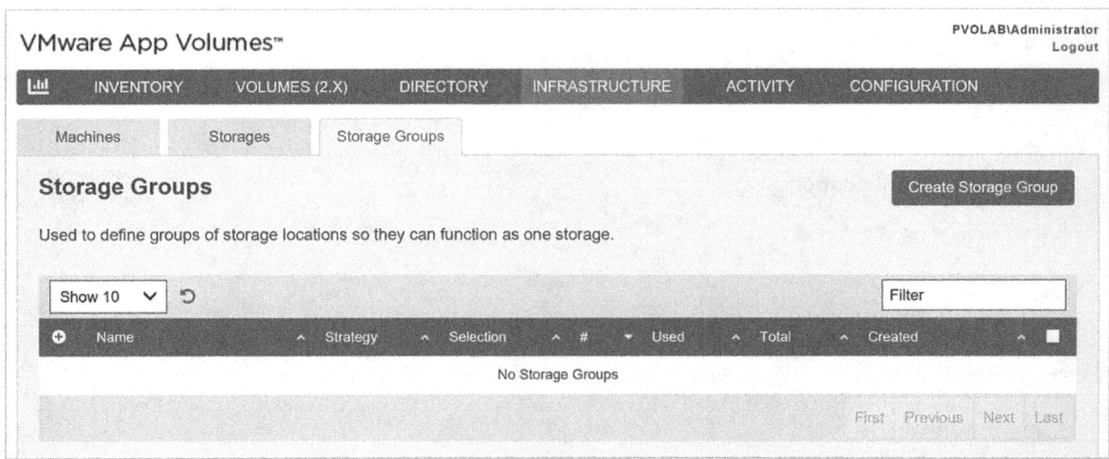

***Figure 4-33.** Managed Storage Locations screen*

We will cover the configuration of storage groups in greater detail later in this book. The next set of menu options we are going to look at are those that show system activity.

The Activity menu

The Activity menu options are used to show you what is going on with your App Volumes environment. We will start by looking at the Pending Actions tab.

Pending Actions tab

As the name suggests, **Pending Actions** lists all the actions that are still yet to complete. It shows the time of when the action was initiated, what the action is, the message generated, and then the status.

By default, the App Volumes Manager will list 500 pending actions and the **Auto Refresh** box is checked, meaning the actions listed will update automatically.

An example of this screen is shown in Figure 4-34.

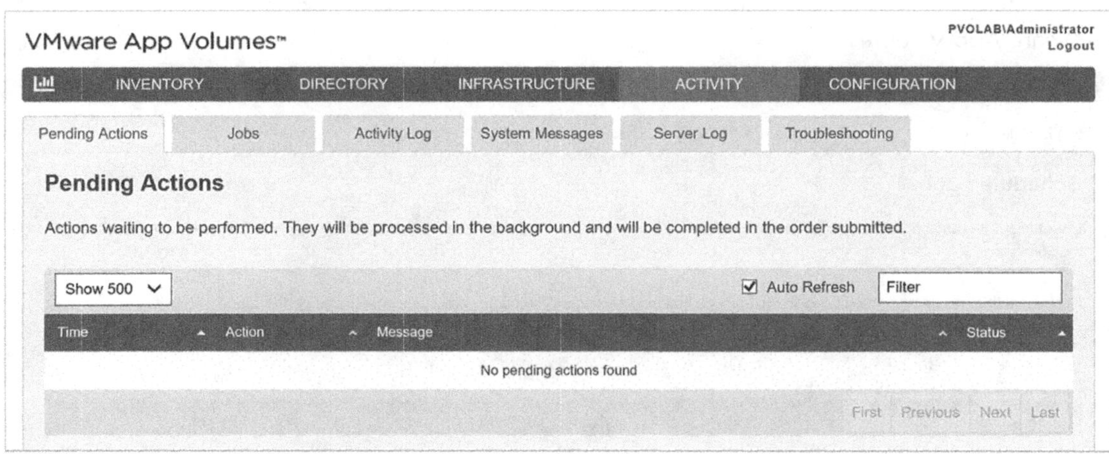

Figure 4-34. *Pending Actions screen*

The next tab is the **Jobs** tab.

Jobs tab

The Scheduled Jobs screen lists the jobs that run automatically at scheduled intervals.

These settings are intended only for advanced tuning and should not require any modification. If you enable, disable, or modify any timing settings, this could cause significant performance or a decrease in functionality to your app Volumes environment.

In the test lab environment, we have expanded the Audit vms option to show you. You can see that the job is enabled and runs every 9 hours and 21 minutes. It last ran about 3 hours ago.

You will see that you can click the Enabled button to disable the job and prevent it from running, as well as being able to change the frequency in which it runs and the down time.

This example is shown in Figure 4-35.

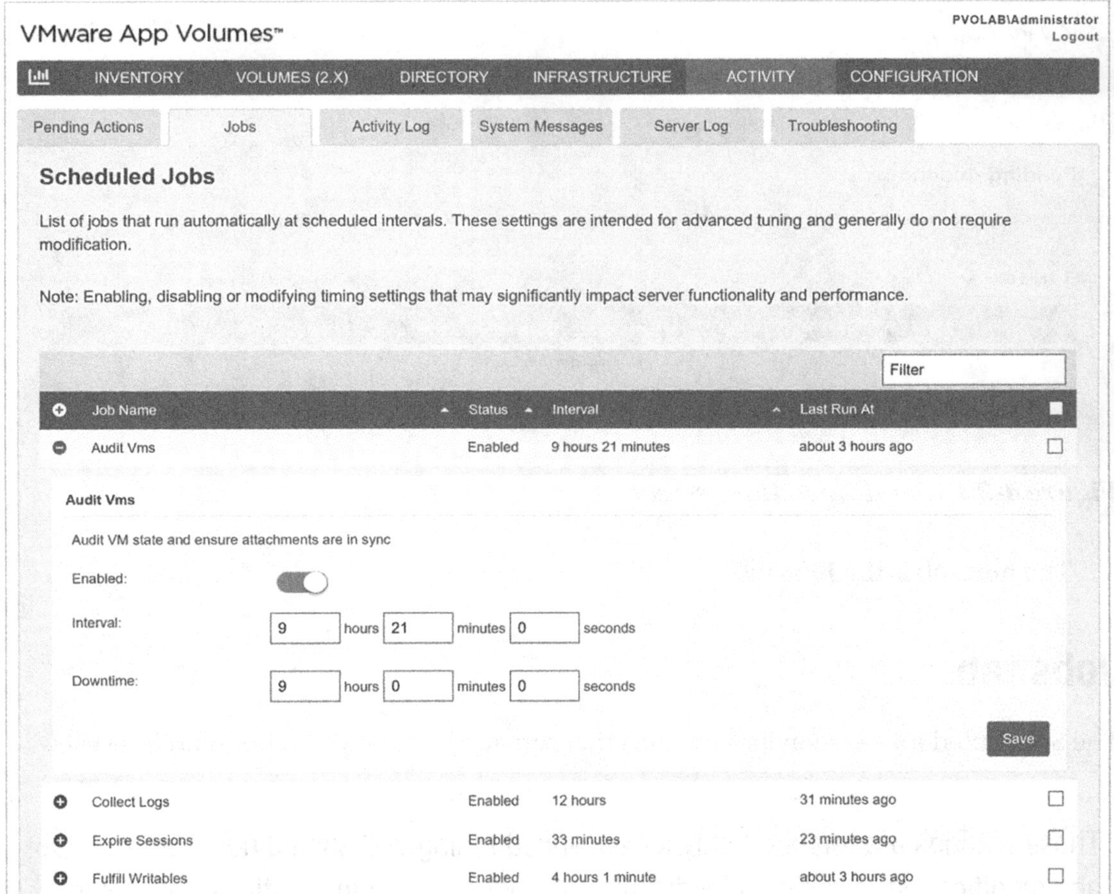

Figure 4-35. *Scheduled Jobs screen*

If you do make any changes, click the **Save** button to accept them.

Next is the **Activity Log** tab.

Activity Log tab

The **Activity Log** screen provides you a record of all activity within your App Volumes environment.

It logs the time of the activity, who initiated the activity, what the activity was, the entity, and the target.

An example of the Activity Log screen is shown in Figure 4-36.

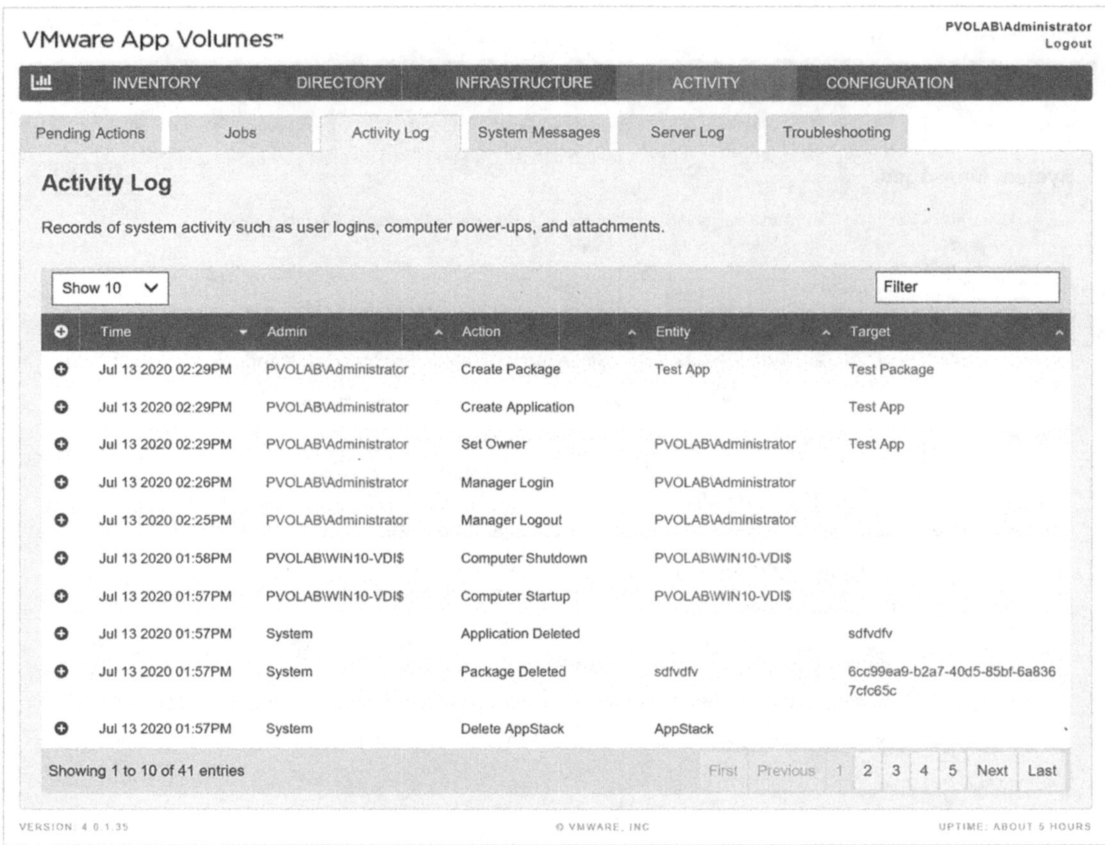

Figure 4-36. *Activity Log screen*

The next tab to look at is the **System Messages** tab.

System Messages tab

On the System Messages screen, you will see a list of all system-generated messages as shown in Figure 4-37.

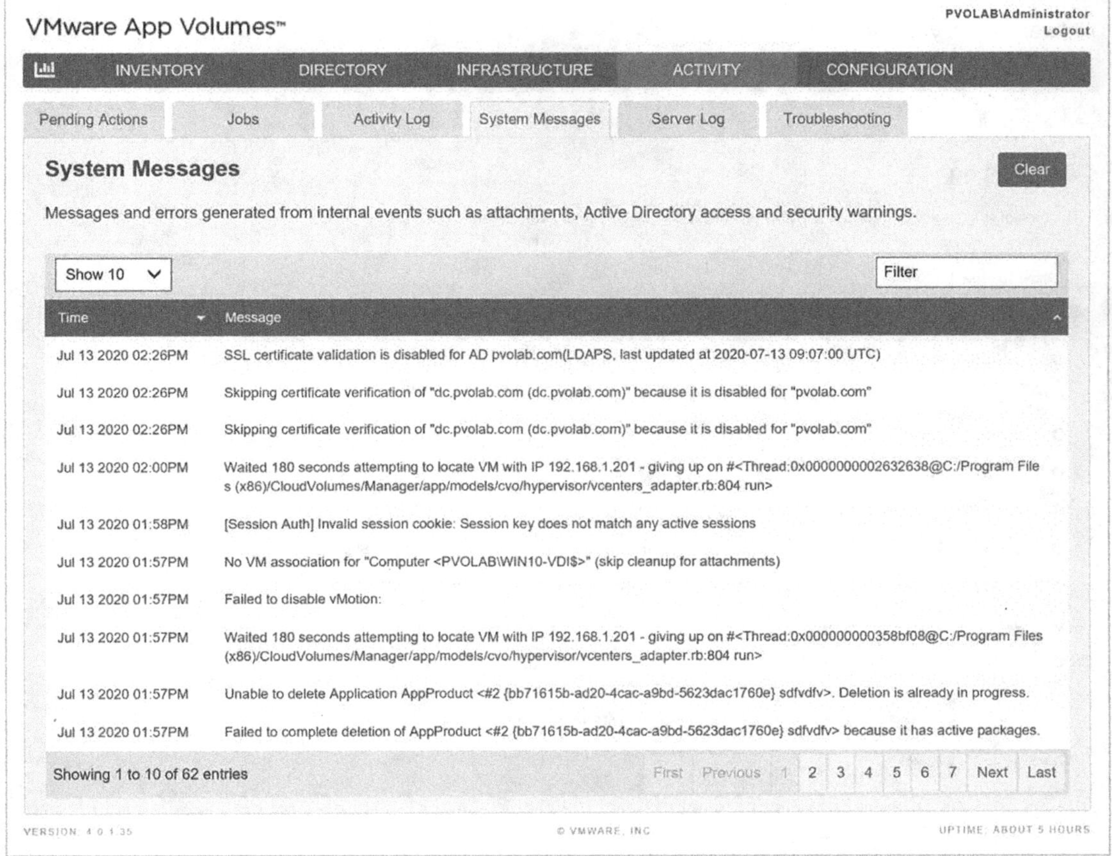

Figure 4-37. *System Messages screen*

You can clear the activity log by clicking the **Clear** button.

Next is the **Server Log** tab.

Server Log tab

The Server Log screen shows the end of the current file. This is shown in Figure 4-38.

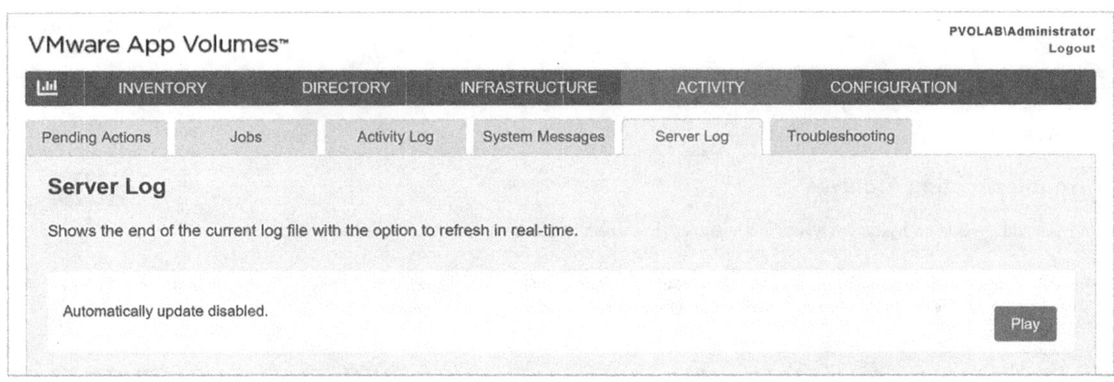

Figure 4-38. *Server Log screen*

If you click the Play button, you will see the server log in real time, as shown in Figure 4-39.

```
[2020-07-13 13:49:31 UTC]    P1312DJ84  INFO       Cvo: [AdapterState] Active - &quot;Hypervisor &lt;VMware vCenter#37291320 administrator@vsphere.local@vcsa.pvolab.com&gt;&quot;
[2020-07-13 13:49:31 UTC]    P1312DJ84  INFO       Cvo: [AdapterState] Not Connected - &quot;Hypervisor &lt;Multiple vCenters&gt;&quot; - 3461 secs old
[2020-07-13 13:49:34 UTC]    P4280R269  INFO Started GET &quot;/log?&amp;color=1&amp;html=1&amp;bytes=50000&amp;_=1594647966852&quot; for ::1 at 2020-07-13 14:49:34 +0100
[2020-07-13 13:49:34 UTC]    P4280R269  INFO Processing by LogsController#tail as TEXT
[2020-07-13 13:49:34 UTC]    P4280R269  INFO   Parameters: {&quot;color&quot;=&gt;&quot;1&quot;, &quot;html&quot;=&gt;&quot;1&quot;, &quot;bytes&quot;=&gt;&quot;50000&quot;, &quot;
[2020-07-13 13:49:34 UTC]    P4280R269  INFO Referred by https://localhost/activity using Mozilla/5.0 (Windows NT 10.0; WOW64; Trident/7.0; rv:11.0) like Gecko
[2020-07-13 13:49:34 UTC]    P4280R269  INFO Current Request roles: [&quot;Administrators&quot;], user: Administrator (1)
[2020-07-13 13:49:34 UTC]    P4280R269  INFO   Rendering html template
[2020-07-13 13:49:34 UTC]    P4280R269  INFO   Rendered html template (0.0ms)
[2020-07-13 13:49:34 UTC]    P4280R269  INFO Completed 200 OK in 33ms (Views: 3.7ms | ActiveRecord: 7.5ms)
[2020-07-13 13:49:34 UTC]    P4280R269  INFO


[2020-07-13 13:49:39 UTC]    P4988R182  INFO Started GET &quot;/log?&amp;color=1&amp;html=1&amp;bytes=50000&amp;_=1594647966853&quot; for ::1 at 2020-07-13 14:49:39 +0100
[2020-07-13 13:49:39 UTC]    P4988R182  INFO Processing by LogsController#tail as TEXT
[2020-07-13 13:49:39 UTC]    P4988R182  INFO   Parameters: {&quot;color&quot;=&gt;&quot;1&quot;, &quot;html&quot;=&gt;&quot;1&quot;, &quot;bytes&quot;=&gt;&quot;50000&quot;, &quot;
[2020-07-13 13:49:39 UTC]    P4988R182  INFO Referred by https://localhost/activity using Mozilla/5.0 (Windows NT 10.0; WOW64; Trident/7.0; rv:11.0) like Gecko
[2020-07-13 13:49:39 UTC]    P4988R182  INFO Current Request roles: [&quot;Administrators&quot;], user: Administrator (1)
```

Figure 4-39. *Server Log played in real time*

The final tab under the Activity menu is the Troubleshooting tab.

Troubleshooting tab

The Troubleshooting Archives screen is used to create an archive on a specific App Volumes Manager server. This is used should you need to log a support call with VMware.

An example of the Troubleshooting Archives screen is shown in Figure 4-40.

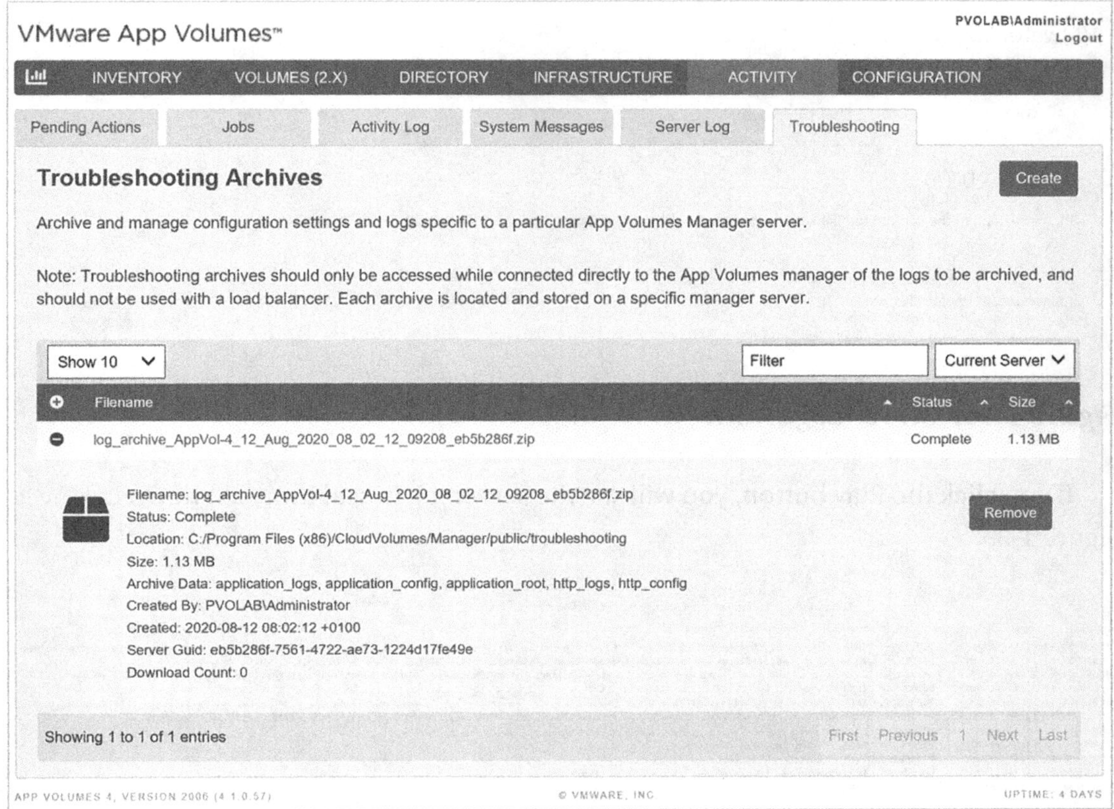

Figure 4-40. *Troubleshooting Archives screen*

By clicking the + button next to the log you want to see information about, you will see the details of the archive log - details such as the filename, size, who created it, the time and date it was created, and the ID of the server it relates to.

It also displays the location of the archive file so that you can use it for support should you need to email it. To create the archive, follow the described steps:

1. Click the **Create** button.

2. You will see the **Create Troubleshooting Archive** dialog box as shown in Figure 4-41.

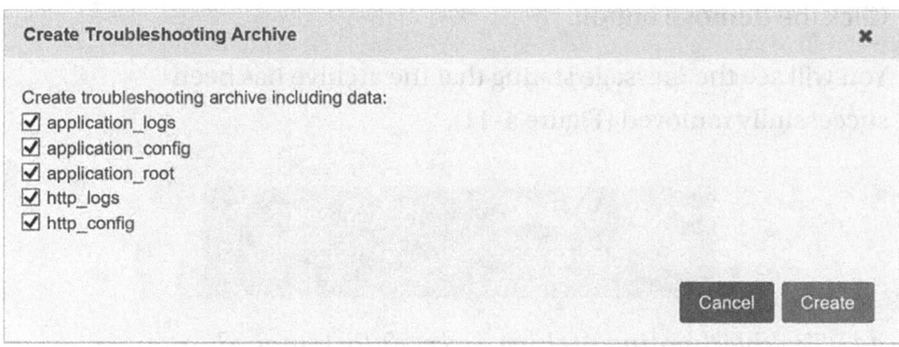

***Figure 4-41.** Creating a Troubleshooting Archives screen*

3. Check the boxes for each log you want to add to the archive.
4. Click the **Create** button.
5. You will see the message stating that the archive has been successfully created (Figure 4-42).

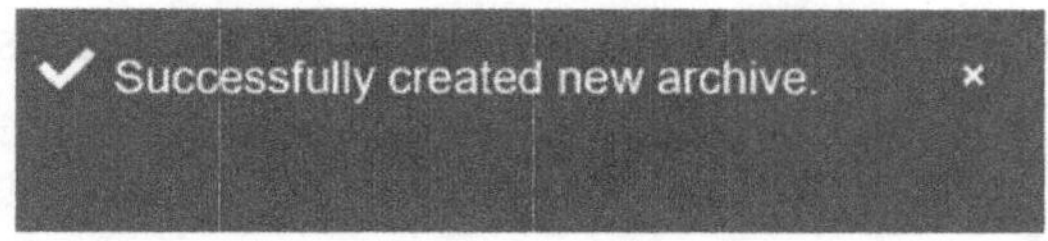

***Figure 4-42.** Successful creation of a Troubleshooting Archive*

6. If you want to remove an archive log, then click the **Remove** button.
7. You will see the dialog box in Figure 4-43.

***Figure 4-43.** Confirm removal of Troubleshooting Archive*

8. Click the **Remove** button.
9. You will see the message stating that the archive has been successfully removed (Figure 4-44).

✓ log_archive_AppVol-4_12_Aug_2020_08_11_41_12400_eb5b286f.zip removed! ×

Figure 4-44. *Troubleshooting Archive successfully removed*

Next, we are going to look at the **Configuration** menu.

The Configuration menu

You will have already seen the **Configuration** menu. This is the configuration and settings screen you completed as part of the initial setup of the App Volumes Manager, with the tabs for License, AD Domains, Admin Roles, and so on, as shown in Figure 4-45.

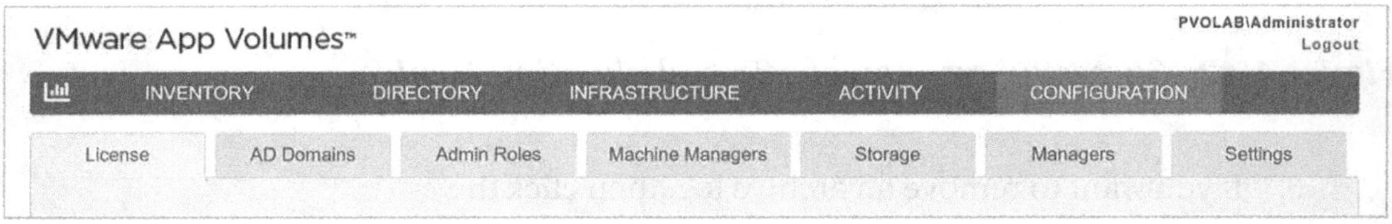

VMware App Volumes™ PVOLAB\Administrator Logout
INVENTORY DIRECTORY INFRASTRUCTURE ACTIVITY CONFIGURATION
License AD Domains Admin Roles Machine Managers Storage Managers Settings

Figure 4-45. *Configuration menu*

As we have already covered this menu in detail, when we set up the App Volumes Manager server, then please refer to Chapter 3.

The final screen we are going to look at is the dashboard screen.

The Dashboard screens

The last screens we are going to look at are the dashboard screens. These can be found at the start of the menu bar, before the INVENTORY option, shown by the icon in Figure 4-46.

Figure 4-46. *Dashboard page icon*

If you click the icon, you will see the dashboard page. We are going to look at this in three sections. The first section shows you a breakdown of the licensed options for App Volumes. So, in this example, we have 50,000 users and the ability to use both desktops and servers for attaching volumes. It also shows the utilization of those licenses, as shown in Figure 4-47.

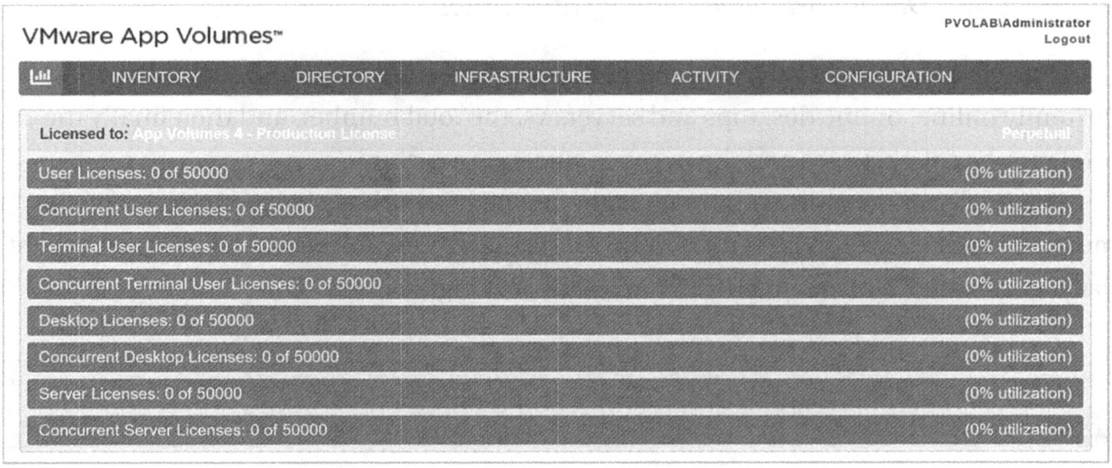

VMware App Volumes™
PVOLAB\Administrator
Logout
INVENTORY DIRECTORY INFRASTRUCTURE ACTIVITY CONFIGURATION
Licensed to: App Volumes 4 - Production License Perpetual
User Licenses: 0 of 50000 (0% utilization)
Concurrent User Licenses: 0 of 50000 (0% utilization)
Terminal User Licenses: 0 of 50000 (0% utilization)
Concurrent Terminal User Licenses: 0 of 50000 (0% utilization)
Desktop Licenses: 0 of 50000 (0% utilization)
Concurrent Desktop Licenses: 0 of 50000 (0% utilization)
Server Licenses: 0 of 50000 (0% utilization)
Concurrent Server Licenses: 0 of 50000 (0% utilization)

Figure 4-47. *Dashboard page showing license utilization*

The next section of the dashboard screen shows a graphical representation of the utilization of users, computers, and packages as shown in Figure 4-48.

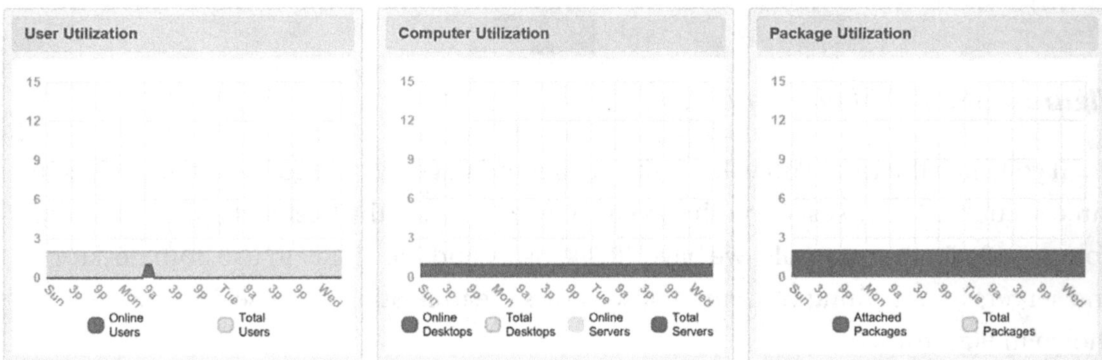

Figure 4-48. *Dashboard page showing utilization*

Here, you can see, briefly, the total number of users and the number of users currently online, online desktops and servers vs. the total number, and then finally the total number of packages and the number currently attached.

The final section shows information about which users have logged in recently, the most recent machines to boot up that are managed by App Volumes, and the most recent packages that have been attached. This is shown in Figure 4-49.

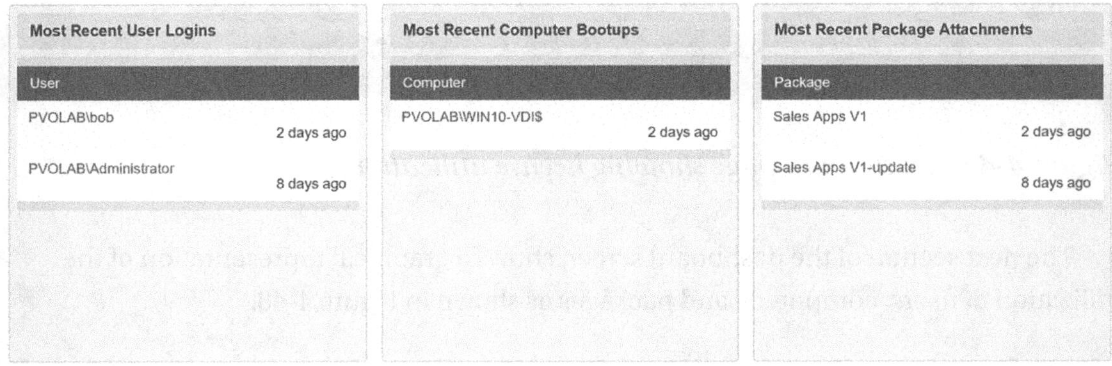

Figure 4-49. *Dashboard page showing user logins, machine boots, and packages*

We have now completed our guide through the management console.

Chapter summary

In this chapter, we have taken a complete guided tour of the App Volumes Manager management console. We have looked at each one of the menu options, and the submenus within, along with the various icons used to identify the various components, showing you exactly where to find the different tasks and actions that you need to manage your App Volumes environment.

Now, with this information, in the next chapter, we can start to build the environment, starting with App Volumes Applications and Packages.

CHAPTER 5

Applications, Packages, and Programs

At this stage in the book, we have talked about how the solution works, have installed and configured all the component parts, and then taken a guided tour of the management console in preparation for using App Volumes to deliver apps to end users.

In this fifth chapter, we are now going to use the knowledge gained, along with the test lab we have built, to start creating our applications and packages and deliver those to end users.

But before we get onto the practical side of creating our applications and packages, we need to have a packaging machine available on which we can install the applications and capture that installation process to create the packages from. In the first section of this chapter, we are going to look at the requirements for the packaging machine.

Building a packaging machine

To package an application, you will need to use a packaging machine. The application you want to package is installed onto the packaging machine, which has the new virtual hard disk attached. During the installation, the application files and settings are installed using the packaging machine but are redirected to the attached virtual hard disk.

P. von Oven, *Delivering Applications with VMware App Volumes 4*,
https://doi.org/10.1007/978-1-4842-6689-2_5

There are a few requirements to be aware of when it comes to the packaging machine and its configuration:

- Application Packages must be packaged using a clean base image, which ideally is the same OS, patches, service packs, and security levels as the virtual machines that you are going to deploy within your environment. So, if those machines are Windows 10 and a specific version of Windows 10, then use that very same OS and version for the packaging machine. Although some Windows 10 apps with work on a server OS, if you are packaging an application.
- Install the correct version of the App Volumes Agent on the packaging machine. This is required for the packaging machine to register with the App Volumes Manager and be available to select as a packaging machine.
- If you are going to have applications that are going to be delivered in the base image, then ensure that these are already installed before you start the packaging process. This ensures that there is no conflict with shared files between the apps you are packaging and the apps already installed.
- Ensure that the packaging machine has no other volumes attached when you start the packaging process. That includes Writable Volumes.
- Only one packaging process per virtual machine.
- Include all the app dependencies within the package. So, if the app needs a particular version of Java, then ensure that that version of Java gets installed as part of the packaging process.
- Ensure that there is no antivirus software running on the packaging machine.
- Ensure that the packaging machine is not running the Horizon Agent or the VMware Dynamic Environment Manager (DEM) agent when you are packaging.

- When installing apps, ensure that they are installed for all users and not the user you are using for the install. Otherwise, you could end up preventing users from having access to their apps.
- Do not package apps that need a common SID to a desktop pool or to a virtual machine that have had Sysprep run on them.
- Virtual machines used for packaging should have a snapshot dedicated to the state of a user's desktop and should be taken before you start the packaging process.
- Once you have completed creating your package, revert the packaging machine back to the snapshot taken before you started the packaging process, that is, before you install your apps.
- Disable Windows update and Windows search.

Logging in to the management console

The first step of the process is to log in to the management console. You can do this remotely using the browser on an IT admin's desktop or directly from the App Volumes Manager by double-clicking the icon.

Now follow the steps described:

1. You will now see the App Volumes Manager login box as shown in Figure 5-1.

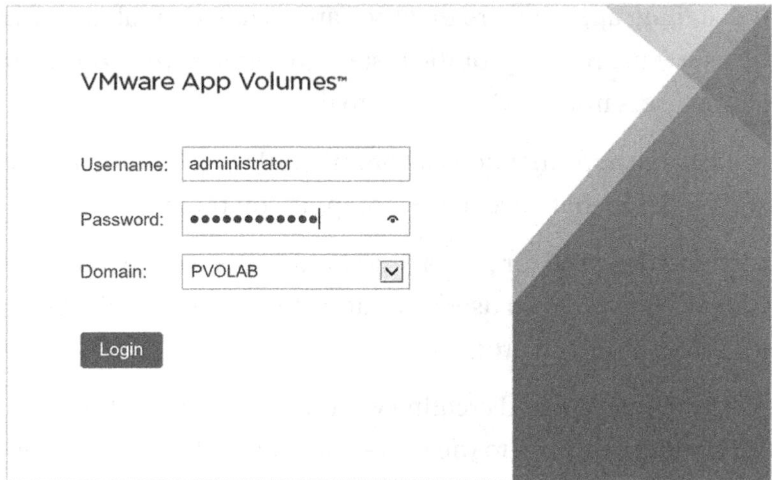

***Figure 5-1.** Logging in to the App Volumes Manager console*

2. Enter your **Username** and **Password** in the boxes. In the test lab, we are using the administrator user account.
3. In the Domain drop-down menu box, click and select the domain for this user account. In the test lab, this is the PVOLAB domain.
4. Click the **Login** button.
5. You will now see the **INVENTORY** screen and the **Applications** tab as shown in Figure 5-2.

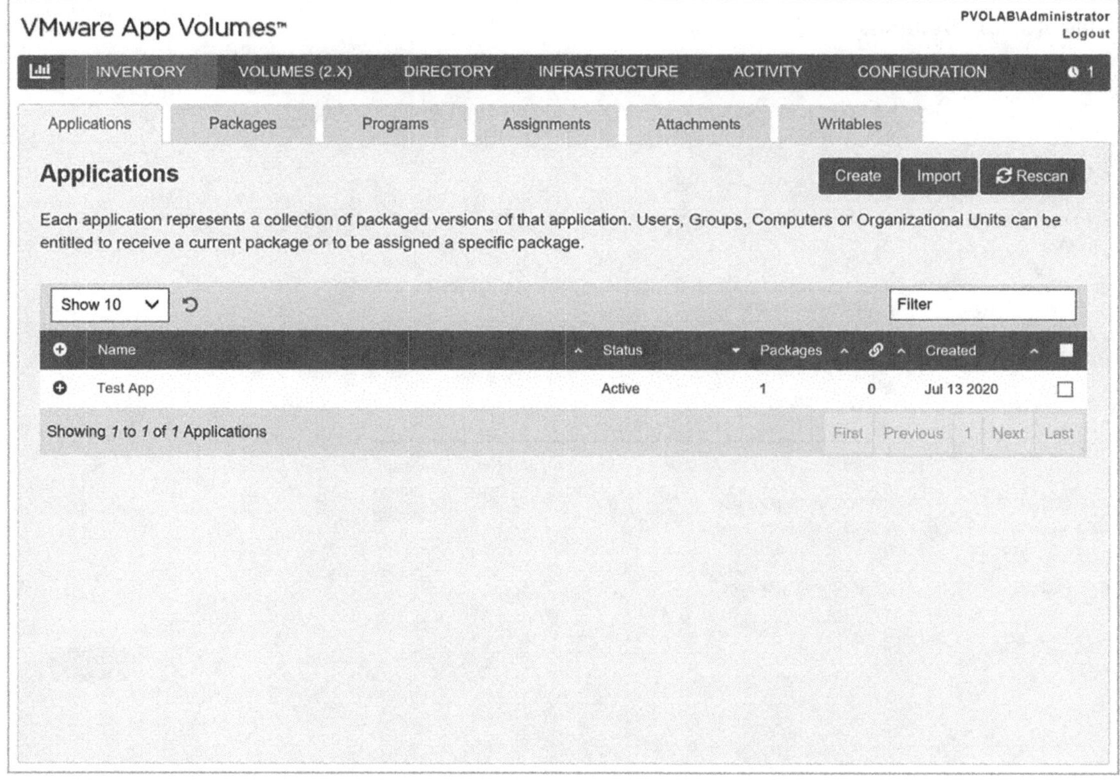

***Figure 5-2.** The INVENTORY menu and Applications tab*

Now that you have logged in to the App Volumes Manager console, in the next section, we are going to create the application.

Creating an Application

In this section, we are going to create an application.

As a quick reminder, an application in App Volumes terminology refers to a logical construct for an individual application or a group of applications. It is the application that is assigned to your end users.

An application could also be made up of multiple different packages.

To create an application, follow the steps as described:

1. Click the **Create** button at the top right-hand side of the screen.

   You will see the Create Application screen as shown in Figure 5-3.

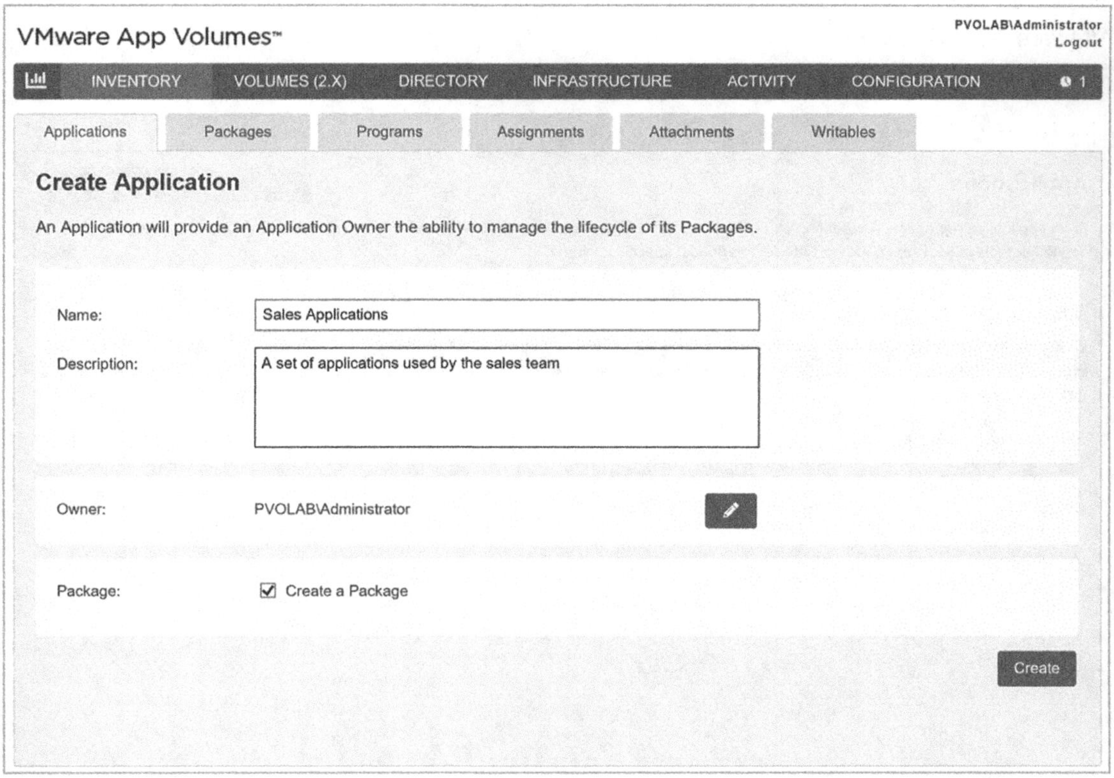

Figure 5-3. *Creating an Application*

2. In the **Name** box, type in a name for this application. In the test lab example, we have called this **Sales Applications** as these applications will be assigned to the sales teams.
3. Next, in the **Description** box, type in a description that easily identifies this application.
4. The next section allows you to add an application owner. To add an owner, click the pencil icon next to the **Owner**. You will see the section expand and give you the option to search Active Directory to select an owner, as shown in Figure 5-4.

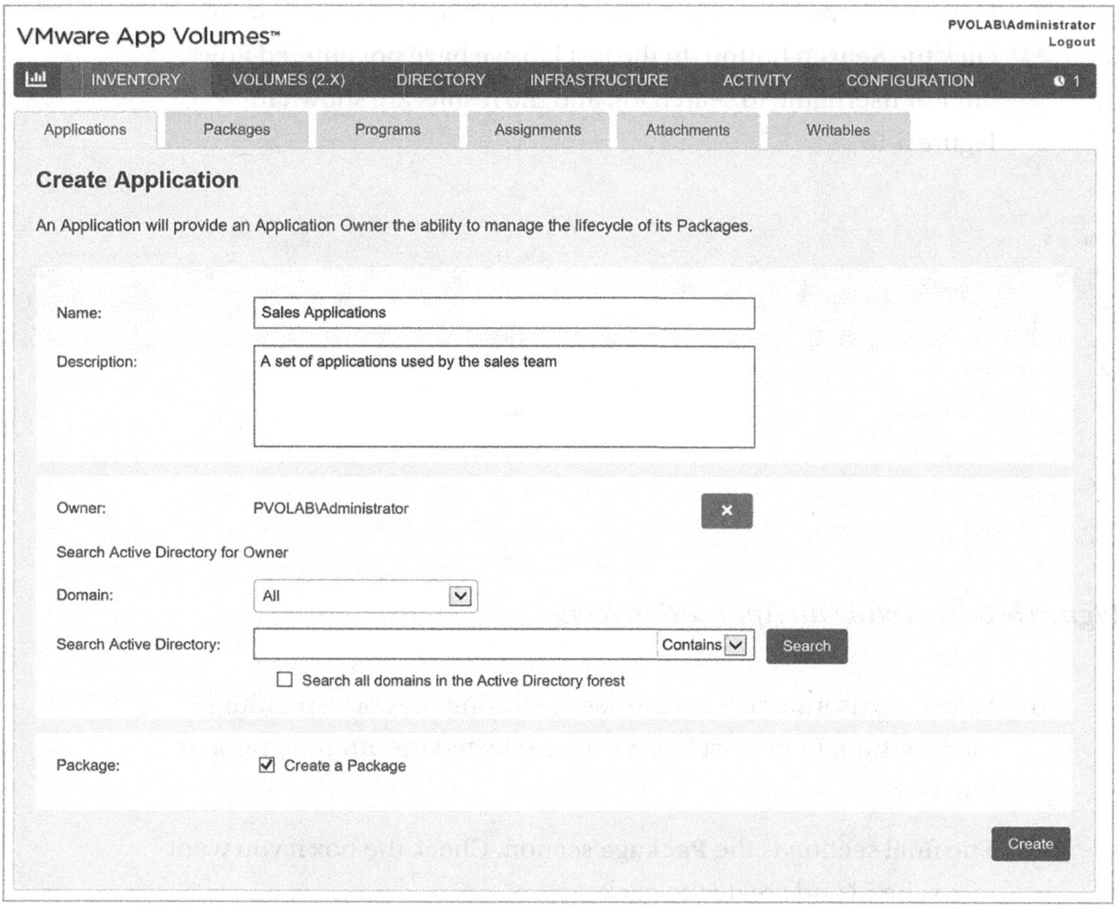

VMware App Volumes™
PVOLAB\Administrator
Logout
INVENTORY VOLUMES (2.X) DIRECTORY INFRASTRUCTURE ACTIVITY CONFIGURATION 1
Applications Packages Programs Assignments Attachments Writables
Create Application
An Application will provide an Application Owner the ability to manage the lifecycle of its Packages.
Name: Sales Applications
Description: A set of applications used by the sales team
Owner: PVOLAB\Administrator
Search Active Directory for Owner
Domain: All
Search Active Directory: Contains Search
Search all domains in the Active Directory forest
Package: Create a Package
Create

Figure 5-4. *Adding an Application owner*

5. In the **Domain** drop-down box, click and select the domain in which you want to search for the user you want as the owner. In the test lab, we are going to leave this as the default setting of **All** and therefore search all domains registered with the App Volumes Managers.

6. The **Search Active Directory** box is a filter that allows you to search for specific users. In the box, you can start to type in the name you want to search for, and then in the drop-down box on the right, you can select a filter. You can select **Contains**, **Begins**, **Ends**, and **Equals** to apply to the text you enter to help find the username.

7. Once you have entered your text for searching for the username, click the **Search** button. In the test lab, we have not entered any filter or username to search for, and the results are shown in Figure 5-5.

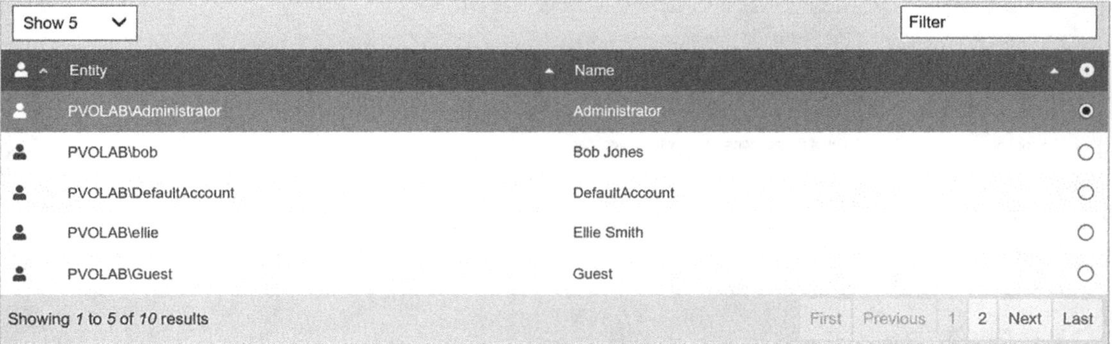

Figure 5-5. *Selecting an Application owner*

8. Select the username from the list by clicking the corresponding radio button. In the test lab, we have selected the administrator as the user.

9. The final section is the **Package** section. Check the box if you want to go ahead and create the package.

10. Now click the **Create** button.

11. You will see the **Confirm Create Application** box as shown in Figure 5-6.

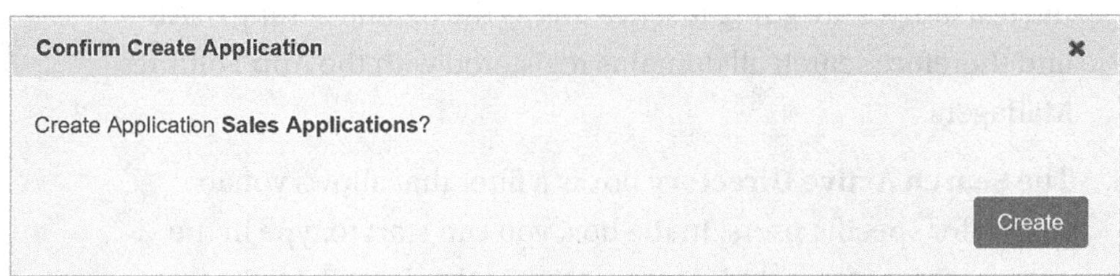

Figure 5-6. *Confirming the creation of an Application*

12. Click the **Create** button.

13. You will see the Creating Application progress bar appear as the process runs, as shown in Figure 5-7.

Figure 5-7. *Application creation process running*

14. Once successfully completed, you will see the message appear as shown in Figure 5-8.

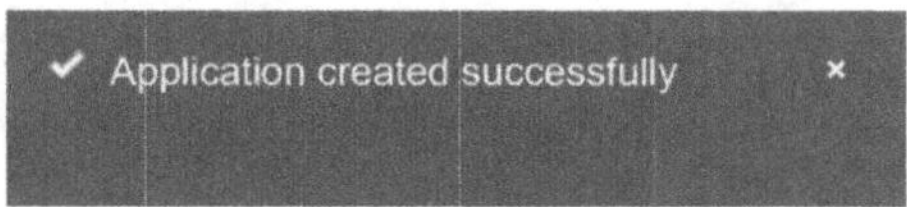

Figure 5-8. *Application creation process successfully completed*

You have now successfully created your Application. The next step of the process, covered in the next section, is to create the package by capturing the applications you want to include within the package. You will automatically be taken to the **Create Package** screen.

Creating a Package

Now that you have created the application, the next step is to add a package to the application by capturing the program or programs you want to include as part of that package. This is where your packaging machine will be used.

As you completed the creation of the application, you will automatically see the **Create Package for Sales Applications** screen. To configure and create the package, complete the following steps:

1. In the **Name** box, enter a name you want to give to this package. Remember, call this something that easily identifies what the package is. If it contains multiple programs, then do not name it after the individual programs and instead call it something more related to the department or what the set of programs are used for. In the test lab, we have called the package **Sales Apps V1**.

2. The next box is for selecting the **Base Package**. From the drop-down menu, select the base package you want to use to add the programs to. In this example, as there are no programs in the package yet, then the only option is for **Create New Package**.

3. **Storage** is the next option. From the drop-down menu, choose the datastore on which you want to create this package. This is where the VMDK file that gets created will be stored. In the test lab, we have selected the **Datastore-App-Vol** datastore on the **PVO Datacenter**.

4. As part of the storage, the next option is the **Path** option which allows you to select where to store the newly created VMDK file on the datastore. The default path is the **appvolumes/packages** folder, but you can change that to suit.

5. From the **Template** box, from the drop-down menu options, select the template file from which you are going to create this new VMDK file. In the test lab, we are going to use the standard **template.vmdk** file.

6. The next box is to select the **Stage** of the package. You can select from the stages shown in Figure 5-9 to reflect where the package is in its lifecycle.

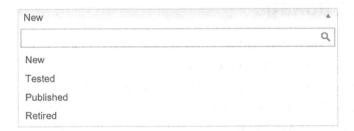

Figure 5-9. *Selecting the Package lifecycle stage*

7. In the test lab, as this is a new package, we are going to select the option for **New.**

8. Finally, there is the **Description** box. In this box, you can enter any additional information that helps describe what the package is used for and what it contains.

9. You have now completed the configuration screen for creating the package, and you should see something like Figure 5-10.

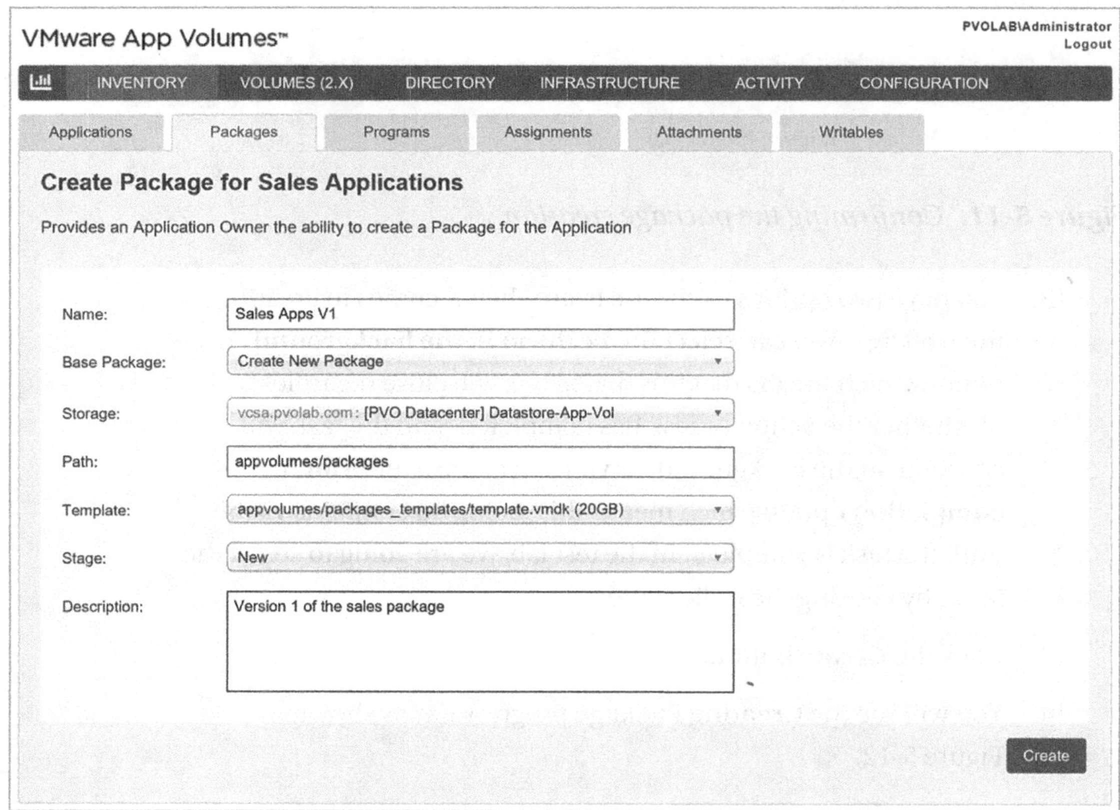

Figure 5-10. *Creating a Package*

10. Now click the **Create** button.

11. You will see the Confirm Create Package message as shown in Figure 5-11.

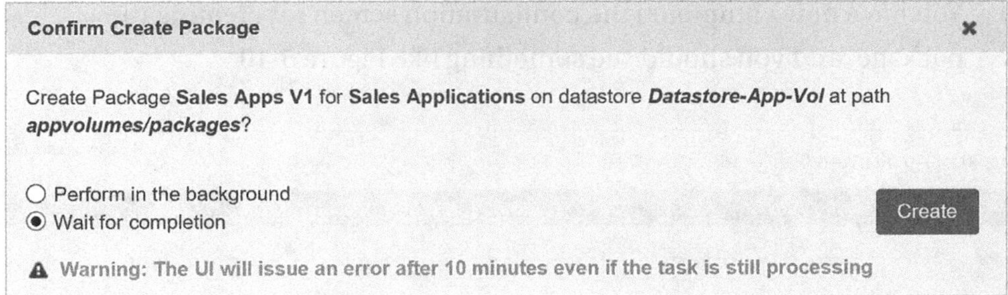

***Figure 5-11.** Confirming the package creation*

12. You have two options to choose from when it comes to creating the package. You can select the **Perform in the background** option which means that this dialog box will close regardless of whether the action or task has completed, and the task will continue in the background, or you can choose the **Wait for completion** option which means this dialog box remains visible until the task is complete. In the test lab, we are going to select the latter by clicking the radio button.

13. Click the **Create** button.

14. You will see the **Creating Package** progress bar as shown in Figure 5-12.

***Figure 5-12.** Package creation process running*

15. In the background, App Volumes is now taking a copy of the template.vmdk file.

16. Once completed, you will be taken to the **Package for Sales Apps V1** screen as shown in Figure 5-13.

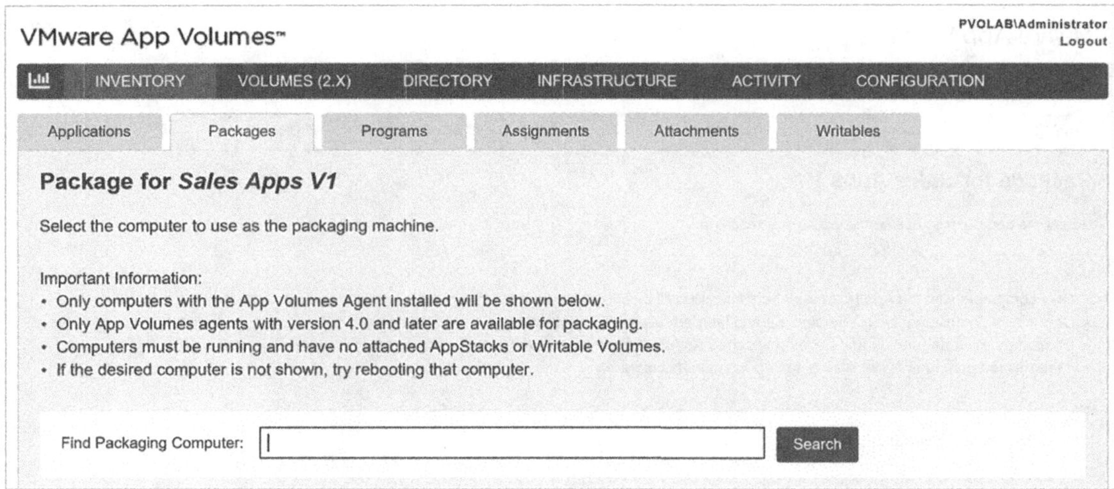

***Figure 5-13.** Finding the packaging machine*

17. On this screen, you select the machine you want to use to create the package on.

18. In the Find Packaging Computer box, type in the name or part of the name of the machine you want to use, and then click the **Search** button.

19. In the test lab, we have just clicked Search without entering any specific machine details. You will see the screenshot in Figure 5-14.

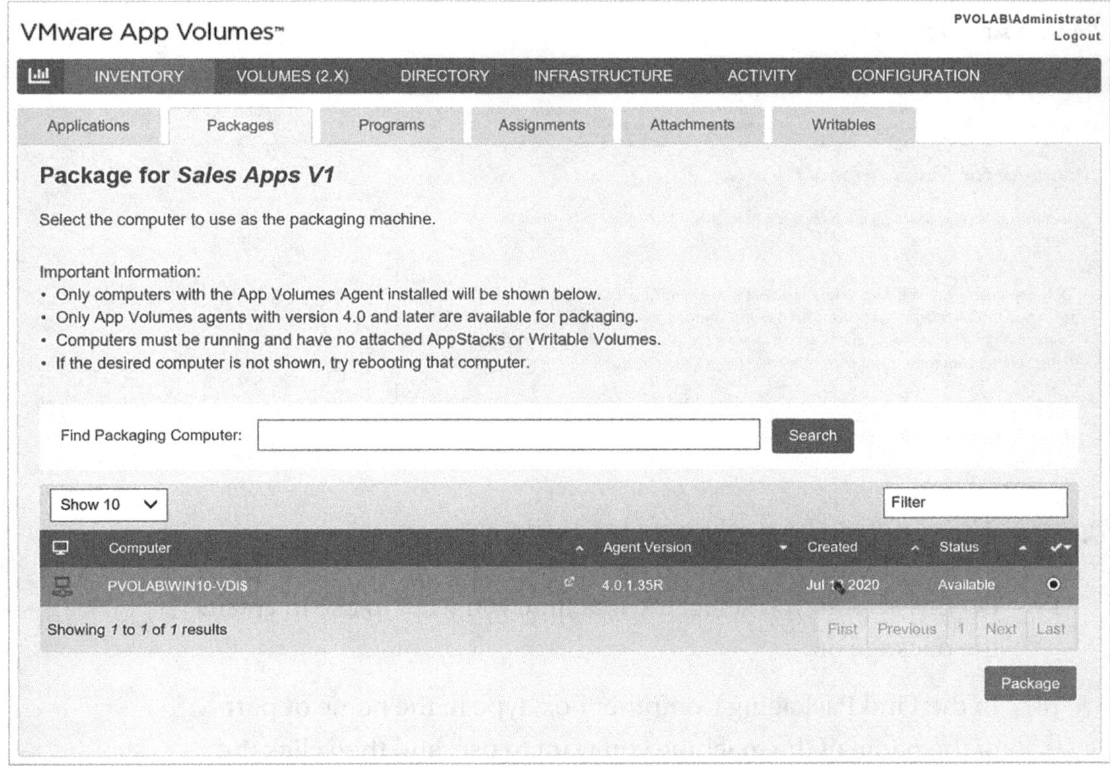

***Figure 5-14.** Selecting the packaging machine*

20. You will see the **PVOLAB\WIN10-VDI** machine listed. This machine is running the App Volumes Agent and has been optimized as the packaging machine. If you have other machines running the App Volumes Agent, they will also appear on this screen so take care to select the correct machine.

21. You will also see the agent version that the machine is running and its status. In this example, its status is set to available, meaning it can be used.

22. Click the radio button to select the machine. You will see the **Confirm Start Packaging** message as shown in Figure 5-15.

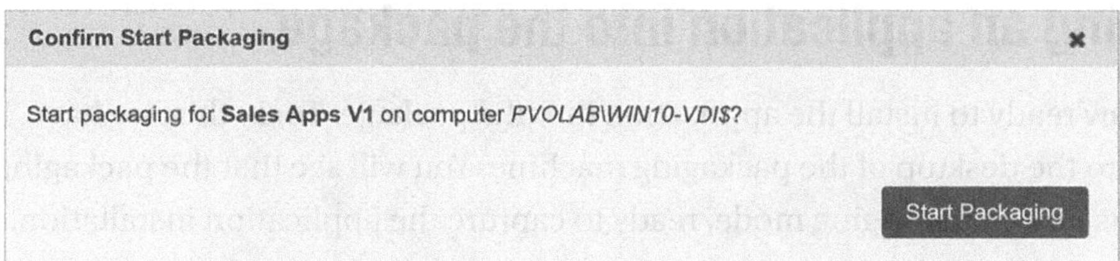

Figure 5-15. *Confirming the packaging process*

23. Now click the **Start Packaging** button.

24. You will see the **Attaching Package to Computer** progress bar appear as shown in Figure 5-16.

Figure 5-16. *Attaching the package to the packaging machine*

25. In the background, App Volumes is attaching the new VMDK file to the packaging machine, ready to capture the installation process and redirect the program files to the new virtual hard disk file.

26. You will now see the screenshot in Figure 5-17.

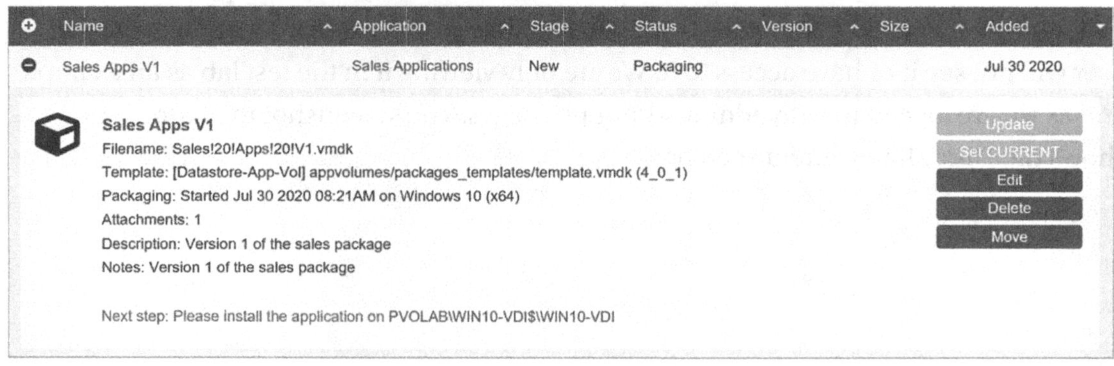

Figure 5-17. *Ready to create the package*

The next stage of the process is to install the program on the packaging machine, and so to complete that, we are now going to switch over to the packaging machine and install the application.

Installing an application into the package

We are now ready to install the application into the package. To do this, we have switched to the desktop of the packaging machine. You will see that the packaging machine is now in packaging mode, ready to capture the application installation. You will see the message in Figure 5-18.

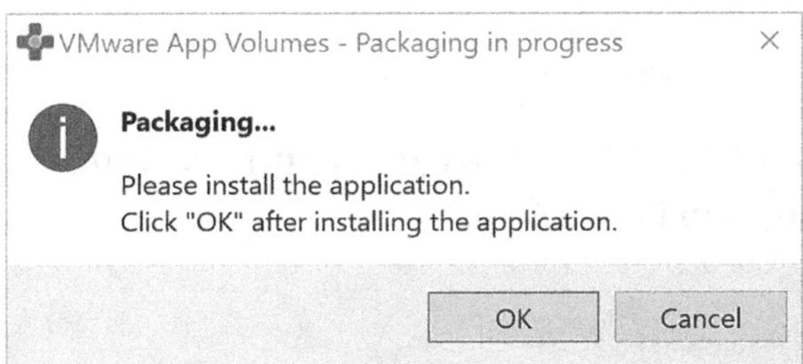

Figure 5-18. *Packaging in progress message box*

Do not click the OK button until you have finished installing all the applications for this package.

To see what is going on behind the scenes, if you launch the **Disk Management** utility on the packaging machine, you will see that the new virtual hard disk (the 20 GB thin provisioned template.vmdk file) has been attached ready for the capture.

You will also note that the hard disk does not have a drive letter, meaning the end user will not see it or have access to it. We are only viewing it in the test lab as an example and as we are logged in with administrator privileges. The screenshot in Figure 5-19 shows the Disk Management screen.

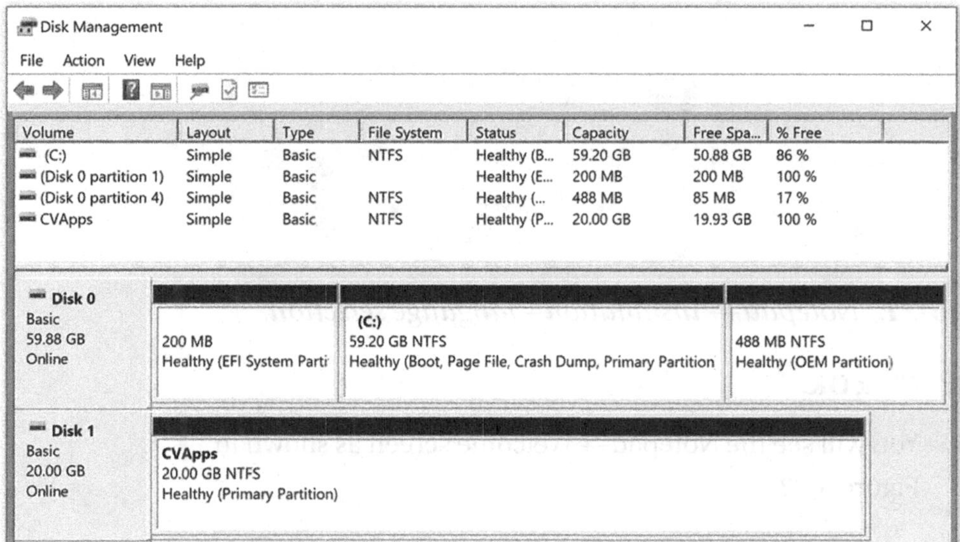

***Figure 5-19.** Disk Manager showing the attached virtual hard disk for packaging*

We can now start the application installation on the packaging machine, following the steps described:

1. From the packaging machine, locate the installer for the application you want to install. In the test lab, we are going to install Notepad++ as shown in Figure 5-20.

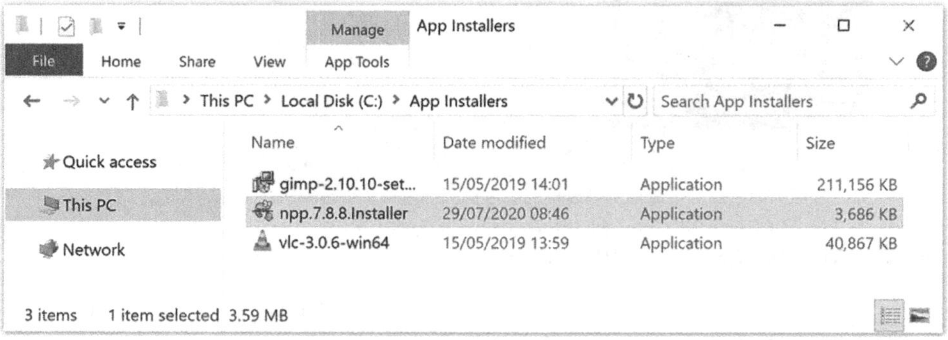

***Figure 5-20.** Notepad++ installer*

2. Double-click to launch the installer.

3. You will see the screenshot in Figure 5-21.

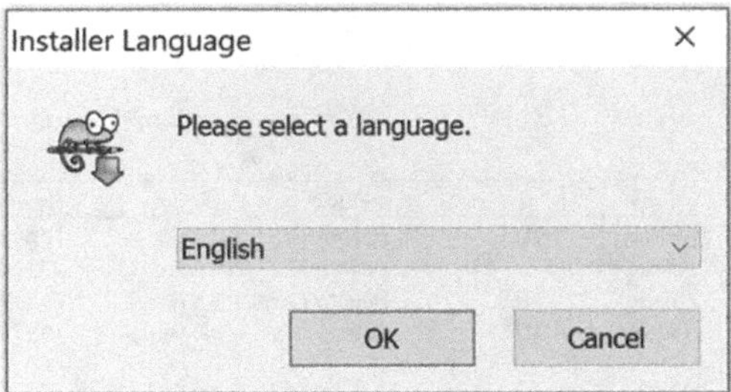

Figure 5-21. *Notepad++ installation – language selection*

4. Click **OK.**
5. You will see the Notepad++ Welcome screen as shown in Figure 5-22.

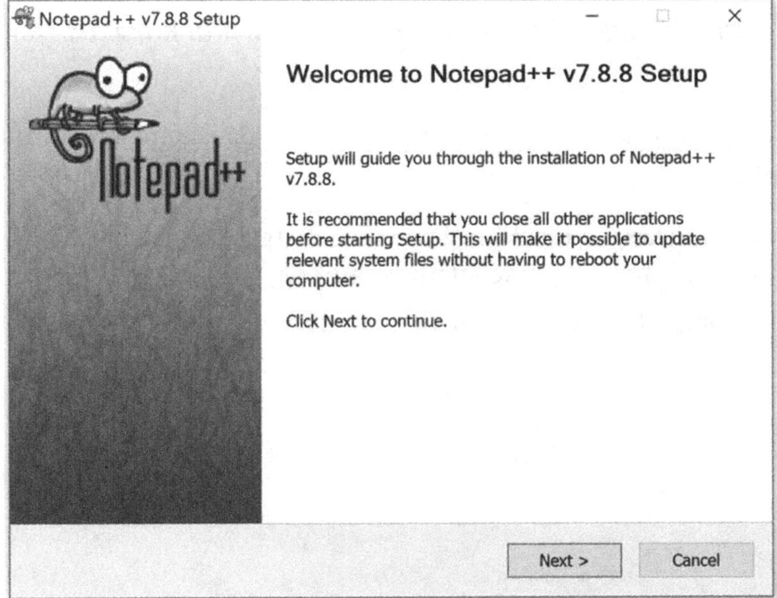

Figure 5-22. *Notepad++ Welcome screen*

6. Click **Next ►** to continue the installation.

We are not going to run through the complete installation of Notepad++ step by step, so continue installing the application as you would do normally, or the application you have chosen for this exercise.

The installation process has been "accelerated" as shown in Figure 5-23.

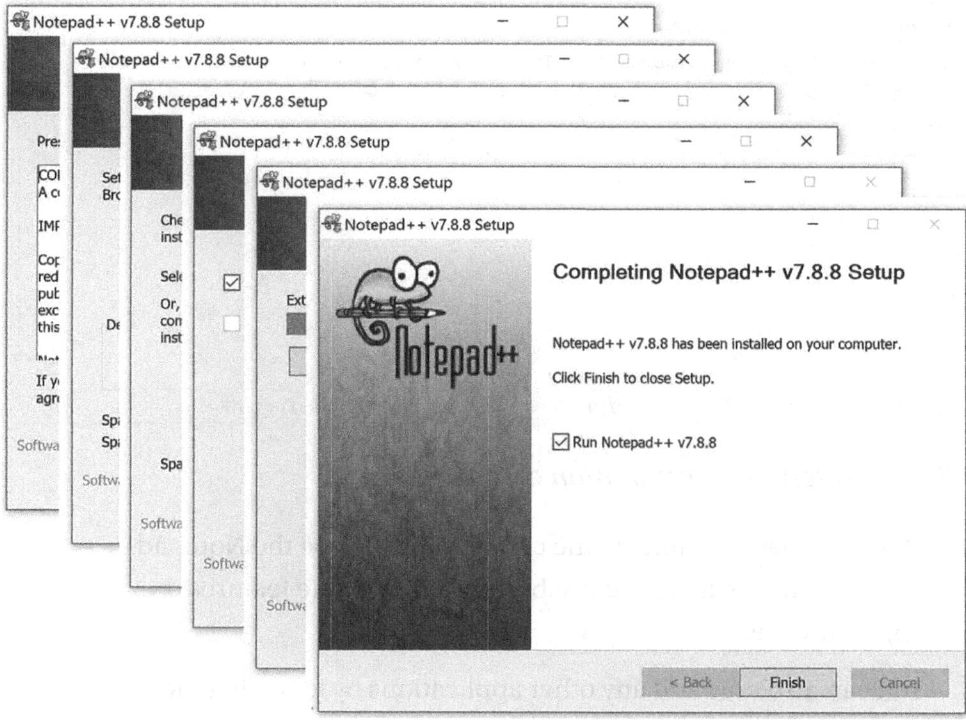

Figure 5-23. *Notepad++ installation completed*

7. Click the **Run Notepad++ v7.8.8** check box, and then click the **Finish** button.

8. Before we complete the installation, we are going to configure the settings we want users to have for Notepad++ as these will be captured as part of the capture process; therefore, every user will have access to the correctly configured version.

9. You will see Notepad++ launch so that you can make these configuration and user setting changes, as shown in Figure 5-24.

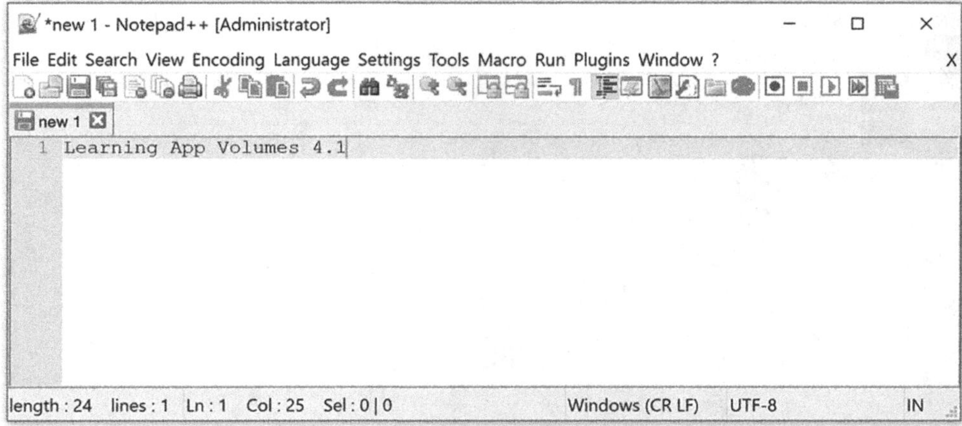

***Figure 5-24.** Notepad++ installation completed*

10. Once you have completed the configuration, close the Notepad++ application, ensuring you disable any auto-update features the app may have.

11. You can also now add any other applications by following the installation process of each additional app you want to add. In this example, we will install just a single app.

12. Now return to the **Packaging in progress** dialog box as shown in Figure 5-25.

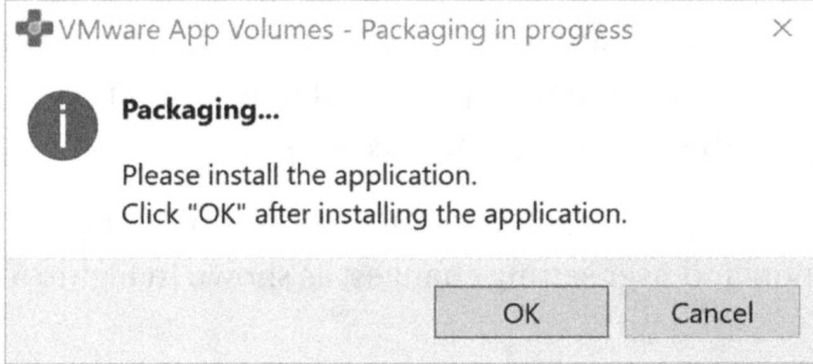

***Figure 5-25.** Packaging in progress message box for completion*

13. Click the **OK** button to continue.

14. You will now see the **Installation complete?** dialog box as shown in Figure 5-26.

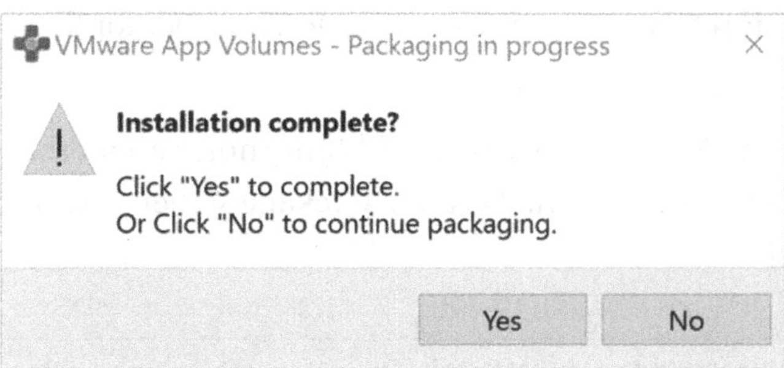

Figure 5-26. *Installation complete dialog box*

15. Click the **Yes** button to continue. If you have not finished configuring the installed application, or you want to add more applications to this package, then click the **No** button. Clicking no will return you to the desktop of the packaging machine where you can continue installing and configuring.

16. You will now see the **Packaging...** dialog box as shown in Figure 5-27.

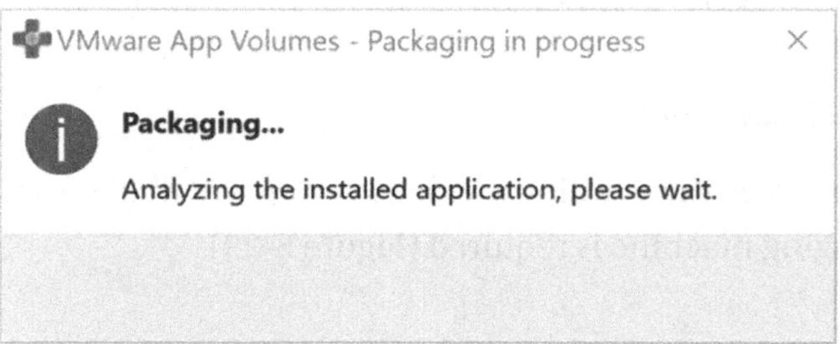

Figure 5-27. *Packaging dialog box for app analyzing*

17. App Volumes now analyzes the installation of the applications you installed.

18. Next, you will see the **Finalize Package** screen, with some additional options to configure.

19. In the **Name** box, you can enter a name for the program installed in the package. You will see that there is a drop-down menu from where you can select the name. In the test lab, we only have one program installed, and so this is entered by default.

20. In the **Version** box, you can enter a version number for the program.

21. Finally, in the **Notes** box, you can add some notes about the program you installed. The **Finalize Package** screen is shown in Figure 5-28.

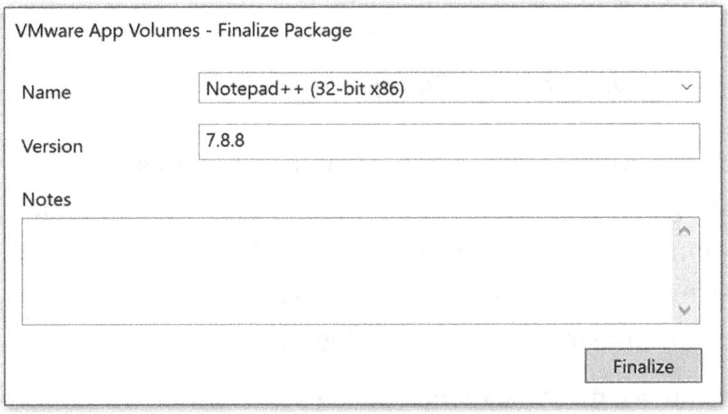

Figure 5-28. *Finalizing the package*

22. Click the **Finalize** button.

23. You will now see the warning message telling you that a restart of the packaging machine is required (Figure 5-29).

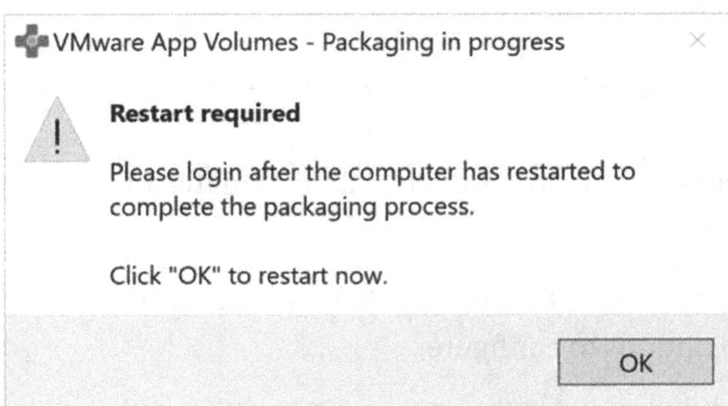

Figure 5-29. *Restart of the packaging machine is required*

24. Click **OK**. The packaging machine will restart so that the VMDK file is unmounted from the packaging machine.

25. Once it has restarted, log back in and you will see the message displayed in Figure 5-30.

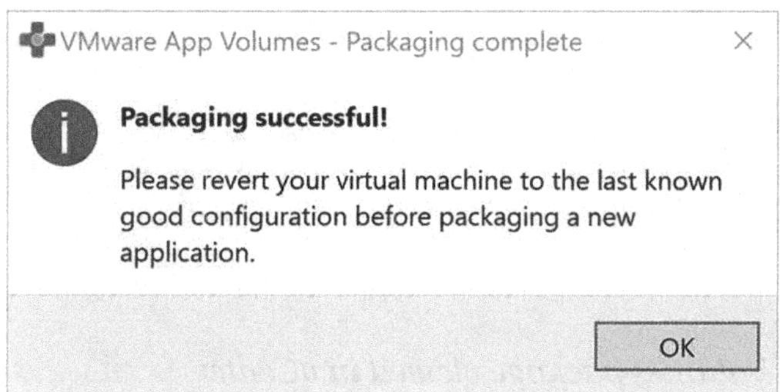

Figure 5-30. *Packaging successful message*

26. If you again launch the **Disk Management** utility, you will see that the App Volumes virtual hard disk is no longer attached (Figure 5-31).

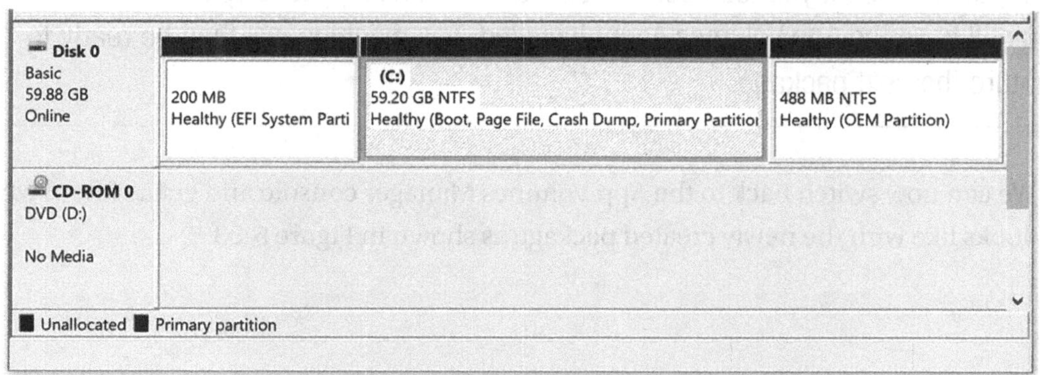

Figure 5-31. *App Volumes package no longer attached*

The newly created package has been finalized and is now stored within the datastore on your vSphere infrastructure, ready to be assigned and attached to end users.

If you open your vCenter management console and browse the **Datastore-App-Vol** datastore, you will see that three files have been created. These three files make up the new package and are shown in Figure 5-32.

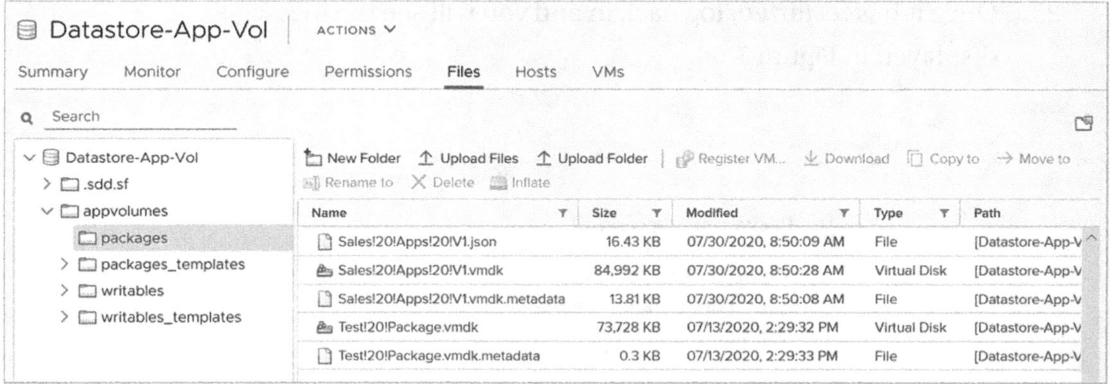

Figure 5-32. *App Volumes package viewed in vCenter*

You have now completed the installation and creation of the package.

You should now restore the packaging machine back to its prepackaging state, using the snapshot you took before you started installing your apps. Make sure you still have the App Volumes Agent installed. The machine will then be ready to capture the next package.

We can now switch back to the App Volumes Manager console and get a view of what that looks like with the newly created package as shown in Figure 5-33.

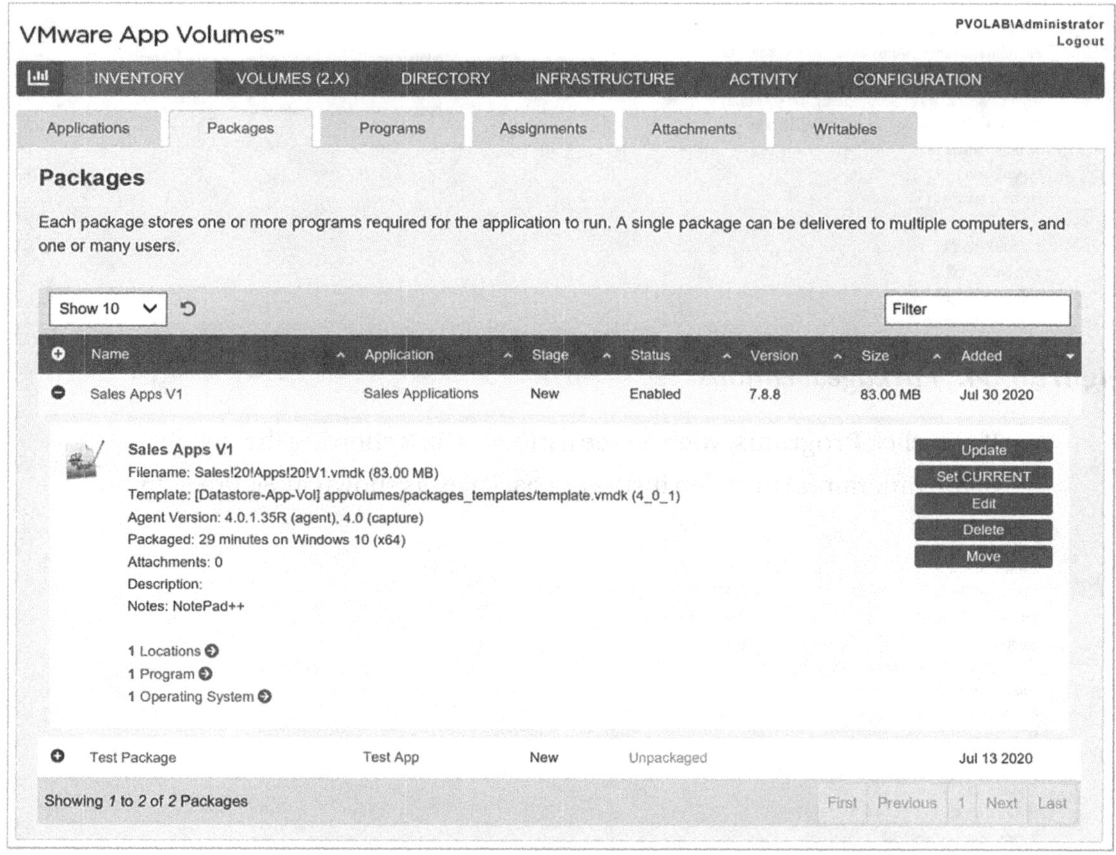

***Figure 5-33.** App Volumes Manager showing the new package*

On the main screen, you will now see information about the package, such as the filename, template, the App Volumes Agent version used, the description, and any notes you added when you finalized the package.

You will also see three links in the bottom-left corner of the screen. These links show the following information:

- If you click **Locations**, you will see a message box showing the details of the vCenter Server and the datastore where the package virtual hard disk file resides, as shown in Figure 5-34.

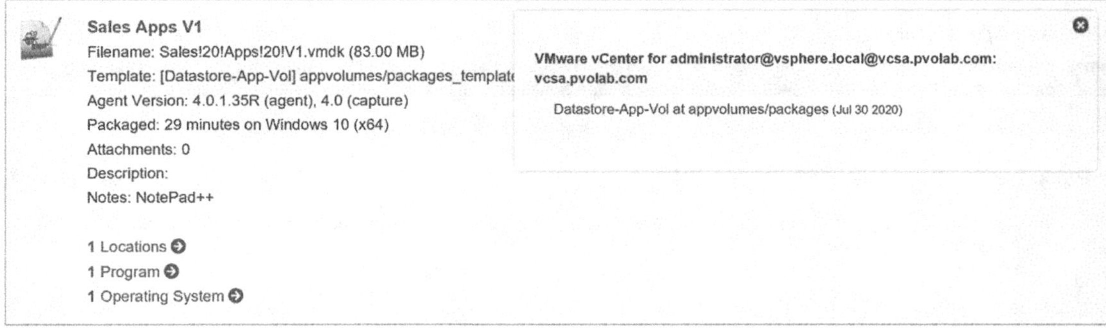

Figure 5-34. *Package locations*

- If you click **Programs**, you will see a message box showing the details of the program(s) installed inside the package, as shown in Figure 5-35.

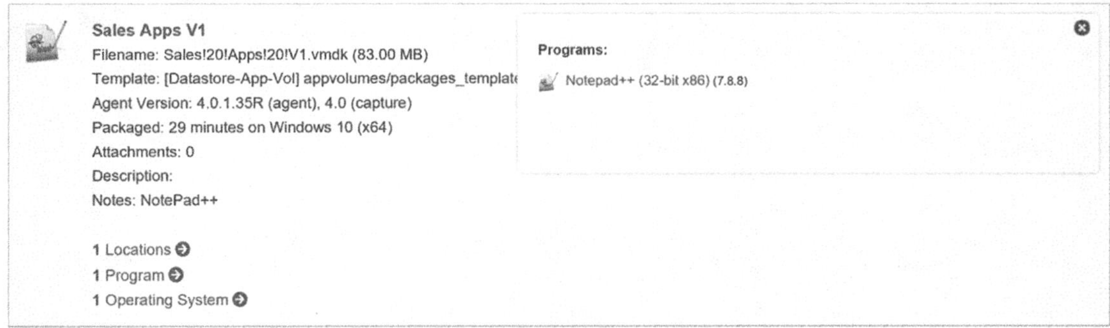

Figure 5-35. *Package programs list*

- Finally, if you click **Operating System**, you will see a message box showing the details of the OS used to capture the package, as shown in Figure 5-36.

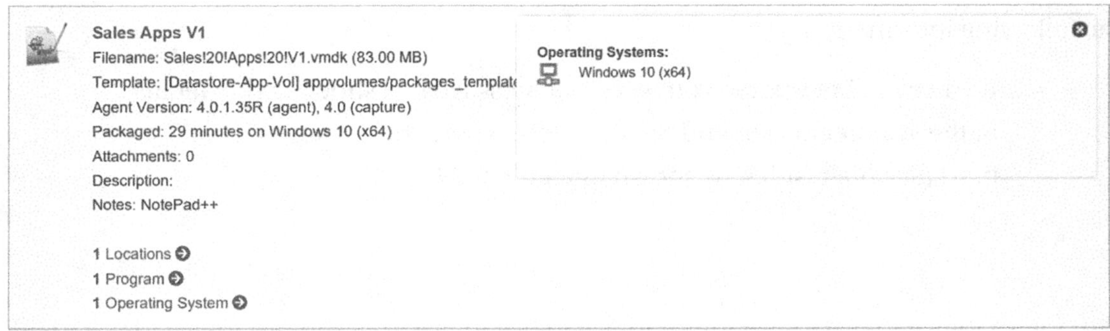

Figure 5-36. *Package operating system*

As well as this screen, there are a couple of other views of the package and programs that you can look at. Let us start by clicking the **Programs** tab. You will see the screenshot in Figure 5-37.

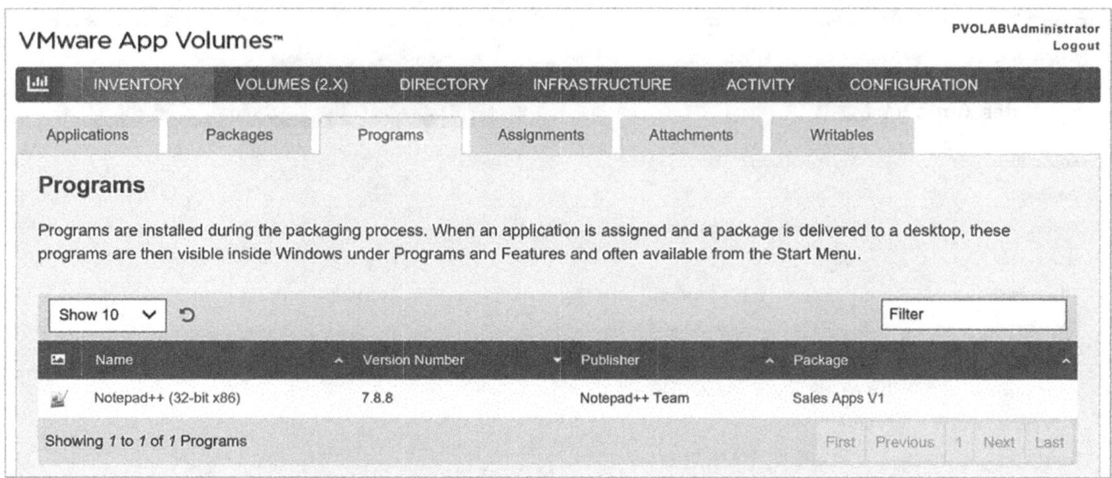

Figure 5-37. *The Programs tab view*

You will see that the program is listed, along with the version number, the publisher, and which App Volumes package the program is part of. The name and the version of the program are both taken from the information you entered when you created the package.

You will also notice that the name and package are also links to other screens. Under the **Name** heading, if you click **Notepad++ (32-bit x86)**, you will see the screen in Figure 5-38.

VMware App Volumes™
PVOLAB\Administrator
Logout
INVENTORY
VOLUMES (2.X)
DIRECTORY
INFRASTRUCTURE
ACTIVITY
CONFIGURATION
Applications
Packages
Programs
Assignments
Attachments
Writables
Notepad++ (32-bit x86)
Publisher: Notepad++ Team
Package: Sales Apps V1
Publisher: Notepad++ Team
Install Location:
Version Number: 7.8.8
Created: Jul 30 2020 08:50:14 AM GMT Daylight Time

Figure 5-38. *The Programs tab view - program details*

The other link, the package link, will take you to the screen shown in Figure 5-39.

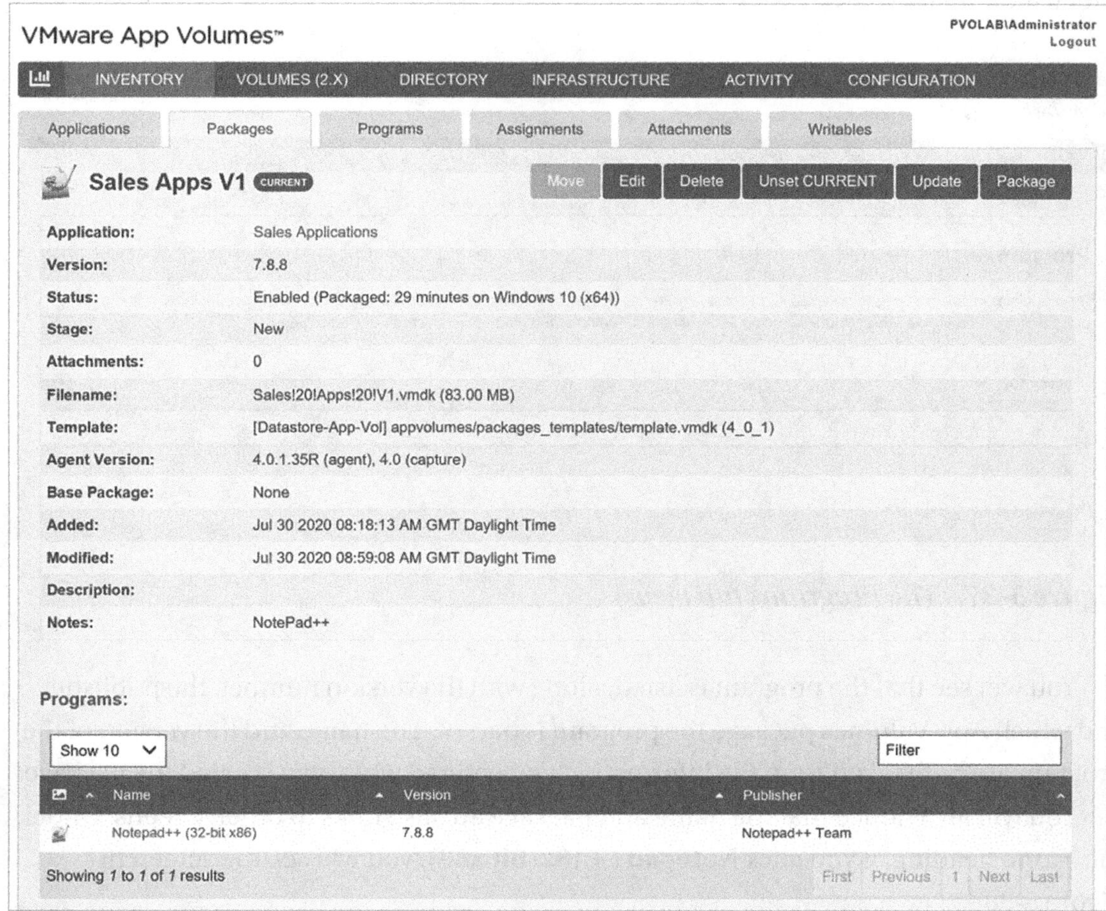

Figure 5-39. *Detailed package view*

You have now completed the creation process for creating an application and a package, as well as packaging a program, in this example, using Notepad++ as the program.

With a package and application built and ready to go, you can now assign this to your end users, which we will cover in the next section.

Assigning applications

Now that you have packages and applications built and configured, you can assign them to end users so that they get attached to the end user's virtual desktop machines where they can run the applications. Or you can assign the applications to an RDSH server.

In this section, we are going to look at how to assign an application to an end user's virtual desktop machine. To do this, follow the steps described:

1. From the App Volumes Manager console, ensure you are in the **INVENTORY** menu, and then select the **Applications** tab as shown in Figure 5-40.

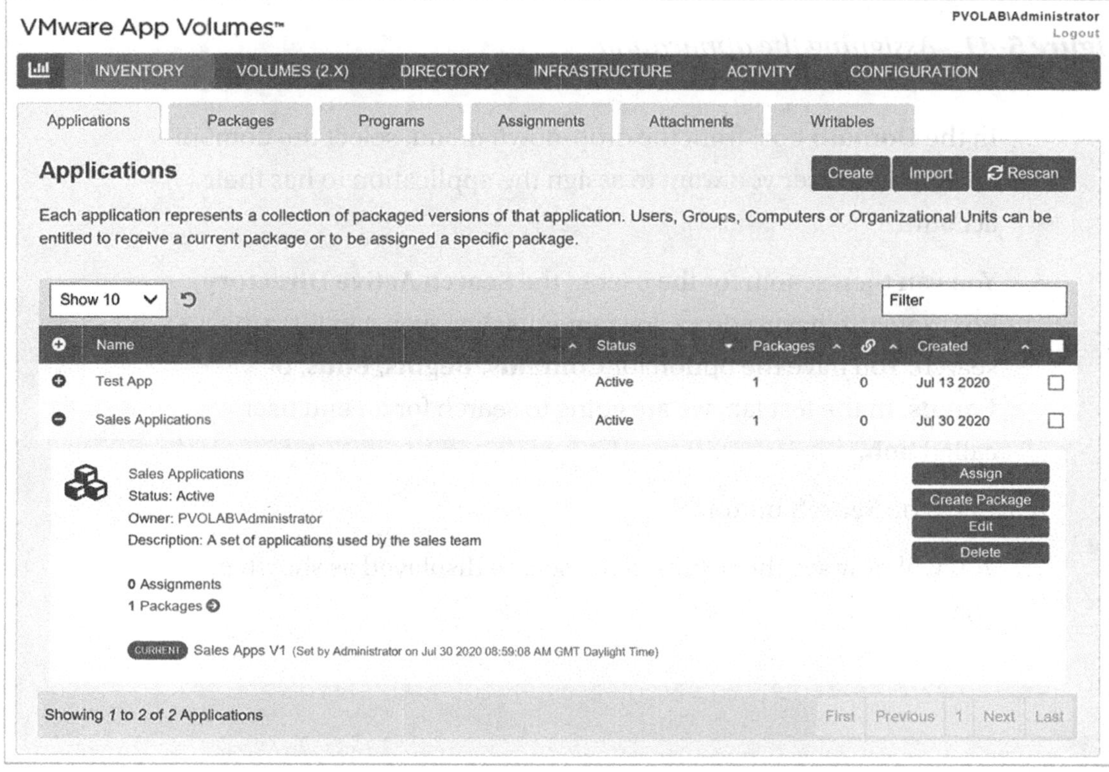

Figure 5-40. *The Applications tab*

2. Click the **Assign** button.

3. You will see the **Assign Application: Sales Applications** screen as shown in Figure 5-41.

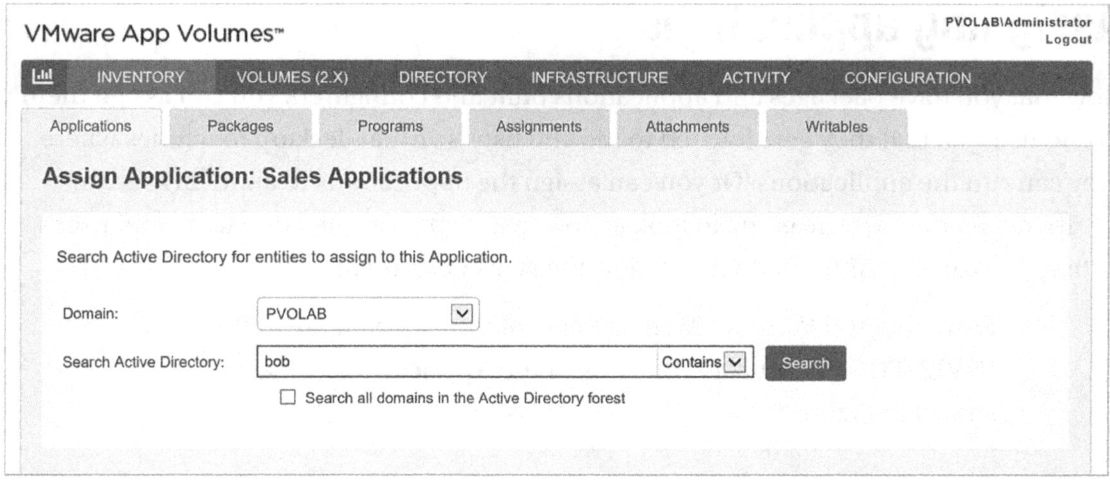

***Figure 5-41.** Assigning the application*

4. In the **Domain** box, from the drop-down menu, select the domain in which the user you want to assign the application to has their account.

5. You can then search for the user in the **Search Active Directory** box. You also have a drop-down menu where you can filter the search. You have the option for **Contains**, **Begins**, **Ends**, or **Equals**. In the test lab, we are going to search for an end user called **bob.**

6. Click the **Search** button.

7. You will now see the results of the search displayed as shown in Figure 5-42.

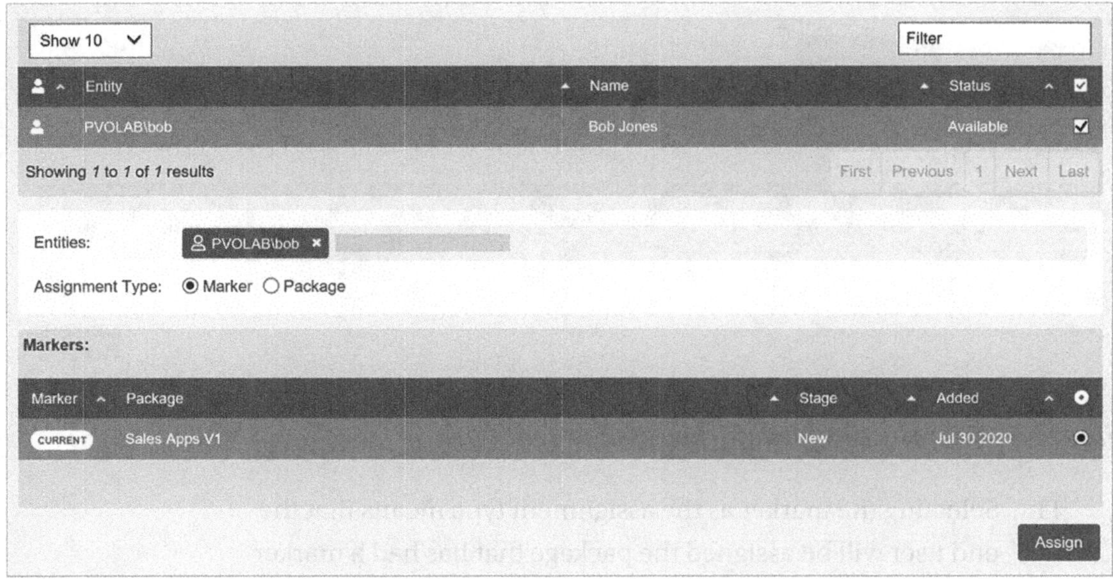

***Figure 5-42.** Results of the user search*

8. You will see that the username is now listed under **Entity**, along with their full name. Under the **Status** heading, you will see that the user is listed as **Available**, meaning that they have an active account in Active Directory.

9. Check the box to select the user. You now see the username listed next to **Entities.**

10. Under Entities, you will see you can select the **Assignment Type**, either using a marker or a package. If you click the radio button for **Markers,** you will see the screenshot in Figure 5-43.

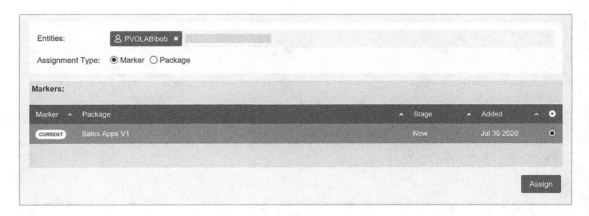

Figure 5-43. *Selecting the Marker assignment type*

11. Selecting the marker as the assignment type means that the end user will be assigned the package that has had a marker added. The marker refers to the package having been marked as **Current**. We will look at how to do this in the managing existing applications and packages section of this chapter.

12. To select this assignment, click the radio button and then the **Assign** button.

13. The other assignment option is for **Package**, selected by clicking the radio button as shown in Figure 5-44.

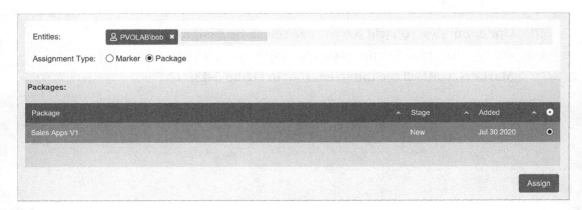

Figure 5-44. *Selecting the Package assignment type*

14. You will see the packages listed. In this example, you will see the **Sales Apps V1** package. Click the radio button to select the package and then click the **Assign** button.

15. You will see the **Confirm Assign** dialog box as shown in Figure 5-45.

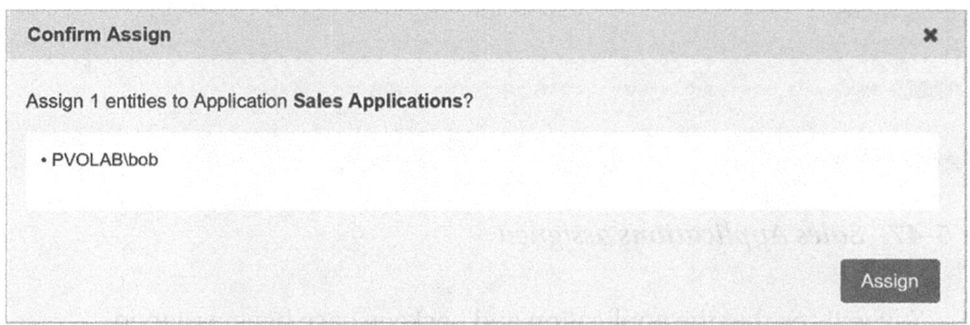

Figure 5-45. *Confirm the assignment*

16. As you can see, we are assigning one entity, the end user with the username Bob, to the Application called Sales Applications.

17. Click the **Assign** button. You will see the Saving Assignment progress bar appear as the save process completes as shown in Figure 5-46.

Figure 5-46. *Saving the assignment*

18. Once the assignment has been saved, then you will return to the main **Applications** page.

19. If you expand the **Sales Application** section by clicking the + button, then clicking the link for **Assignments** in the bottom left of the screen, then you will see the screenshot in Figure 5-47.

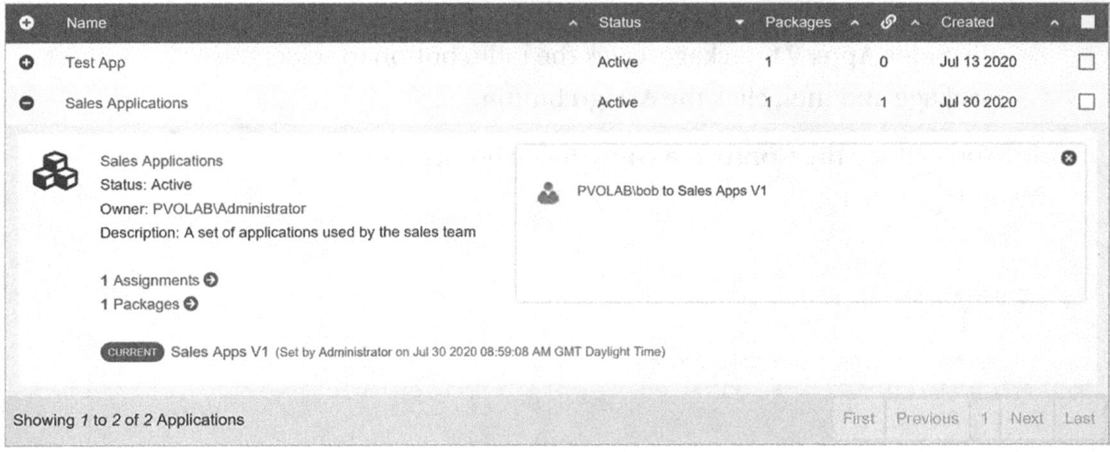

Figure 5-47. *Sales Applications assigned*

20. You will see that the application and package have been assigned to **PVOLAB\bob**.

21. Also, under the menu title headings, you will see the icon in Figure 5-48.

Figure 5-48. *Icon for assigned applications*

22. This icon in the menu heading shows that **Sales Applications** currently has one assignment.

In the preceding example, we have shown you how to assign an application to one specific end user. You could of course assign multiple users, by adding them individually on the assignment screen, or you could assign a user group, an OU, or a virtual machine depending on your use case.

In the following example, shown in the **Assign Application: Sales Applications** screenshot (Figure 5-49), we have selected our application and clicked the **Assign** button.

But this time, in the **Search Active Directory** box, we have entered the name of a group called **sales**, which we have created in Active Directory, and then clicked the **Search** button.

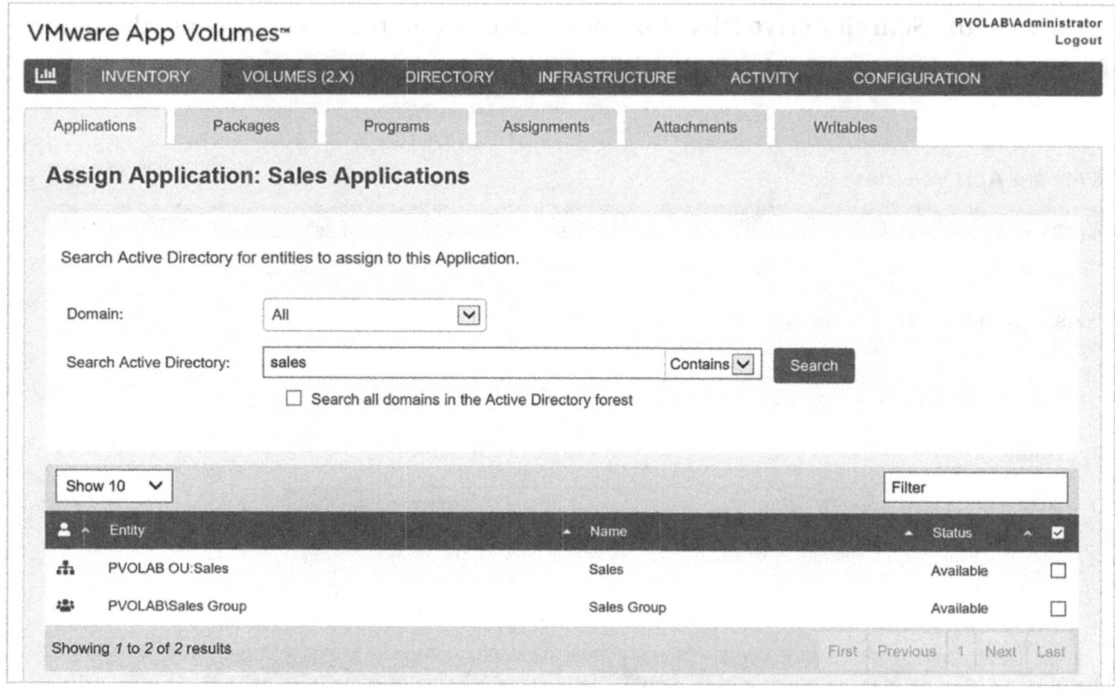

Figure 5-49. Assigning an application to a group

In the results, you will see **OU:Sales** and the **Sales Group**. Each one is also identified by an icon as shown in Figure 5-50.

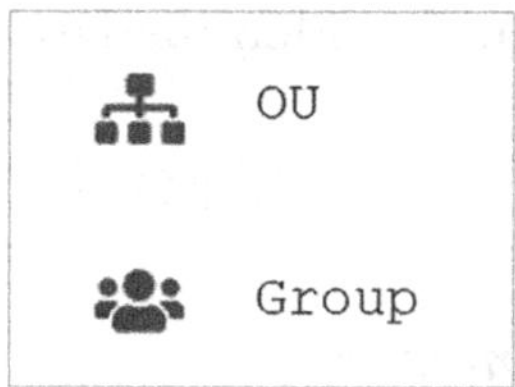

Figure 5-50. Entity icons

To assign the application to a group, simply check the box next to the group or groups you want to assign the application to, select the assignment type, and then click the **Assign** button.

It is a similar process for assigning an application to a machine. From the **Assign Application: Sales Applications** screenshot (Figure 5-51), we have selected our application and clicked the **Assign** button.

Now, in the **Search Active Directory** box, we have entered the first part of the name of a machine starting with **win10**, then clicked the **Search** button.

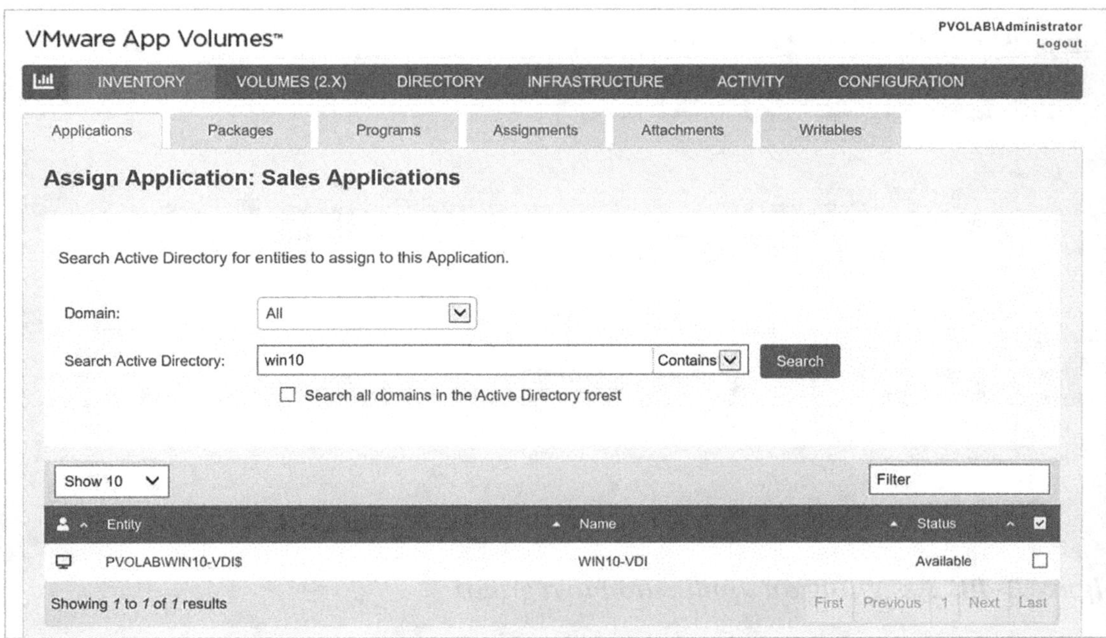

Figure 5-51. *Assigning an application to a machine*

In the results, you will see **PVOLAB/WIN10-VDI$** and the status set to **Available**. A machine assignment in App Volumes is identified by an icon as shown in Figure 5-52.

Figure 5-52. *Machine assignment icon*

To assign the application to a machine, simply check the box next to the name of the machine you want to assign the application to, select the assignment type, and then click the **Assign** button.

In the next section, we are going to test that the application works by logging in as the assigned user.

Testing the newly created package

Now that the application has been assigned to an end user, in this section, we are going to test to make sure that the application works as expected, and to do that we are going to log in as the end user to whom we assigned the application to.

To do this, we are going to follow the steps described here:

1. Log in to a virtual desktop machine as the end user that has the application assigned to them. In the test lab, we assigned the application to the user Bob Jones, as shown in Figure 5-53.

***Figure 5-53.** Logging in as the end user*

2. The user will now be logged in, and as the login process runs, the App Volumes Agent is checking in with the App Volumes Manager to check the assignment. As there is an application assigned to this particular end user, then it will be attached as part of the login process.

3. Once logged in, the end user will have a shortcut icon on their desktop for Notepad++, which was configured as part of the packaging process. In this example, we have also launched the disk management utility by running it as the administrator, to show that the package is attached to the end user's virtual desktop machine.

4. Finally, we have launched Notepad++ to show that it runs as if it were natively installed, as shown in Figure 5-54.

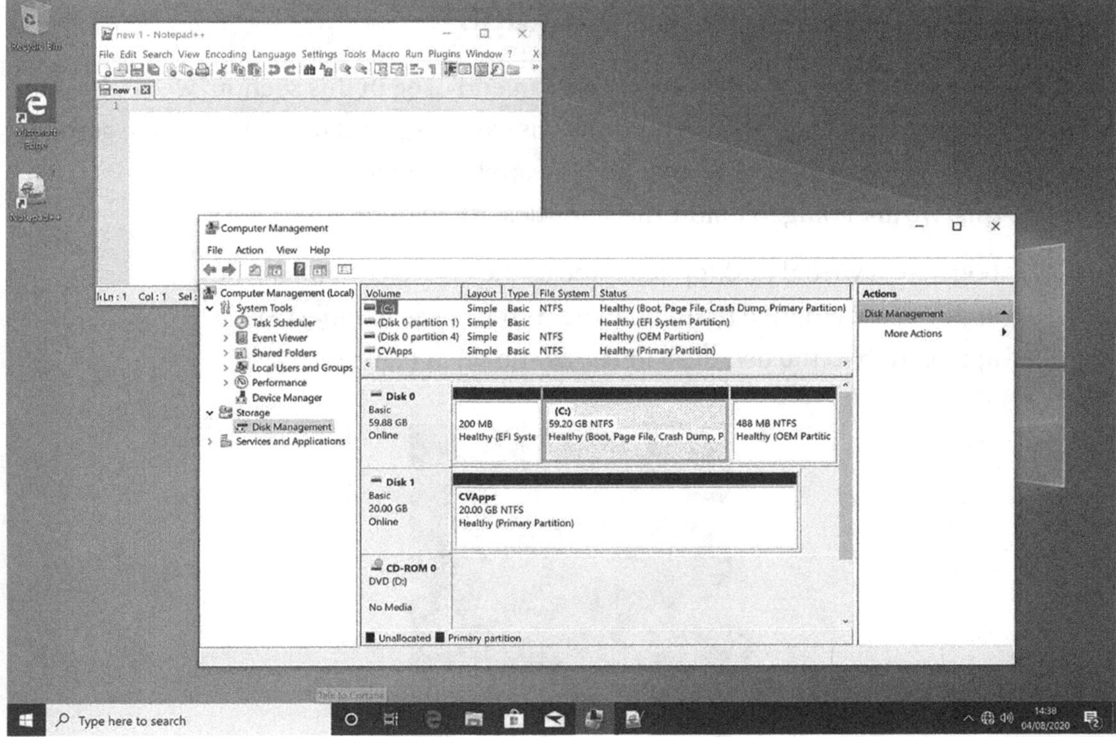

Figure 5-54. Virtual desktop machine with application attached and running

Now that you have applications and packages in place, with end users being assigned to use them and using them, in the next section, we are going to look at the ongoing management of these elements, starting with packages.

Managing existing packages

In this section, we are going to look at how to manage existing packages, starting with the updating process.

Updating an existing package

The update an existing package option, as the name suggests, allows you to make updates and changes to an already existing package. This is done by attaching the existing package to a packaging machine, which then allows you to install a new version of the programs within the package, or to add security patches and updates, or to make configuration changes to the programs.

To update a package, follow the steps described:

1. Log in to the App Volumes Manager console, and then from the **INVENTORY** menu, select the **Packages** tab as shown in Figure 5-55.

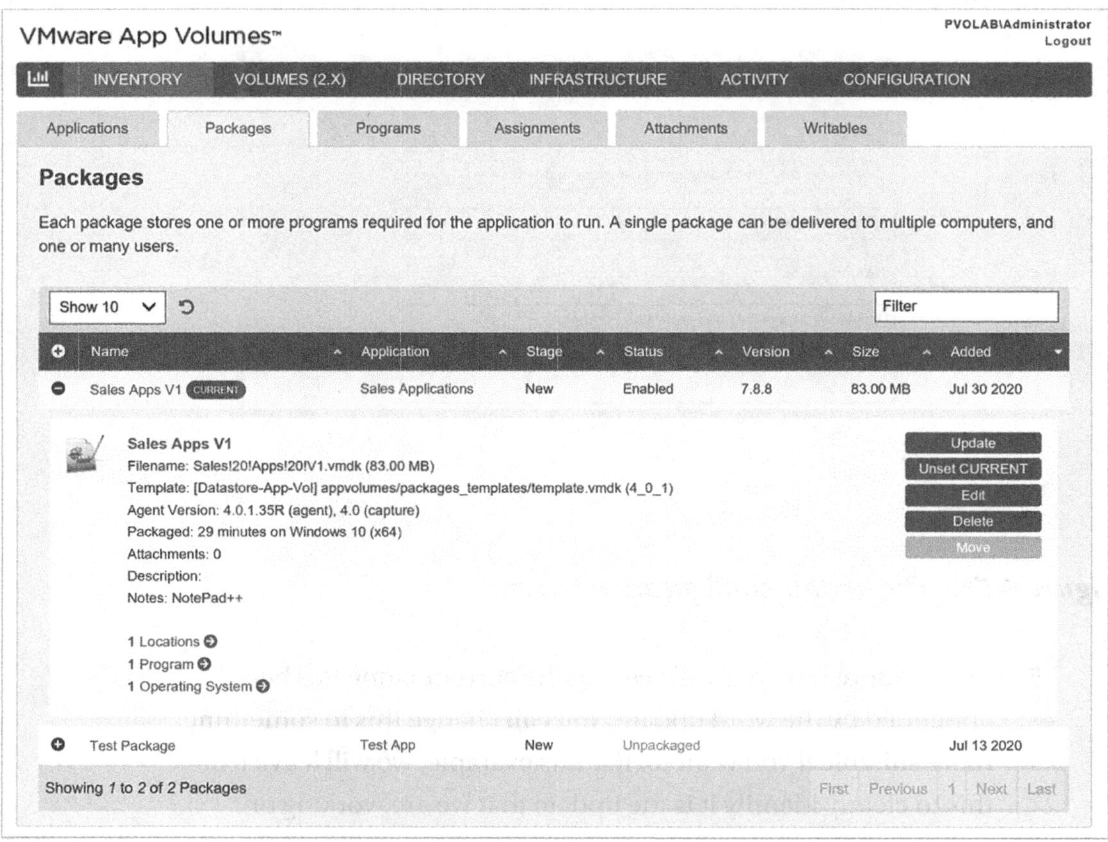

Figure 5-55. *Updating an existing package*

2. Expand the details of the package you want to update by clicking the + button. In this example, it is **Sales Apps V1**.

3. From the blue action buttons shown on the right-hand side of the screen, click the **Update** button.

4. You will see the **Update Sales Apps V1 for Sales Applications** screen as shown in Figure 5-56.

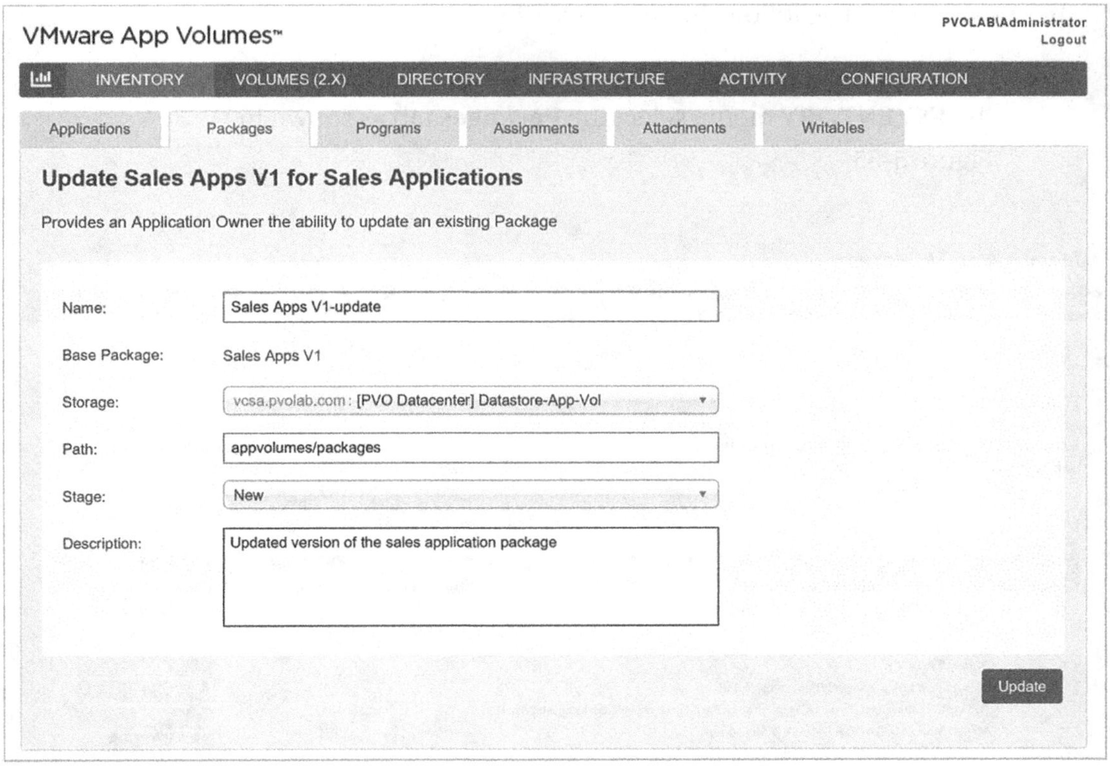

Figure 5-56. *The update configuration screen*

5. In the **Name** box, you will see that the current name has been appended by the word update. You can change this to something more suitable if you want to. For this example, we will leave it as this to clearly identify it is the update that we are working on.

6. The **Base Package** box shows the name of the package that we are using to update. In this example, this is the **Sales Apps V1** package that we are going to make the updates to.

7. Enter the location in the **Storage** box. This is the datastore location for where the new updated package will be stored. From the drop-down menu, select the datastore with this example using the **Datastore-App-Vol** datastore. You can choose a different datastore to save the updated package to.

8. Then, in the **Path** box, select which folder to save the updated package to. This is a folder on the datastore.

9. Next, in the **Stage** box, from the drop-down menu list, select the package stage. We are going to select New for this example as it is essentially a new package.

10. Finally, in the **Description** box, you can type in a description to help identify this package. As this is an update, then it would be a good idea to describe what the update contains.

11. Now click the **Update** button. You will see the **Confirm Update Package** dialog box as shown in Figure 5-57.

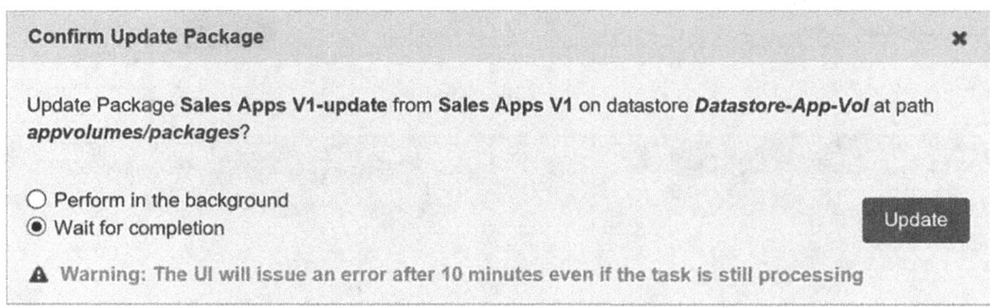

Figure 5-57. *Confirm the package update dialog box*

12. Click the radio button for **Wait for completion**, and then click the **Update** button. A clone of the original package VMDK file is created.

13. You will see the **Updating Package** progress bar as shown in Figure 5-58.

Figure 5-58. *Updating the package progress bar*

14. You will now see the **Package for Sales Apps V1-update** screen, where you can select the packaging machine you want to use to make the updates, as shown in Figure 5-59.

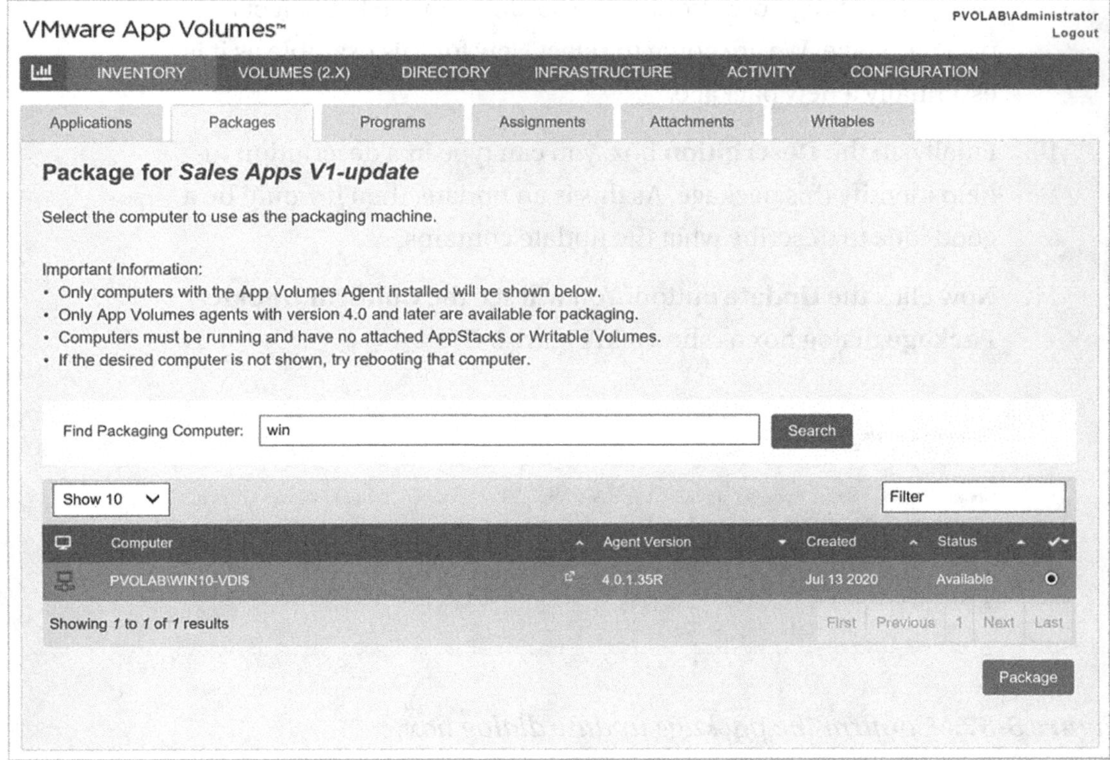

Figure 5-59. *Selecting the packaging machine for the updates*

15. In the **Find Packaging Computer** box, we are going to type in **win**, which is part of the name of the packaging machine we are going to use. Click the **Search** button.

16. You will see the results later with the **PVOLAB\WIN10-VDI$** machine listed as being available.

17. Click the radio button next to the machine name to select it, and then click the **Package** button. You will see the Confirm Start Packaging dialog box in Figure 5-60.

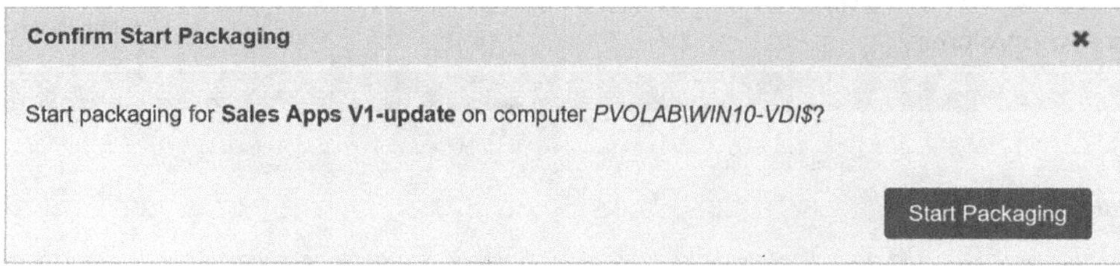

Figure 5-60. *Confirm the start of the packaging process*

18. You will see the **Attaching Package to Computer** progress bar as shown in Figure 5-61.

Figure 5-61. *Attaching the package progress bar*

As we are updating a package, then at this stage, the copy of the existing package is attached to the packaging machine. If you remember when we created a new package, it was the blank template file that was copied and attached to the packaging machine.

The package is now attached and is ready for packaging. In this example, that packaging process refers to the updates we are going to make to this package. This is shown in Figure 5-62.

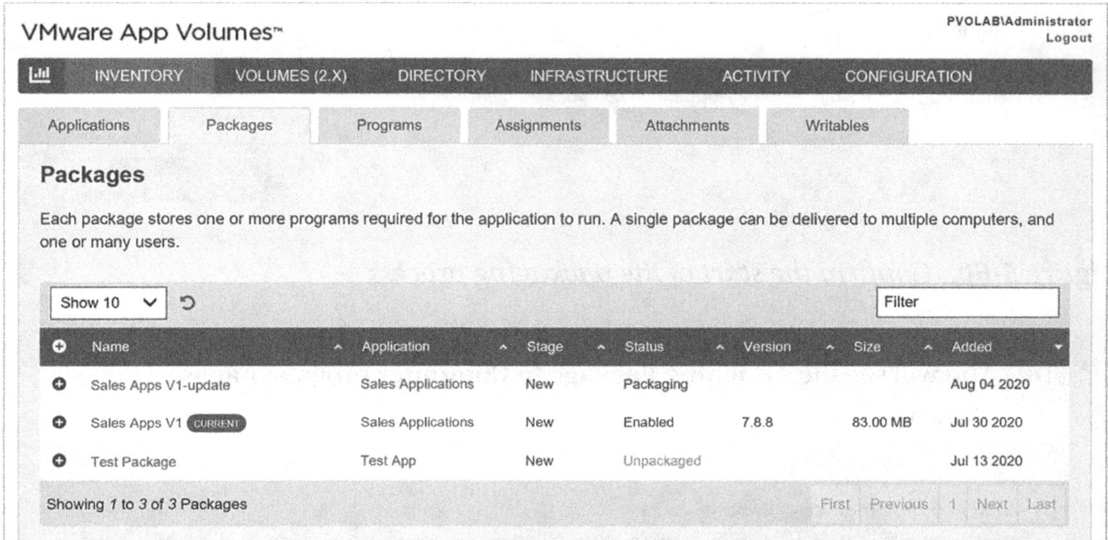

Figure 5-62. *Updated package ready for packaging the updates*

With the package now attached to the packaging machine in readiness for making the updates, you can now switch to the desktop of the packaging machine to start the update process.

The first thing to check when you switch to the packaging machine is that the existing package has been attached. In this example, you will see that the icon for Notepad++ appears on the desktop, as shown in Figure 5-63. You could also check in Disk Manager.

Figure 5-63. *Existing package attached ready for the updates*

You will also see the **Packaging in progress** dialog box appears too, as shown in Figure 5-64.

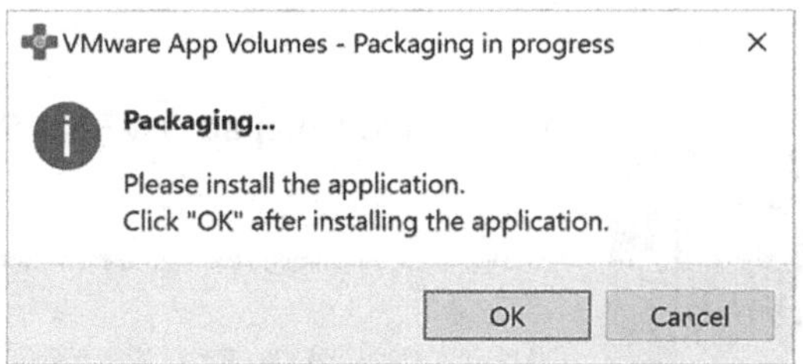

***Figure 5-64.** Packaging in progress dialog box*

You can now start the updating of the package process as described in the following:

1. In this example, we are going to install a new version of Notepad++, so locate the installer as shown in Figure 5-65.

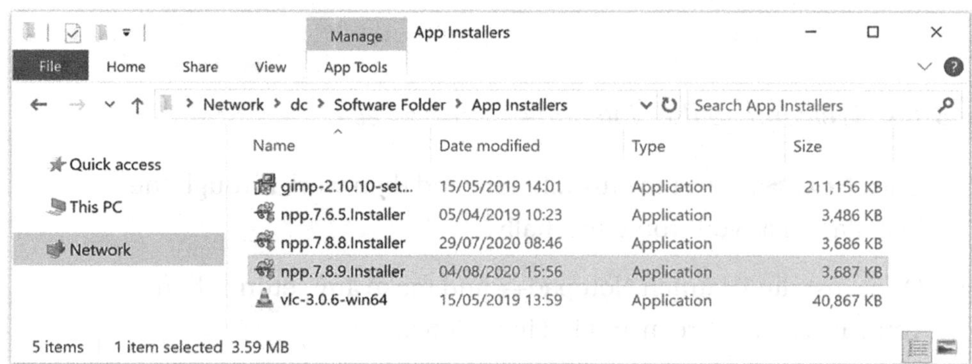

***Figure 5-65.** Launch the Notepad++ installer*

2. Double-click to launch the installer. You will see the screenshot with the new version of Notepad++ in Figure 5-66.

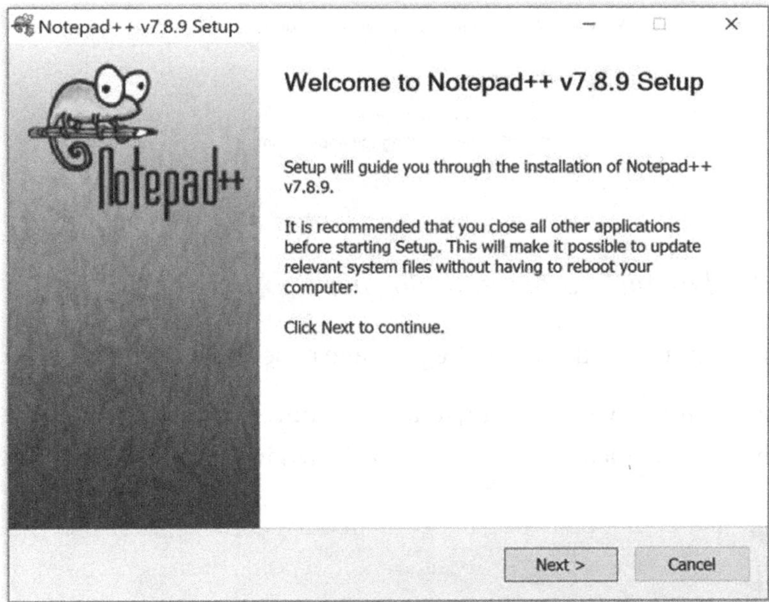

Figure 5-66. *Welcome to the Notepad++ setup screen*

3. Click **Next ▶** to start the installation, and then work through the installation as you would normally.

4. Once installed, launch Notepad++ and make any setting changes. You will see the screenshot in Figure 5-67.

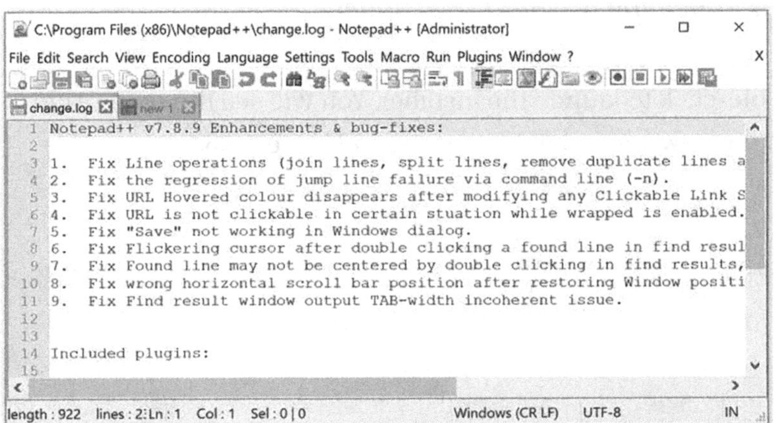

Figure 5-67. *New version of Notepad++ installed*

5. You can now complete the packaging process. In the **Packaging in progress** dialog box, click the ***Yes*** button to tell App Volumes that you have completed the installation and update (Figure 5-68).

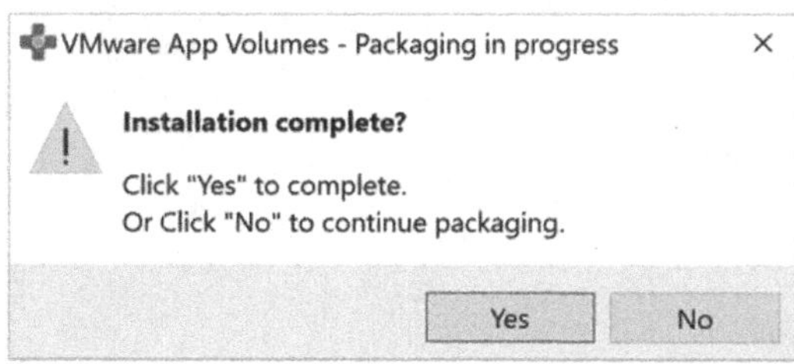

Figure 5-68. *New version of Notepad++ installed*

6. You will now see the **Packaging...** dialog box as the application you installed is analyzed, as shown in Figure 5-69.

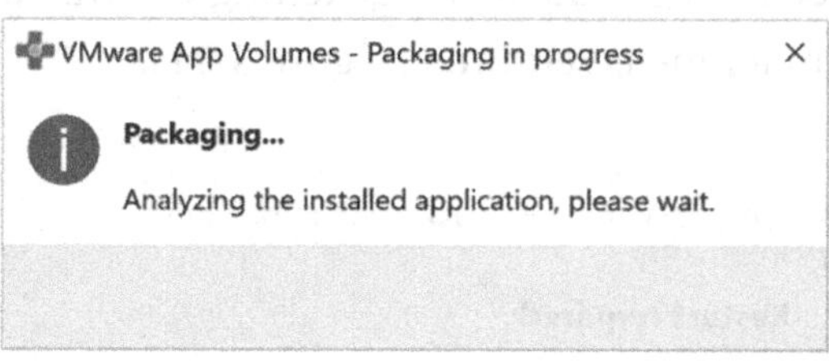

Figure 5-69. *Updated package being analyzed*

7. Next, you will see the **Finalize Package** screen, with some additional options to configure.
8. In the **Name** box, you can enter a name for the program installed in the package. You will see that there is a drop-down menu from where you can select the name. In the test lab, we have selected Notepad++ (32-bit x86).
9. In the **Version** box, you can enter a version number for the program. In this example, we are going to update the version number to reflect the updated version installed.
10. Finally, in the **Notes** box, you can add some notes about the program you installed – in this example, what this update contains. The **Finalize Package** screen is shown in Figure 5-70.

VMware App Volumes - Finalize Package

Name Notepad++ (32-bit x86)

Version 7.8.9

Notes

Latest 7.8.9 version.

Finalize

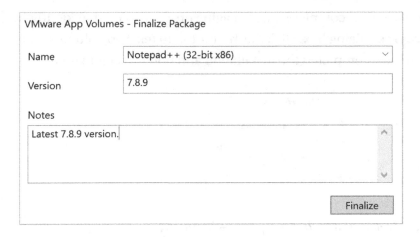

Figure 5-70. *Finalizing the package screen*

11. Click the **Finalize** button.

12. You will now see the warning message telling you that a restart of the packaging machine is required (Figure 5-71).

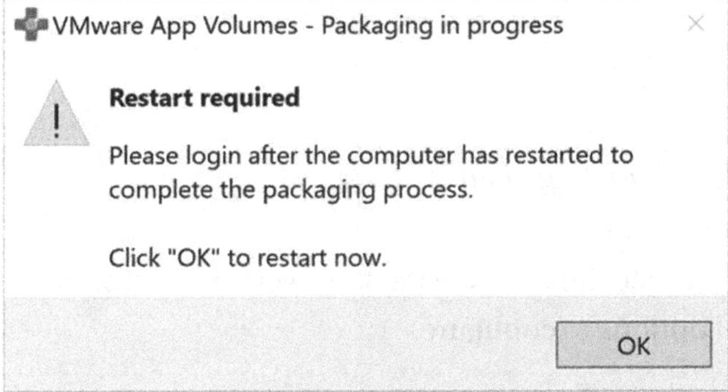

Figure 5-71. *Restart of the packaging machine is required*

13. Click **OK**. The packaging machine will restart.

14. Once it has restarted, log back in and you will see the message displayed in Figure 5-72.

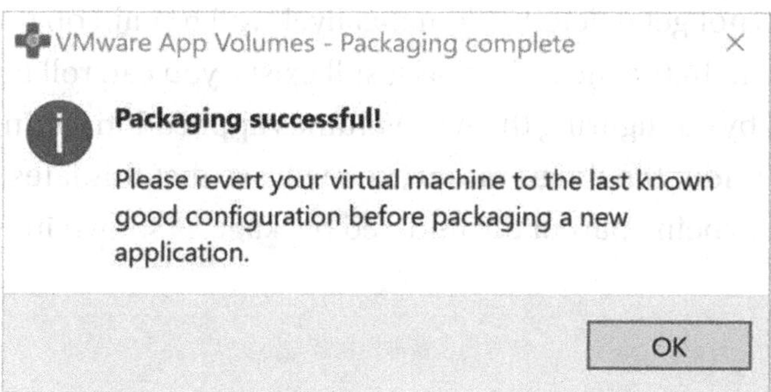

***Figure 5-72.** Packaging successful message*

15. You can now, as the message prompts, roll back the packaging machine to the snapshot you took prior to starting the packaging process.

16. Now switch back to the App Volumes Manager console. You will now see the screenshot in Figure 5-73.

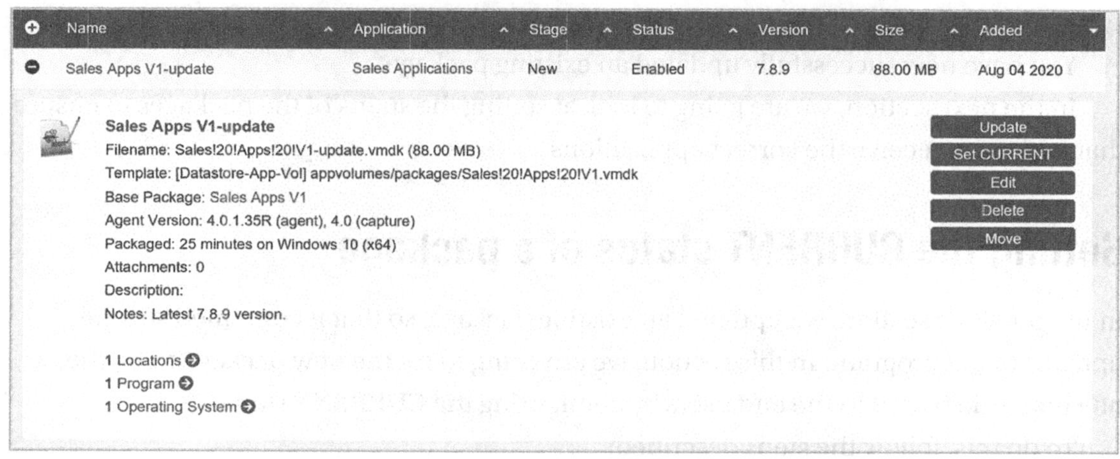

***Figure 5-73.** Updated package successfully created*

As you can see, the update has a new filename for the VMDK file, appended by the word **update** in the test lab example. In fact, this is a completely new file, a copy of the original package but now containing your updates.

You will see the original file listed on this screen as the template. This is because the update was based on using this file as a starting point.

The old file does not get deleted automatically. It will remain on the datastore until you go in and delete it. In the meantime, as it still exists, you can roll back and use it should you need to, by configuring the App Volumes application settings.

If you now look under the Programs tab, you will see that this latest version of Notepad++ is listed as being part of the updated package as shown in Figure 5-74.

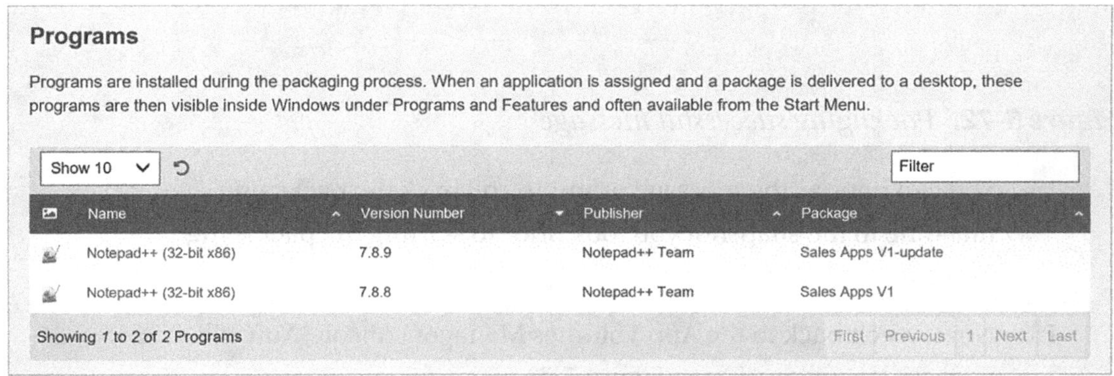

Figure 5-74. *The Programs screen*

You have now successfully updated an existing package.

In the next section, we are going to look at setting the status of the packages to ensure that end users receive the correct applications.

Setting the CURRENT status of a package

In the previous section, we updated an existing package, so that it contained several updates to the program. In this section, we are going to set the new package to be the one that is delivered to the end users by configuring the CURRENT status.

To do this, follow the steps described:

1. Click the **INVENTORY** menu, and then click the **Packages** tab.
2. You will see the screenshot in Figure 5-75.

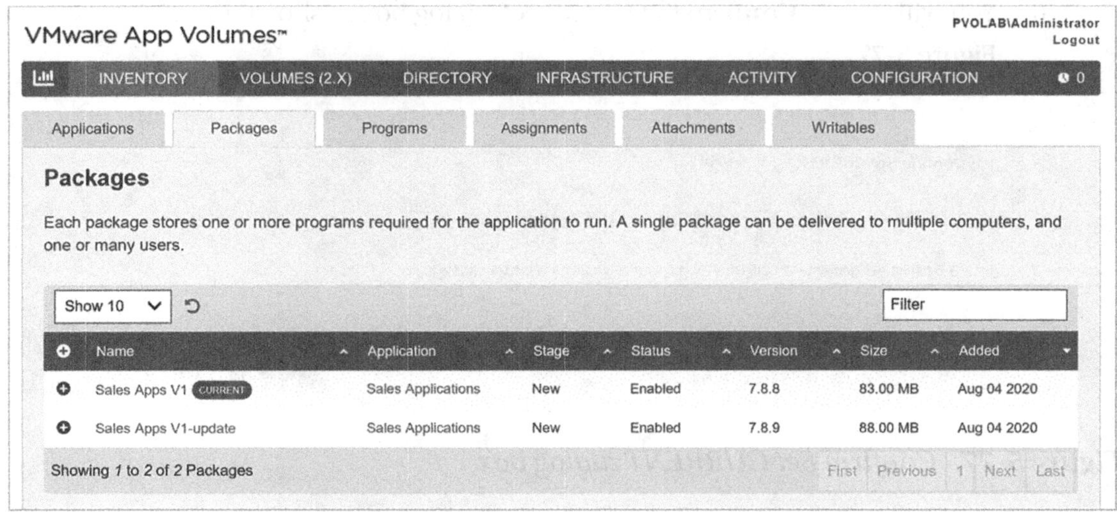

***Figure 5-75.** The Packages screen*

You will see that the two packages are listed - the previous version, which is set to current, and the new updated package.

3. Click the + button next to **Sales Apps V1-update** to expand the detail.

4. You will see the screenshot in Figure 5-76.

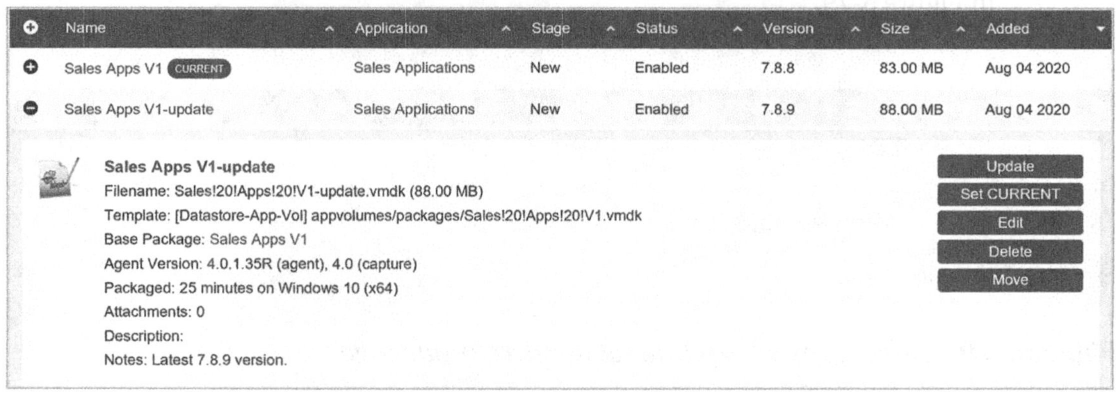

***Figure 5-76.** Expanded view of the Sales Apps V1-update package*

5. Click the **Set CURRENT** button.

6. You will see the **Confirm Set CURRENT** dialog box as shown in Figure 5-77.

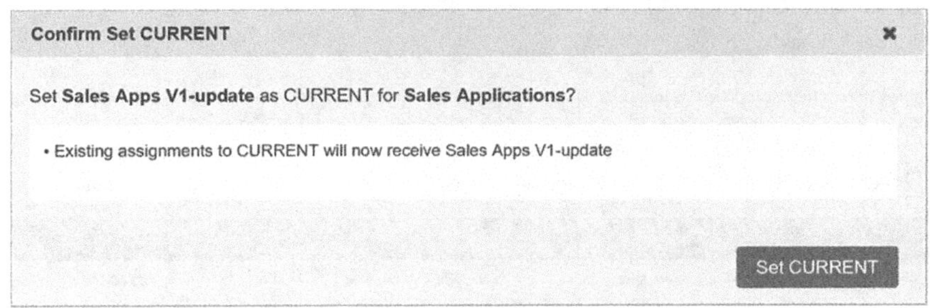

Figure 5-77. *Confirm Set CURRENT dialog box*

7. You will briefly see the progress bar appear, and then the message will pop up (Figure 5-78).

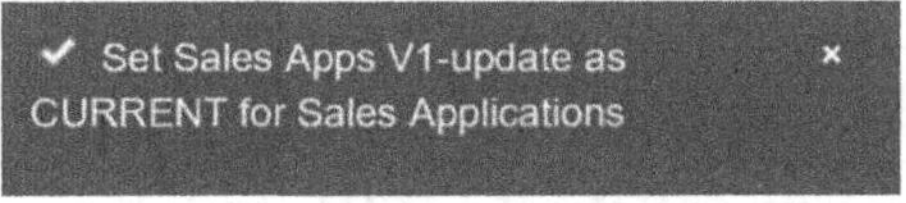

Figure 5-78. *Confirm Set CURRENT dialog box*

8. The new package will now be set as current, as shown in Figure 5-79.

Name	Application	Stage	Status	Version	Size	Added
Sales Apps V1-update CURRENT	Sales Applications	New	Enabled	7.8.9	88.00 MB	Aug 04 2020
Sales Apps V1	Sales Applications	New	Enabled	7.8.8	83.00 MB	Jul 30 2020
Test Package	Test App	New	Unpackaged			Jul 13 2020

Showing 1 to 3 of 3 Packages First Previous 1 Next Last

Figure 5-79. *Sales Apps V1-update set as current package*

If you want to remove the current status of the package, then simply click the Unset CURRENT button as shown in Figure 5-80.

Unset CURRENT

***Figure 5-80.** Removing the current status from a package*

You have now successfully set the status of the new package to be the current package. This means that end users automatically receive this package as part of their application assignment. You do not need to do anything else in terms of giving them access.

In the next section, we are going to look at editing an existing package.

Editing an existing Package

In this section, we are going to look at the process for editing the package. This editing feature is purely for editing some of the package details, and not the actual contents of the package. To edit the package, follow the steps described:

1. Click the **INVENTORY** menu, click the **Packages** tab, and expand the **Sales Apps V1** package as shown in Figure 5-81.

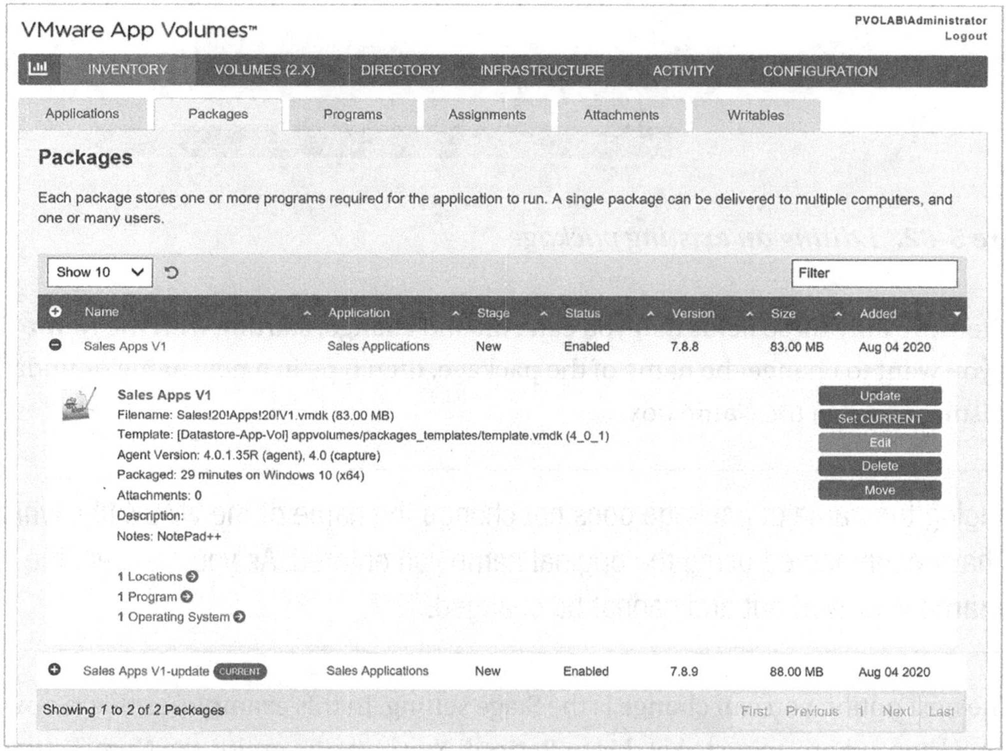

***Figure 5-81.** Editing an existing package*

2. Click the **Edit** button.
3. You will see the **Edit Package: Sales Apps V1** as shown in Figure 5-82.

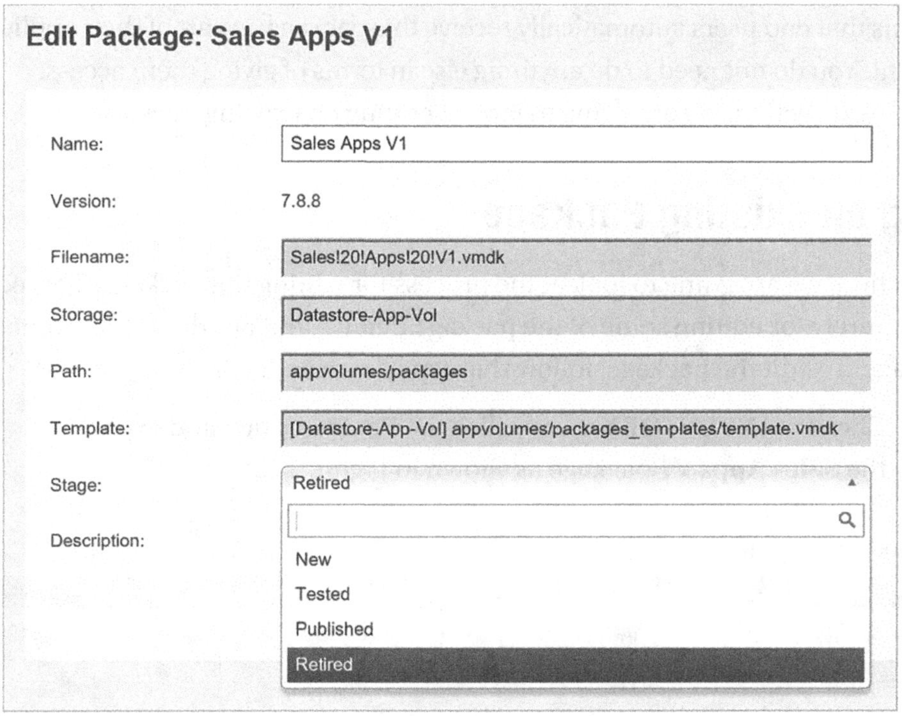

Figure 5-82. *Editing an existing package*

There are only three fields that you can edit and change, starting with the **Name** field.

If you want to change the name of the package, then type in a new name or update the existing name in the **Name** box.

Changing the name of package does not change the name of the VMDK file, which will have been named using the original name you entered. As you can see, the **Filename** is grayed out and cannot be changed.

The next option you can change is the Stage setting. In this example, as this is now the older package, we are going to set this to **Retired**. You have the options of New, Tested, and Published to choose from. This allows you to work with the lifecycle of the package.

Finally, you can edit the description in the **Description** box.

When you have completed your editing, click the Save button to save any changes you have made.

In the next section, we are going to delete a package.

Deleting a Package

In this section, we are going to delete an existing package.

To delete a package, follow the steps described:

1. Click the **INVENTORY** menu, then click the **Packages** tab.
2. Expand the **Test Package** package as shown in Figure 5-83.

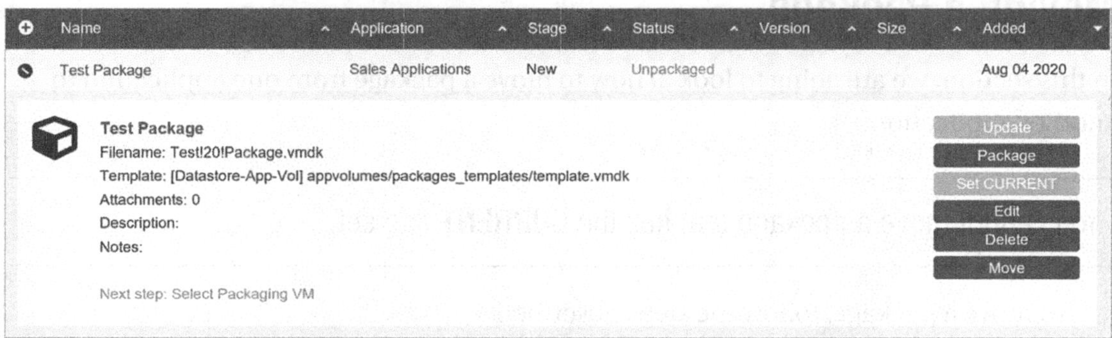

***Figure 5-83.** Deleting an existing package*

3. Click the **Delete** button. You will see the **Confirm Delete** dialog box as shown in Figure 5-84.

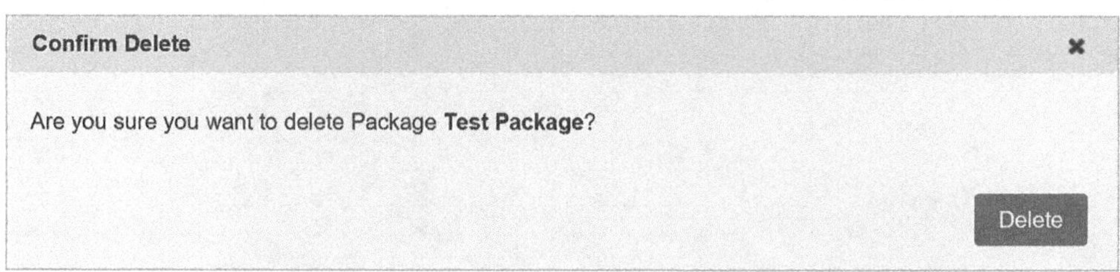

***Figure 5-84.** Confirm the deleting of a package*

4. Click the **Delete** button.
5. You will see the **Deleting Package Test Package** progress bar as shown in Figure 5-85.

Deleting Package Test Package

Figure 5-85. *Progress of the package being deleted*

The package will now have been successfully deleted and removed from the inventory. In the next section, we are going to look at moving an existing package.

Moving a Package

In this section, we are going to look at how to move a package from one application to another application.

You cannot move a package that has the **CURRENT** flag set.

To move a package, follow the steps described:

1. Click the **INVENTORY** menu, then click the **Packages** tab.
2. Expand the details for the **Sales App V1,** then click the **Move** button.
3. You will now see the **Move Package: Sales App V1** screen as shown in Figure 5-86.

VMware App Volumes™
PVOLAB\Administrator
Logout
INVENTORY VOLUMES (2.X) DIRECTORY INFRASTRUCTURE ACTIVITY CONFIGURATION
Applications Packages Programs Assignments Attachments Writables
Move Package: Sales Apps V1
This package will be moved to a different Application
Application: Test App
Assignments:
The following assignments to this package will be updated
Show 10 Filter
Name Created Modified
PVOLAB\bob Aug 04 2020 Aug 04 2020
Showing 1 to 1 of 1 results First Previous 1 Next Last
Move

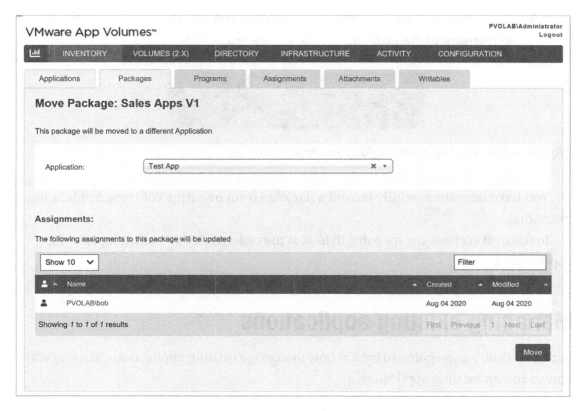

***Figure 5-86.** Moving a package to another application*

4. In the **Application** box, from the drop-down menu, select the Application to where you want to move the package. In this example, we are going to move the **Sales Apps V1** package to the **Test App** application, so from the Application drop-down menu, select **Test App**. You will also see that this package has a current assignment, which will be updated as part of the move process.

5. Click the **Move** button.

6. You will see the **Moving Package** progress bar as shown in Figure 5-87.

***Figure 5-87.** Moving a package progress bar*

7. Once the move has successfully completed, you will see the screenshot in Figure 5-88.

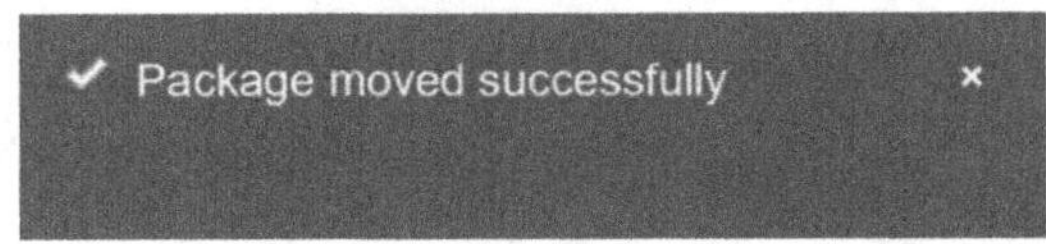

Figure 5-88. *Package successfully moved*

You have now successfully moved a package from one App Volumes Application to another.

In the next section, we are going to look at the tasks related to managing existing applications.

Managing existing applications

In this section, we are going to look at how to manage existing applications, starting with how to edit an existing application.

Editing an existing Application

In this section, we are going to edit an existing application.

To do this, we are going to follow the steps as described:

1. Click the **INVENTORY** menu, then click the **Applications** tab.
2. Check the box next to the application you want to edit. In the test lab example, we are going to use an application called **Test App** for this task.
3. With the application now highlighted, click the **Edit** button from the buttons along the bottom as shown in Figure 5-89.

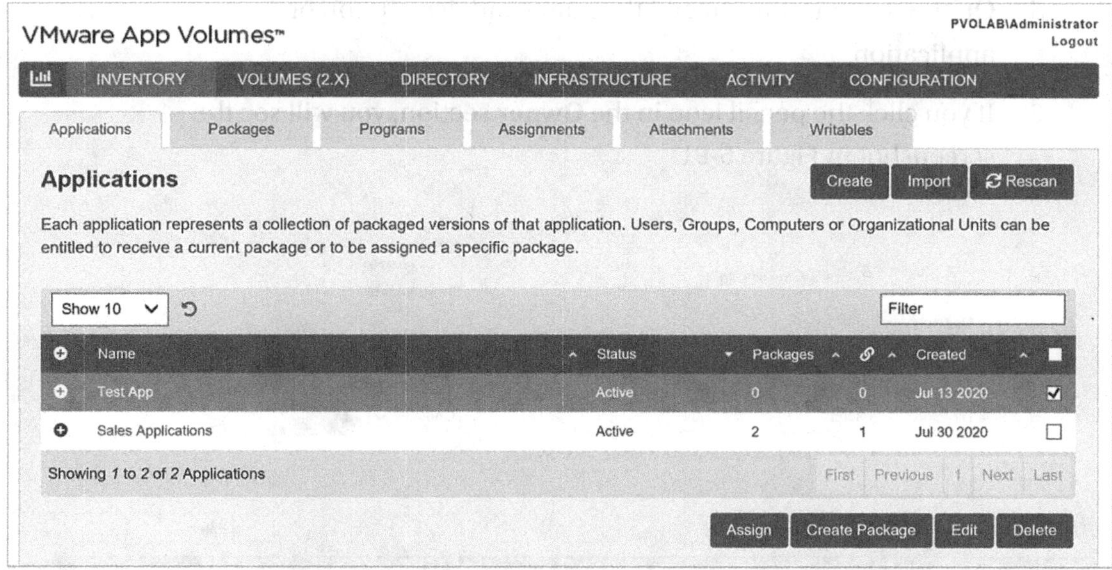

Figure 5-89. *Editing an existing application*

4. You will now see the **Edit Application: Test App** screen as shown in Figure 5-90.

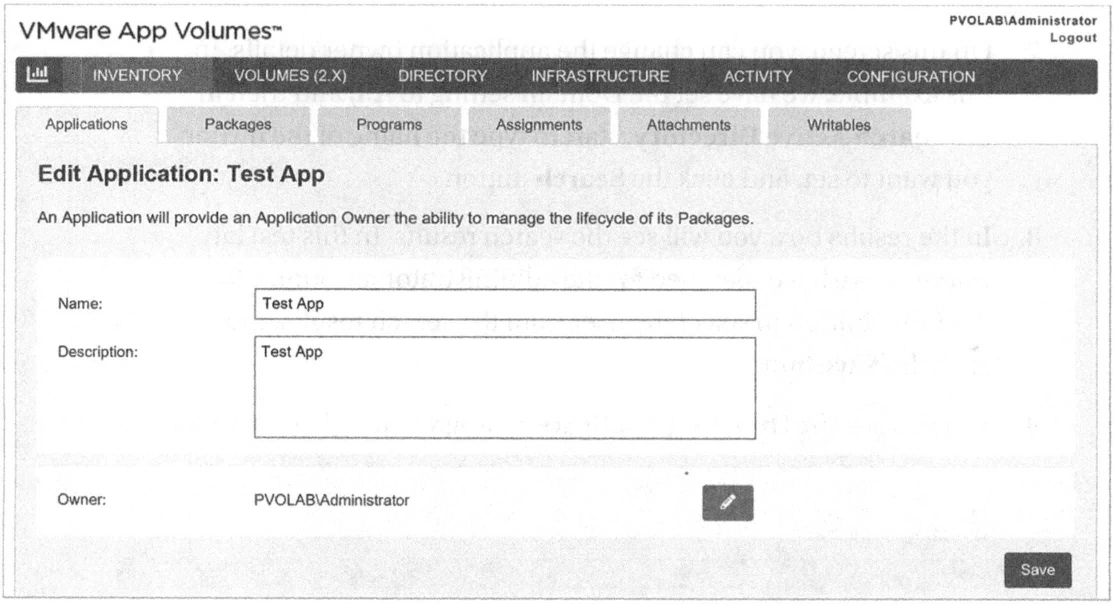

Figure 5-90. *Editing the application details*

5. On this screen, you can edit the name and description of the application.
6. If you click the pencil icon in the **Owner** section, you will see the screenshot in Figure 5-91.

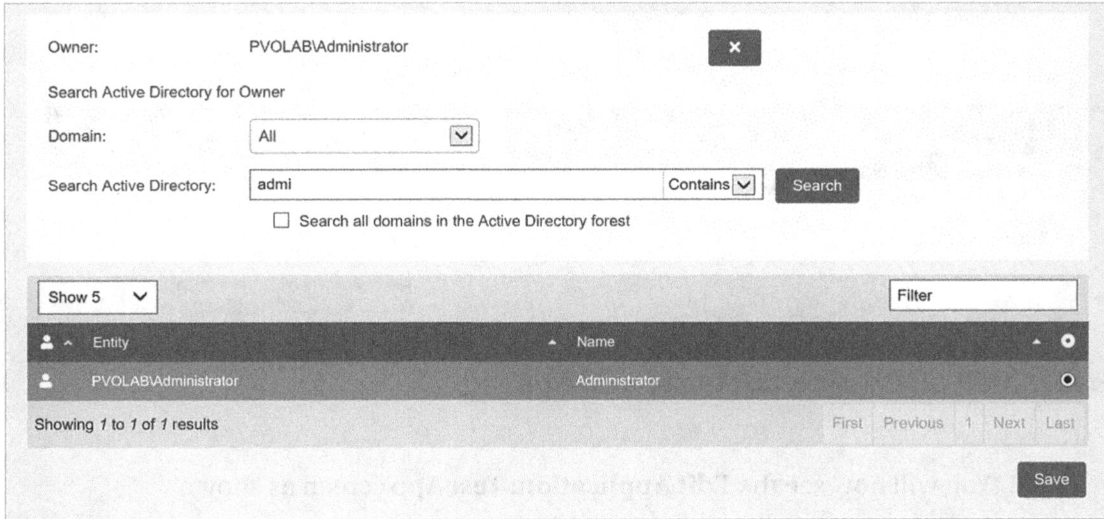

***Figure 5-91.** Editing owner details for the application*

7. On this screen, you can change the application owner details. In this example, we have set the Domain setting to **All,** and then in the **Search Active Directory**, start to type the name of the owner you want to set, and click the **Search** button.
8. In the results box, you will see the search results. In this test lab example, we have searched for the administrator account. Click the radio button to select the user from the search results, then click the **Save** button.
9. You will see the **Updating Application** progress bar (Figure 5-92).

***Figure 5-92.** Application updating process*

10. You will then see that the application has been successfully updated as shown in the message in Figure 5-93.

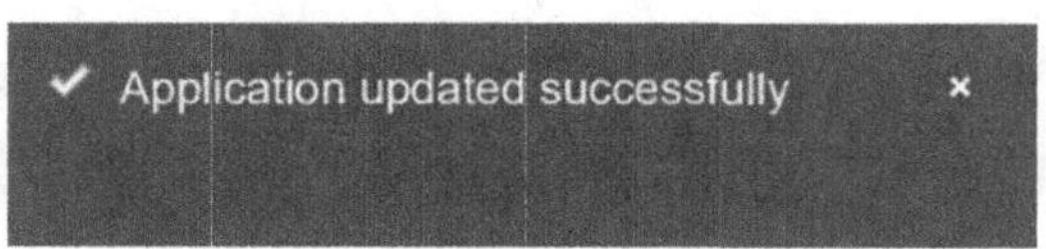

Figure 5-93. *Application update completed successfully*

You have now successfully edited an existing application.

In the next section, we are going to delete an existing application.

Deleting an existing Application

The final management task we are going to look at is deleting an existing application.

To delete an application, follow the steps as described:

1. Click the **INVENTORY** menu, and then click the **Applications** tab.
2. Check the box next to the application you want to delete, as shown in Figure 5-94.

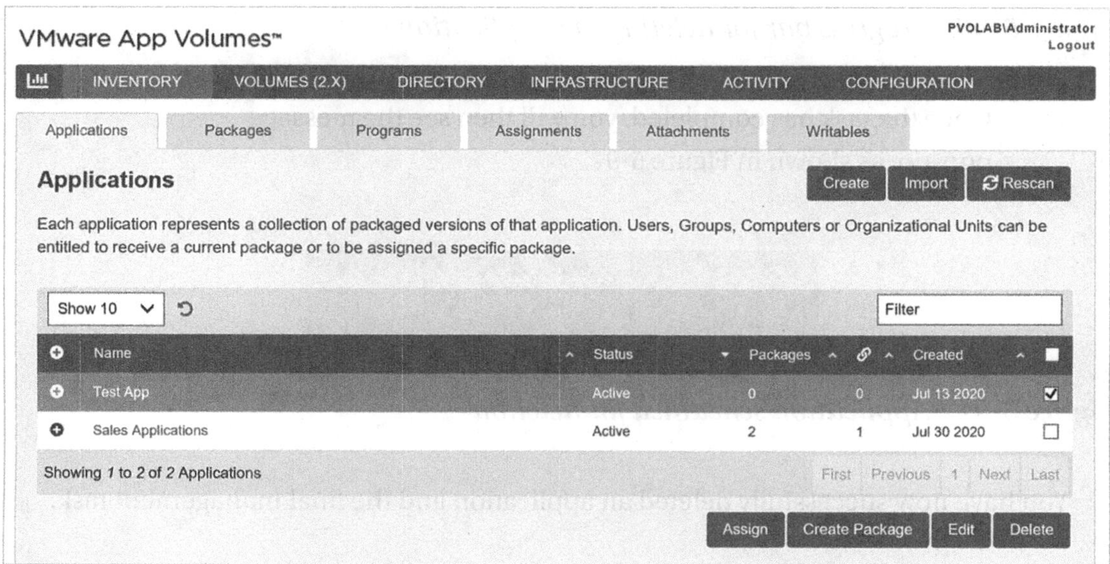

Figure 5-94. *Deleting an application*

3. Click the **Delete** button.

4. You will see the **Confirm Delete** dialog box as shown in Figure 5-95.

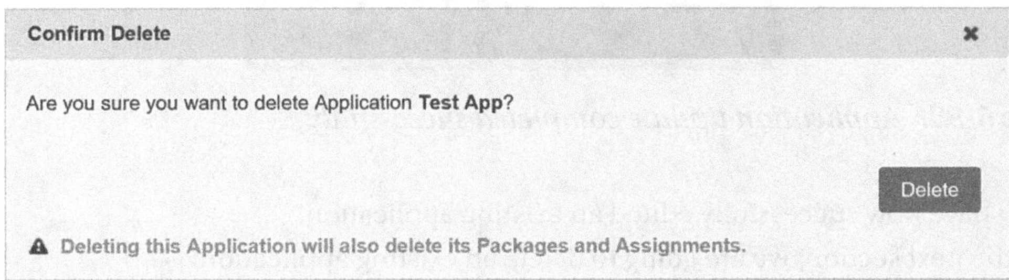

Figure 5-95. *Deleting an application*

5. Click the **Delete** button.

6. You will see the **Deleting Application** progress bar as shown in Figure 5-96.

Figure 5-96. *Progress bar for deleting the application*

7. Once the task has completed, you will then see the message pop-up, as shown in Figure 5-97.

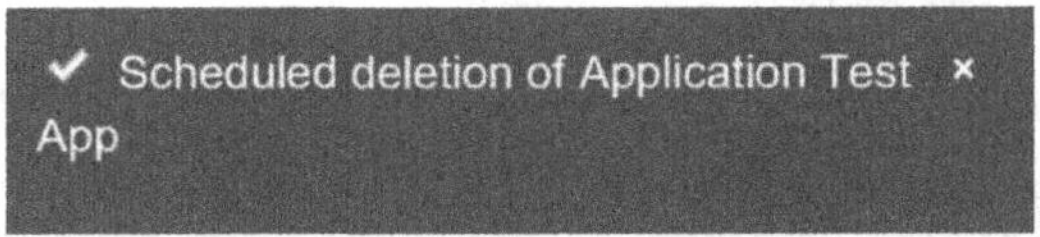

Figure 5-97. *Application scheduled for deletion*

You have now successfully deleted an application and the final management task.

Chapter summary

In this chapter, we have focused on Applications, Packages, and Programs, taking a much deeper look into how to configure these elements of the App Volumes solution.
We started by creating and configuring applications, then looking into creating a package and installing end user applications.

Once built, we then assigned the application to an end user to test functionality.

Finally, we looked at the ongoing management of the existing applications and packages.

In the next chapter, we will look at how to create and manage Writable Volumes.

CHAPTER 6

Writable Volumes

In the previous chapter, we created our first App Volumes Application to deliver applications to your end users. The Application consisted of App Volumes Packages as well as the actual Programs that you installed. So that is the delivery of applications taken care of, but what if the end user wants to install their own apps?

The end user cannot do this in the application package, as it is a read-only virtual hard disk. They could just install their app onto their virtual desktop, but if you deploy stateless virtual desktops, then when the end user logs out, the app will be deleted as the virtual desktop image will be reset.

The answer is Writable Volumes.

Let us quickly rewind and remind ourselves what a Writable Volume is. A Writable Volume is essentially a blank virtual hard disk (other than containing the drivers required by App Volumes), created as a VMDK file, that is then attached to the end user's virtual desktop machine when they log in. End users can now install their own applications onto this virtual hard disk, or it can be used to store user profile information, in conjunction with VMware Dynamic Environment Manager.

Once an end user has a Writable Volume assigned to them, it will be attached to any virtual desktop machine that they log in to. It is like them having an external USB memory stick, as the Writable Volume effectively becomes portable across any virtual desktop they use, meaning that any applications they install themselves will be available on any desktop they use.

The building process for a Writable Volume for the desktop admin team is far simpler, that of the application and packaging process, simply because the desktop admin team have nothing to install. All they need to do is to create and assign a Writable Volume.

The process can be summarized using the graphic shown in Figure 6-1.

P. von Oven, *Delivering Applications with VMware App Volumes 4*,
https://doi.org/10.1007/978-1-4842-6689-2_6

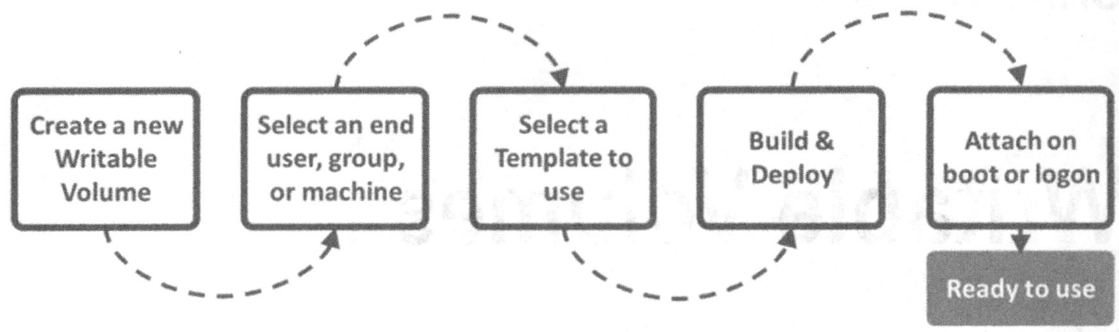

Figure 6-1. *Creating a Writable Volume – the process*

Now that we have refreshed your memory on what Writable Volumes are and their use case, in the next section, we are going to create a Writable Volume using the process we described.

Creating a Writable Volume

In this section, we are going to cover the practical side of creating a Writable Volume. To do this, we are going to follow the steps as described:

1. Log in to the App Volumes Manager, by either double-clicking the icon on the desktop of the App Volumes Manager server or via a browser from a desktop administrator's machine, typing in the address of the App Volumes Manager in the address bar.

2. You will see the login box as shown in Figure 6-2.

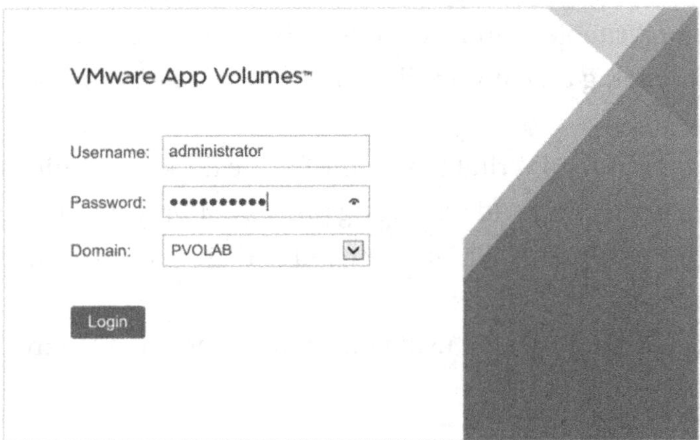

Figure 6-2. *App Volumes Manager login screen*

3. In the test lab, we are going to log in using the administrator account, selecting the PVOLAB domain, and then clicking the **Login** button.

4. You will see the **INVENTORY** screen and by default the **Applications** tab. Click the **Writables** tab as shown in Figure 6-3.

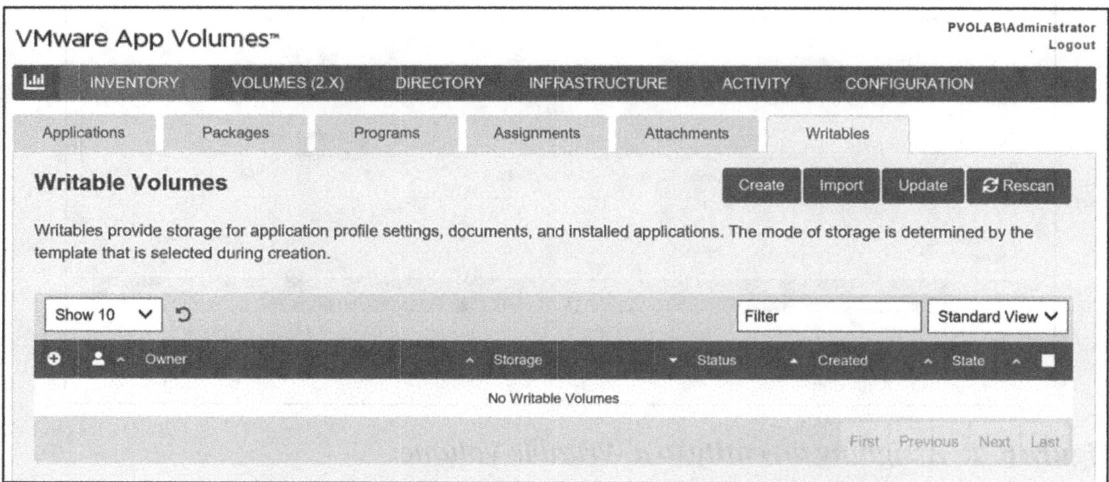

Figure 6-3. *Writables configuration screen*

5. Click the **Create** button.

6. You will now see the **Create Writable Volume** screen.

7. The first thing to configure is the entity you want to add the Writable Volume to. The entity in this context is who or what you want to assign a Writable Volumes to. This can be a user, a group of users, or a machine.

8. In the **Domain** box, from the drop-down menu, select the domain in which you want to search for the entity. In the test lab, this is the PVOLAB domain.

9. Then, in the **Search Active Directory** box, start to type in the name of the entity you want to assign the Writable Volume to. In the test lab, we are going to use the same end user as we used previously, so type **Bob** into the box.

10. Click the **Search** button. You will see something like Figure 6-4.

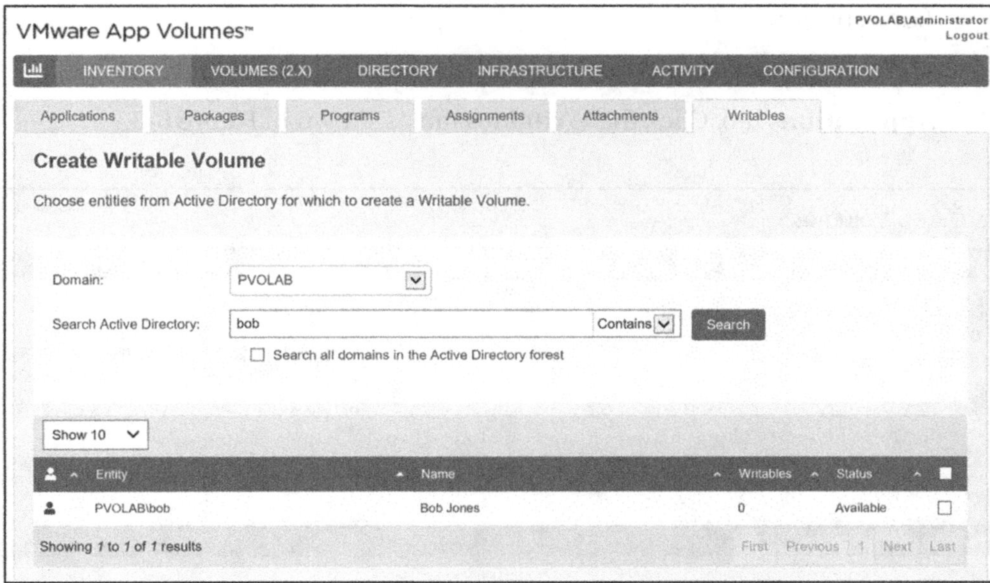

Figure 6-4. *Assigning an entity to a Writable Volume*

11. Check the box next to the username **PVOLAB\bob** to select it. You will see the screenshot in Figure 6-5.

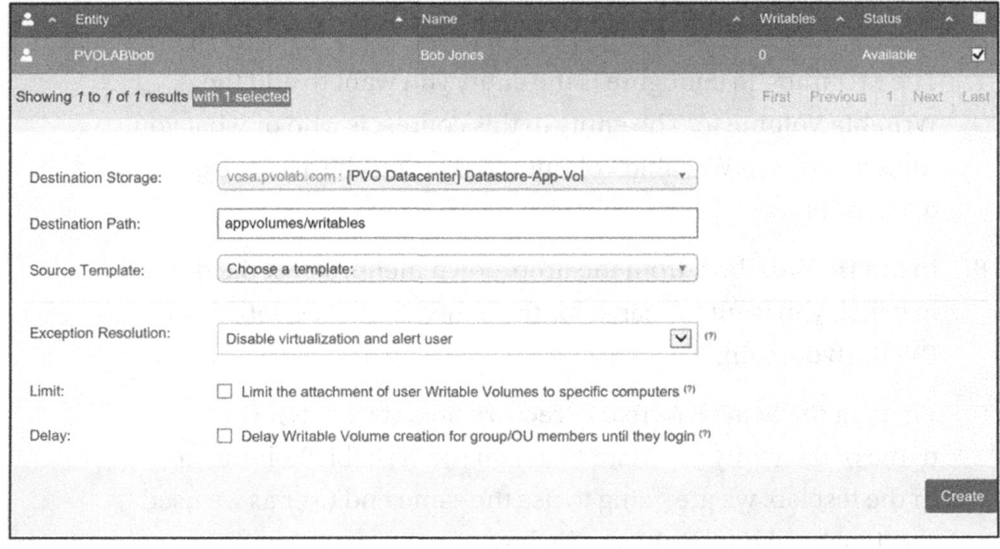

Figure 6-5. *Selecting the entity and configuring the Writable Volume*

You can now configure the Writable Volume.

12. The first thing to configure is the Destination Storage. This is the datastore on which the Writable Volume is going to be saved and stored. In the test lab, this is the **Datastore-App-Vol** datastore, so from the drop-down menu, click and select that datastore from those listed.
13. Next is the **Datastore Path** option. This is the folder on the datastore in which the Writable Volume will be created and stored. In the test lab, we are going to leave this as the default setting of **appvolumes/Writables.**
14. You then need to choose the **Source Template** from which to create the Writable Volume. This is the blank virtual hard disk that contains the necessary files dependent on the use case of the template. You have the choice of the following template options:
    a. User profile only
    b. User installed application only
    c. User profile and user installed applications
15. These options are shown in full, with the name and file size details, as shown in Figure 6-6.

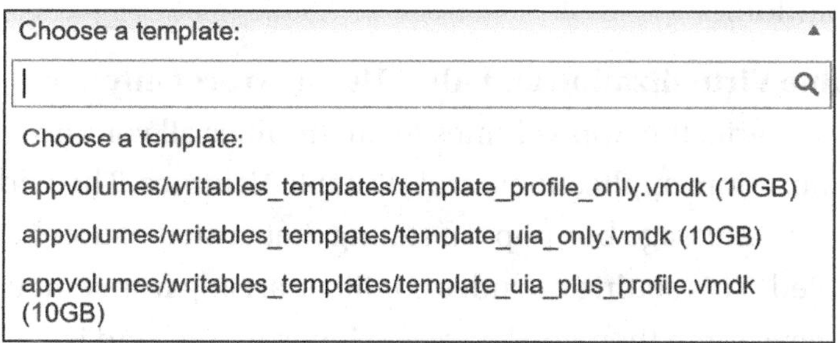

***Figure 6-6.** Writable Volumes template options*

16. In the test lab, we are just going to create a Writable Volume for user installed applications, so from the list of options, we are going to select the option for **Writables_templates/template_uia_only.vmdk**.

17. The next option is for **Exception Resolution**. This setting is used to manage conditions whereby an end user's Writable Volume cannot be attached for some reason. For example, they are logged in to another virtual desktop which has the Writable Volume already attached. The Exception Resolution setting allows you to set what happens, should this happen when an end user logs in to their virtual desktop.

18. If you click the drop-down menu, you will see that there are three options to choose from. These options are as follows:

    a. **Disable Virtualization and Alert User**: In this scenario, the App Volumes Agent disables all volume virtualization, meaning that no volumes will be attached to the end user's virtual desktop machine. This includes applications and packages, as well as the Writable Volume. If this scenario is triggered, the end user will see a pop-up message box, stating that virtualization has been disabled.

    b. **Block User Login**: This setting means that the end user cannot log in. It means that when there is conflict, due to a Writable Volume already being attached to another virtual desktop machine, the end user will not be able to log in to another machine. This feature is especially useful if their Writable Volume is also being used to store their Windows profile and prevents conflicts and profile corruption.

    c. **Disable Virtualization and Alert User (Errors Only)**: In this scenario, the App Volumes Agent disables all volume virtualization, applications, and Writable Volumes. The end user will see a message box pop-up stating that virtualization has been disabled. This setting excludes conflicts, arising from end users who have more than one active session at a time, and is the default behavior in App Volumes 2.14 and earlier.

19. The next setting is for **Limit**. The limit setting is used when an end user does not need their Writable Volume attached to all virtual desktop machines they use. Some users may also require a separate Writable Volume that is attached to specific virtual desktop machines only. This option enables you to specify the prefix of a computer name. Any computer names that then start with this prefix are the only computers that can then have a Writable Volume attached to them.

20. The final setting is the **Delay** setting. If you create a Writable Volume for a group of users or for an entire Organizational Unit (OU), then the Writable Volume will be created for every member of that group or OU. If you have hundreds of end users within the group or OU, then this could potentially cause a performance issue on your infrastructure, as it will go and create a Writable Volume for those hundreds of end users. It may also be a case that not every one of those end users needs a Writable Volume in the first place. The delay option will delay the creation of the Writable Volumes for group and OU members until an end user logs in. So, it is in effect a build on demand option, with Writable Volumes being created as and when the end user logs in to their virtual desktop machine. Writable Volumes for individual end users will still be created immediately after they have been configured, with no delay. It is worth noting that this could slow login times the first time it runs.

21. Once you have configured your Writable Volume, click the **Create** button.

22. You will see the Confirm Create Writable Volumes dialog box, as shown in Figure 6-7.

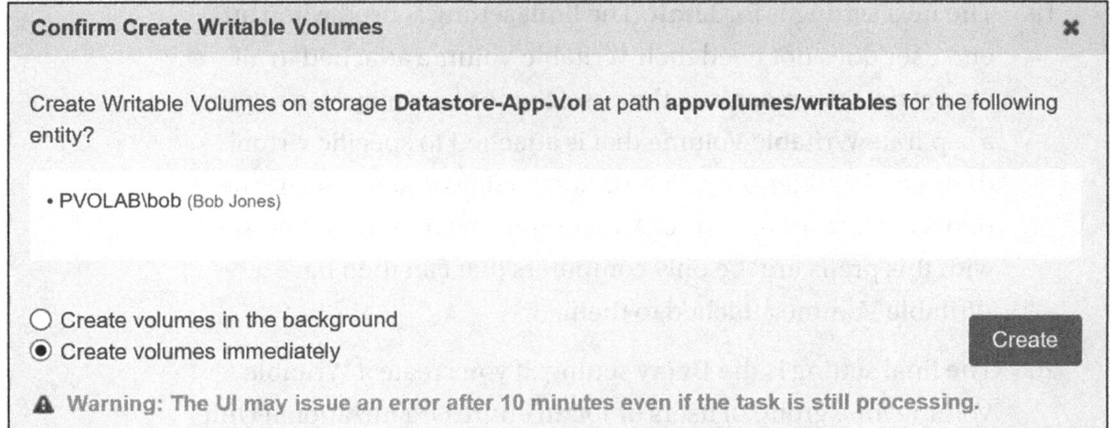

Figure 6-7. *Confirm Create Writable Volumes*

23. Click the radio button for **Create volumes immediately**, and then click the **Create** button.

24. You will see the Creating Writable Volumes progress bar, as shown in Figure 6-8.

Figure 6-8. *Creating Writable Volumes progress bar*

25. Once completed, you will see a message appear, stating that one Writable Volume has been created (Figure 6-9).

Figure 6-9. *Writable Volume successfully created*

You will return to the main **Writable Volumes** screen which now shows the newly created volume, as shown in Figure 6-10.

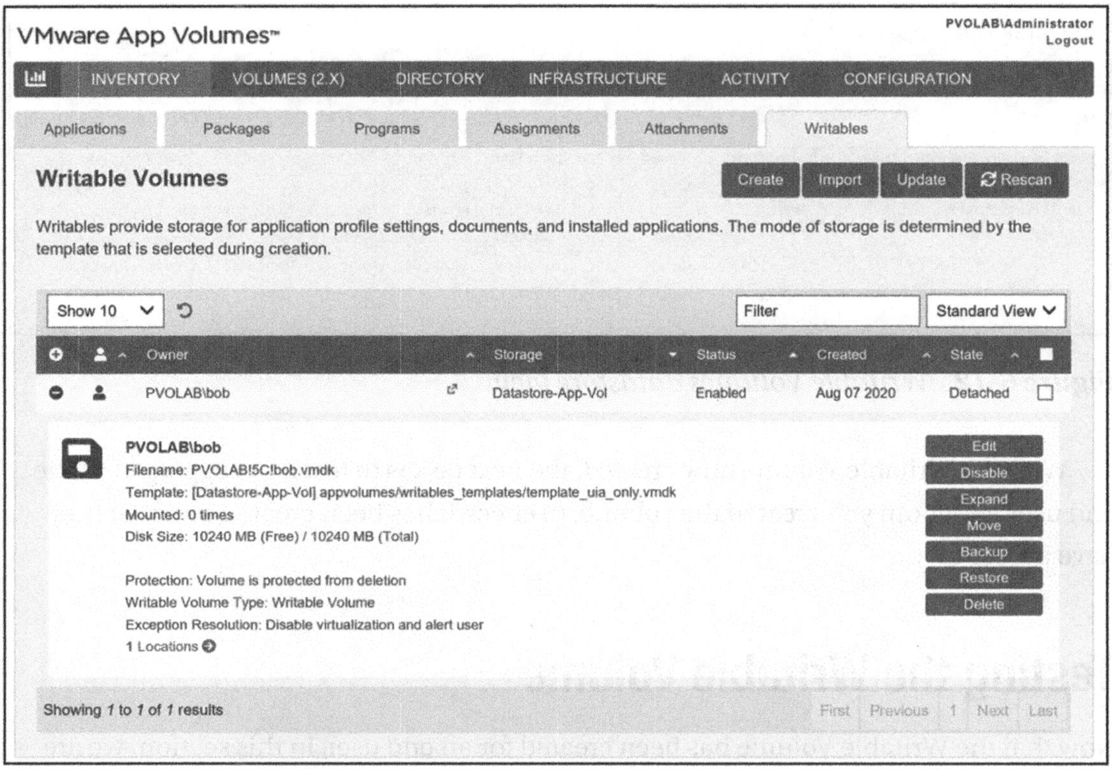

Figure 6-10. Writable Volumes screen with newly created volume

If you click the **Locations** link, you will see the location of where the Writable Volume has been created, as shown in Figure 6-11.

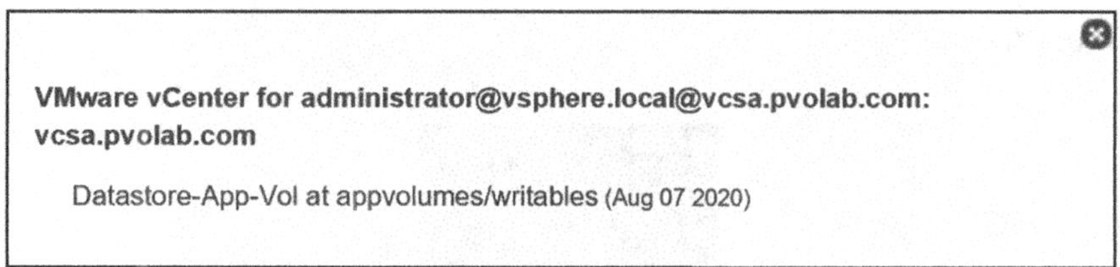

Figure 6-11. Writable Volumes datastore location

It would be useful here to show what the newly created Writable Volume looks like from the datastore perspective. The screenshot in Figure 6-12 is from the vCenter Server and shows the Datastore-App-Vol datastore and the Writables folder.

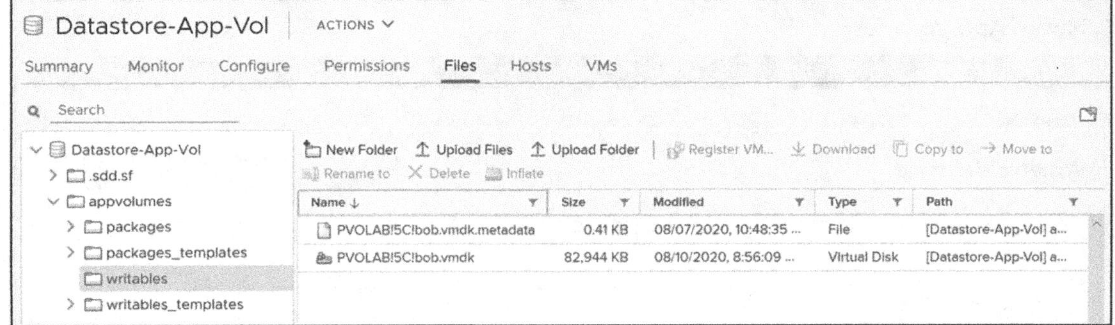

Figure 6-12. *Writable Volumes datastore view*

With the Writable Volume now created, the next task is to test it by logging in as the end user for whom you created the volume, to check it has been created and that they have access to it.

Testing the Writable Volume

Now that the Writable Volume has been created for an end user, in this section, we are going to test to make sure that the volume works as expected; to do that, we are going to log in as the end user for whom we created the Writable Volume.

To do this, we are going to follow the steps described here:

1. Log in to a virtual desktop machine as the end user that we created the Writable Volume for. This user needs to have admin rights. In the test lab, this is the user called **Bob Jones**, as shown in Figure 6-13.

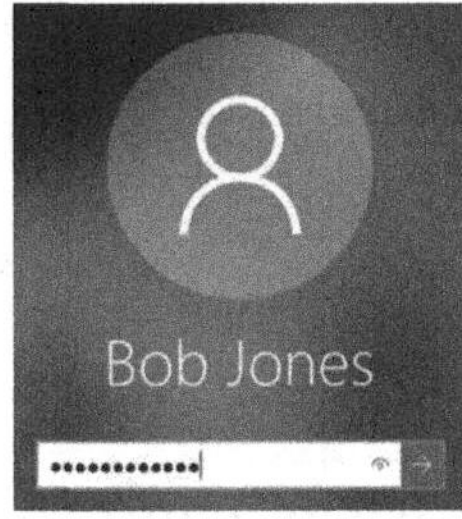

Figure 6-13. *Logging in as the end user*

2. The user will now be logged in, and as the login process runs, the App Volumes Agent is checking in with the App Volumes Manager to check what volumes the end user has been. In this example, it is the Writable Volume we just created, as well as the application package they still have assigned to them, which was configured in the previous chapter. Figure 6-14 shows the Disk Management view.

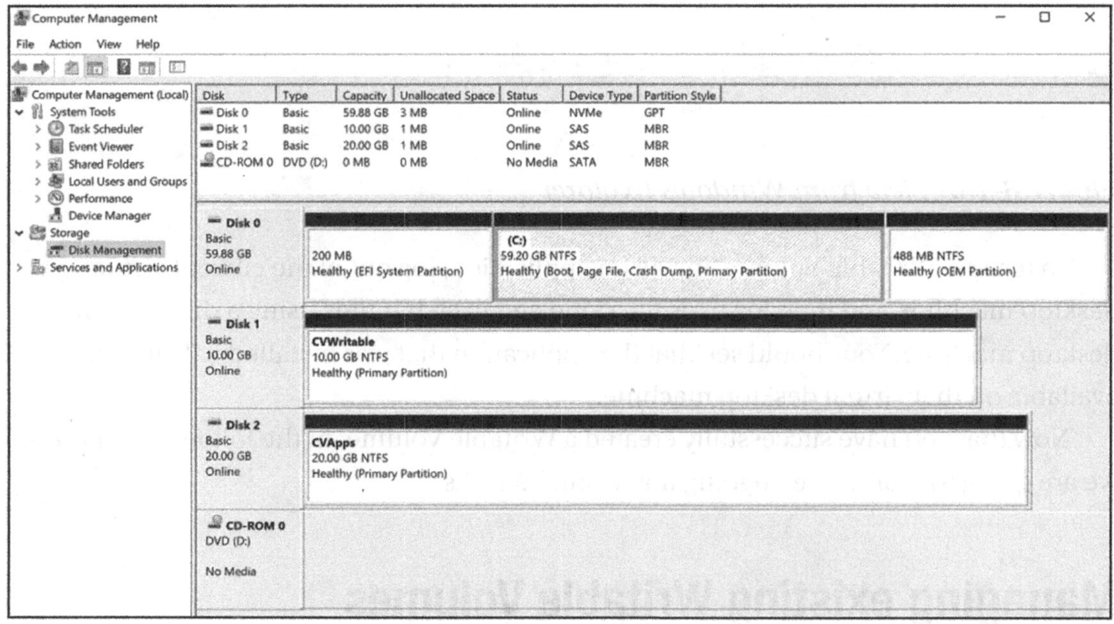

Figure 6-14. *Writable Volume from Windows disk manager*

As you can see, **Disk 1** is a 10 GB disk with the name **CVWritable**. This is the Writable Volume that we created. The "CV" part of the name refers to the solution's previous name of Cloud Volumes.

You will also see **Disk 2** listed still. This is the application packages and therefore has the name **CVApps**.

The other point to highlight here is that neither of those virtual hard disks has drive letters assigned to them, meaning the end user cannot access them. In any case, the disk containing the packages is read only, and the App Volumes Agent will take care of redirecting any user installed apps to the Writable Volume. The user will just see something like Figure 6-15 should they open Windows Explorer.

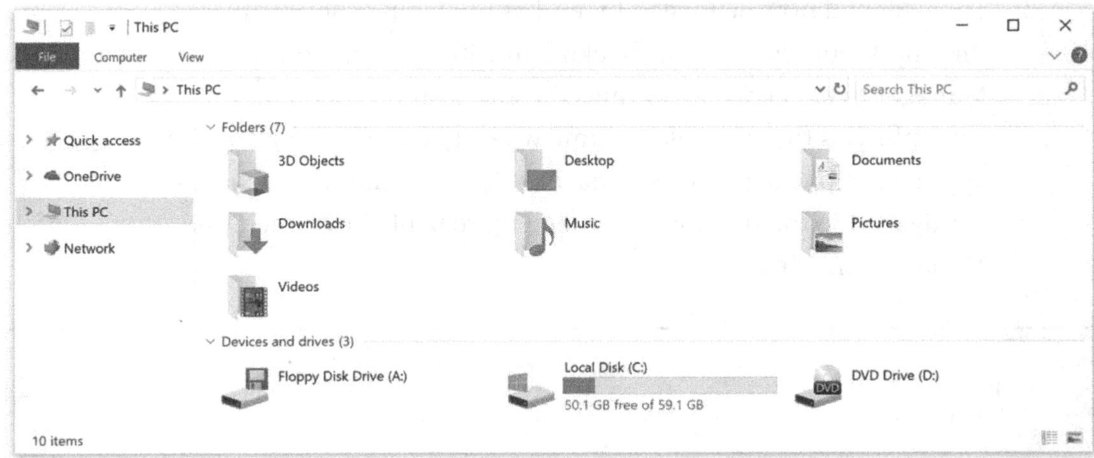

Figure 6-15. *View from Windows Explorer*

To test the Writable Volume, install an application, log out of the current virtual desktop machine, and then log in as the same end user, but now using a different virtual desktop machine. You should see that the application that was installed will also be available on that virtual desktop machine.

Now that you have successfully created a Writable Volume, in the following sections, we are going to look at the ongoing management tasks.

Managing existing Writable Volumes

In this section, we are going to look at the ongoing management and maintenance tasks associated with Writable Volumes.

As you can see from the blue task buttons on the right-hand side of the screen, available once you have Writable Volumes in your environment, and shown in Figure 6-16, there are a few tasks.

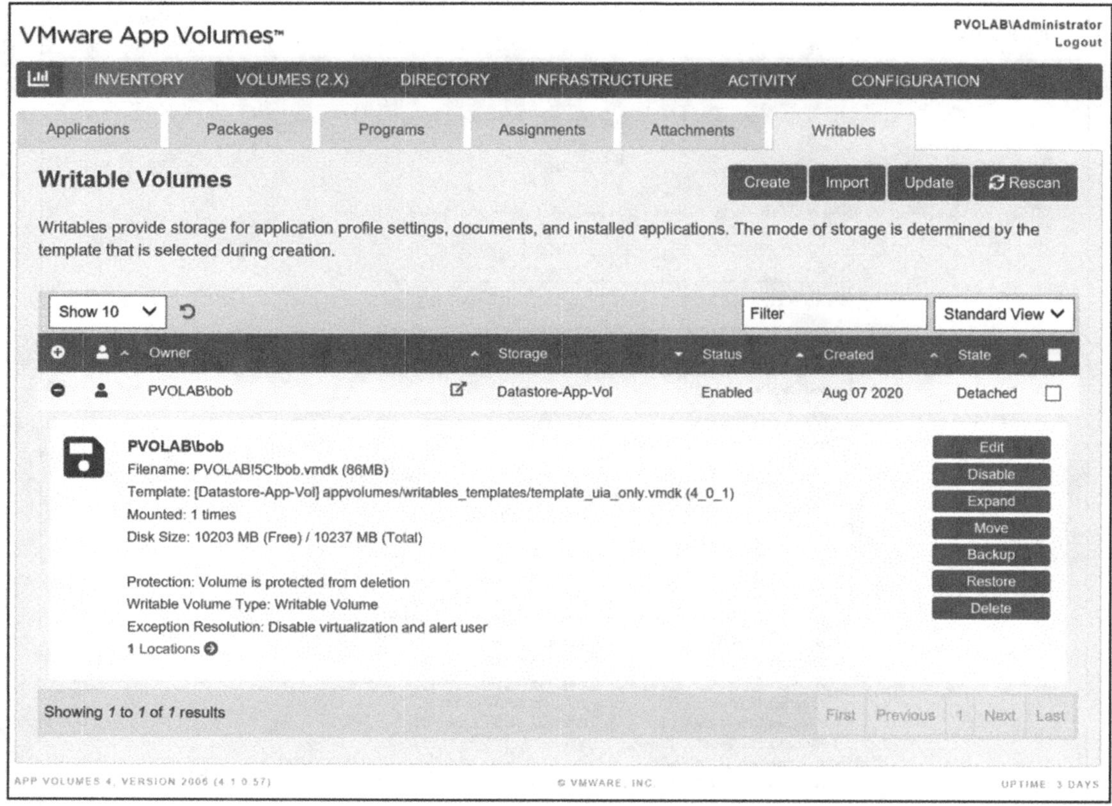

Figure 6-16. *Writable Volumes main screen*

In the following sections, we are going to look at these tasks in more detail.

Editing an existing Writable Volume

Once a Writable Volume has been created, you can edit certain information about the Writable Volume. To do this, follow the steps described:

1. Click the + button to expand the details and the options for the Writable Volume you want to edit.

2. Click the **Edit** button.

3. You will see the **Edit Writable Volume** screen, as shown in Figure 6-17.

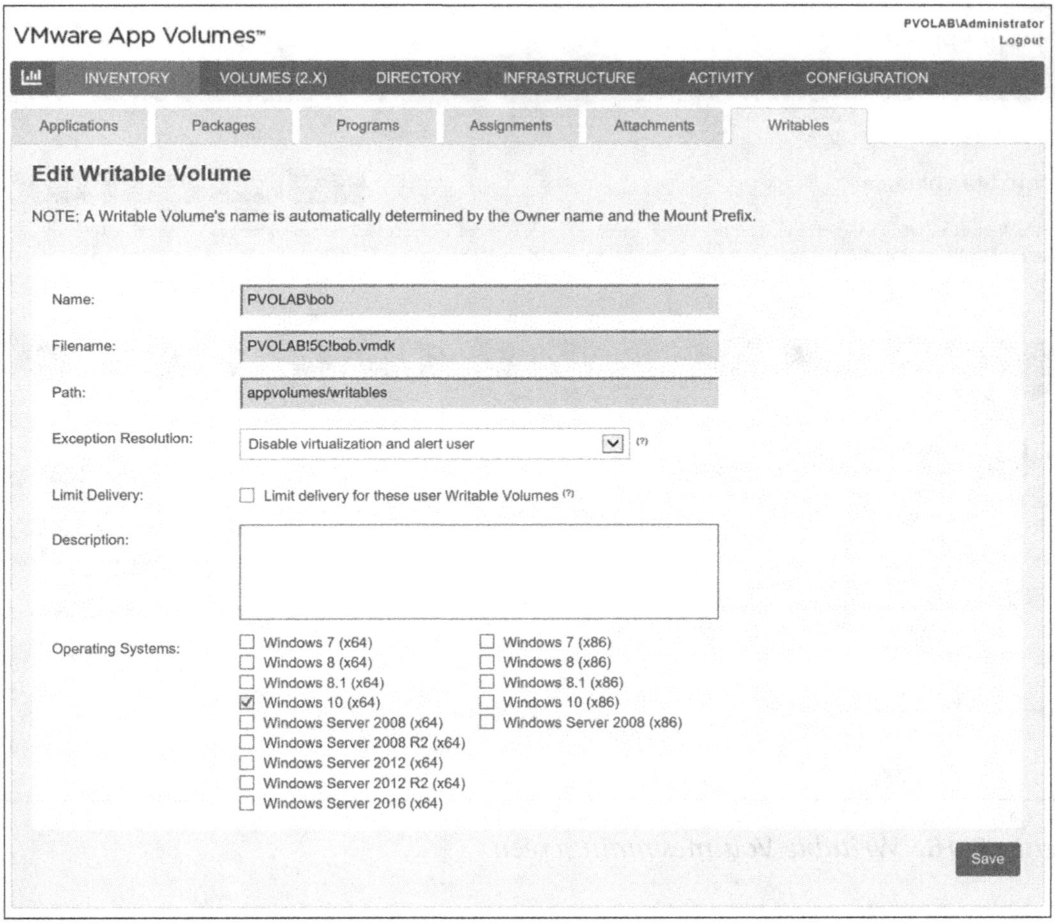

Figure 6-17. *Writable Volumes edit screen*

4. The boxes for **Name**, **Filename**, and **Path** are grayed out and therefore cannot be edited or changed. The filename is created based on the username you create the Writable Volume for.

5. The next option is for **Exception Resolution**. We have discussed this setting previously, and it is used to manage conditions whereby an end user's Writable Volume cannot be attached for some reason. This is shown in Figure 6-18.

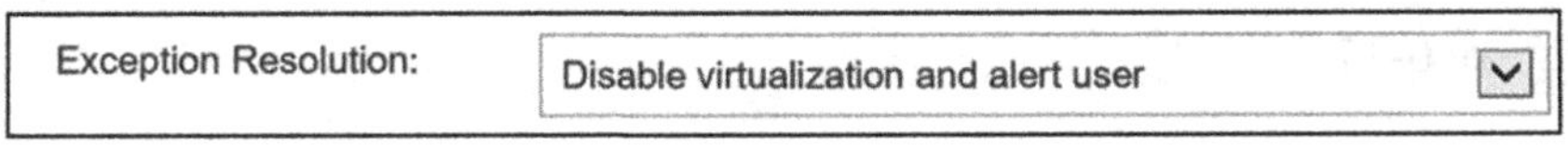

Figure 6-18. *Exception Resolution options*

6. If you click the drop-down menu, you will see that there are three options to choose from. These options are as follows:

    a. **Disable Virtualization and Alert User**: In this scenario, the App Volumes Agent disables all volume virtualization, meaning that no volumes will be attached to the end user's virtual desktop machine. This includes applications and packages, as well as the Writable Volume. If this scenario is triggered, then the end user will see a pop-up message box stating the virtualization has been disabled.

    b. **Block User Login**: This setting means that the end user cannot log in. It means that when there is conflict, due to a Writable Volume already being attached to another virtual desktop machine, the end user will not be able to log in to another machine. This feature is especially useful if their Writable Volume is also being used to store their Windows profile and thereby prevents conflicts and profile corruption.

    C. **Disable Virtualization and Alert User (Errors Only)**: In this scenario, the App Volumes Agent disables all volume virtualization, bit applications, and Writable Volumes. The end user will see a message box pop-up, stating that virtualization has been disabled. This setting excludes conflicts arising from end users who have more than one active session at a time and is the default behavior in App Volumes 2.14 and earlier.

7. The next option is to Limit Delivery, as shown in Figure 6-19.

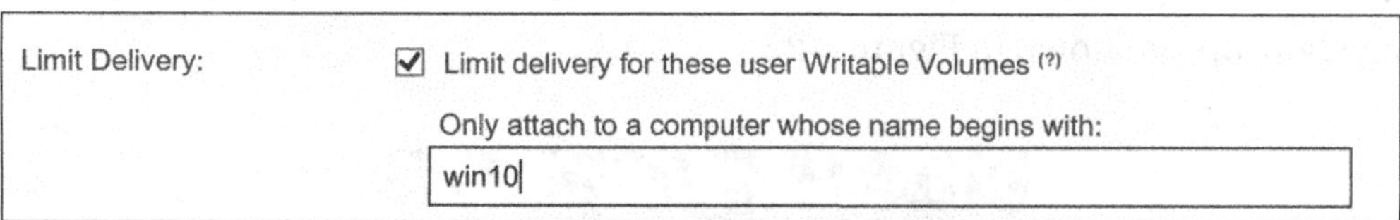

Figure 6-19. *Limit Delivery configuration*

8. If you check the **Limit delivery for these user Writable Volumes** box, you can then, in the box below, enter the first part of the name of the machines you want only to have a Writable Volume attached. In the preceding example, the machine names will need to start with **win10**.

9. The final option on the edit Writable Volumes screen is to select the operating system to which the Writable Volumes can be attached. Check the box next to the OS you want to allow. You can select multiple OSs should you need to.

10. Once you have completed your edits, click the **Save** button.

11. You will see the **Confirm Save** message, as shown in Figure 6-20.

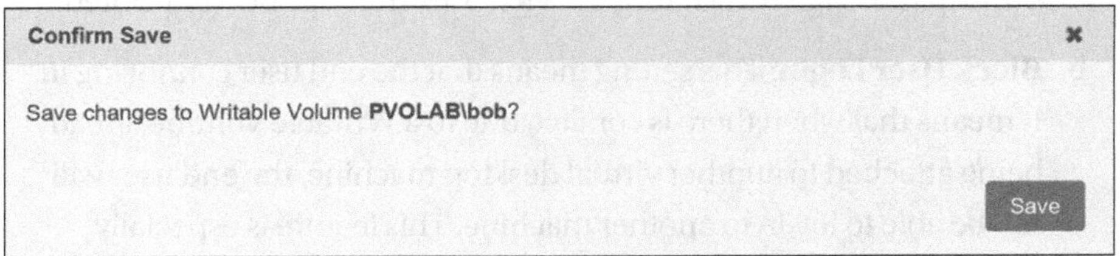

***Figure 6-20.** Confirm Save dialog box*

12. You will see the **Saving Writable Volume** progress bar as shown in Figure 6-21.

***Figure 6-21.** Saving Writable Volume progress bar*

Once the changes have been saved, you will see the **Saved Writable changes** message pop-up, as shown in Figure 6-22.

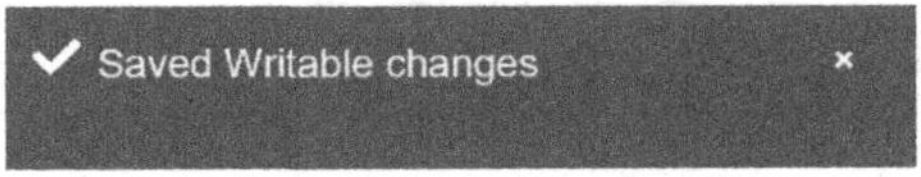

***Figure 6-22.** Writable changes successfully saved*

In the next section, we are going to look at how to disable an existing Writable Volume.

Disabling an existing Writable Volume

The disable feature allows you to basically switch off the Writable Volume for an end user, meaning that they will no longer have access to it. It does not delete it from the datastore, and it can easily be enabled again.

To disable a Writable Volume, follow the steps described:

1. Select the Writable Volume you want to disable by clicking the + button next to it to expand the detail.
2. Click the **Disable** button.
3. You will see the **Confirm Disable** dialog box, as shown in Figure 6-23.

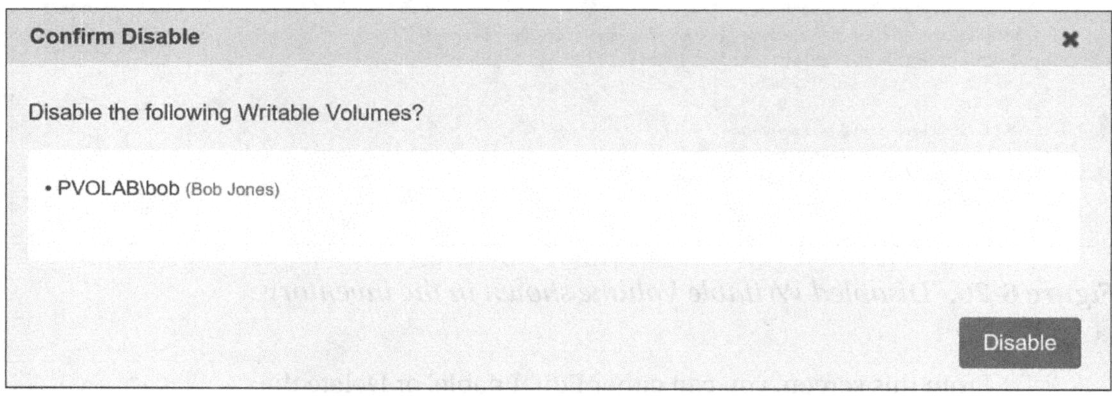

Figure 6-23. *Confirm Disable dialog box*

4. Check you have selected the correct Writable Volume to disable - in this example, we are disabling the Writable Volumes assigned to the user **PVOLAB\bob** - and click the **Disable** button.
5. You will see the Disabling Writable Volumes progress bar (Figure 6-24).

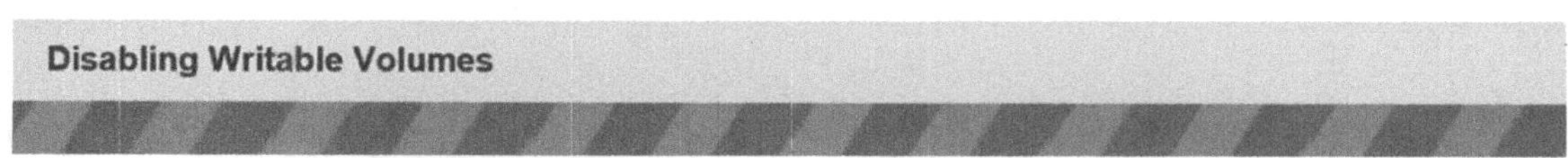

Figure 6-24. *Disabling Writable Volumes progress bar*

6. Once disabled, you will see the message pop-up in Figure 6-25.

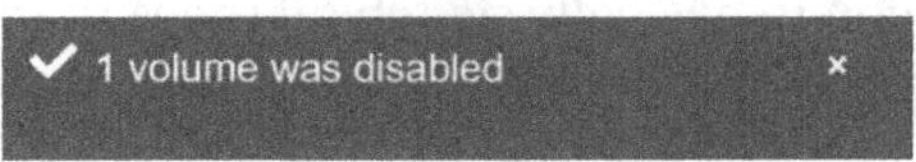

Figure 6-25. *Writable Volume disabled message*

7. You will now see the entry for the Writable Volume for the end user PVOLAB\bob as shown in Figure 6-26.

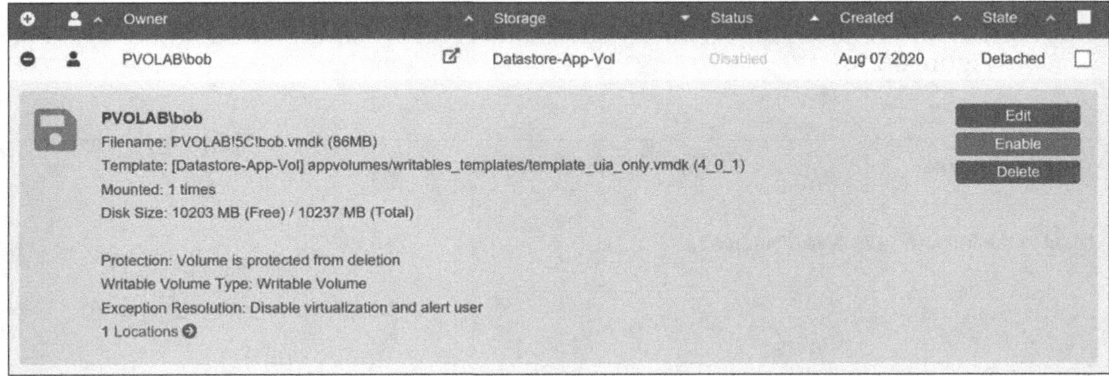

Figure 6-26. *Disabled Writable Volume shown in the inventory*

From this screen, you can either Edit, Enable, or Delete the Writable Volume. We are going to enable it so that the end user has access again.

8. Click the **Enable** button. You will see the **Confirm Enable** dialog box, as shown in Figure 6-27.

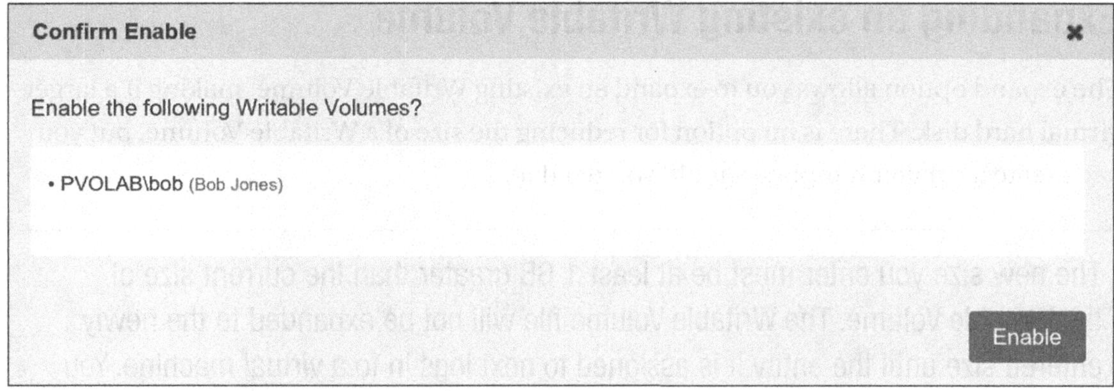

Figure 6-27. *Confirm Enable of Writable Volume*

9. Click the **Enable** button.
10. You will see the **Enabling Writable Volumes** progress bar (Figure 6-28).

Figure 6-28. *Enabling Writable Volumes progress bar*

11. Once enabled, you will see the message pop-up in Figure 6-29.

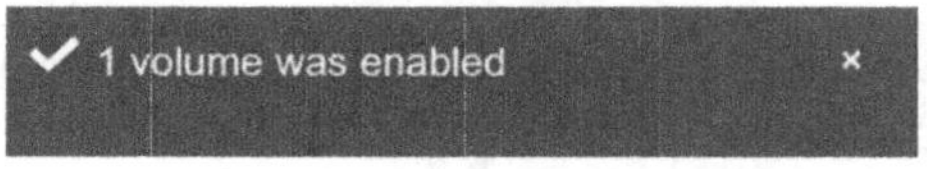

Figure 6-29. *Writable Volume enabled message*

You have now successfully disabled and enabled a Writable Volume.

In the next section, we are going to look at how to expand the size of an existing Writable Volume.

Expanding an existing Writable Volume

The expand option allows you to expand an existing Writable Volume, making it a larger virtual hard disk. There is no option for reducing the size of a Writable Volume, but you can create a smaller template should you need to.

The new size you enter must be at least 1 GB greater than the current size of the Writable Volume. The Writable Volume file will not be expanded to the newly entered size until the entity it is assigned to next logs in to a virtual machine. You also need to ensure that you have the correct permission in vCenter to expand a virtual hard disk.

To expand an existing Writable Volume, follow the steps described:

1. Click the + button to expand the details and the options for the Writable Volume you want to expand.
2. Click the **Expand** button.
3. You will see the Confirm Expand dialog box as shown in Figure 6-30.

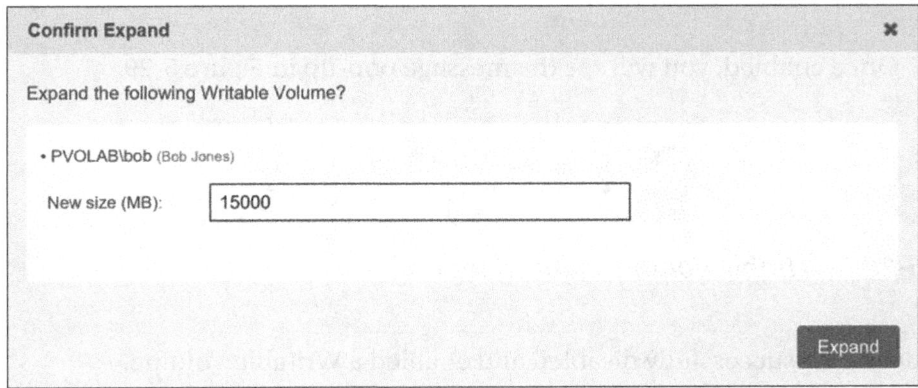

Figure 6-30. *Confirm the expansion of a Writable Volume*

4. In the **New size (MB)** box, type in the new size of the Writable Volume. Note that you enter the new size and not how much you want to expand the volume by. In this example, we are going to resize the volume to 12000 MB, or 12 GB.

5. Click the **Expand** button.

6. You will see the **Expanding Writable Volume** progress bar (Figure 6-31).

Figure 6-31. *Expanding Writable Volume progress bar*

Once successfully completed you will see the following message shown in Figure 6-32.

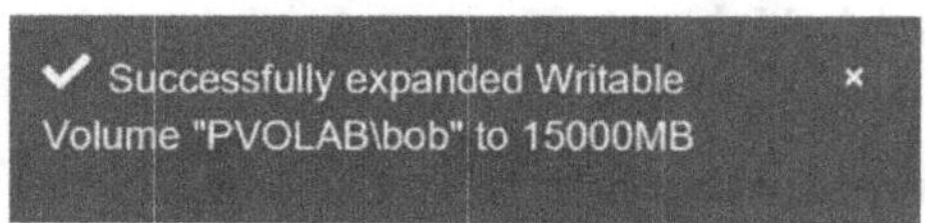

Figure 6-32. *Writable Volume successfully expanded*

You have now successfully expanded the size of a Writable Volume.

In the next section, we are going to look at how to move a Writable Volume.

Moving an existing Writable Volume

The Writable Volume move feature allows you to move the Writable Volume virtual hard disk file from one datastore to another datastore.

To do this, follow the steps described:

1. Click the + button to expand the details and the options for the Writable Volume you want to move.

2. Click the **Move** button.

3. You will see the **Move Writable Volume** screen as shown in Figure 6-33.

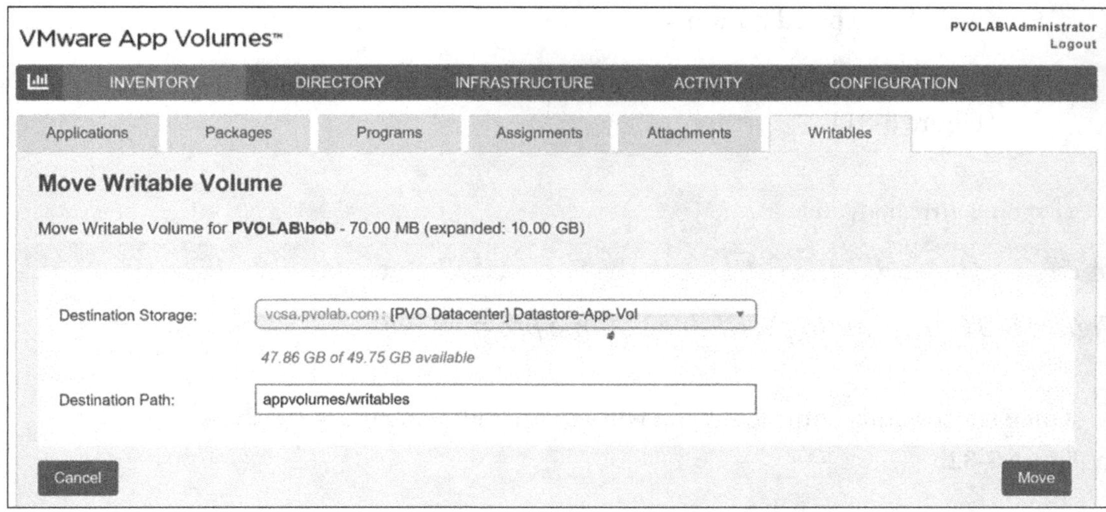

***Figure 6-33.** Move Writable Volume screen*

4. In the **Destination Storage** box, from the drop-down menu options, select the datastore you want to move the Writable Volume to. The options are shown in Figure 6-34.

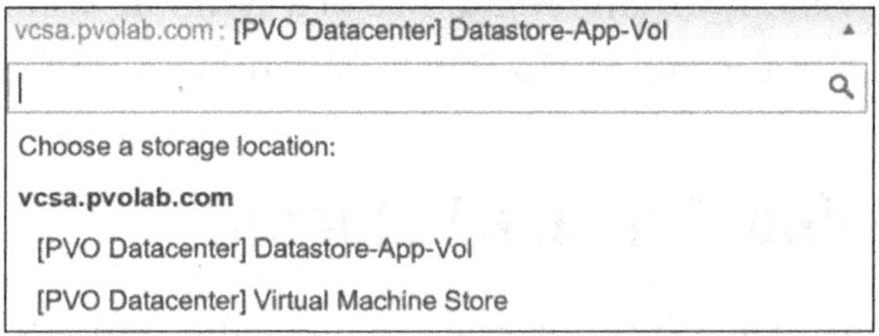

***Figure 6-34.** Selecting the destination datastore*

5. In the test lab, we are going to select the **Datastore-App-Vol** datastore.

6. Then, in the **Destination Path** box, type in the name of the folder within the datastore you want to move the Writable Volume to.

7. Click the **Move** button. You will see the **Confirm Move Writable Volume** dialog box as shown in Figure 6-35.

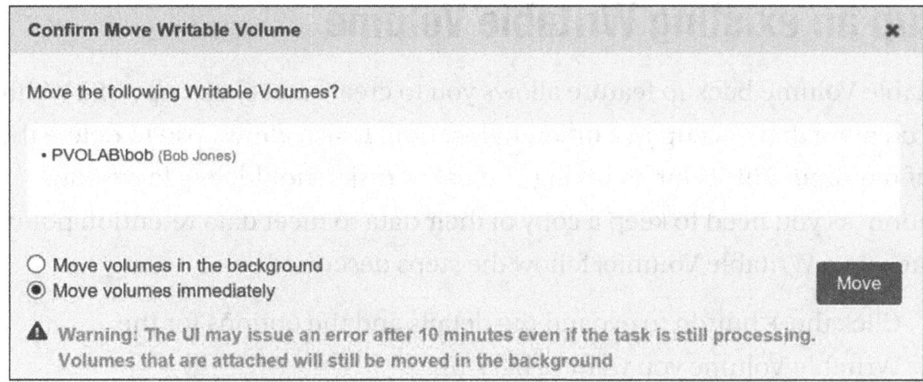

***Figure 6-35.** Confirm Move Writable Volume dialog box*

8. Click the radio button for **Move volumes immediately**, and then click the **Move** button.
9. You will see the **Moving Writable Volumes** progress bar as shown in Figure 6-36.

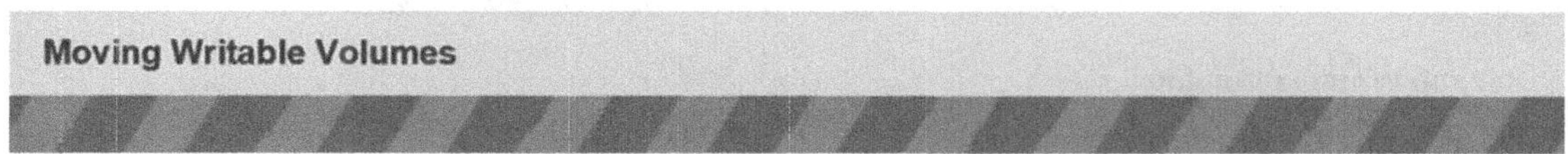

***Figure 6-36.** Moving Writable Volumes progress bar*

10. Once completed, you will see the message pop-up in Figure 6-37.

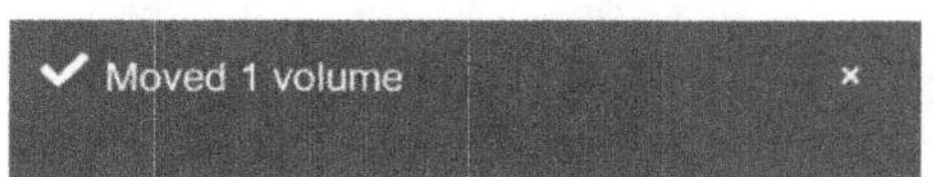

***Figure 6-37.** Writable Volume successfully moved message*

You have now successfully moved a Writable Volume.

In the next section, we are going to look at how to back up a Writable Volume.

Back up an existing Writable Volume

The Writable Volume backup feature allows you to create a backup copy of a Writable Volume, creating that backup in a different location. It also allows you to delete the original if required. This is for archiving end users' disks should they leave your organization, as you need to keep a copy of their data to meet data retention policies.

To back up a Writable Volume, follow the steps described:

1. Click the + button to expand the details and the options for the Writable Volume you want to back up.
2. Click the **Backup** button.
3. You will see the **Backup Writable Volume** screen as shown in Figure 6-38.

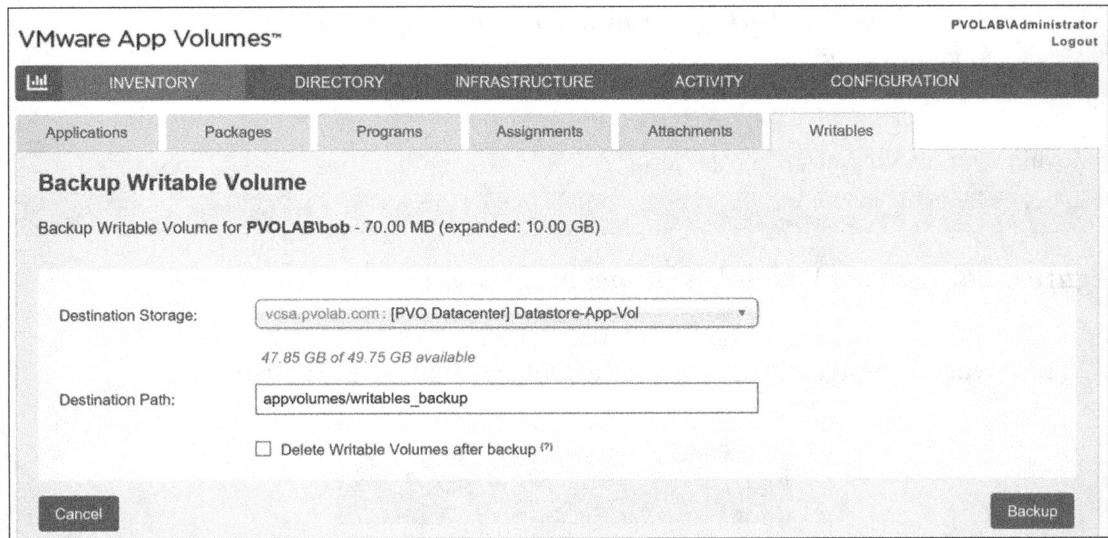

Figure 6-38. *Writable Volume backup screen*

4. In the **Destination Storage** box, from the drop-down menu options, select the datastore you want to back up the Writable Volume to. The options are shown in Figure 6-39.

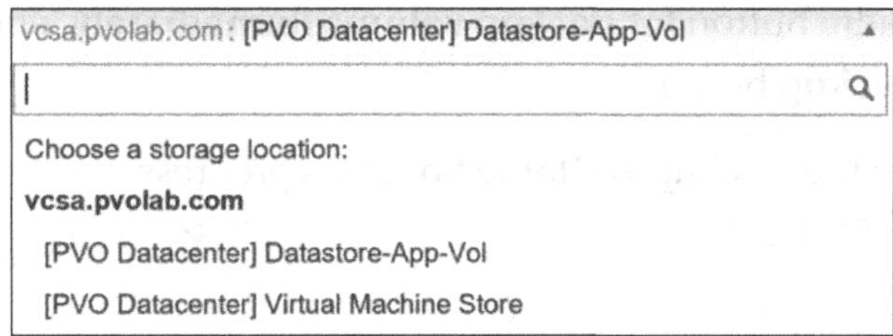

***Figure 6-39.** Selecting the destination datastore*

5. In the test lab, we are going to select the **Datastore-App-Vol** datastore.

6. Then, in the **Destination Path** box, type in the name of the folder on the datastore you want to back the Writable Volume up to. By default, this folder is **ppvolumes/writables_backup** folder.

7. You then have a check box for **Delete Writable Volumes after backup**. As the name suggests, if you check this box, then the volume will be deleted after being backed up.

Deleting the volume cannot be reversed.

---

8. Click the **Backup** button. You will see the Confirm Backup Writable Volume screen (Figure 6-40).

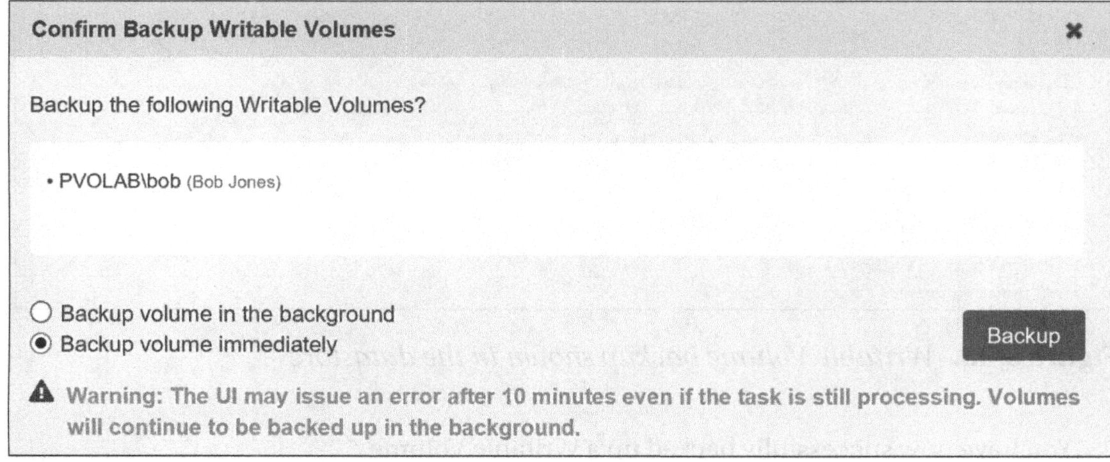

***Figure 6-40.** Confirm backup of Writable Volume screen*

9. Click the radio button for **Backup volume immediately**, and then click the **Backup** button.

10. You will see the **Backup Writable Volumes** progress bar (Figure 6-41).

Figure 6-41. *Backup of Writable Volumes progress bar*

11. Once completed, you will see the message pop-up in Figure 6-42.

Figure 6-42. *Writable Volume successfully backed up*

You have now successfully backed up a Writable Volume. If you log in to the vCenter Server and browse the datastore and the backup folder, you will see the screenshot in Figure 6-43.

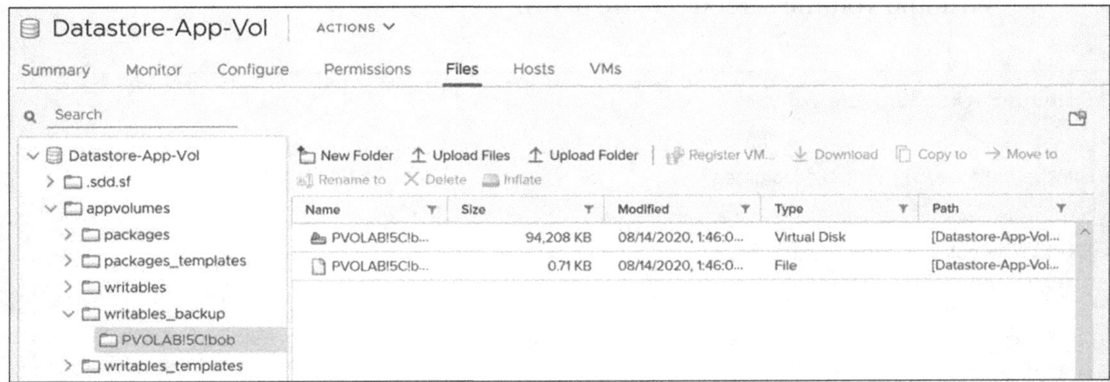

Figure 6-43. *Writable Volume backup shown in the datastore*

You have now successfully backed up a Writable Volume.

In the next section, we are going to look at how to restore a Writable Volume.

Restoring a Writable Volume

The restore feature allows you to restore a Writable Volume backup back into your production environment. To do this, follow the steps described:

1. Click the + button to expand the details and the options for the Writable Volume you want to restore.

2. Click the **Restore** button.

3. You will see the screenshot in Figure 6-44.

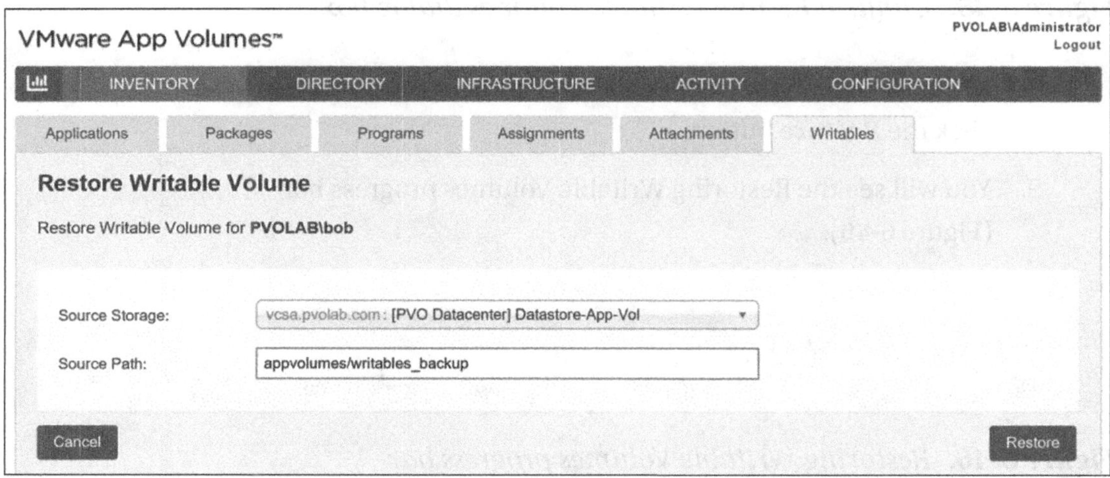

Figure 6-44. *Restore Writable Volume screen*

4. In the **Source Storage** box, from the drop-down menu, select the datastore that contains the Writable Volume you want to restore.

5. Then in the **Source Path**, enter the folder in the datastore where the backup is stored. By default, this is the **appvolumes/writables_backup** folder.

6. Click the **Restore** button.

7. You will see the **Confirm Restore Writable Volumes** dialog box as shown in Figure 6-45.

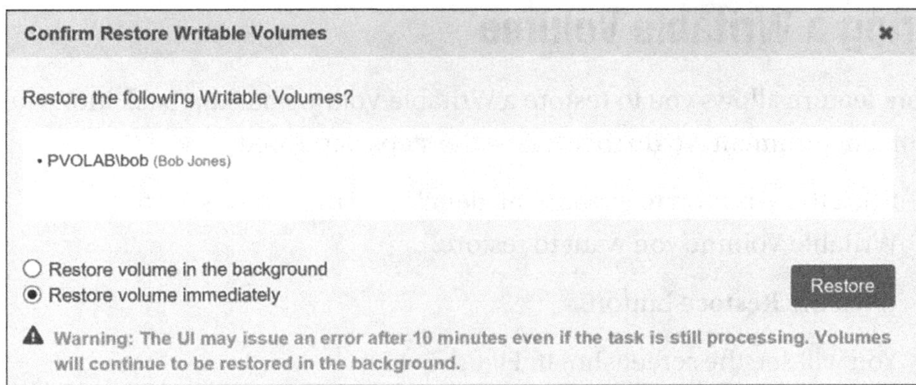

***Figure 6-45.** Confirm Restore Writable Volumes dialog box*

8. Click the radio button for **Restore volume immediately** and then click the **Restore** button.
9. You will see the Restoring Writable Volumes progress bar (Figure 6-46).

***Figure 6-46.** Restoring Writable Volumes progress bar*

10. Once completed, you will see the message pop-up stating that the Writable Volume has successfully been restored (Figure 6-47).

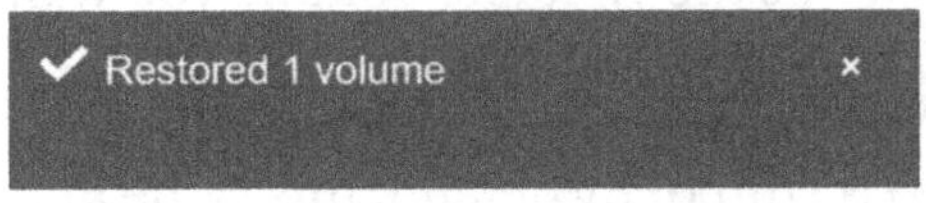

***Figure 6-47.** Writable Volumes successfully restored*

You have now successfully restored a Writable Volume.

In the next section, we are going to look at the final management task and how to delete a Writable Volume.

Deleting a Writable Volume

The final management task you can perform on a Writable Volume is to delete it from the datastore. To do this, follow the steps described:

1. Click the + button to expand the details and the options for the Writable Volume you want to delete.
2. Click the **Delete** button.
3. You will see the **Confirm Delete** screen as shown in Figure 6-48.

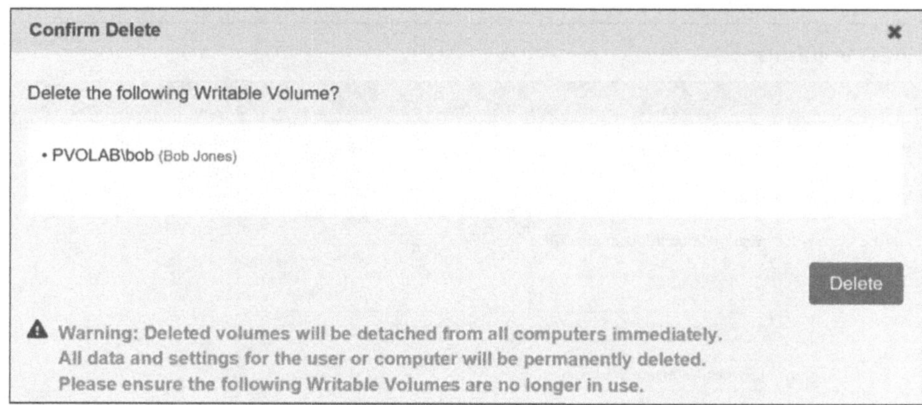

Figure 6-48. *Writable Volumes Confirm Delete dialog box*

4. Click the **Delete** button.

You have now successfully deleted a Writable Volume.

We have now discussed in detail the task buttons that are available when you select an existing Writable Volume. However, there are other buttons in addition to the Create button that we have not yet covered, as shown in Figure 6-49.

Figure 6-49. *Writable Volumes action buttons*

We will cover these in the last few sections of this chapter, starting with the **Import** button.

Importing a Writable Volume

The Import button allows you to import an existing Writable Volume. This could be from another App Volumes environment or could be stored elsewhere. In this example, we are going to use our backup copy to demonstrate the import function.

To import a Writable Volume, follow the steps described:

1. Click the **Import** button.
2. You will see the Import Writable Volumes screen as shown in Figure 6-50.

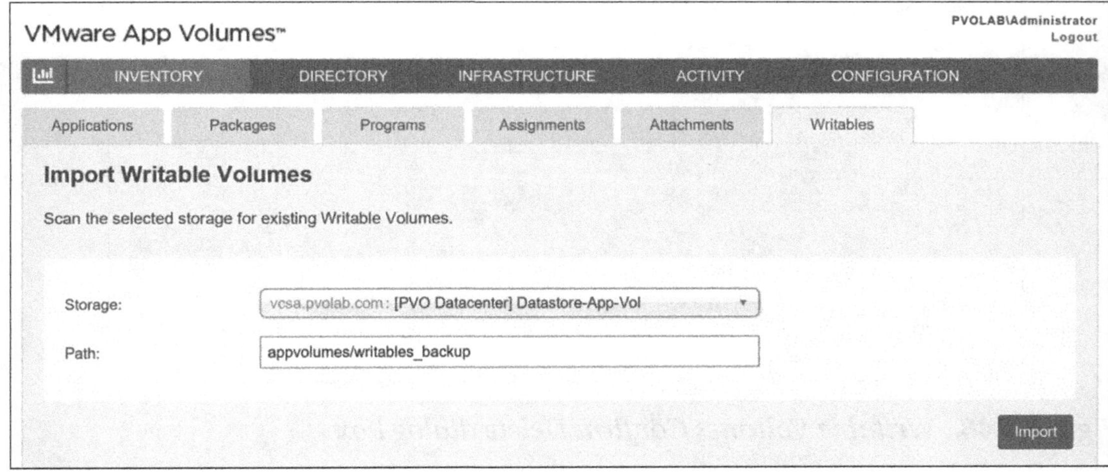

Figure 6-50. *Import Writable Volumes screen*

3. In the **Storage** box, from the drop-down menu, select the datastore on which the volume you want to import resides.
4. Then in the **Path** box, enter the details of the folder on that datastore where the volume resides. In this example, we are going to import the backup copy we took earlier, so the path to this file is **appvolumes/Writable_backup**.
5. Click the **Import** button.
6. You will see the **Confirm Import Writable Volumes** dialog box, as shown in Figure 6-51.

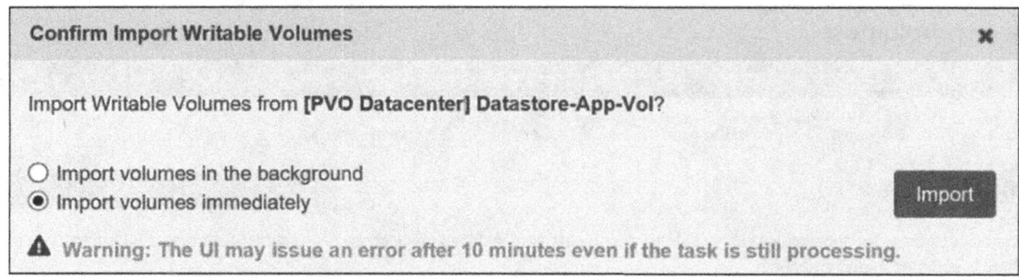

***Figure 6-51.** Confirm Import Writable Volumes dialog box*

7. Click the **Import** button.
8. You will see the Importing Writable Volumes progress bar, as shown in Figure 6-52.

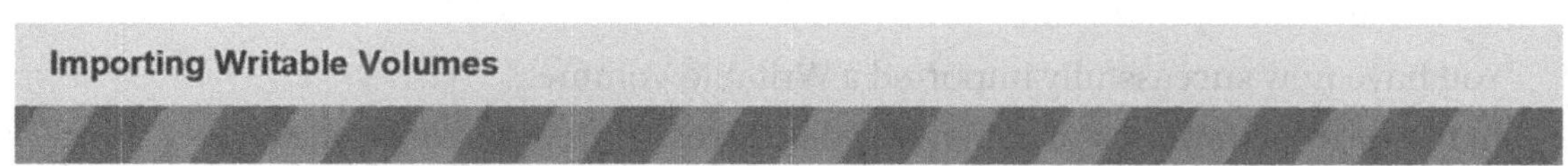

***Figure 6-52.** Importing Writable Volumes progress bar*

9. Once imported, you will see the message pop-up stating that the volume has been successfully imported (Figure 6-53).

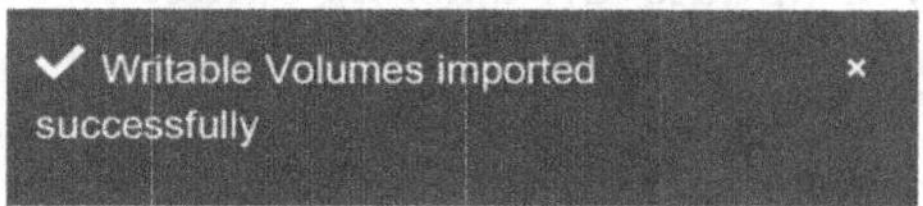

***Figure 6-53.** Writable Volumes imported successfully*

With the Writable Volume now successfully imported, you will see it listed on the Writable Volume screen, as shown in Figure 6-54.

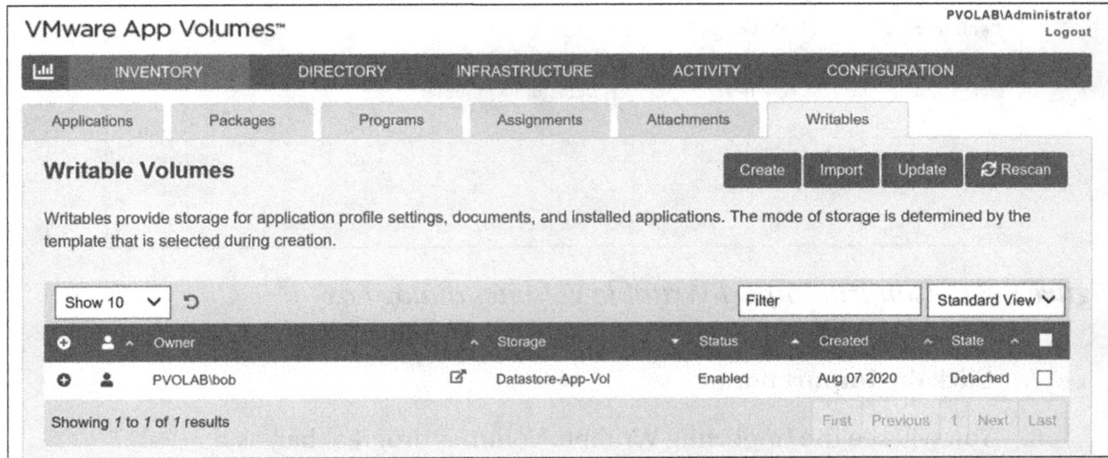

***Figure 6-54.** Writable Volume displayed in the inventory view*

You have now successfully imported a Writable Volume.

In the next section, we are going to update an existing Writable Volume.

Updating an existing Writable Volume

The updating of a Writable Volume is not quite as it is described. The update basically allows the IT admins to upload a .ZIP file to all existing Writable Volumes. They cannot change, edit, or update any existing contents, such as any apps that end users have installed.

The ZIP file you upload to the Writable Volume as the update must be smaller than 5 MB in size.

The Writable Volume can be managed by adding policies around what the end users can and cannot do, controlled using the snapvol.cfg file which is present on every volume. This will be covered in Chapter 7.

To update a Writable Volume, follow the steps described:

1. Click the **Update** button.

2. You will see the **Update Writable Volumes** screen as shown in Figure 6-55.

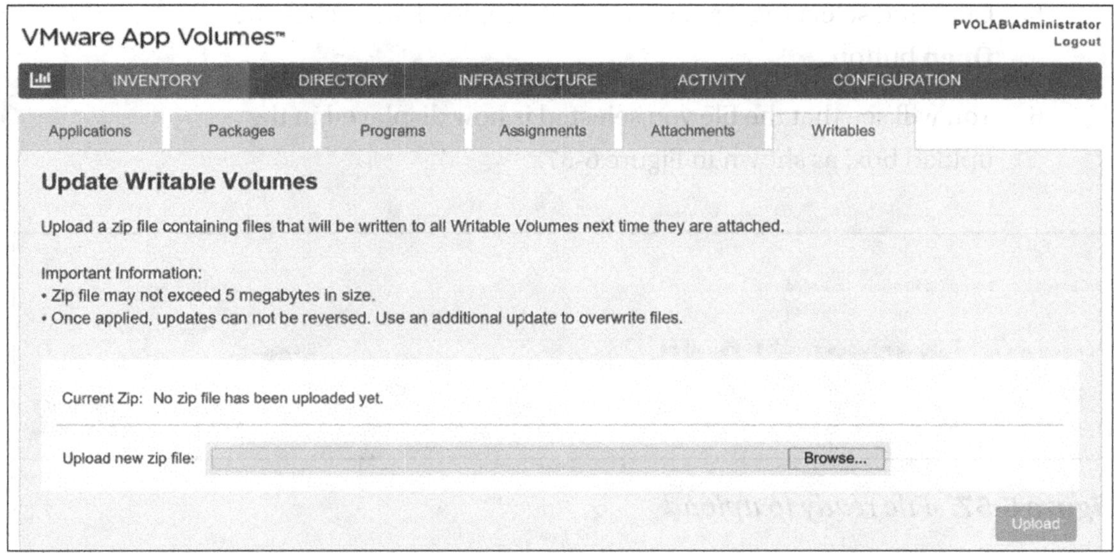

Figure 6-55. *Update Writable Volumes screen*

3. In the **Upload new zip file** box, click the **Browse...** button to find the file you want to upload.

4. You will see a Windows Explorer window launch, as shown in Figure 6-56.

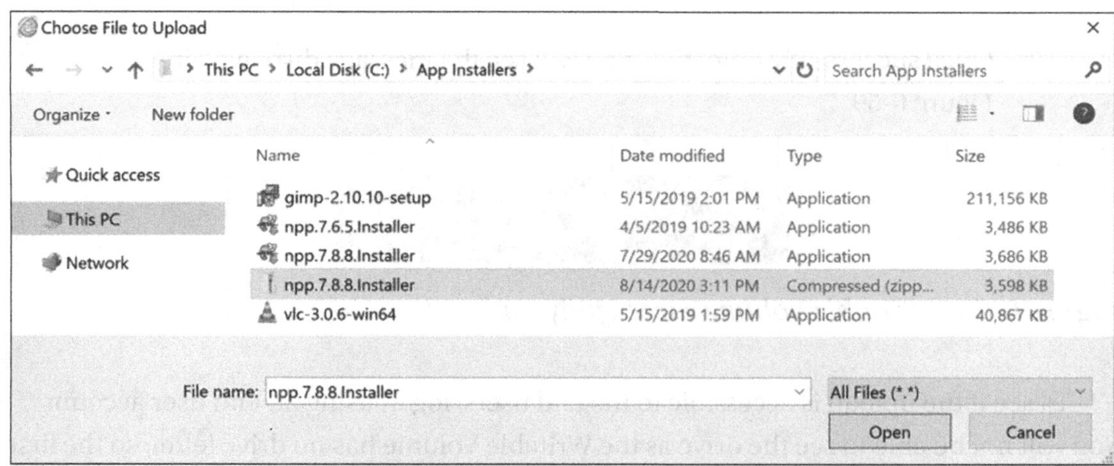

Figure 6-56. *Choose the file to upload*

5. Click and select the zip file you want to upload, then click the **Open** button.

6. You will see that the file you selected is now displayed in the upload box, as shown in Figure 6-57.

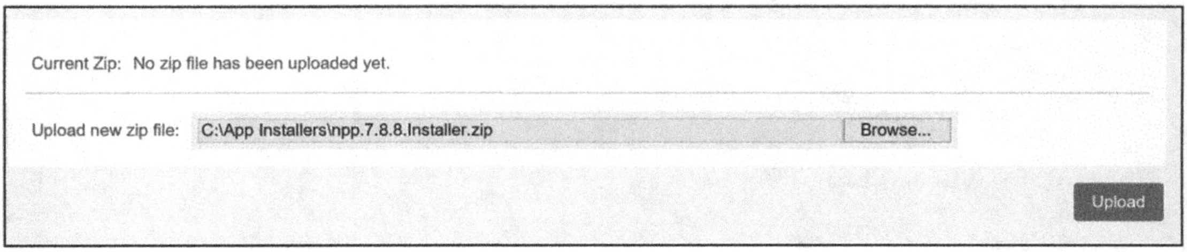

Current Zip: No zip file has been uploaded yet.

Upload new zip file: C:\App Installers\npp.7.8.8.Installer.zip Browse...

Upload

Figure 6-57. *File ready to upload*

7. Click the **Upload** button.

8. You will see the **Uploading...** progress bar (Figure 6-58).

Figure 6-58. *File uploading progress bar*

9. Once successfully uploaded, you will see the message displayed in Figure 6-59.

Figure 6-59. *Writable Volume successfully updated*

To see if the upload is accessible to the end users, log in using an end user account. You will not be able to see the drive as the Writable Volume has no drive letter, so the first step is to launch the Disk Management utility and assign a drive letter to the Writable Volume. We will cover that in more detail in Chapter 7, but an example of this is shown in Figure 6-60.

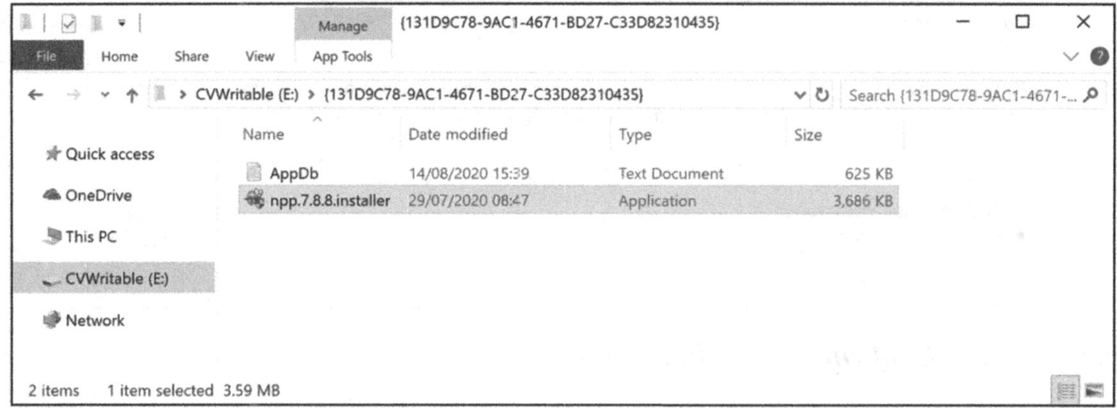

Figure 6-60. *Mounting the Writable Volume and assigning a drive letter*

You will see that the zip file of the Notepad++ installer is now available on the Writable Volumes and has also been extracted.

You have now successfully updated a Writable Volume.

In the next section, we are going to look at the rescanning of the datastore process.

Rescanning the datastore for Writable Volumes

The rescan function is used to perform a scan of the datastores, to check that Writable Volumes exist on the datastore, and to check their status. This can help with troubleshooting when a Writable Volume fails to attach. The rescan will confirm it still exists. If not, then you can always import it again or restore from a backup copy.

To rescan the datastore, follow the steps described:

1. Click the **Rescan** button.

2. You will see the **Confirm Rescan** dialog box as shown in Figure 6-61.

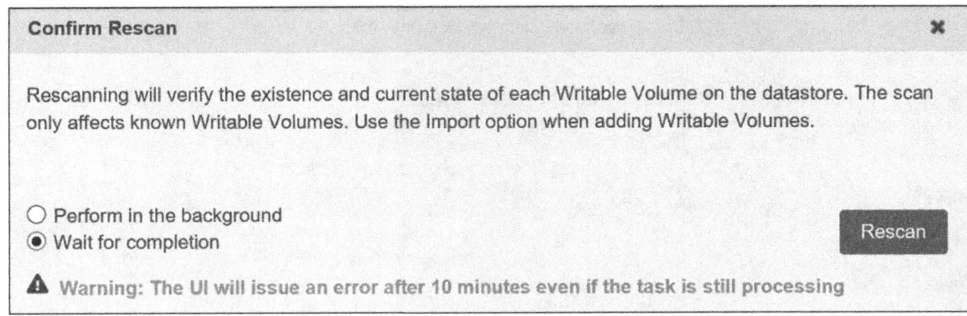

Figure 6-61. *Confirm Rescan dialog box*

3. Click the radio button for **Wait for completion** and then click the **Rescan** button.
4. You will see the **Rescanning Writable Volumes on Storage** as shown in Figure 6-62.

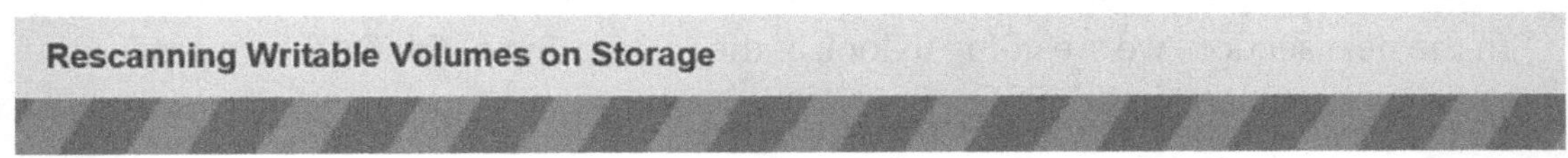

Figure 6-62. *Rescanning Writable Volumes on Storage progress bar*

Once completed, you will see the message pop-up stating that the Writable Volumes have been successfully refreshed, as shown in Figure 6-63.

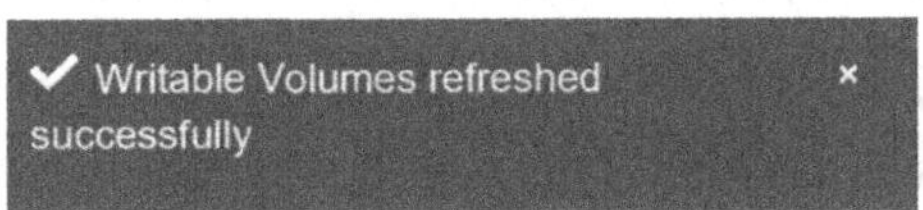

Figure 6-63. *Rescanning Writable Volumes successfully completed*

You have now successfully rescanned the datastore for Writable Volumes.

Writable Volumes and VMware DEM

We have mentioned several times that you can integrate the user profile Writable Volume with VMware Dynamic Environment Manager.

In this section, we are just going to show you a quick example of that integration point from the DEM management console perspective.

VMware DEM has a built-in configuration option for App Volumes already included as shown in Figure 6-64 taken from the DEM management console.

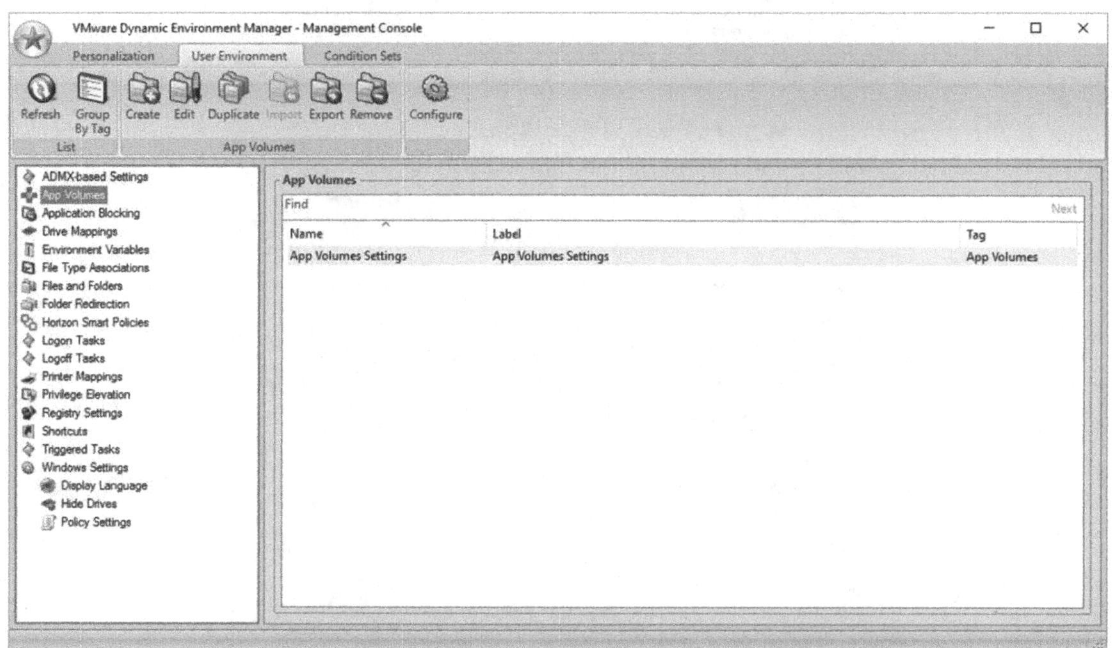

***Figure 6-64.** VMware DEM and the App Volumes configuration*

If you edit the policy settings, you create rules that redirect profile files to the Writable Volume. In the following example, you can see that the Outlook data file or OST file has been configured to be saved on the Writable Volume.

This means that whichever virtual desktop machine the end user logs in to, their Outlook file will be attached and be available each time. There is no need for a file resync, especially useful as OST files can grow to a substantial size, meaning they would take a long time to copy each time the end user logs in.

The App Volumes configuration screen for DEM and Outlook is shown in Figure 6-65.

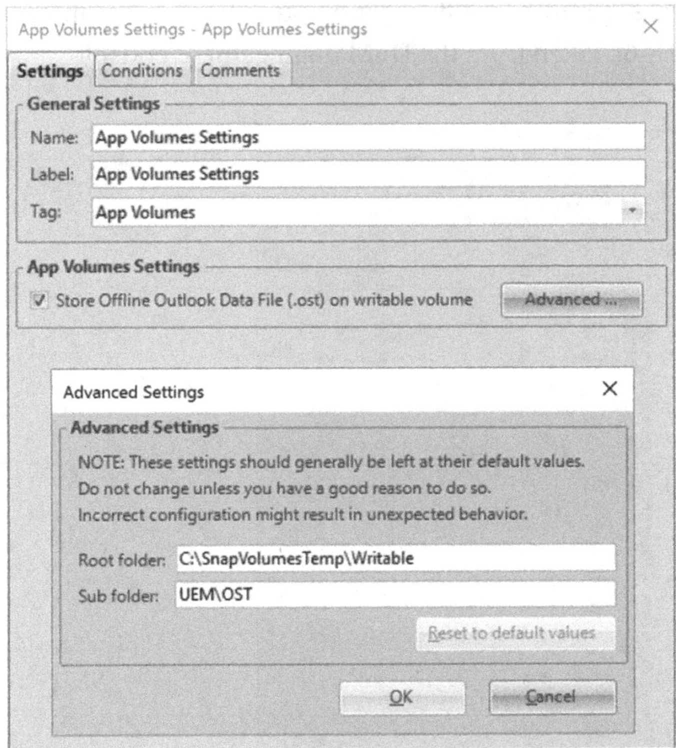

Figure 6-65. *VMware DEM and the App Volumes configuration for Outlook*

Chapter summary

The subject and focus of this chapter have been around Writable Volumes.

We started the chapter with a recap of what a Writable Volume is and what it is used for, then detailing the process of how to create and configure one.

The next part of the chapter was to do exactly that. Create a Writable Volume and assign it to an end user, before then testing its functionality.

The final part of this chapter focused on the ongoing management of Writable Volumes and how to perform those. This included backing up, restoring, and expanding volumes.

In the next chapter, we are going to cover some of the more advanced configuration options around configuring custom templates, App Volumes Agent advanced configuration, and greater depth into the **snapvol.cfg** file for managing volumes.

CHAPTER 7

Advanced Configuration

At this point in the book, we have built application packages containing programs and a Writable Volume. To do this, we have followed the tasks that are available to us in the App Volumes Manager management console. However, there are more management and configuration options available to an administrator by using some of the additional advanced tools that ship with App Volumes as well as some more manual-based tasks.

In this chapter, we are going to go beyond those "standard" management-based tasks in the GUI management console and look at how to perform some of these more advanced configuration and management tasks.

In particular, we are going to look at the following tasks:

- Creating custom templates for packages
- Creating custom Writable Volumes templates
- Storage groups
- Advanced App Volumes Agent configuration
- The snapvol.cfg file

The first advanced configuration task we are going to look at is how to create a custom template for creating application packages.

Creating custom templates for packages

Back in Chapter 5 when we created an application package, you would have seen that when we selected the template from which to create the virtual hard disk, there was only one option available – that option being for a 20 GB virtual hard disk.

There may be a use case or a program that you need to deliver that does not need that amount of disk space, regardless of the disk being thin provisioned. There is no way of doing this in the management console, and so it must be done manually.

P. von Oven, *Delivering Applications with VMware App Volumes 4*,
https://doi.org/10.1007/978-1-4842-6689-2_7

Before we work through the process of doing this, let us recap what the template is used for.

A template is a prebuilt virtual hard disk file (VMDK or VHD depending on your machine management platform) that contains all the files that App Volumes needs to be present for the App Volumes Agent to attach a volume and seamlessly layer it into the operating system of the virtual desktop or server.

Whenever you create a new application package or Writable Volume, App Volumes creates a copy of the relevant template. As it is an exact copy of the virtual hard disk, it will be the same size as the original. So, as we are talking about application packages, this will be an exact copy of the 20 GB application package virtual hard disk template file.

To create a new custom-sized template, we are going to follow the process as described in Figure 7-1.

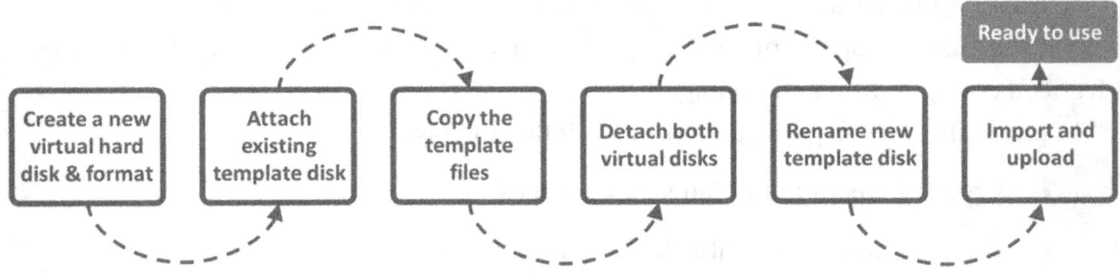

***Figure 7-1.** Process for creating a custom template*

The first step of the process is to create a new virtual hard disk of the size you want the new template to be. So, in this test lab example, we are going to create a new 10 GB virtual hard disk.

The new virtual hard disk will be created on a clean virtual desktop machine. This means a brand-new, clean machine, patched, optimized, and that has never had the App Volumes Agent installed on it.

Creating a new virtual hard disk

The first step of the process is to create a new virtual hard disk, initialize it, and then format it ready for use.

To do this, we are going to use our vCenter Server, so the first step is to log in to vCenter and then navigate to the virtual desktop machine that we will use for creating the new virtual hard disk. Once logged in to vCenter, follow the steps described:

1. Select the virtual desktop machine that is going to be used for creating the new hard disk. In the test lab, we have a machine called **Windows 10 Virtual Desktop** that we will use as shown in Figure 7-2.

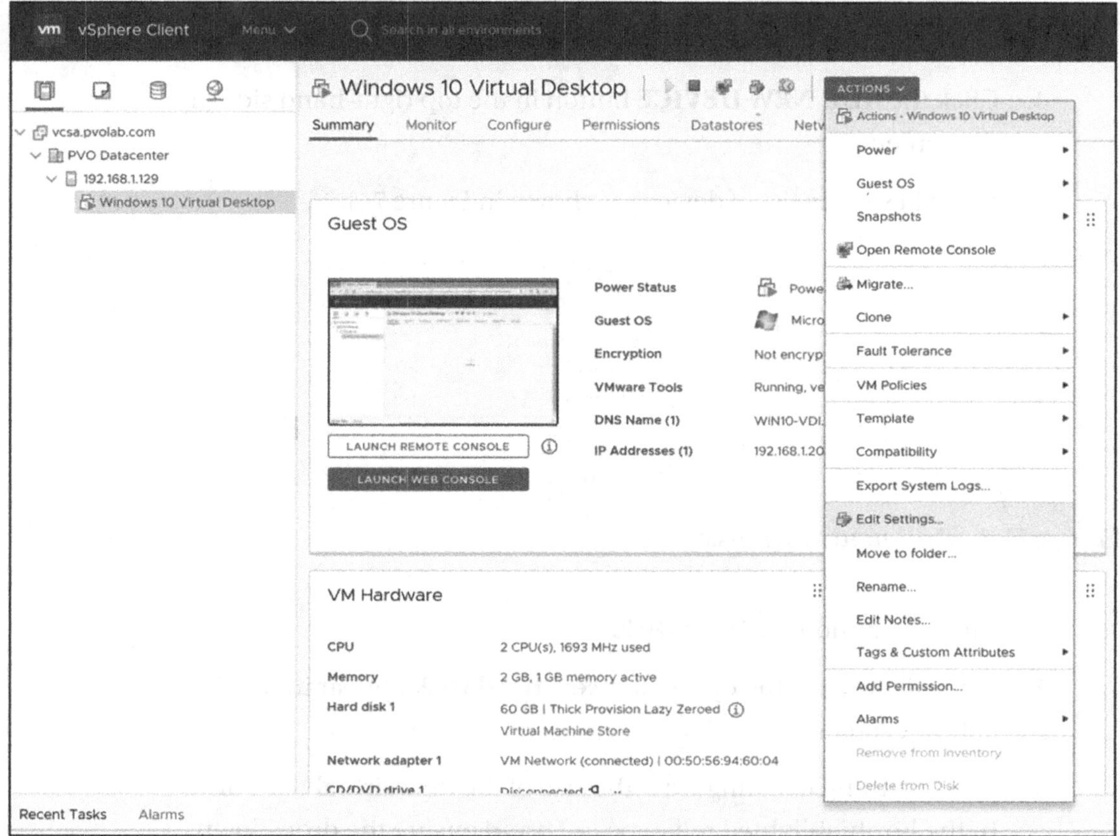

Figure 7-2. *Selecting the virtual machine for creating the new disk*

2. Click the drop-down menu for **Actions**, and select the **Edit Settings...** option.

3. You will see the **Edit Settings** screen as shown in Figure 7-3.

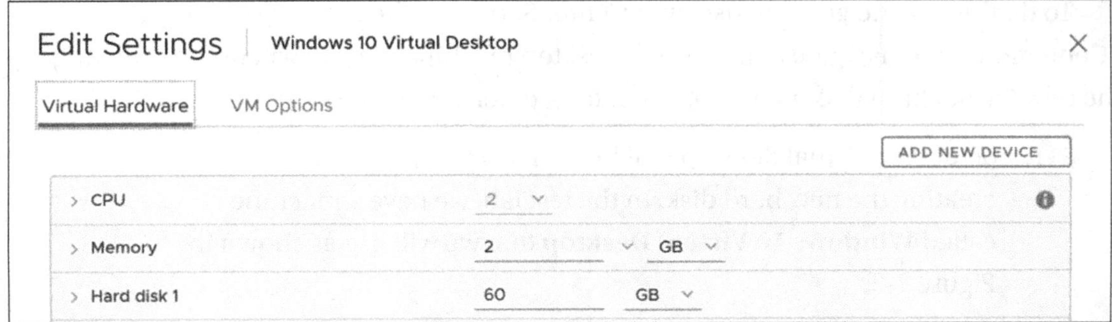

Figure 7-3. *Edit Settings screen*

4. Click the **ADD NEW DEVICE** button in the top right-hand side of the screen.

5. You will see the list of devices as shown in Figure 7-4.

Figure 7-4. *Add new hard disk*

6. Click the option for **Hard Disk.**

7. You will now see the option for **New Hard Disk** appear in the Edit Settings screen.

8. The first thing to configure is the size of the new virtual hard disk. In the box highlighted red, type in **10** and ensure the drop-down next to the box is set to **GB** as shown in Figure 7-5.

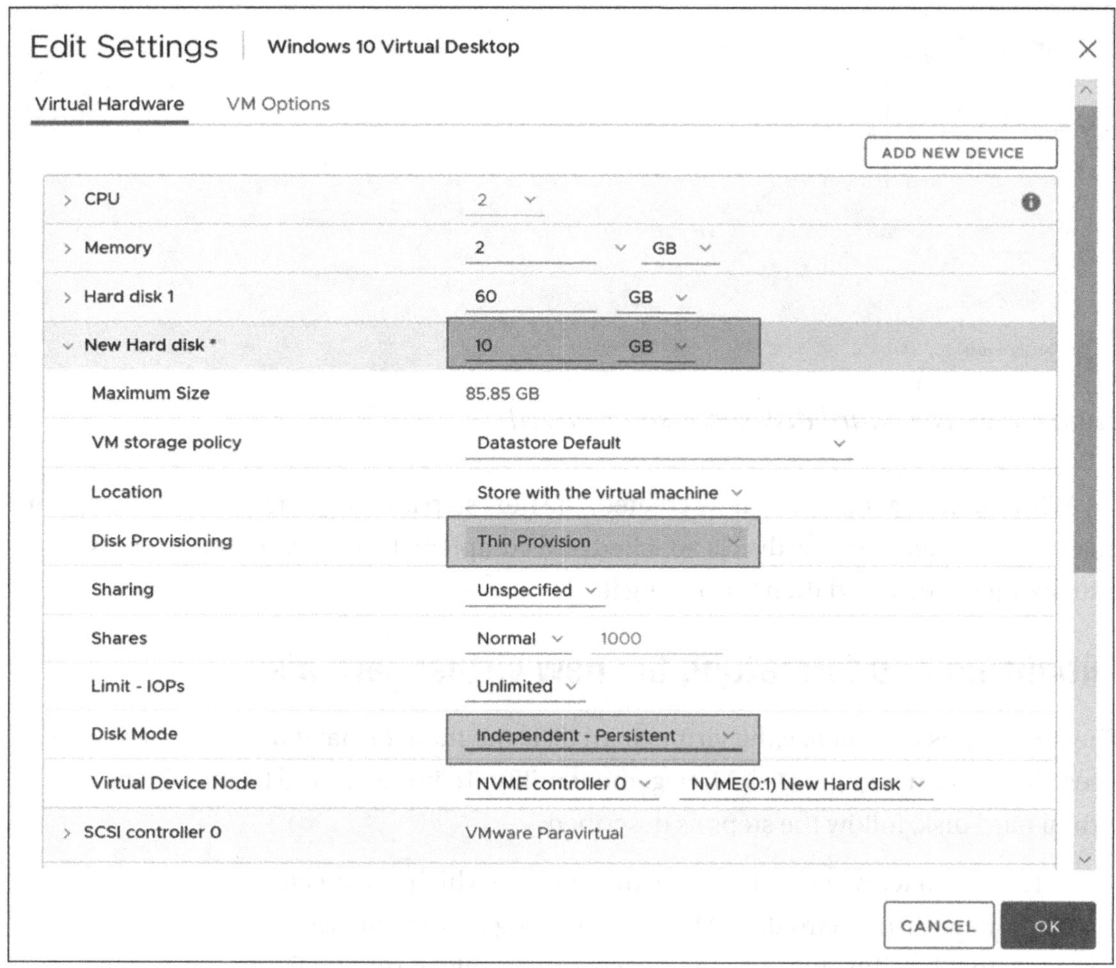

***Figure 7-5.** Configure new virtual hard disk*

9. Then, in the **Disk Provisioning** box highlighted, from the drop-down menu, select the option for **Thin Provision**.
10. Finally, in the **Disk Mode** box, from the drop-down menu, select the option of **Independent - Persistent**.
11. Now click the **OK** button to save the configuration.
12. Once completed, you will see that you have **Hard disk 2** listed as shown in Figure 7-6.

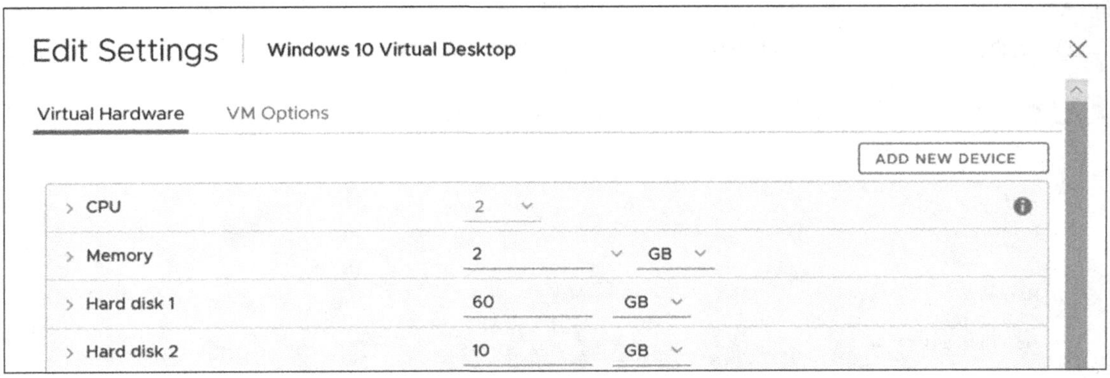

***Figure 7-6.** New hard disk successfully added*

With the virtual hard disk now created, the next step is to log in to the virtual desktop machine to which the new disk is attached and complete the configuration process by initializing the disk and then formatting it.

Initializing and formatting the new virtual hard disk

The next step is to initialize the virtual hard disk and then format it using the Windows operating system and the Disk Management utility. To initialize and format the new virtual hard disk, follow the steps as described:

1. Log in to the virtual desktop machine on which you created the new virtual hard disk. Make sure you log in using an account that has the appropriate privileges to be able to run the Disk Management utility.

2. Right-click the **Start** button, and from the menu options, click **Disk Management.**

3. The Disk Management utility will now launch as shown in Figure 7-7.

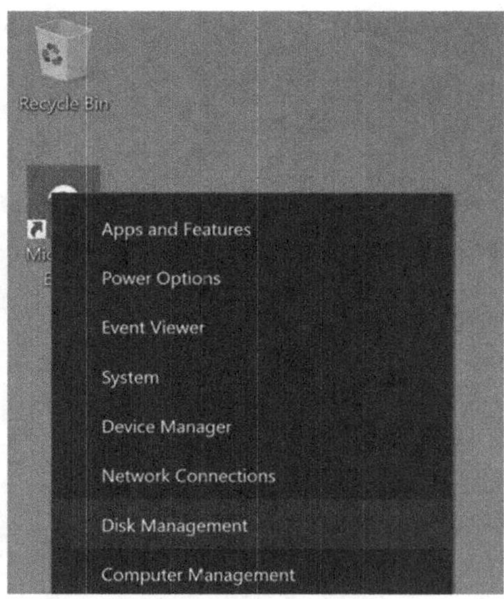

Figure 7-7. *Launch the Disk Management utility*

4. You will see the Disk Management utility where the new disk is available but uninitialized and unformatted as shown in Figure 7-8.

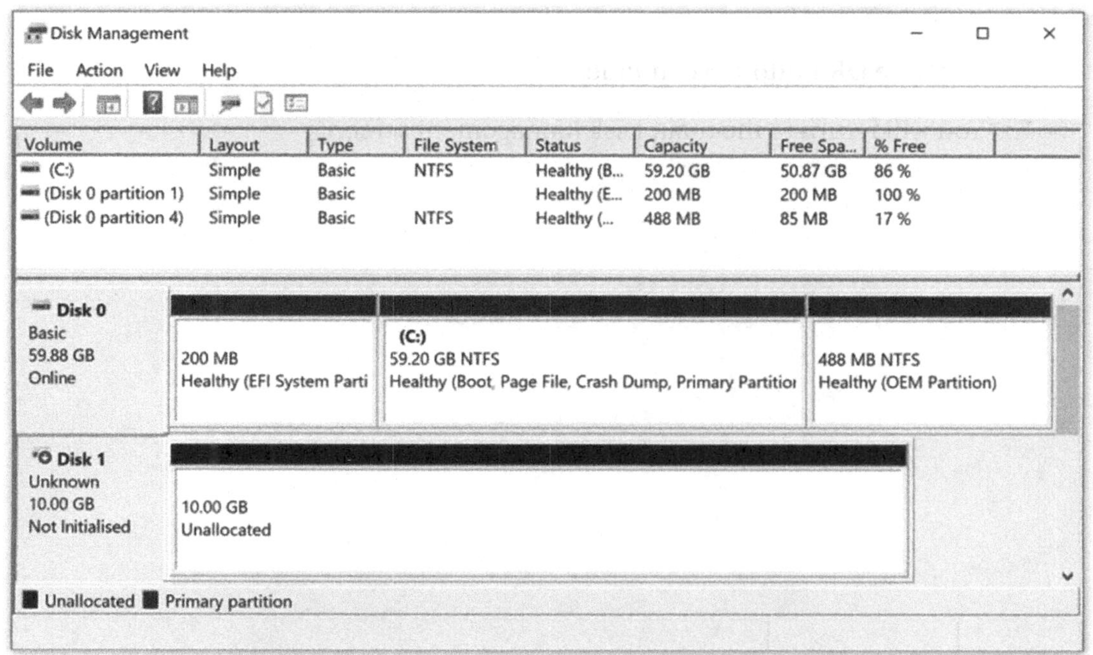

Figure 7-8. *Disk Management utility showing the new hard disk*

5. You will also see the **Initialise Disk** dialog appear as shown in Figure 7-9.

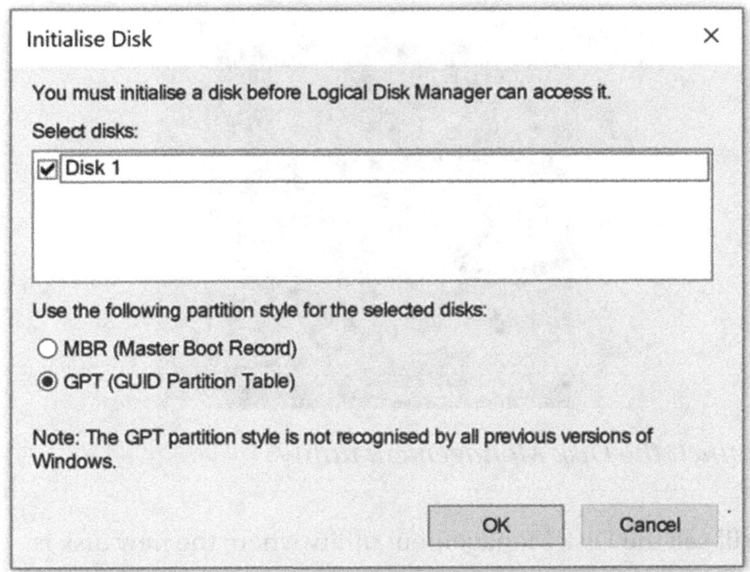

Figure 7-9. *Initializing the new hard disk*

6. Click the **OK** button to continue.
7. You will return to the main Disk Management screen.

This is shown in Figure 7-10 in the following screenshot:

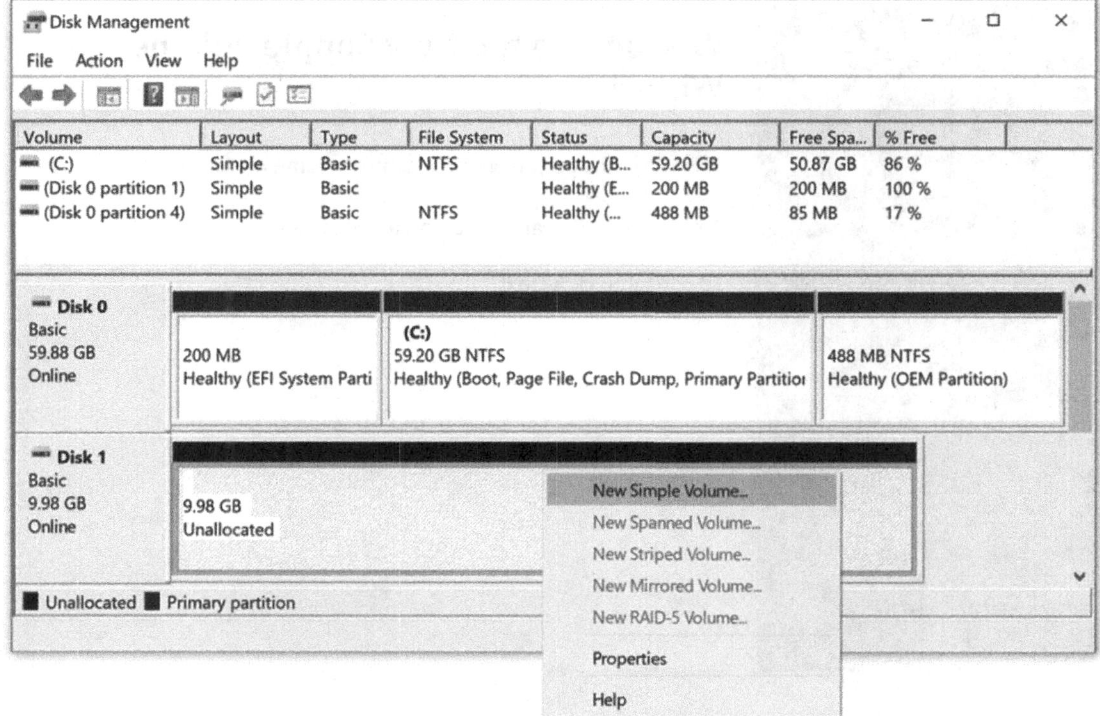

Figure 7-10. *Creating a simple volume*

8. Right-click the entry for **Disk 1**, the new disk, and then select the option for **New Simple Volume....**
9. You will see the **Welcome to the New Simple Volume Wizard** screen as shown in Figure 7-11.

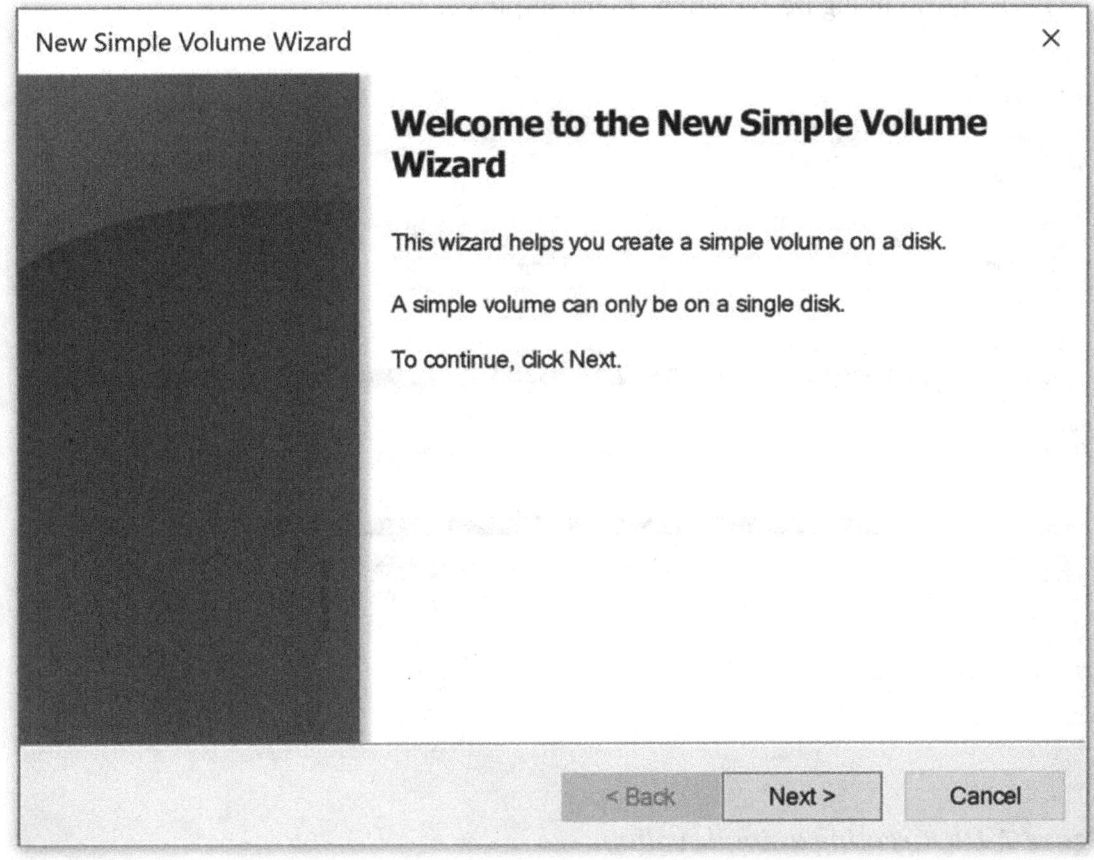

Figure 7-11. *Welcome to the New Simple Volume Wizard screen*

10. Click **Next ►** to continue.
11. You will see the **Specify Volume Size** screen.
12. Leave the **Simple volume size in MB** box as the default size. In this example, it is the 10222 MB, so the full size of the new disk that was created as shown in Figure 7-12.

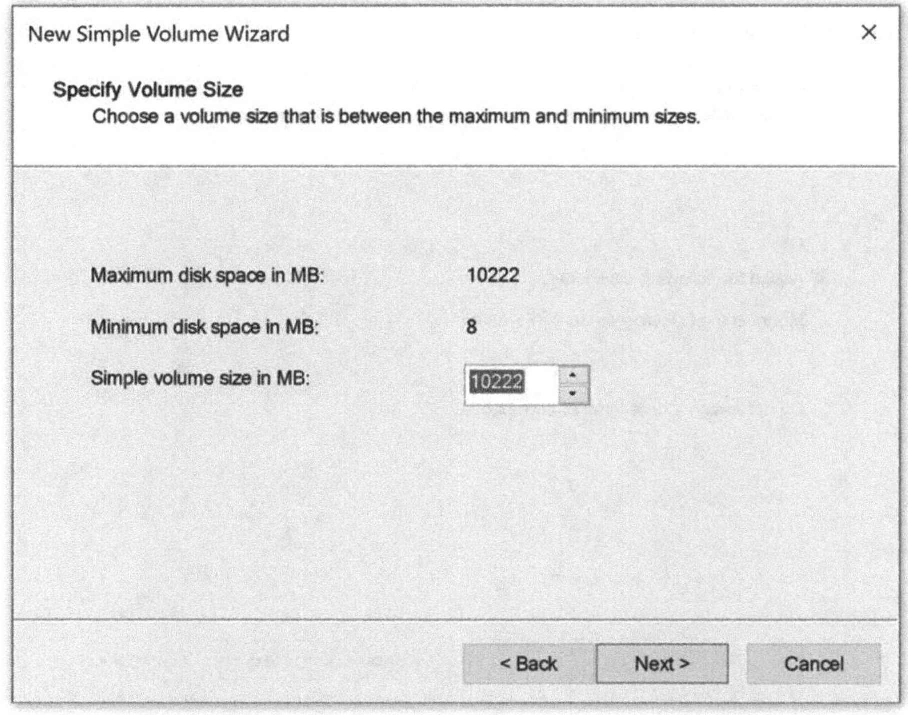

***Figure 7-12.** Specify the volume size*

13. Click **Next ►** to continue.
14. You will see the **Assign Drive Letter or Path** screen.
15. Click the radio button for **Assign the following drive letter**, and then, from the drop-down menu, select a free drive letter. In the text lab example, we have selected **E**. This means that the new hard disk will appear with the E:\ drive letter when we come to open it in Windows Explorer in a later step.
16. This is shown in Figure 7-13.

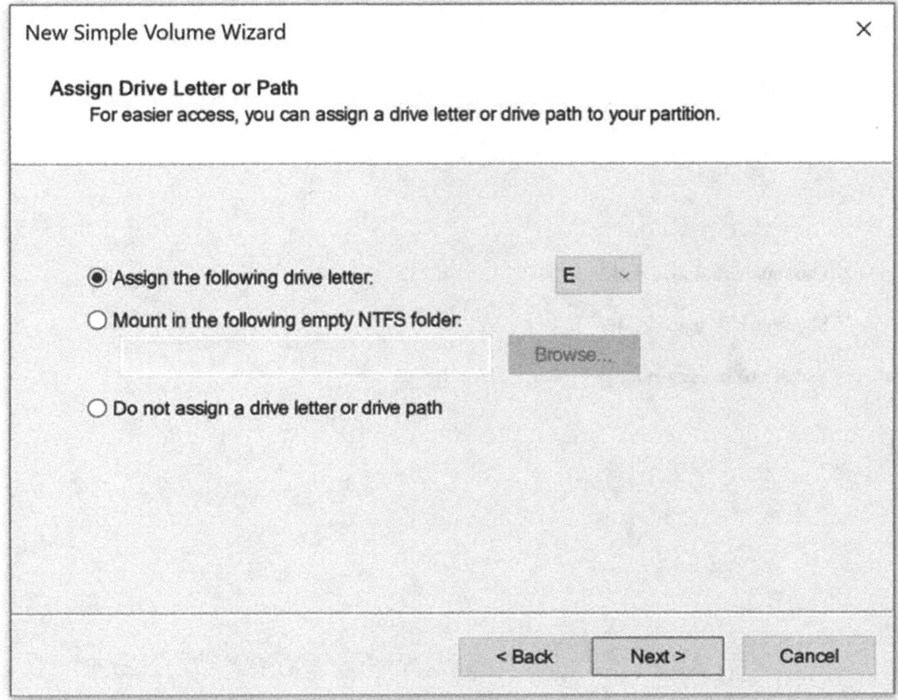

Figure 7-13. *Assigning a drive letter*

17. Next, you will see the **Format Partition** screen (Figure 7-14).

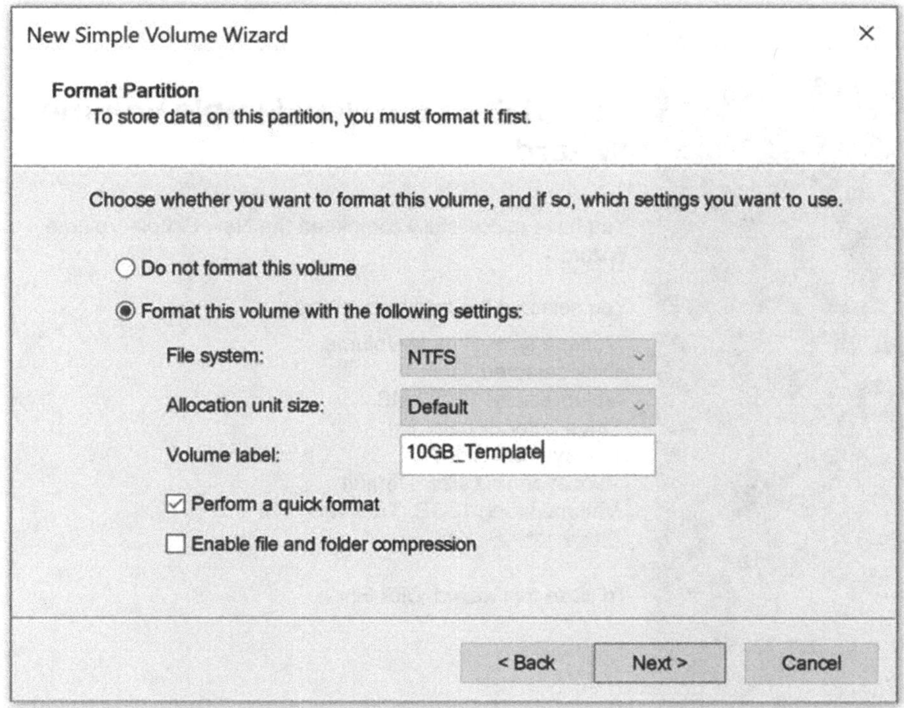

***Figure 7-14.** Format partition*

18. Click the radio button for **Format this volume with the following settings.**

19. Leave the **File system** setting as the default **NTFS** and the **Allocation unit** size as **Default.**

20. In the **Volume label** box, type in a name to identify this volume. In the test lab example, we have called this **10GB_Template**. This will help identify it later in this chapter when we come to copy the template files.

21. Finally, check the box for **Perform a quick format** and then click **Next ►**.

22. You will see the **Completing the New Simple Volume Wizard** screen as shown in Figure 7-15.

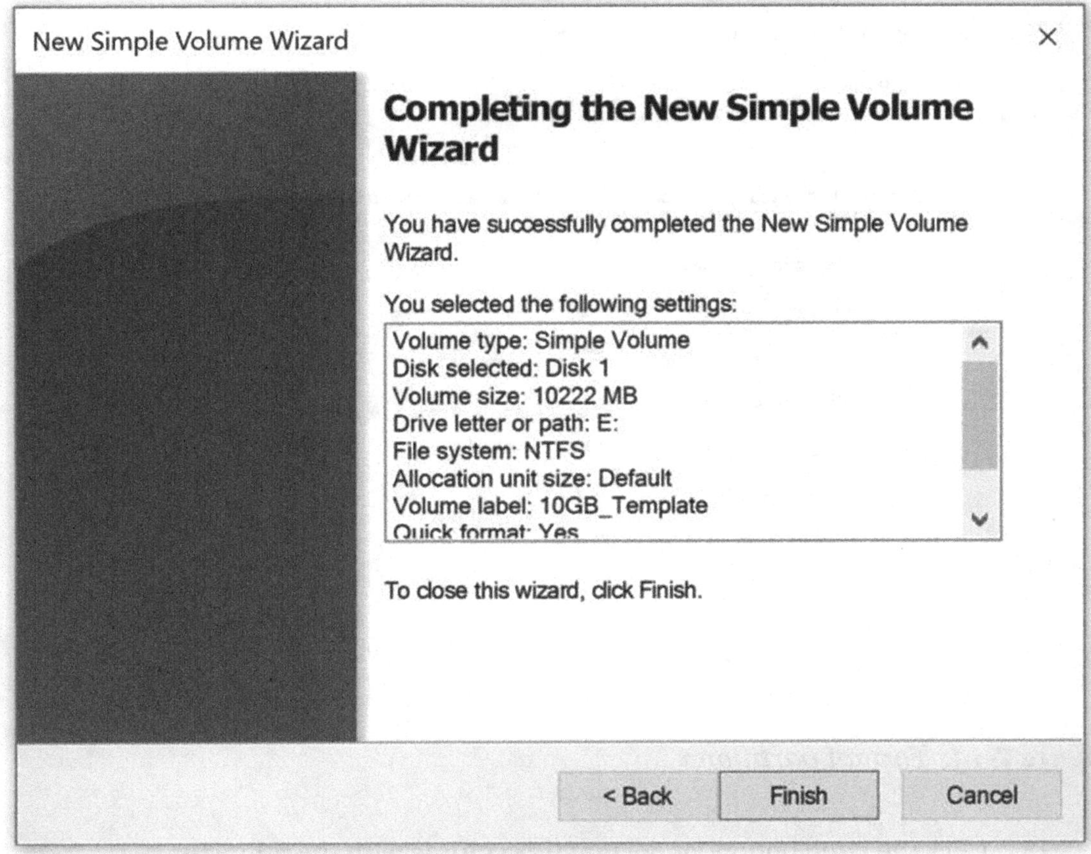

Figure 7-15. *Completing the new simple volume wizard*

You will return to the main Disk Management screen where you will see that the new hard disk has been initialized, formatted, assigned the drive letter E, and named 10GB_Template. It is now ready to use as shown in Figure 7-16.

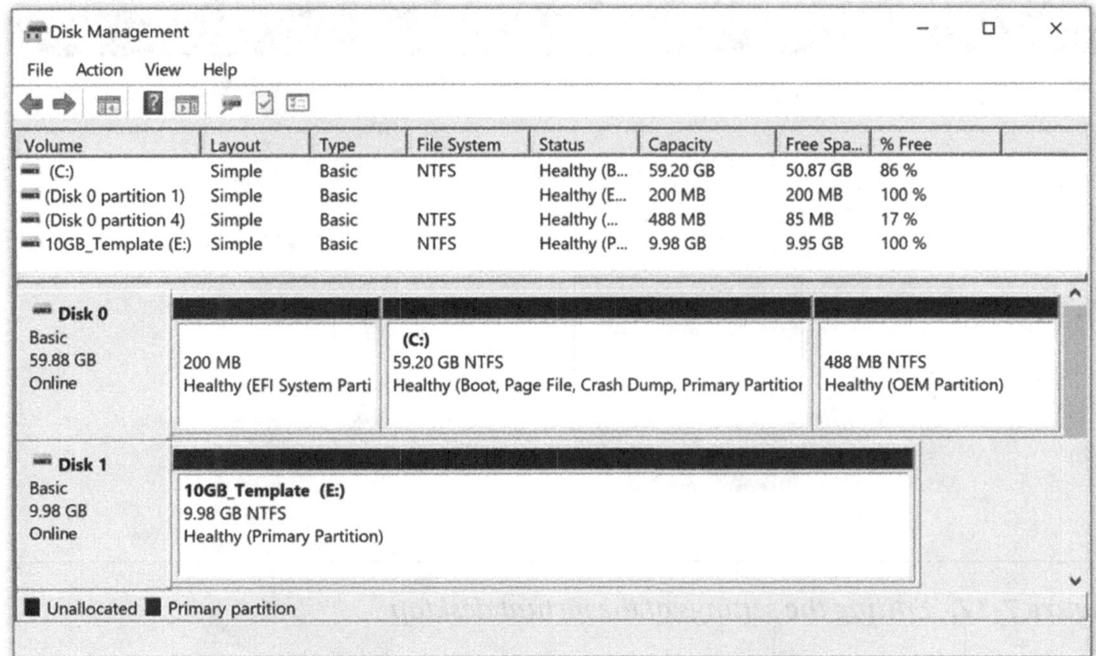

Figure 7-16. *Disk Manager view of the new hard disk ready for use*

The next step is to attach an existing template hard disk ready to copy the template files from.

Attaching an existing template hard disk

The next step is to attach an existing template hard disk to the same virtual desktop machine and copy the files from the existing template to the one we are creating. These files are those that are required in order to attach the volumes to the virtual machine.

To do this, from vCenter, follow the steps described:

1. Select the same virtual desktop machine you created the new virtual hard drive on in the previous step. This is the machine called **Windows 10 Virtual Desktop**.

2. Click the drop-down menu for **Actions**, and select the **Edit Settings...** option.

3. This is shown in Figure 7-17.

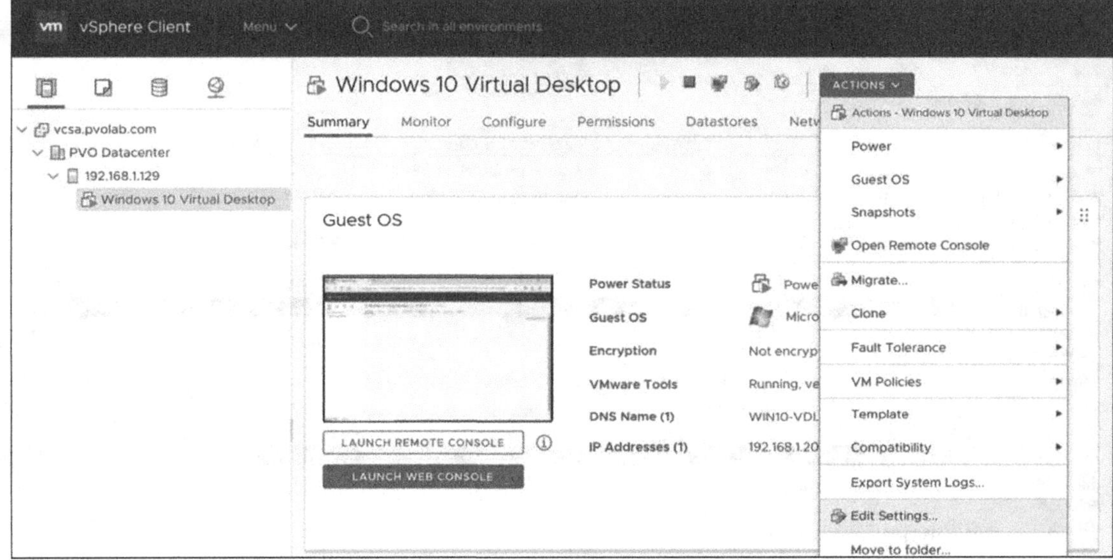

Figure 7-17. Editing the settings of the virtual desktop

4. Click the **ADD NEW DEVICE** button in the top right-hand side of the screen.
5. You will see the list of devices as shown in Figure 7-18.

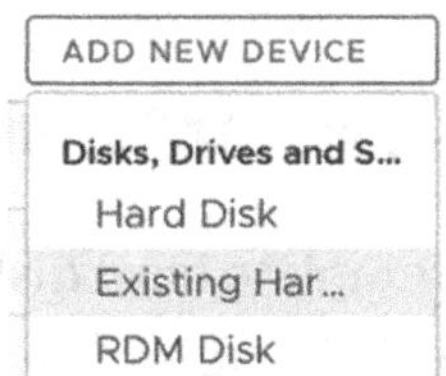

Figure 7-18. Add exisitng hard disk

6. Click the option for **Existing Hard Disk.**
7. You will now see the **Select File** screen as shown in Figure 7-19.

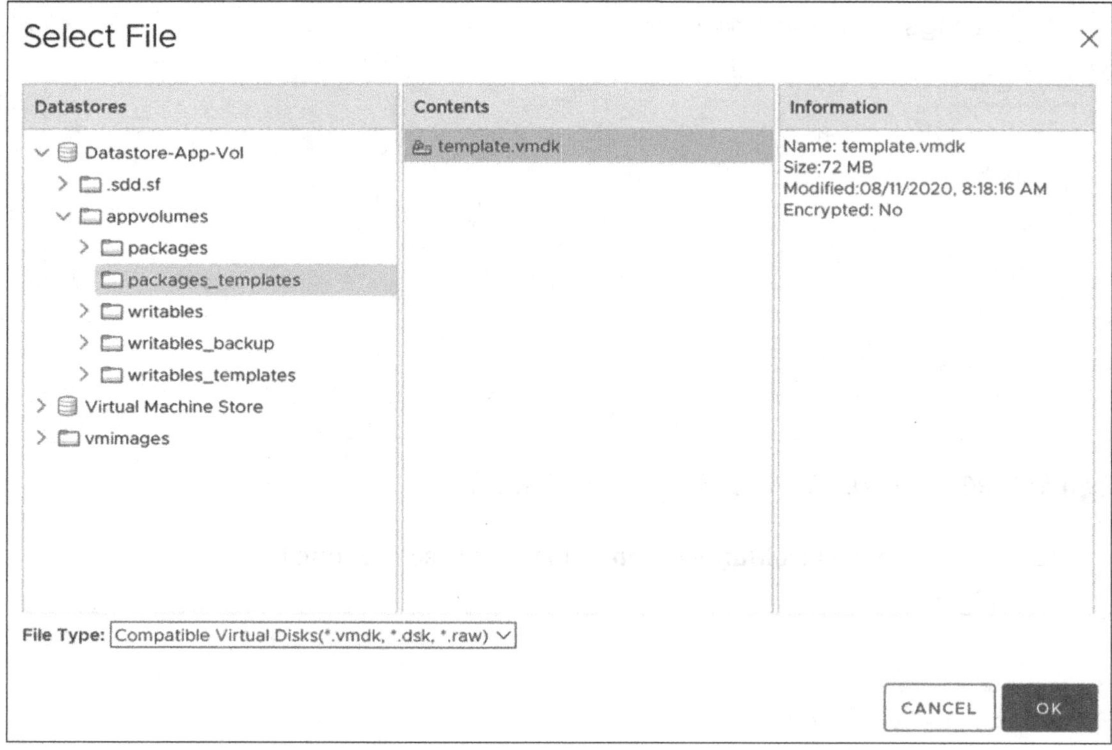

Figure 7-19. *Selecting an existing template*

8. Expand the **Datastore-App-Vol** datastore, **appvolumes**, and then click the **packages_templates** folder.
9. In the Contents pane, you will see a list of the template files. In this example, we have the original application package template called template.vmdk.
10. Click to highlight the template, and then click the **OK** button.
11. You will now return to the **Edit Settings** screen where you will see **New Hard Disk** has been added as shown in Figure 7-20.

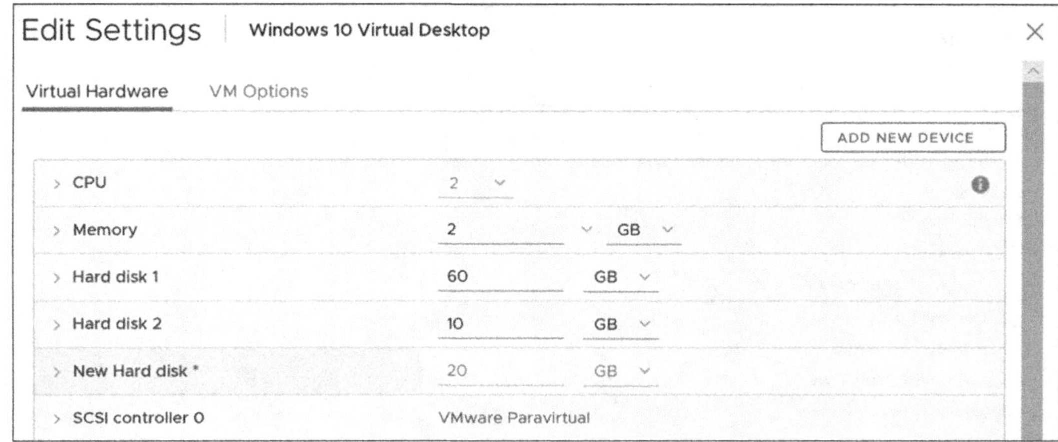

Figure 7-20. Existing hard disk successfully added

12. Now launch **Disk Management** and you will see the one in Figure 7-21.

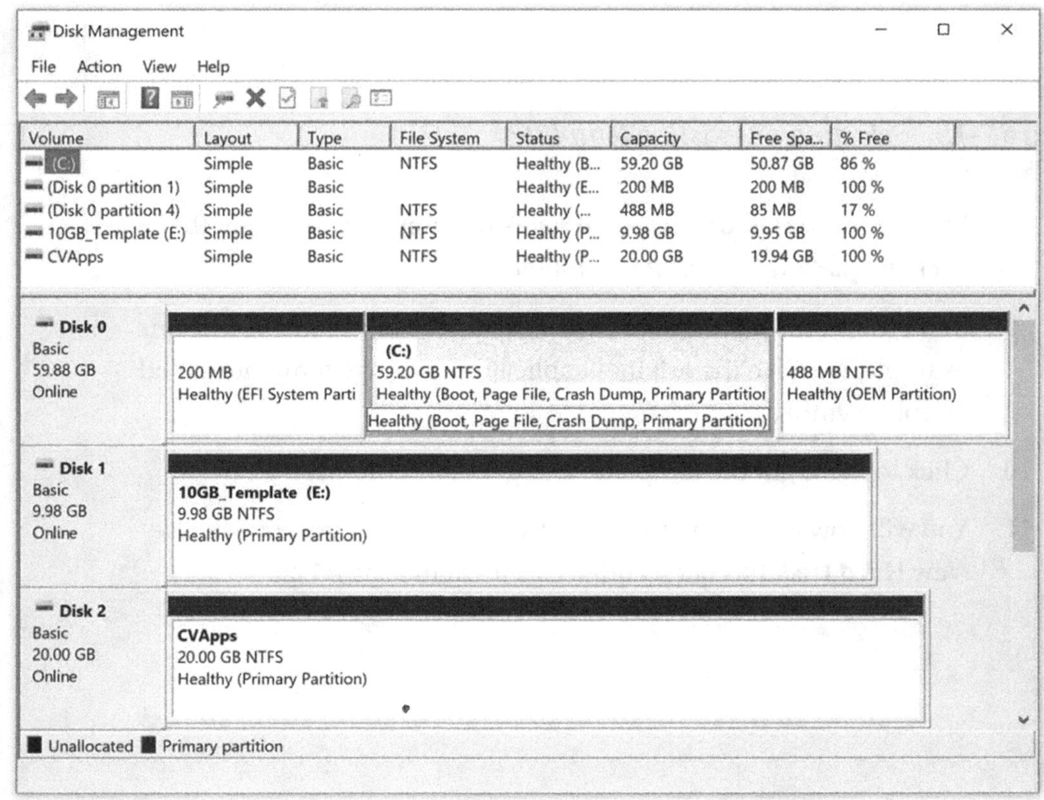

Figure 7-21. Disk Management screen showing new hard drive

13. You will see that **Disk 2** is attached. This is the existing template as you can see as it is called **CVApps**. You will also see that currently this disk has no drive letter.

14. Right-click the **CVApps** disk, and from the contextual menu, select the option for **Change Drive Letter and Paths...** as shown in Figure 7-22.

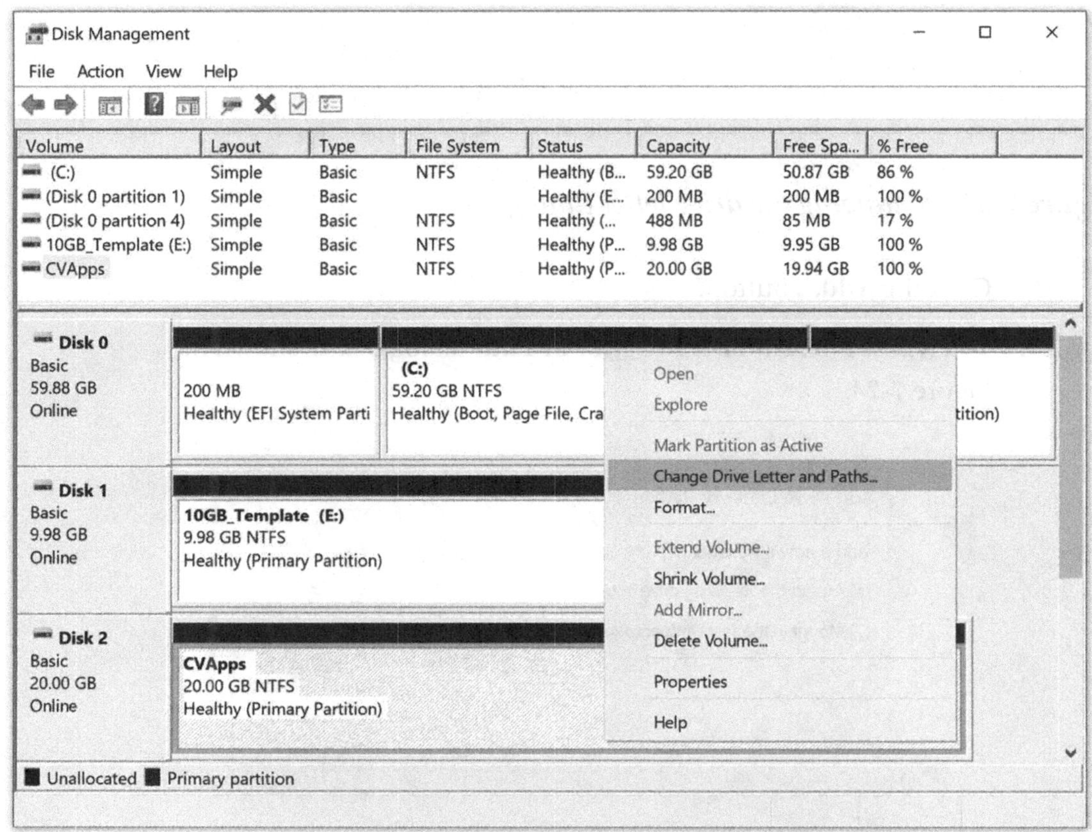

***Figure 7-22.** Adding a drive letter to the existing template hard disk*

15. You will see the **Change Drive Letter and Paths for CVApps** dialog box as shown in Figure 7-23.

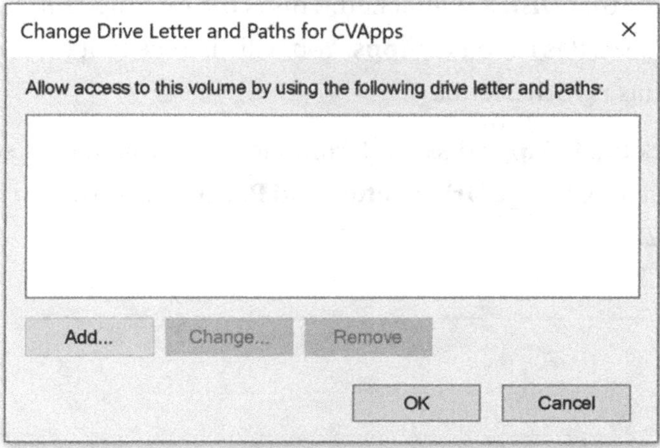

Figure 7-23. *Changing the drive letter dialog box*

16. Click the **Add...** button.
17. You will see the **Add Drive Letter or Path** dialog box as shown in Figure 7-24.

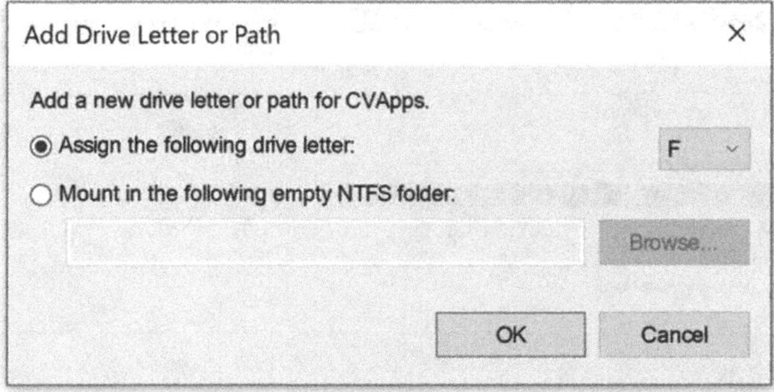

Figure 7-24. *Assigning a drive letter dialog box*

18. Click the **Assign the following drive letter** radio button, and then from the drop-down, select a drive letter. In this example, the drive letter selected is **F.**
19. Click the **OK** button.
20. You will now return to the **Disk Management** screen where you will see the newly added drive letter as shown in Figure 7-25.

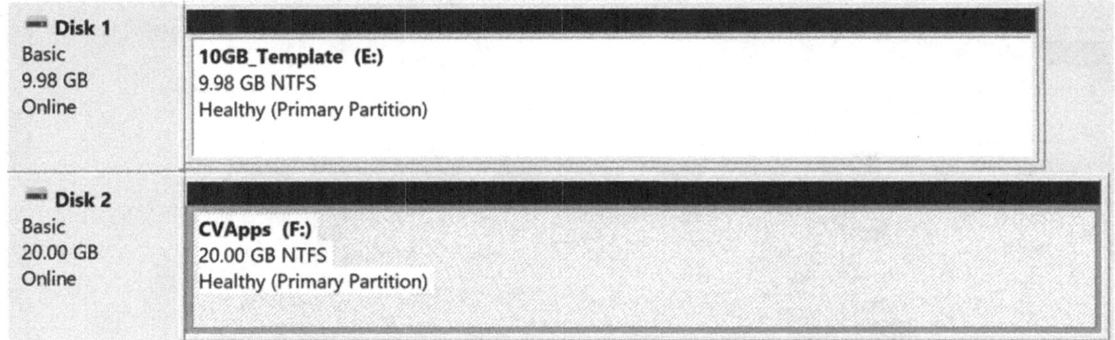

***Figure 7-25.** Drive letter now added*

21. Next, open Windows Explorer as shown in Figure 7-26.

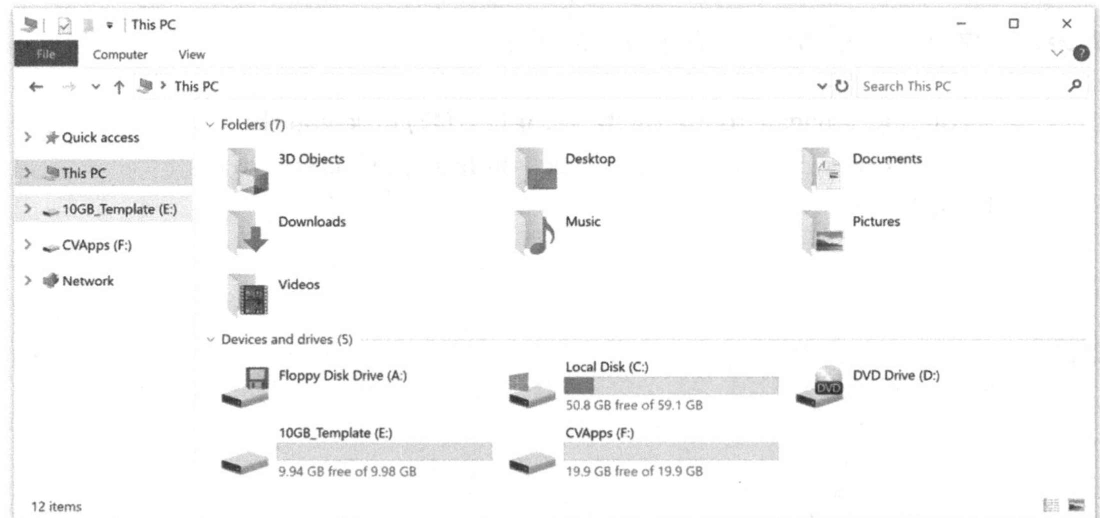

***Figure 7-26.** Windows Explorer with all drives available*

22. You will see that both the new disk and the old disk are available.

23. Double-click the **CVApps (F:)** disk.

24. Select all the files in the folder (CTRL+A), and then right-click. From the contextual menu displayed, click **Send to** and then select the option for **10GB_Template (E:)** as shown in Figure 7-27.

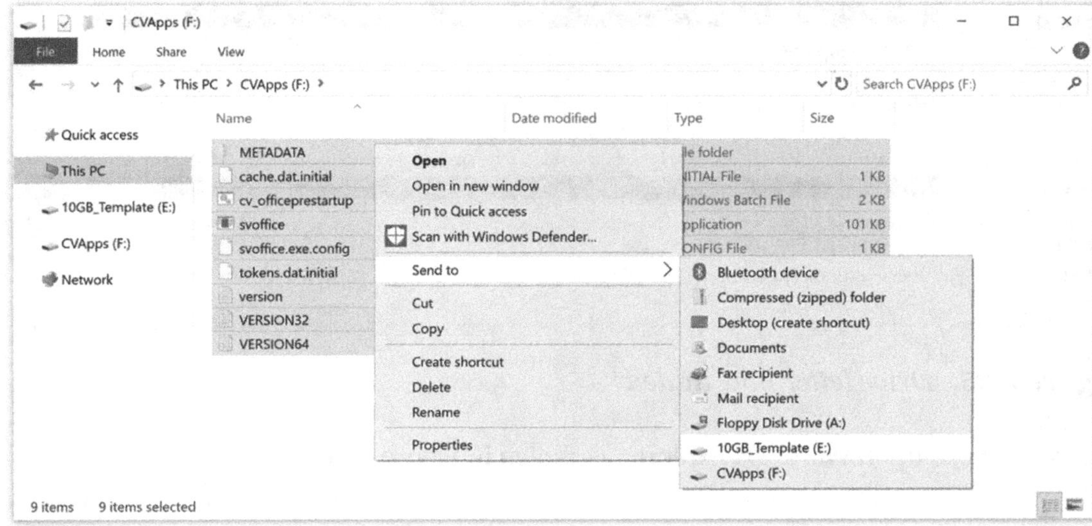

Figure 7-27. Copying the existing template files

25. If you now navigate to the **10GB_Template (E:)** disk, you should see that the contents have been successfully copied as shown in Figure 7-28.

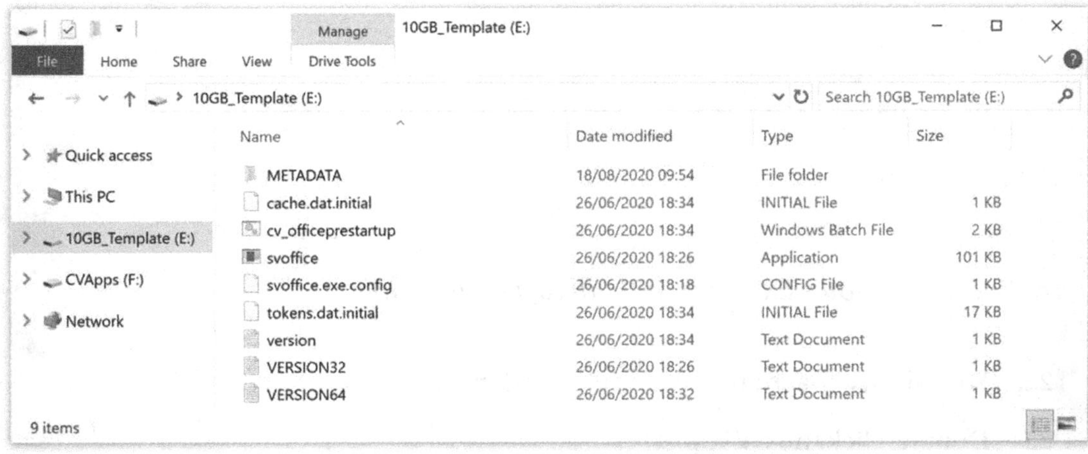

Figure 7-28. Contents of the new template virtual hard disk

26. With the file successfully copied, you can disconnect both virtual hard disks.

27. From vCenter, select the **Windows 10 Virtual Desktop** machine and click **Edit Settings** as shown in Figure 7-29.

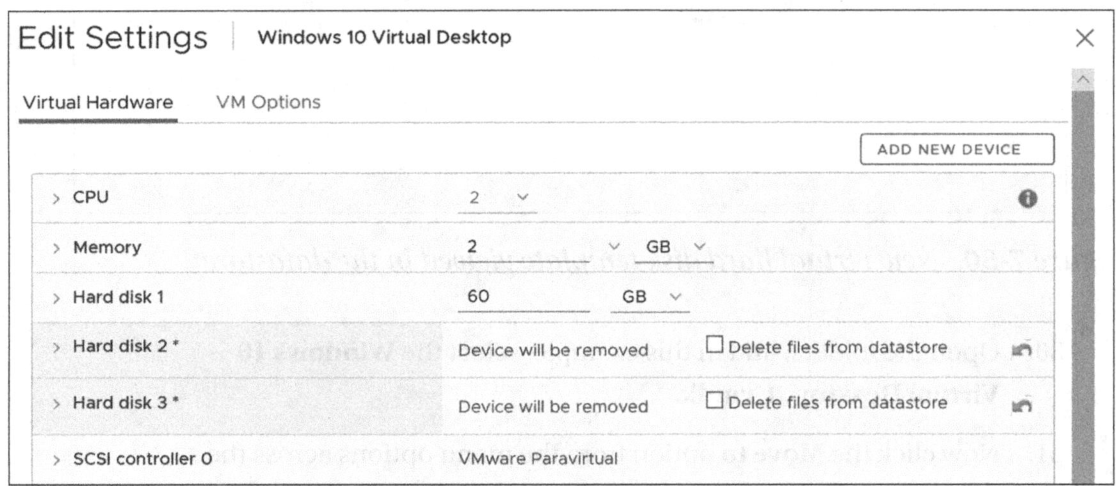

***Figure 7-29.** Disconnecting the virtual hard disk templates*

28. Click to disconnect both virtual hard disks, ensuring that you DO NOT click to delete them from the datastore.

Next, you need to move the new virtual hard disk template to the correct folder with App Volumes.

29. In vCenter, open the datastore where the new virtual hard disk template was created. You will find it under the folder that bears the name of the virtual desktop machine on which the virtual hard disk was created. In this example, this is in the **Virtual Machine Store** and the **Windows 10 Virtual Desktop** folder as shown in Figure 7-30.

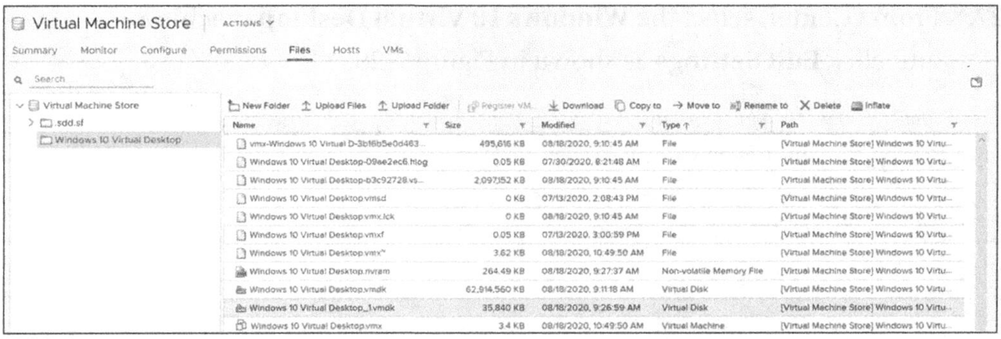

Figure 7-30. New virtual hard disk template viewed in the datastore

30. Open the folders, and in this example, select the **Windows 10 Virtual Desktop_1.vmdk.**

31. Now click the **Move to** option from the menu options across the top of the folder list.

32. You will see the **Select Destination** dialog box as shown in Figure 7-31.

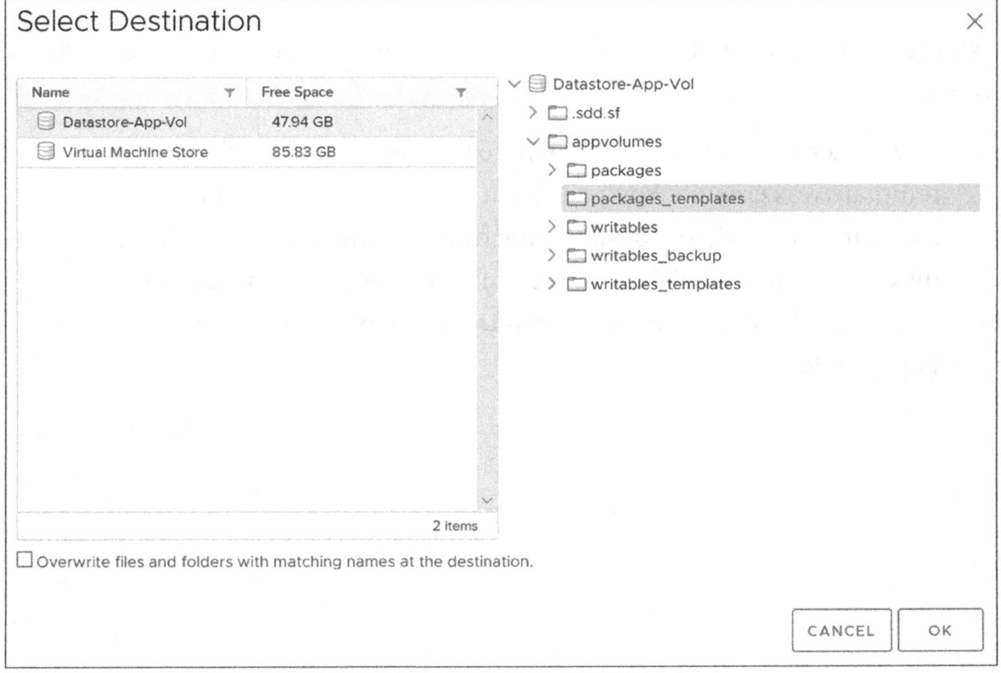

Figure 7-31. Select the destination folder

33. Navigate to the destination folder you want to use. In this example, as it is an application package template, move this to the default folder location of **appvolumes** and **packages_templates.**

34. Click **OK** to continue.

35. You will now return to the datastore view where if you navigate to the Datastore-App-Vol folder and then the **packages_templates** folder, you will see the newly created template as shown in Figure 7-32.

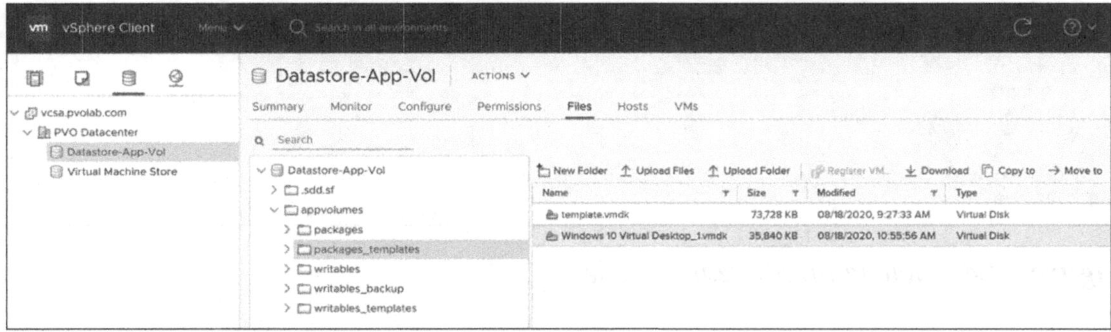

Figure 7-32. *Datastore view of the new template in the correct location*

Next, you need to rename the new virtual hard disk template. By default, it will have been named using the machine name of the machine on which it was created, so in this case **Windows 10 Virtual Desktop_1.vmdk,** as shown in the previous screenshot.

36. To rename the new template, click to highlight the template file and then click the **Rename to** option.

37. You will see the **Rename Selection** dialog box as shown in Figure 7-33.

Rename Selection | Datastore-App-Vol

Selection path: [Datastore-App-Vol] appvolumes/packages_templates/Windo...

New name: 10GB_Template.vmdk

CANCEL OK

Figure 7-33. *Renaming the new template*

38. In the **New name** field, type in a new name for the template. This will appear in the App Volumes Manager when you create an application package and select the template to use. In this example, we have called the template 10GB_Template.vmdk.

39. Once renamed, you will see the screenshot in Figure 7-34.

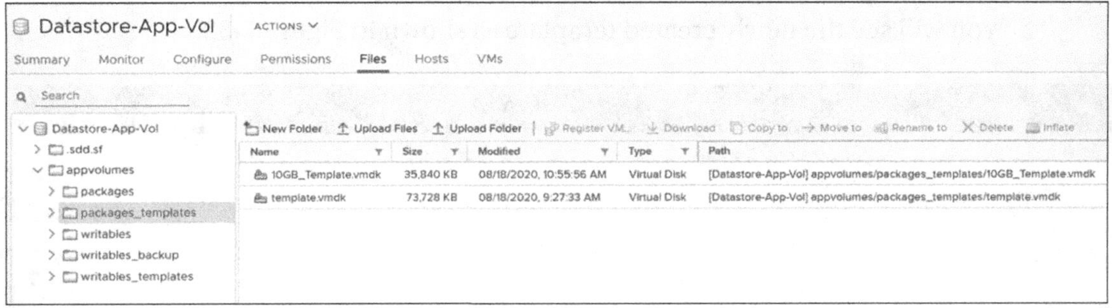

Figure 7-34. *New template ready to use*

You have now successfully created a custom template for creating application packages.

In the next section, we are going to look at how to create a custom-sized Writable Volume using the same process.

Creating custom Writable Volumes templates

In the previous section, we defined the process for creating a custom-sized application package template. In this section, we are going to look at defining the same process but this time for creating a custom-sized Writable Volumes template.

As App Volumes already has the ability to expand an existing Writable Volume, the use case for creating a custom-sized Writable Volume is when you want it to start off as a smaller disk size, or if you will only ever need less disk space. Do not forget that the virtual hard disk is always thin provisioned in any case.

Unlike the application package template, there are three different templates for Writable Volumes, and all start at 10 GB in size. These templates are listed as follows:

- Writable Volumes template for user installed applications
- Writable Volumes template for user profiles only
- Writable Volumes for user profiles and user installed applications

As with the creation of custom-sized application packages, the process for creating a custom-sized Writable Volumes uses the same manual process with just a few differences based on the fact that we are now dealing with Writable Volumes. Those differences are, as we just described, the three different template types and then the location the files are saved in on the datastore. Ensuring you select the correct template is important as each one contains different files depending on the use case. You will also need to do this to each of the three existing template files individually if you want to create a custom size for each one.

The following diagram illustrates the process for creating a custom-sized Writable Volume.

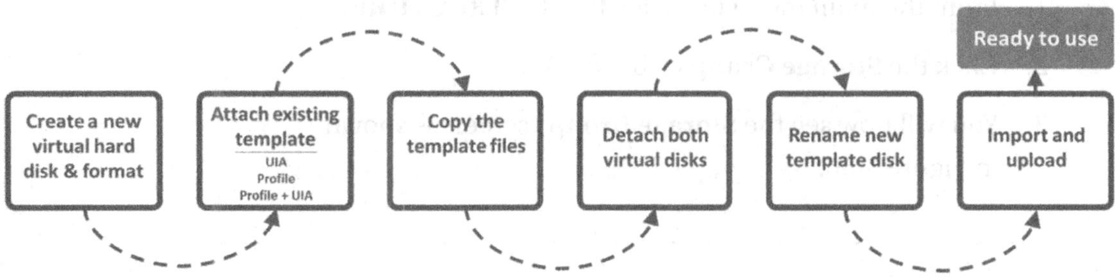

Figure 7-35. *Process for creating a custom-sized Writable Volume*

With the preceding information and following the steps described in the "Creating custom templates for packages" section, you can now create a custom-sized Writable Volume.

In the next section, we are going to look at how to configure and manage storage groups.

Storage groups

Storage Groups enable you to automatically replicate application packages, App Volumes 2.x AppStacks, and when it comes to Writable Volumes, allow you to distribute them across datastores.

The Storage Groups feature is designed to enable you to configure and define a group of datastores that will be used to hold the same volumes.

However, some of these features are only available when working with Writable Volumes. These are the template location and the distribution strategy.

The distribution strategy setting allows you to configure how Writable Volumes are distributed across the datastore using one of the following two distribution methods:

- **Spread:** Distributes the Writable Volumes files evenly across all storage locations. When a file is created, the storage with the most available space is selected.
- **Round Robin:** Sequential distribution of Writable Volumes files across the storage locations. When a Writable Volume is created, the storage with the oldest time since it was last used is selected.

To configure a Storage Group, follow the steps described:

1. From the main menu bar, click **INFRASTRUCTURE.**
2. Click the **Storage Groups** tab.
3. You will now see the **Storage Groups** screen as shown in Figure 7-36.

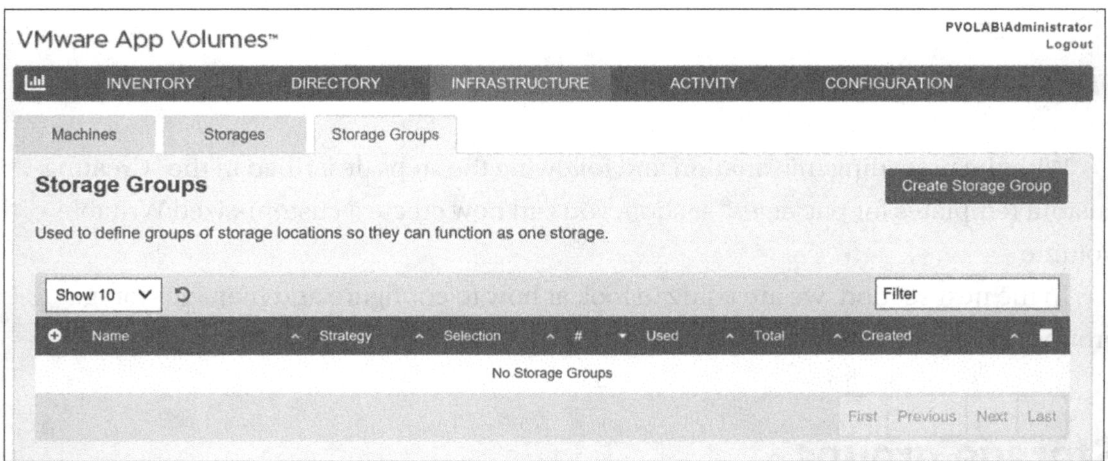

Figure 7-36. *Storage Groups screen*

4. Click the **Create Storage Group** button.
5. You will see the **Create Storage Group** screen as shown in Figure 7-37.

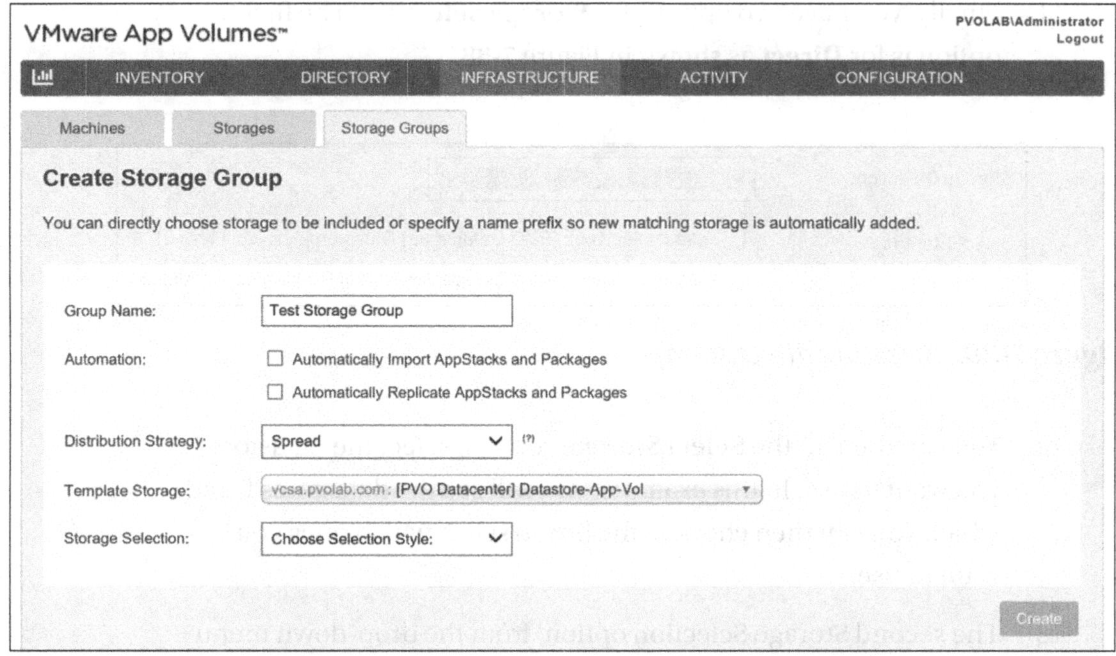

Figure 7-37. *Creating a Storage Group*

6. In the **Group Name** field, type in a name for this group. In this example, we have called it **Test Storage Group.**

7. In the **Automation** section, you have two options. You can either automatically import AppStacks (v2.x) and application packages or automatically replicate AppStacks (v2.x) and application packages. Check the box for which options you want to select.

8. The next setting is for **Distribution Strategy** and is for Writable Volumes.

9. In the **Distribution Strategy** box, select how you want the Writable Volumes distributed across the datastores. This is where you choose from **Spread** or **Round Robin.**

10. Next is the **Template Storage** location option. From the drop-down menu, select the datastore where the volume templates are located. In this example, they are in the **Datastore-App-Vol** folder within the PVO Datacenter.

11. Finally, you have two options for **Storage Selection**. The first option is for **Direct** as shown in Figure 7-38.

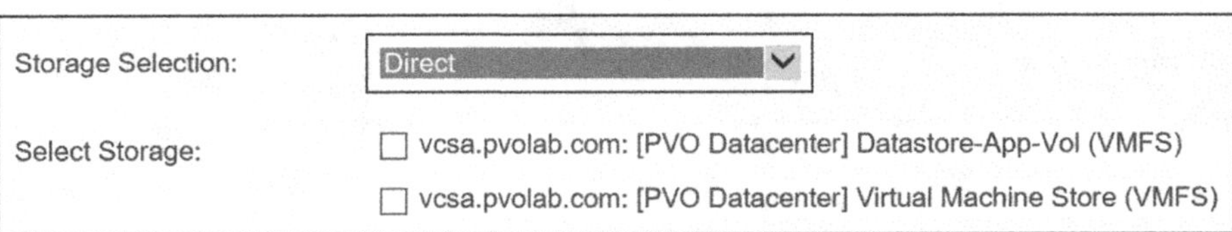

Figure 7-38. *Selecting direct storage*

12. You can then, in the **Select Storage** section, select the datastores you want to use. In this example, you will see the datastores listed which you can then check to the box to select which ones you want to use.
13. The second Storage Selection option, from the drop-down menu list, is for **Automatic** as shown in Figure 7-39.

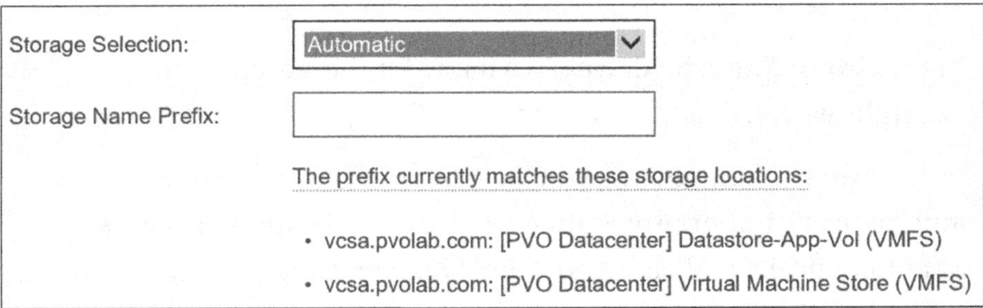

Figure 7-39. *Selecting automatic storage*

14. In the **Storage Name Prefix** box, you can type in the first part of the name of the storage. You will see the matching datastores listed.
15. Now click the **Create** button.
16. You will see the **Confirm Create Storage Group** dialog box as shown in Figure 7-40.

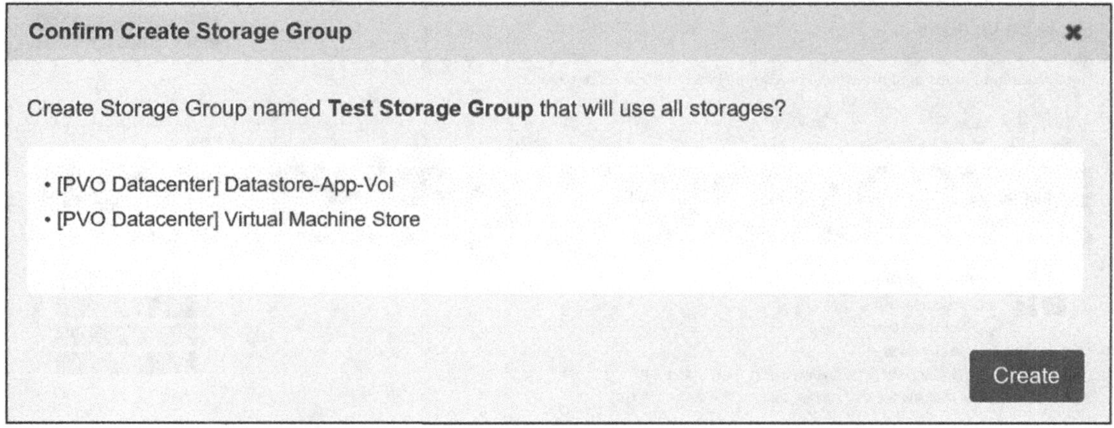

Figure 7-40. *Confirming the Storage Group creation*

17. You will see the progress bar as shown in Figure 7-41.

Figure 7-41. *Storage Group creation progress*

18. Once completed, you will see the pop-up message in Figure 7-42.

Figure 7-42. *Storage Group successfully created*

19. You will now return to the **Storage Groups** screen where you will see the **Test Storage Group** has successfully been created as shown in Figure 7-43.

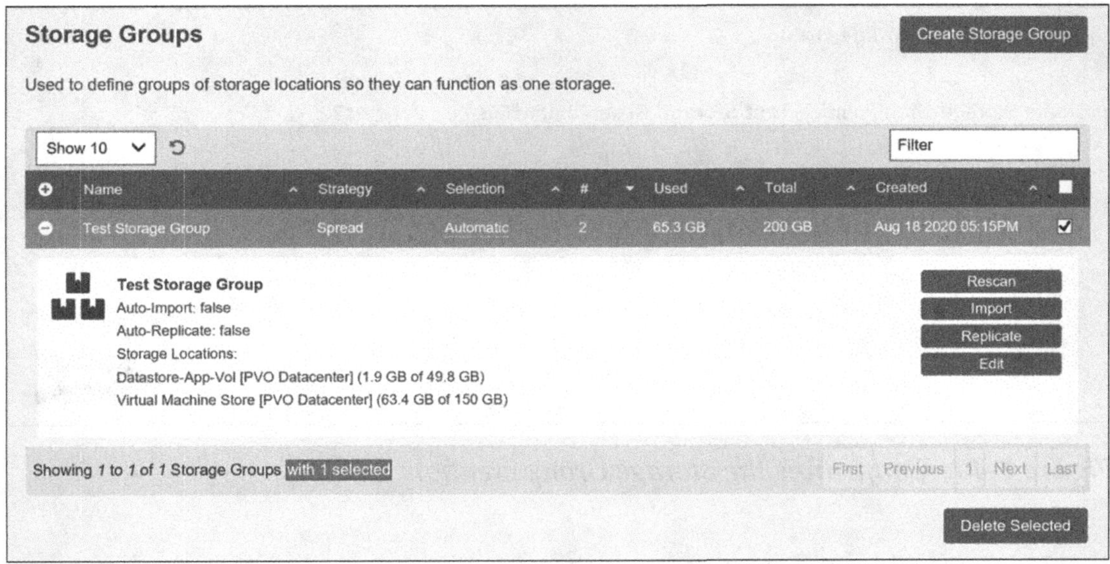

***Figure 7-43.** Storage Group view in the App Volumes Manager*

You will also see that you now have the options for **Rescan**, **Import**, **Replicate**, and **Edit**. You can also delete the storage group.

You have now successfully created a storage group. In the next section, we are going to look at the advanced configuration of the App Volumes Agent.

Advanced App Volumes Agent config

The App Volumes Agent gets installed onto the virtual desktop machines or servers which you want to be able to attach application packages and Writable Volumes. It comprises two distinct elements. One element is for communicating with the App Volumes Managers, and the other element is responsible for the layering into the OS. These are described in the following:

- **SVdriver:** Manages the virtualization and layering of the volumes into the operating system and is also referred to as the filter driver and therefore ensures that the application layers are seamlessly attached to the OS and make them appear as though they were locally installed on the machine.
- **SVservice:** Controls and manages the volumes and the communication with the App Volumes Manager.

The App Volumes Agent can also be configured to make use of batch scripts. These scripts enable you to select specific configuration options such as registry settings, services, and drivers that the programs delivered as an application package require to be able to run. Scripts are executed on startup of a virtual desktop machine or when users log in to their virtual desktop machines when a volume is attached.

Batch script options

The script files are in the application package and Writable Volumes templates, hence the reason they are executed when a volume is attached.

The following scripts are available:

- **OnPreLoadApp.bat**: Called before an application is initialized for the first user session
- **OnPostLoadApp.bat**: Called after an application is initialized for the first user session
- **OnPreEnableApp.bat**: Called before an application is enabled for each user session
- **OnPostEnableApp.bat**: Called after an application is enabled for each user session
- **OnPreDisableApp.bat**: Called before an application is disabled for each user session
- **OnPostDisableApp.bat**: Called after an application is disabled for each user session
- **OnPreUnloadApp.bat**: Called before an application is uninitialized for the last user session
- **OnPostUnloadApp.bat**: Called after an application is uninitialized for the last user session

In addition to the script files themselves, there are also scope elements that can define the behavior of the scripts and when and where they run. These are listed as follows:

- **Global Scope**: With the global scope, the scripts will run for every application when a script is present in the following locations:
    - %SVAgent%\Custom

- %SVAgent%\Custom\system
- %SVAgent%\Custom\provisioning
- %SVAgent%\Custom\app

- **User Writable Volume Scope**: Scripts will run for an assigned end user when a script is present at
  - \[Writable VolumeID GUID]\Config\Writable
- **Application Package Scope**: Scripts when present at this location are run only for that application.

Batch scripts run one after the other, with any new scripts not executing until the previous script has fully completed.

In the case of needing to prevent a script from blocking end users from logging in or logging out, a timeout can be specified by using the following registry entry:

- HKLM\SYSTEM\CurrentControlSet\services\svservice\Parameters

Simply add the time, in seconds, that you want to add for the configured timeout. To do this add the **REG_DWORD** type to the registry key.

You have now successfully configured your advanced App Volumes Agent settings. In the next section, we are going to look at the snapvol.cfg policy configuration file.

The snapvol.cfg file

The snapvol.cfg policy configuration file in App Volumes 4.x is now part of the App Volumes Agent. Previously in App Volumes 2.x version, the file was in the root folder of each individual volume. It would then be available once the volume was attached.

However, to make it easier to manage and update, in App Volumes 4.x, it now gets installed as part of the App Volumes Agent onto the App Volumes managed machines.

Snapvol.cfg contains keywords that must not be modified by the end users as well as those that can be customized. It contains not only paths to folders in the end user's C: drive but also registry locations to capture (include) (or not to capture (exclude)), file types in a given path, specific process names, and so on.

To edit the snapvol.cfg file, it is simply a case of opening and editing using something like Windows Notepad. To do this, follow the steps described:

1. Open Windows Explorer on the virtual desktop machine that is running the App Volumes Agent.

2. Navigate to the folder **CloudVolumes\Agent\Config** as shown in Figure 7-44.

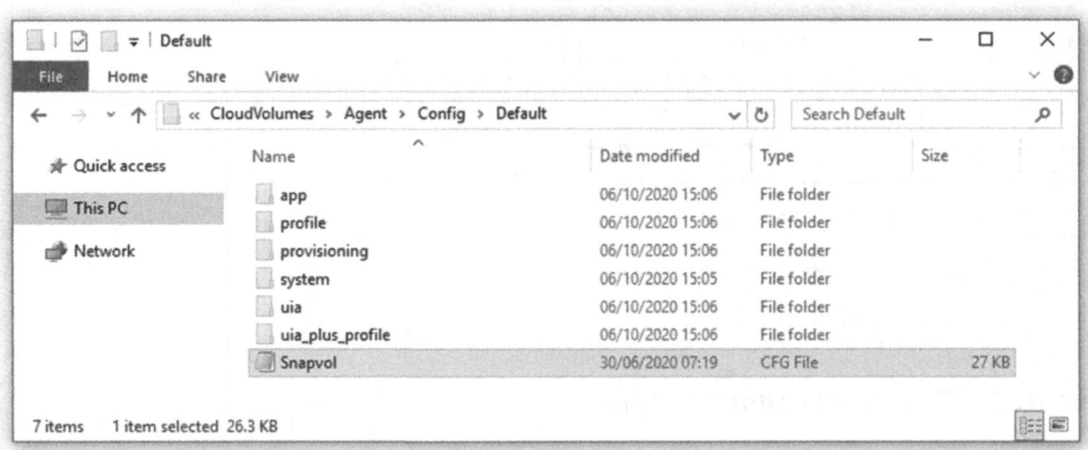

***Figure 7-44.** Navigating to the snapvol.cfg file*

3. You will now see the snapvol.cfg file.

4. Click to highlight the file, right-click, and select **Open with**, and then select **Notepad.**

5. The file will open and will look something like the file shown in Figure 7-45.

Snapvol - Notepad

File Edit Format View Help

```
####################################################################
# File system
####################################################################

#virtualize=\

####################################################################
# Registry
####################################################################

#virtualize_registry=\REGISTRY\MACHINE\SOFTWARE
#virtualize_registry=\REGISTRY\MACHINE\COMPONENTS\CanonicalData
#virtualize_registry=\REGISTRY\MACHINE\COMPONENTS\DerivedData
#virtualize_registry=\REGISTRY\MACHINE\COMPONENTS\ServicingStackVersions
#virtualize_registry=\REGISTRY\MACHINE\COMPONENTS\Installers
#virtualize_registry=\REGISTRY\MACHINE\COMPONENTS\Configuration
#virtualize_registry=\REGISTRY\MACHINE\COMPONENTS\ccpinterface
#virtualize_registry=\REGISTRY\MACHINE\SYSTEM\ControlSet001\control
#virtualize_registry=\REGISTRY\MACHINE\SYSTEM\ControlSet001\services
#virtualize_registry=\REGISTRY\USER\S-1-5-20\SOFTWARE\Microsoft\OfficeSoftwareProtectionPlatform
#virtualize_registry=\REGISTRY\USER\S-1-5-20\SOFTWARE\Microsoft\Windows NT\CurrentVersion\SoftwareProtectionPlatform
#virtualize_registry_notify_change=\REGISTRY\MACHINE\Software\Microsoft\.NetFramework
#virtualize_registry_notify_change=\REGISTRY\MACHINE\Software\Wow6432Node\Microsoft\.NetFramework

####################################################################
# File system exclusions
####################################################################

# Should never virtualize $Recycle.Bin folder
exclude_path=\$RECYCLE.BIN

# Profile delivered via roaming profile or folder redirection
exclude_path=\Users

exclude_path=\ProgramData\ntuser.pol
exclude_path=\ProgramData\tempntuser.pol
```

***Figure 7-45.** Example snapvol.cfg file*

You can now edit the file to add your specific settings. However, before you do, there are some that you *should not* modify. These are listed as follows:

- virtualize
- virtualize_registry
- virtualize_registry_notify_change
- reverse_replicate_file
- delete_local_profile

In the next section, we will look at those that can be configured and modified.

Configuration options for application packages

When configuring the snapvol.cfg file, you can modify the following:

- **exclude_path**: During a read or write operation, App Volumes excludes looking for any file or folder in the path specified in this keyword in either the application package or the Writable Volume. Instead, if the file or folder specified in the path is present in the base image, then the read or write operation is performed in the base image.

  For example: exclude_path=\ProgramData\Microsoft

  App Volumes excludes looking for Microsoft in either the application package or Writable Volume. Instead, if Microsoft is present in the base image, then the read or write operation on the folder is performed in the base image.

- **include_path**: App Volumes reads any file or folder in the path specified in this keyword in the following order: Writable Volumes, application package, and the base image. Any write operation in this path is performed on the Writable Volume.

  For example: include_path=\Users

  App Volumes reads all subfolders of Users from all volumes: Writable Volume, application package, and the base image. If an end user creates a folder or file within Users, then the file or folder is created on the Writable Volume.

- **exclude_registry**: During a read or write operation, App Volumes excludes looking for any registry key or registry value in the path specified in this keyword in either the application package or Writable Volume. Instead, if the registry key or registry value specified in the path is present in the base image, then the read or write operation is performed in the base image.

  For example: exclude_registry=\REGISTRY\MACHINE\SOFTWARE\Policies

App Volumes excludes looking for any registry key or registry value specified within Policies in either the application package or Writable Volume. Instead, if the path is present in the base image, then the read or write operation is performed on the registry key or registry value in the base image.

- **include_registry**: App Volumes reads any registry key or registry value in the path specified in this keyword in the following order: Writable Volume, application package, and the base image. Any write operation in this path is performed on the Writable Volume.

  For example: include_registry=\REGISTRY\MACHINE\SOFTWARE\Microsoft\Windows Search

  App Volumes reads all registry keys and registry values at \REGISTRY\MACHINE\SOFTWARE\Microsoft\Windows Search from all volumes: Writable Volume, application package, and base image. If a registry key or registry value is created at this path, then this operation is performed on the Writable Volume.

- **exclude_process_path**: All processes that are run from an executable file in this path or subpath only see the file system and registry content from the base image.

  For example: exclude_process_path=\Program Files\VMWare\AppCapture

  Any executable file run from the AppCapture folder or its subfolders only sees the file system and registry content from the base image. If the process spawns a new child process, the child process sees contents from the Writable Volume, AppStack, and base image.

- **include_process_name**: The process specified in this keyword sees the file system and registry content from the Writable Volume, AppStack, and base image.

  For example: include_process_name=SearchIndexer.exe

  The SearchIndexer process sees the file system and registry content from all volumes.

- **exclude_process_name**: The process specified in this keyword sees the file system and registry content only from the base image.

  For example: exclude_process_name=chkdsk.exe

  The chkdsk process sees the file system and registry content only from the base image.

In the following section, we are going to look at the keywords that can only be used when customizing Writable Volumes.

Writable Volumes

The following keywords can be used when customizing Writable Volumes:

- **exclude_uwv_file**: App Volumes reads any file or folder in the path specified in this keyword in the following order: Writable Volume, application package, and the base image.

  Any write operation to the file or folder in this path is performed on the Writable Volume, which persists for that session, but gets deleted when the user logs off from their virtual desktop machine.

- **exclude_uwv_reg**: App Volumes reads any registry key or registry value in the path specified in this keyword in the following order: Writable Volume, application package, and the base image.

  Any write operation to the registry key or registry value in this path is performed on the Writable Volume, which persists for that session, but gets deleted when the user logs off from their virtual desktop machine.

  For example: exclude_uwv_reg=\REGISTRY\MACHINE\SOFTWARE\Microsoft\\

  App Volumes reads any registry key or registry value within Microsoft from all the volumes: Writable Volume, application package, and the base image.

  If a new registry key or registry value is created within Microsoft, then the new key or value persists for that session. When the end user logs off, the key or value is deleted.

You have now successfully looked at the options for configuring the snapvol.cfg file.

Chapter summary

In this chapter, we have discussed the more advanced features of App Volumes, that is, some of the configuration options that are not available within the App Volumes management console.

Most of these features have been more manual-based processes.

We looked at how to create custom templates for application packages and Writable Volumes, configuring storage groups, configuring the App Volumes Agent to use some more advanced features, and then finally the snapvol.cfg file.

CHAPTER 8

Just-in-Time Management Platform

The Just-in-Time Management Platform (JMP) brings together all the different virtual desktop components such as OS (delivered by Horizon with Instant Clone desktops), applications (delivered by App Volumes), and user data and profile management (managed by VMware Dynamic Environment Manager).

It acts as the orchestration layer in that it brings all these different components together and delivers them to end users on demand. The end user receives a complete desktop environment including all their application and all their end user–specific data, all built on demand as the end user logs in. Taking this approach enables organizations to deliver a completely stateless virtual desktop environment.

One of the key components of JMP platform is delivering the end user applications, and this is where App Volumes comes in to play.

In this chapter, we are going to concentrate on how to configure the App Volumes to work with the JMP platform. We are going to start by looking at the architecture and how all the component parts fit together.

The architecture

As we have already discussed, the Just-in-Time Management Platform is not just an individual product (unless you talk about the JMP Server itself), but it is the automation engine that orchestrates the VMware EUC technologies in delivering on-demand virtual desktop machines, applications, and end user data and profiles.

Although this sounds like it will be complex to bring all these components together and configure them, in reality it is very straightforward, and it all uses the standard Horizon admin console, so you keep that single point of management even though JMP consists of lots of moving parts.

P. von Oven, *Delivering Applications with VMware App Volumes 4*,
https://doi.org/10.1007/978-1-4842-6689-2_8

Figure 8-1 shows how all these components come together under the JMP platform solution.

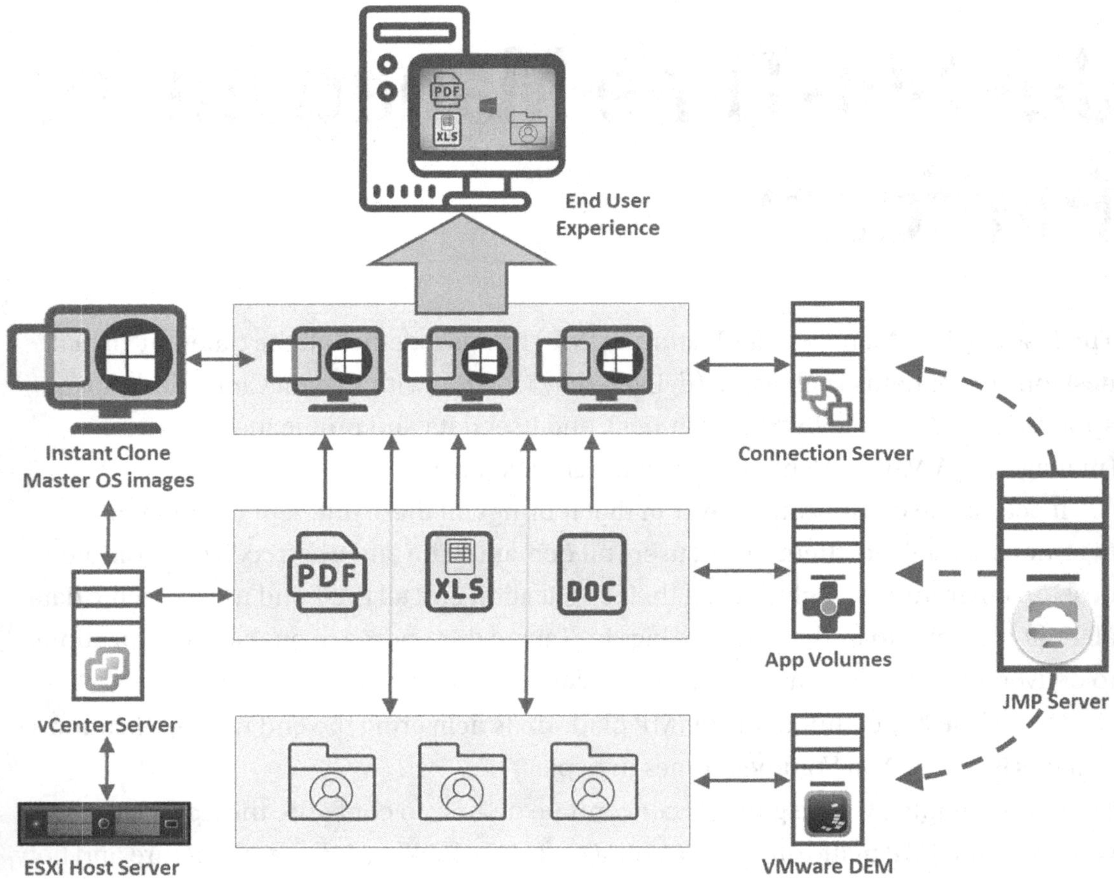

***Figure 8-1.** JMP architecture and components*

How it works

We've previously described the JMP platform as an automation engine that orchestrates the on-demand delivery of the complete end user workspace. This includes virtual desktops, apps, profiles, and user data. So how does it work and what exactly does it automate?

The first part is in building the virtual desktop machine the end user is going to use. As the end user logs in to their Horizon Client or Workspace ONE and requests a desktop or workspace, the JMP Server initiates this using Horizon View and the Connection Server, which in turn builds an Instant Clone desktop ready for the end user to use.

With the new desktop built on demand, as the end user login process continues, if the end user has been entitled to applications delivered using App Volumes, these will now be attached to the virtual desktop machine ready to be launched when the end user is logged in.

The final piece is to deliver the end user personalization or profile using VMware Dynamic Environment Manager. This makes the newly created desktop personal to the end user in that it will deliver all their settings and data.

JMP orchestration components

As you can see from the preceding description on how JMP works, there are several components that go to make up the complete solution, in addition to App Volumes. These are described in the following sections.

VMware Workspace ONE

VMware Workspace ONE is a digital workspace solution that allows IT admins to centrally manage end users' mobile devices, virtual desktops, and applications. It allows end users to access their resources securely using a device of their choice regardless of whether it is a corporate device or a personal BYOD and regardless of whether that device is joined to the corporate domain. Taking this approach also means that a VPN is no longer required.

End users access their resources from a single portal or workspace, which also provides a catalog of self-service apps that a user can access and entitle themselves to use. From an App Volumes or JMP perspective, apps accessed from the workspace could be delivered using App Volumes with the apps being delivered via either a virtual desktop, hosted desktop, or an app publishing solution.

VMware Dynamic Environment Manager (DEM)

VMware DEM is responsible for delivering the personalization of the end user's virtual desktop machine by adding their personal settings and data. The virtual desktop machine can also be dynamically configured using standard Windows policies enabling end user–specific setting to be applied to both the OS and the apps. For example, a standard application could be delivered using App Volumes and then configured for a specific use case using DEM.

VMware Instant Clones

Instant Clone is a feature of the vSphere platform, used by Horizon to build virtual desktop machines on demand.

It uses VMware VM Fork technology that allows you to provision virtual desktop machines very quickly, from a gold image. Rather than cloning a powered off virtual desktop machine and then having to power it on and customize it, with Instant Clones the clone of the virtual desktop machines is created from an already powered on and running virtual desktop machine. This means that Instant Clones are very quick to provision and deploy.

The clone uses the parent's shared memory but then, once created, has no dependency on it. It shares its disk not with the parent but the replica. Once virtual desktops are created, you can then turn off the parent machine without affecting anything in the newly created machines. The parent is only used for creation.

Installing the JMP Server

In this section, we are going to install the JMP Server software. Before we do, we are going to cover the prerequisites of what you need to have in place before you start the install.

Prerequisites

Before we start the installation, in this section, we are going to discuss what you need to have in place before you get started. First up are the components in addition to App Volumes that you will need to deploy the complete solution. These are not all mandatory, and you may well have another solution in place that already provides the functionality. For example, you may already have a third-party user environment management solution in place.

Orchestration component prerequisites

To gain the advantage of the full set of JMP Integrated Workflow features that allow you to automate the entire process of building fully stateless virtual desktop machines, the following versions of the VMware products need to be installed before you install the JMP Server:

- VMware Horizon 7 version 7.5 or later
- VMware App Volumes 2.14 or later
- VMware Dynamic Environment Manager (DEM) 9.2.1 or later
- VMware Identity Manager (vIDM) 2.9.2 or later (for integration with VMware Workspace ONE)

JMP Server requirements and prerequisites

The JMP Server software can be installed on either a physical or virtual server just so long as it meets the following minimum requirements for hardware and software.

Hardware

Hardware requirements for the JMP Server:

- 4 CPUs or vCPUs
- 8 GB memory (minimum of 4 GB for proof of concept)
- 100 GB disk space (25 GB for proof of concept)

Software

Software requirements for the JMP Server:

- Windows Server 2008 R2 SP1 64-bit Standard, Enterprise, or Datacenter
- Windows Server 2012 R2 64-bit Standard or Datacenter
- Windows Server 2016 64-bit Standard or Datacenter

In addition to the operating system, you also need a SQL database for the configuration information. The JMP Server supports the following SQL versions:

- SQL Server Express 2014 64-bit (for POC deployments)
- SQL Server 2012 (SP1, SP2, SP3, and SP4) 64-bit Standard and Enterprise
- SQL Server 2014 (SP1 and SP2 with CU7 or later) 64-bit Standard and Enterprise
- SQL Server 2016 (SP1 with CU6 or later)

JMP Server installation process

With the prerequisites in place, we can now install the JMP Server software. Configuring App Volumes to work with JMP will be completed once the JMP Server is up and running.

To install the JMP Server, follow the steps described:

1. Navigate to the location of the JMP Server installer file. In the test lab, this was downloaded and saved to a shared folder and is shown in Figure 8-2.

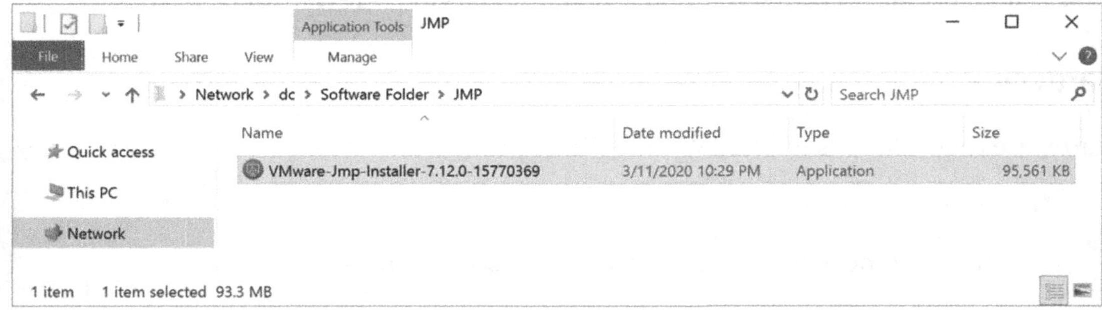

***Figure 8-2.** Navigating to and launching the JMP installer*

2. Double-click the **VMware-Jmp-Installer-7.12.0-15770369** file to launch the installer. The long number at the end is the release number which may differ even if the version number is the same. As the installer launches, you may well see the **Open File – Security Warning** box pop-up. If you do see this warning message, then click the **Run** button to continue.

3. The installer will now launch, and you will see the **Welcome to the InstallShield Wizard for VMware JMP** as shown in Figure 8-3.

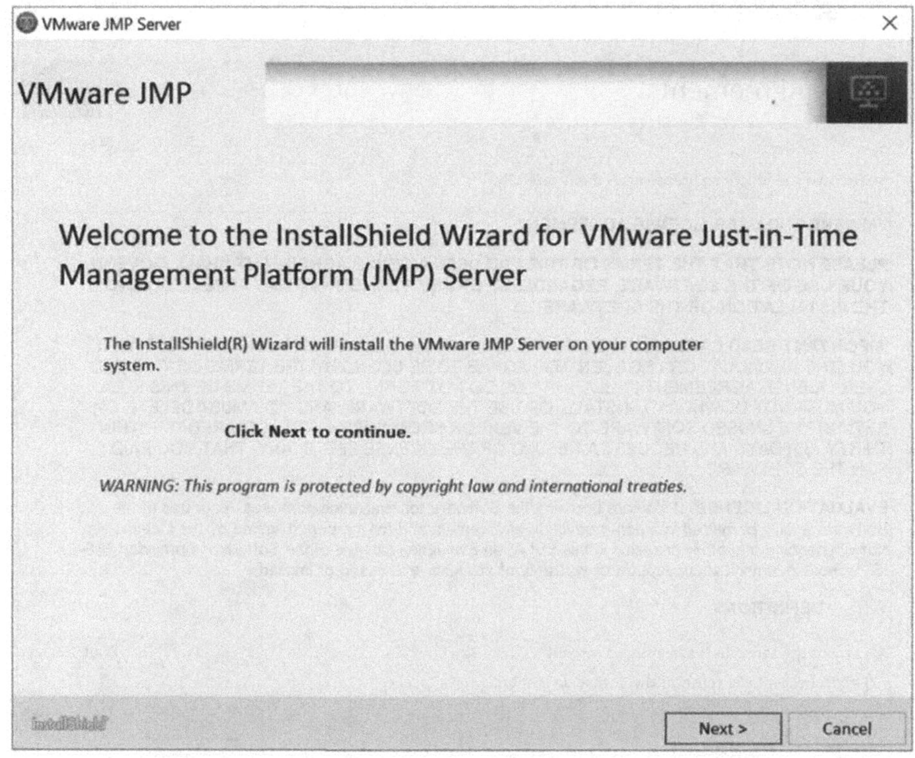

Figure 8-3. *VMware JMP installer welcome screen*

4. Click **Next ►** to continue.

5. You will now see the **License Agreement** screen as shown in Figure 8-4.

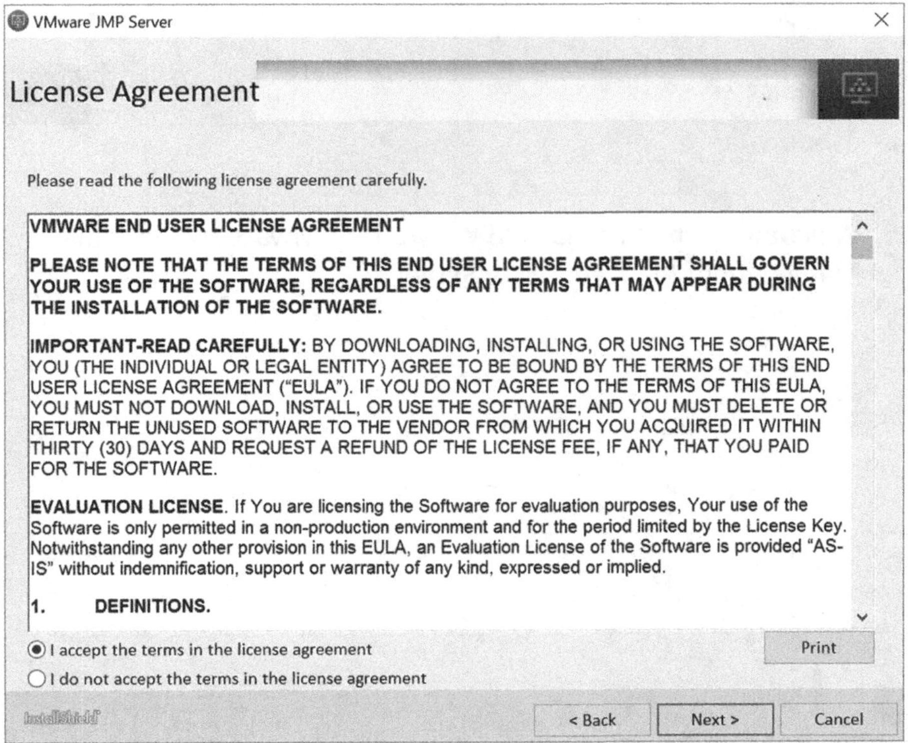

Figure 8-4. *JMP license agreement screen*

6. Click the radio button for **I accept the terms in the license agreement** and then click **Next ►**.
7. You will now see the **Allow HTTP traffic on Port 80** configuration screen as shown in Figure 8-5.

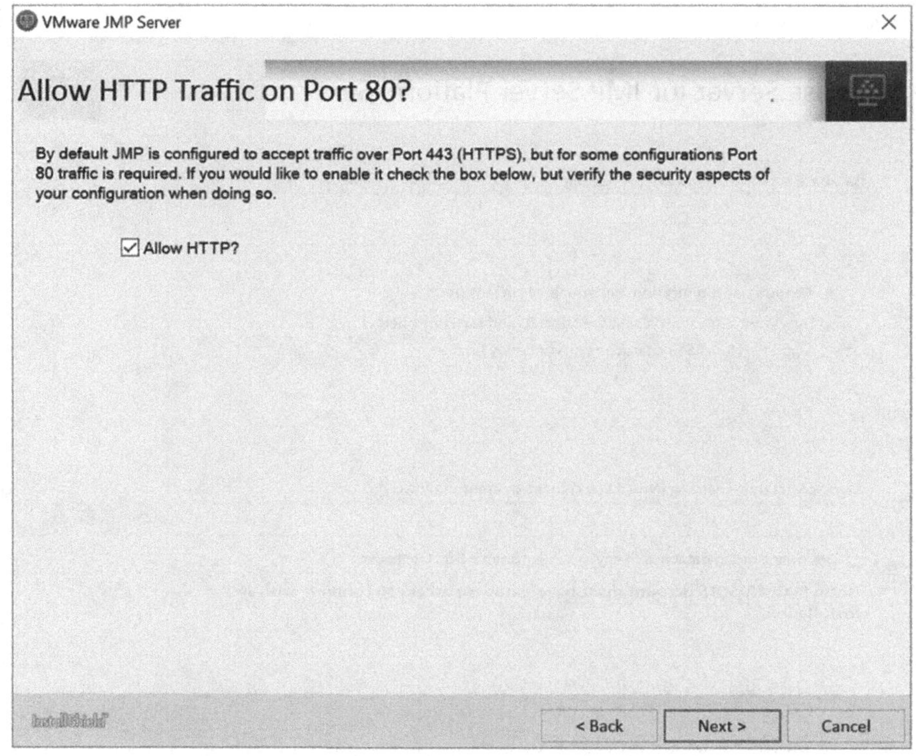

Figure 8-5. *Configuring HTTP traffic*

8. Check the **Allow HTTP** box if you want to use HTTP port 80 for JMP traffic, and then click **Next ►**.
9. You will now see the **Database Server for JMP Server Platform Services** screen as shown in Figure 8-6.

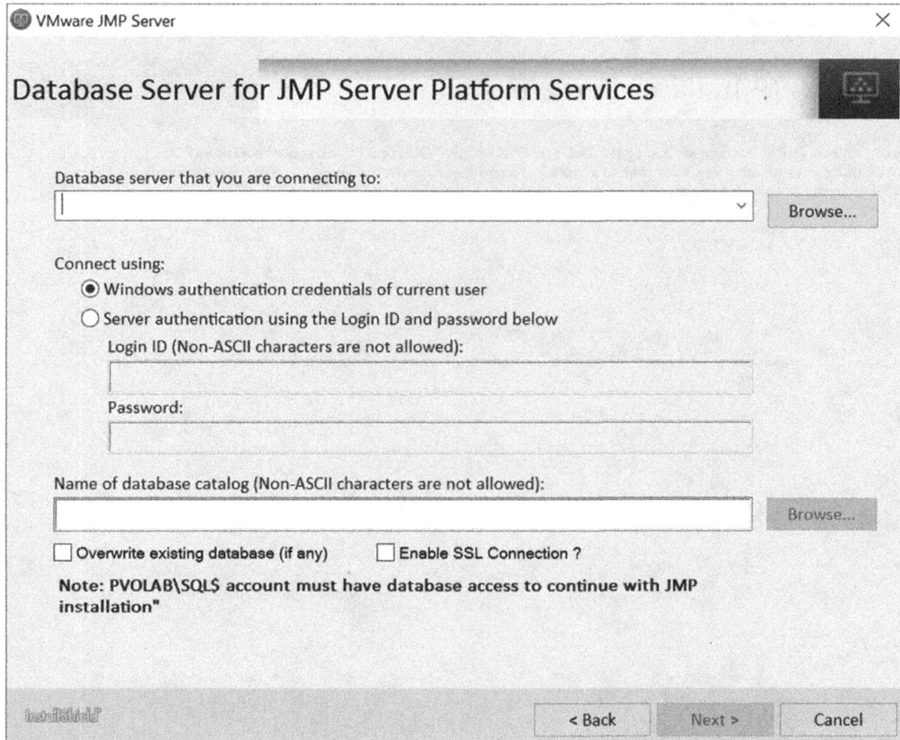

Figure 8-6. *JMP database configuration screen*

10. Click the **Browse...** button to select the database server that you want to connect to. You will now see the list of database servers as shown in Figure 8-7.

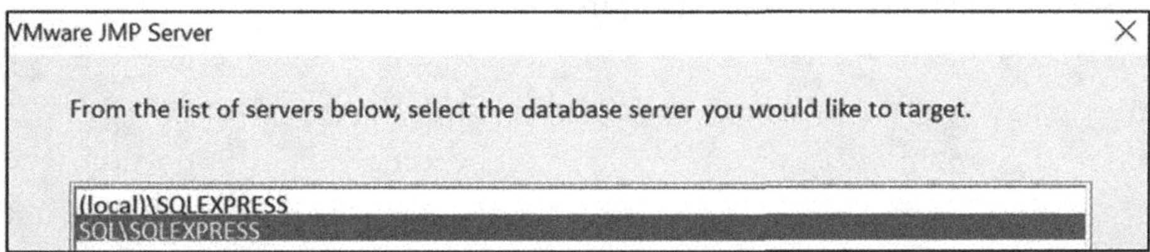

Figure 8-7. *Selecting the JMP database*

11. Click to select the database server from the list. In the test lab, we only have a single SQL Server which is called **SQL\SQLEXPRESS**.

12. Click **OK** to continue.

13. You will return to the database configuration screen where you will see that the selected database server **SQL\SQLEXPRESS** has now been added as shown in Figure 8-8.

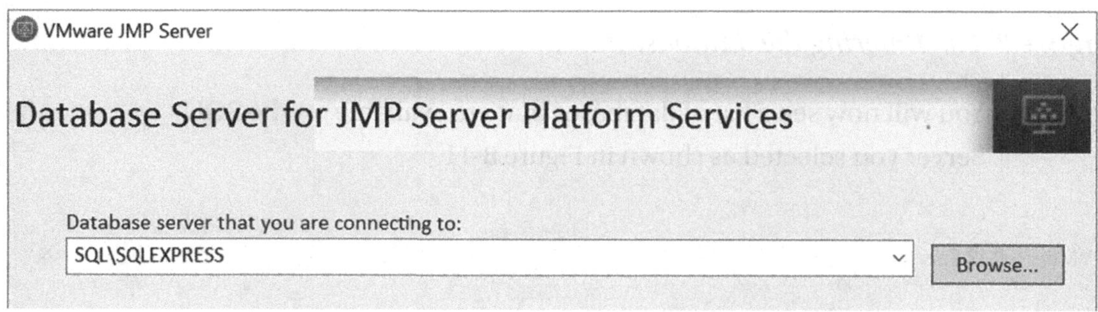

Figure 8-8. *Database now added*

14. Next, you need to add the connection details for this database server. In this example, we have already created a user called JMP within SQL. Click the radio button for **Server authentication using the Login ID and password below**, and then in the **Login ID** box, type in the login name, jmp in this example, followed by the password for this account in the **Password** box, as shown in Figure 8-9.

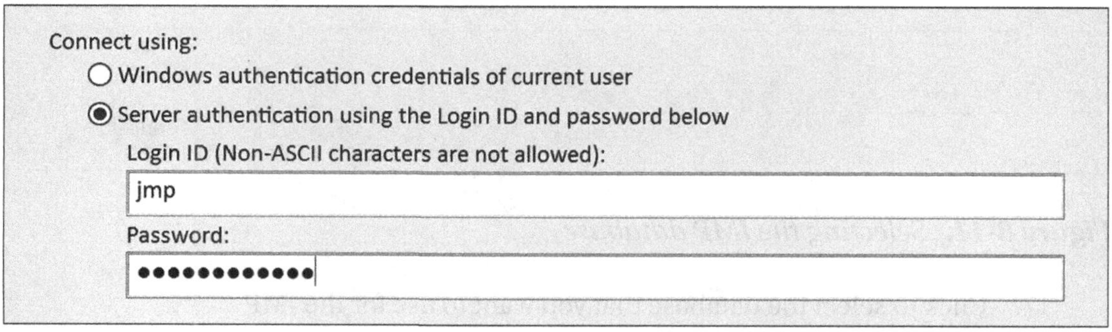

Connect using:
Windows authentication credentials of current user
Server authentication using the Login ID and password below
Login ID (Non-ASCII characters are not allowed):
jmp
Password:
●●●●●●●●●●●●

Figure 8-9. *SQL Server authentication*

15. Next, you need to select the database that you want to use for the JMP Server. In the **Name of database catalog** box, click the **Browse...** button as shown in Figure 8-10.

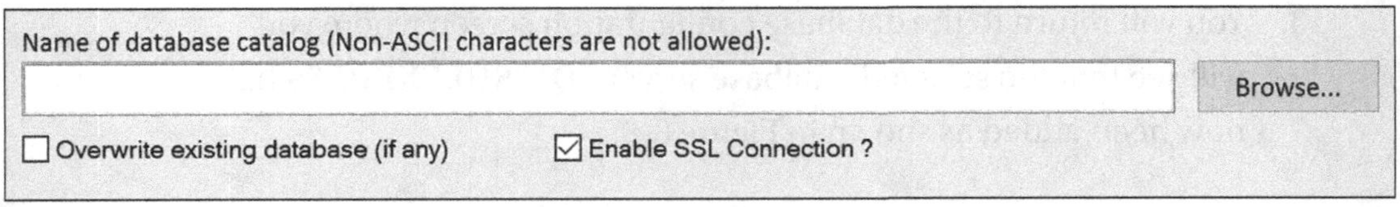

Figure 8-10. *Entering the database name*

16. You will now see a list of databases that are available on the SQL Server you selected as shown in Figure 8-11.

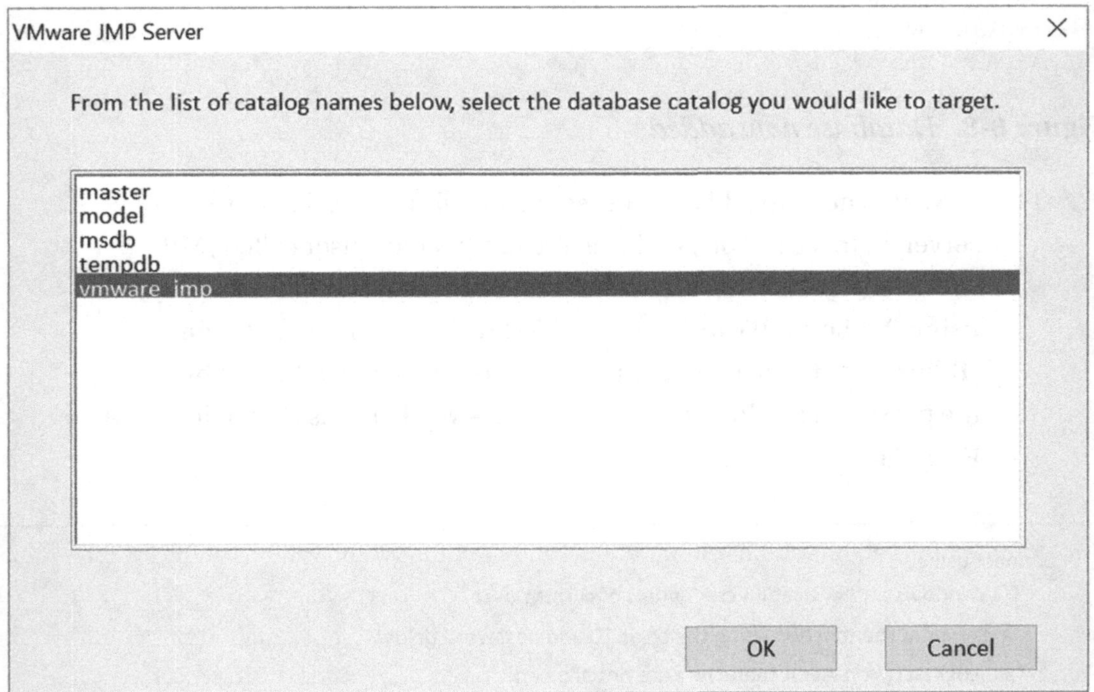

Figure 8-11. *Selecting the JMP database*

17. Click to select the database that you want to use for the JMP Server. In the test lab example, this database has been called **vmware_jmp**.
18. Click the **OK** button.
19. You will now return to the database configuration screen which will now show that the **vmware_jmp** database has been successfully added as shown in Figure 8-12.

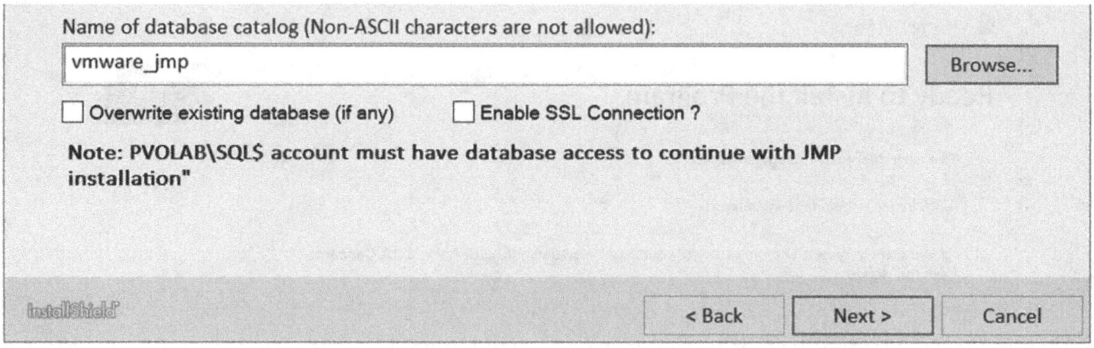

Name of database catalog (Non-ASCII characters are not allowed):
vmware_jmp
Browse...
Overwrite existing database (if any)
Enable SSL Connection ?
Note: PVOLAB\SQL$ account must have database access to continue with JMP installation"
InstallShield
< Back
Next >
Cancel

Figure 8-12. *JMP database now selected*

20. You will also see that there are two check boxes underneath the box containing the database name. The first check box is for **Overwrite existing database (if any)**. If you check this box, then if there is an existing database, then it will be overwritten during the installation.

If you are performing an upgrade of your existing JMP Server, then ensure that this check box is left unchecked; otherwise, you will overwrite the current configuration information.

---

21. The second check box is to **Enable SSL Connection**. Checking this option ensures that the traffic between the JMP Server and the SQL Server database is secured over SSL.

If you enable SSL, then you need to ensure that the TLS/SSL certificate installed on the SQL Server also gets imported into the Windows local certificate store on the JMP Server. If you do not do this, then the JMP Server installation will fail.

---

22. Once you have configured your options and entered the database details, click **Next ►**.

23. You will see the **Ready to Install the Program** screen as shown in Figure 8-13.

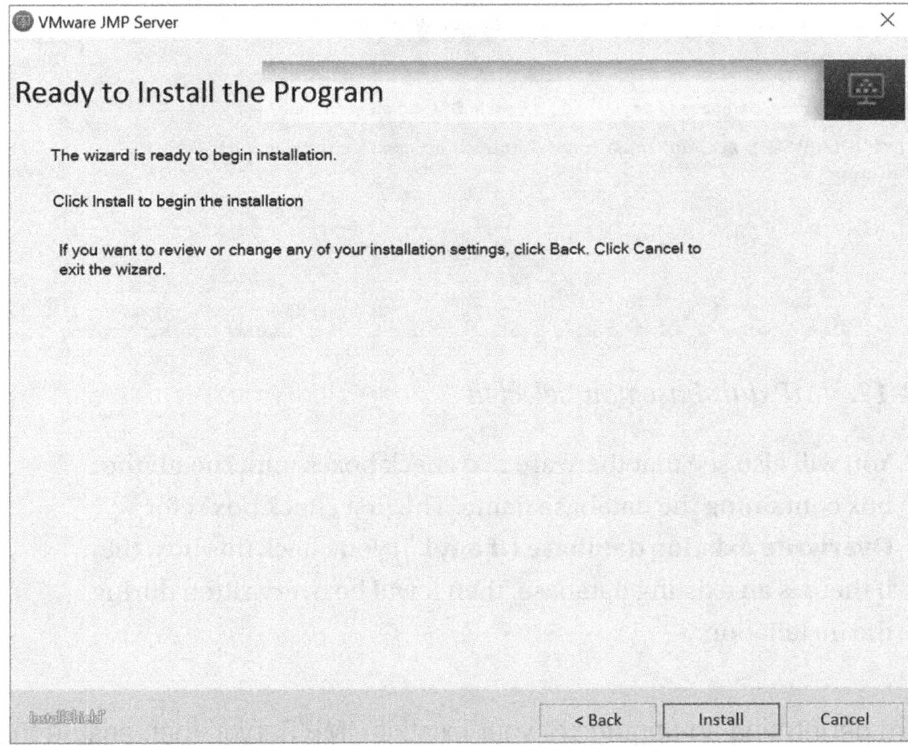

***Figure 8-13.** JMP Server ready to be installed*

24. Click the **Install** button.

25. You will now see the Installing VMware JMP Server screen as shown in Figure 8-14.

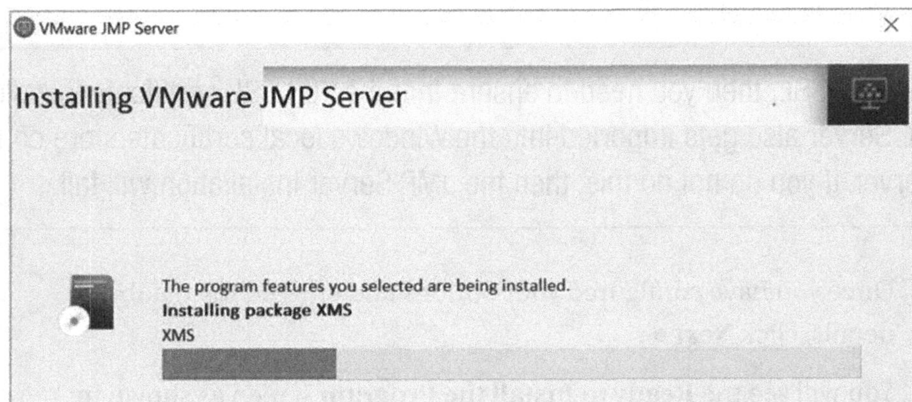

***Figure 8-14.** JMP Server installation progress*

26. Once the installation has completed, you will see the **Installation Complete** screen as shown in Figure 8-15.

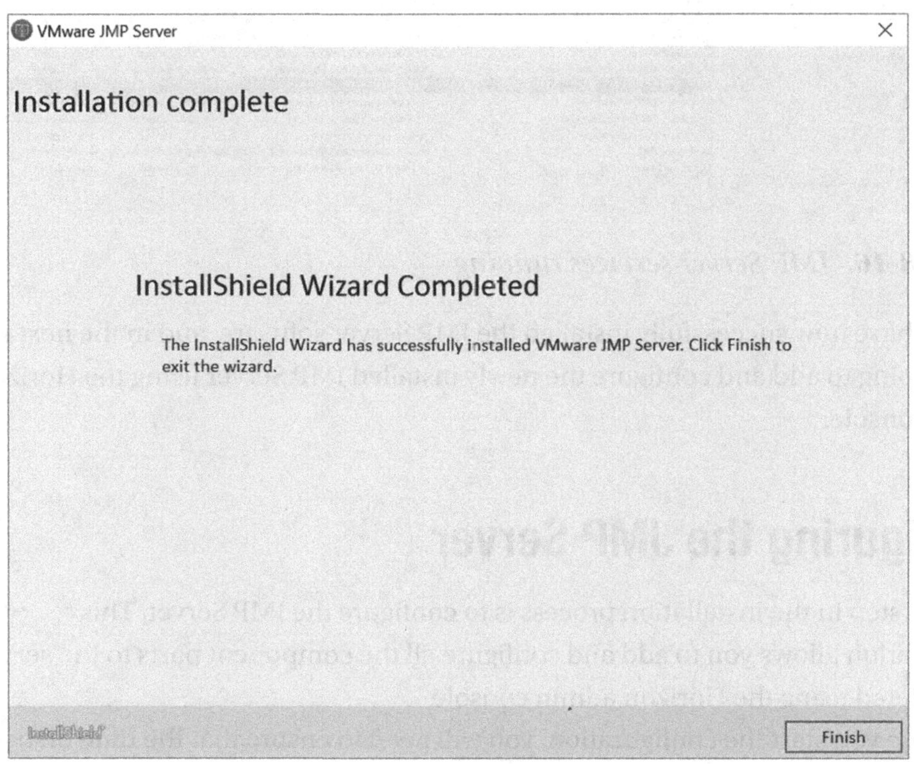

***Figure 8-15.** JMP Server successfully installed*

27. Click **Finish** to complete the installation.

28. The JMP Server runs as a service and is managed using the Horizon Console. Therefore, you will not see any program icons on the desktop of the server. To ensure it is installed correctly and is up and running, launch the Service management console and scroll down to your VMware services. Out of those listed, you will see the VMware JMP services as shown in Figure 8-16.

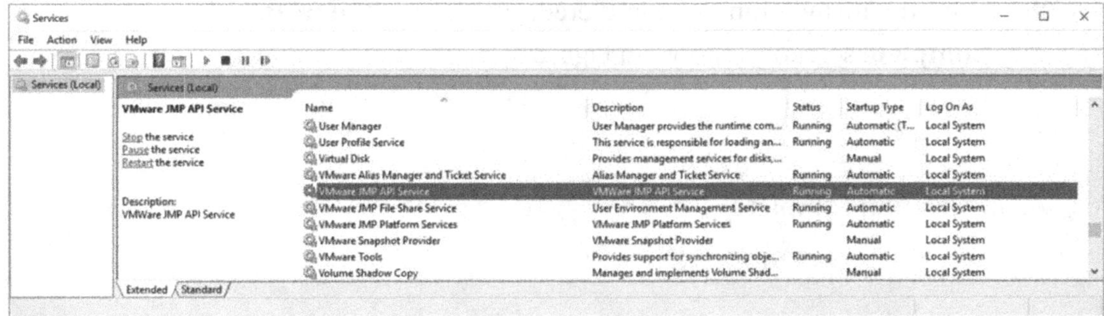

Figure 8-16. *JMP Server services running*

You have now successfully installed the JMP Server software, and in the next section, we are going to add and configure the newly installed JMP Server using the Horizon admin console.

Configuring the JMP Server

The next step in the installation process is to configure the JMP Server. This configuration allows you to add and configure all the component parts to the server and is completed using the Horizon admin console.

Before you start the configuration, you will need to ensure that the time on both the Horizon Connection Server and the JMP Server are synchronized with each other. We will complete this task in the next section.

Time synchronization

The delivery of virtual desktop machine happens in real time, so the Horizon Connection Server and the JMP Server must have their clocks synchronized. This is so that the authentication process between the two servers is successful. If it is not in sync, then the workflow features will simply not work.

When using the JMP Integrated Workflow features delivered using the Horizon Console, the JMP Server authenticates a token that it receives from the Horizon Connection Server. A token is then sent in return from the Connection Server back to the JMP Server. If the time between the Connection Server and the JMP Server is not synchronized, then the token will be rejected, and therefore the workflow will fail.

It is a recommended best practice to synchronize the time by using the ESXi host server hosting the Horizon Connection Server and the JMP Server as the time source. In turn, these should use an Internet-based time service. You also need to make sure that on your ESXi host servers, you have the Time Configuration option configured and that it is using a Network Time Protocol (NTP) client as well as an external time source such as ntp.org.

To configure the time synchronization on each of the servers, follow the steps described:

1. On the Horizon Connection Server, open a command prompt by pressing Windows key + R, and typing **cmd** in the **Run** box, followed by the Enter key.

2. From the command line, change to the following directory: **C:\Program Files\VMware\VMware Tools**

3. Type the following command:

```
VMwareToolboxCmd.exe timesync enable
```

4. You will see something like Figure 8-17.

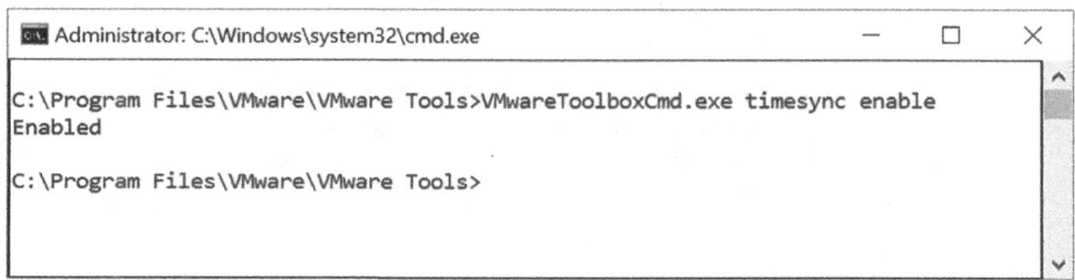

***Figure 8-17.** Enabling timesync on the Horizon and the JMP Server*

5. Once you have done this on the Horizon Connection Server, you need to do exactly the same on the JMP Server.

The JMP Server has now been successfully installed and configured.

The next task is to configure all the different components, including App Volumes, and bring them altogether in the Horizon administration console.

Adding the JMP orchestration components

In this section, we are going to configure the JMP Server using the new Horizon Console. This part of the configuration brings together all the component parts, including App Volumes.

You cannot configure the JMP Server using the old Horizon Administrator. You will need to be running a version of Horizon that includes the new Horizon Console.

To configure the JMP Server, follow the steps as described:

1. From the desktop of the Horizon Connection Server, double-click the Horizon 7 Administrator icon. Alternatively, you could connect via a browser using the address of the server such as `http://horizon-7.pvolab.com/newadmin`. You will see the screenshot in Figure 8-18.

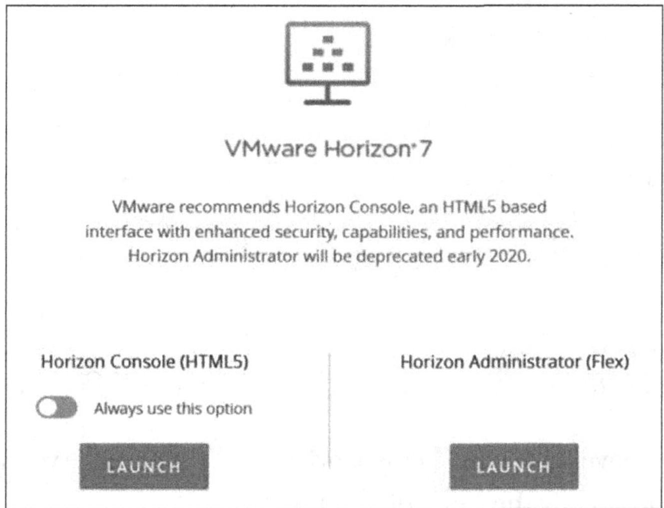

Figure 8-18. *Logging in to the Horizon Connection Server*

2. Click the **LAUNCH** button under **Horizon Console (HTML5).**
3. You will see the login box as shown in Figure 8-19.

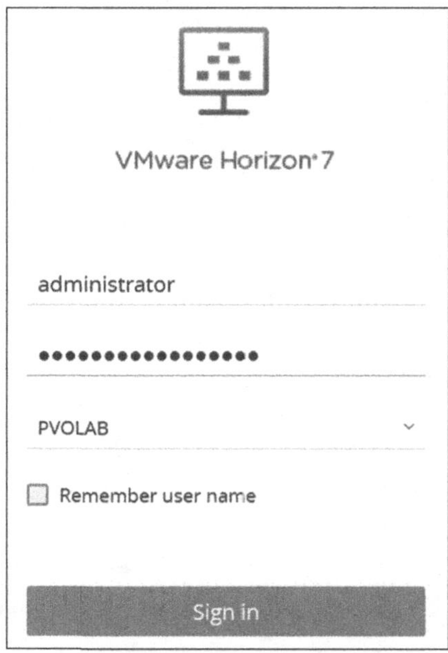

Figure 8-19. *Horizon 7 Connection Server login box*

4. Log in with the administrator account and the administrator password and then click **Sign in.**
5. You will now see the Horizon Console as shown in Figure 8-20.

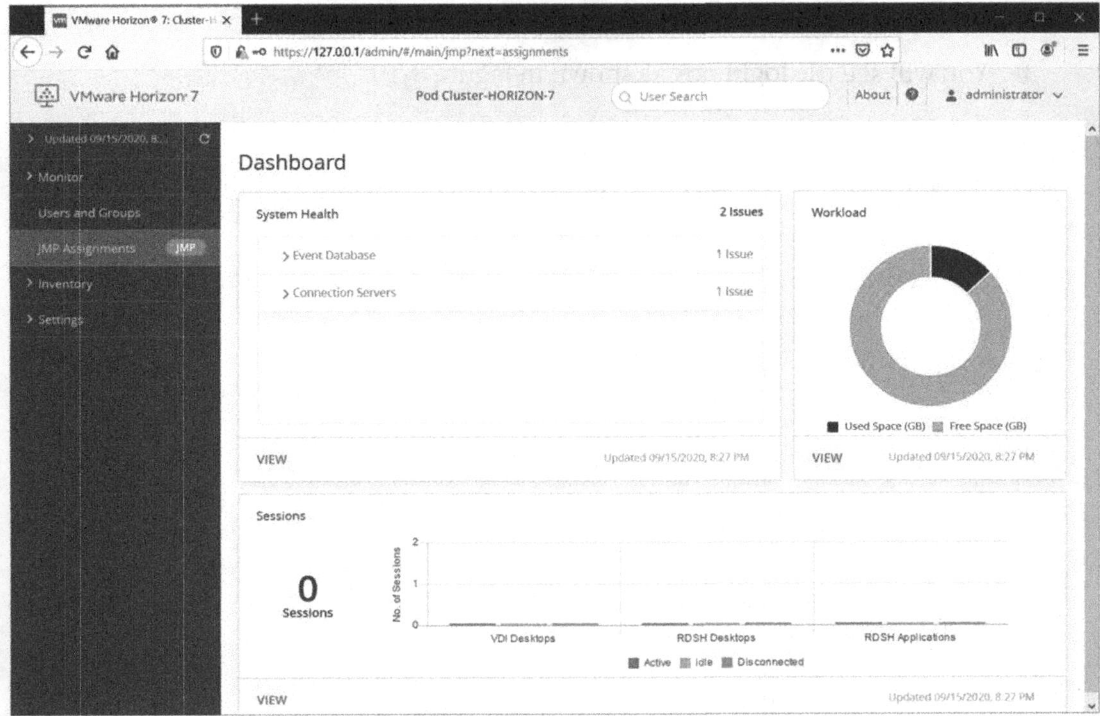

Figure 8-20. *Horizon 7 Connection Server dashboard*

6. In the left-hand menu, navigate to **JMP Assignments** and then click it. You will see the **JMP Settings** screen as shown in Figure 8-21.

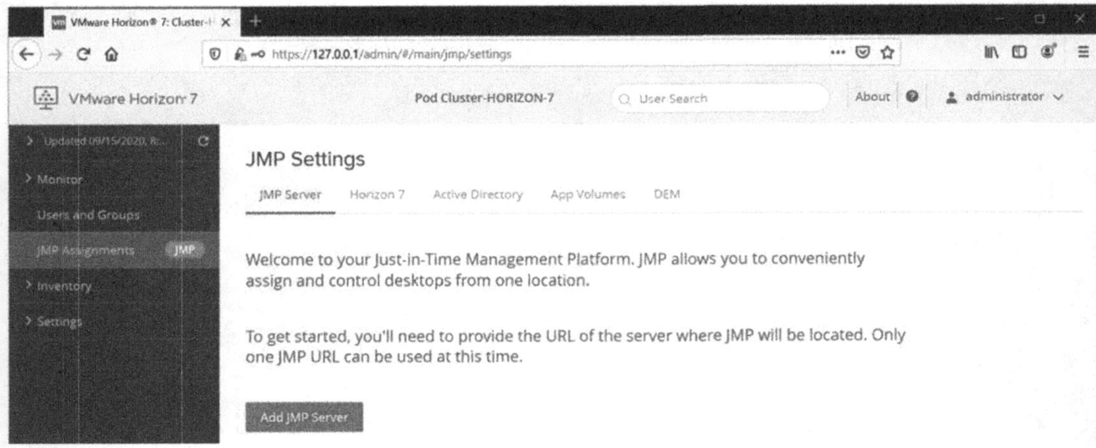

Figure 8-21. *Horizon 7 Connection Server dashboard*

7. Now click the **Add JMP Server** button. You will see the **Add JMP Server** dialog box as shown in Figure 8-22.

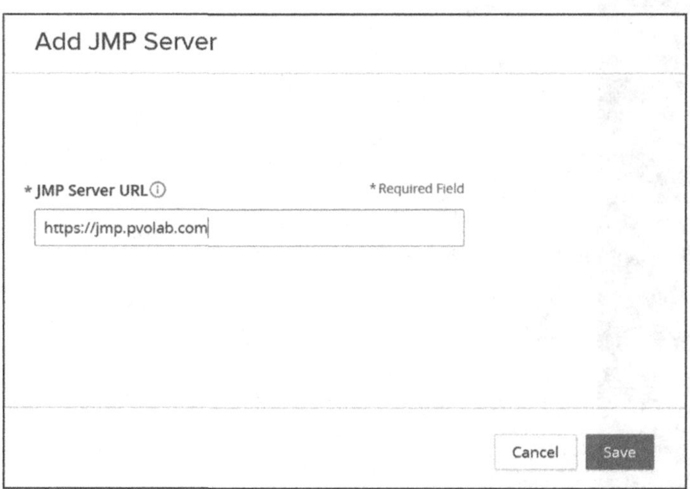

Figure 8-22. *Adding the details of the JMP Server*

8. In the **JMP Server URL** box, enter the address of the JMP Server. In the test lab, this is **`https://jmp.pvolab.com`**.

9. Click the **Save** button.

10. You will now see the **JMP Settings** screen which now shows that the JMP Server is validated. It also lists a number of other components that you will need to have the address, username, and password details of the other components that you plan to install. This screenshot is shown in Figure 8-23.

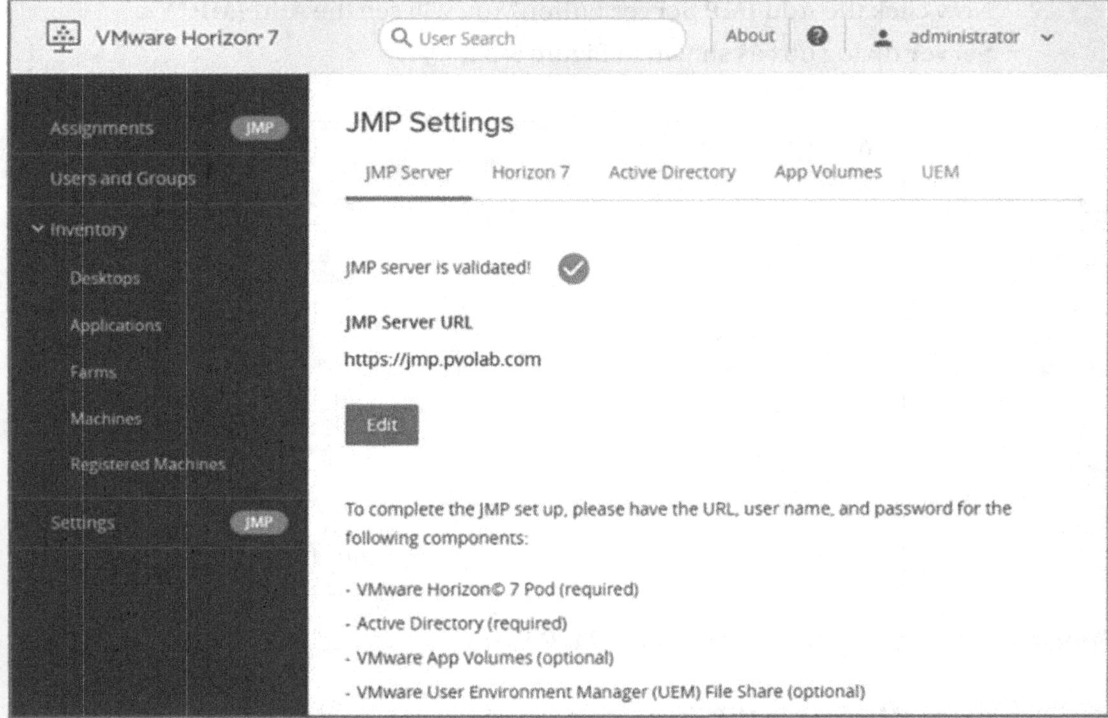

Figure 8-23. *JMP Server successfully added*

11. Next, click **Horizon 7**. You will see the screenshot in Figure 8-24.

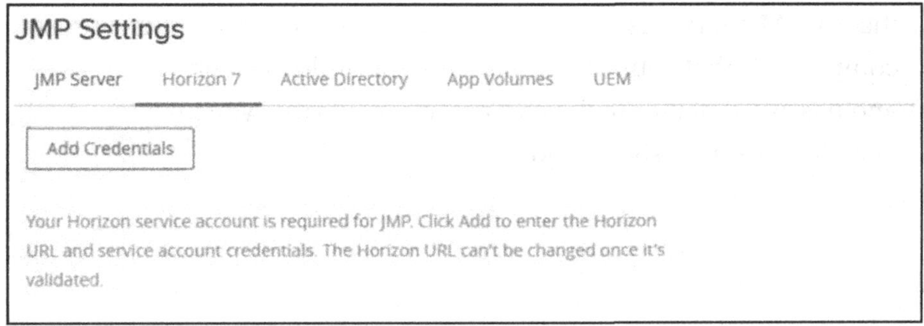

Figure 8-24. *Adding the Horizon 7 details to the JMP Server*

12. Click the **Add Credentials** button.

13. You will now see the **Edit Horizon** dialog box as shown in Figure 8-25.

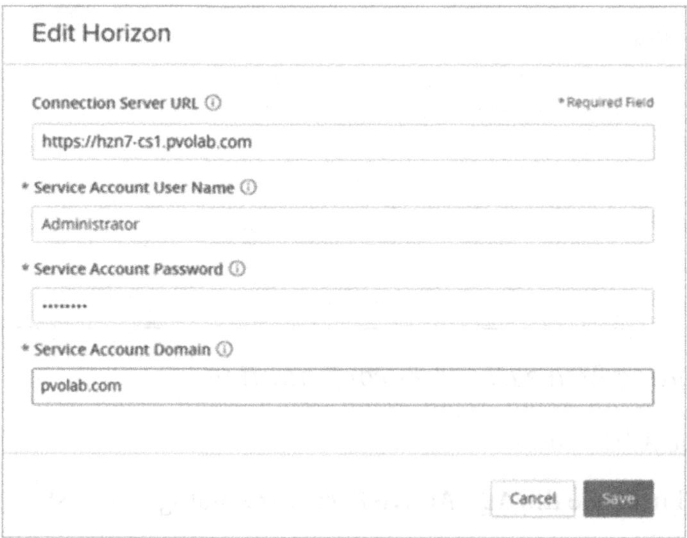

Figure 8-25. *Editing the Horizon Connection Server*

14. In the **Connection Server URL** box, type in the name of the Horizon Connection Server that will be used for creating your stateless virtual desktop machines. In the test lab, the address of the Horizon Connection Server is `https://hzn7-cs1.pvolab.com`.

15. In the **Service Account User Name** box, type in the Horizon service account user, and in the **Service Account Password** box, type in the password for this account. In this example, the Administrator account has been used.

16. The last box is for the **Service Account Domain** name. This is the domain in which the service account lives. In the test lab, the service account is in the pvolab.com domain, so enter this into the box.

17. Now click the **Save** button.

18. Next, click **Active Directory** from the options.

19. You will see the configuration page as shown in Figure 8-26.

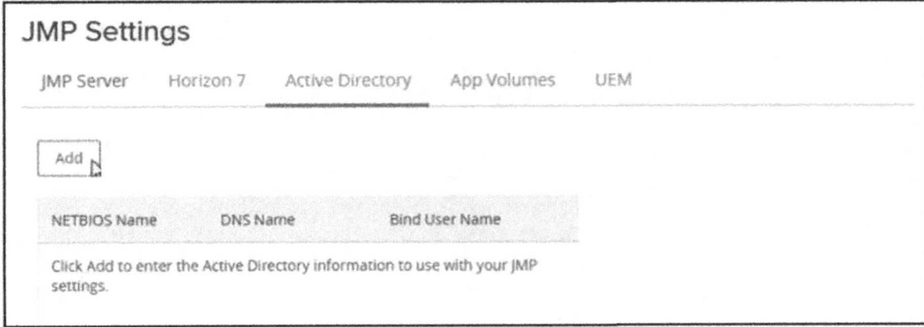

Figure 8-26. *Adding Active Directory configuration*

20. Click the **Add** button.

21. You will now see the **Add Active Directory** dialog box as shown in Figure 8-27.

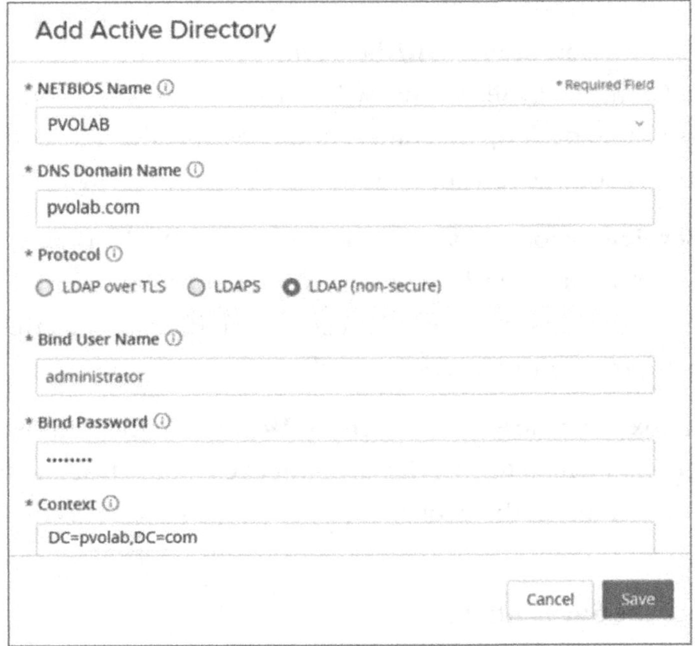

Figure 8-27. *Adding Active Directory configuration*

22. In the **NETBIOS Name** box, type in the NETBIOS name for your domain. In the test lab, the NETBIOS name is **PVOLAB.**

23. Next, in the **DNS Domain Name** box, type in the full name of your domain. For example, in the test lab, this would be **pvolab.com**.

24. In the Protocol section, click the radio button to select the protocol you want to use for communication between the JMP Server and Active Directory. You have the following options to choose from:

    - LDAP over TLS
    - LDAPS
    - LDAP (non-secure)

25. Next, in the **Bind User Name** box, type in the name of a user account that has the appropriate privileges and access to your Active Directory domain. This account will need to be able to create machine and user accounts. This is required so that as new virtual desktop machines are built and deployed dynamically, these accounts will need to be created automatically and dynamically too.

26. In the **Bind Password** box, you need to enter the password for the Bind User Name you entered previously.

27. Finally, you have the **Context** box. In this box, you need to type in the domain naming context for your domain. Enter this using your domain's distinguished name or DN. In the test lab example, you would enter **DC=pvolab, DC=com** as the context.

28. Now click the **Save** button.

29. You will now see the **App Volumes** configuration screen as shown in Figure 8-28.

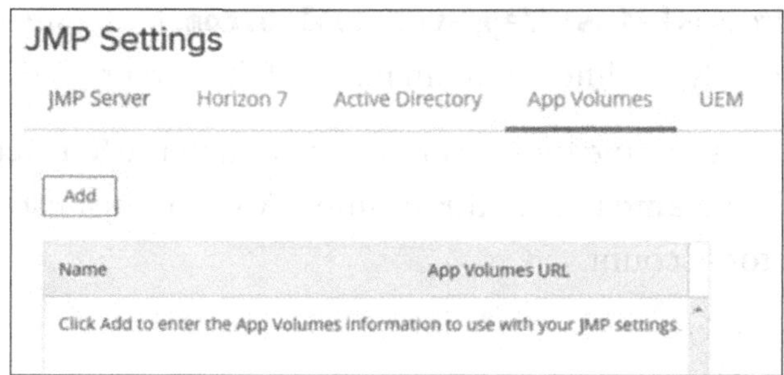

Figure 8-28. *App Volumes configuration for the JMP Server*

30. Click the **Add** button.

31. You will now see the **Add App Volumes Instance** dialog box as shown in Figure 8-29.

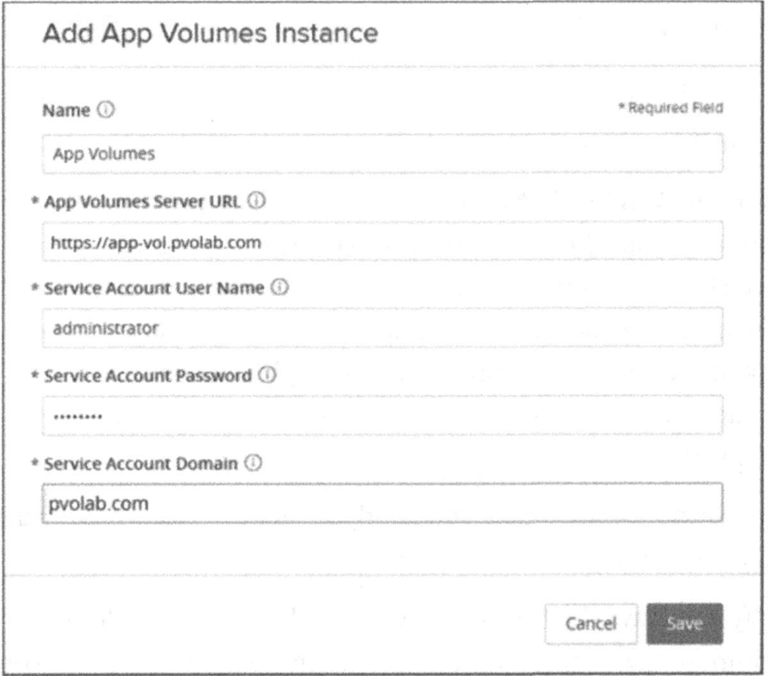

Figure 8-29. *App Volumes configuration dialog box*

32. In the **Name** box, enter the name you want to use to identify your App Volumes Manager. This is optional and so not a required field.

33. Next, in the **App Volumes Server URL** box, type in the address of your App Volumes Manager. In this example, the App Volumes Server address is **`https://app-vol.pvolab.com`**. Make sure that you use the fully qualified domain name of the server (FQDN).

34. Now enter a username for the service account in the **Service Account User Name** box. In this example, we have just used the administrator account.

35. Then in the **Service Account Password** box, type in the password for the service account you used in the previous step.

36. Finally, in the **Service Account Domain**, type in the name of the domain. This is the domain in which the service account exists. In this example, the administrator account resides in the pvolab.com domain.

37. Click the **Save** button.

38. You will now see the final configuration screen for **UEM** as shown in Figure 8-30.

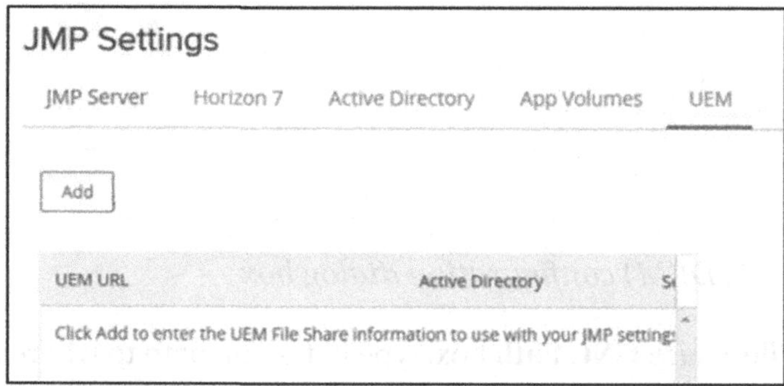

Figure 8-30. *Adding the UEM (DEM) server to JMP*

39. Click the **Add** button. You will see the **Add UEM File Share** dialog box as shown in Figure 8-31.

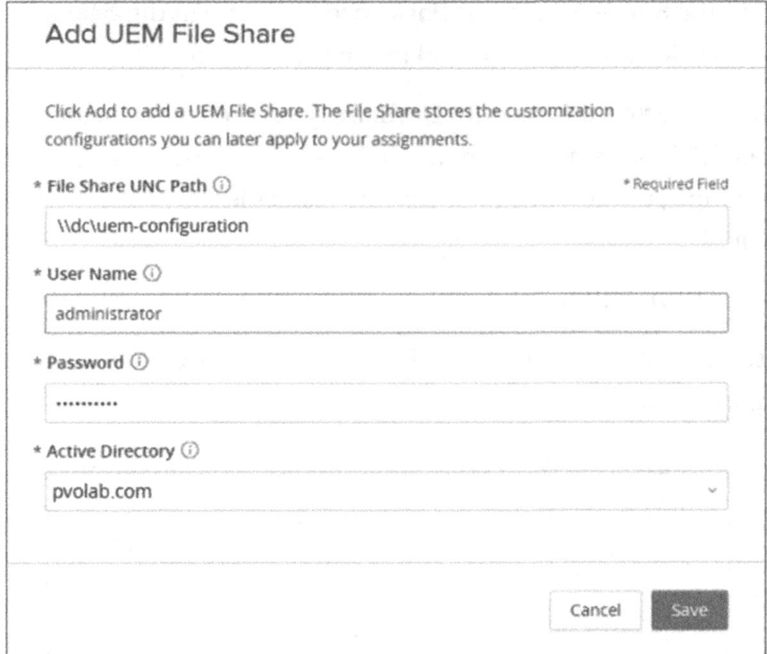

Figure 8-31. *UEM (DEM) configuration dialog box*

40. In the **File Share UNC Path** box, type in the full path to where the UEM configuration files folder is located. In this example, the path we have used is \\dc\uem-configuration.

41. Then, in the **User Name** box, enter a username that has access to the shared UEM configuration folder.

42. In the **Password** box, type in the password for this username account you used in the previous step.

43. Finally, in the **Active Directory** box, type in the name of the Active Directory domain.

44. Now click the **Save** button.

You have now successfully installed and configured the JMP Server including adding the additional orchestration components such as UEM/DEM and Instant Clone virtual desktop machines.

Chapter summary

This chapter has focused on the VMware Just-in-Time Management Platform, or JMP. JMP has been designed to orchestrate a number of VMware components to deliver just-in-time virtual desktops, built using vSphere Instant Clones, applications by adding layered applications delivered by App Volumes, and finally the user personalization and date piece via VMware UEM or DEM.

The JMP Server, which we installed and configured throughout this chapter, delivers the automation engine that brings all these existing and preinstalled component solutions together so that an end user receives a complete desktop experience.

For the IT admin teams, it reduces the management overheads of managing individual component parts as well as costs now that desktops and apps are delivered as and when required and on demand using stateless virtual desktop machines. Moving to a stateless environment reduces the amount of infrastructure that is required.

In terms of App Volumes, it plays a key role in the overall solution. App Volumes is responsible for delivering applications to the end users in a stateless environment. These applications are attached to the virtual desktop machines as the end user logs in and can be added and removed dynamically.

In the next chapter, we are going to look at delivering published apps with Microsoft RemoteApp with the apps delivered by App Volumes.

CHAPTER 9

RDSH and App Volumes

The focus of this book so far has been how App Volumes delivers layered applications to virtual desktop machines, enabling the seamless delivery of applications to stateless virtual desktops.

But App Volumes is not just limited to desktop operating systems. It can also be used within a server environment when delivering published applications. As applications are abstracted from the underlying operating system and delivered as application layers, then this enables App Volumes to provide the same functionality to RDSH servers. The published applications in this case are not installed directly onto the RDSH server, but instead the applications are delivered as layers that get attached to the RDSH server.

There are numerous reasons for deploying App Volumes to deliver applications within an RDSH environment. The first reason is to enable scalability. Previously, when you added RDSH servers to your environment, you would need to install the apps on each server. With App Volumes, the apps are abstracted and delivered on demand. This means that you can easily deploy new RDSH servers enabling scalability with App Volumes automatically and dynamically adding the applications as you grow and scale. You are effectively building a stateless RDSH farm.

Applications are far easier to update and manage. You only need to update the individual application layer and not every app on every server, individually, which also means you get consistency across your server farm as you will be using the same version of the applications.

In this ninth chapter, we are going to first look at setting up an RDSH environment in the test lab, install the App Volumes Agent so that we can create an application layer, and then test the solution using the RemoteApp feature. This will then give us the foundation to use RDSH within other application publishing solutions such as VMware Horizon Apps or Citrix Virtual Apps and Desktops.

P. von Oven, *Delivering Applications with VMware App Volumes 4*,
https://doi.org/10.1007/978-1-4842-6689-2_9

The architecture

We are going to start by looking at the high-level architecture of how App Volumes and RDSH servers fit together.

Figure 9-1 shows how App Volumes delivers applications in an RDSH environment.

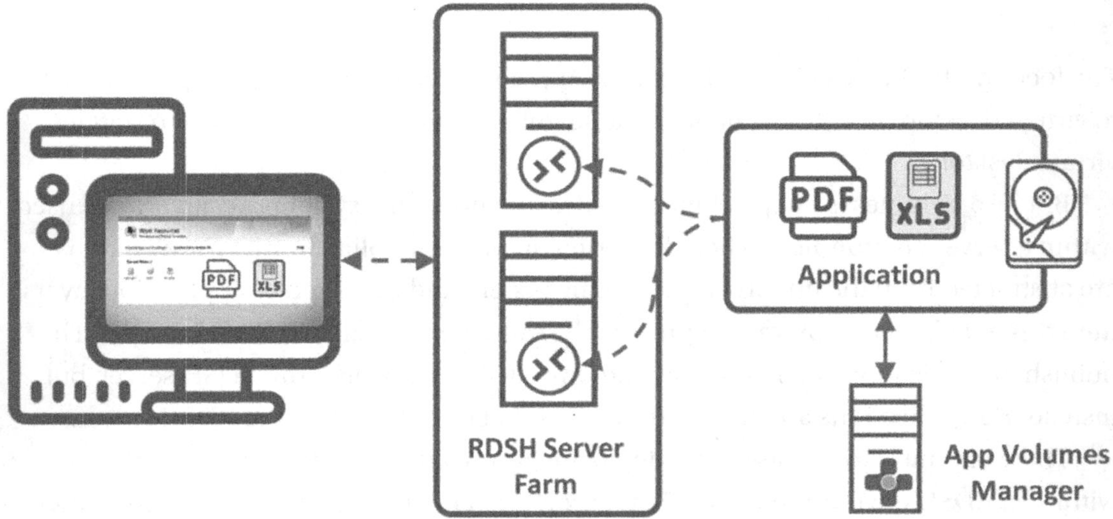

Figure 9-1. *RDSH servers and App Volumes delivered applications*

Now that we have discussed the use cases and the high-level architecture, in the next section, we will work through the process of building an application and then delivering it to your end users.

We are going to describe this as a two-step process and will start by describing the workflow of building RDSH, creating an application by capturing it using a capture machine, resulting in an application ready to be assigned.

In the second step, we are going to assign the application that was captured and then assign it to an RDSH server and then ensure the apps are available for end users to launch.

Capturing applications for RDSH

The first step we need to complete is to capture the application you want the RDSH server to deliver to the end users. In an earlier chapter, we captured applications that were going to be used by individual users via their virtual desktop machine - in this case, virtual desktop machine running the Windows 10 operating system. Therefore, applications were captured using a Windows 10 virtual desktop machine as the capture machine.

In this chapter, as the applications are going to be delivered using an RDSH server, then the applications will need to be captured using the same OS. So, in this example, we will use a Windows Server 2016 virtual machine with the RDSH role installed as our capture machine.

The process we are going to follow for capturing the application for RDSH is illustrated in Figure 9-2.

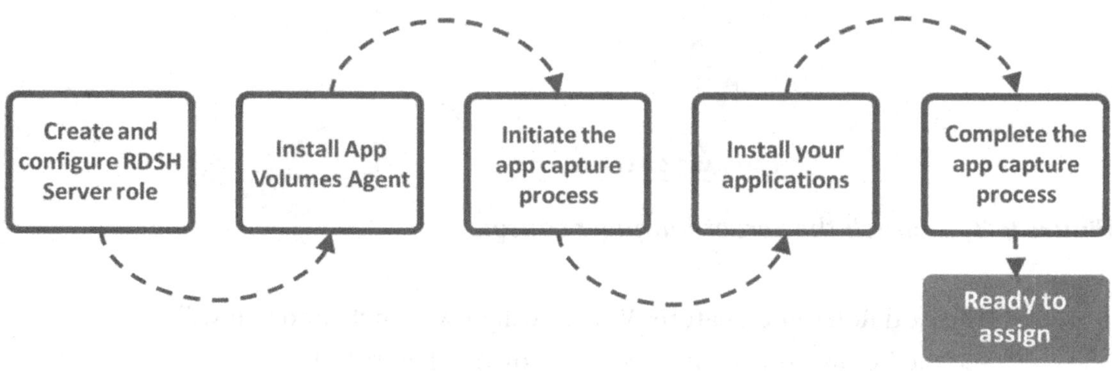

Figure 9-2. *Step 1: Configuring RDSH and capturing an application*

We are going to start with the configuring of the RDSH role on a server that has already been set up with an OS, hostname, IP address, and networking.

Installing and configuring the RDSH role

To set up the RDSH role, follow the steps as described:

1. Open a console to the server on which you are going to add the RDSH role. In the test lab example, we have built and configured a server called rdsh-apps.pvolab.com.

2. From the **Server Manager** console, and the **Dashboard** page, click **(2) Add roles and features** as shown in Figure 9-3.

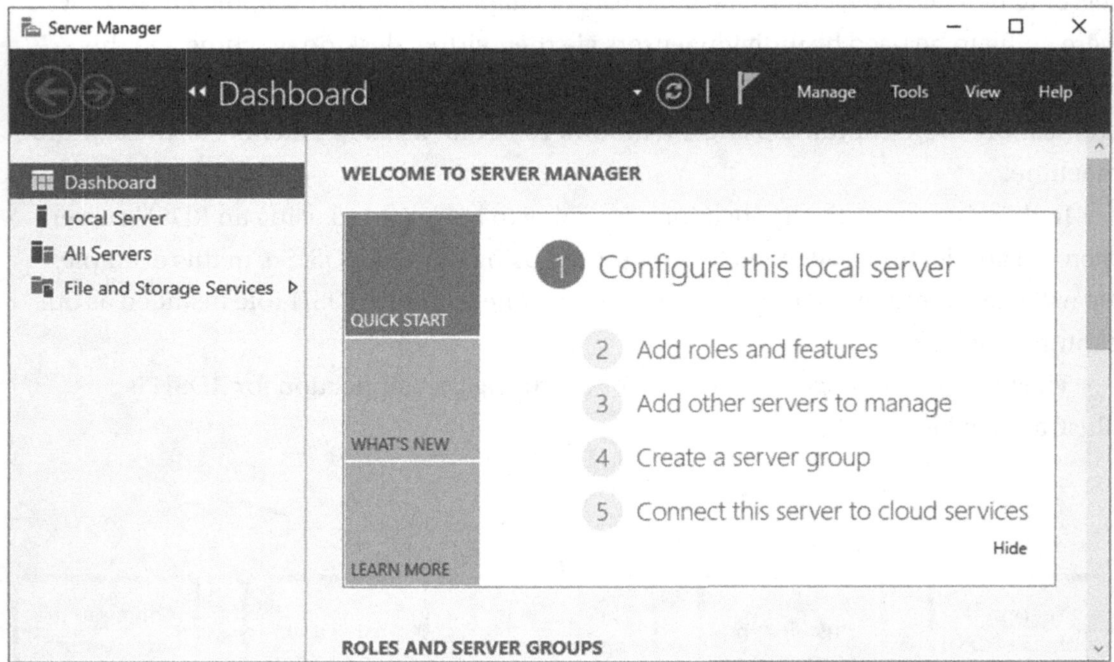

Figure 9-3. *Launch the Server Manager console*

3. The Add Roles and Features Wizard will now launch, and you will see the Before you begin screen as shown in Figure 9-4.

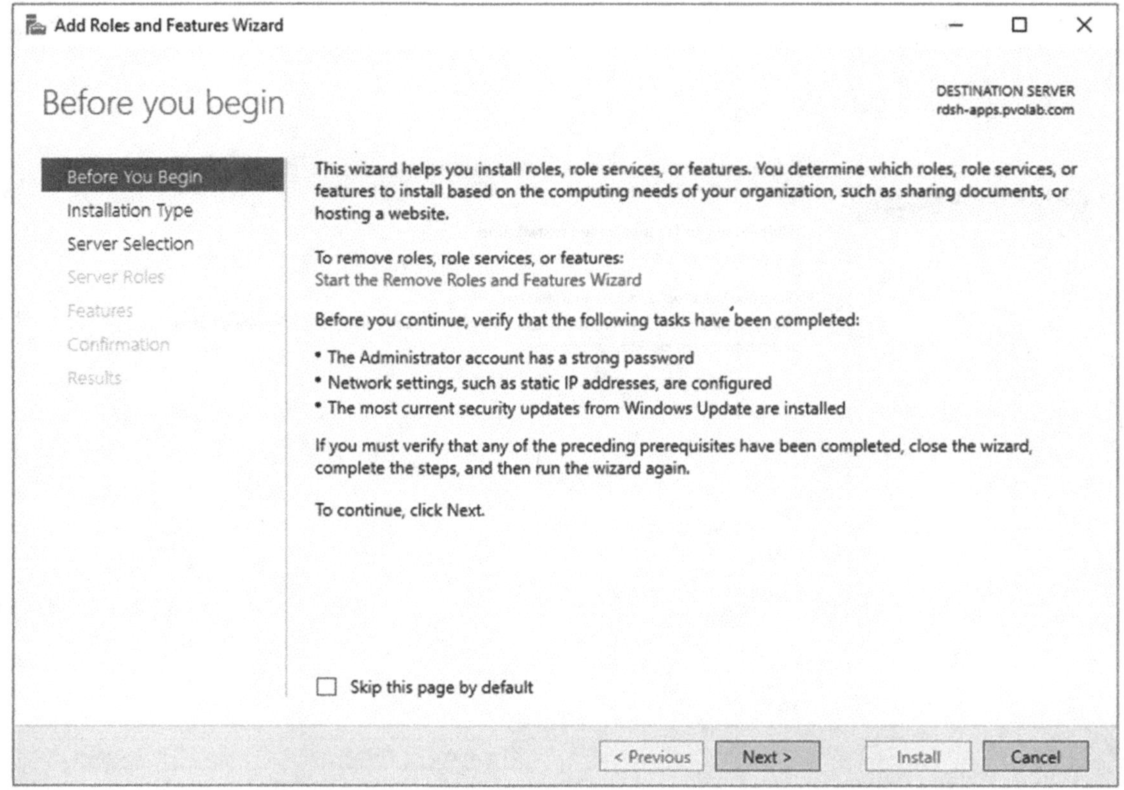

Figure 9-4. *Add Roles and Features Wizard - Before you begin screen*

4. You can opt to skip this page in future by checking the **Skip this page by default** box.
5. Click **Next ➤** to continue.
6. You will see the **Select installation type** screen as shown in Figure 9-5.

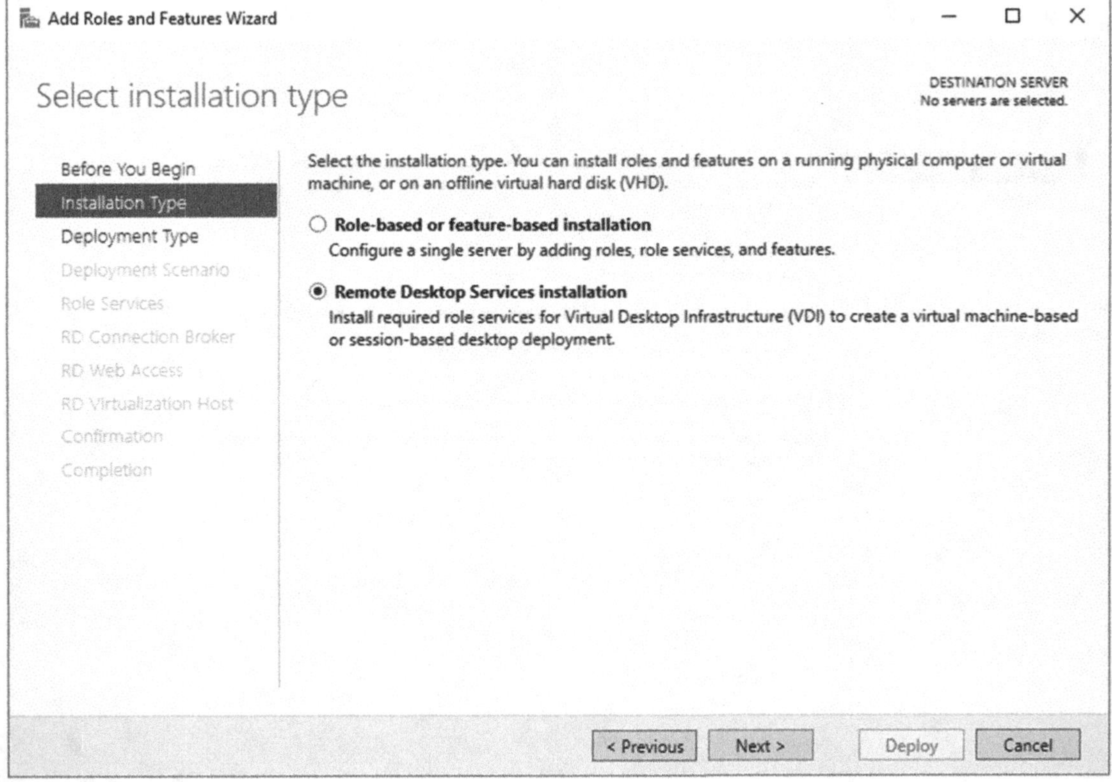

Figure 9-5. *Selecting the installation type screen*

7. Click the **Remote Desktop Services installation** radio button and then click **Next ➤** to continue.

8. You will now see the **Select deployment type** screen as shown in Figure 9-6.

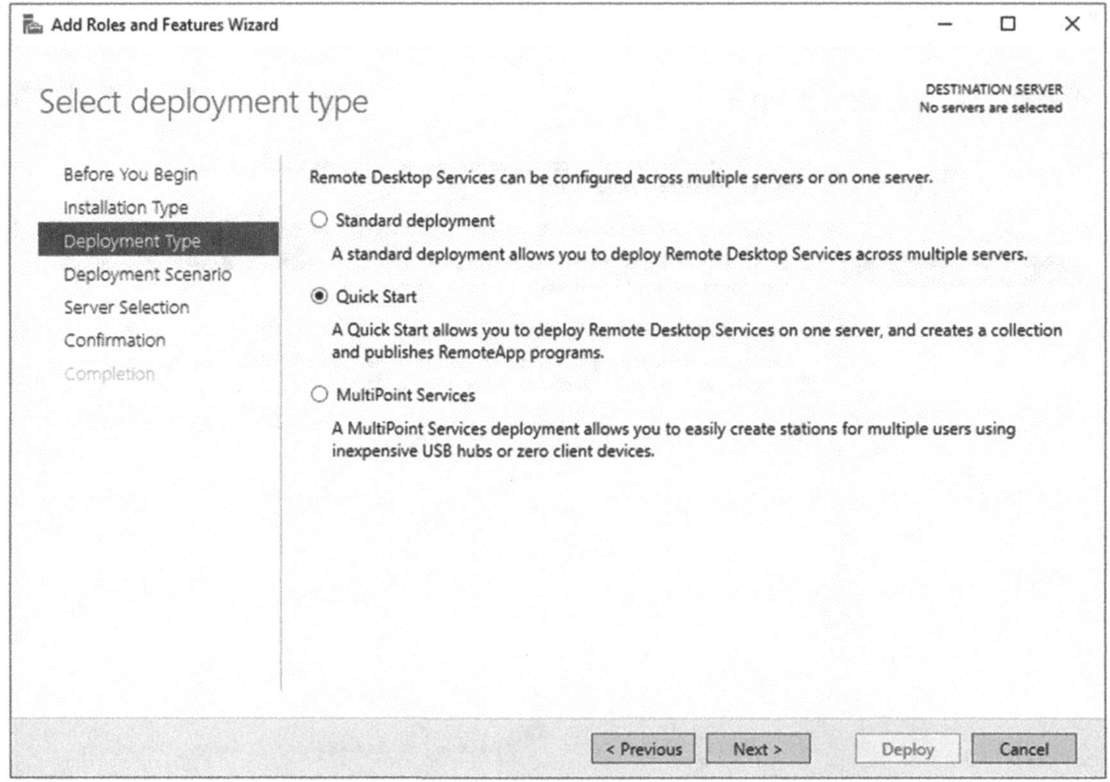

Figure 9-6. *Selecting the deployment type screen*

9. Click the **Quick Start** radio button. Quick start allows you to quickly and simply set up the RDSH role on a single server and automatically set up several applications that are already installed as part of the OS, namely, WordPad, Calculator, and Paint. This helps with testing before adding the App Volumes applications and demonstrates that the RDSH server is functioning correctly. It also therefore aids troubleshooting when the App Volumes apps are added.

10. Click **Next ➤** to continue.

11. You will now see the **Select deployment scenario** screen as shown in Figure 9-7.

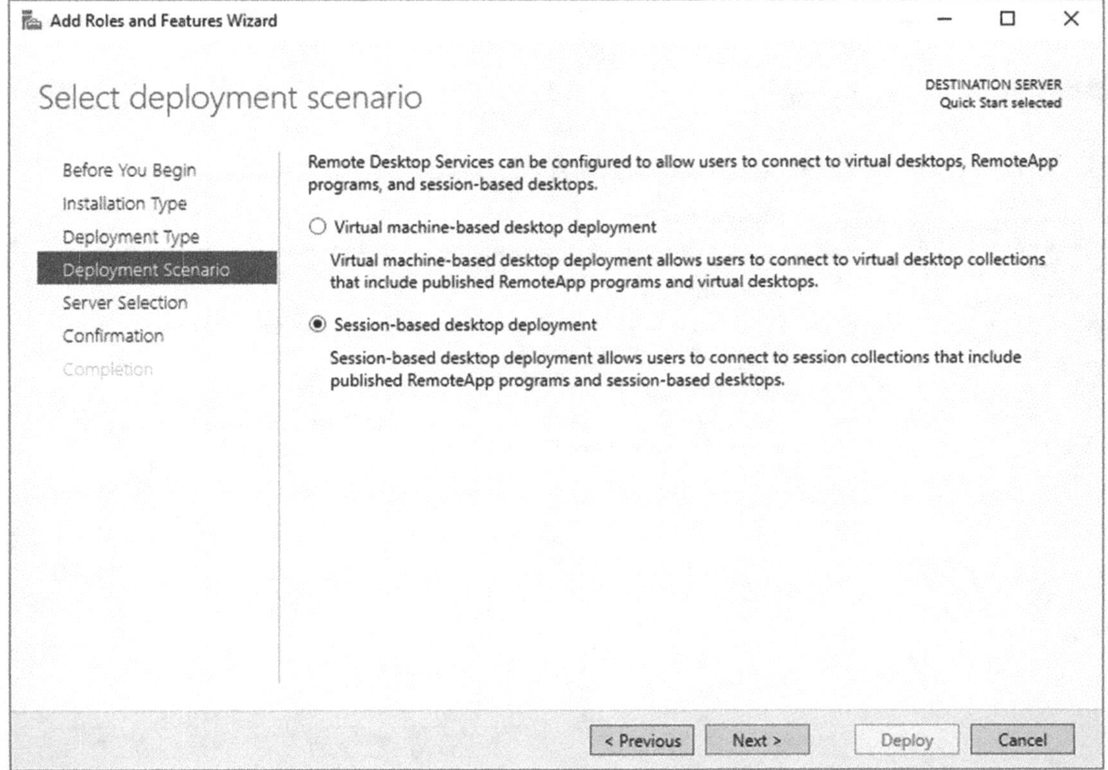

Figure 9-7. *Selecting the deployment scenario screen*

12. Click the **Session-based desktop deployment** radio button. This enables end users to connect to session collections (collections of available applications) that are published using the RDSH server and the RemoteApp feature. We will use RemoteApp to test the applications are available and launch correctly before replacing that with Horizon Apps as the broker in a future chapter.

13. Click **Next ➤** to continue.

14. You will now see the **Select a server** screen.

15. Select the server which you are going to use for capturing the App Volumes applications. Select the server name by clicking to highlight it from the list shown in the Server Pool box. In the test lab example, this is the server called **rdsh-apps.pvolab.com**.

16. Click the right arrow next to the box to add the server to the Selected box as shown in Figure 9-8.

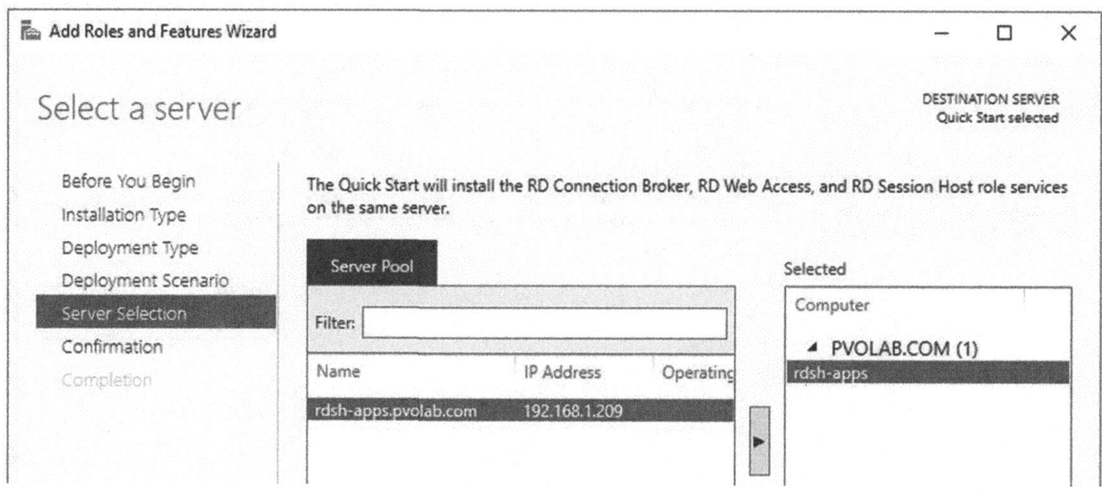

Figure 9-8. *Select a server to install the RDSH role to*

17. Click **Next ➤** to continue.

18. You will now see the **Confirm selections** screen. On this screen, you will see a summary of what is going to be installed on the server. This will be the RD Connection Broker, RD Web Access, and RD Session Host. You will also see that there is a warning message highlighted by the yellow triangle. This states that the server will be restarted once the installation of the role services has been completed.

19. Check the **Restart the destination server automatically if required** box. This means as the server will need to be restarted as part of the installation, then it will be done automatically.

20. This is shown in Figure 9-9.

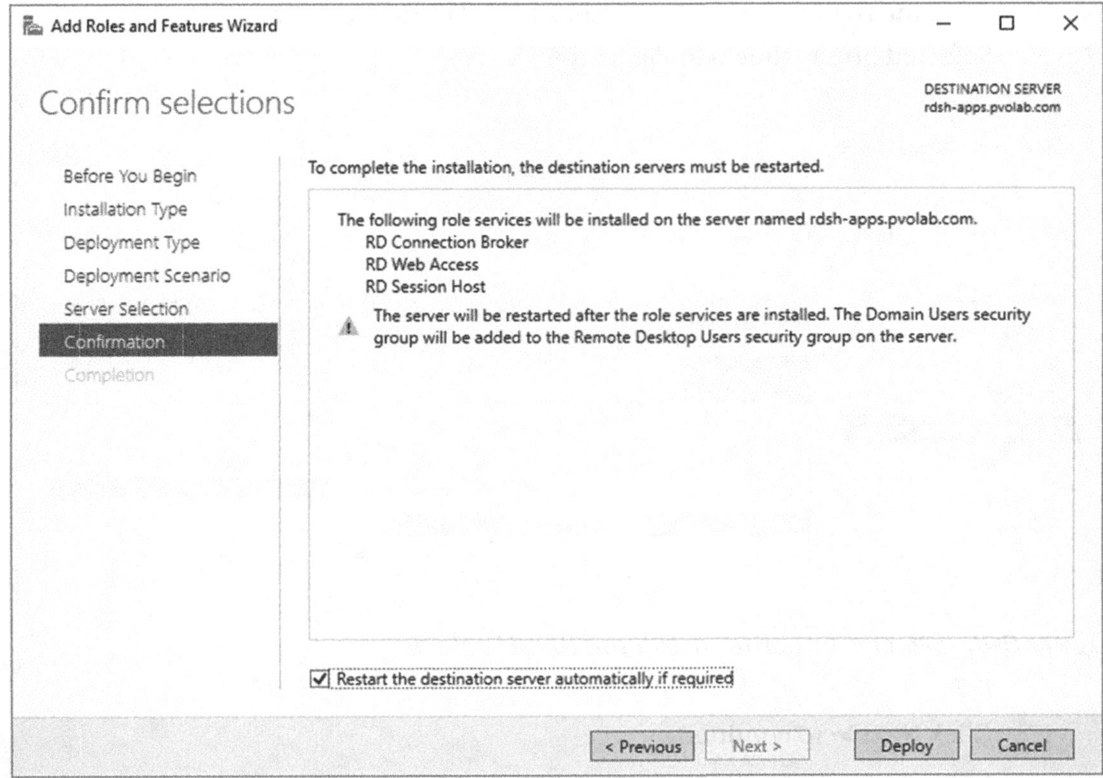

Figure 9-9. *Confirm the installation of the RDSH server roles*

21. Click the **Deploy** button.

22. You will now see the **View progress** screen that shows the progress of each of the individual tasks and features. As we are installing the RDSH role, the installation will include the Remote Desktop Service role services, the Session collection, and the RemoteApp programs that get added by default when the quick start option is selected.

23. This screen is shown in Figure 9-10.

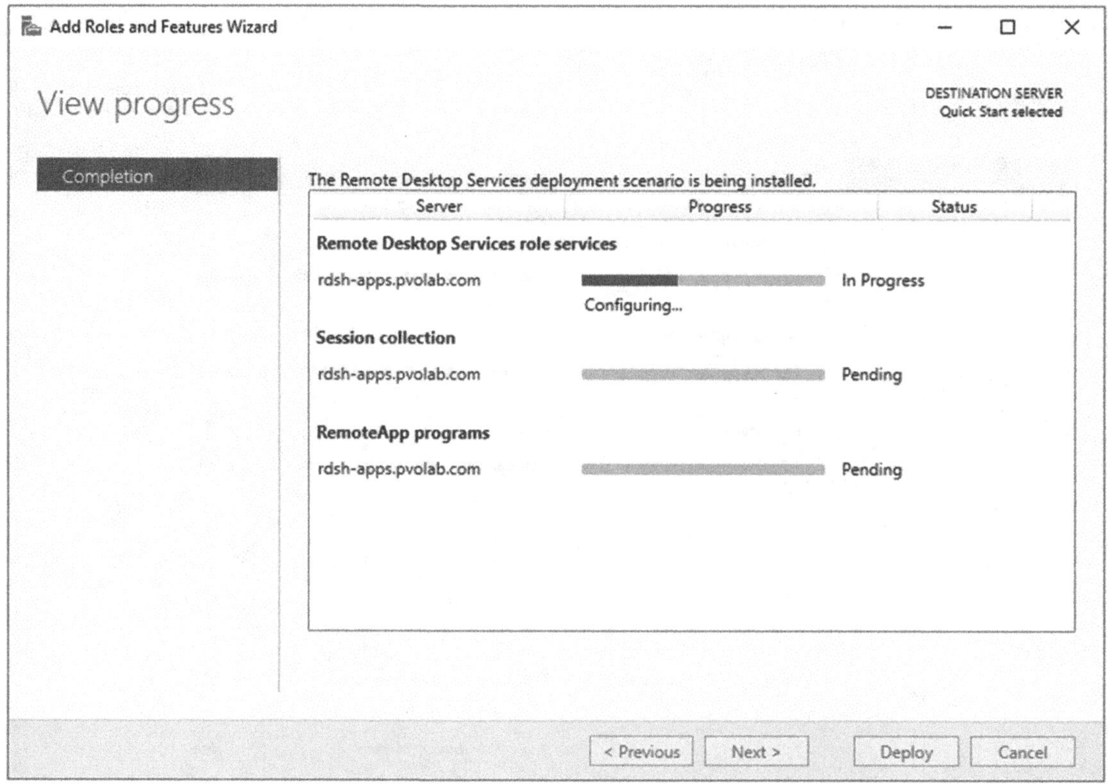

Figure 9-10. *Progress of the RDS deployment*

24. The server will restart during the installation process, and once successfully completed, you will see **Succeeded** against each task as shown in Figure 9-11.

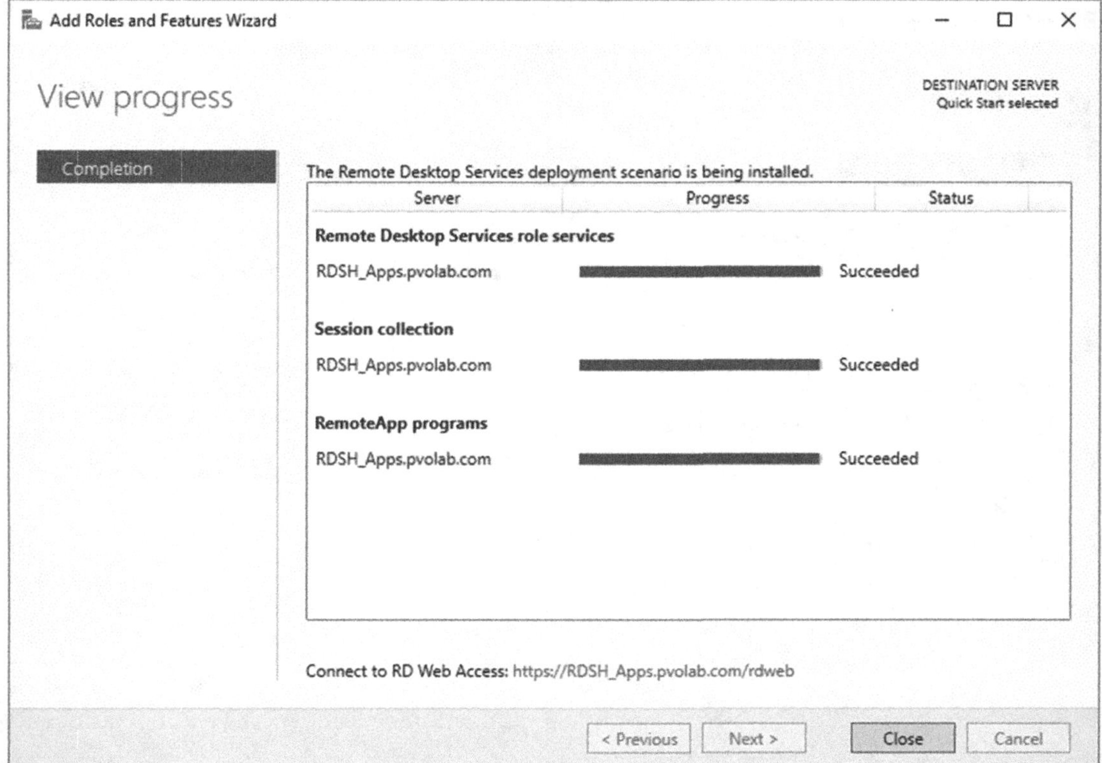

Figure 9-11. *Installation and configuration successfully completed*

25. Finally, you will return to the **Server Manager Dashboard** where you will see that the **Remote Desktop Services** role has been successfully deployed as shown in Figure 9-12.

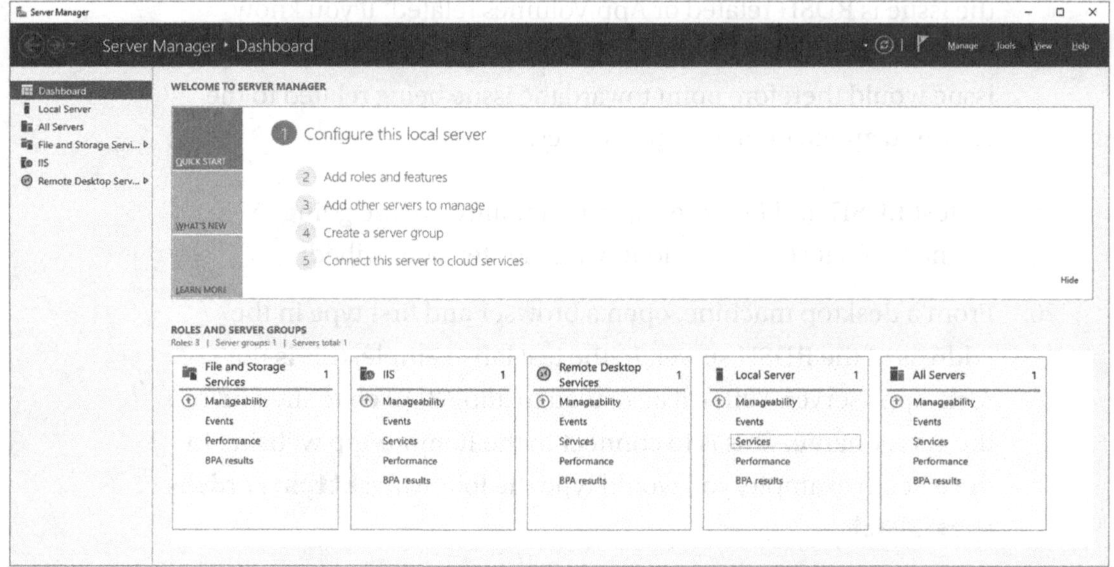

Figure 9-12. *Remote Desktop Services installed and running*

Now that you have completed the installation of the Remote Desktop Services role and it is up and running, you will also need to ensure you have the appropriate licensing in place as shown in the message box that will appear (Figure 9-13).

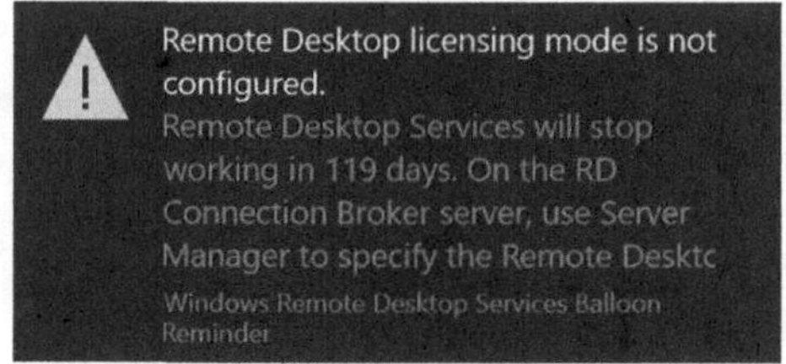

Figure 9-13. *Remote Desktop licensing mode not configured warning*

The next thing to do before we start to use the server to capture an application is to ensure that an end user can connect and launch the applications that were published as part of the quick start application collection.

This approach ensures that the RDSH and RemoteApp elements are running correctly before capturing App Volumes applications. It can help with any future troubleshooting later as to whether the issue is RDSH related or App Volumes related. If you know that RDSH and RemoteApp are functioning as expected, then any issue would therefore point toward the issue being related to the captured application in App Volumes.

To test RDSH and RemoteApp functionality, we are going to connect as a test using by following the steps described:

26. From a desktop machine, open a browser and first type in the address of the RDSH server. In the test lab example, this is the rdsh-apps server. You will also need to add /RDWeb to the end of the server name. This is to connect to the RemoteApp website. In the test lab example, you would type the following: **`https://rdsh-apps/RDWeb`**.

27. You will see the login box as shown in Figure 9-14.

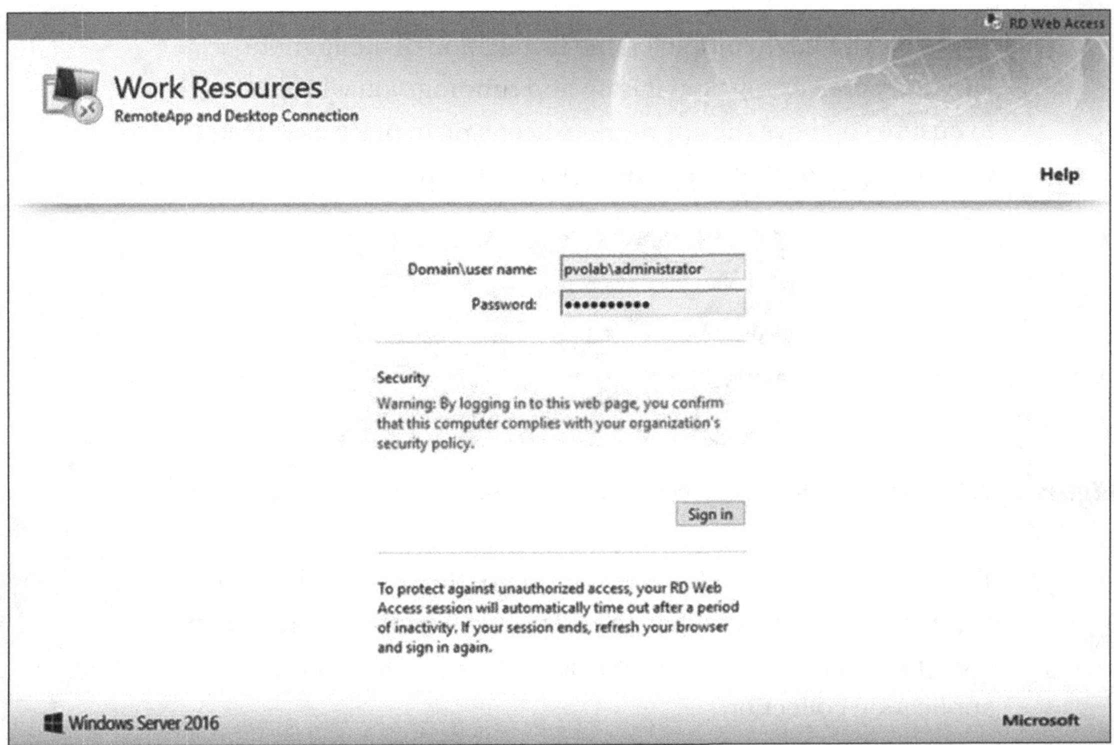

***Figure 9-14.** Logging in to the RemoteApp website*

28. In the **Domain\username** box, type the username in the format specified; in this example, we are going to log in as the administrator, so in the box, type **pvolab\administrator**.

29. Then, in the **Password** box, type in the password for the account you used in the previous step.

30. Click **Sign in.**

31. You will see the RemoteApp screen showing the available apps. In this example, we have WordPad, Calculator, and Paint available as the published apps, as shown in Figure 9-15.

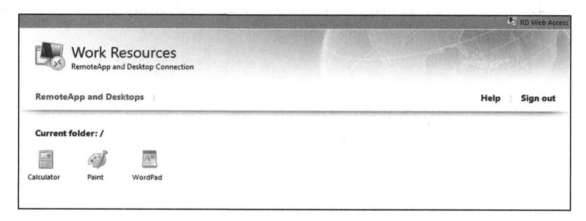

Figure 9-15. *RemoteApp applications*

32. Test that an application launches, and the end user can connect and run it, by double-clicking one of the app icons, in this example, Calculator.

33. You will see the RemoteApp pop-up box showing that the end user is being connected to the application as shown in Figure 9-16.

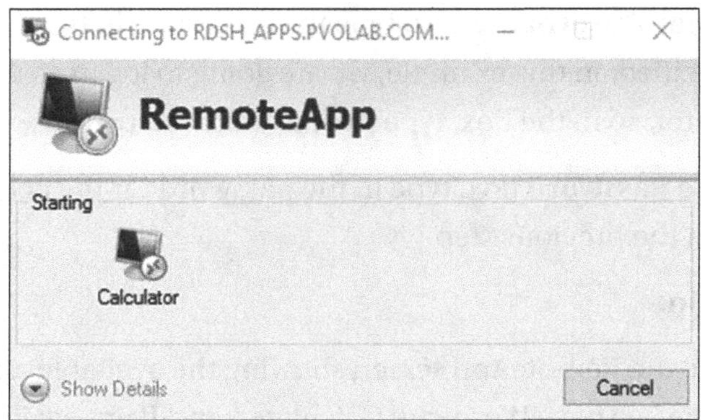

Figure 9-16. *Calculator launching via RemoteApp*

34. Once connected and the app has launched, the end user will see the one in Figure 9-17.

Figure 9-17. *Calculator running as a published app via RemoteApp*

35. Close the Calculator app.

You have now successfully installed the RDSH role on your server that is going to be used to publish your applications.

The next step, as these applications are going to be delivered as App Volumes layers, is to install the App Volumes Agent onto the server.

Installing the App Volumes Agent

Like any other machine to which you want to add App Volumes layered applications, you need to install the App Volumes Agent onto the RDSH server. This enables it to become an App Volumes managed machine. In this example, it will be used to capture applications.

To install the App Volumes Agent, follow the steps described:

1. Navigate to the location of where you have saved the App Volumes Agent installation software. In the example lab, we have a folder called **Software Folder** on the Domain Controller as shown in Figure 9-18.

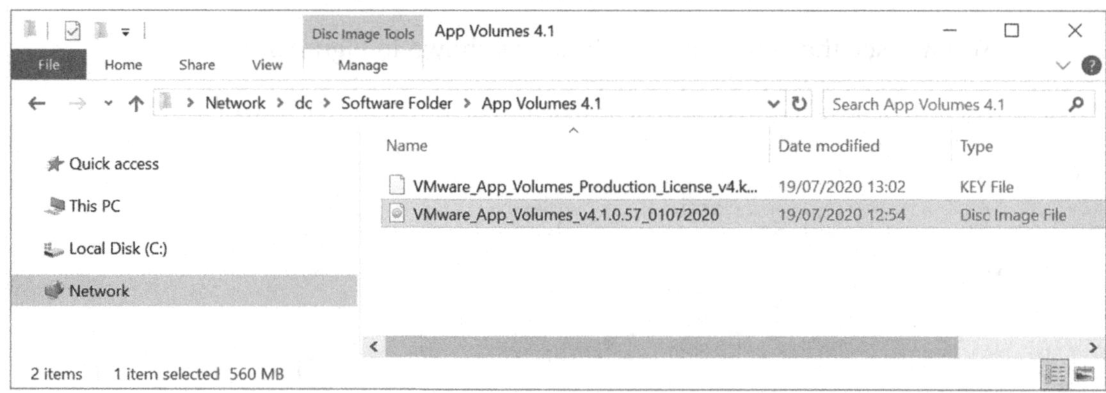

Figure 9-18. *Navigating to the App Volumes installation software*

2. Double-click the **VMware_App_Volumes_v4.1.0.57_01072020.ISO** file to mount it.

3. You will see the .ISO file mount and appear as a DVD Drive with the driver letter of E: as shown in Figure 9-19.

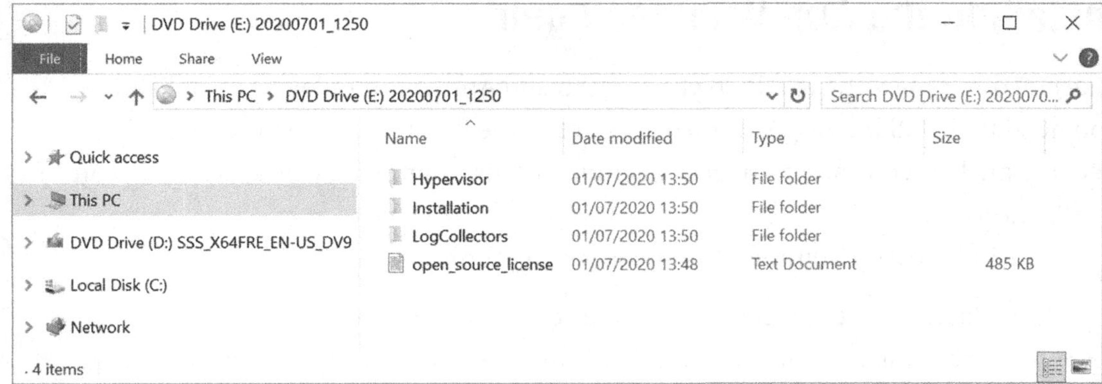

***Figure 9-19.** App Volumes installation software ISO mounted*

4. Double-click and open the **Installation** folder.

5. You will see the contents of the folder as shown in Figure 9-20.

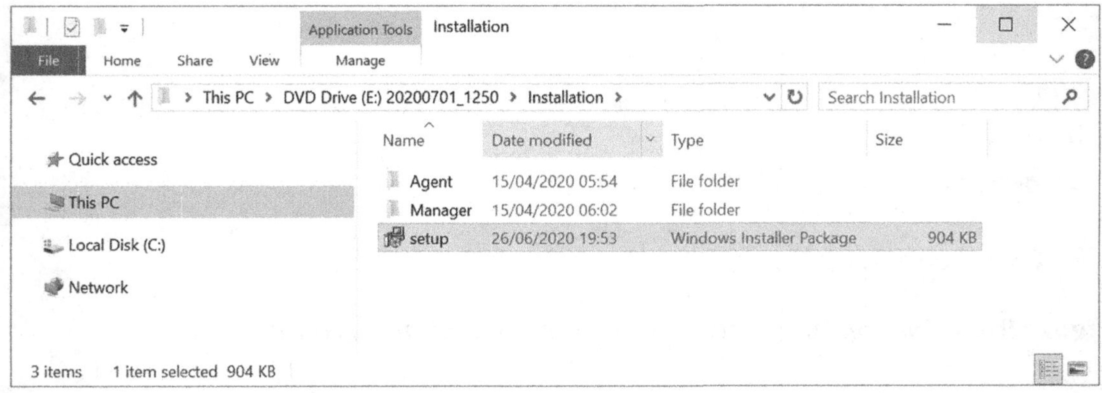

***Figure 9-20.** App Volumes setup installer package*

6. Double-click the **setup** Windows Installer Package.

7. The installer will launch, and you will see the **Welcome to the App Volumes Installer Setup Wizard** screen as shown in Figure 9-21.

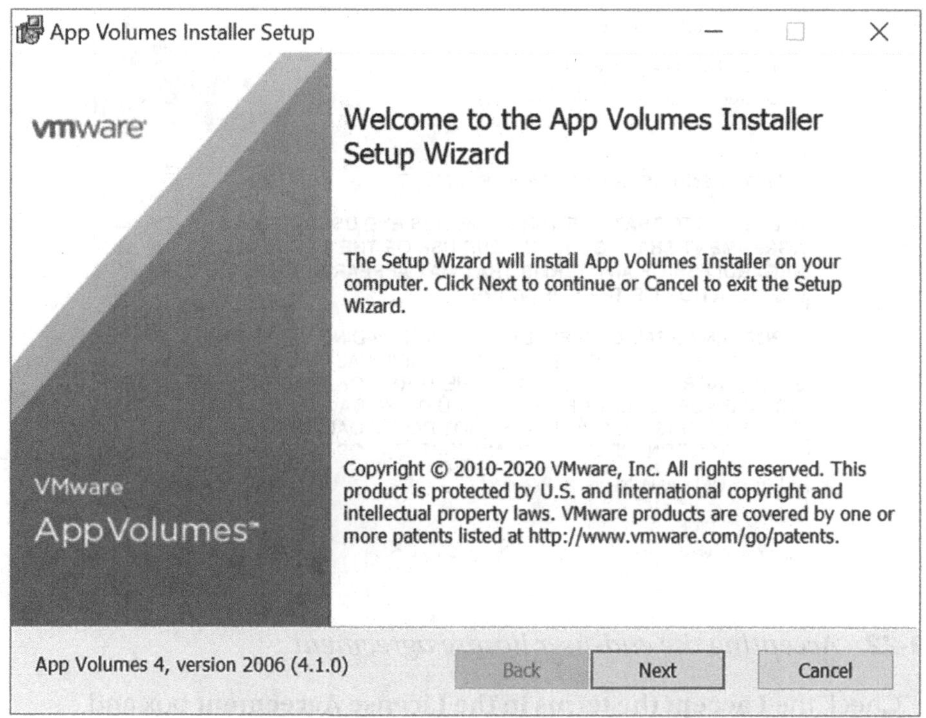

Figure 9-21. *App Volumes installer - Welcome screen*

8. Click **Next** to continue.
9. You will see the **End-User License Agreement** screen as shown in Figure 9-22.

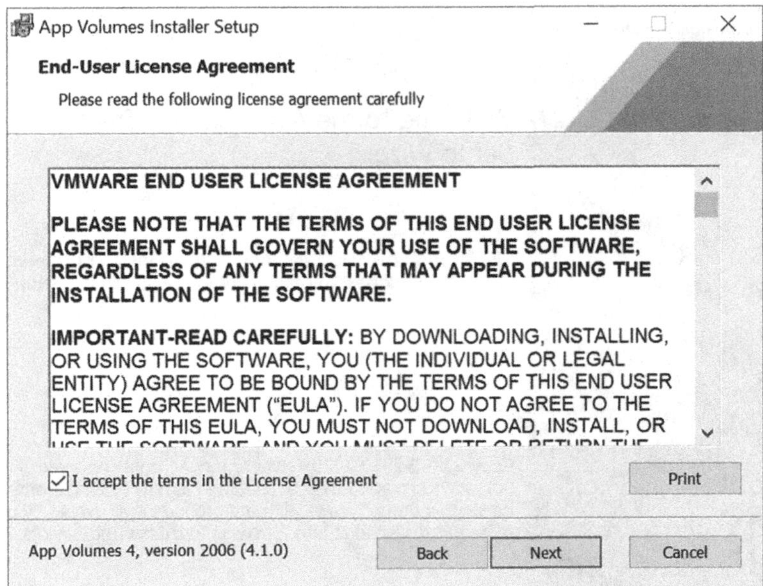

Figure 9-22. *Accepting the end-user license agreement*

10. Check the **I accept the terms in the License Agreement** box and then click **Next.**

11. You will see the App Volumes Install Screen as shown in Figure 9-23.

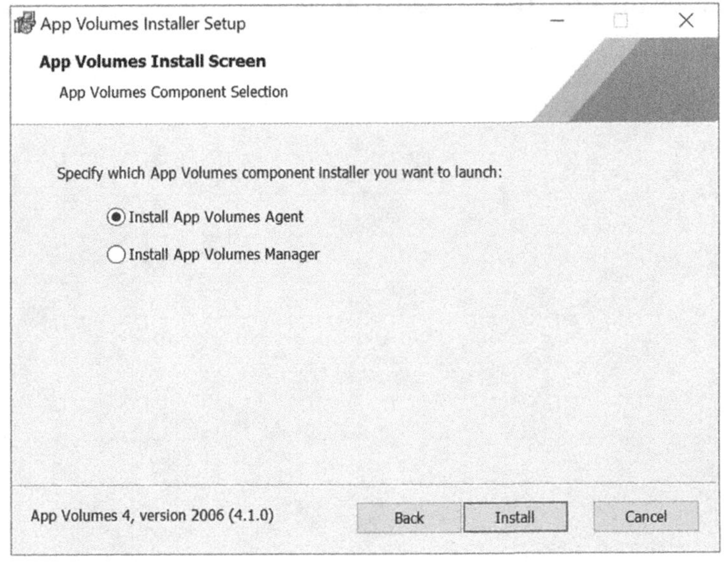

Figure 9-23. *App Volumes Installer screens*

12. Click the radio button for **Install App Volumes Agent**, and then click **Install.**

13. You will see the **Welcome to the App Volumes Agent Setup Wizard** screen as shown in Figure 9-24.

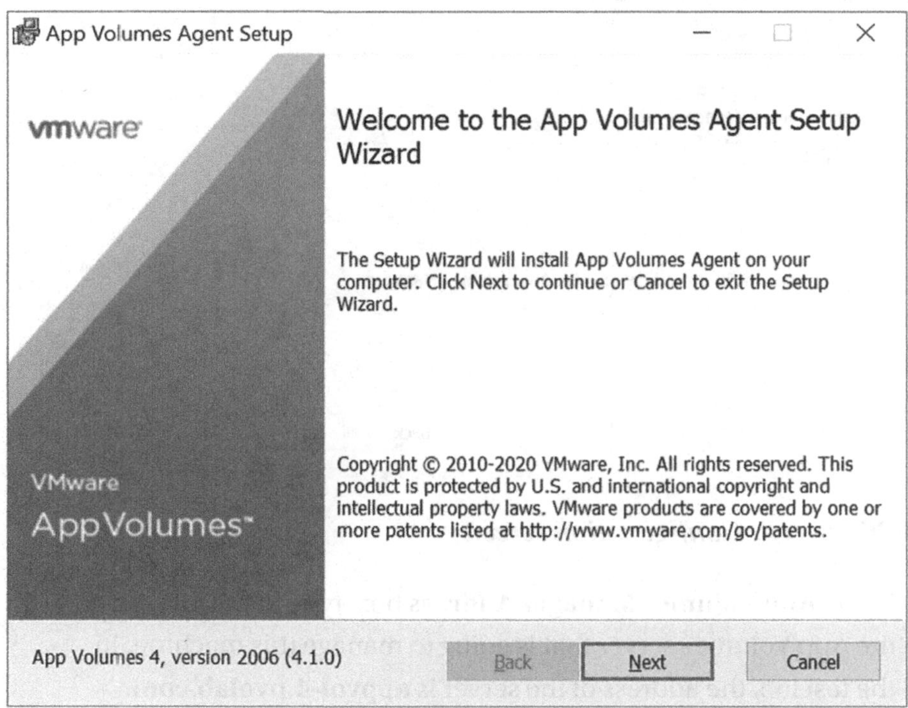

Figure 9-24. *Welcome to the App Volumes Agent Wizard screen*

14. Click the **Next** button.

15. You will see the **Server Configuration** screen as shown in Figure 9-25.

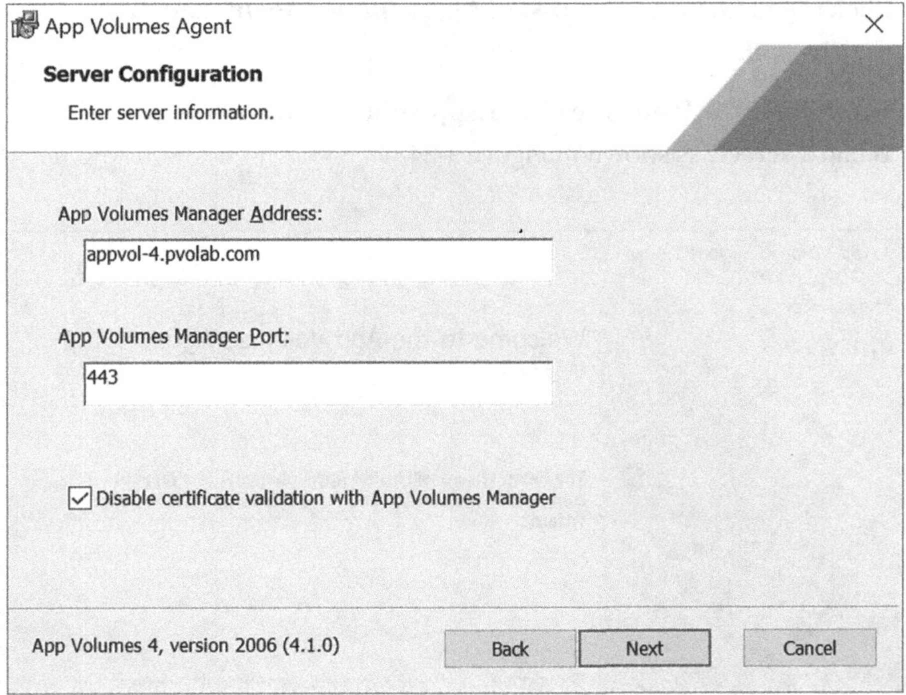

Figure 9-25. *Server Configuration screen*

16. In the **App Volumes Manager Address** box, type in the address to the App Volumes server that is going to manage this machine. In the test lab, the address of the server is **appvol-4.pvolab.com**.

17. Next, in the **App Volumes Manager Port** box, enter the port number that will be used for communication between the agent and the server. In the test lab, we will use the default setting of port **443**.

18. Finally, you have the option of checking a box to **Disable certificate validation with App Volumes Manager**. Note that this reduces the level of security between the agent and the server as it will not check the certificate.

19. Click **Next** to continue.

20. You will see the **Ready to install App Volumes Agent** screen as shown in Figure 9-26.

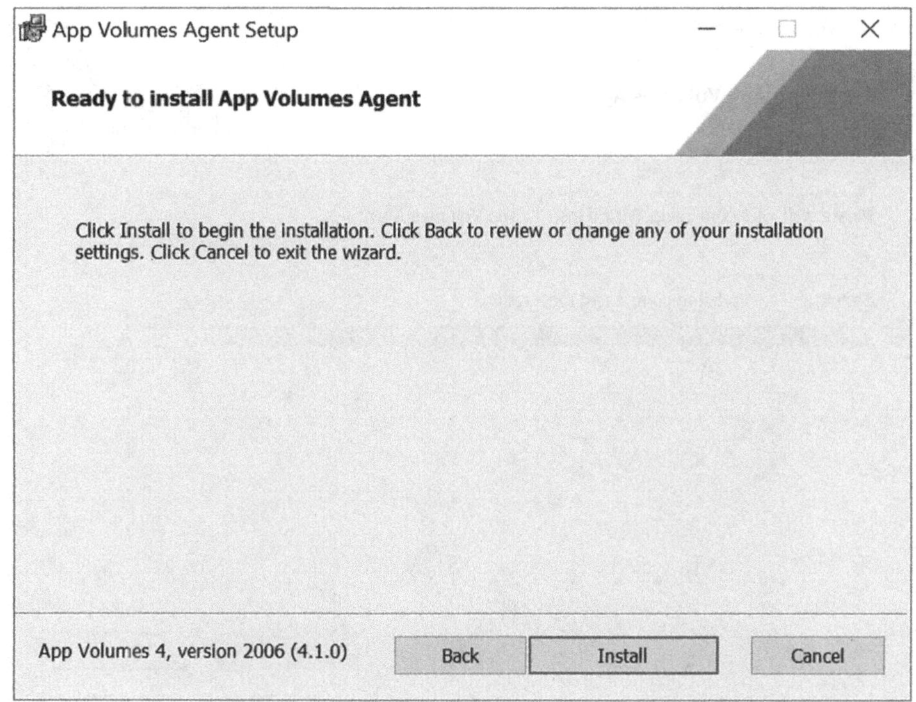

***Figure 9-26.** Ready to install the App Volumes Agent screen*

21. Now click the **Install** button.

22. You will see the screenshot that shows the status and progress of the installation (Figure 9-27).

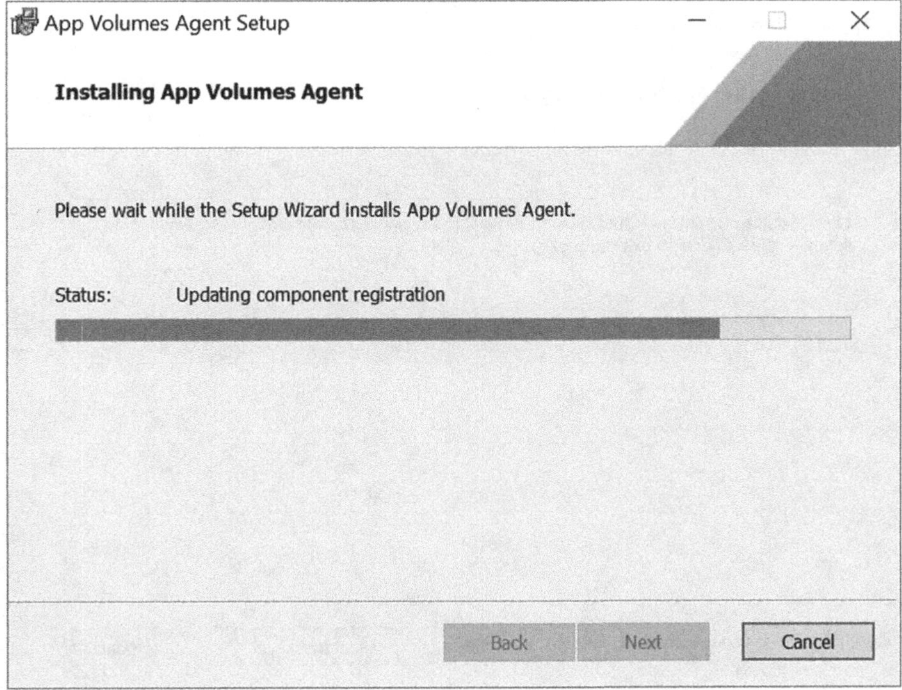

Figure 9-27. *App Volumes Agent installation status screen*

23. Once completed, you will see the **Completed the App Volumes Agent Setup Wizard** screen as shown in Figure 9-28.

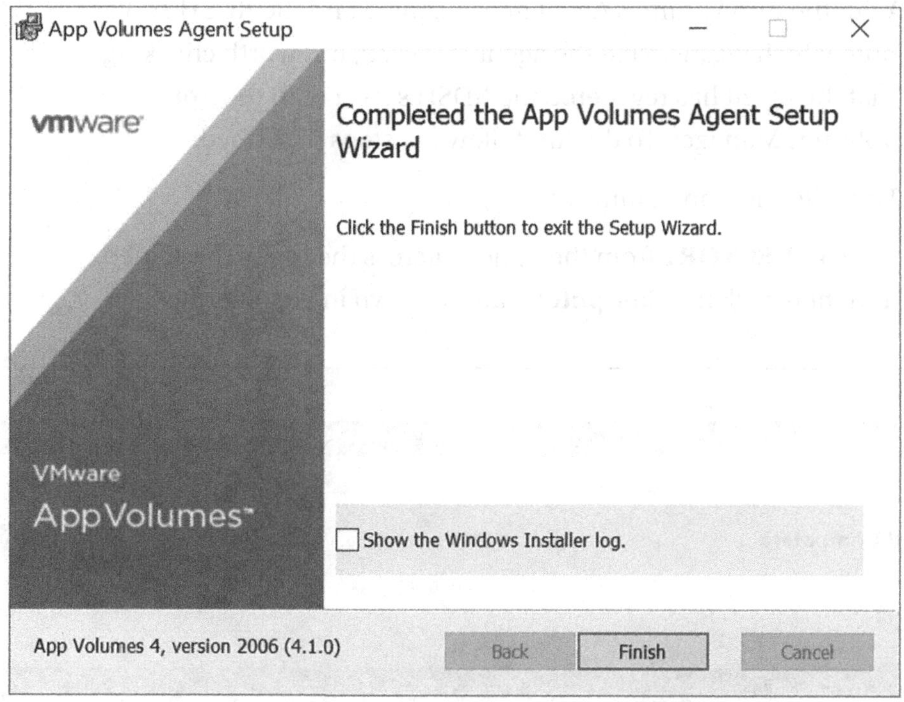

Figure 9-28. *App Volumes Agent installation completed screen*

24. Click **Finish** to complete the installation and to close the installer.
25. You will then see the pop-up dialog box stating that you need to restart the computer to complete the installation (Figure 9-29).

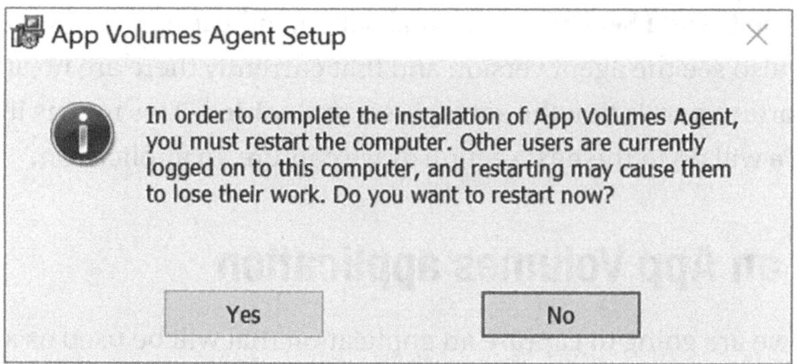

Figure 9-29. *Restart the computer after installation*

26. Click **Yes** to restart the computer.

With the App Volumes Agent now installed and the RDSH server onto which we installed the agent restarted, it is worth checking that the agent has registered the RDSH server with the App Volumes Manager. To do this, follow the steps described:

27. Log in to the App Volumes Manager.

28. Click **DIRECTORY** from the options across the top of the screen, and then click the **Computers** tab as shown in Figure 9-30.

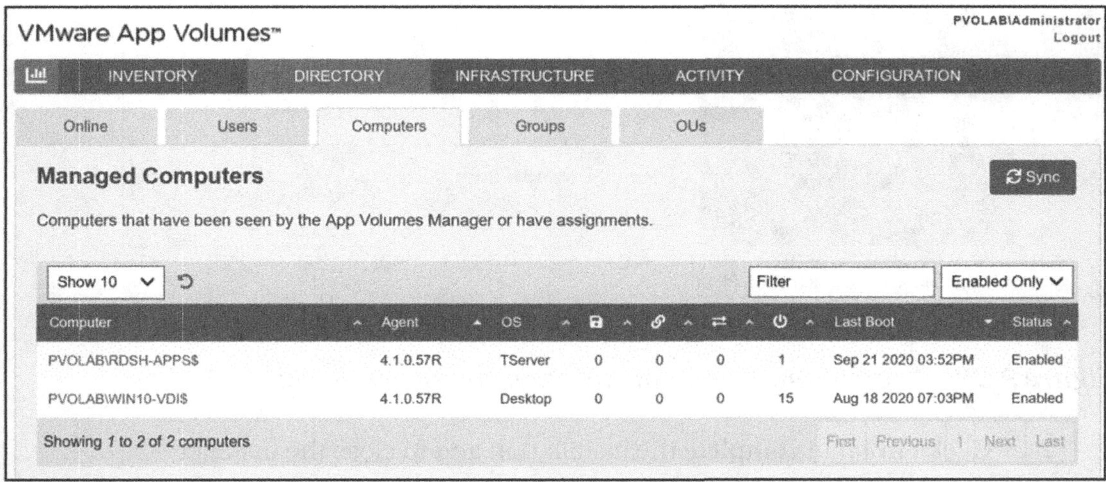

Figure 9-30. *App Volumes Manager - Managed Computers screen*

You will see from the list of computers that the **PVOLAB\RDSH-APPS$** server is listed. It shows the OS as **TServer** or Terminal Server, indicating that this is an RDSH server. You can also see the agent version and that currently there are no attachments or users. The important part is that the server is set to **Enabled**. This means it is available for use which we will do in the next section as we capture an application.

Capturing an App Volumes application

In this section, we are going to capture an application that will be used as a published application in RDSH environments.

To capture the application, we are going to use the RDSH server we configured in the previous section. This is the server called RDSH-APPS.

To start the capture process, follow the steps described:

1. Log in to the App Volumes Manager console.
2. From the top menu, click **INVENTORY**, and then click the **Applications** tab as shown in Figure 9-31.

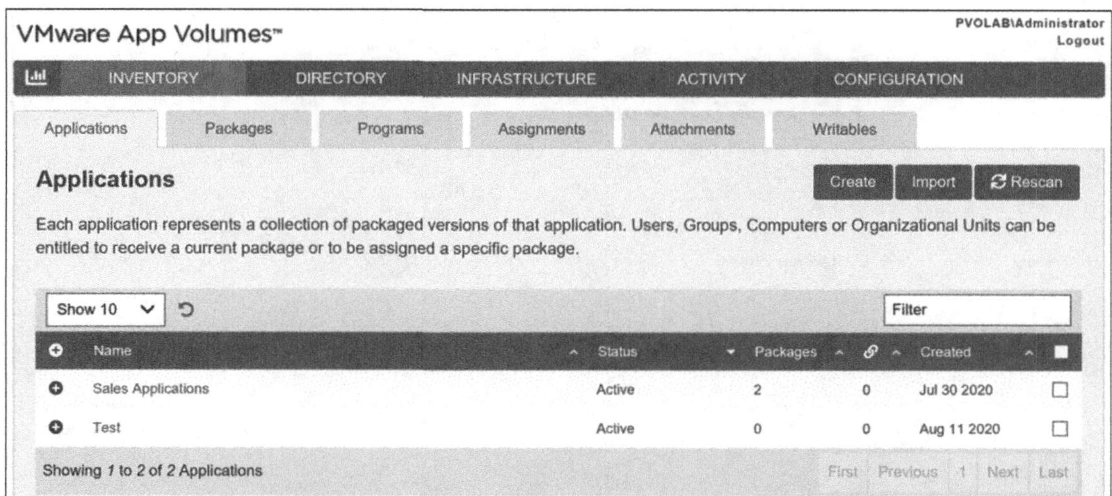

***Figure 9-31.** Creating an Application for RDSH*

3. Click the **Create** button.
4. You will see the **Create Application** screen as shown in Figure 9-32.

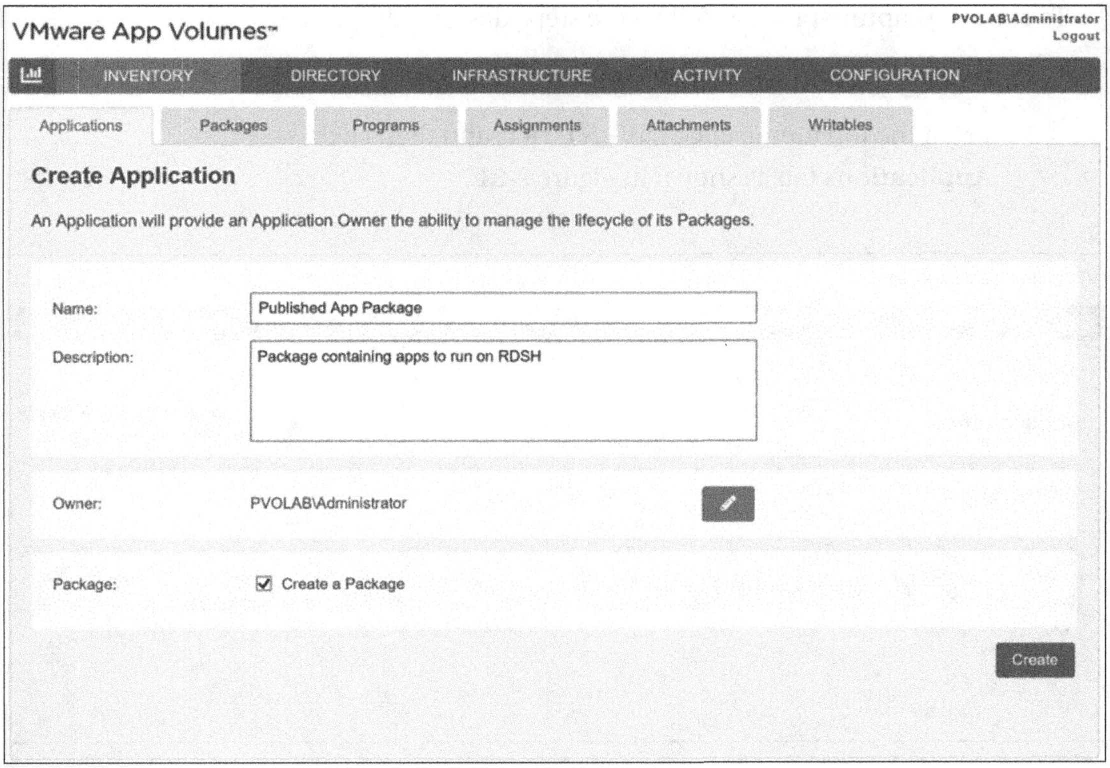

Figure 9-32. *Create an Application screen*

5. In the **Name** box, type in a name for this application package. In this example, we have called it **Published App Package.**

6. Then, in the **Description** box, you can optionally enter a description to describe this application package.

7. In the **Owner** box, you can select an owner for this application package. In this example, we will leave this as the default user (this is the currently logged in user) of **PVOLAB\Administrator**. If you want to change the owner, then click the pencil icon and search for and select the user you want to designate as the owner.

8. Finally, in the **Package** box, check the box for **Create a Package**.

9. Click the **Create** button.

10. You will see the **Confirm Create Application** dialog box as shown in Figure 9-33.

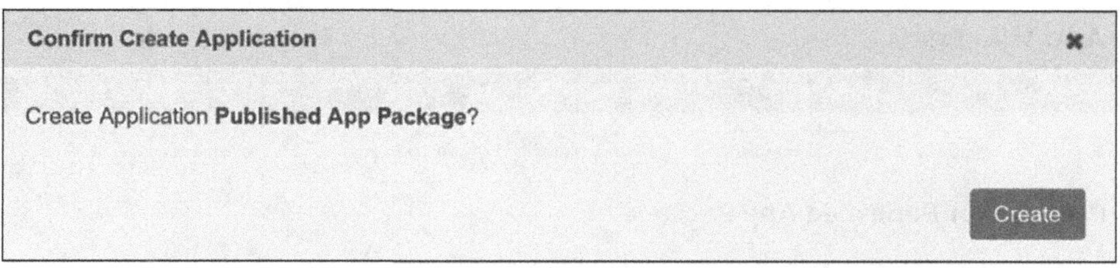

Figure 9-33. Confirm the Application creation dialog box

11. Click the **Create** button.

12. You will see the **Creating Application** progress bar as shown in Figure 9-34.

Figure 9-34. Progress of the Application creation

13. Once created, you will see the message stating that the application was successfully created as shown in Figure 9-35.

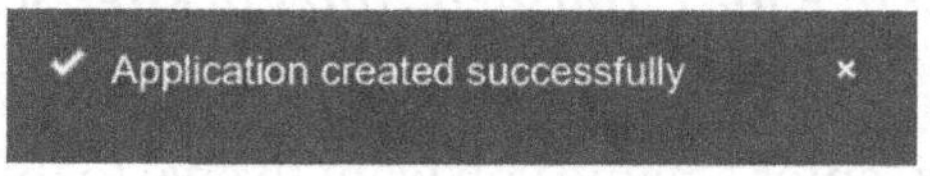

Figure 9-35. Application created successfully

14. You will now see the **Create Package for Published App Package** as shown in Figure 9-36.

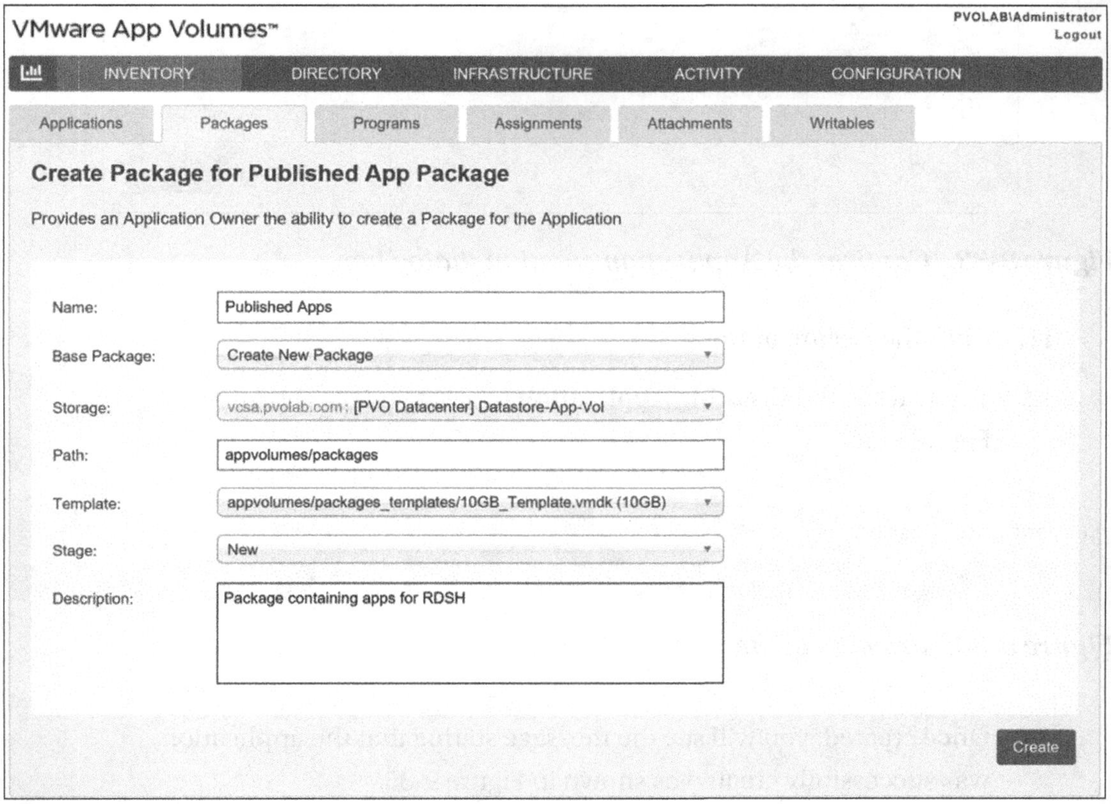

Figure 9-36. *Create Package for Published App Package screen*

15. In the **Name** box, enter a name you want to give to this package. Remember, call this something that easily identifies what the package is. If it contains multiple programs, then do not name it after the individual programs and instead call it something more related to the department or what the set of programs are used for. In the test lab, we have called the package **Published Apps.**

16. The next box is for selecting the **Base Package**. From the drop-down menu, select the base package you want to use to add the programs to. In this example, as there are no programs in the package yet, then the only option is for **Create New Package**.

17. **Storage** is the next option. From the drop-down menu, choose the datastore on which you want to create this package. This is where the VMDK file that gets created will be stored. In the test lab, we have selected the **Datastore-App-Vol** datastore on the **PVO Datacenter.**

18. As part of the storage, the next option is the **Path** option which allows you to select where to store the newly created VMDK file on the datastore. The default path is the **appvolumes/packages** folder, but you can change that to suit.

19. From the **Template** box, from the drop-down menu options, select the template file from which you are going to create this new VMDK file. In the test lab, we are going to use the **10GB_template.vmdk** file we created in Chapter 7.

20. The next box is to select the **Stage** of the package. You can select from New, Tested, Published, or Retired. In the test lab, as this is a new package, we are going to select the option for **New.**

21. Finally, there is the **Description** box. In this box, you can enter any additional information that helps describe what the package is used for and what it contains.

22. You have now completed the configuration screen for creating the package.

23. Now click the **Create** button.

24. You will see the **Confirm Create Package** message as shown in Figure 9-37.

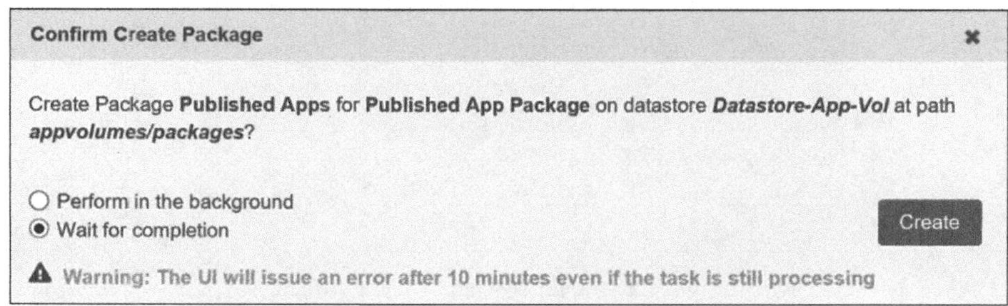

***Figure 9-37.** Confirming the creation of the package screen*

25. Click the **Wait for completion** button, and then click the **Create** button.

26. You will see the package creation process start with the progress bar in Figure 9-38.

Figure 9-38. *Creating package progress bar*

27. Once completed, you will see the message pop-up stating the package has successfully been created (Figure 9-39).

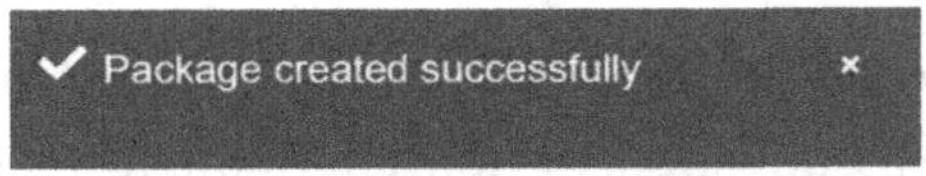

Figure 9-39. *Package successfully created*

28. You will now return to the **Package for Published Apps** screen (Figure 9-40).

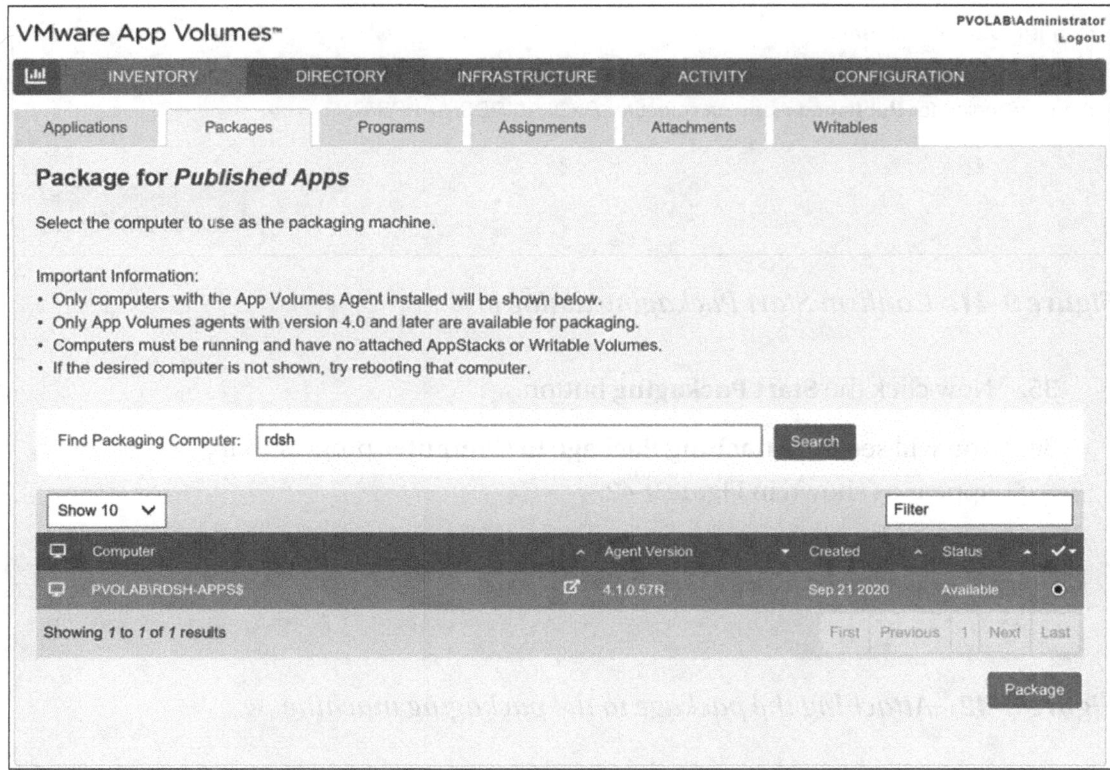

Figure 9-40. *Package for Published Apps screen*

29. On this screen, you need to select the machine you want to use to create the package on – in this example, the RDSH server.

30. In the **Find Packaging Computer** box, type in the name or part of the name of the machine to use for packaging. So, in this example, this is the RDSH server, so type in **RDSH** in the box and then click the **Search** button.

31. You will see the **PVOLAB\RDSH-APPS$** machine listed.

32. You will also see the agent version that the machine is running and its status. In this example, its status is set to **Available,** meaning we can go ahead and use this machine for creating our package.

33. Click the **Package** button.

34. You will see the **Confirm Start Packaging** screen as shown in Figure 9-41.

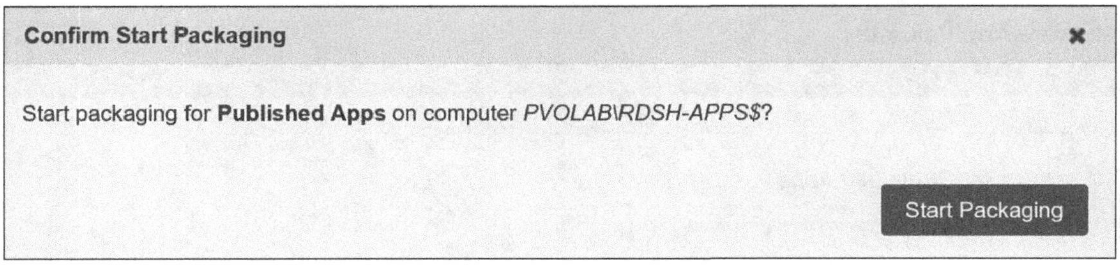

Confirm Start Packaging ✖

Start packaging for **Published Apps** on computer *PVOLAB\RDSH-APPS$*?

Start Packaging

Figure 9-41. *Confirm Start Packaging dialog box*

35. Now click the **Start Packaging** button.

36. You will see the **Attaching Package to Computer** progress bar appear as shown in Figure 9-42.

Figure 9-42. *Attaching the package to the packaging machine*

37. As with capturing an application on a virtual desktop machine, in the background, App Volumes has taken a copy of the 10GB_template.vmdk file and now attaches it to the packaging machine, ready to capture the installation process and redirect the application program files to the new virtual hard disk file.

38. If you check the **Activity Log** under the **ACTIVITY** menu, then you will see the task has successfully completed (Figure 9-43).

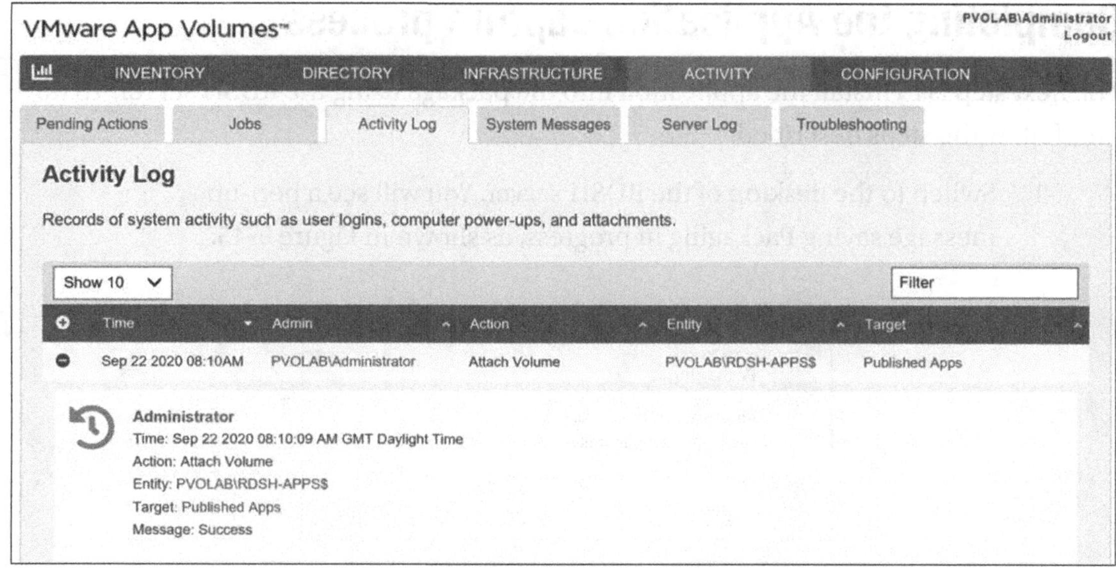

***Figure 9-43.** Activity Log showing attached volume for packaging*

39. If you return to the **INVENTORY** screen and the **Packages** tab, you will now see the screenshot in Figure 9-44.

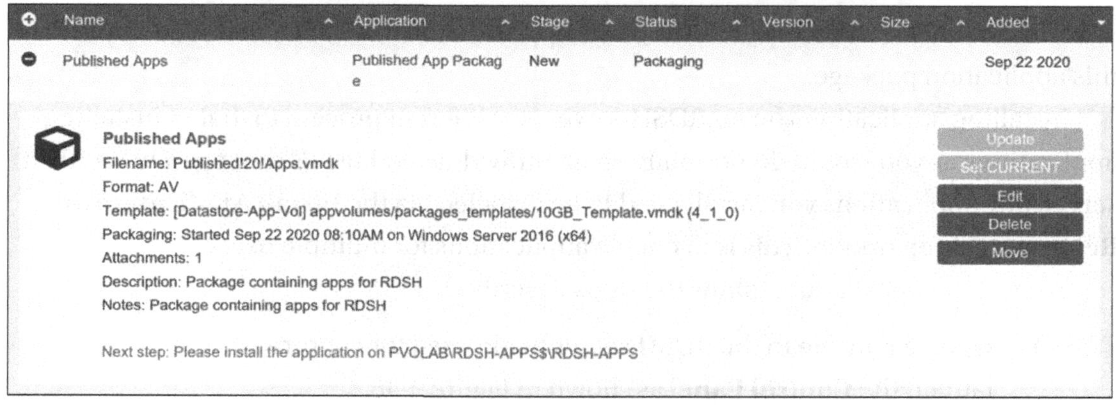

***Figure 9-44.** Published Apps ready for application installation*

The next stage of the process is to install the program on the packaging machine, and so to complete that, we are now going to switch over to the packaging machine and install the application.

Completing the Application capture process

The next step is to install the application into the package using the RDSH server. To do this, follow the steps described:

1. Switch to the desktop of the RDSH server. You will see a pop-up message saying Packaging in progress, as shown in Figure 9-45.

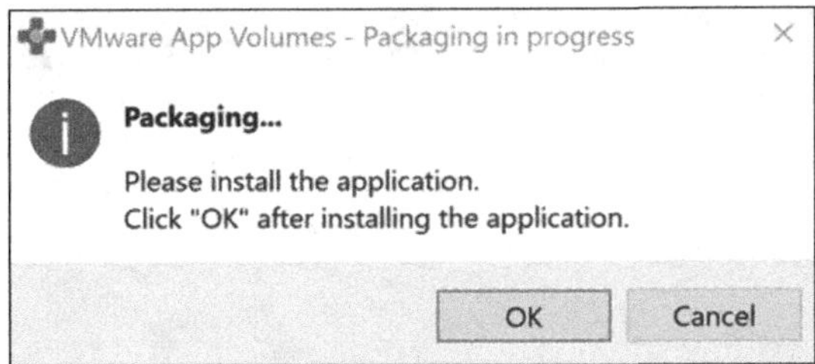

Figure 9-45. *Packaging in progress message box*

Do not click the **OK** button until you have finished installing all the applications for this package.

You can now start the installation of the applications that will be included as part of this application package.

Installing applications on an RDSH server is a different process to that of installing applications as you would do normally on an individual end user's desktop. On an RDSH server, any applications you install need to be installed via the **Install Application on Remote Desktop** option. This is to enable applications for multiple users.

To start the installation, follow the steps described:

1. Open a console to the RDSH server being used for capture, and launch the **Control Panel** as shown in Figure 9-46.

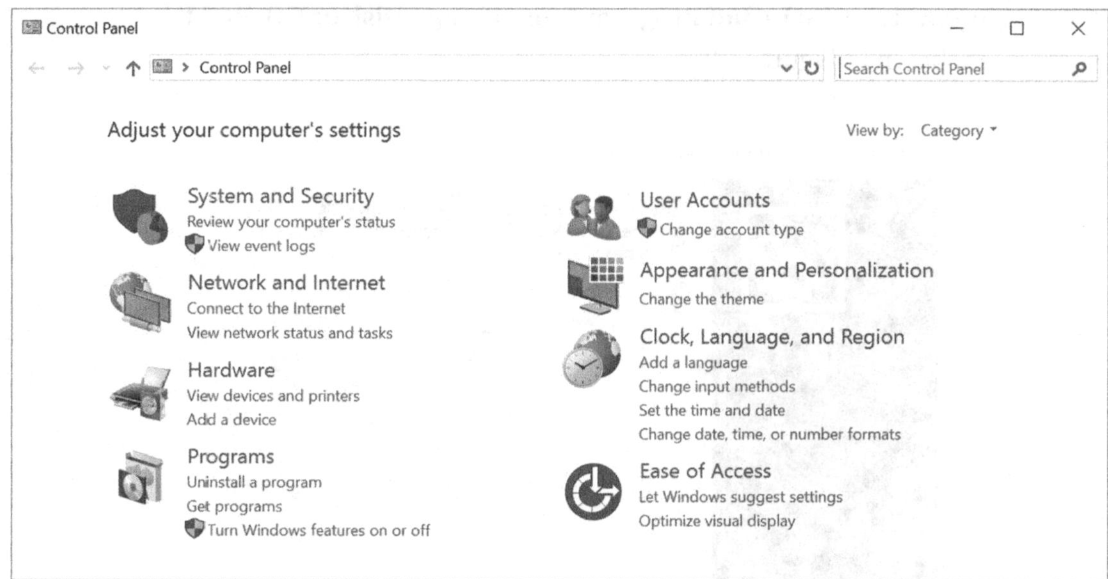

***Figure 9-46.** Launching the Control Panel on the RDSH server*

2. Click **Programs** in the bottom left-hand corner of the Control Panel main screen.

3. You will now see the **Programs** screen of the Control Panel as shown in Figure 9-47.

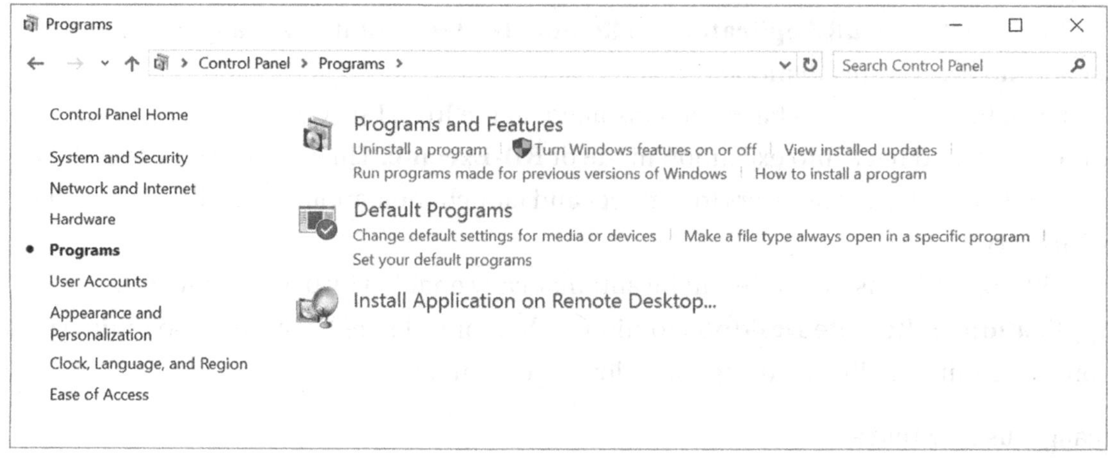

***Figure 9-47.** Programs section of the Control Panel*

4. Now click **Install Application on Remote Desktop....**

5. You will see the **Install Program From Floppy Disk or CD-ROM** as shown in Figure 9-48.

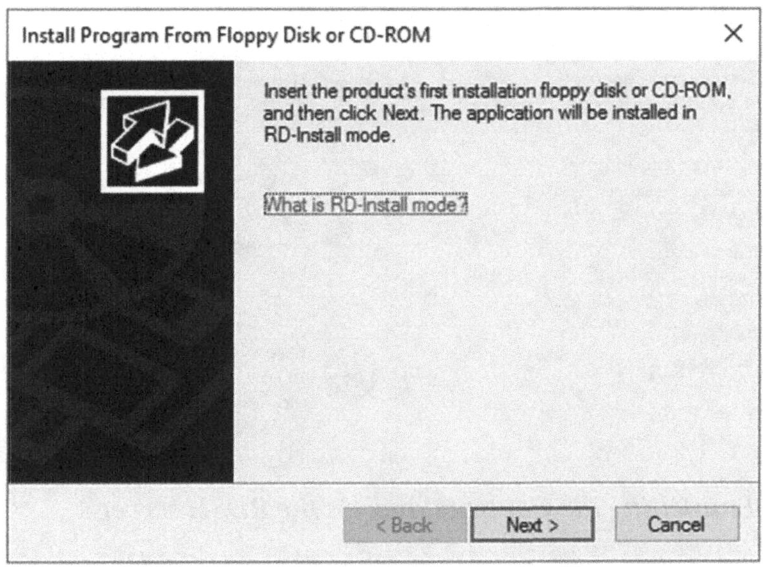

Figure 9-48. *Installing a program using RD-Install mode*

Before we get started with the actual application installation, we mentioned at the start of this section that the installation process for applications running on RDSH is different to a normal installation. That is where the **RD-Install** option comes in.

Clicking the **Install Application on Remote Desktop...** automatically switches the server into the RD-Install mode.

Once the applications have been installed on the RDSH server, the RDSH server is then switched back into execution mode or **RD-Execute**. This mode is for normal operation and allows end users to connect and launch their applications hosted on the RDSH server.

Although RD-Install mode can be automatically enabled by using the **Install Application on Remote Desktop...** option in the Control Panel, you can also initiate this from the command line by using the following commands:

```
change user /install
change user /execute
```

To check which mode the RDSH server is currently using, you can use the following command:

```
change user /query
```

In this example, we are going to continue using the automated method that is initiated from the Control Panel. To do this, follow the steps as described:

1. On the **Install Program From Floppy Disk or CD-ROM** dialog box, click **Next** to start the application installation.
2. You will see the **Run Installation Program** dialog box as shown in Figure 9-49.

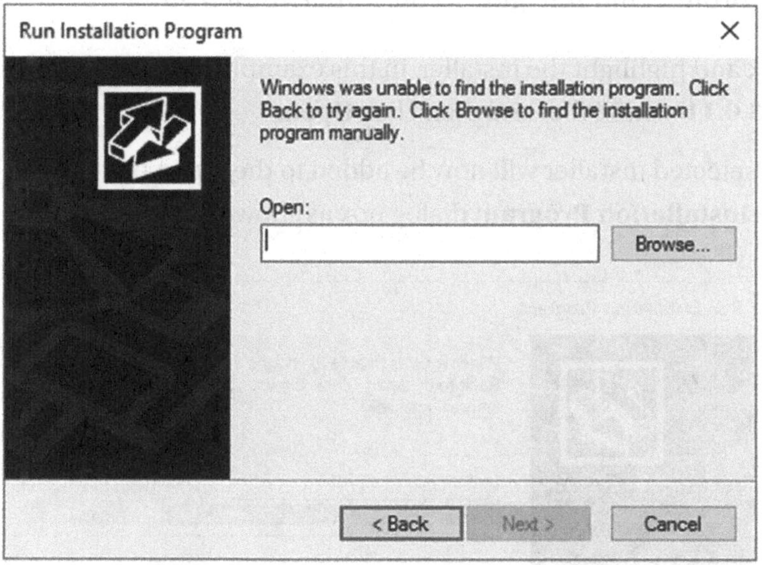

Figure 9-49. *Run Installation Program dialog box*

3. Click the **Browse...** button.
4. You will see a Windows Explorer open from where you can navigate to the application installer for the required application. In this example, we are going to install VLC media player as the application we are going to publish as shown in Figure 9-50.

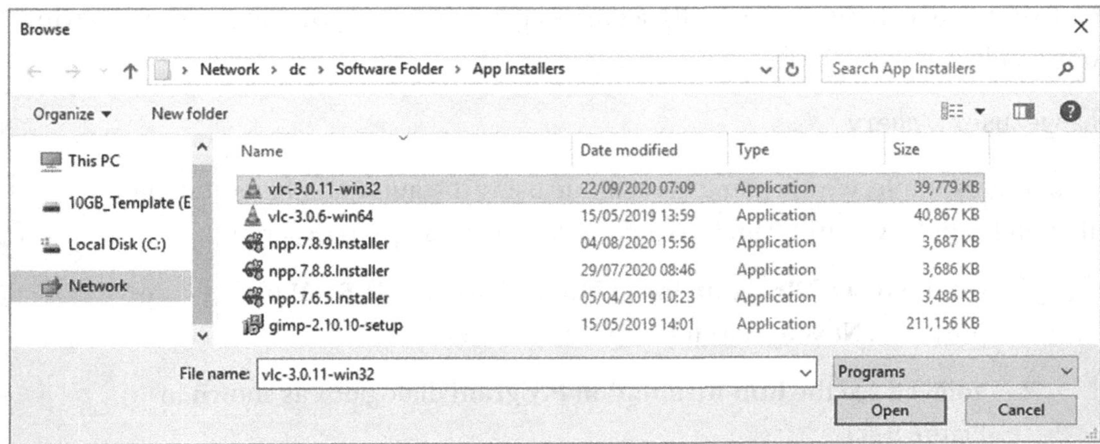

Figure 9-50. *Browse and navigate to the application installer*

5. Click and highlight the installer, in this example, the **vlc-3.0.11-win32** file, and then click **Open.**

6. The selected installer will now be added to the **Open** box in the **Run Installation Program** dialog box as shown in Figure 9-51.

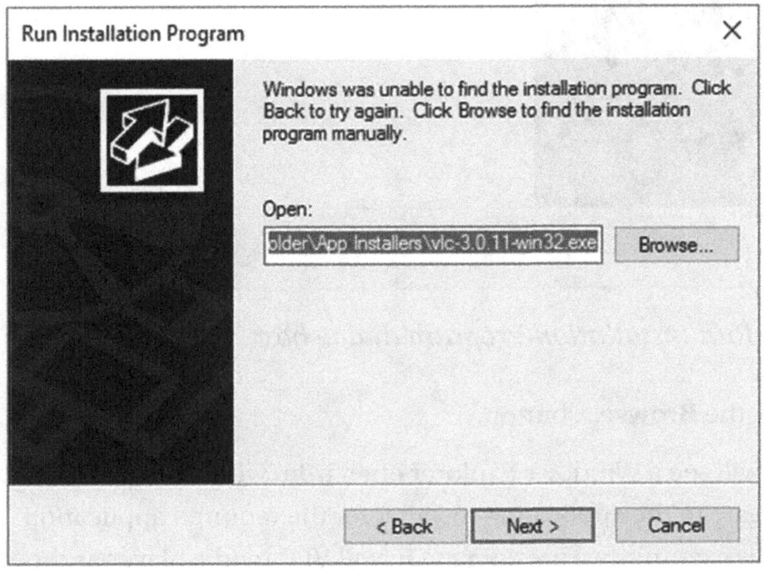

Figure 9-51. *Application installer added*

7. Now click the **Next ➤** button.

8. You will see the **Finish Admin Install** dialog box appear, which will be grayed out for the time being. This will be used once the installation has been completed and is shown in Figure 9-52.

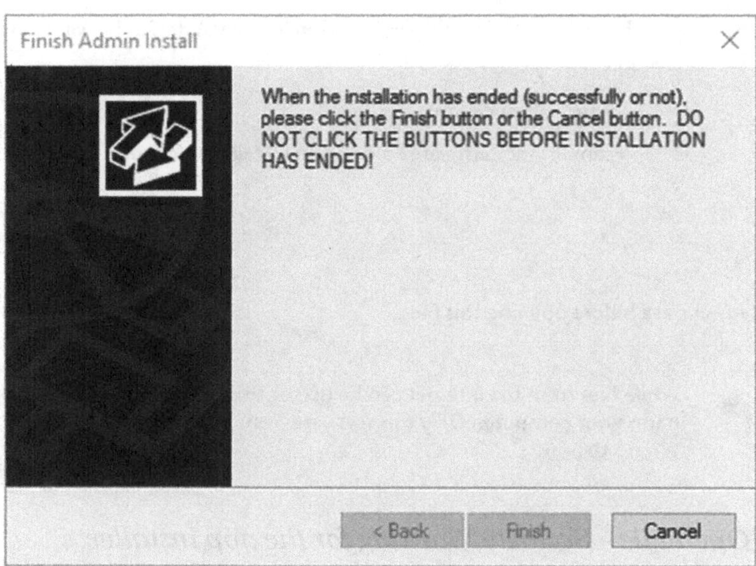

***Figure 9-52.** The Finish Admin Install dialog box*

9. At the same time, the application installer will have also launched as you will see with the **Open File - Security Warning** dialog box shown in Figure 9-53.

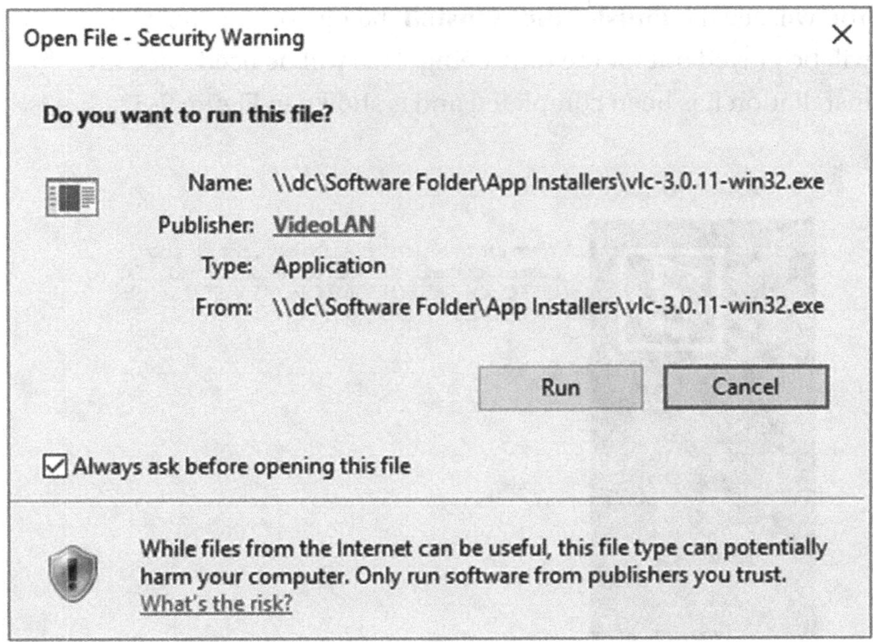

***Figure 9-53.** Open File – Security Warning for the app installer*

10. Click the **Run** button.
11. You will now see the first installation screen for VLC media player as shown in Figure 9-54.

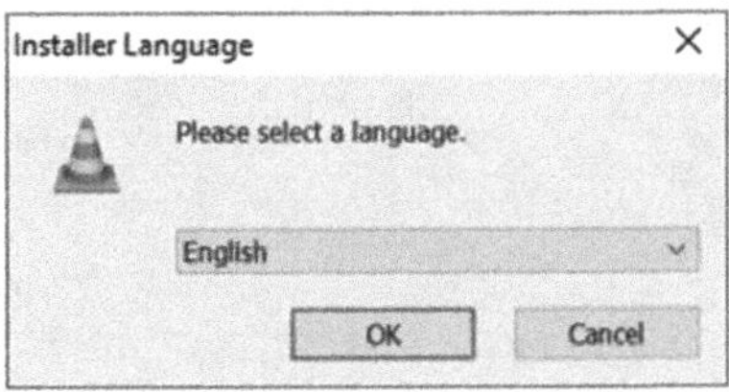

***Figure 9-54.** Application installer launches*

12. Run through the installer as you would with any other installation of the app as shown in Figure 9-55.

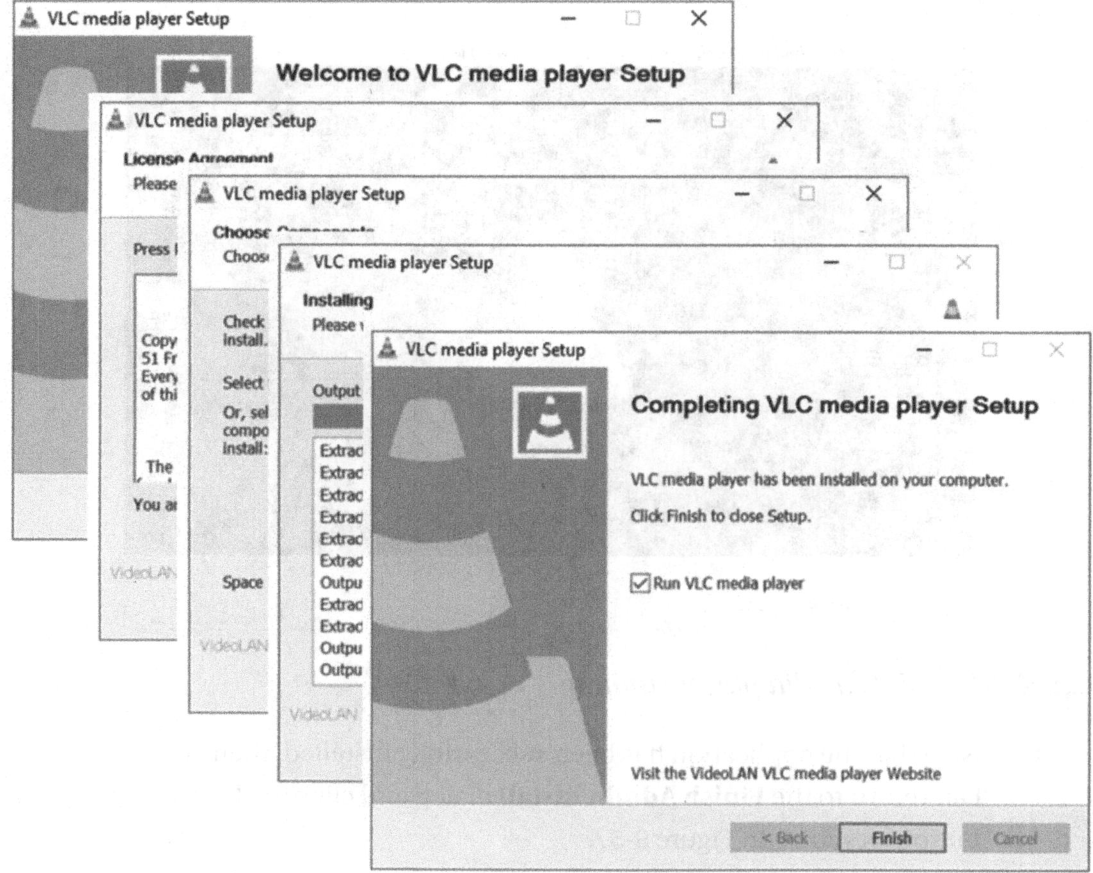

Figure 9-55. *Installing VLC media player*

13. Once installed, launch the app and test that it runs as well as make any settings or configuration changes as shown in Figure 9-56.

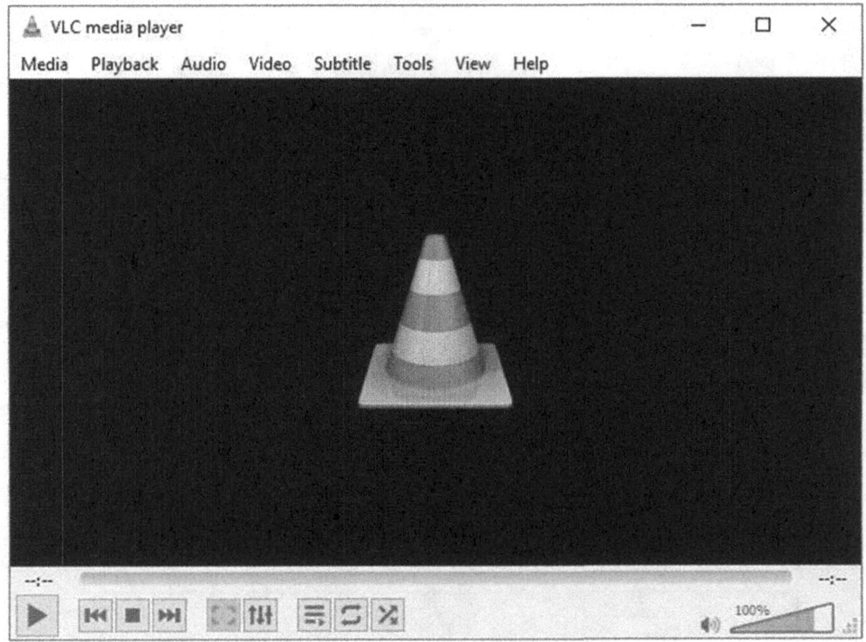

***Figure 9-56.** VLC media player running*

14. Now that the application has been successfully installed, then you can return to the **Finish Admin Install** dialog and click the **Finish** button as shown in Figure 9-57.

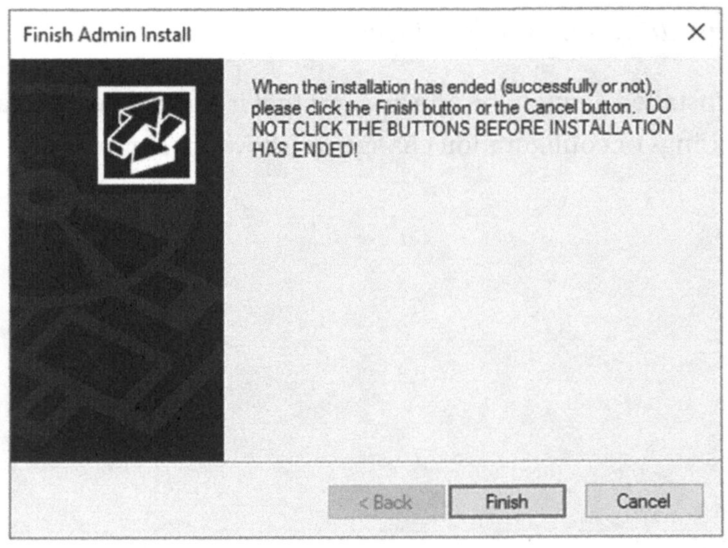

***Figure 9-57.** Finish Admin Install dialog box to complete installation*

15. Next, on the **Packaging in progress** dialog box, click **OK** to complete the application installation as shown in Figure 9-58.

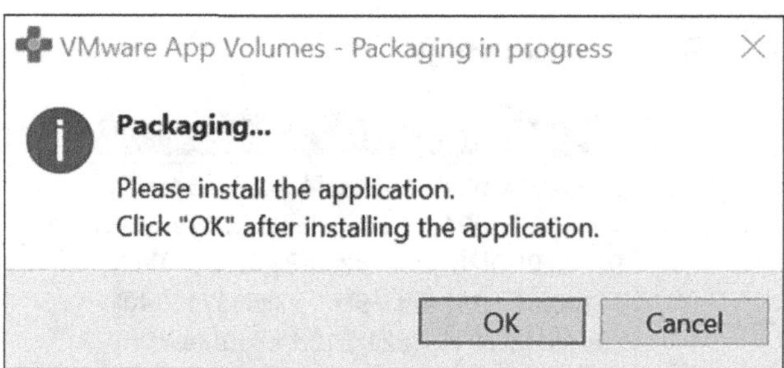

Figure 9-58. *Finish Admin Install dialog box to complete installation*

16. You will then see the **Installation complete?** dialog box as shown in Figure 9-59.

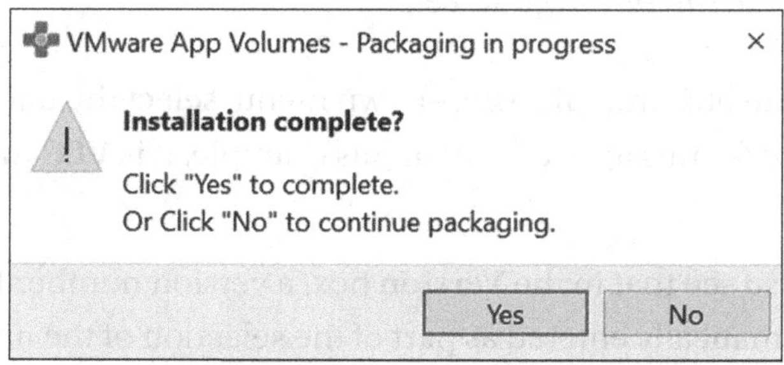

Figure 9-59. *The installation complete dialog box*

17. Click the **Yes** button to complete the installation.

18. You will also see the **VMware App Volumes - Packaging in progress** screen as shown in Figure 9-60.

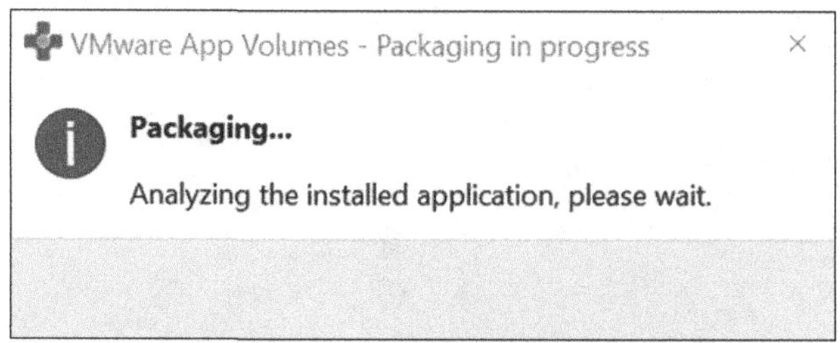

Figure 9-60. *Installed application being analyzed ready for packaging*

19. You will also see the **VMware App Volumes - Finalize Package** screen as shown in Figure 9-61.

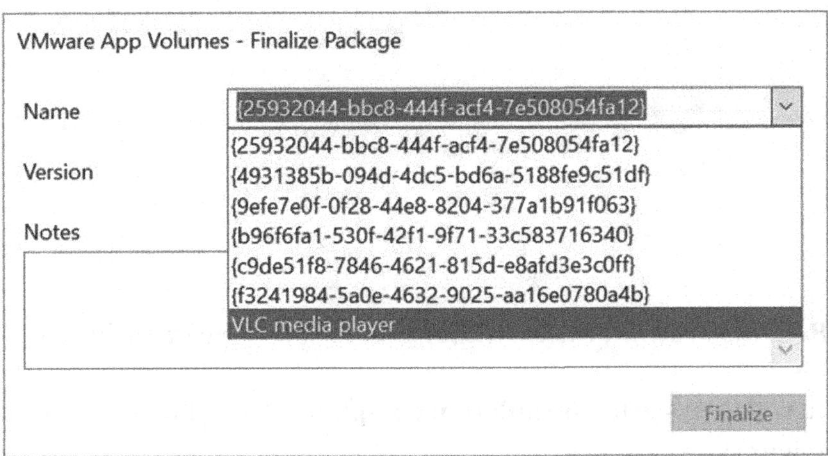

Figure 9-61. *Finalize the package screen*

20. In the **Name** box, from the drop-down menu, select the name you want to use for this application. In this example, it is **VLC media player.**

21. You will also see that in the **Version** box, a version number has been automatically entered as part of the selection of the name, in this example, **3.0.11.**

22. Optionally, in the **Notes** box, you can type in some notes about this application as shown in Figure 9-62.

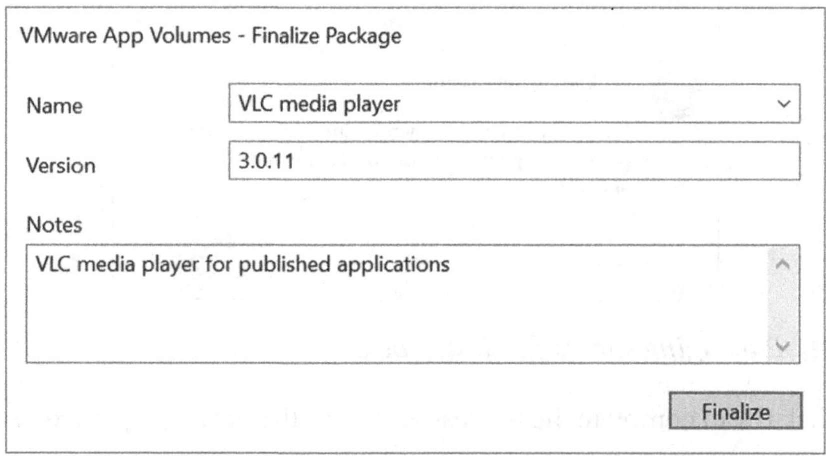

Figure 9-62. *Completing the details in the finalize package screen*

23. Click the **Finalize** button.

24. You will see the **Restart required** dialog box as shown in Figure 9-63.

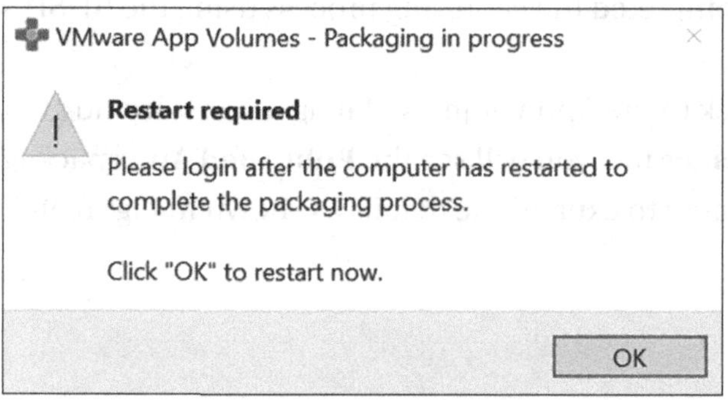

Figure 9-63. *Restart required dialog box*

25. Click the **OK** button.

26. The RDSH server will now restart. Once it is back up and running and you log in, you will see the **Packaging successful!** dialog box as shown in Figure 9-64.

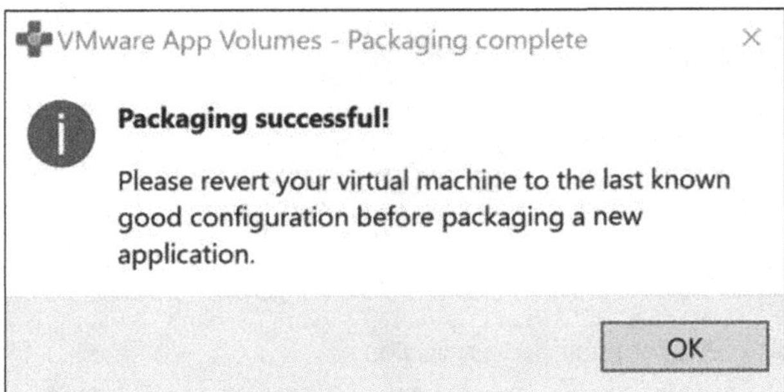

Figure 9-64. *Packaging successful dialog box*

27. Click **OK** to complete the process and close the packaging process.

With the application capturing process complete, you should now revert to the original snapshot of the RDSH server before the application was installed. This will ensure that you have a clean machine ready for the next capture.

You have now completed the capturing process using the RDSH server to capture your application.

If you switch back to the App Volumes Manager console and go to the **INVENTORY** menu and the **Packages** tab, you will see the **Published Apps** package listed. Click the + button next to the name to expand the details as shown in Figure 9-65.

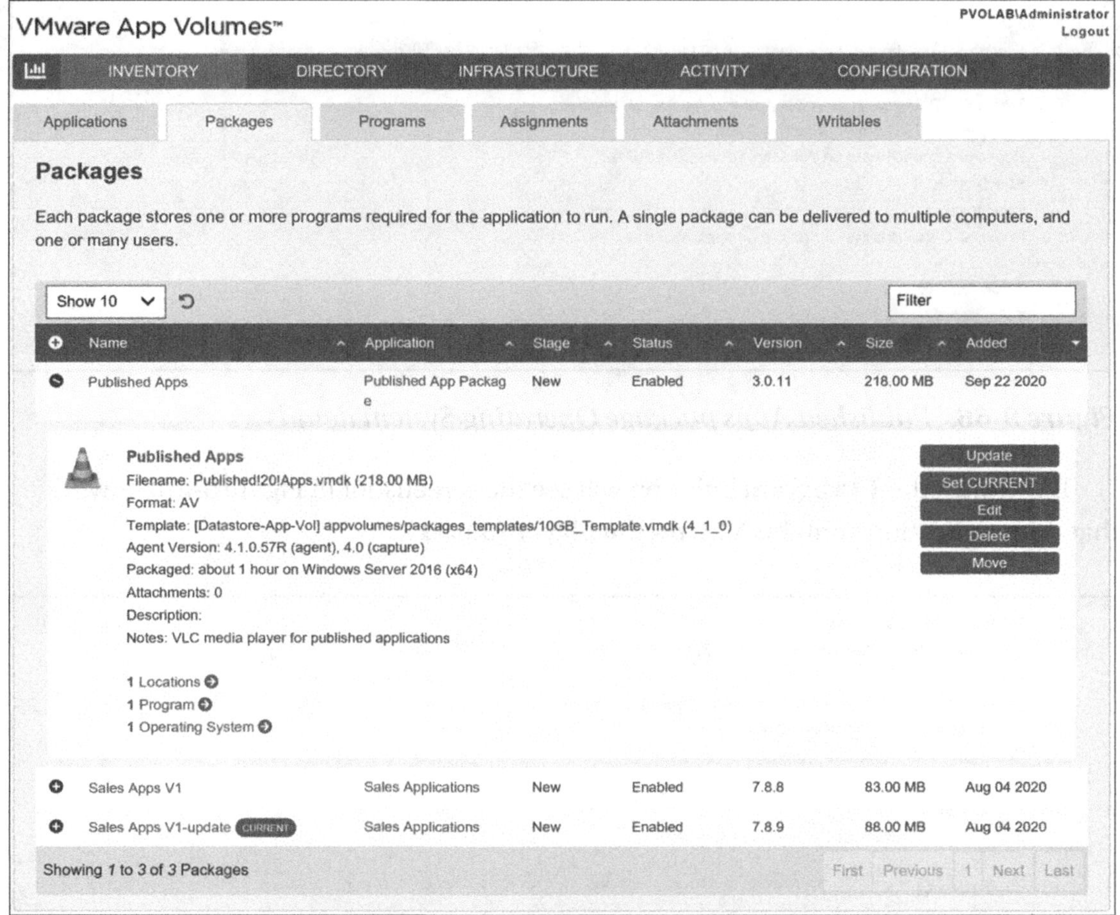

***Figure 9-65.** Published App package viewed in App Volumes Manager*

If you click the **1 Operating System** link, you will see the screenshot in Figure 9-66 showing that this application was captured using **Windows Server 2016 (x64)**.

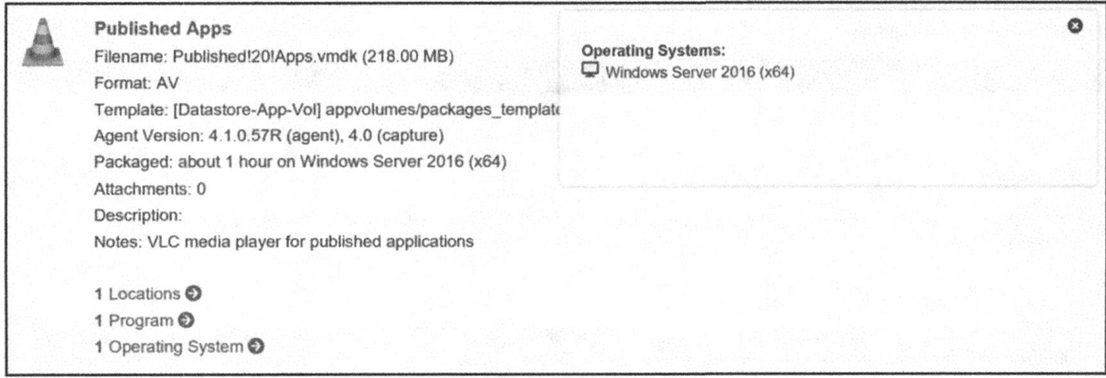

Figure 9-66. *Published Apps package Operating System details*

If you click the **1 Program** link, you will see the screenshot in Figure 9-67 showing that this application contains **VLC media player (3.0.11)**.

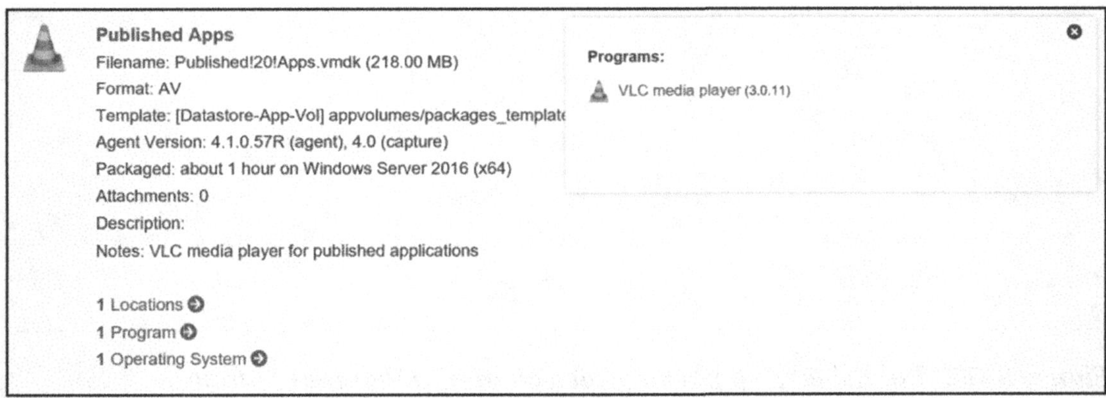

Figure 9-67. *Published Apps package Programs detail*

You will also see the program listed if you click **INVENTORY** and then the **Programs** tab as shown in Figure 9-68.

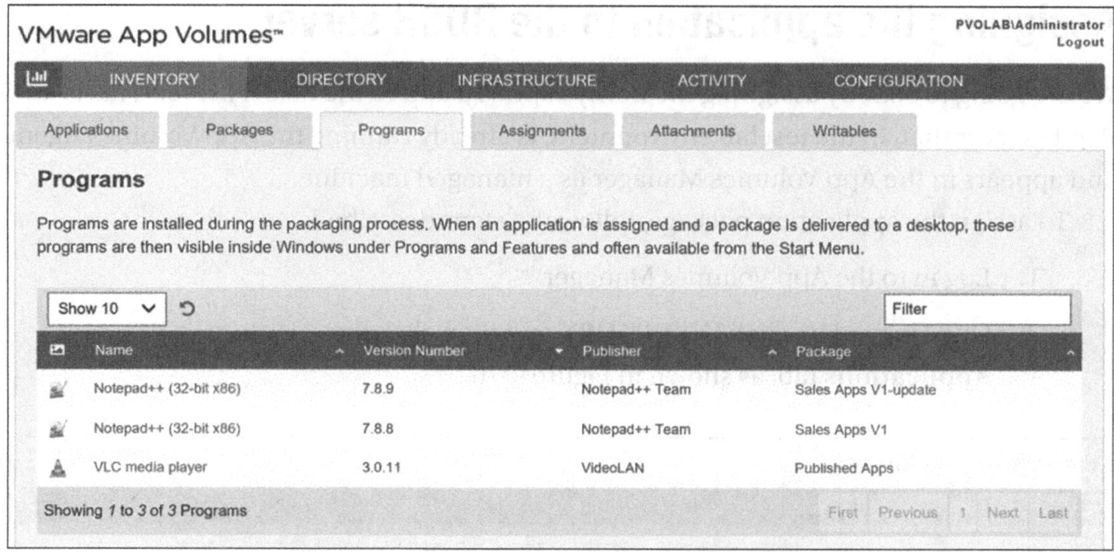

Figure 9-68. *Programs view showing the newly captured program*

You have now successfully captured an application package that can be used within RDSH server environments. In the next section, we are going to look at how to configure RDSH to deliver the application package and test that the end user can launch and run the application.

Assigning and delivering applications with RDSH

The next step, now that we have our application package built and configured, is to configure the RDSH server so that the app can be delivered to end users. Figure 9-69 illustrates the steps we are going to follow to do this.

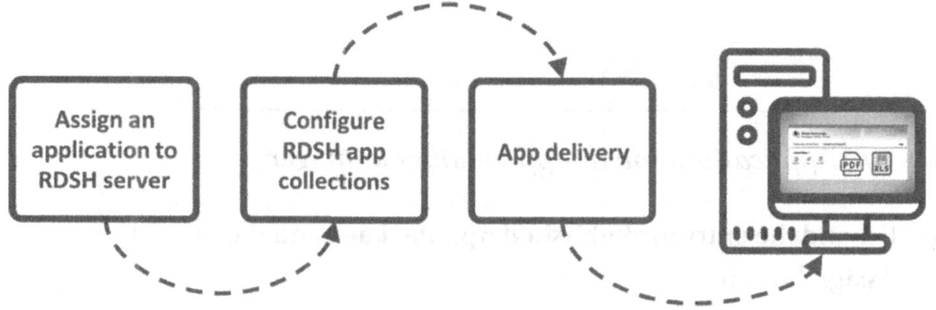

Figure 9-69. *Process for assigning and delivering an app package*

Assigning the application to the RDSH server

We are going to start by assigning the newly captured app to the RDSH server. This is an RDSH server that, in the test lab environment, is already running the App Volumes Agent and appears in the App Volumes Manager as a managed machine.

To assign the application package, follow the steps described:

1. Log in to the App Volumes Manager.
2. Once logged in, click **INVENTORY** and then click the **Applications** tab, as shown in Figure 9-70.

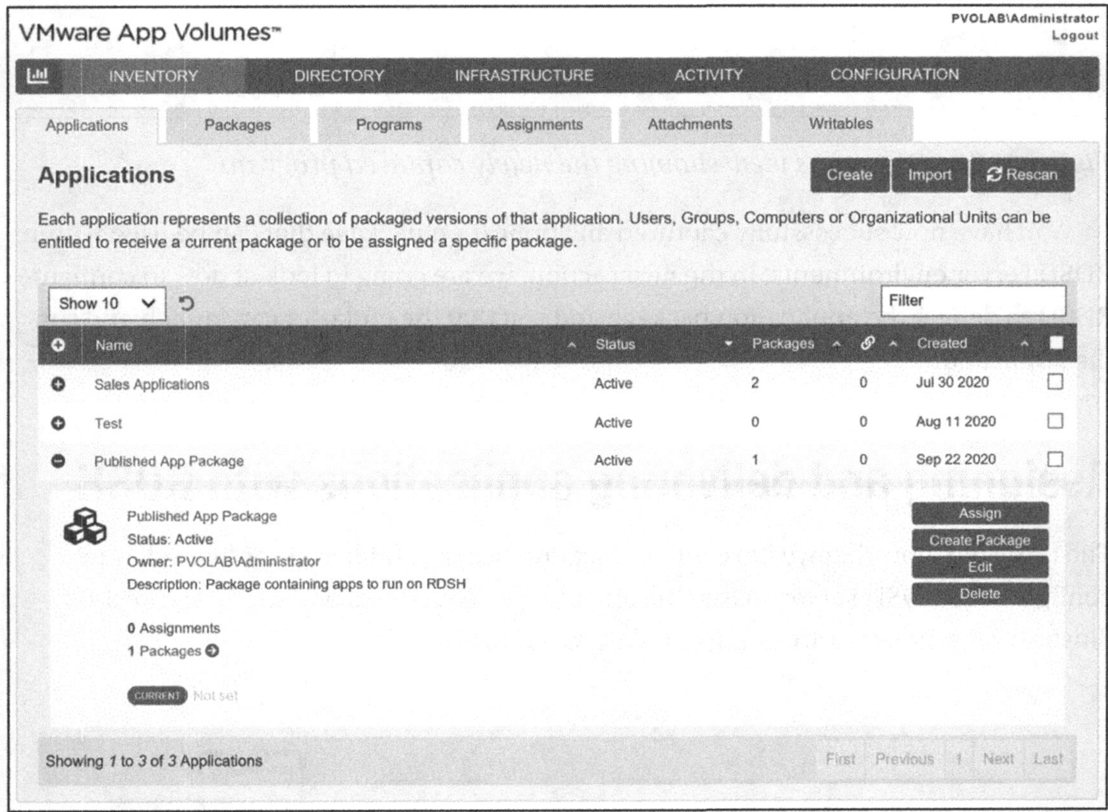

Figure 9-70. *Applications tab in App Volumes Manager*

3. Expand the entry for **Published App Package** and then click the **Assign** button.
4. You will see the **Assign Application: Published App Package** screen as shown in Figure 9-71.

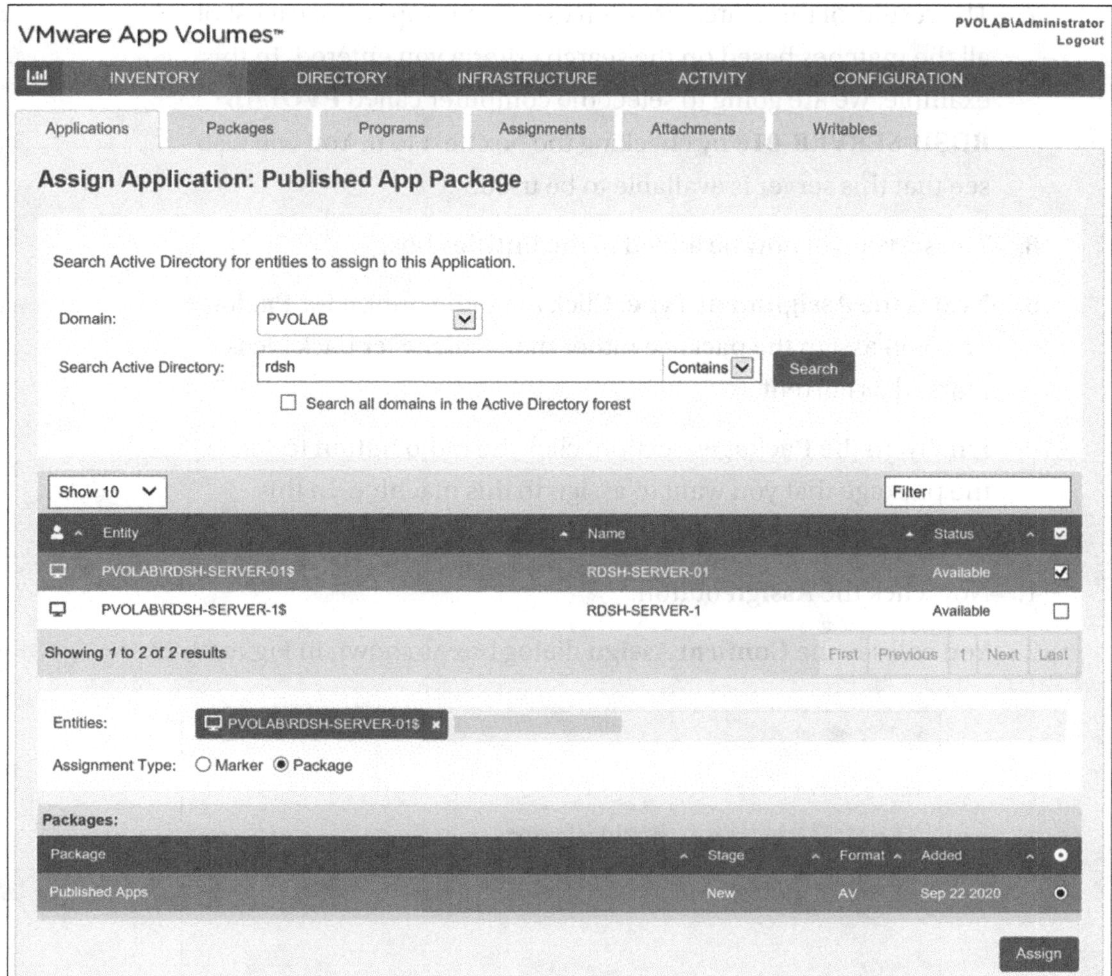

Figure 9-71. *Assign application screen*

5. In the **Domain** box, from the drop-down menu, select the domain in which the machine you want to assign the application to lives. In this example, the domain is called PVOLAB.

6. Next, in the **Search Active Directory** box, type the first part of the name of the machine you want to assign to. In this example, we are going to assign the application to the server called **RDSH-SERVER-01**, so type rdsh, which is the first part of the machine name, in the box and then click the **Search** button.

7. The results of the search are then displayed. You will see a list of all the matches based on the search criteria you entered. In this example, we are going to select the computer called **PVOLAB\RDSH-SERVER-01$** by checking the box next to it. You will also see that this server is available to be used.
8. The server will now be added to the **Entities** box.
9. Next is the **Assignment Type**. Click the radio button for **Package**. This will assign the package rather than whichever package is marked as current.
10. Finally, in the **Packages** section, click the radio button to select the package that you want to assign to this machine. In this example, we are assigning the **Published Apps** package.
11. Now click the **Assign** button.
12. You will see the **Confirm Assign** dialog box as shown in Figure 9-72.

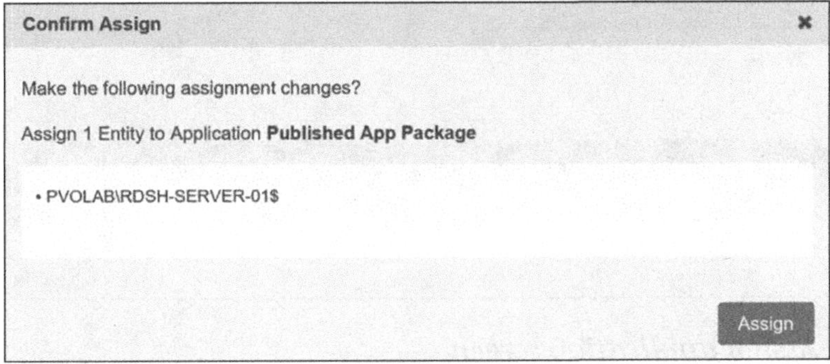

Figure 9-72. *Confirming the application assignment*

13. Check the details and then click the **Assign** button.
14. You will see the **Saving Assignment** progress bar (Figure 9-73).

Figure 9-73. *Saving Assignment progress bar*

15. Once successfully assigned, you will see the message in Figure 9-74.

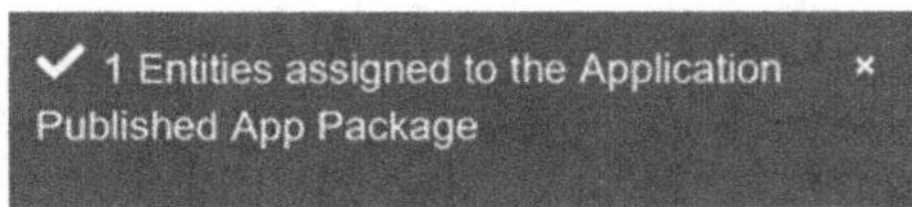

Figure 9-74. Application successfully assigned message

16. This is also shown in Figure 9-75.

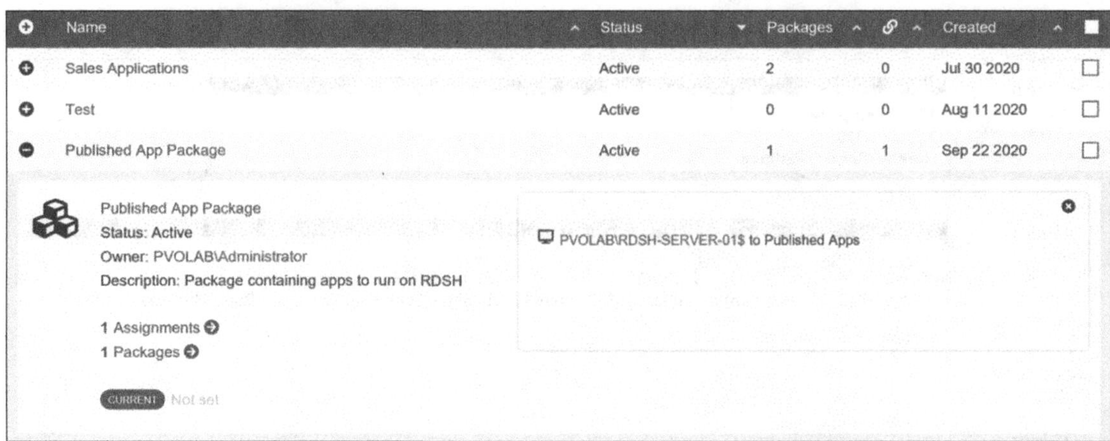

Figure 9-75. Assignment of Published App Package to the RDSH server

Now that the application package has been assigned, we can now switch to the RDSH server and ensure the app has been attached and then configure the RDSH elements to publish the app to the end users.

Configuring the app package for RDSH

Before starting the configuration, it is worth checking that the assigned application is attached and available. To do this, complete the following:

1. Log in to the RDSH server, and from the desktop, launch **Disk Management**. You will see the screenshot in Figure 9-76.

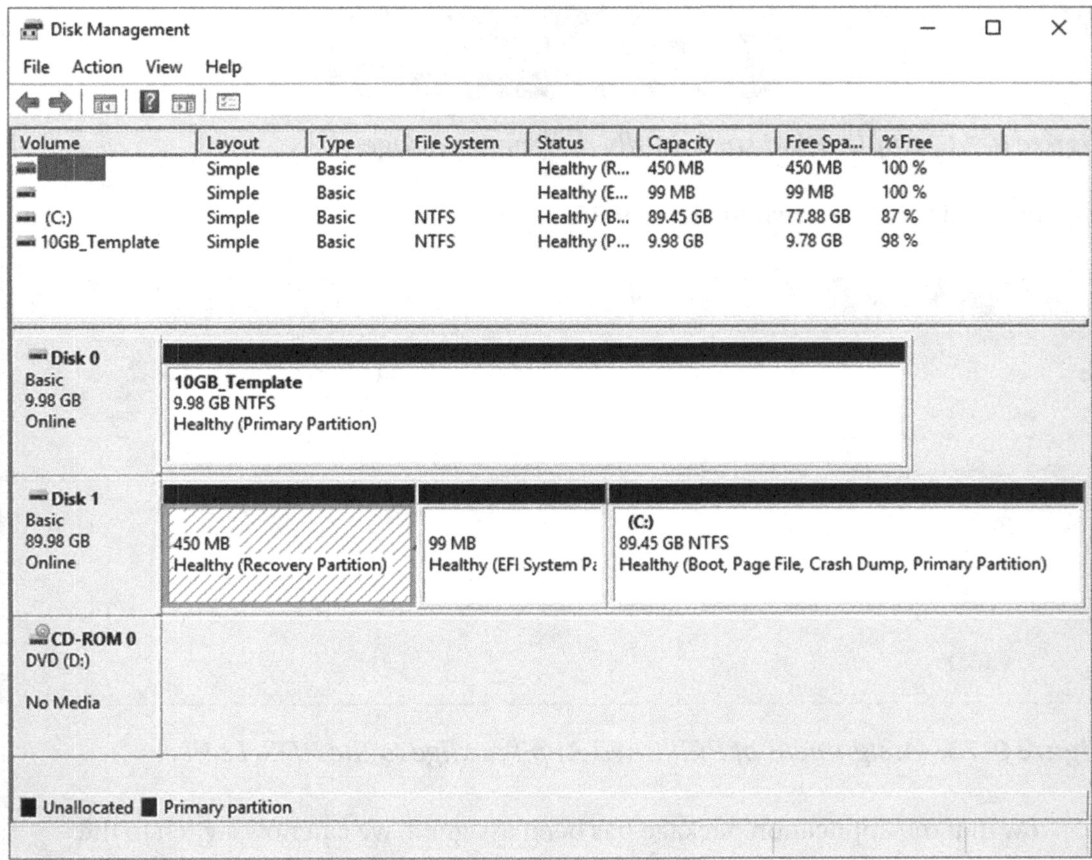

Figure 9-76. *Disk Management showing the application package attached*

2. If you switch back to the App Volumes Manager console briefly and click INVENTORY and then the Attachments tab, you will see the screenshot in Figure 9-77.

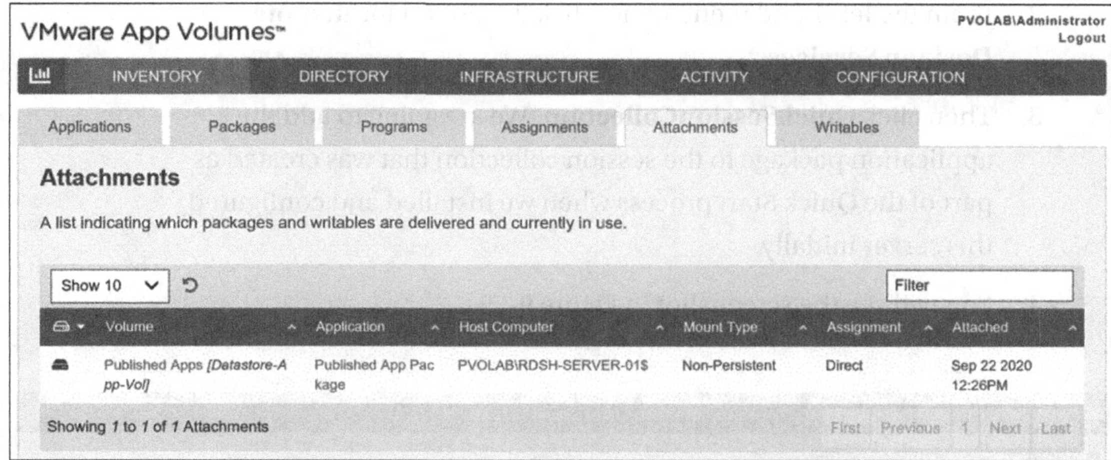

***Figure 9-77.** Application package attached – App Volumes Manager view*

Once you are happy that the application package is attached and available, then you can start to configure the app for publishing by following the steps described:

1. From the desktop of the RDSH server, launch the **Server Manager** as shown in Figure 9-78.

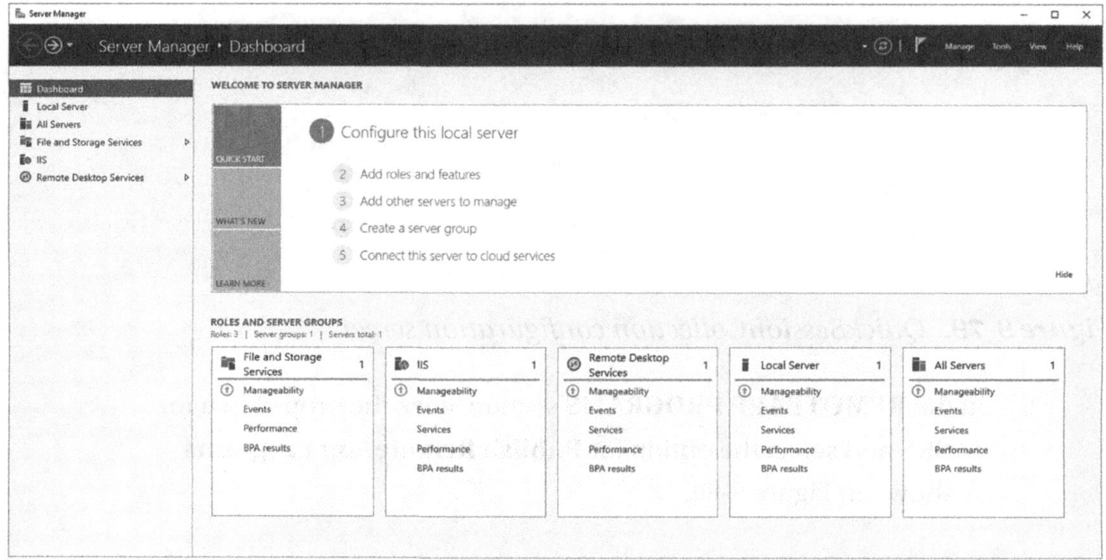

***Figure 9-78.** Server Manager on the RDSH server*

2. From the left-hand menu pane, click the option for **Remote Desktop Services.**

3. Then click **QuickSessionCollection**. We are going to add the application package to the session collection that was created as part of the Quick Start process when we installed and configured this server initially.

4. You will see the screenshot in Figure 9-79.

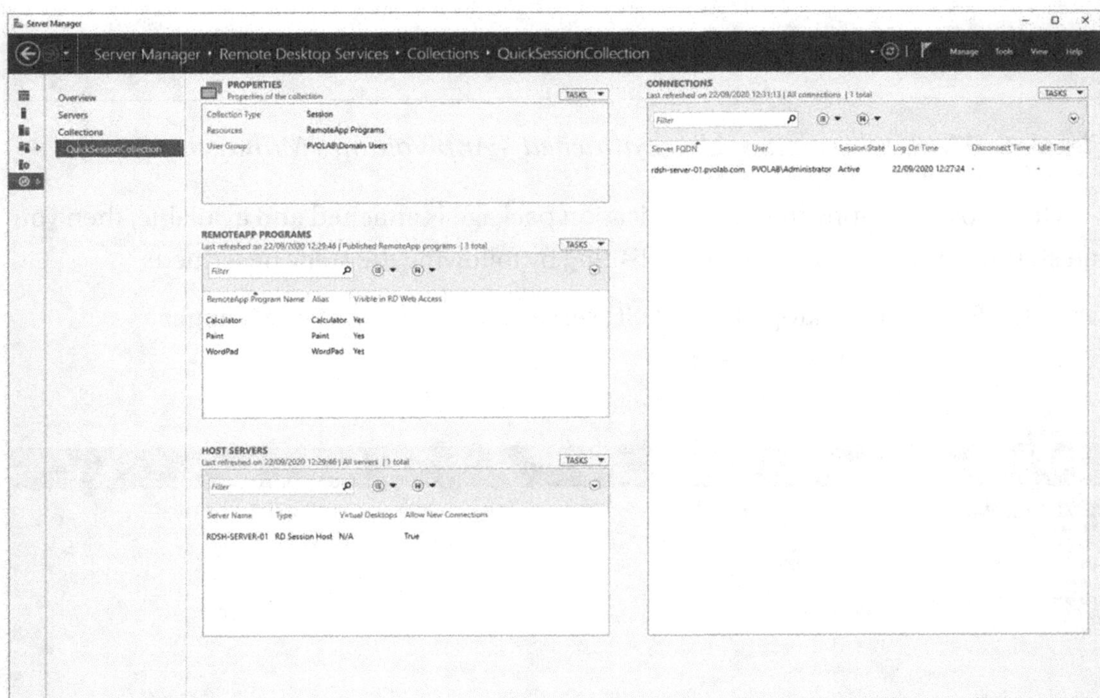

Figure 9-79. QuickSessionCollection configuration screen

5. In the **REMOTEAPP PROGRAMS** section, click the drop-down for **TASKS** and select the option for **Publish RemoteApp Programs** as shown in Figure 9-80.

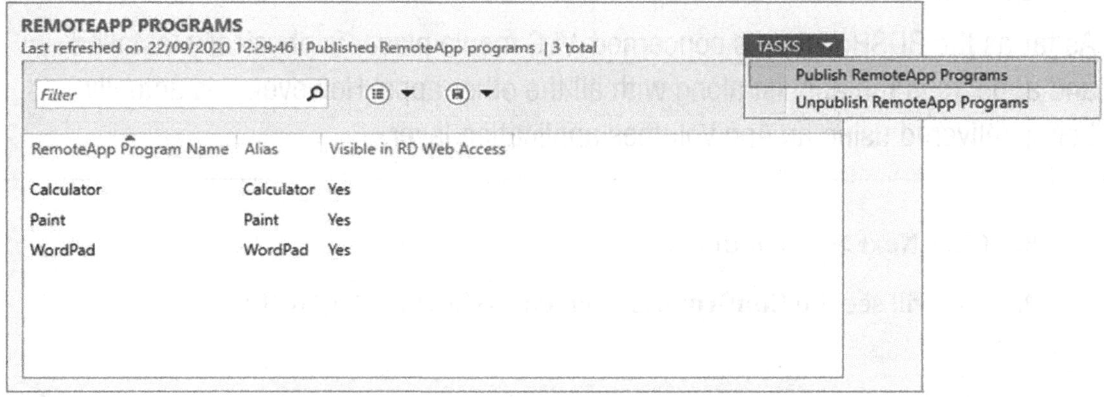

***Figure 9-80.** QuickSessionCollection RemoteApp Programs*

6. You will now see the **Select RemoteApp Programs** screen as shown in Figure 9-81.

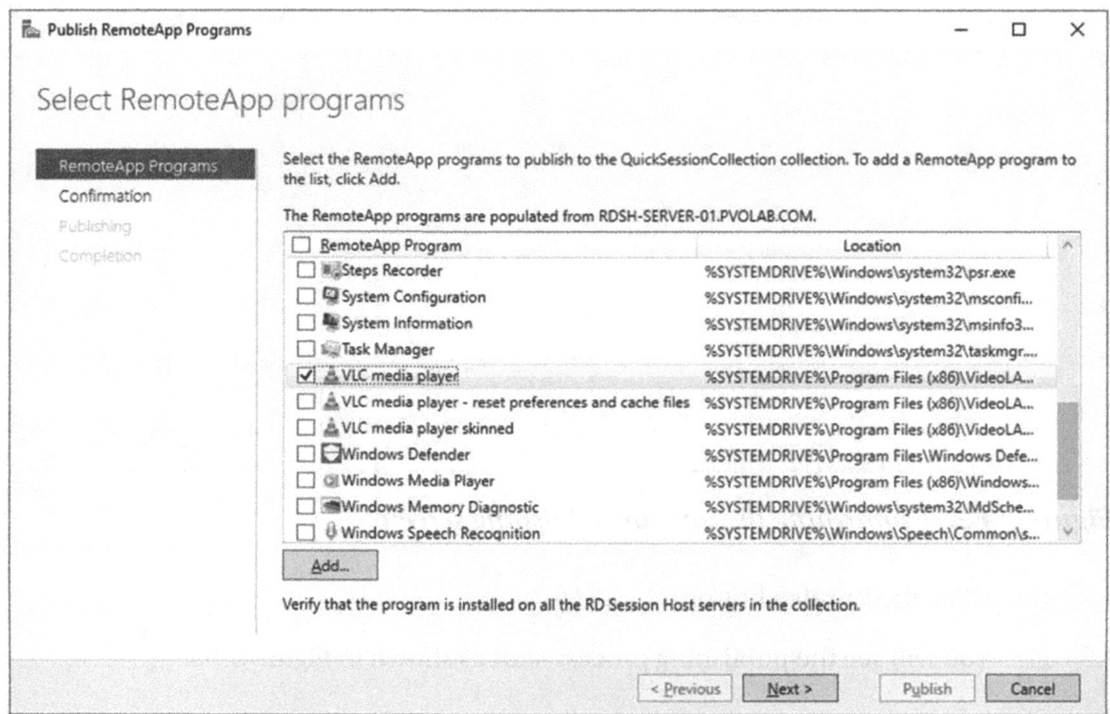

***Figure 9-81.** Selecting the programs to be published via RemoteApp*

7. Scroll down and check the box for **VLC media player**.

As far as the RDSH server is concerned, VLC media player is physically installed and appears in the app list along with all the other apps. However, it is actually being delivered using an App Volumes application layer.

8. Click **Next ➤** to continue.

9. You will see the **Confirmation** screen as shown in Figure 9-82.

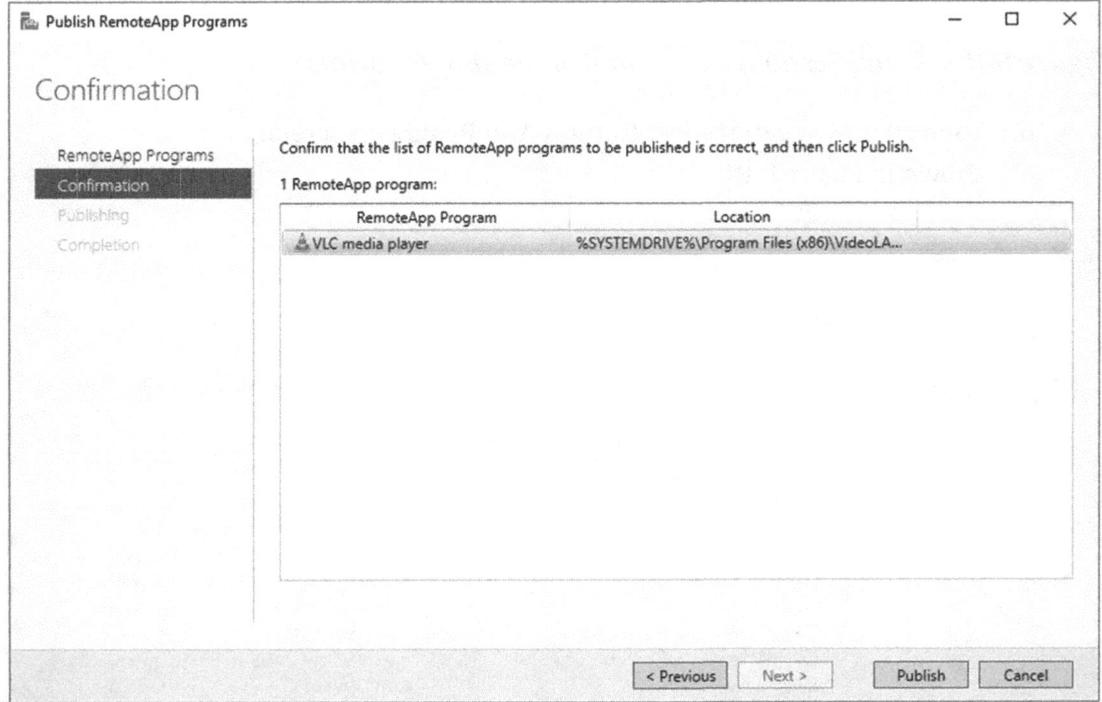

Figure 9-82. *Confirming the app for publishing screen*

10. Click the **Publish** button.

11. You will see the publishing process start as shown in Figure 9-83.

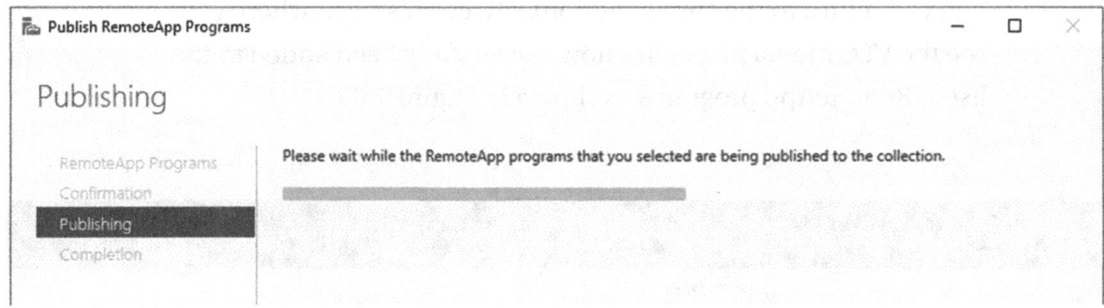

***Figure 9-83.** Application publishing progress screen*

12. Once the publishing process has completed, you will see the **Completion** screen as shown in Figure 9-84.

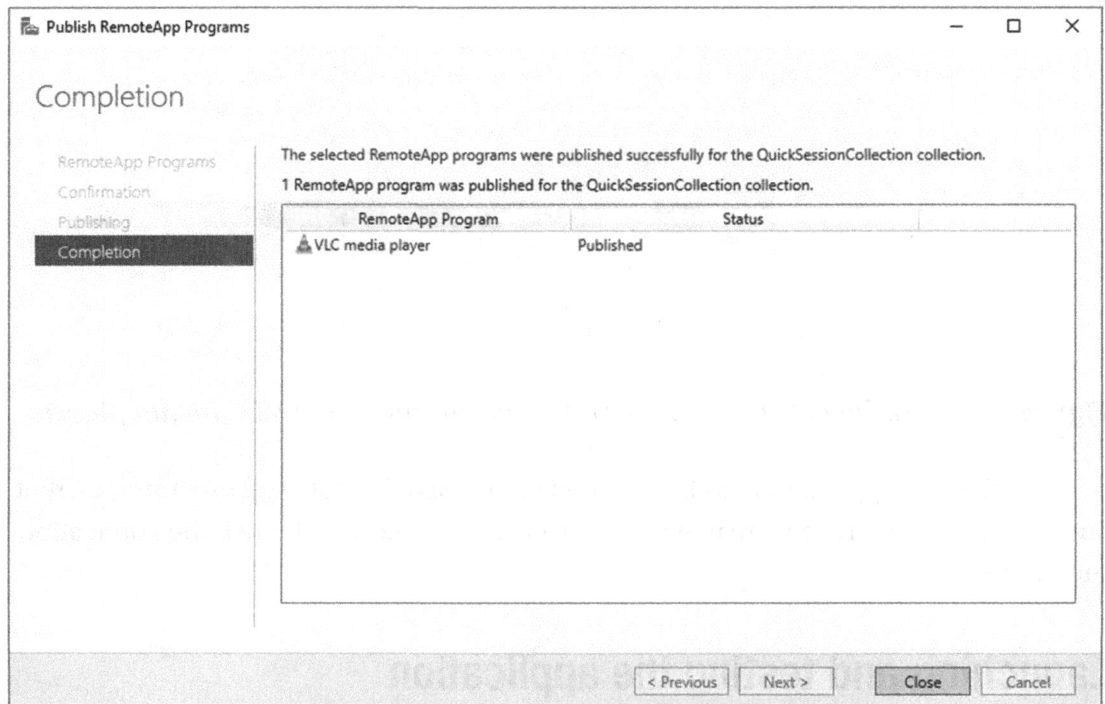

***Figure 9-84.** Application publishing progress completion screen*

13. Click the **Close** button.

14. You will return to the **QuickSessionCollection** screen where you see the VLC media player has now successfully been added to the list of RemoteApp programs as shown in Figure 9-85.

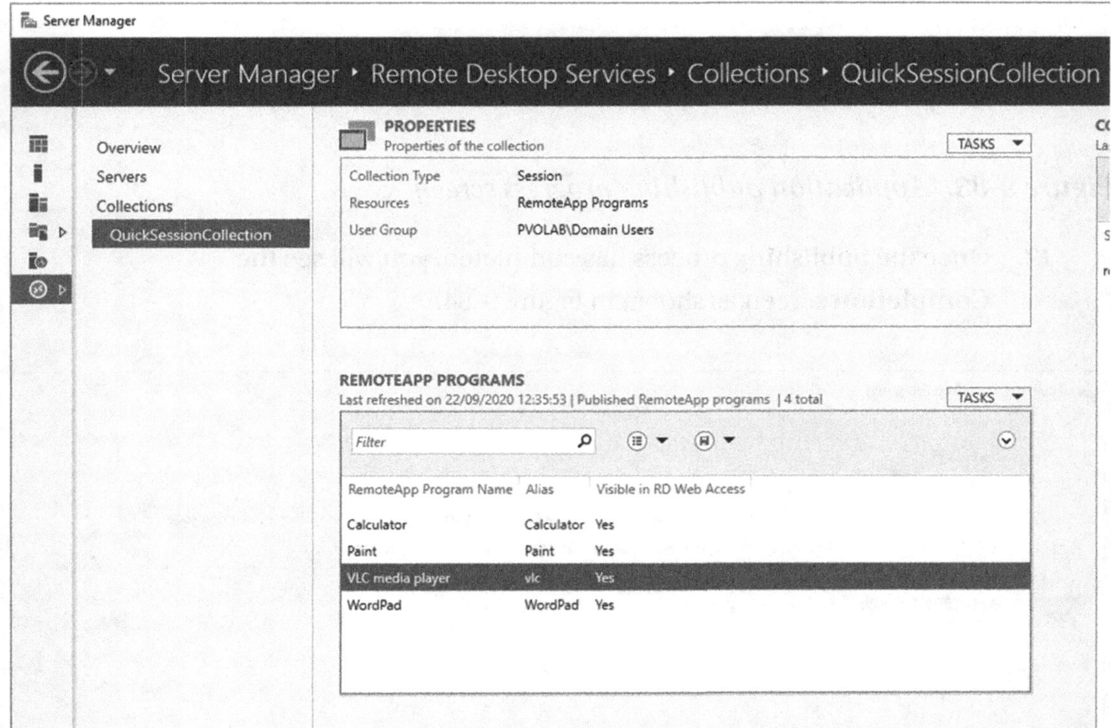

***Figure 9-85.** Updated list of RemoteApp programs including VLC media player*

Now that the application has been added to the list of RemoteApp programs, all that remains is to test it and ensure that an end user can connect and launch the application successfully.

Launching and testing the application

In this final section, we are going to test that an end user can log in and launch the application that is being delivered to the RDSH server using App Volumes application layers.

To do this, follow the steps described:

1. Log in to the RemoteApp server. The address to use in this example is **https:\\rdsh-server-01\rdweb.**

2. Once successfully logged in, you will see the **RemoteApp and Desktops** screen as shown in Figure 9-86.

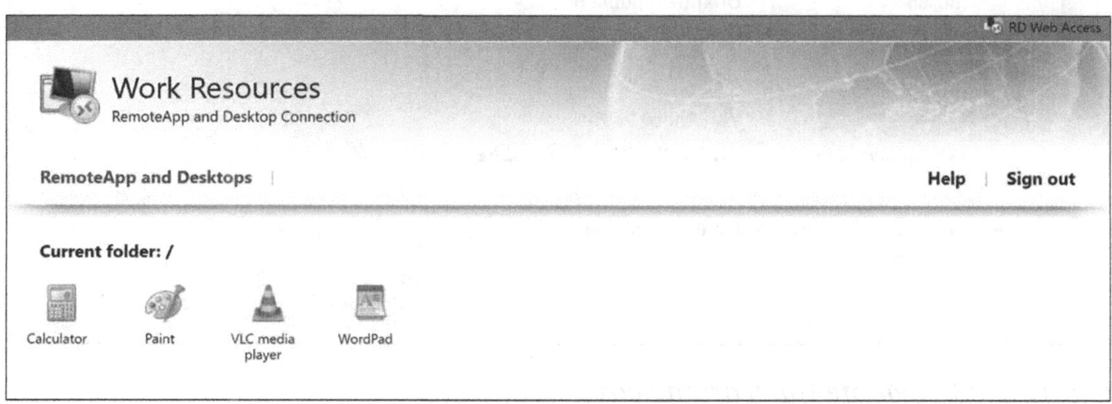

Figure 9-86. *RemoteApp and Desktops screen*

3. Double-click the **VLC media player** icon to start the session and launch the application.

4. You will see an RDP connection file download as shown in Figure 9-87.

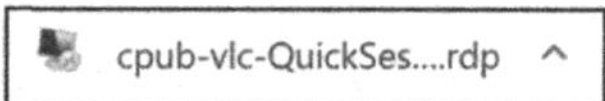

Figure 9-87. *Download the RDP connection file*

5. Double-click and launch the RDP file. You will see the RemoteApp warning box as shown in Figure 9-88.

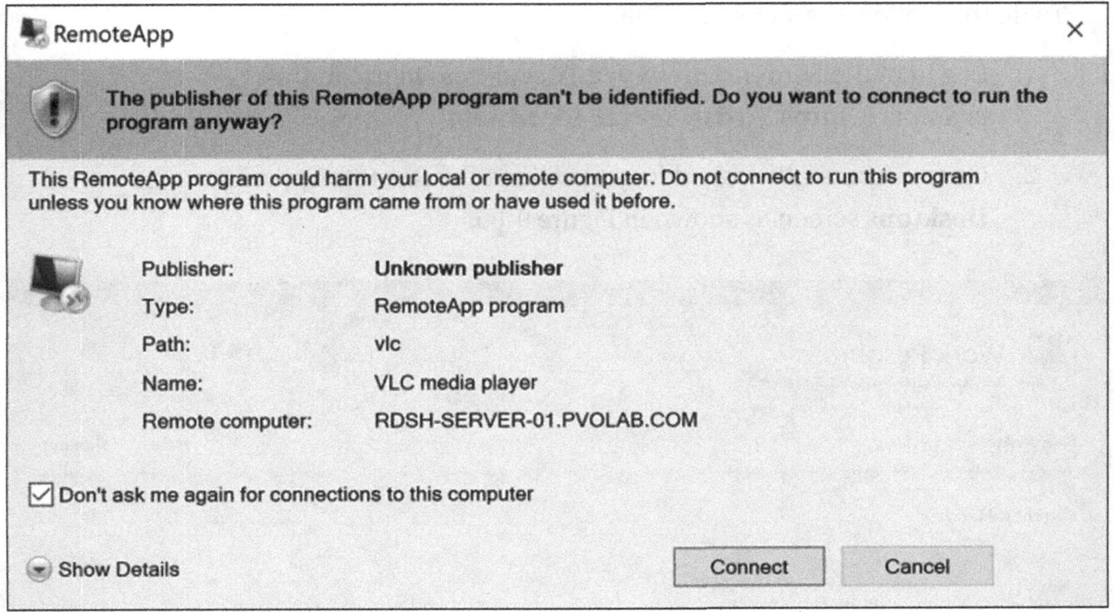

Figure 9-88. *RemoteApp warning box*

6. Click the **Connect** button.
7. You will see that the VLC media player app has launched as shown in Figure 9-89.

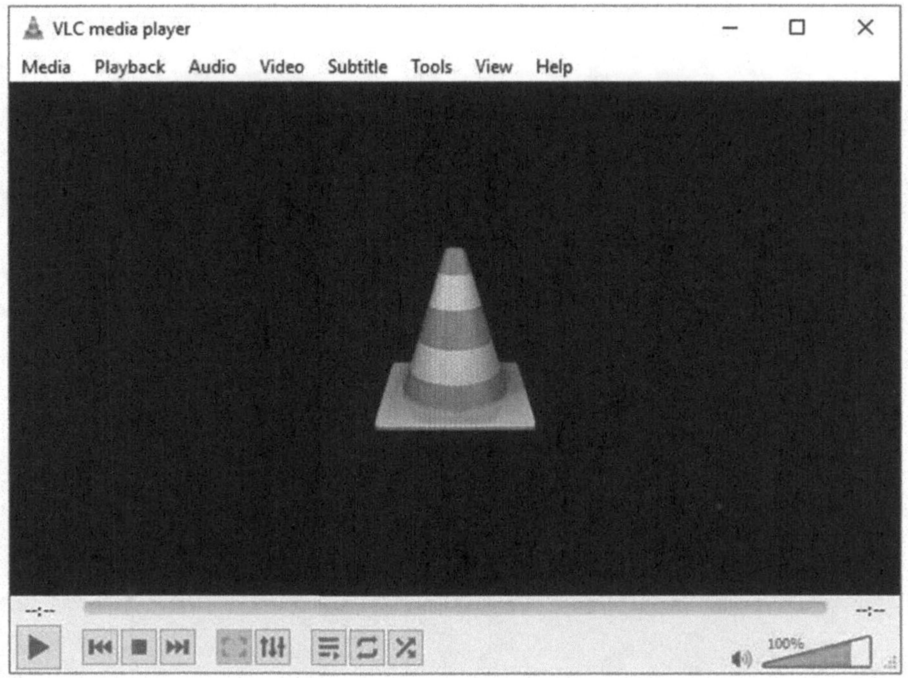

***Figure 9-89.** VLC media player running as a published app*

You have now successfully tested that the application launches.

Chapter summary

This chapter has focused on how to deliver App Volumes layered applications that are then published to end users with Microsoft RDSH server solutions and RemoteApp.

We started the chapter by discussing the use case as to why you would consider using layered application within an app publishing environment. The key reasons are scalability, manageability, and costs. Next, we looked at the infrastructure and how the solution fits together.

Armed with the knowledge of why you would take this approach, we moved to the how and built out a solution using the example lab. This enabled us to follow all the steps required in getting App Volumes to deliver apps that are then published to the end user.

Chapter summary

CHAPTER 10

Horizon Apps and App Volumes

This chapter, in effect, follows on from the previous chapter in that it builds upon what we covered in Chapter 9 by replacing the standard Microsoft connection broker elements and the RemoteApp website with the Horizon Connection Server. This enables published applications, published desktop sessions, and full virtual desktop machines to be delivered from the same platform. In this case, that platform is VMware Horizon.

This means that to gain access to their applications, end users will now use the Horizon Client or the Horizon browser connection.

As far as the back-end infrastructure is concerned, there is no change other than installing the Horizon Agent onto the RDSH server so that the Horizon Connection Server can access the published applications.

In this tenth chapter, we are going to first recap on the previous chapter so as to ensure you have the prerequisites in place before adding the Horizon-specific components, and then work through the process of setting up Horizon to deliver the applications that in turn are delivered by App Volumes.

We will start by looking at the architecture.

The architecture

We are going to start by looking at the high-level architecture of how App Volumes, RDSH servers, and the Horizon Connection Server fit together.

Figure 10-1 shows how App Volumes delivers applications to the RDSH server farm which is then brokered to the end users using the Horizon Connection Server.

P. von Oven, *Delivering Applications with VMware App Volumes 4*,
https://doi.org/10.1007/978-1-4842-6689-2_10

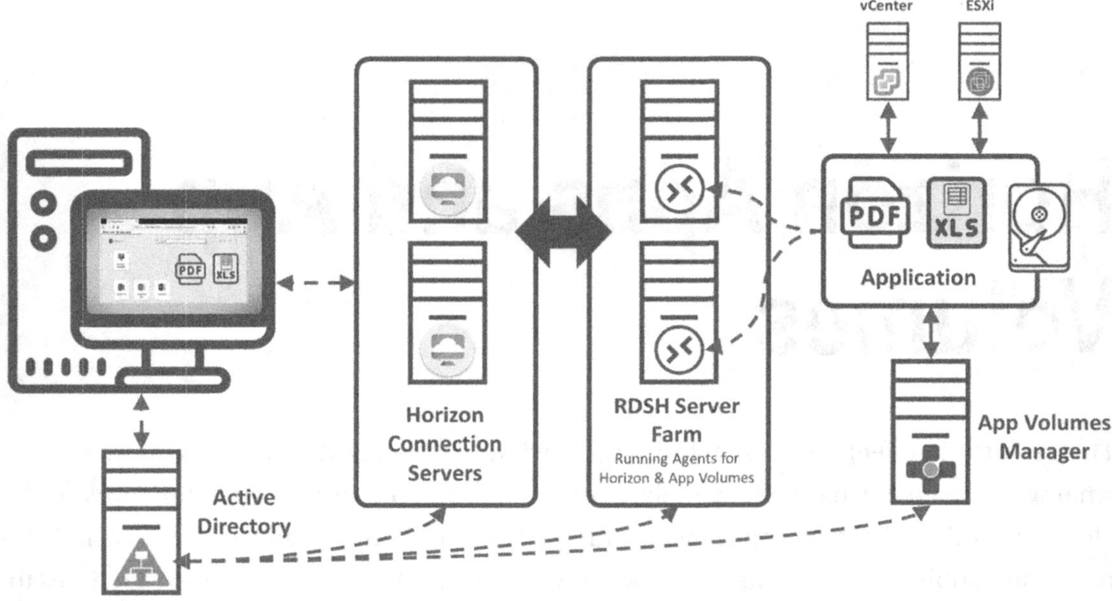

Figure 10-1. *RDSH, VMware Horizon, and App Volumes architecture*

Now that we have looked at the high-level architecture, in the next sections, we are going to work through the process of configuring the Horizon components to deliver published App Volumes applications.

Installing App Volumes with VMware Horizon

We are going to describe this as a three-step process. The first two steps are covered in detail in Chapter 9, and the focus of this chapter will be the configuration of the Horizon components. Before we do that, we will recap as to where we are and how we got to this stage. Figure 10-2 shows the first stage in capturing an application for App Volumes.

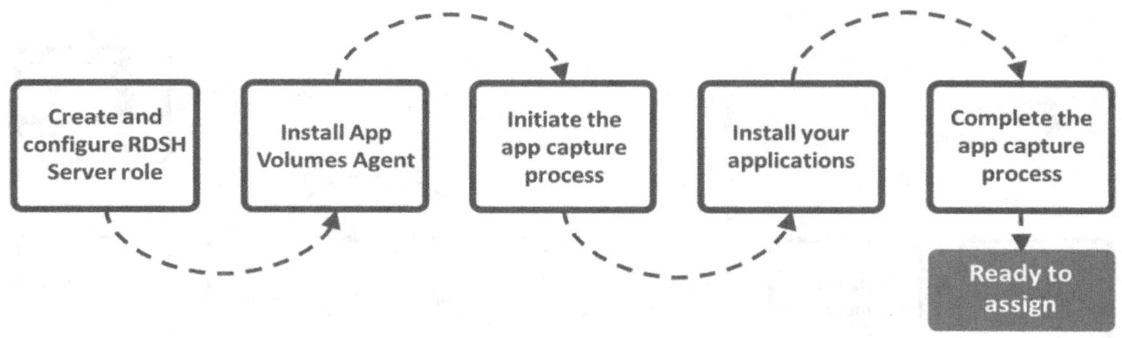

***Figure 10-2.** Step 1: Capturing an App Volumes application package*

In the second step, we take the newly captured application package, assign it to an RDSH server, configure the application collection within Remote Desktop Services, and test that the app is available.

This is shown in Figure 10-3.

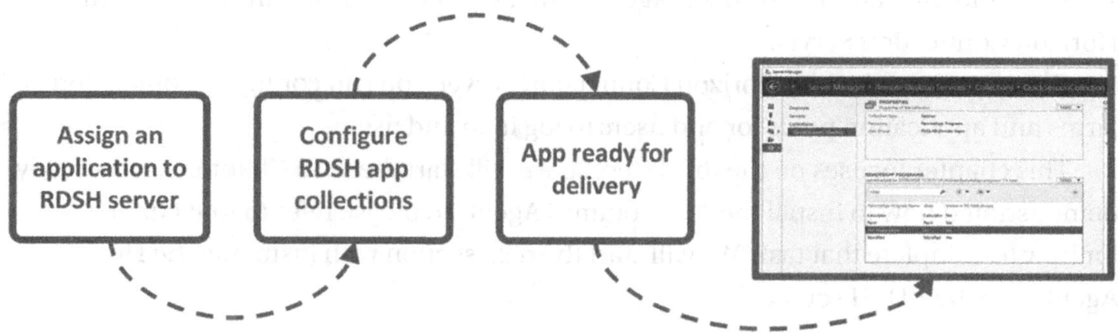

***Figure 10-3.** Step 2: Assigning and configuring application packages*

The third step is what this chapter will focus on, as this is the piece that adds to the previous steps that were covered in Chapter 9.

In this step, we add the Horizon components to the solution to enable Horizon to act as the broker for delivering apps to end users. This is shown in Figure 10-4.

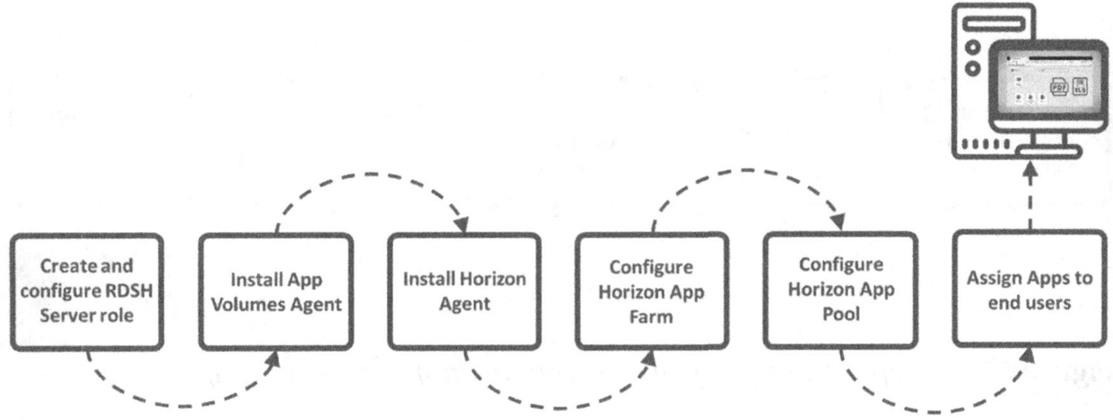

Figure 10-4. *Step 3: Installing and configuring the Horizon components*

We take an RDSH server (not the one used for capturing, but a production server) and install the App Volumes Agent so that it becomes a managed machine in App Volumes and then also the Horizon Agent so that the server can communicate with the Horizon Connection Server.

Once connected to the Horizon Connection Server, you can configure application farms and application pools for end users to log in to and use.

This chapter focuses on the third step, so we will start there. In Chapter 9, we already demonstrated how to install the App Volumes Agent, so please refer to that chapter for how to complete that task. We will start the next section with installing the Horizon Agent onto the RDSH server.

Installing the Horizon Agent

In this section, we are going to install the Horizon Agent onto the RDSH server in addition to the App Volumes Agent that has already been installed. For this example, we are using VMware Horizon 7.12.

The Horizon Agent allows the RDSH server to be accessed from the Horizon Connection Server that in turn enables administrators to build and configure application farms and pools using the applications already published by the RDSH server. Those applications in this case are delivered as layers by App Volumes.

To install the Horizon Agent, follow the steps described:

1. On the RDSH server, navigate to the Horizon Agent installer as shown in Figure 10-5.

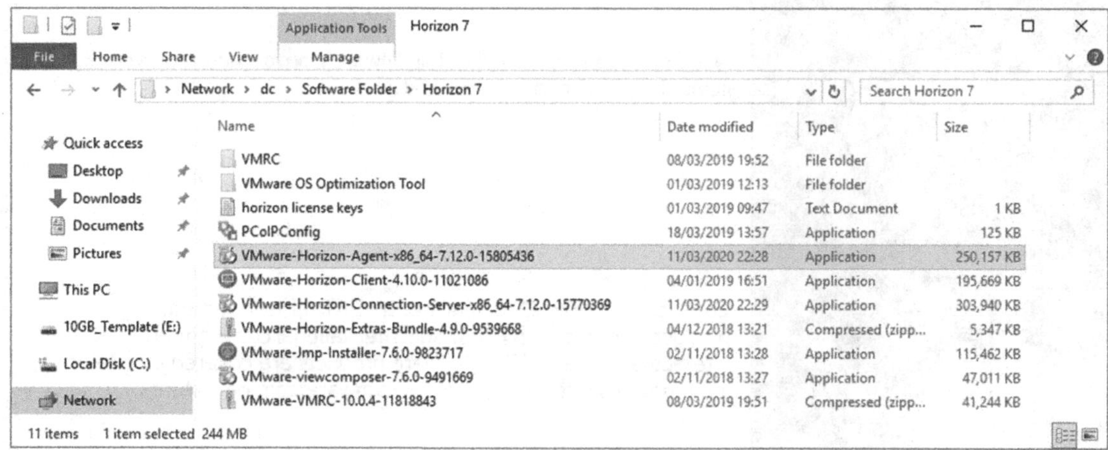

Figure 10-5. *Navigate to the Horizon Agent installer*

2. Double-click **VMware-Horizon-Agent-x86_64-7.12.0** to launch the installer. In this example, we are using Horizon 7.12.

3. You will see the **Welcome to the Installation Wizard for VMware Horizon Agent** as shown in Figure 10-6.

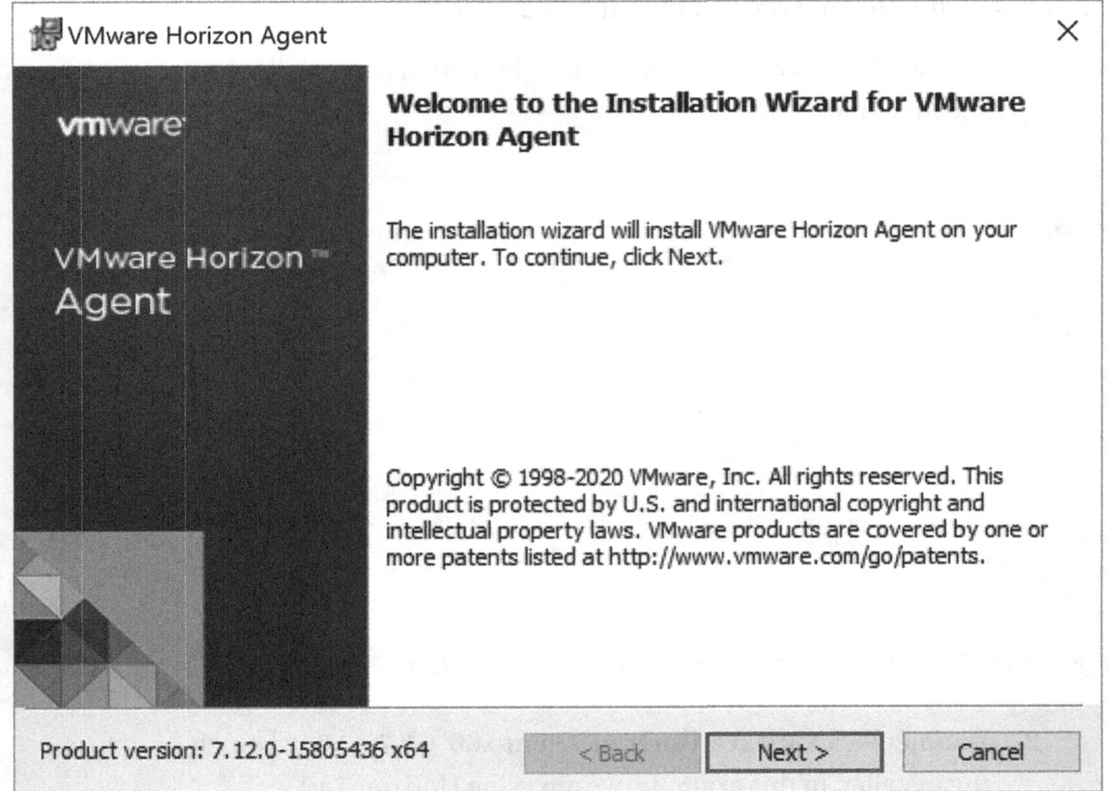

***Figure 10-6.** Horizon Agent installer welcome screen*

4. Click **Next** ► to continue.
5. You will see the **License Agreement** screen as shown in Figure 10-7.

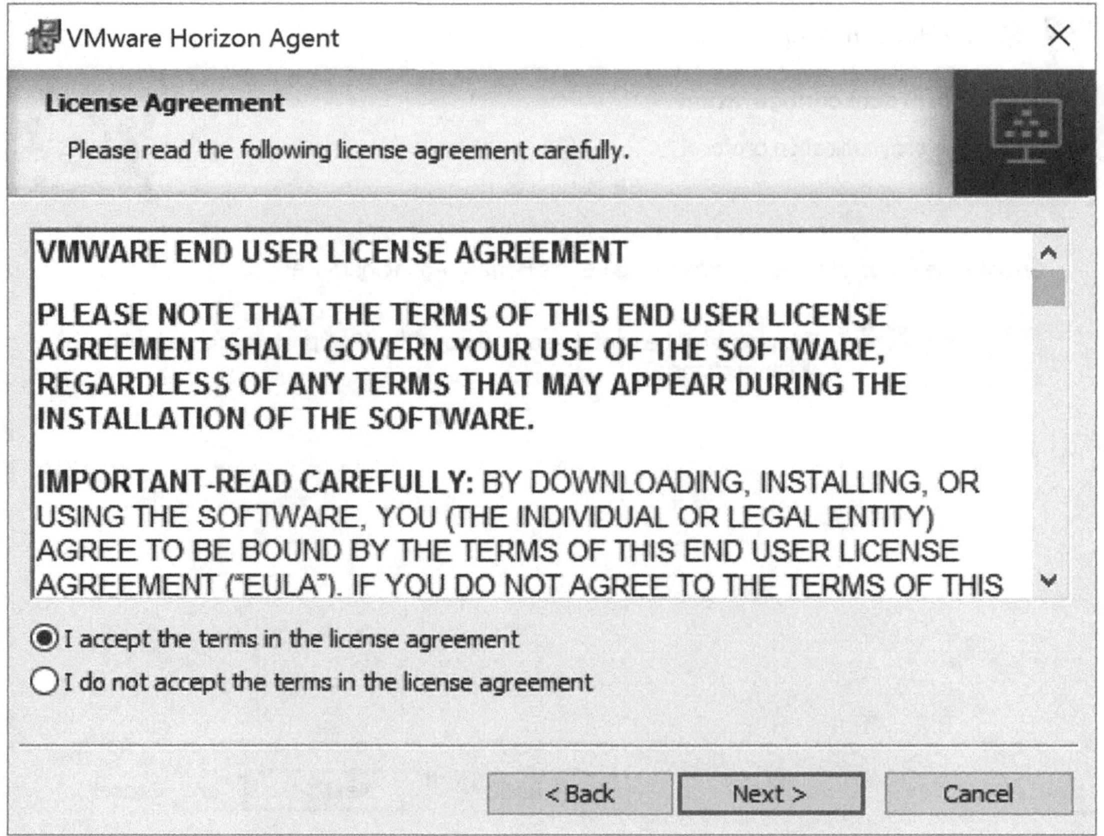

Figure 10-7. *License Agreement screen*

6. Click the **I accept the terms in the license agreement** radio button.
7. Click **Next ►** to continue.
8. You will see the **Network Protocol configuration** screen as shown in Figure 10-8.

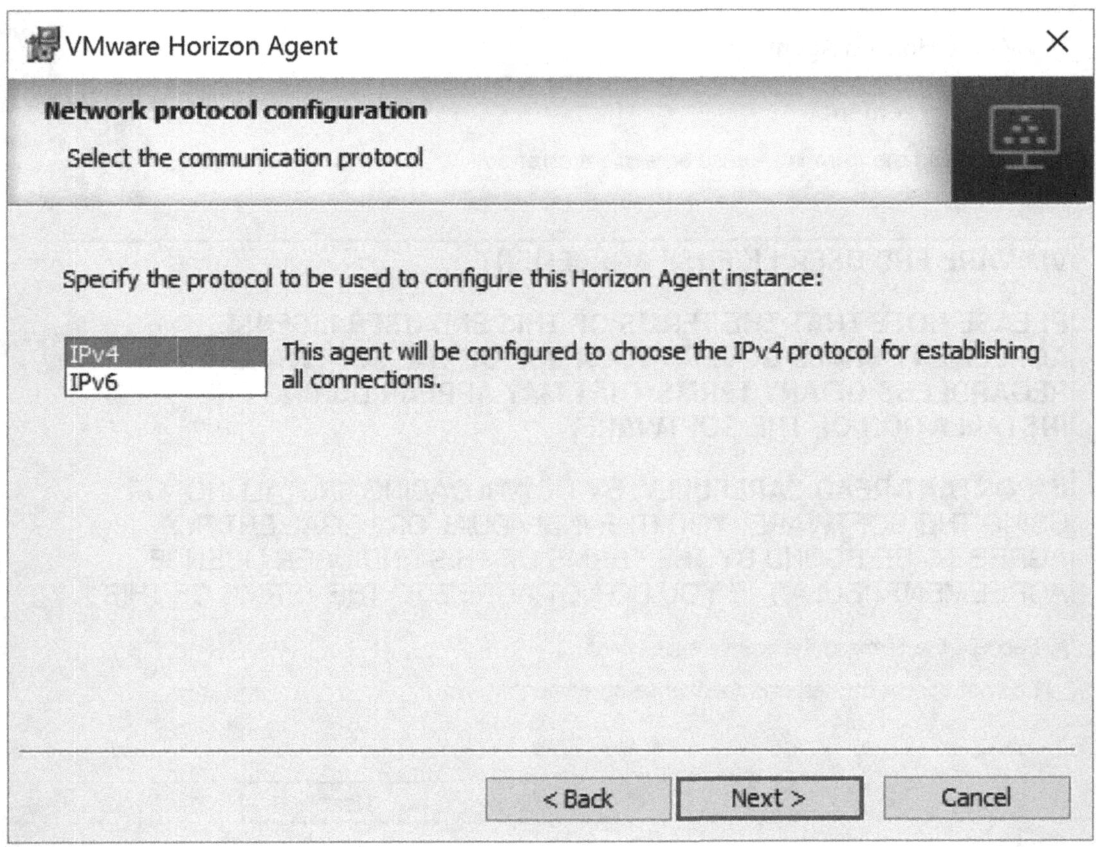

Figure 10-8. *Network protocol configuration screen*

9. From the list, select the IP version that you are going to use. In this example, our Horizon environment uses IPv4.

You cannot mix and match IP versions in a Horizon environment, so you need to ensure that all components use the same version.

---

10. Click **Next** ► to continue.

11. You will now see the **Custom Setup** screen. On this screen, you can select the various features you want to include in the install. These are shown in Figure 10-9.

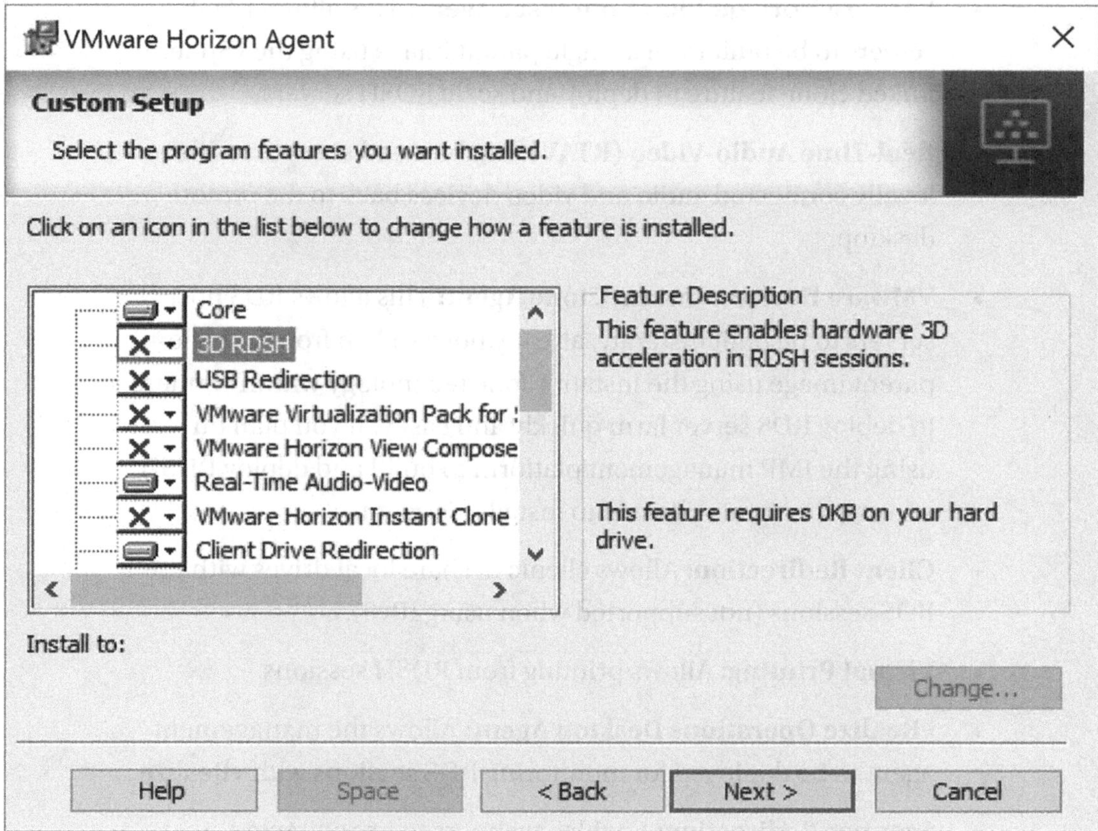

Figure 10-9. *Custom Setup screen*

In this example, we are going to accept the default option selection. You will note that there are some other features you can add to the Horizon Agent, including a **3D RDSH** option to allow for 3D graphics acceleration during the RDSH session.

The other available features are listed as follows:

- **Core:** Installs the core features that are required for running on an RDSH server.
- **USB Redirection:** Redirects USB devices from the Horizon Client on the endpoint device to the RDSH session.
- VMware Virtualization Pack for Skype for Business: Delivers an optimal end user experience between end points

- **VMware Horizon View Composer Agent:** This allows RDSH servers to be built from a single parent image using the vSphere linked clone feature to deploy and scale RDSH servers.
- **Real-Time Audio-Video (RTAV):** Enables end users to redirect locally connected audio and video devices back to the remote desktop.
- **VMware Horizon Instant Clone Agent:** This allows RDS host servers to be built instantly, already powered on from a single parent image using the Instant Clone technology within vSphere to deploy RDS server farm quickly and easily. If you plan on using the JMP management platform to build and deploy RDSH servers, then you will need to install this agent.
- **Client Redirection:** Allows clients to share local drives with the RDS sessions (not supported when using IPv6).
- **Virtual Printing:** Allows printing from RDSH sessions.
- **vRealize Operations Desktop Agent:** Allows the management agent to be deployed for monitoring RDS sessions with vRealize.
- **Scanner Redirection:** Enables scanners to be redirected.
- **Serial Port Redirection:** Enables serial ports to be redirected.
- **Flash Redirection:** Enables Flash to be redirected.
- **Device Bridge BAS Plugin:** Enables fingerprint scanners that are supported by the BAS system.
- **Geolocation Redirection:** Enables redirection of the client's geolocation to the remote session.
- **VMware Client IP Transparency:** Allows remote connections to Internet Explorer to use the client IP address instead of the IP address of the RDSH server. This is not supported when using IPv6.
- **Horizon Performance Tracker:** Enables the performance tracker.

- **Hybrid Logon:** Allows unauthenticated users to have access to network resources without having to enter their credentials.
- **VMware Integrated Printing:** Enables printer redirection.
- **Help Desk Plugin for Horizon:** Enables the help desk feature.

12. Once you have selected all the features you want to install with the Horizon Agent, click the **Next ►** button to continue.
13. You will now see the **Register with Horizon 7 Connection Server** as shown in Figure 10-10.

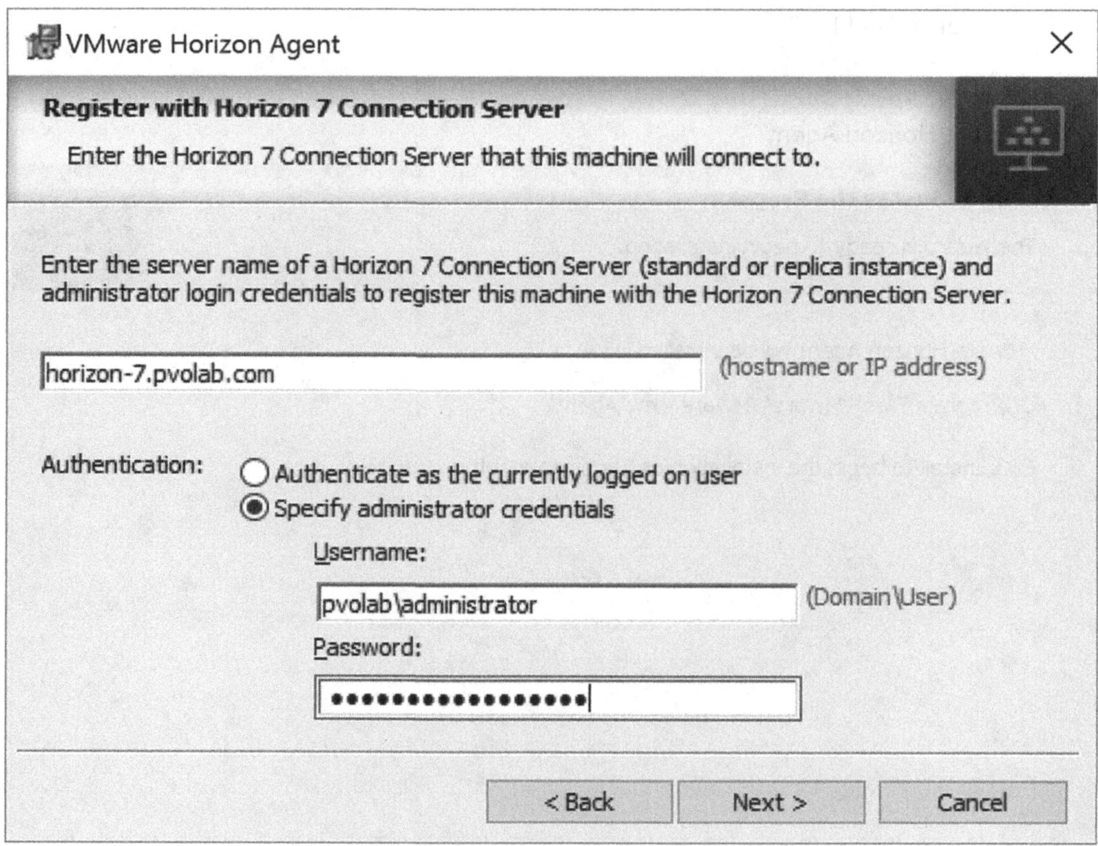

***Figure 10-10.** Registering with the Horizon Connection Server*

14. In the **(hostname or IP address)** box, type in the address of the Horizon Connection Server you want to register this machine with. In this example, the address is horizon-7.pvolab.com.

15. In the **Authentication** section, click the radio button for **Specify administrator credentials.**

16. Then, in the **Username** box, type in the username using the domain\user format. In this example, the username would be entered as **pvolab\administrator.**

17. Finally, in the **Password** box, type in the password for the username you used in the previous step.

18. Click the **Next ►** button to continue.

19. You will see the **Ready to Install the Program** screen as shown in Figure 10-11.

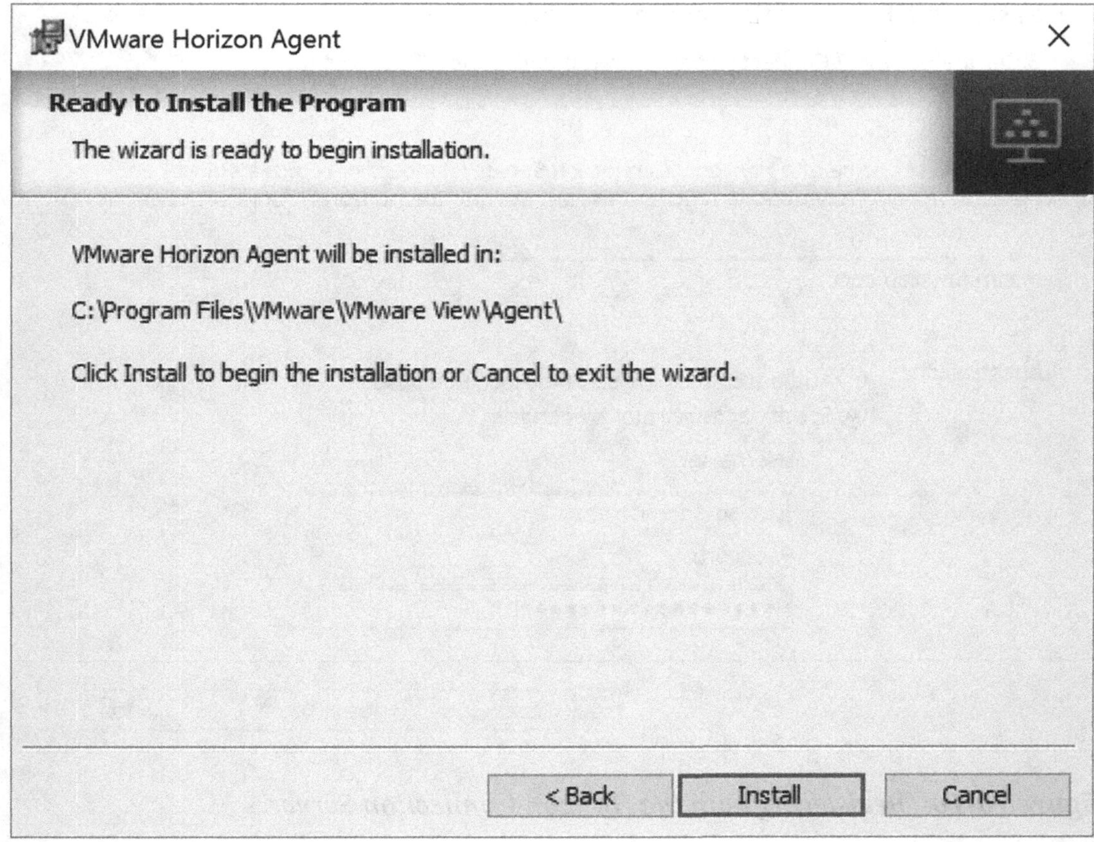

Figure 10-11. *Ready to Install the Program screen*

20. Click the **Install** button. You will see the Horizon Agent being installed as shown in Figure 10-12.

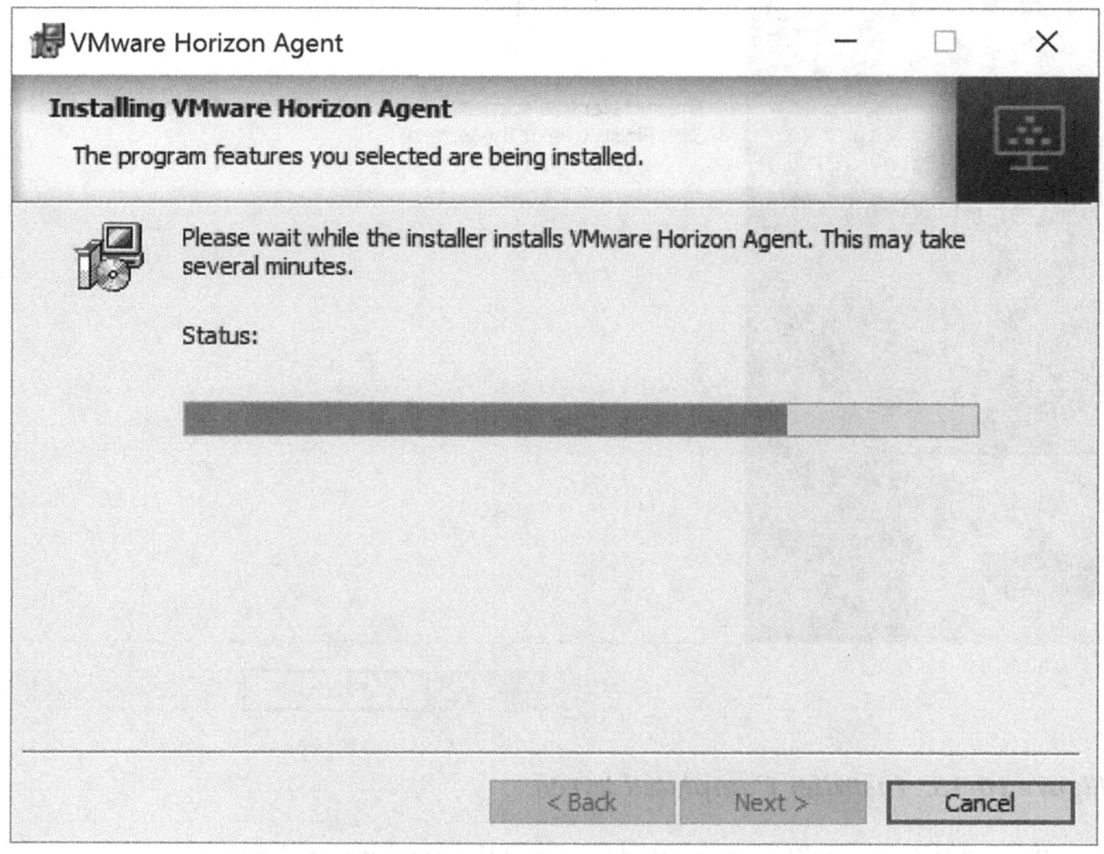

***Figure 10-12.** Horizon installation progress*

21. Once the installation has successfully completed, you will see the **Installer Completed** screen as shown in Figure 10-13.

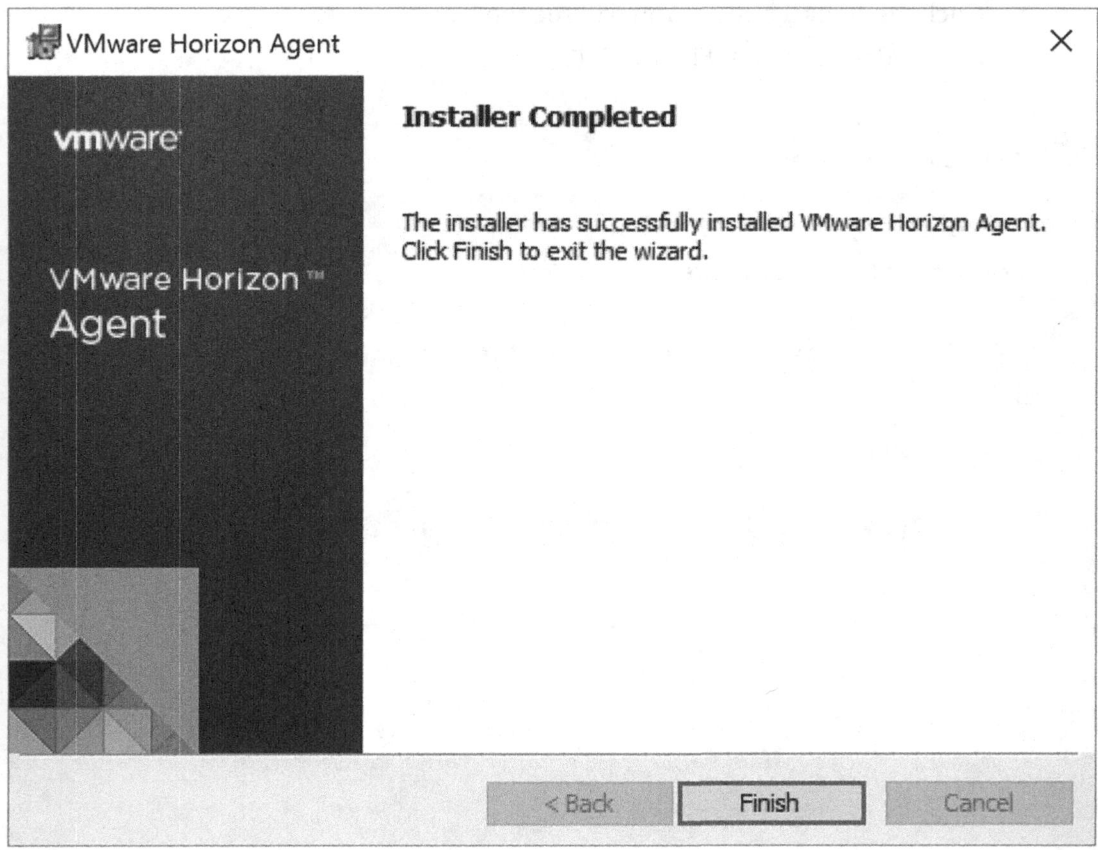

***Figure 10-13. Installer Completed** screen*

22. Finally, you will be prompted to restart the machine as shown in Figure 10-14.

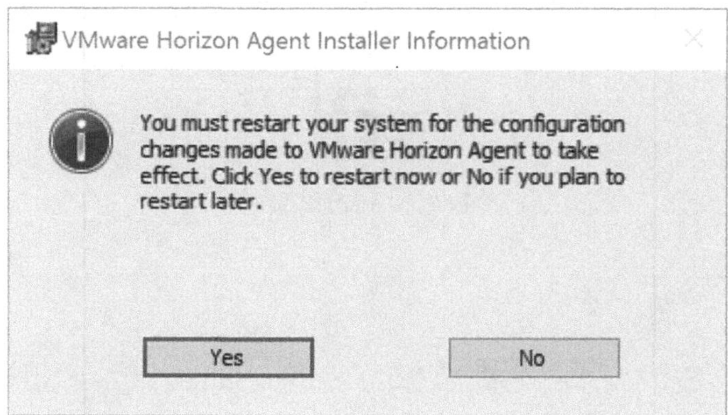

Figure 10-14. *Horizon Agent Installer restart dialog box*

23. Click the **Yes** button to restart.

You have now successfully installed the Horizon Agent so that the RDSH server can connect to the Horizon Connection Server. In the next section, we are going to start configuring the applications, starting with the application farm.

Configuring a Horizon App farm

With the Horizon Agent now installed, the RDSH server can communicate with the Horizon Connection Server. So now we can switch to the admin console on the Horizon Connection Server and complete the next task. That next task is creating an application farm. The application farm is a construct that contains the RDSH servers that are hosting the applications.

In Horizon terms, it is the equivalent to building a desktop pool where the desktop pool contains a number of virtual desktop machines that can be accessed and used by the end users.

To configure an application farm, follow the steps described:

1. Log in to the Horizon administration console via a browser and using the address of the Horizon Connection Server. In this example, the server is called horizon-7.pvolab.com.

2. You will see the login screen as shown in Figure 10-15.

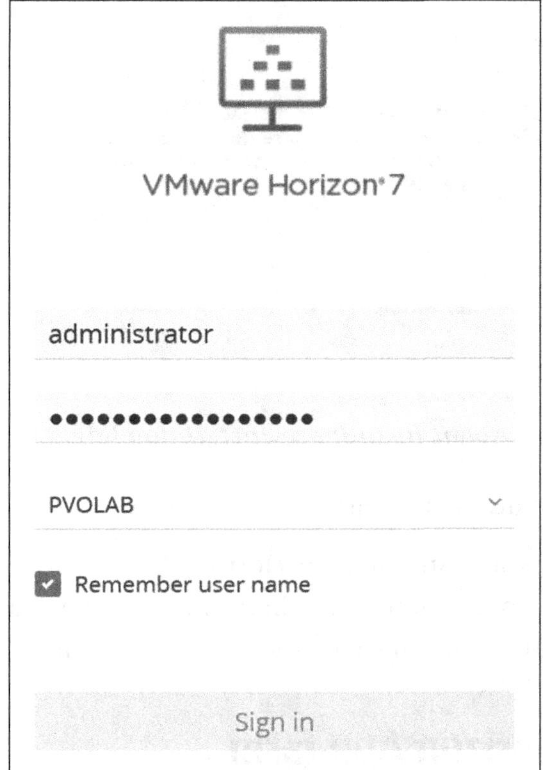

Figure 10-15. *Login to the Horizon admin console*

3. Log in using the administrator account, and then in the box below, enter the password for the administrator account.

4. From the drop-down menu, select the domain for this user, in this example, the PVOLAB domain, and then click **Sign in**.

5. You will see the main dashboard screen.

6. From the left-hand side menu, expand the **Inventory** option and then click **Farms** as shown in Figure 10-16.

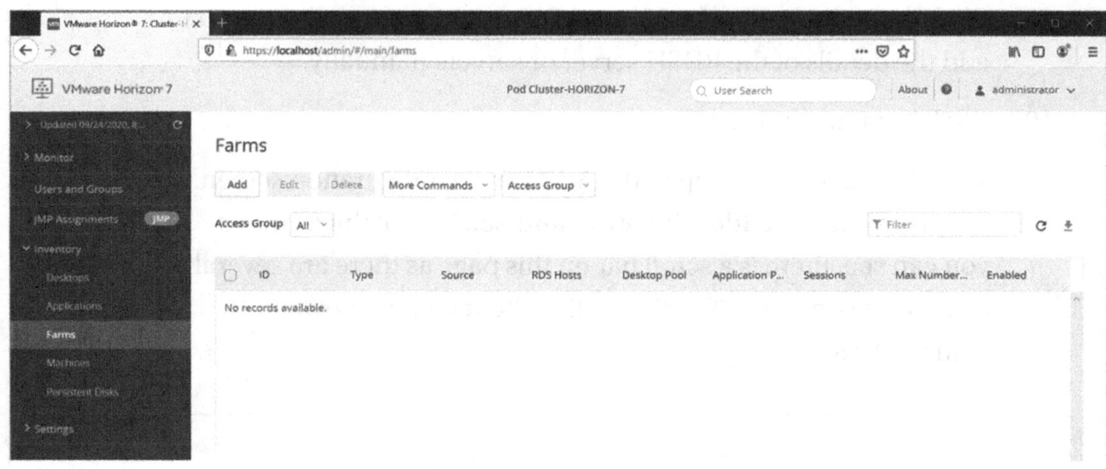

Figure 10-16. *Farms configuration screen*

7. From the top row of the menu options, click the **Add** button.
8. You will now see the **Add Farm** configuration screen as shown in Figure 10-17.

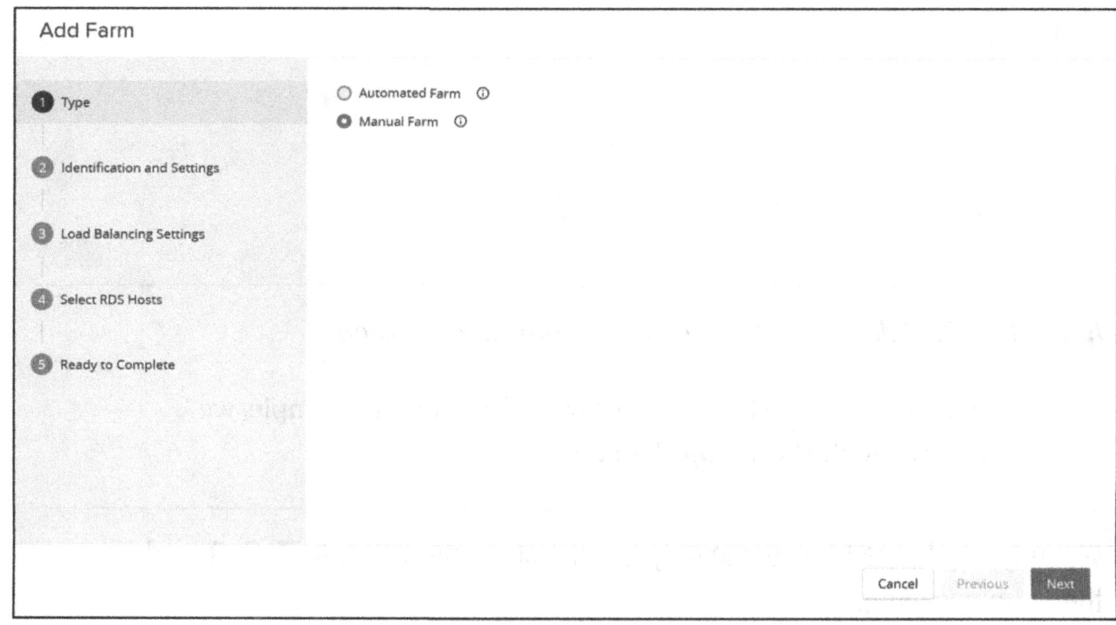

Figure 10-17. *Adding the farm configuration screen – step 1*

9. Click the radio button for **Manual Farm**. This option allows you to add the details of the RDSH server or servers manually.

10. Click **Next** to continue.

11. You will see the next step of the **Add Farm** configuration screen. This is to enter the **Identification and Settings** of the farm. As you can see, there is a scroll bar on this page as there are several options to configure. The first half of the screen is shown in Figure 10-18.

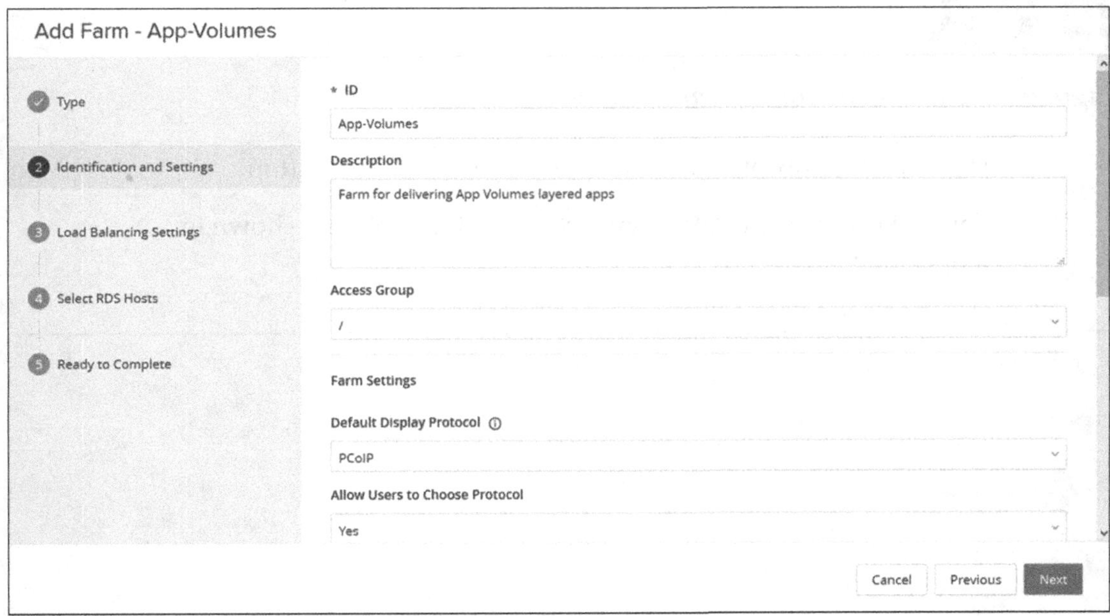

Figure 10-18. *Adding the farm configuration screen - step 2*

12. In the **ID** box, type in the name for the farm. In this example, we have called the farm **App-Volumes**.

When typing in the ID, you can only use the characters **a–z**, **A–Z**, **0–9**, and the – (minus sign).

---

13. Next, you can enter a description for the farm so that you easily recognize what it is used for. This is an optional field.

14. In the **Access Group** box, you can choose an access group for this farm if you have configured one. Access Groups are used to review the desktop pools and machines that have been configured as part of an access group. In this example, we will leave the default setting.

15. You now have the **Farm Settings** section and the first setting for selecting the **Default Display Protocol**. From the drop-down menu, choose the protocol you want to use. In this example, we have chosen PCoIP so the published App Volumes apps will be delivered to the client using PCoIP.

16. In the next drop-down menu, **Allow Users to Choose Protocol**, you can choose whether you want to allow end users to be able to change the default display protocol.

    Now scroll down to the second half of the configuration screen as shown in Figure 10-19.

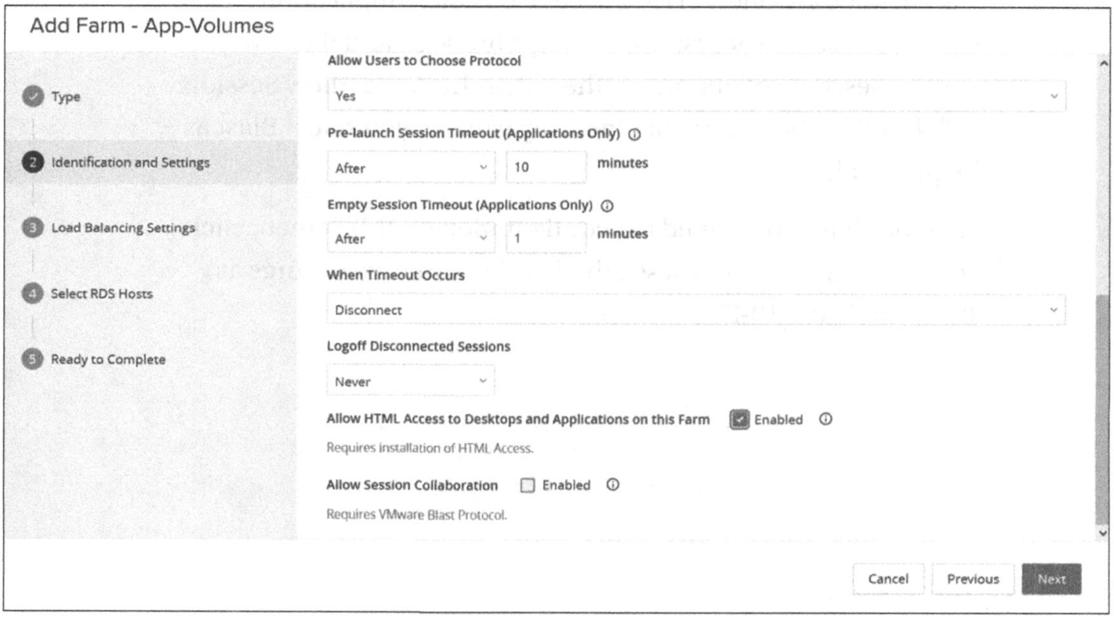

Figure 10-19. *Adding the farm configuration screen – step 3*

17. In the **Pre-launch Session Timeout (Applications Only)** section, enter a time after which any prelaunched application should time-out if they are not used.

18. Then in the **Empty Session Timeout (Applications Only),** enter a time after which any empty or unused sessions should time-out if they are not used.

19. In the **When Timeout Occurs** box, from the drop-down menu, select what action should be taken should a timeout event occur. In this example, we have opted to **Disconnect** the user from the session.

20. The **Logoff Disconnected Sessions** option allows you to log off any disconnected sessions. In this example, this is set to **Never**, so disconnected sessions remain, and the user will not be logged off. This means they can easily reconnect to the same session again.

21. Check the **Allow HTML Access to Desktops and Applications on this Farm** box to allow HTML access to hosted applications if you want your users to access apps using a browser, and if you want to allow session collaboration, then also check the Allow Session Collaboration box. Note that this only works if you select Blast as the protocol.

22. Once you have completed the configuration on this screen, click **Next** to continue. You will see the **Load Balancing Settings** as shown in Figure 10-20.

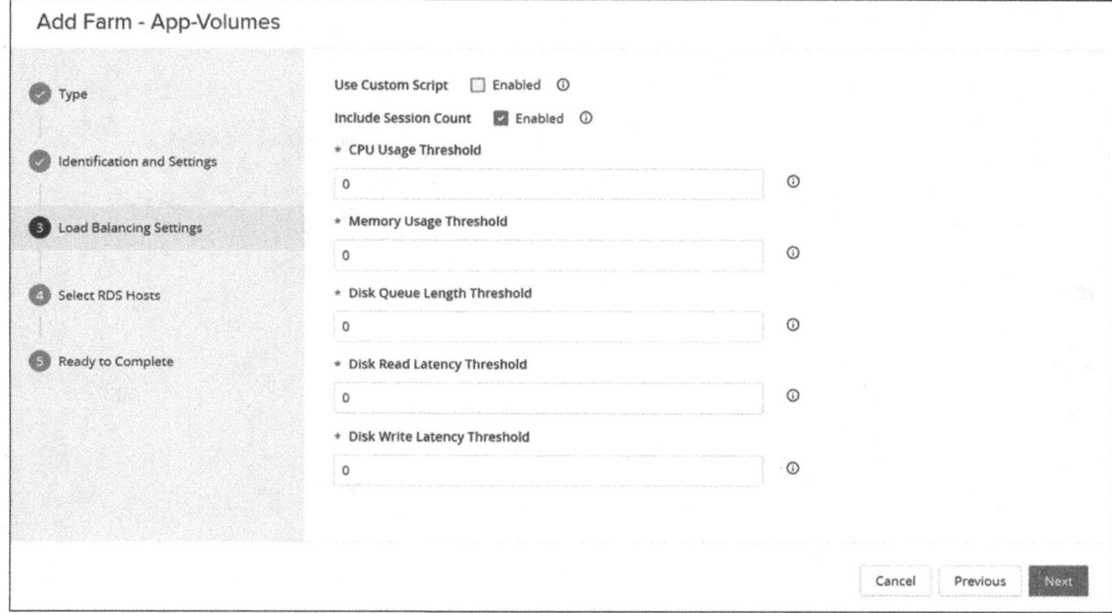

Figure 10-20. *Load balancing configuration screen*

23. On the **Load Balancing Settings** screen, you can configure the load balancing across the server in the farm. You can configure the thresholds at which point the application sessions are delivered by other servers in the farm. You can configure the CPU, memory, disk queue length, disk read latency, and disk write latency. The default setting for all these components is 0, so we will leave this as the default in this example.
24. Click **Next** to continue.
25. You will see the **Select RDS Hosts** screen as shown in Figure 10-21.

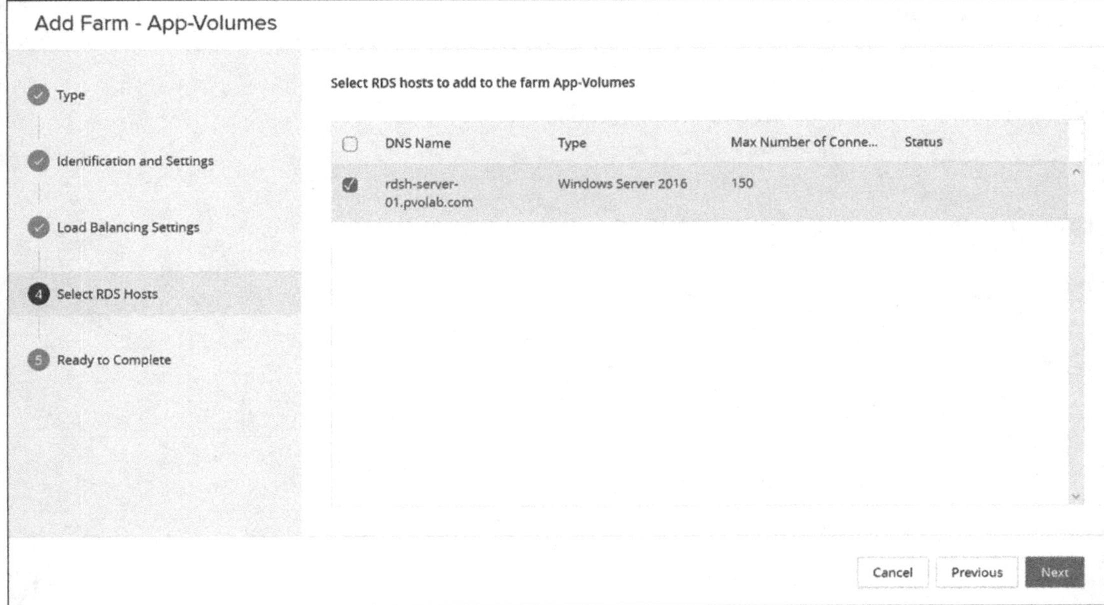

Figure 10-21. *Selecting the RDS hosts for the App Volumes farm*

26. Check the box next to the RDS servers you want to add to the App Volumes farm. In this example, we just have the server called **rdsh-server-01.pvolab.com** to choose from.

27. Click **Next** to continue.

28. You will now see the Ready to Complete screen as shown in Figure 10-22.

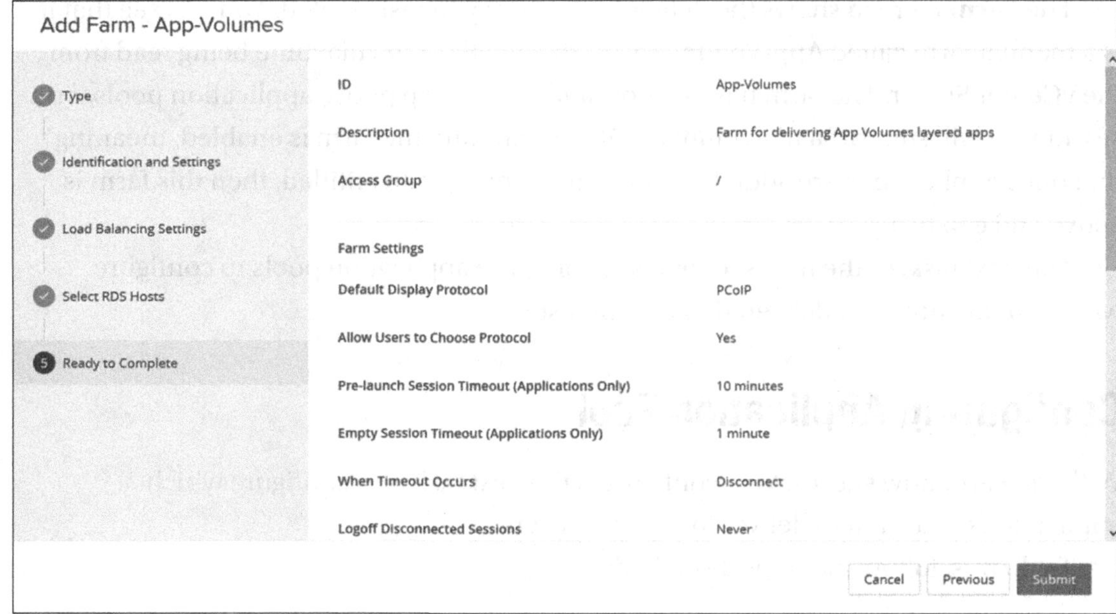

Figure 10-22. *Ready to Complete screen*

29. Check the configuration details you have entered and then click the **Submit** button.

30. You will now return to the **Farms** screen as shown in Figure 10-23.

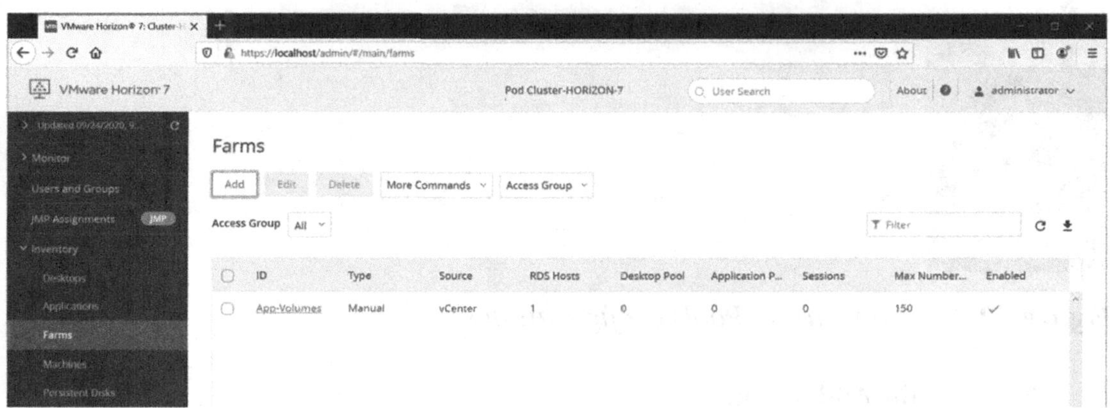

Figure 10-23. *Farms screen now showing the newly created App Volumes farm*

31. You have now successfully configured a farm.

The **Farms** screen shows the details of the farm you just created. You can see that it is a manual farm called App-Volumes, with the details of the machine being read from the vCenter Server. The farm has one host and no desktop pools, application pools, or sessions. It will support a maximum of 150 sessions and the farm is enabled, meaning that once applications are added and once users have been entitled, then this farm is active and can be used.

The next task, in the next section, is to configure application pools to configure which applications are delivered to the end users.

Configuring Application Pool

With the Farm now successfully configured, the next task is to configure which applications you want to deliver to your end users.

To do this, follow the steps described:

1. From the Horizon admin console and the left-hand navigation menu, click to expand **Inventory**, and then click **Applications**. You will see the **Application Pools** configuration screen as shown in Figure 10-24.

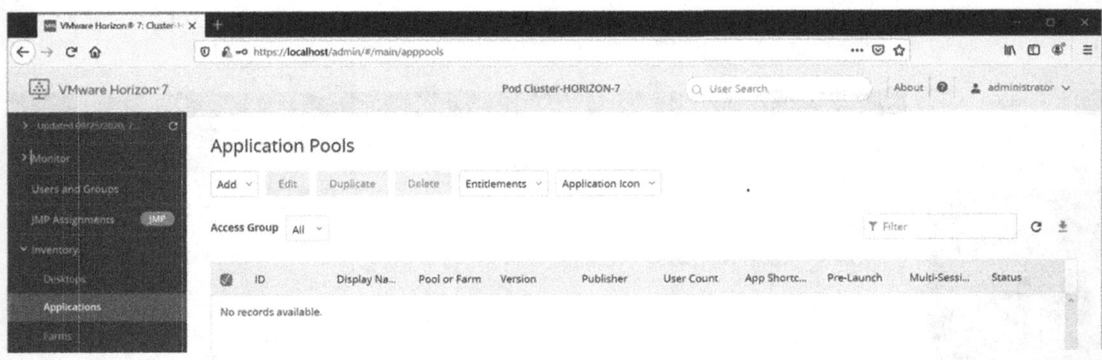

Figure 10-24. *Application Pools configuration screen*

2. Click the **Add** button.

3. The button in this case is a drop-down menu with two options, **Add Manually** or **Add from Installed Applications,** as shown in Figure 10-25.

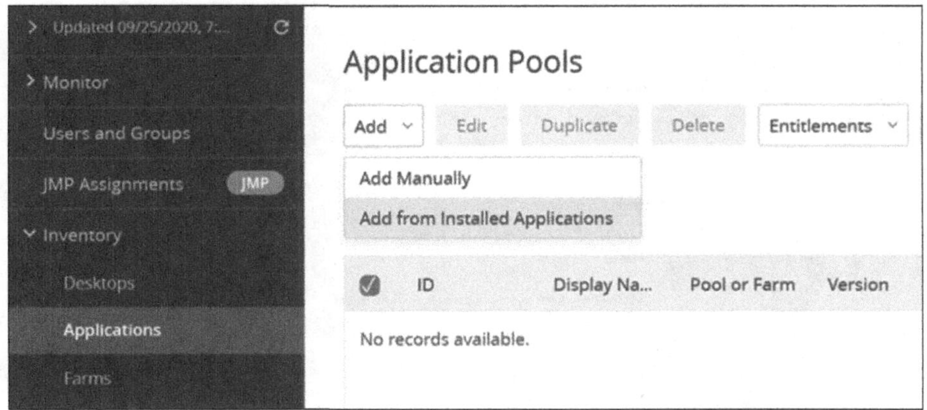

Figure 10-25. Adding an Application Pool

4. Click the **Add from Installed Applications** option.

5. You will see the next screen - the **Add Application Pool** configuration screen.

6. In the **Application Pool Type** section, click the radio button for **RDS Farm.**

7. From the drop-down box below the pool type, click and select the name of the farm. In this example, we only have one farm to choose from. The **App-Volumes** farm, so select this from the list.

   Next, you can select the applications. In this example, we are going to select the VLC media player as this is the app that is being delivered to the RDSH server using App Volumes.

8. In the **Select Installed Applications** box, there is a filter box on the right-hand side. In the box, type **vlc** and then click to search.

9. You will see the results of the search displayed as shown in Figure 10-26.

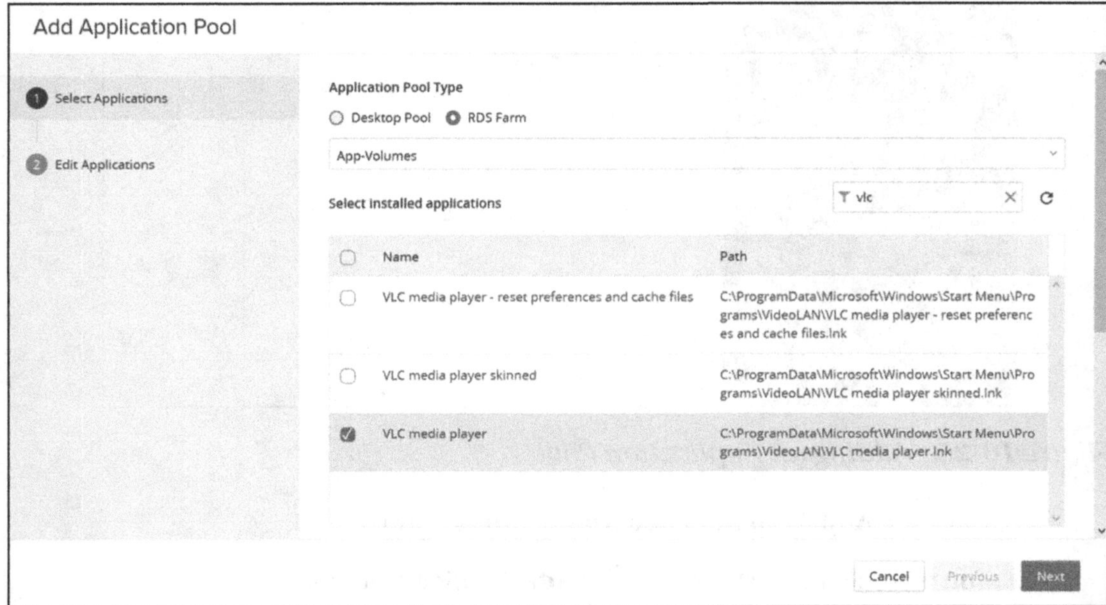

Figure 10-26. *Selecting the applications for delivery*

10. Click the button to select **VLC media player** and then click the **Next** button.

11. You will now see the **Edit Applications** screen.

12. By default, these fields have already been populated with the information presented by the RDSH server; however, in the ID box, you can enter a new ID for this application along with the ability to edit the Display Name. The ID is used within Horizon to identify the pool as with any other desktop or application pool. The display name is what the end users will see on their device when they connect to Horizon.

13. The **Edit Applications** screen is shown in Figure 10-27.

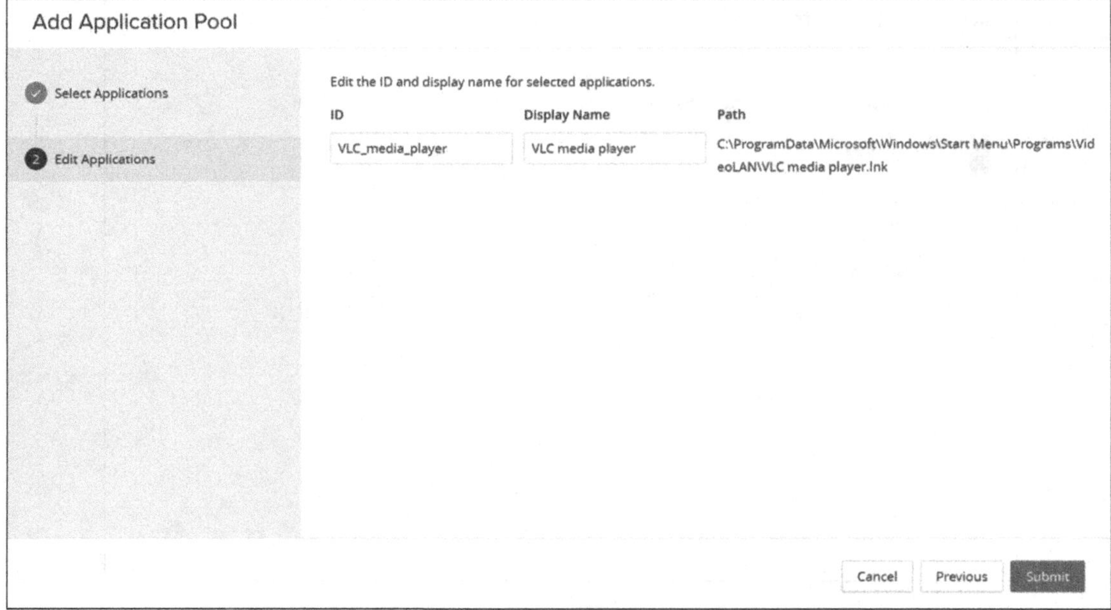

Figure 10-27. *Edit the applications*

14. Now click the **Submit** button.

15. You will now see the **Add Entitlements** screen where you can choose which users and groups can access the application pool, as shown in Figure 10-28.

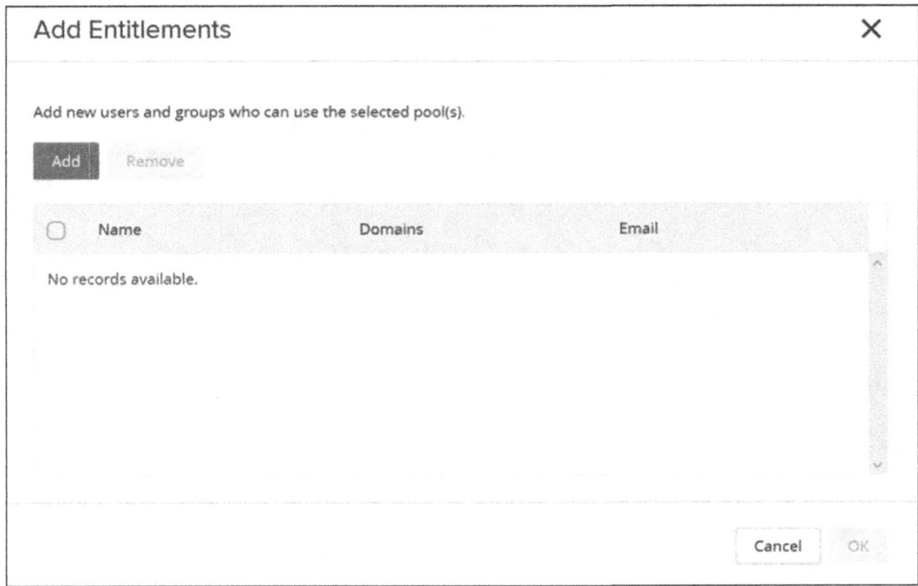

Figure 10-28. *Add Entitlements configuration screen*

16. Click the **Add** button. You will now see the **Find User or Group** configuration screen.

In this example, we are going to add the user Peter von Oven and so will use this username as the search criteria.

1. In the **Type** box, check the boxes for what you want to search for, **Users**, **Groups**, or **Unauthenticated Users.**

2. In the **Domain** box, from the drop-down menu, select the domain in which this user resides. In this example, this is the **pvolab.com** domain.

3. You can then filter the results on either the **Name/User Name** or **Description.** In this example, we are going to search using the **Name** field, selecting **Contains** from the filter options. Then in the box, we will type the name to search for, in this example, the name peter. So, we will search the domain for usernames that contain peter in them.

4. Click the **Find** button. You will see the results listed below as shown in Figure 10-29.

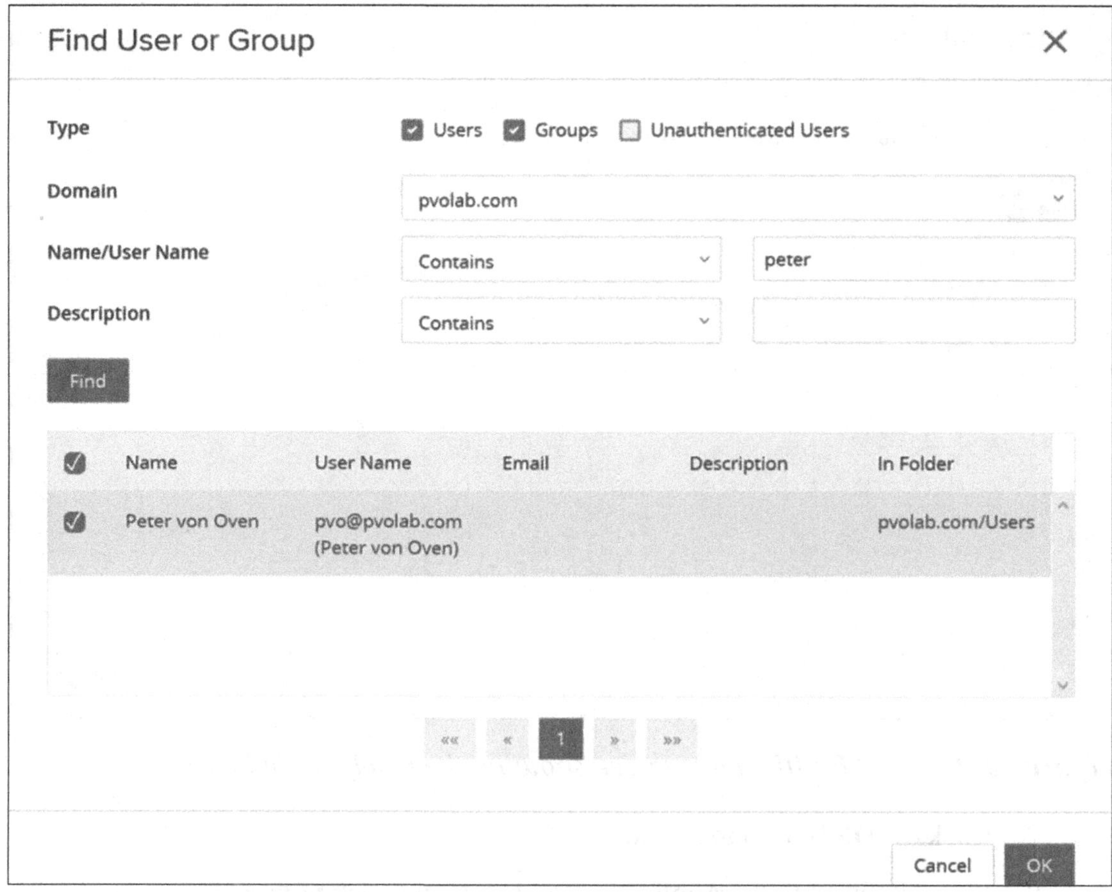

Figure 10-29. *Searching for an end user*

5. Check the box to select the user, and then click the **OK** button to continue.

6. Once added, you will return to the **Add Entitlements** screen which will now show the newly added user and the ability to continue adding more users as shown in Figure 10-30.

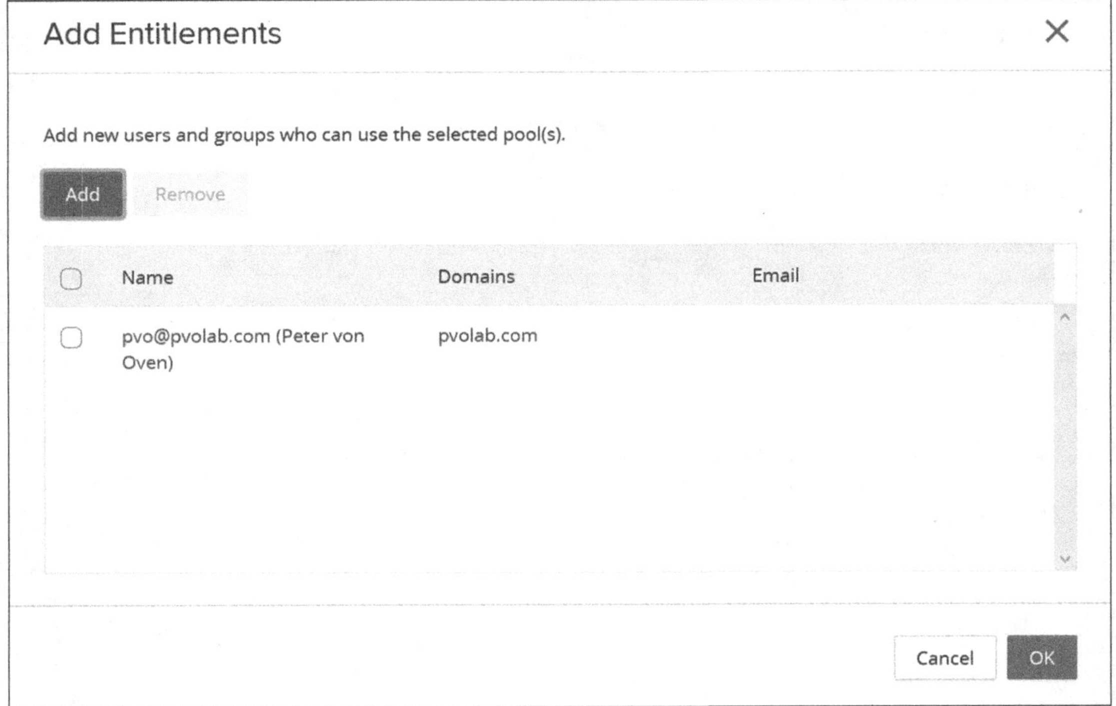

***Figure 10-30.** Add Entitlements screen showing the newly added user*

7. Click the **OK** button to continue.

8. You will return to the Application Pools screen which now shows the details of the application that you just added to the pool as shown in Figure 10-31.

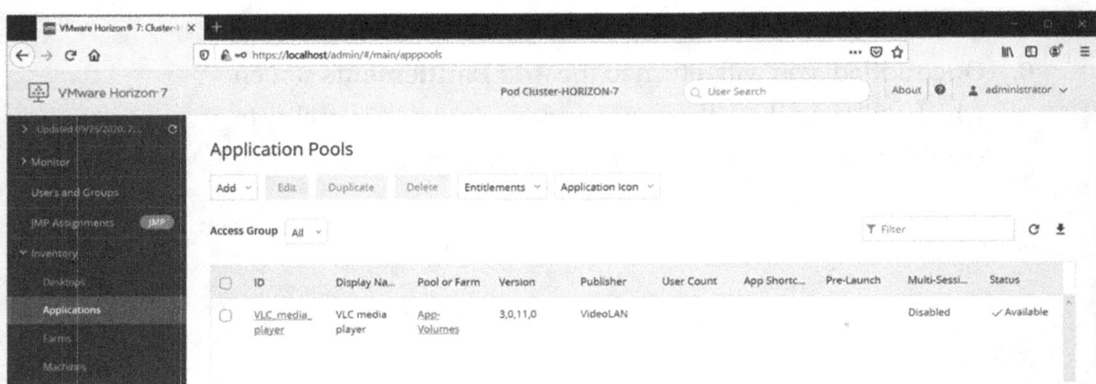

***Figure 10-31.** Application Pools screen showing the newly added application*

You have now successfully added an Application Pool and entitled an end user to be able to access the pool and the applications within it.

To make sure everything is working as expected and that end users can connect and launch the application, in the next section, we are going to assume the role of the end user and test the application.

Testing the application

In this last section, now that we have finished configuring everything, we are going to take on the role of the end user and ensure that they can log in, connect, and launch the newly published application that is being delivered to the RDSH servers using App Volumes.

We are going to connect using a browser. To do this, complete the following steps as described:

1. Log in to VMware Horizon as an end user. To do this, open a browser and in this example enter the address to the Horizon Connection Server - `https:\\horizon-7.pvolab.com`.
2. You will see the login box as shown in Figure 10-32.

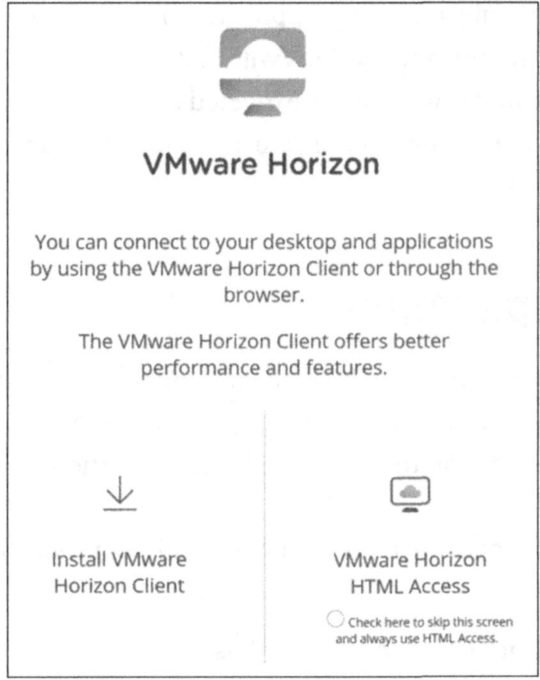

Figure 10-32. *VMware Horizon end user login screen*

3. As we are going to connect using the browser, click **VMware Horizon HTML Access.**

4. You will now see the login box for the end user to enter their credentials. In this example, we are logging in as the end user **pvo**, so type in **pvo@pvolab.com** into the username box followed by the password for this user. This is the user that was entitled to this application pool earlier in this chapter.

5. This is shown in Figure 10-33.

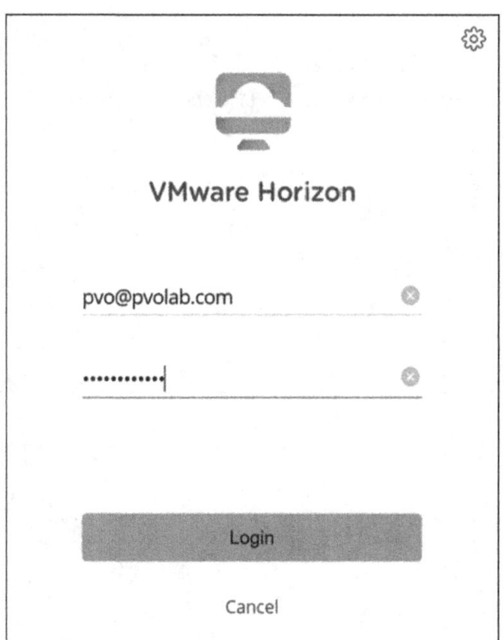

Figure 10-33. *Logging in as the end user*

6. Click the **Login** button to log in. You will now see the Horizon web page showing the entitled application (Figure 10-34).

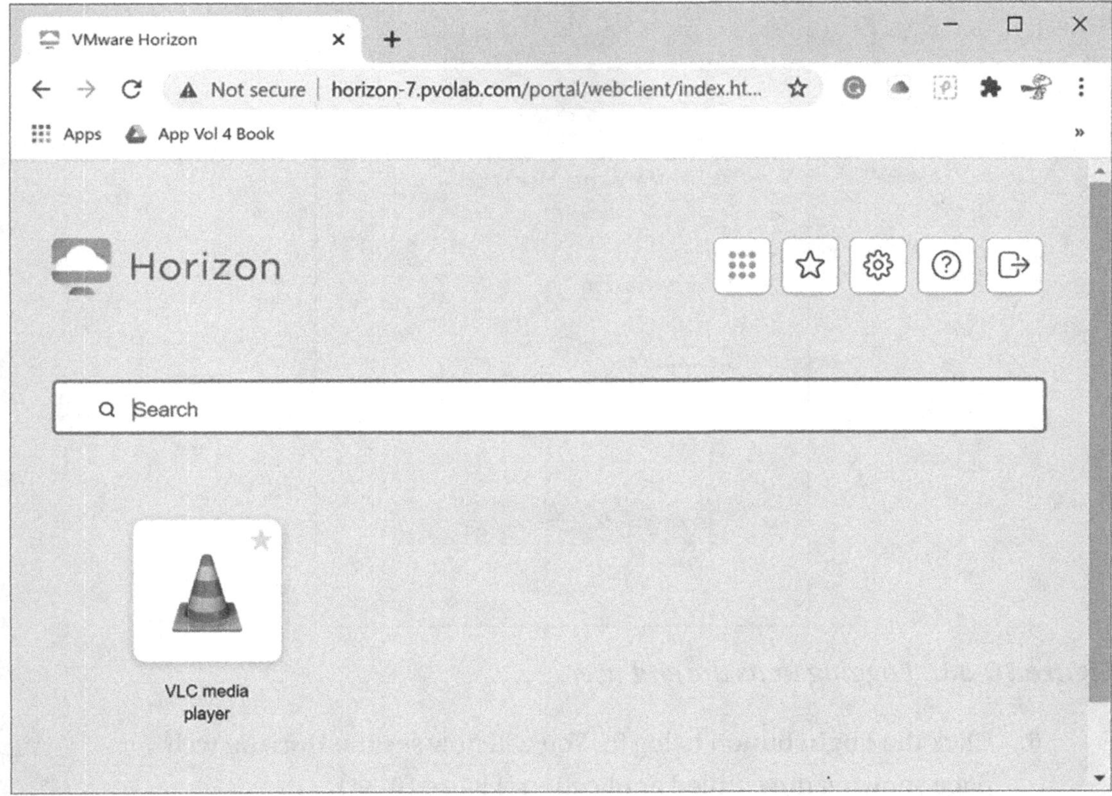

Figure 10-34. *Horizon web page showing the newly published application*

7. Double-click to launch the app.
8. You will see the screenshot in Figure 10-35 as the app launches.

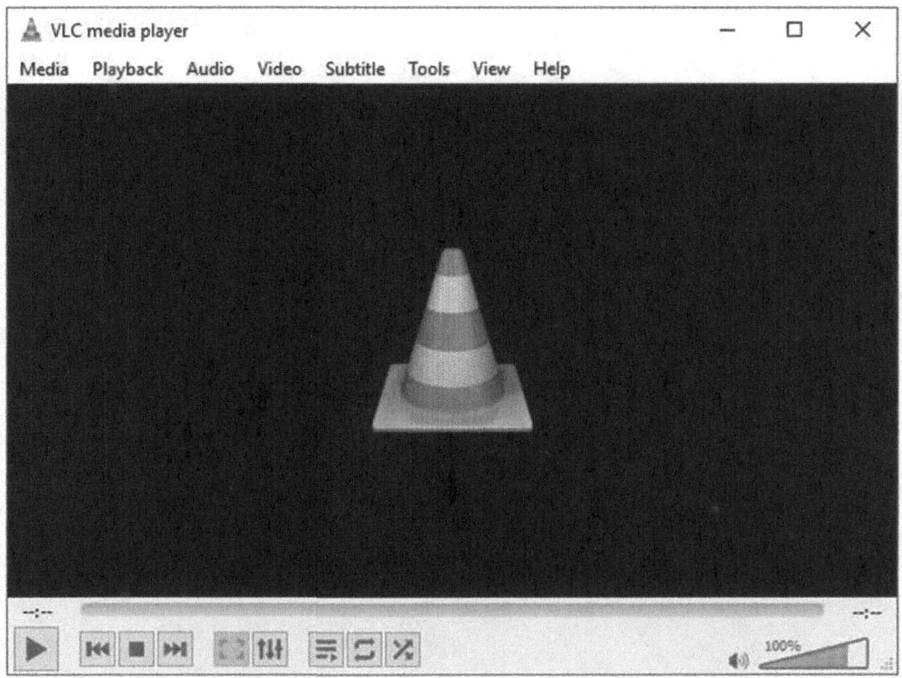

Figure 10-35. *VLC media player successfully launching*

You have now successfully installed and configured an App Volumes layered application to be delivered using RDSH and Horizon.

Chapter summary

In this chapter, we have looked at how to configure App Volumes application packages to be attached to RDSH servers and delivered to end users using Horizon Apps.

We started the chapter with an overview of the architecture and how the solution works before then going on to install and configure all the required components of the solution.

Finally, we entitled an end user to have access to the application before then testing that they could connect and launch the application.

As this book focuses on VMware technology, it is also worth noting that App Volumes can also deliver the same benefits to other app publishing solutions such as Citrix Virtual Apps and Desktops.

In the next chapter, we are going to look at App Volumes and Horizon View–based virtual desktop machines.

CHAPTER 11

Horizon View and App Volumes

In the previous chapter, we looked at how to deliver App Volumes application layers within an RDSH environment, using Horizon to broker the published applications to the end users.

In this chapter, we are going to look at how App Volumes integrates into the VMware Horizon View virtual desktop solution to enable the App Volumes application layers to be attached to virtual desktop machines instead of the RDSH servers we discussed in the previous chapter. However, the process is similar.

We have already looked at creating application packages using a virtual desktop machine, but in this chapter, we will look at the process in preparing the virtual desktop and configuring the Horizon admin console to deliver the desktop complete with the App Volumes layered applications.

As we have already covered some of these in earlier chapters, we are going to provide a high-level overview of those parts already discussed and just focus on those not previously discussed.

Let's start with the architecture and what the solution looks like.

The architecture

We are going to start by looking at the high-level architecture of how App Volumes and the Horizon Connection Server fit together.

Figure 11-1 shows how App Volumes delivers applications to the RDSH server farm which is then brokered to the end users using the Horizon Connection Server.

P. von Oven, *Delivering Applications with VMware App Volumes 4*,
https://doi.org/10.1007/978-1-4842-6689-2_11

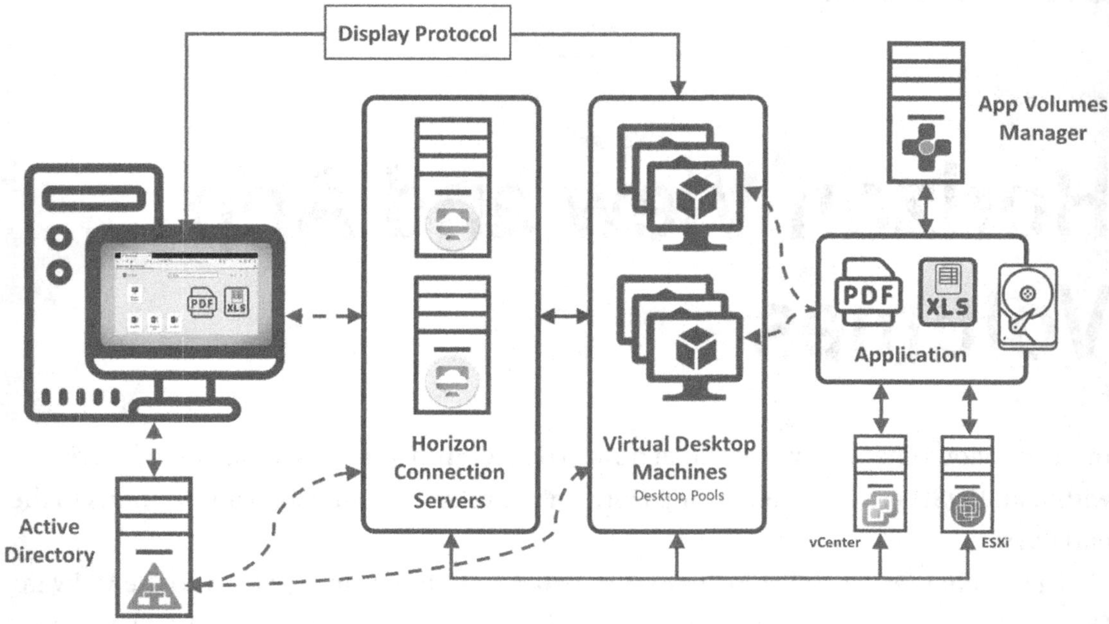

Figure 11-1. App Volumes and Horizon View architecture

As you can see from the diagram, the App Volumes application packages are now attached to virtual desktop machines, which in turn are part of desktop pools with Horizon View.

The applications are attached to a virtual desktop machine as the end user logs in and is allocated a virtual desktop machine by the Horizon Connection Server, based on their entitlement. The virtual desktop machine, complete with the applications, is then delivered to the end user's client device using a display protocol.

In this scenario, the end user has a full desktop operating system complete with the applications delivered by App Volumes, rather than access to just the application.

In the next section, we are going to look at how to create and configure the virtual desktop machine as well as configuring Horizon View.

Installing App Volumes with Horizon View

The process for configuring App Volumes starts off the same way as described in Chapter 5, and that is by creating an app package for delivery.

This task is carried out using a capture machine, a virtual desktop machine running the same operating system that you are using for your Horizon View delivered virtual desktop machines complete with the App Volumes Agent installed so that it appears as a managed machine within the App Volumes Manager. At this stage, there is no need for the Horizon Agent to be installed. You can now create the application package.

This is summarized in Figure 11-2.

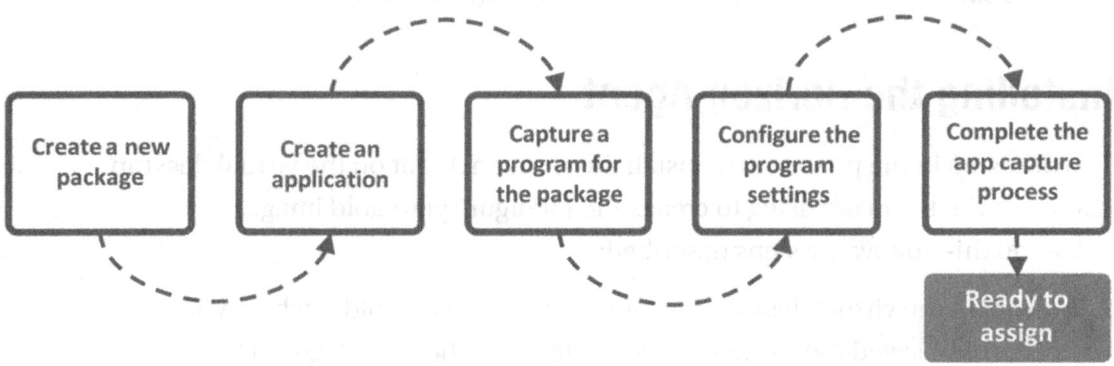

***Figure 11-2.** Creating an application package for virtual desktops*

In this chapter, we have assumed that you have already completed this task and have applications already for assigning, and so we will move on to the next step and look at creating the gold image. This is the virtual desktop machine image that will be rolled out to end users with Horizon View and so now includes the Horizon Agent as well as the App Volumes Agent as shown in Figure 11-3.

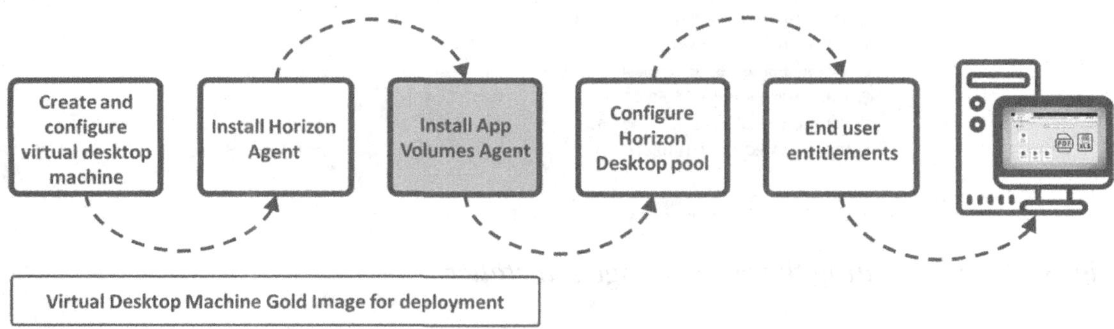

***Figure 11-3.** Creating the gold image and configuring Horizon View*

The final part of the configuration is carried out using the Horizon admin console and is where you create a desktop pool using the image that was built with the App Volumes Agent. The final part is the end user entitlement.

In this example, we have assumed that you have already built, configured, and optimized a virtual desktop machine to use. In the test lab, we have built a machine called **WIN10-VDI** for this purpose.

In the next section, we will install the Horizon Agent so that the virtual desktop machine can communicate with the Horizon Connection Server.

Installing the Horizon Agent

The next step in the process is to install the Horizon Agent on the virtual desktop machine which you are using to create and configure your gold image.

To do this, follow the steps described:

1. On the virtual desktop machine, navigate to the folder where you have saved the Horizon Agent installer as shown in Figure 11-4.

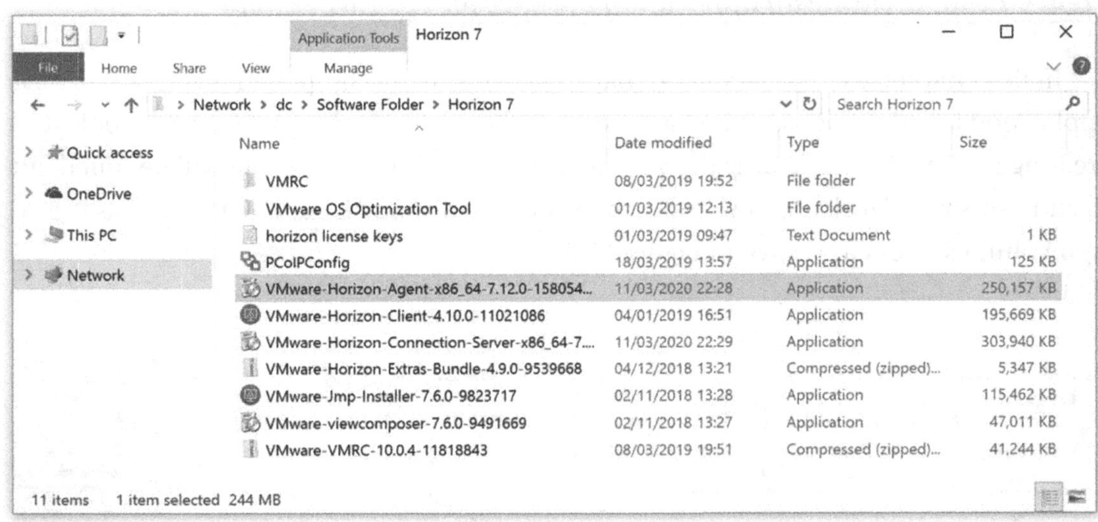

Figure 11-4. *Locating the Horizon Agent installer*

2. Double-click the **VMware-Horizon-Agent-x86_64-7.12.0** file to launch the installer. In this example, we are running Horizon 7.12.

3. You will see the Welcome to the Installation Wizard for VMware Horizon Agent screen as shown in Figure 11-5.

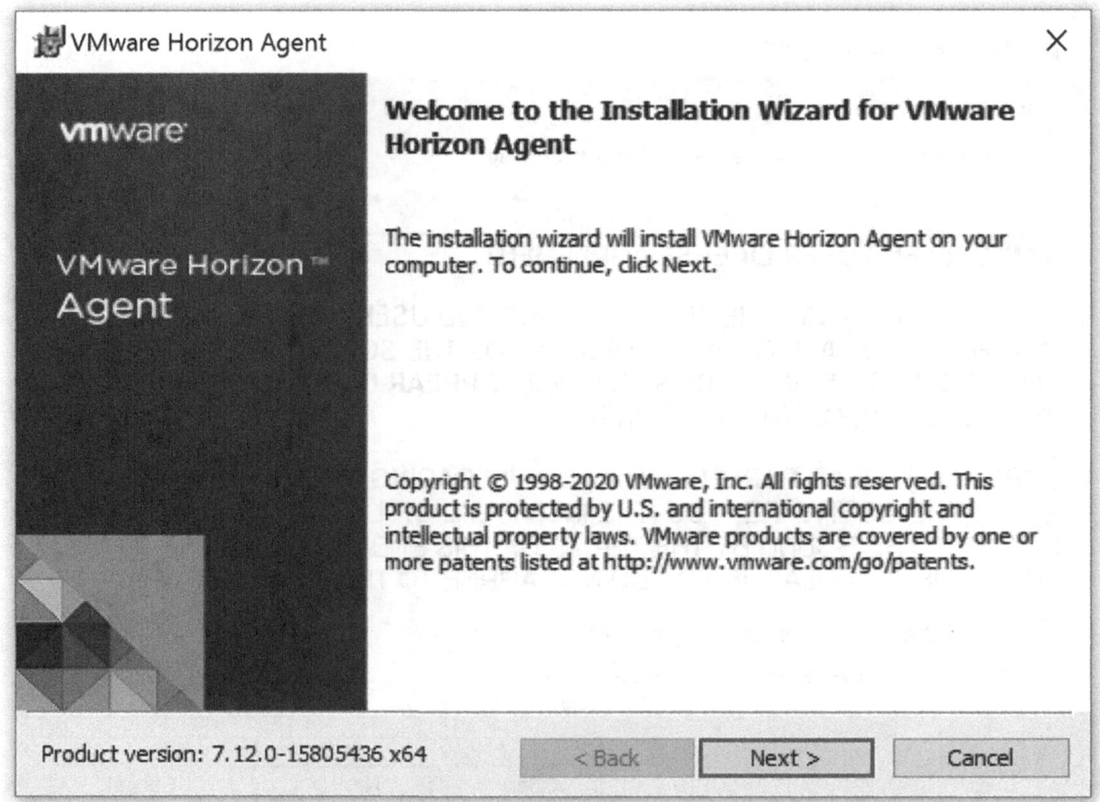

Figure 11-5. *Horizon Agent welcome screen*

4. Click **Next ►** to continue.

5. You will see the **License Agreement** screen as shown in Figure 11-6.

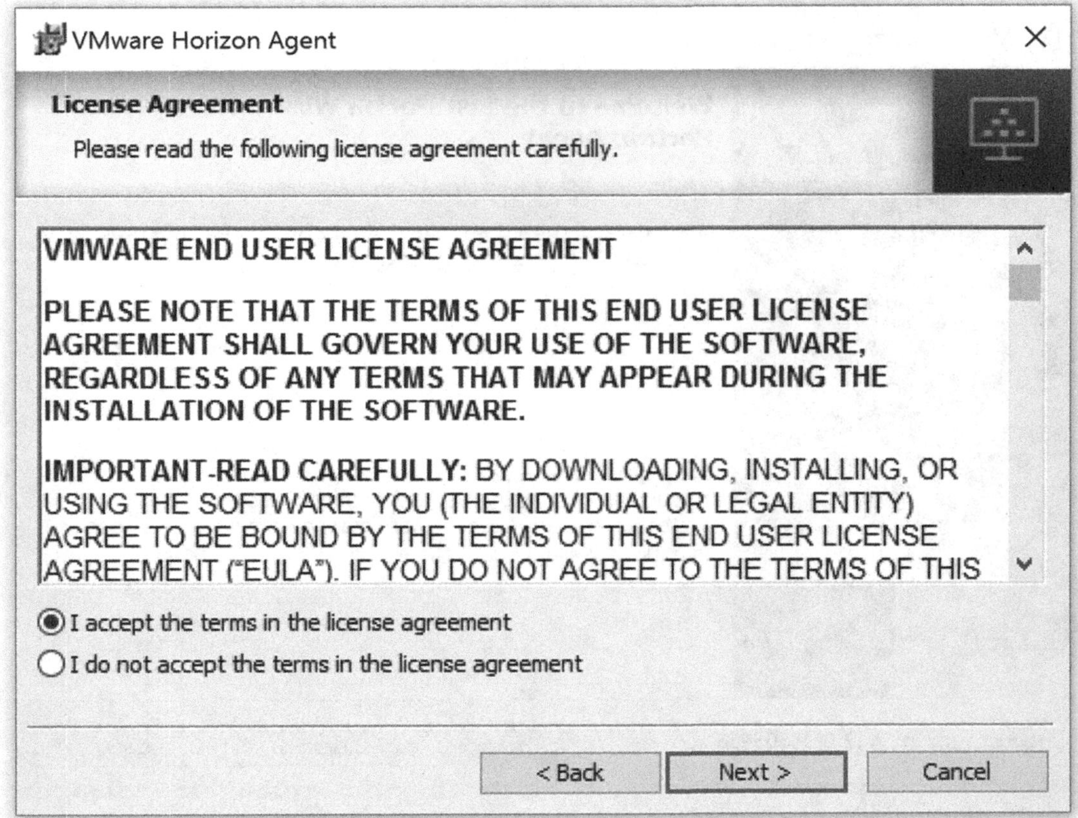

Figure 11-6. *Horizon Agent License Agreement screen*

6. Click the radio button for **I accept the terms in the license agreement** and then click the **Next ▶** button to continue.

7. You will now see the **Network protocol configuration** screen as shown in Figure 11-7.

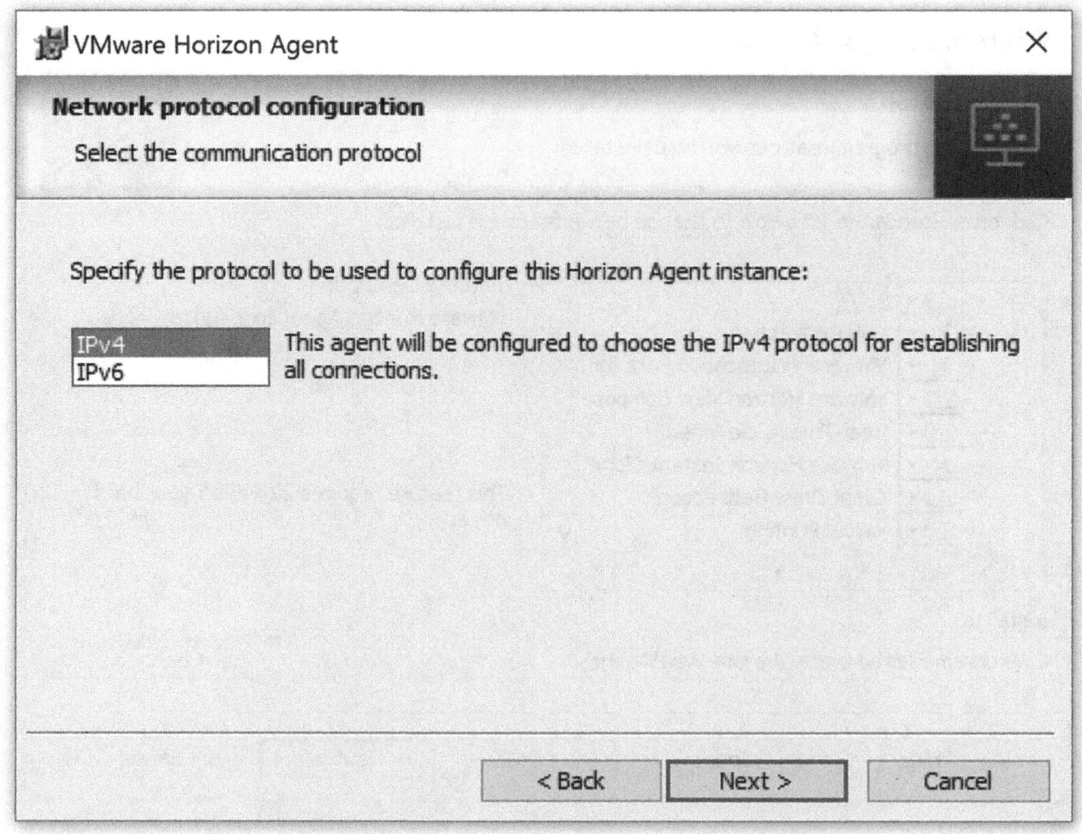

***Figure 11-7.** Network protocol configuration screen*

8. Select **IPv4** from the list and click **Next ►** to continue.
9. You will now see the **Custom Setup** screen as shown in Figure 11-8.

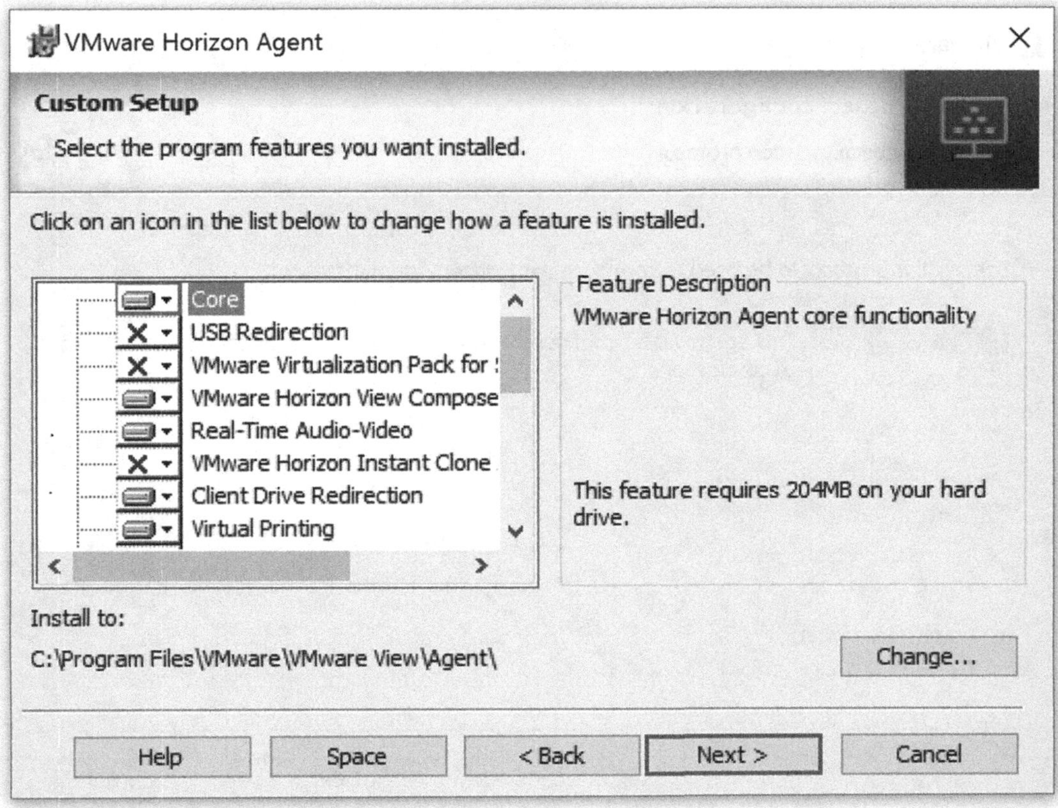

Figure 11-8. *Custom Setup screen*

10. From the **Custom Setup** screen, select the features you want to be installed with the agent. In this example, we are just going to go with the defaults.
11. Click **Next ►** to continue.
12. You will now see the **Remote Desktop Protocol Configuration** screen as shown in Figure 11-9.

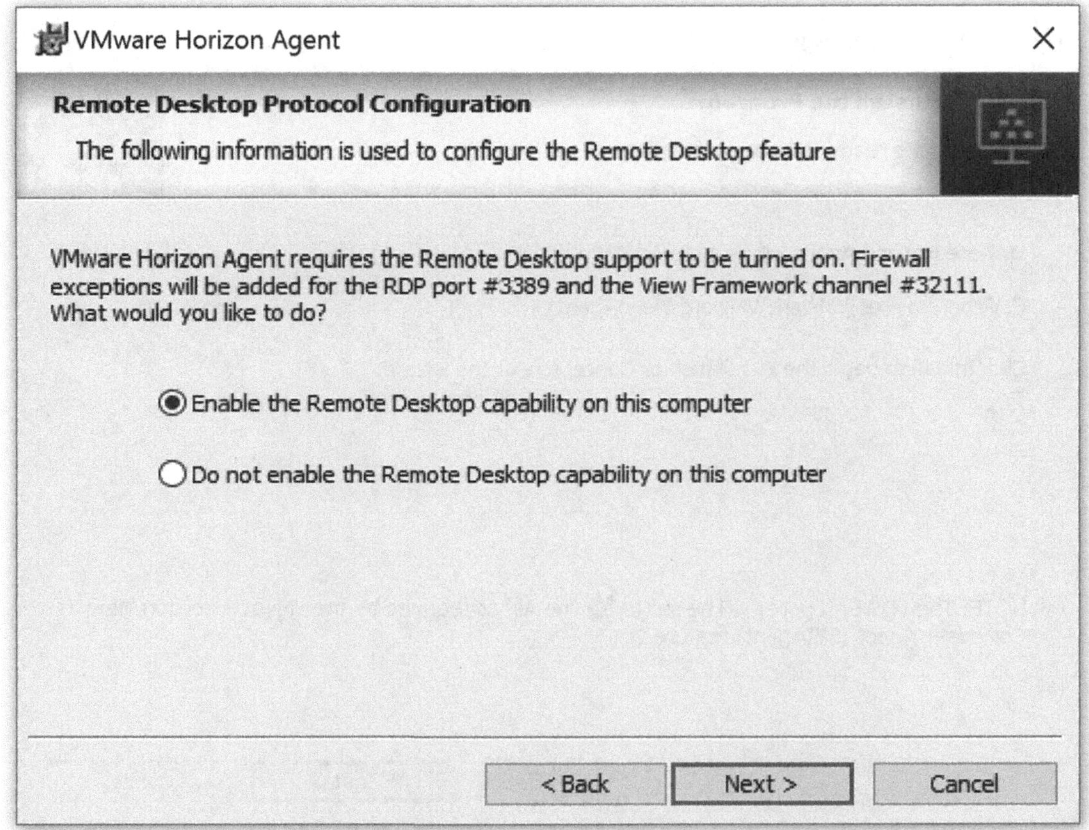

Figure 11-9. *Remote Desktop Protocol Configuration screen*

13. Click the radio button to select **Enable the Remote Desktop capability on this computer.**
14. Click **Next** ► to continue.
15. You will see the **Ready to Install the Program** screen as shown in Figure 11-10.

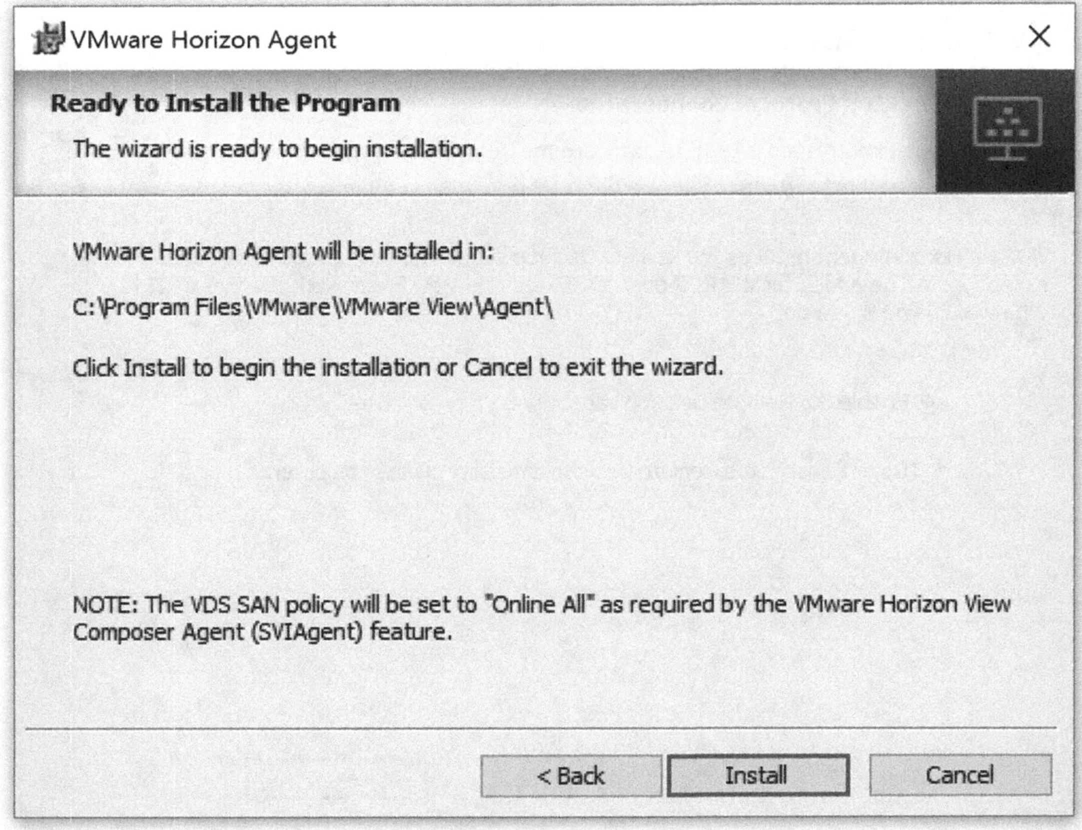

Figure 11-10. *Ready to Install the Program screen*

16. Click the **Install** button to start the installation.

17. You will see the **Installing VMware Horizon Agent** screen detailing the progress of the installation as shown in Figure 11-11.

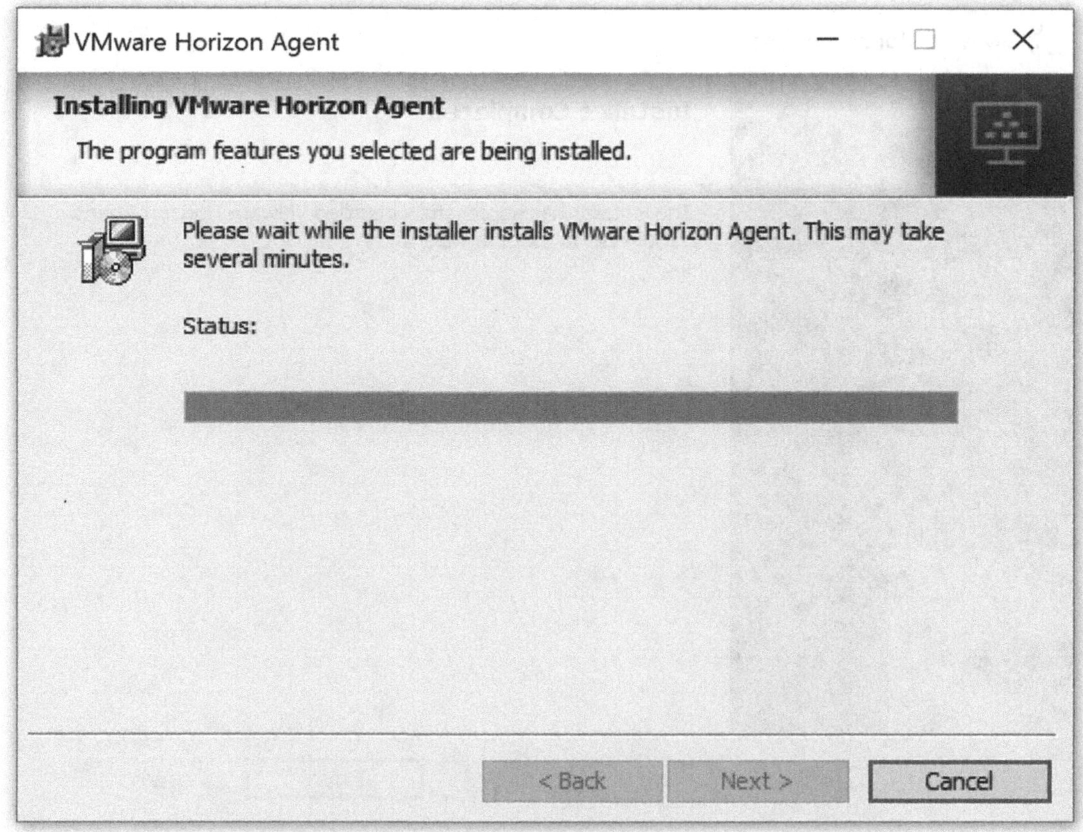

Figure 11-11. *Installing the Horizon Agent*

18. Once successfully installed, you will see the **Installer Completed** screen as shown in Figure 11-12.

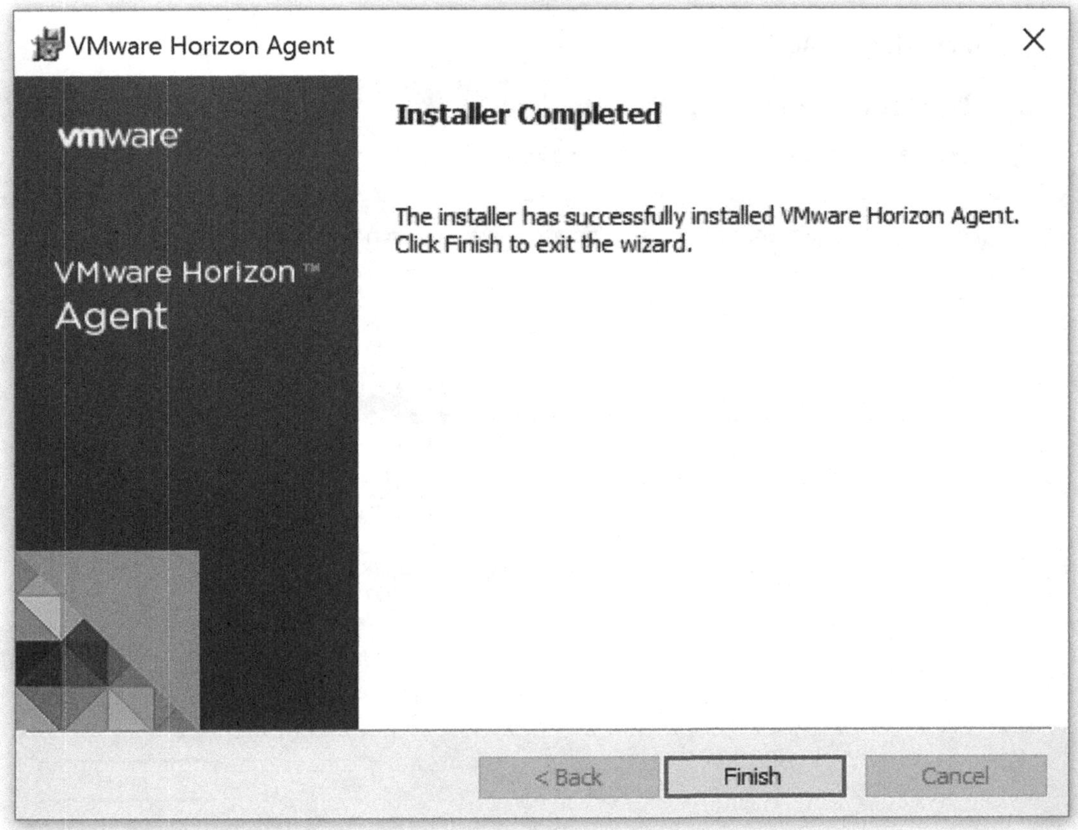

Figure 11-12. *Installer Completed screen*

19. Click the **Finish** button.

20. You will be prompted to restart the machine as shown in Figure 11-13.

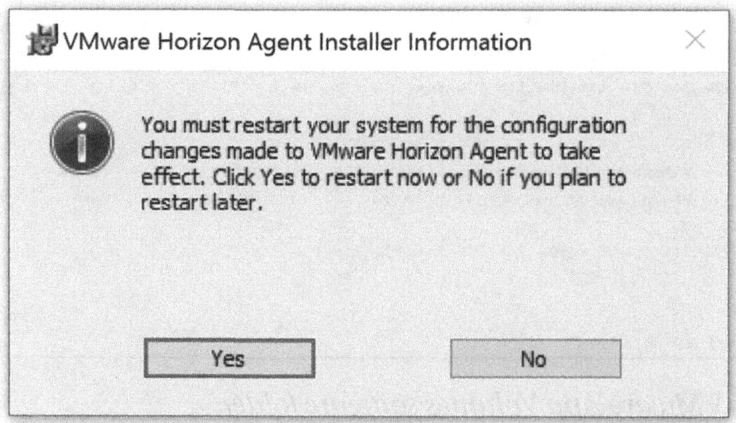

Figure 11-13. *Restarting the machine after install*

21. Click **Yes** to restart the machine.

You have now successfully installed the Horizon Agent onto the virtual desktop machine that will be used as the gold image template. This will allow the machine to be managed and delivered using Horizon View.

The next step is to install the App Volumes Agent.

Installing the App Volumes Agent

In this section, we are going to install the Horizon Agent onto the virtual desktop machine that will be used as the gold image template.

To install the software, follow the steps described:

1. Open a console to the **WIN10-VDI** virtual desktop machine.

2. Navigate to the location where you downloaded the App Volumes software to. In the test lab, this was saved in a folder called **App Volumes 4.1** as shown in Figure 11-14.

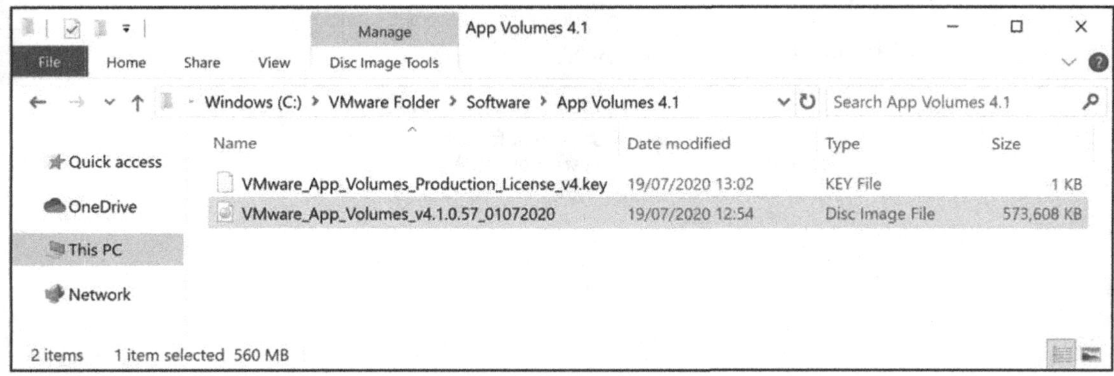

***Figure 11-14.** VMware App Volumes software folder*

3. Double-click the **VMware_App_Volumes_v4.1.0.57_01072020.iso** file to mount the iso image. You will see the screenshot in Figure 11-15.

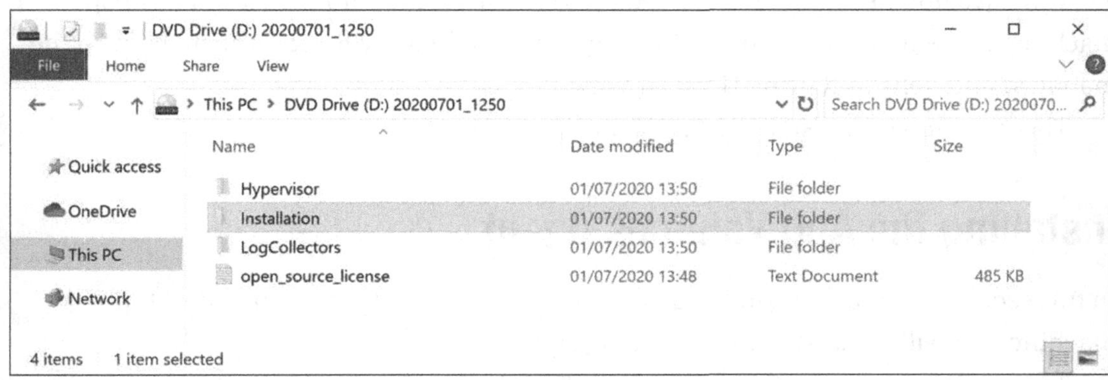

***Figure 11-15.** VMware App Volumes software iso image mounted*

4. Double-click to open the **Installation** folder. You will see the folders in Figure 11-16.

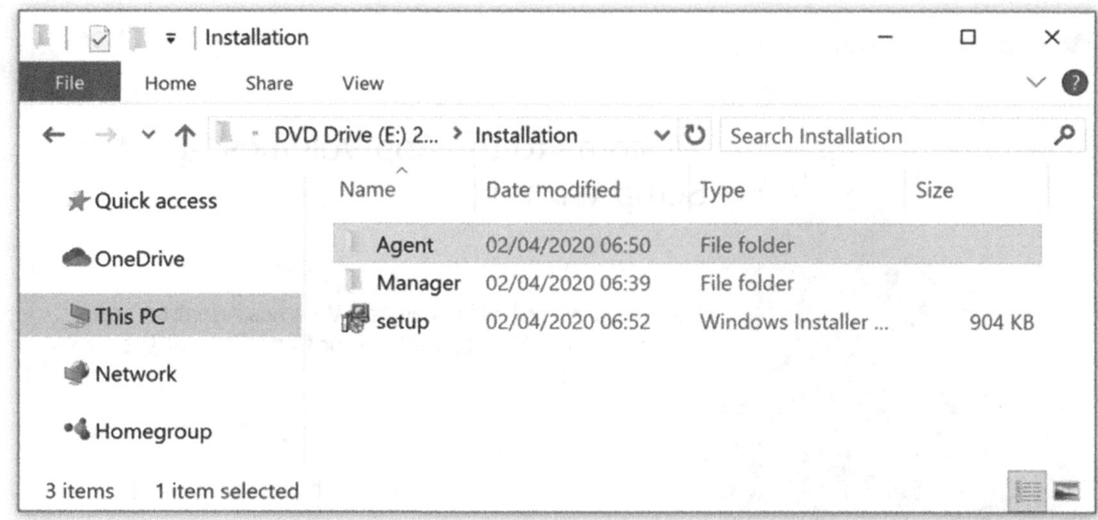

***Figure 11-16.** VMware App Volumes Agent software – installation folder*

5. Double-click the **Agent** folder. You will now see the contents of the folder as shown in Figure 11-17.

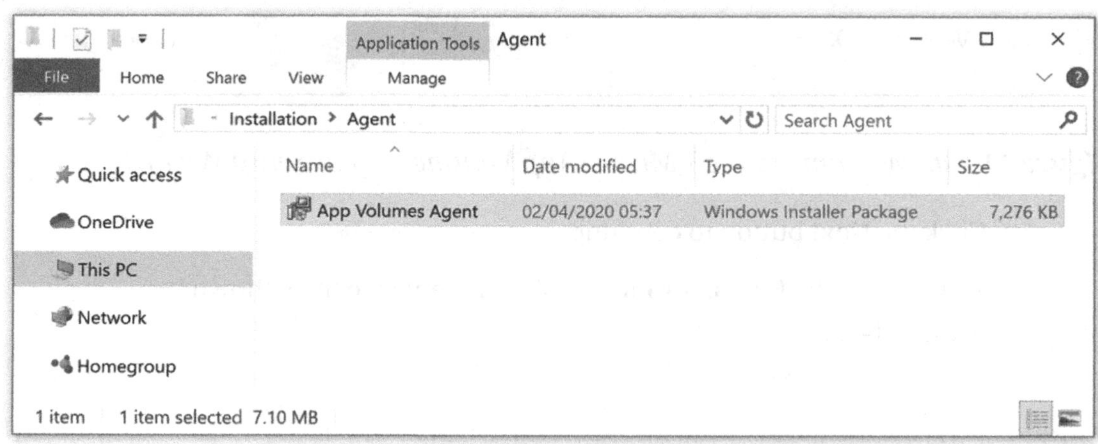

***Figure 11-17.** VMware App Volumes Agent installer*

6. Double-click **App Volumes Agent** to launch the installer. You will see the screenshot in Figure 11-18.

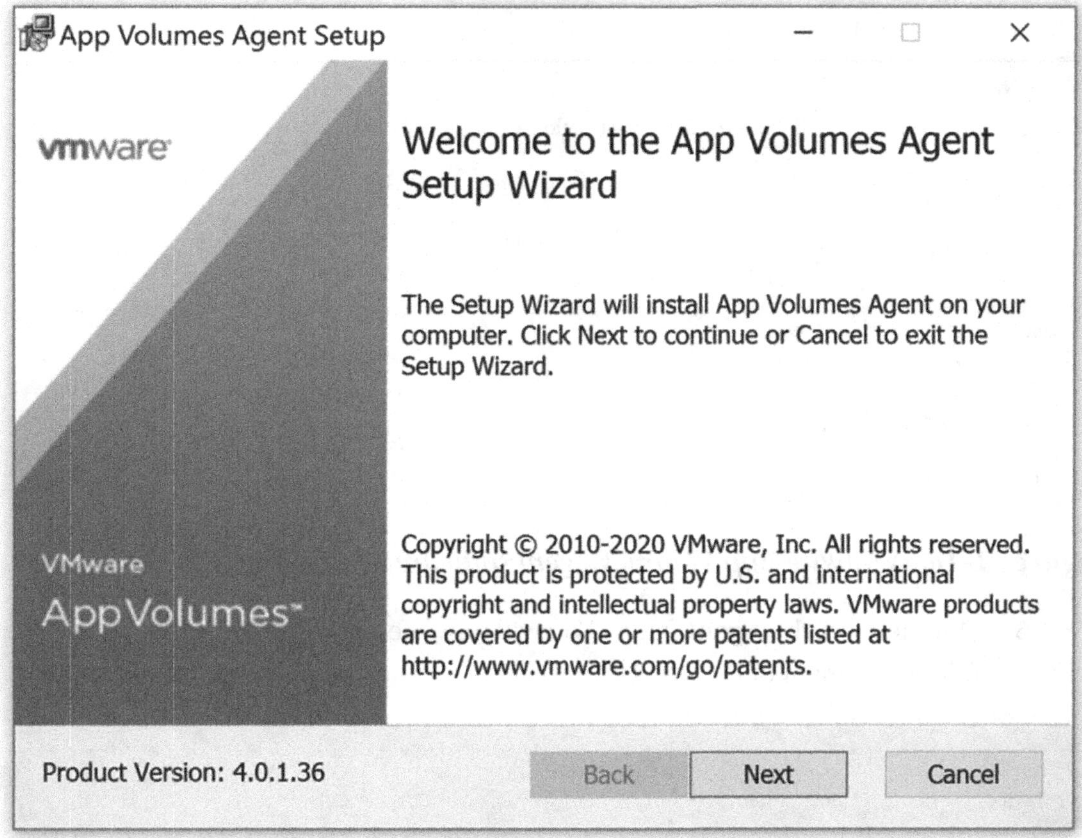

Figure 11-18. *Welcome to the VMware App Volumes Agent Setup Wizard*

7. Click the **Next** button to continue.

8. You will see the **End-User License Agreement** screen as shown in Figure 11-19.

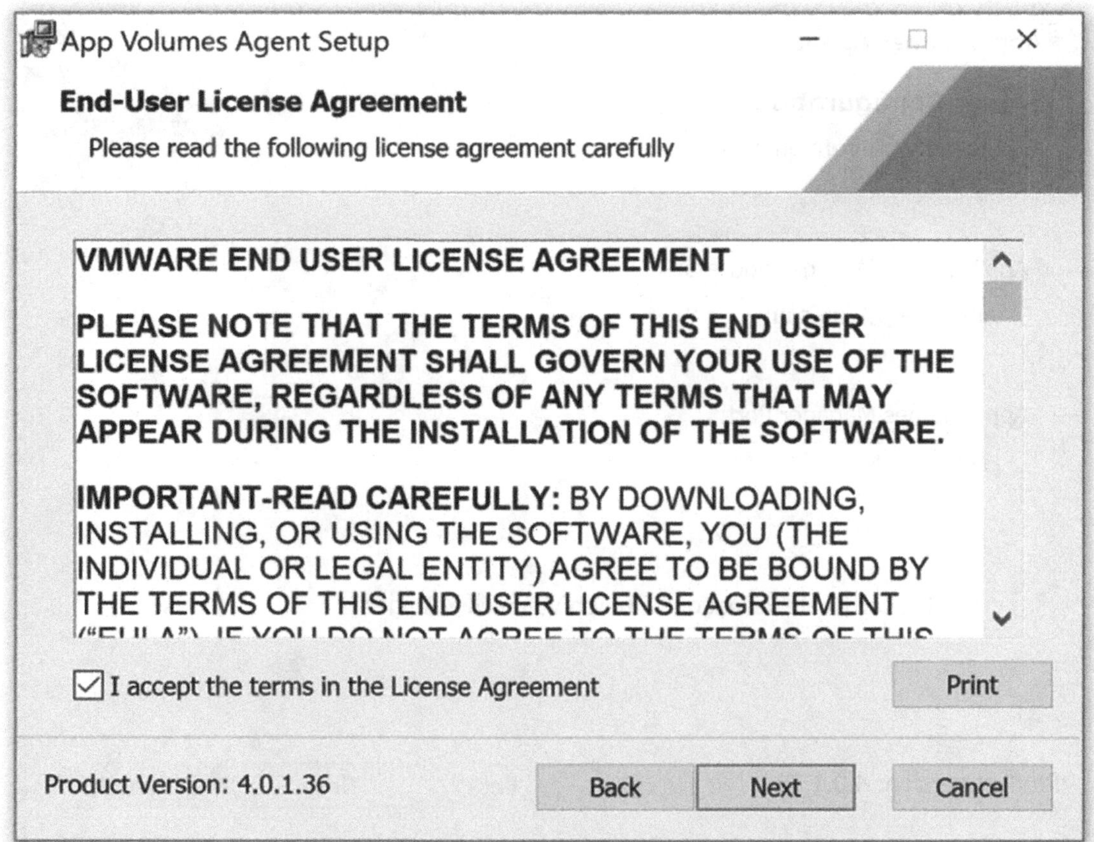

Figure 11-19. *End-User License Agreement screen*

9. Check the box to accept the terms, and click **Next** to continue to the next screen for **Server Configuration** as shown in Figure 11-20.

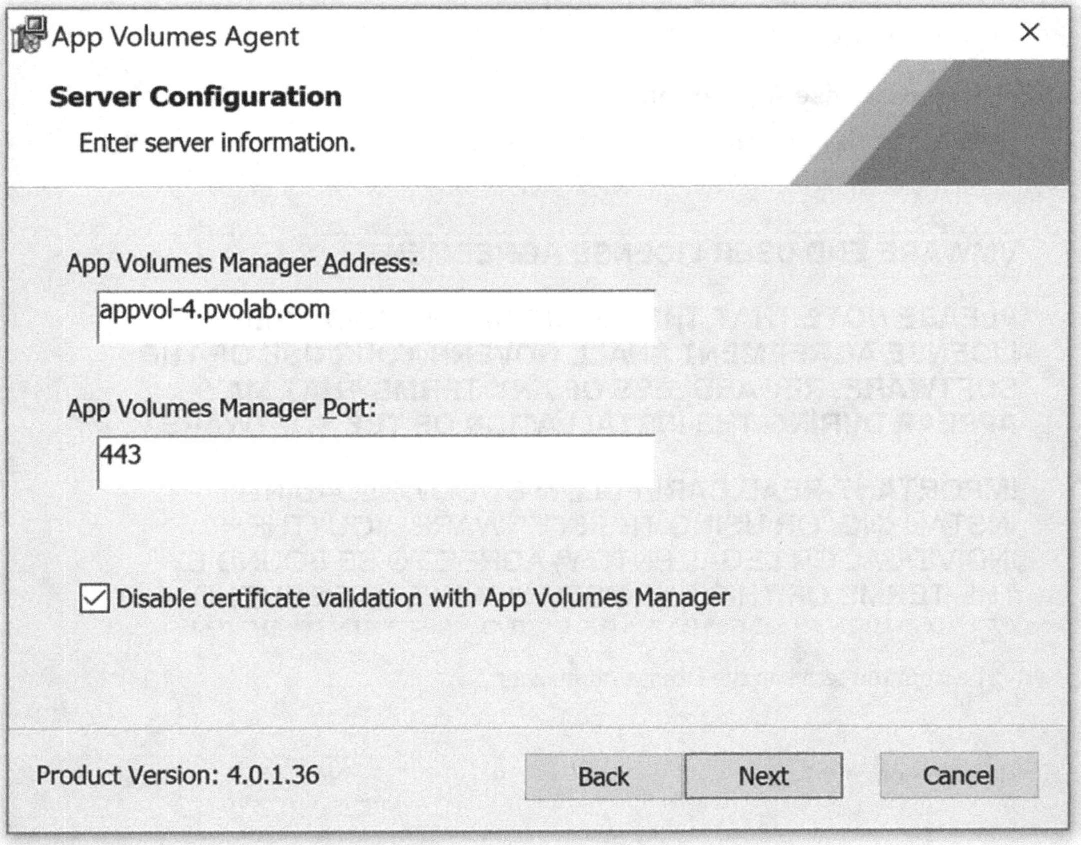

Figure 11-20. Server configuration screen

10. In the **App Volumes Manager Address** box, enter the address to the App Volumes Manager. In the test lab, the address of the App Volumes Manager is appvol-4.pvolab.com. You could also use the IP address.

11. Leave the **App Volumes Manager Port** as **443,** but ensure that this matches the port number you configured the App Volumes Manager with. If you changed the port number, then you will need to change the port number here too.

12. The final option on this screen is the check box to **Disable Certificate Validation with App Volumes Manager**. Check this box if you want to disable certificate checking; however, this is not recommended for production environments.

13. Click the **Next** button to continue the installation. The next screen is the **Ready to install App Volumes Agent** as shown in Figure 11-21.

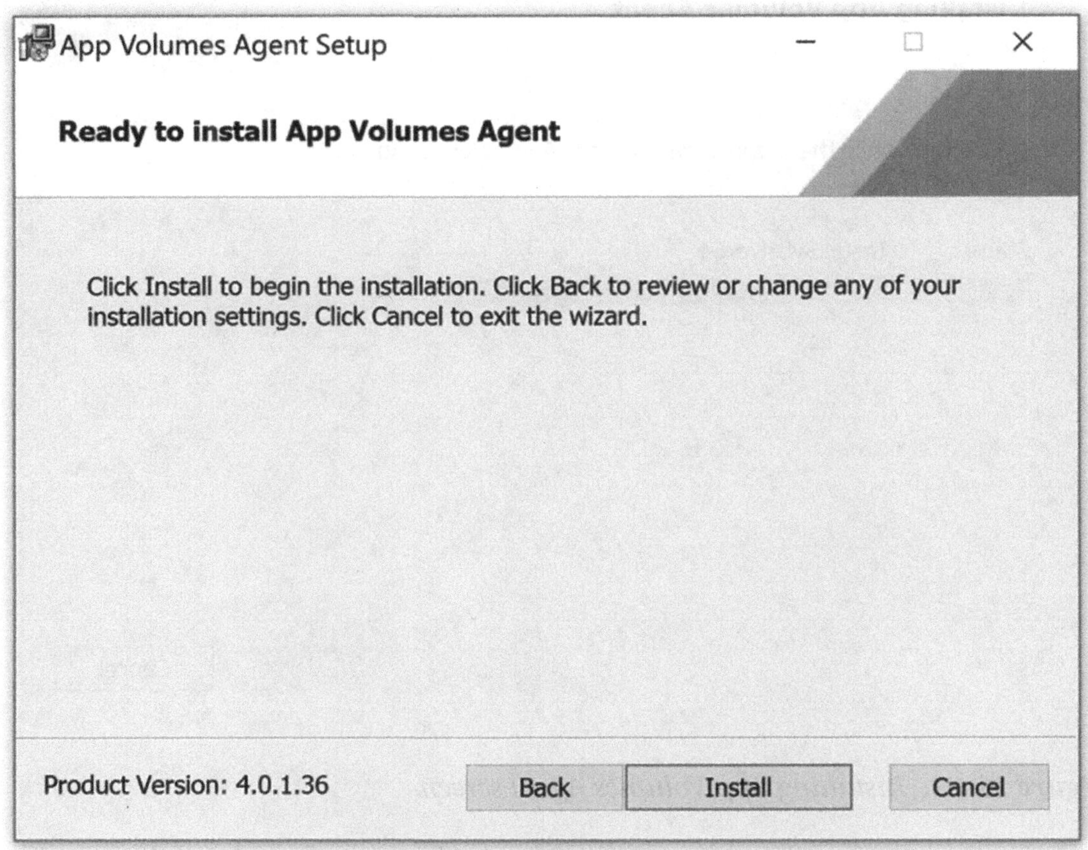

***Figure 11-21.** Ready to install App Volumes Agent screen*

14. Click the **Install** button to start the installation process.

15. You will now see the **Installing App Volumes Agent** screen showing the progress and the status of the installation (Figure 11-22).

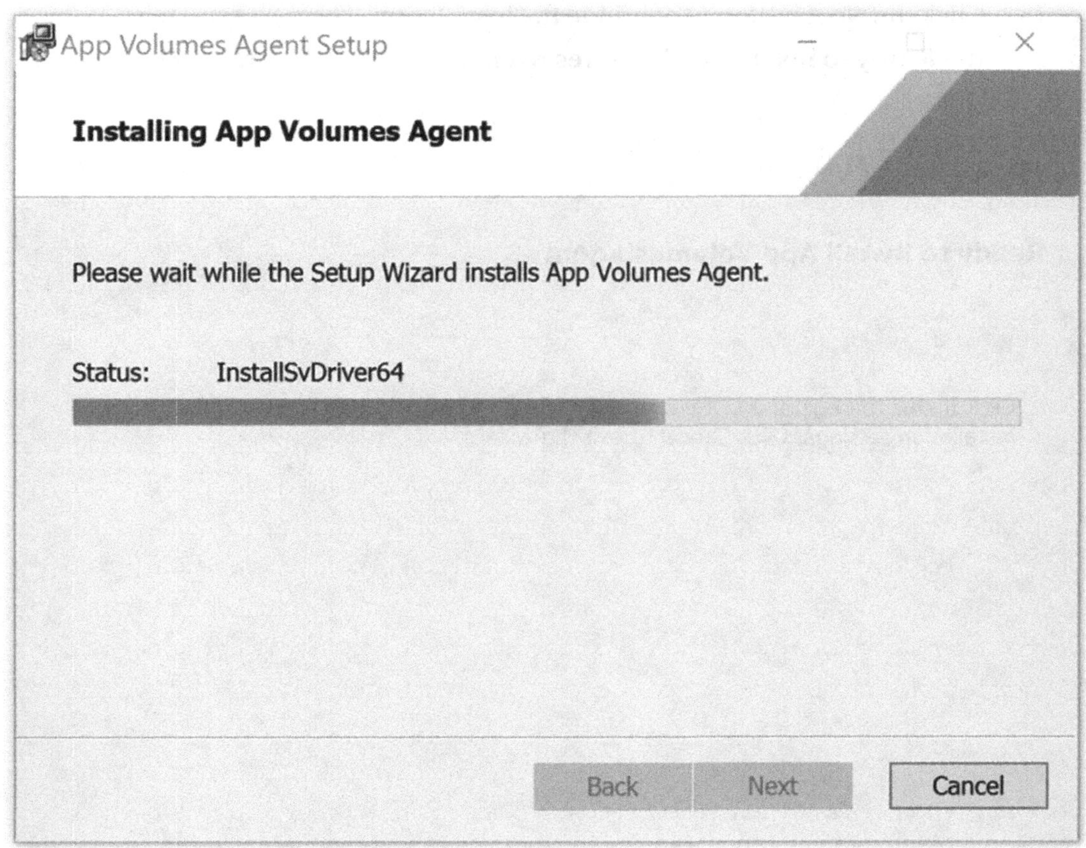

Figure 11-22. *Installing App Volumes Agent screen*

16. Once the installation has completed, you will see the **Completed the App Volumes Agent Setup Wizard** screen as shown in Figure 11-23.

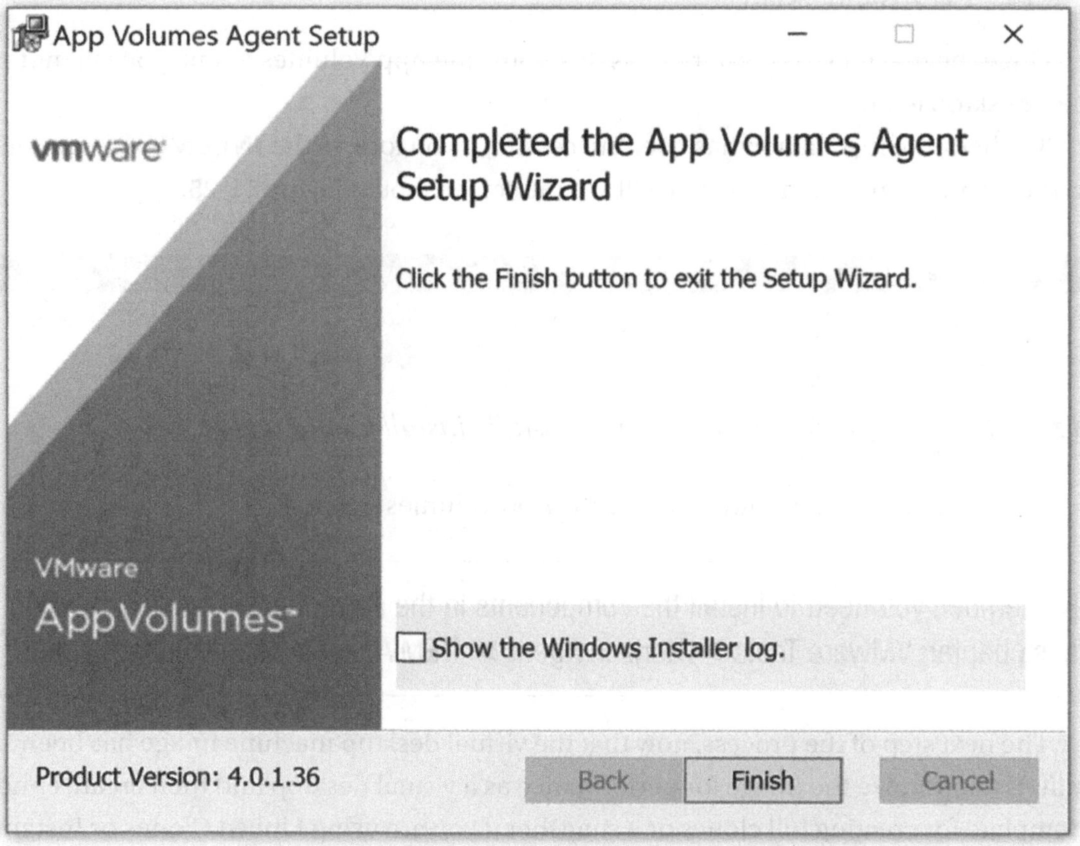

Figure 11-23. Completed the App Volumes Agent Setup Wizard screen

17. Click the **Finish** button to complete the installation.

18. You will now be prompted to restart the system as shown in Figure 11-24.

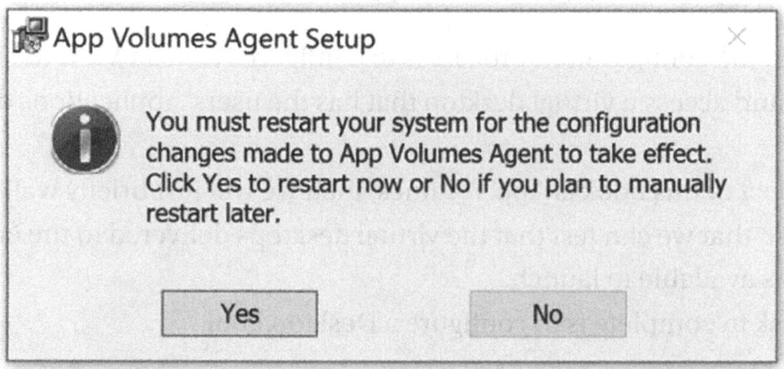

Figure 11-24. Restarting the App Volumes Agent

19. Click **Yes** to restart.

Once the machine has restarted, as this is just the App Volumes Agent, you will not see a desktop icon.

To check the installation has been successful, if you look in the **INVENTORY** section on the App Volumes Manager, you will see the screenshot in Figure 11-25.

Computer	Agent	OS					Last Boot	Status
PVOLAB\WIN10-VDI$	4.0.1.35R	Desktop	0	0	0	5	Jul 13 2020 01:57PM	Enabled

Showing 1 to 1 of 1 computers First Previous 1 Next Last

Figure 11-25. *App Volumes Agent successfully installed and registered*

You have now successfully installed the App Volumes Agent.

Remember, you need to install the components in the correct order, as described in this chapter: VMware Tools ➤ Horizon Agent ➤ DEM Agent ➤ App Volumes Agent

---

The next step of the process, now that the virtual desktop machine image has been built, is to optimize the image for performance as a virtual desktop and then create either a template for creating full clones or a snapshot if you are using Linked Clones or Instant Clones. As this is a vSphere feature, then this is not covered in this book.

The next step is to configure Horizon View to deliver virtual desktop machines using the newly created App Volumes–enabled image.

Configuring the Horizon Console

The next step in the configuration process is to configure Horizon View to enable end users to log in and access a virtual desktop that has the users' applications delivered by App Volumes.

As the subject of this book is App Volumes, then we will just briefly walk through the configuration so that we can test that the virtual desktops delivered to the end users have the applications available to launch.

The first task to complete is to configure a Desktop Pool.

Configuring a Desktop Pool for App Volumes desktops

1. From the desktop of the Horizon Connection Server, double-click the Horizon 7 Administrator icon. Alternatively, you could connect via a browser using the address of the server such as `http://horizon-7.pvolab.com/newadmin`. You will see the screenshot in Figure 11-26.

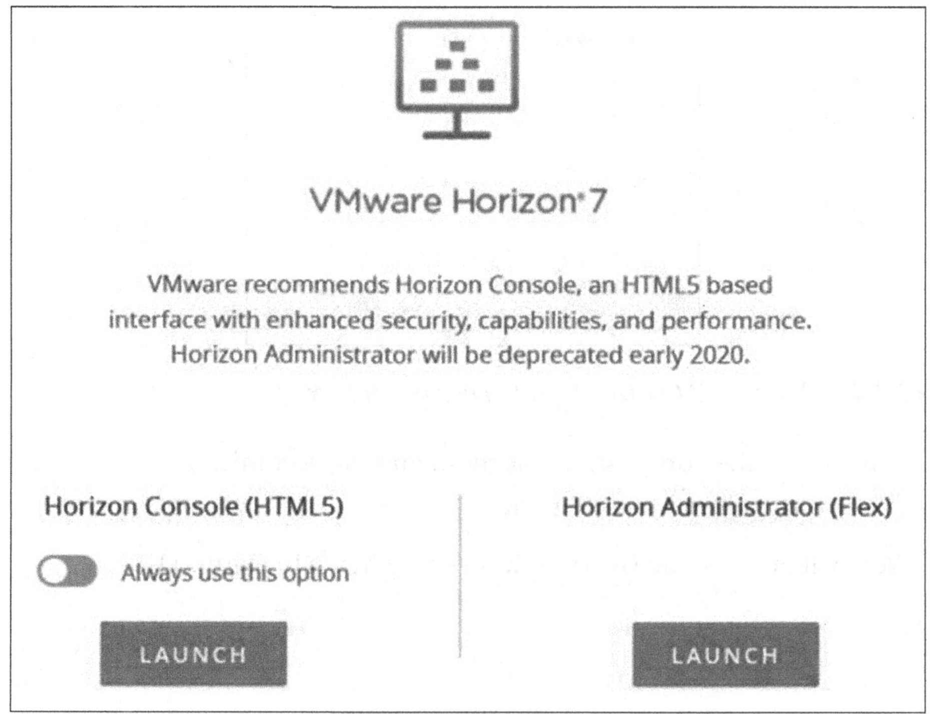

Figure 11-26. *Logging in to the Horizon Connection Server*

2. Click the **LAUNCH** button under **Horizon Console (HTML5).**

3. You will see the login box as shown in Figure 11-27.

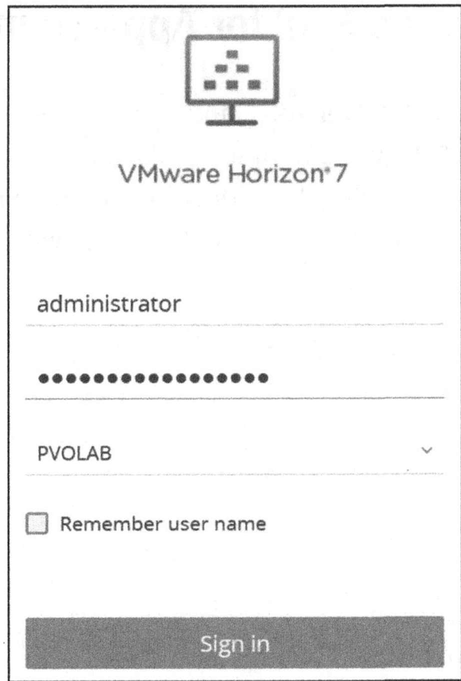

Figure 11-27. *Horizon 7 Connection Server login box*

4. Log in with the administrator account and the administrator password and then click **Sign in.**

5. You will now see the Horizon Console as shown in Figure 11-28.

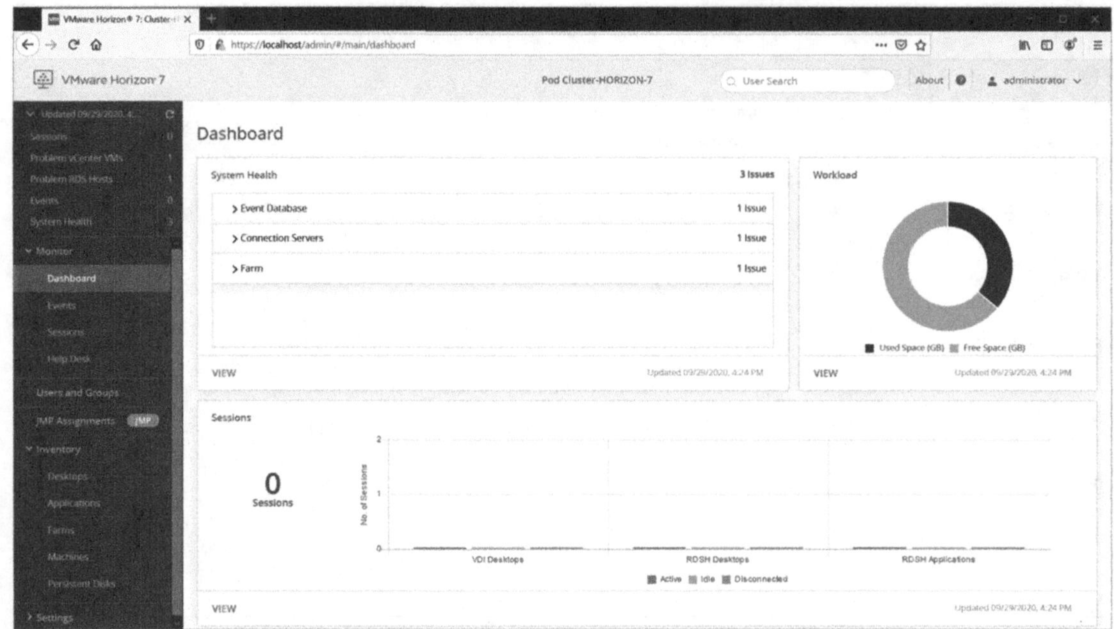

Figure 11-28. Horizon 7 Console

6. From the left-hand navigation pane, under the **Inventory** heading, click the **Desktops** link. You will see the **Desktop Pools** screen as shown in Figure 11-29.

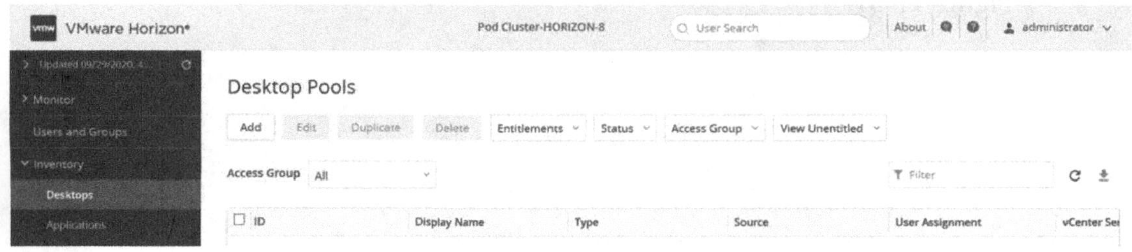

Figure 11-29. Desktop Pools configuration screen

7. Click the **Add** button.

8. You will see the **Add Pool** configuration screen and the first section to configure the **Type** of the desktop pool as shown in Figure 11-30.

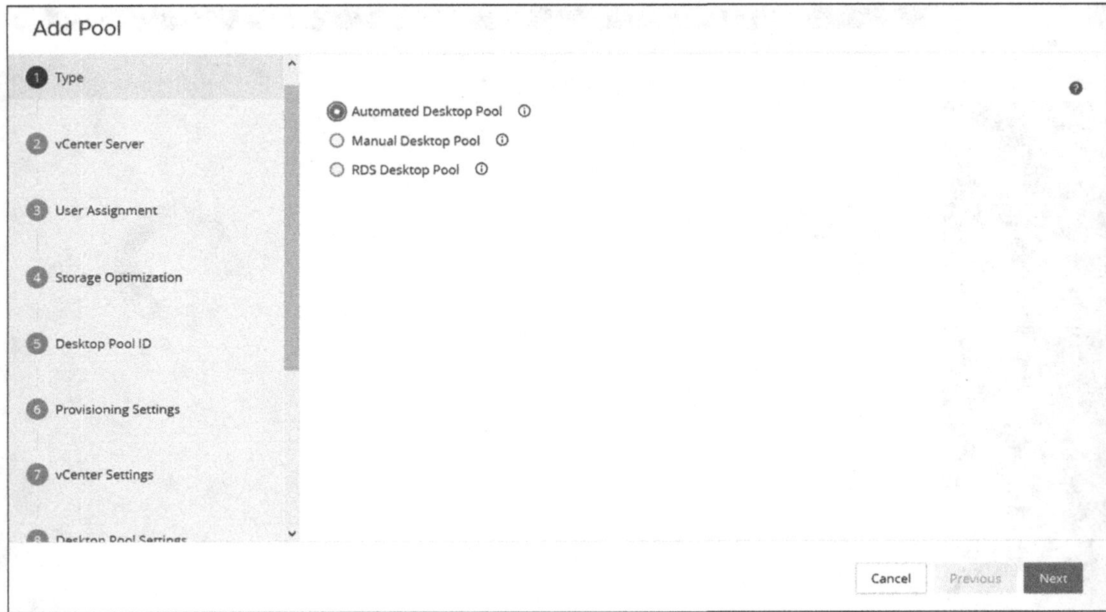

Figure 11-30. *Configuring the desktop pool type screen*

9. Click the radio button for **Automated Desktop Pool.**
10. Click **Next** to continue.
11. You will see the **vCenter Server** configuration screen as shown in Figure 11-31.

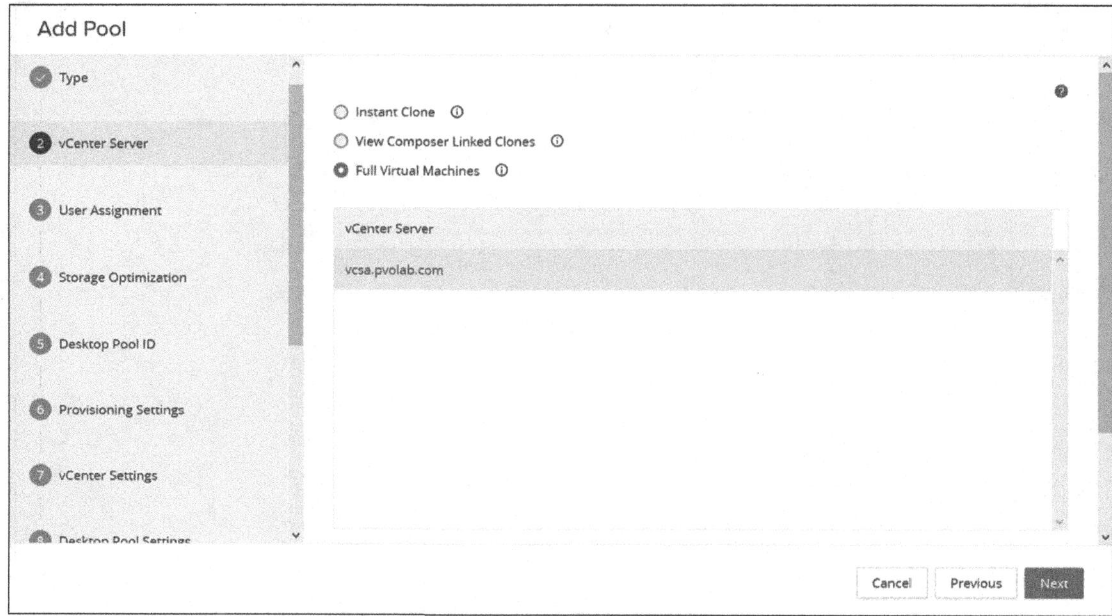

***Figure 11-31.** vCenter Server configuration screen*

12. Click the radio button for **Full Virtual Machines**. We have chosen this option in the test lab purely based on the fact that no cloning has been installed. Select the option most appropriate to your environment.

13. Click to select which vCenter Server you want to use for this virtual desktop pool. In this example, we only have the **vcsa.pvolab.com** vCenter Server to choose from.

14. Click **Next** to continue.

15. You will see the **User Assignment** screen as shown in Figure 11-32.

Figure 11-32. *User Assignment configuration screen*

16. Click the radio button for **Floating.**
17. Click **Next** to continue.
18. You will see the **Storage Policy Management** configuration screen as shown in Figure 11-33.

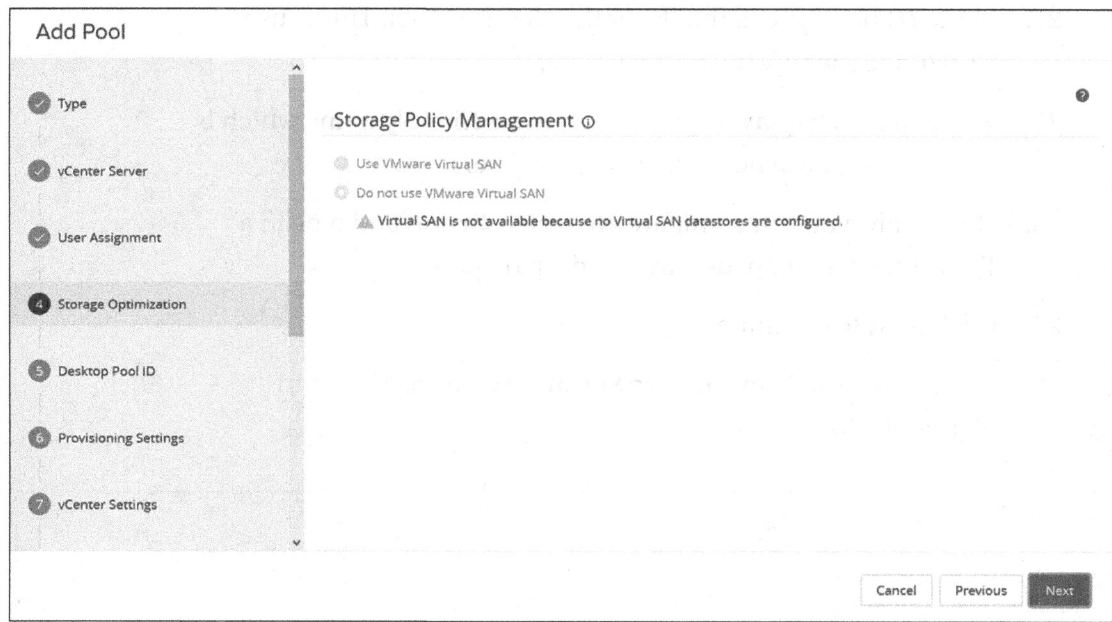

Figure 11-33. *Storage Policy Management configuration screen*

19. Click **Next** to continue.

20. You will see the **Desktop Pool ID** screen as shown in Figure 11-34.

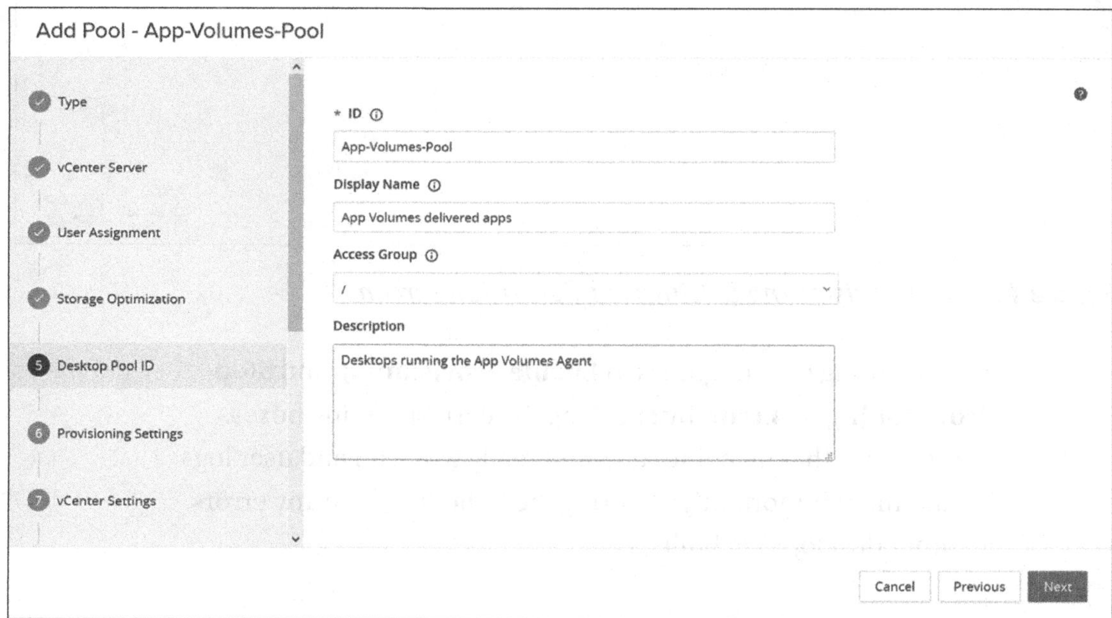

Figure 11-34. *Desktop Pool ID screen*

21. In the **ID** box, type in the ID for this desktop pool. This is used by Horizon to identify the desktop pool.

22. Then, in the **Display Name** box, type in a friendly name which is the name that will be displayed to end users.

23. Optionally, you can configure an **Access Group** and type in a **Description** to help identify this desktop pool.

24. Click **Next** to continue.

25. You will see the **Provisioning Settings** screen as shown in Figure 11-35.

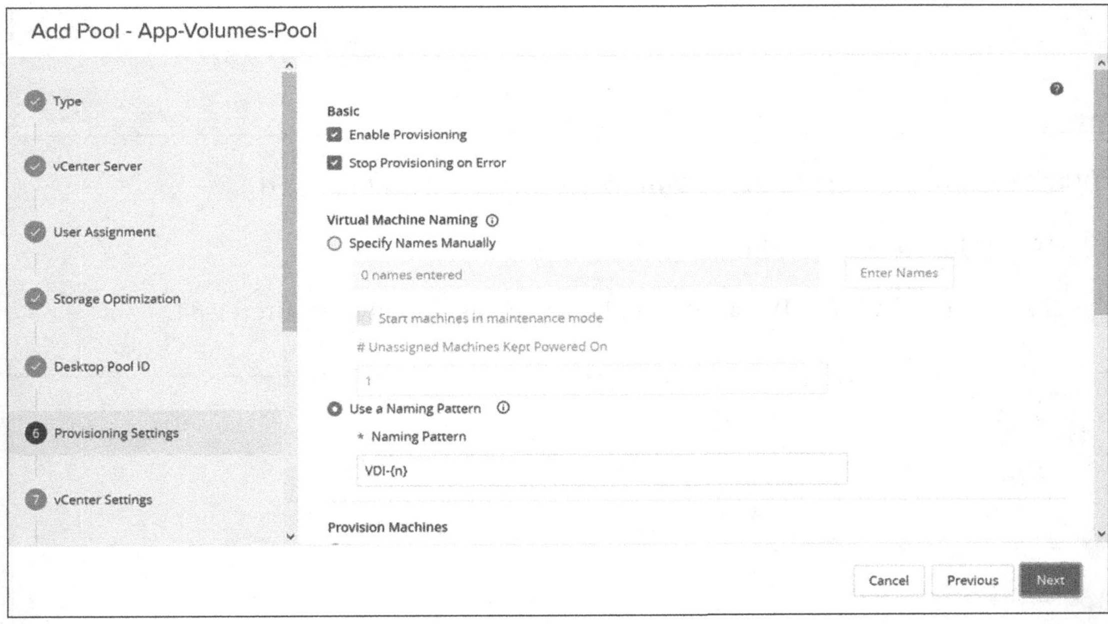

***Figure 11-35.** Provisioning Settings configuration screen*

26. The first thing to configure is to **Enable Provisioning** and **Stop Provisioning on Error**, by checking the corresponding boxes. This ensures that machines are built ready when an end user logs in, and more importantly, if during the build there are any errors, no other desktops get built.

27. Next, in the **Use a Naming Pattern** box, type **VDI-{n}**. This will build desktop machines with the name VDI-1, VDI-2, VDI-3, and so on, up to the maximum number of desktops required.

28. You can configure the other settings based on your environment, but we will just configure the minimum requirements for testing the applications are delivered to the virtual desktops.

29. Click **Next** to continue.

30. You will see the vCenter Settings screen as shown in Figure 11-36.

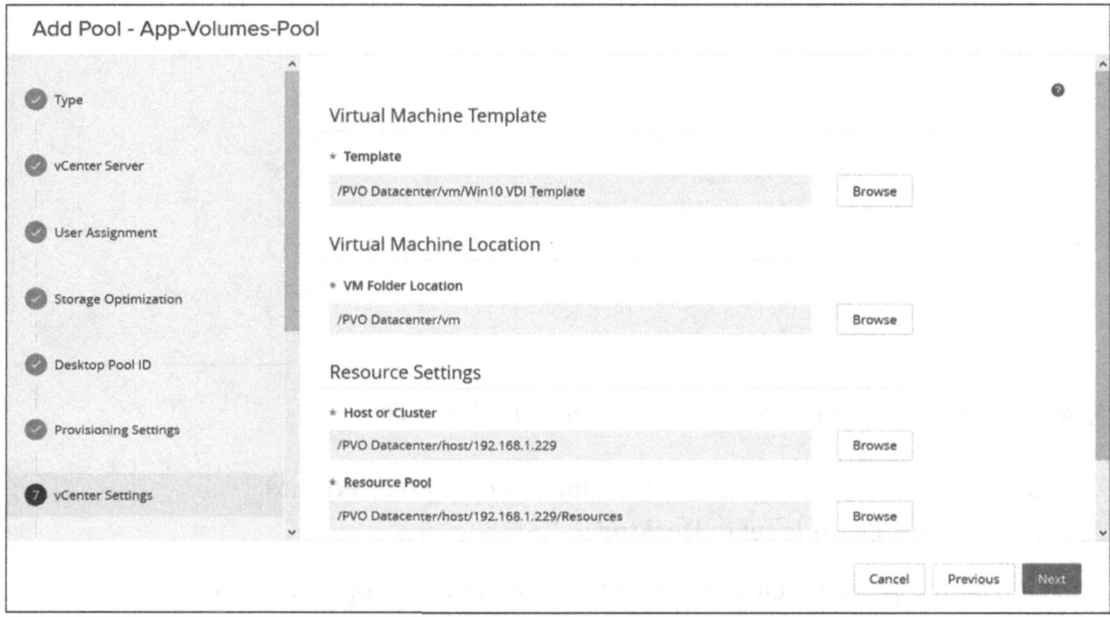

***Figure 11-36.** vCenter Settings configuration screen*

On this configuration screen, you need to configure the virtual machine **Template** (this is the gold image we prepared earlier in this chapter), the **VM Folder Location**, the **Host or Cluster** and the **Resource Pool** that will host the virtual desktop machines, and then finally the **Datastore** where the newly built virtual desktop machines will be stored.

To do this, click the **Browse** button next to each option and then navigate to the required setting.

31. Click **Next** to continue.

32. You will see the **Desktop Pool Settings** screen as shown in Figure 11-37.

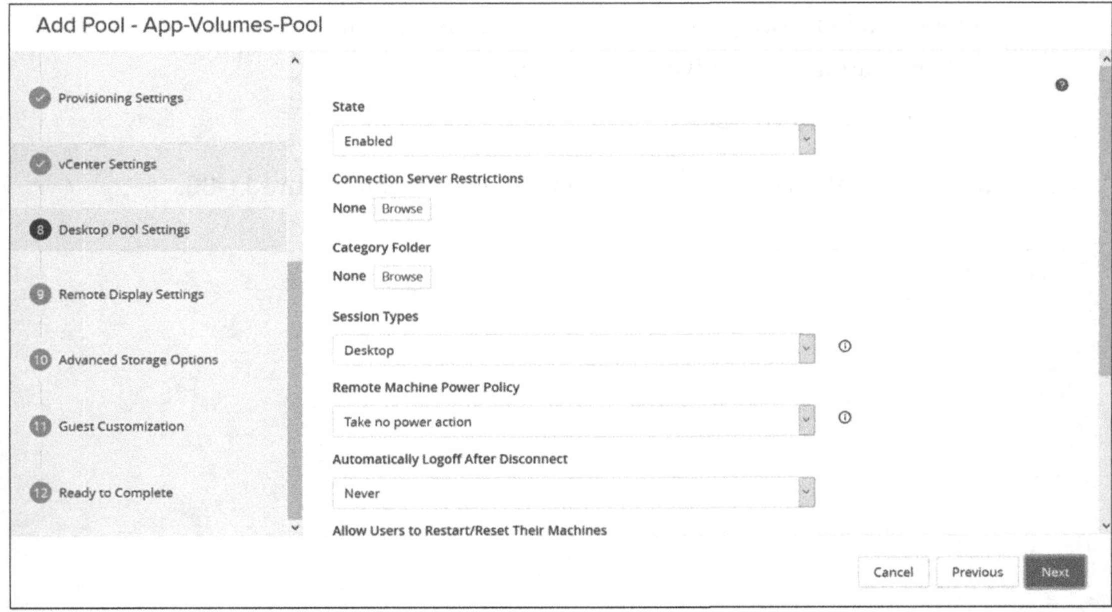

Figure 11-37. *Desktop Pool Settings configuration screen*

33. On this screen, ensure that the **State** is set to **Enabled**, and **Session Types** is set to **Desktop**.

34. We are going to leave the rest of the configuration options on this screen as default.

35. Click **Next** to continue.

36. The next screen you will see is the **Remote Display Protocol** configuration screen as shown in Figure 11-38.

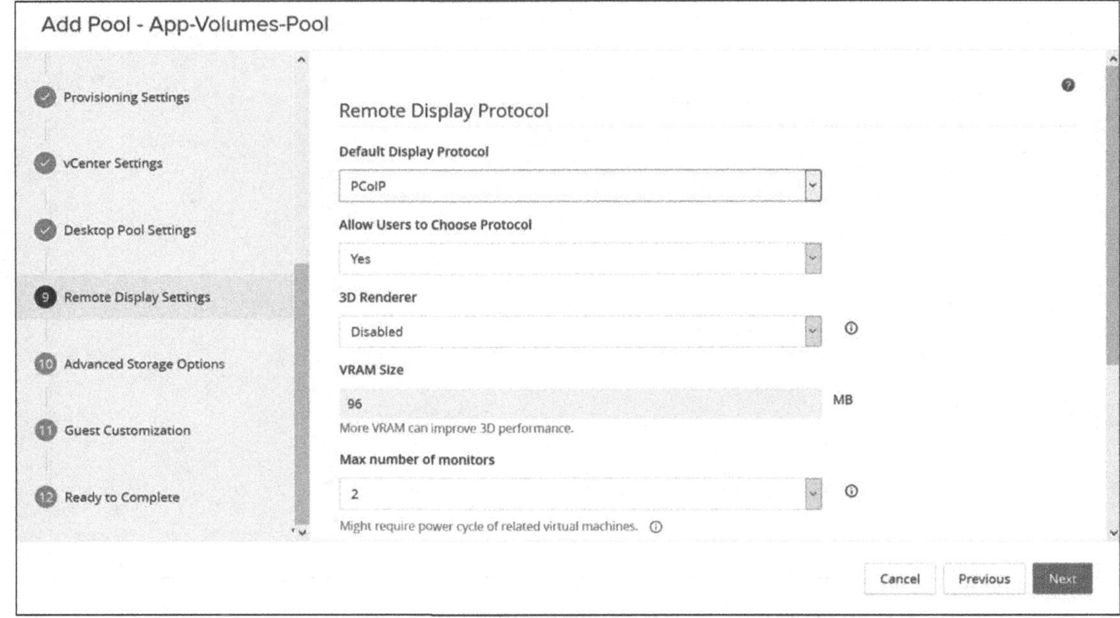

Figure 11-38. *Remote Display Settings configuration screen*

37. On this screen, you can configure how you want the virtual desktop machine to be displayed on the end user's device.

38. Click **Next** to continue.

39. You will see the **Advanced Storage Options** screen as shown in Figure 11-39.

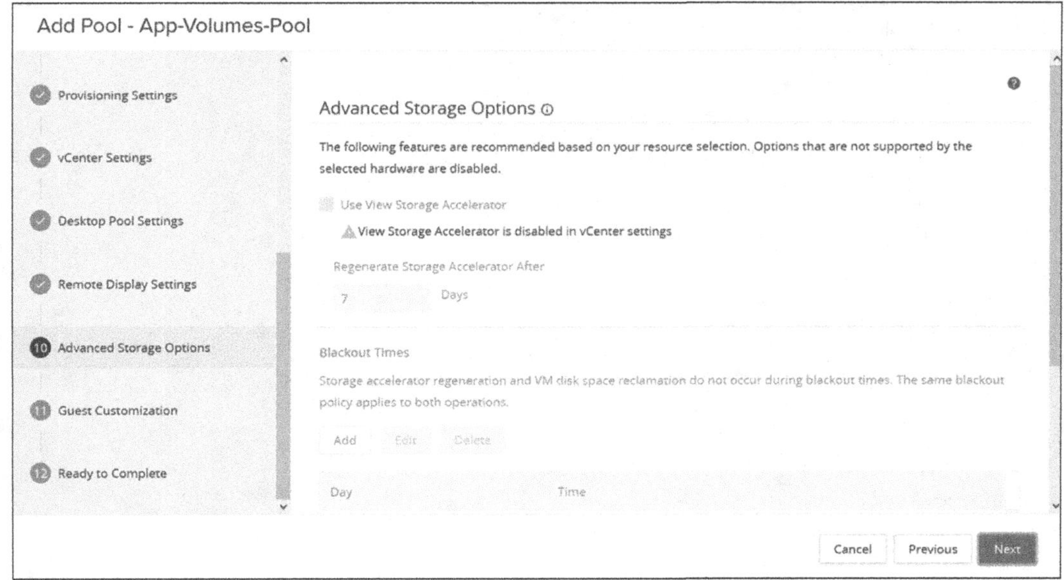

Figure 11-39. Advanced Storage Options configuration screen

40. Click **Next** to continue.

41. You will see the **Guest Customization** configuration screen as shown in Figure 11-40.

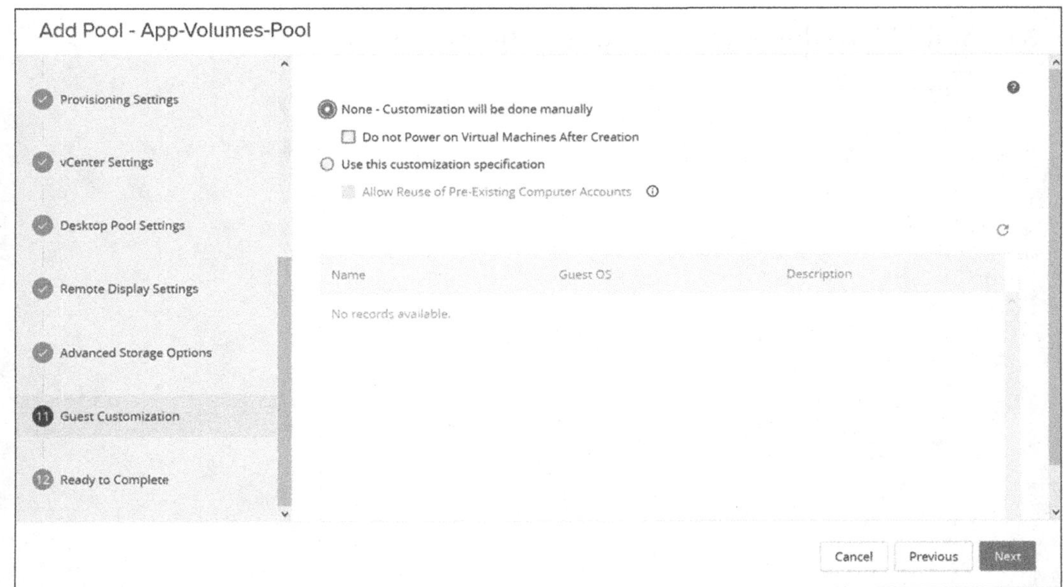

Figure 11-40. Guest Customization configuration screen

42. Click the **None - Customization will be done manually** button for this example, unless you have a customization specification already built within your environment.

43. Click **Next** to continue.

44. The final screen you will see is the **Ready to Complete** screen as shown in Figure 11-41.

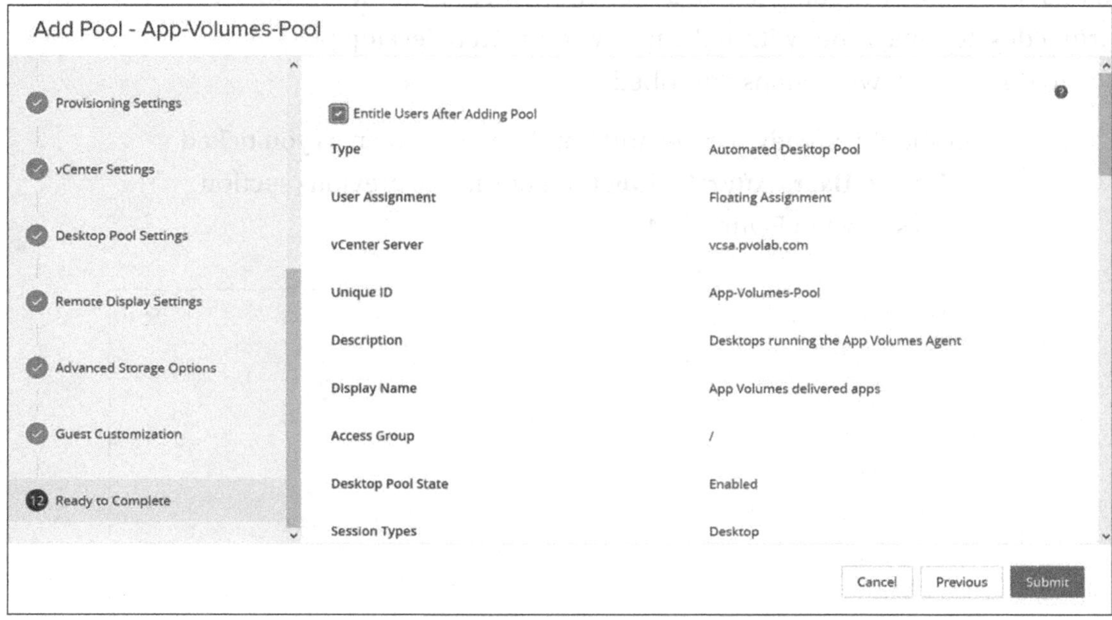

***Figure 11-41.** Ready to Complete screen*

45. Check the details of your configuration.

46. Now check the **Entitle Users After Adding Pool** box. This will automatically take you to the entitlements configuration screen where you can add users that will have access to this desktop pool.

47. Click the **Submit** button.

You have now successfully configured a desktop pool that contains a virtual desktop machine that is App Volumes enabled, meaning that applications can be attached to this virtual desktop machine when the end user logs in.

In the next section, we are going to add an end user entitlement to the desktop pool to enable the end user to connect to a virtual desktop. Even though the end user is already entitled to the application package in App Volumes, they still need to have access to the virtual desktop machine in order to connect to it.

Entitling end users to the Desktop Pool

In this section, we are going to add a user entitlement to allow an end user to access the virtual desktop machines within the newly configured desktop pool.

To do this, follow the steps described:

1. You should already see the Add Entitlements screen as you ticked the **Entitle Users After Adding Pool** box in the previous section. This is shown in Figure 11-42.

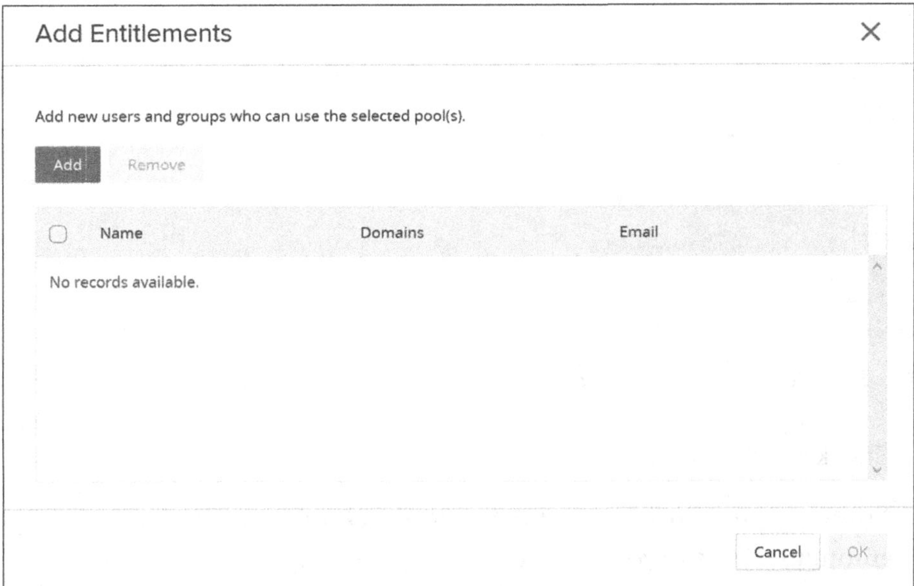

Figure 11-42. *Adding an end user entitlement*

2. Click the **Add** button.

3. You will see the **Find User or Group** configuration screen.

In this example, we are going to add the user Peter von Oven and so will use this username as the search criteria.

1. In the **Type** box, check the boxes for what you want to search for, **Users**, **Groups**, or **Unauthenticated Users.**
2. In the **Domain** box, from the drop-down menu, select the domain in which this user resides. In this example, this is the pvolab.com domain.
3. You can then filter the results on either the **Name/User Name** or **Description**. In this example, we are going to search using the **Name** field, selecting **Contains** from the filter options. Then in the box, we will type the name to search for, in this example, the name peter. So, we will search the domain for usernames that contain peter in them.
4. Click the **Find** button. You will see the results listed below as shown in Figure 11-43.

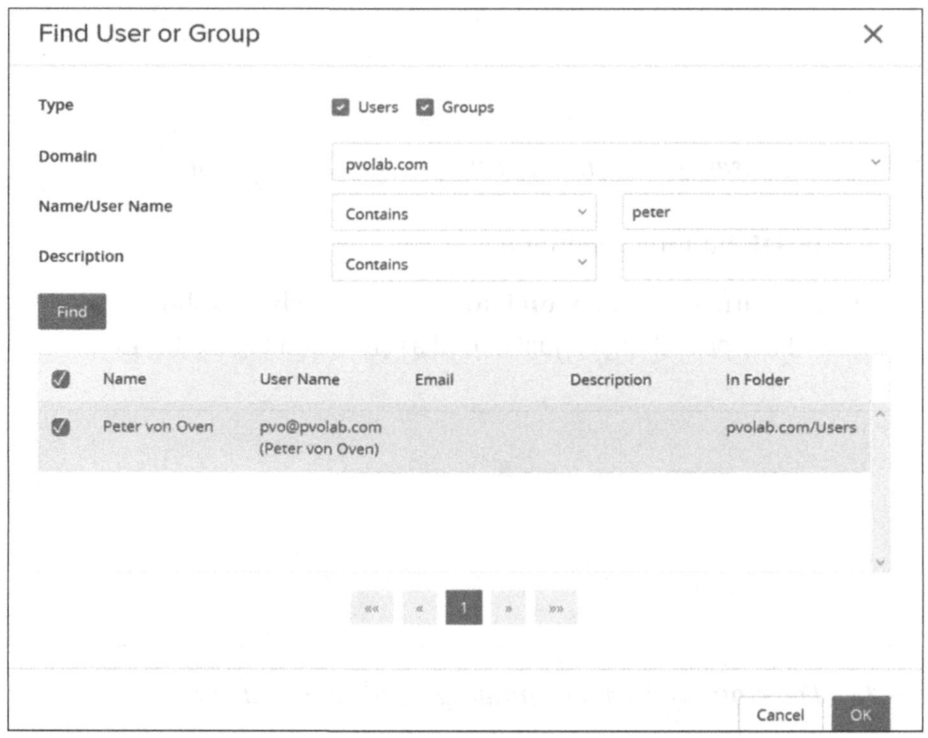

***Figure 11-43.** Finding an end user or group for entitlement*

5. Check the box to select the user, and then click the **OK** button to continue.

6. Once added, you will return to the **Add Entitlements** screen which will now show the newly added user and the ability to continue adding more users as shown in Figure 11-44.

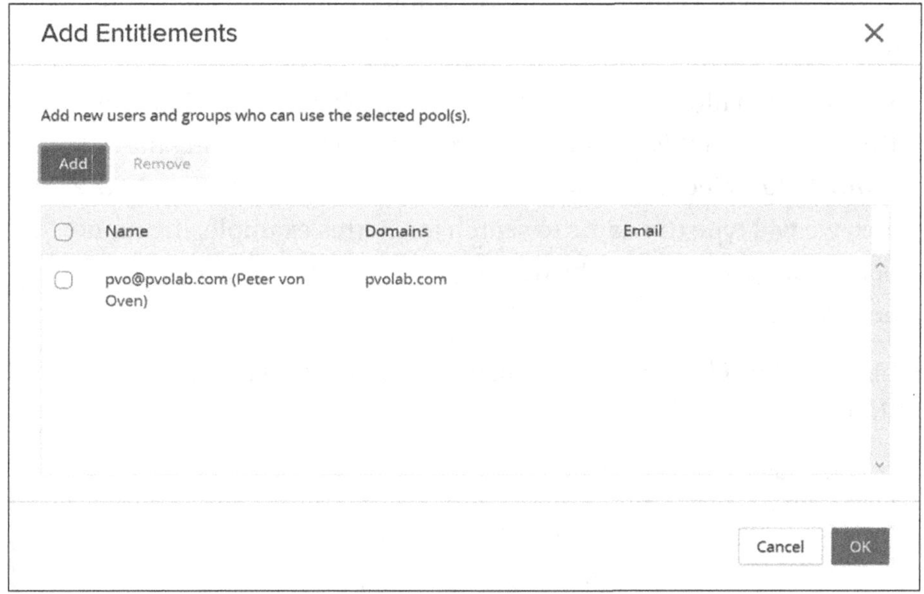

***Figure 11-44.** End user successfully entitled to the Desktop Pool*

7. Click the **OK** button to continue.

8. You will return to the **Desktop Pools** screen which now shows the details of the pool that you just added as shown in Figure 11-45.

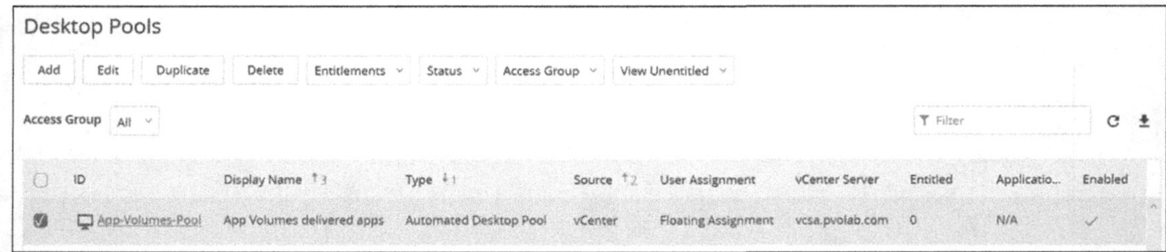

***Figure 11-45.** Desktop Pool screen showing newly entitled end user*

You have now successfully added a Desktop Pool and entitled an end user to be able to access the pool and the virtual desktop machines within it.

To make sure everything is working as expected and that end users can connect and launch a virtual desktop machine, in the next section, we are going to assume the role of the end user and test everything works as expected.

Testing the solution

In this last section, now that we have finished configuring everything, we are going to take on the role of the end user and ensure that they can log in, connect, and launch a virtual desktop machine and that they can successfully launch the application being delivered by App Volumes.

We are going to connect to the virtual desktop machine using a browser.

To do this, complete the following steps as described:

1. Log in to VMware Horizon as an end user. To do this, open a browser and in this example enter the address to the Horizon Connection Server - `https:\\horizon-7.pvolab.com`.
2. You will see the login box as shown in Figure 11-46.

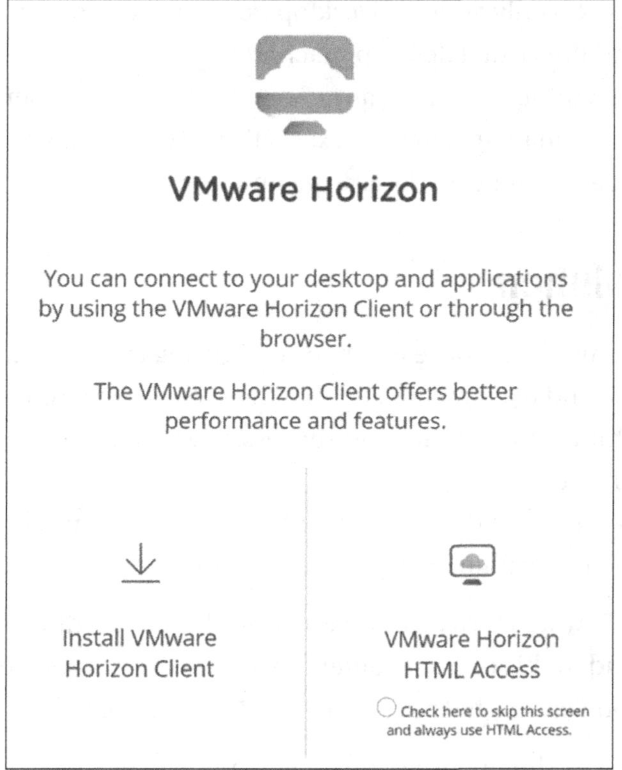

Figure 11-46. *Logging in to a Horizon virtual desktop*

3. As we are going to connect using the browser, click **VMware Horizon HTML Access.**

4. You will now see the login box for the end user to enter their credentials. In this example, we are logging in as the end user **pvo**, so type in **pvo@pvolab.com** into the username box followed by the password for this user. This is the user that was entitled to this desktop pool earlier in this chapter.

5. This is shown in Figure 11-47.

Figure 11-47. *Logging in to Horizon using the browser*

6. Click the **Login** button to log in. You will now see the Horizon web page showing the entitled desktop (Figure 11-48).

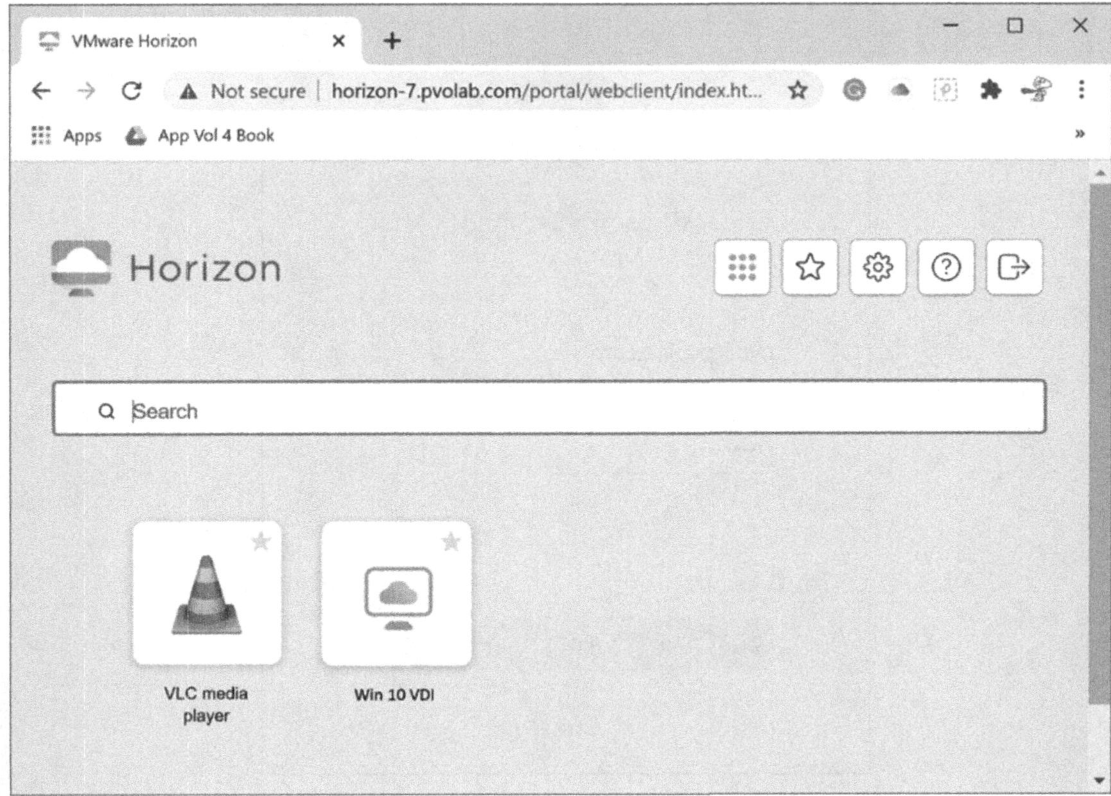

***Figure 11-48.** Horizon web page showing the virtual desktop*

7. You will also notice that you have the published version of VLC available to run as well.

8. Double-click the **Win 10 VDI** desktop.

9. You will then connect to a virtual desktop machine in the pool. This is running the App Volumes Agent. As this user is entitled to VLC, then the app will be delivered to their desktop as shown in Figure 11-49.

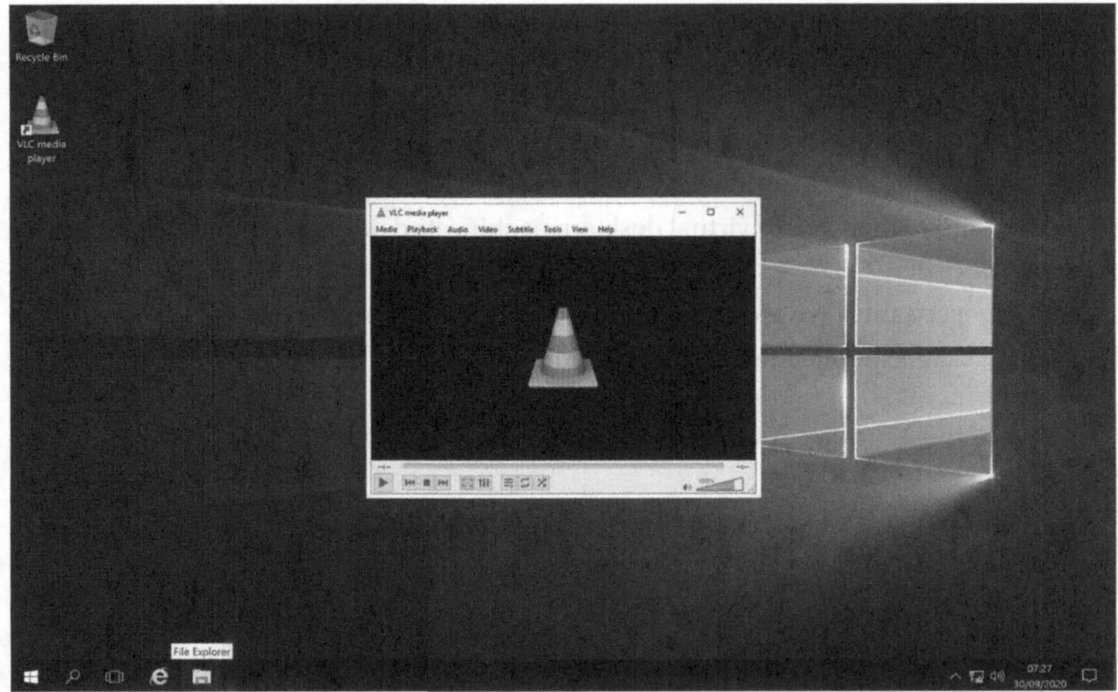

***Figure 11-49.** Virtual desktop machine running VLC delivered by App Volumes*

You have now successfully configured Horizon View to deliver App Volumes-enabled virtual desktop machines, with applications being attached using app layers.

Chapter summary

In this chapter, we have looked at how to configure App Volumes application packages to be attached to virtual desktop machines that are delivered to end users using Horizon View.

We started the chapter with an overview of the architecture and how Horizon View fits in with App Volumes and how that solution works before then going on to install and configure all the required components of the solution.

As part of that configuration, we looked at how to build a virtual desktop machine image that included the components for delivering App Volumes applications, as well as the components required for Horizon View.

Next, we configured desktop pools using this newly created App Volumes–enabled image. Once configured, the pool was entitled to an end user and then tested to ensure that they could launch both a virtual desktop machine and the App Volumes delivered application.

In the next chapter, we are going to look at VMware ThinApp and how to deliver ThinApp packaged applications using App Volumes.

CHAPTER 12

VMware ThinApp and App Volumes

On the surface, ThinApp and App Volumes seem to deliver the same thing. To a certain degree, that is correct; they both deliver applications to end users. However, they work in completely different ways and as such address very different use cases. Let us define what the ThinApp solution delivers as this book being an App Volumes book clearly focuses on App Volumes, and therefore we have defined this.

VMware ThinApp is an application virtualization solution.

As an application virtualization solution, ThinApp decouples applications from the underlying operating system and captures the application dependencies and files required to allow it to run. It then creates a "bubble," referred to as a ThinApp package, that contains all the things the captured application needs to run. This includes OS dependencies, file system, and all the application files. The ThinApp package consists of a single file, either an EXE file or you can create an MSI file.

If you compare this to App Volumes, App Volumes packages are virtual hard drives that contain the application files and settings that then are layered into the operating system. ThinApp is a single file that is launched on the desktop – no layering and no virtual hard drives. It also has no need for an agent to be installed on the desktop either.

ThinApp is designed to eliminate application conflict and so allows you to run nonnative applications on a newer operating system. For example, you could run an older version of a browser that would typically only run on an older version of Windows, package it, and then run it on the latest version of Windows as a ThinApp package.

The ability to do this is in the way that ThinApp creates a level of isolation. As part of the package, it contains all the OS components that the app requires and therefore does not need the host machine OS. App Volumes packages do not contain any virtual OS components.

P. von Oven, *Delivering Applications with VMware App Volumes 4*,
https://doi.org/10.1007/978-1-4842-6689-2_12

In summary, ThinApp and App Volumes complement each other. ThinApp packages can be delivered as App Volumes layers where the layer contains a completely isolated application, allowing it to run on an OS version that ordinarily it was not designed for. Having the ThinApp package deliver as an application layer means that it does not need to be installed in the base image and can be delivered dynamically.

In this chapter, we are going to create a ThinApp package and then create an App Volumes application package containing the ThinApp package.

The first step is to capture the ThinApp package.

Capturing a ThinApp application

Like with App Volumes, the first task is to create an application. Similarly, the process involves capturing the installation process of the application that you want to package and deliver. However, with ThinApp, we are capturing locally to a single file rather than to a virtual hard disk.

In this example, in the test lab, we are going to capture and package Notepad++ as a ThinApp packaged application, using a Windows 10 desktop machine as the capture machine.

To capture the application, follow the steps as described:

1. Open a console to the Windows 10 desktop being used as the capture machine, with ThinApp Setup Capture utility already installed, and then launch the ThinApp Setup Capture application.

2. As the utility launches, you will see the pop-up box in the bottom right-hand side of the screen as shown in Figure 12-1.

***Figure 12-1.** Launching the ThinApp Setup Capture utility*

3. Once loaded, you will see the **Setup Capture - Welcome** screen as shown in Figure 12-2.

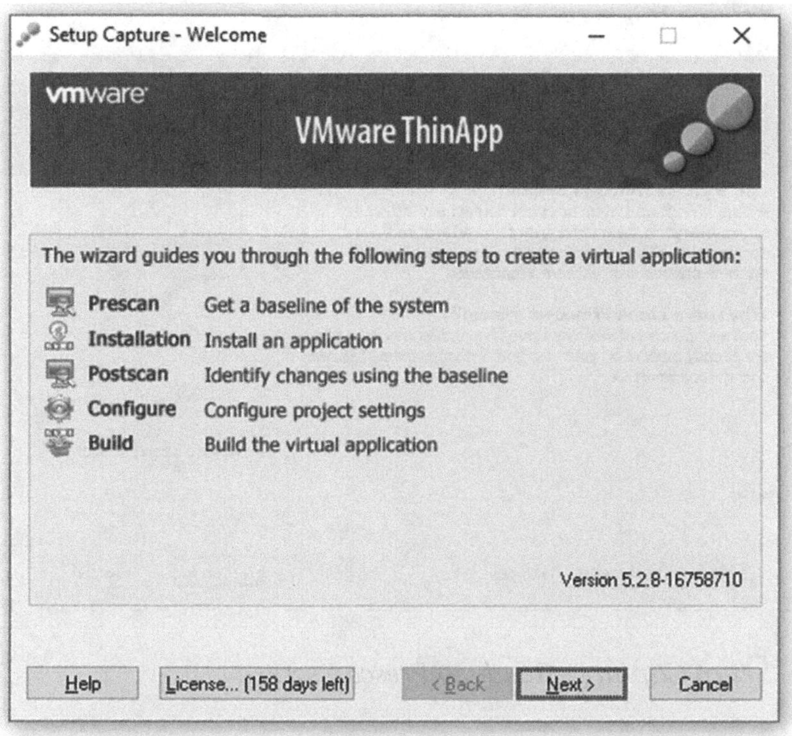

***Figure 12-2.** Setup Capture utility welcome screen*

4. Click **Next ➤** to continue.

5. You will see the **Setup Capture - Ready to Prescan** screen as shown in Figure 12-3.

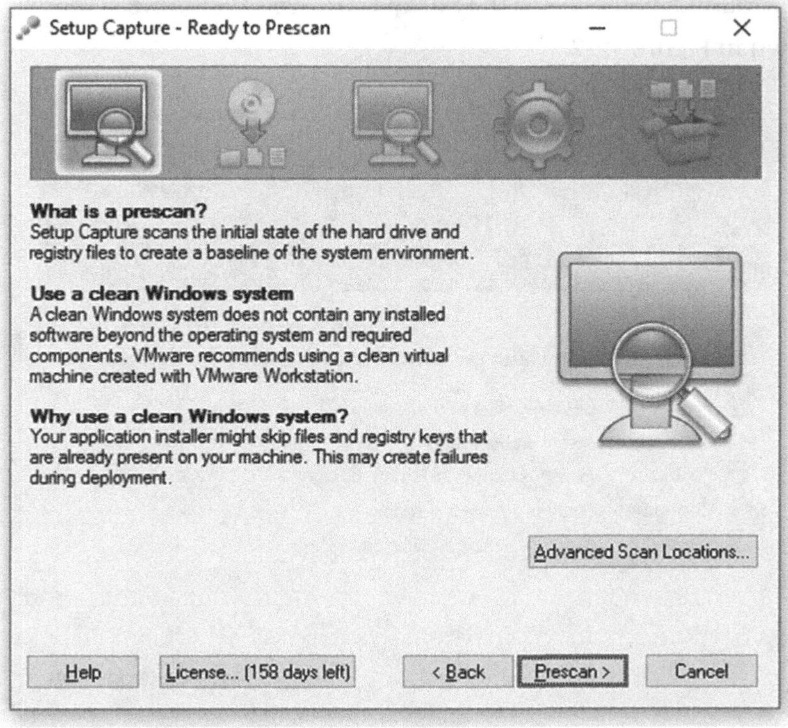

Figure 12-3. *Setup Capture - Ready to Prescan screen*

The prescan performs a scan of the machine state as it is now, before you install the application you want to capture. It creates a before picture of the machine using a snapshot which will then be used to compare the machine state once the application has successfully been installed.

6. Click the **Prescan ➤** button to start the prescan process.
7. You will now see the prescan progress dialog box showing the files that are being scanned. This is shown in Figure 12-4.

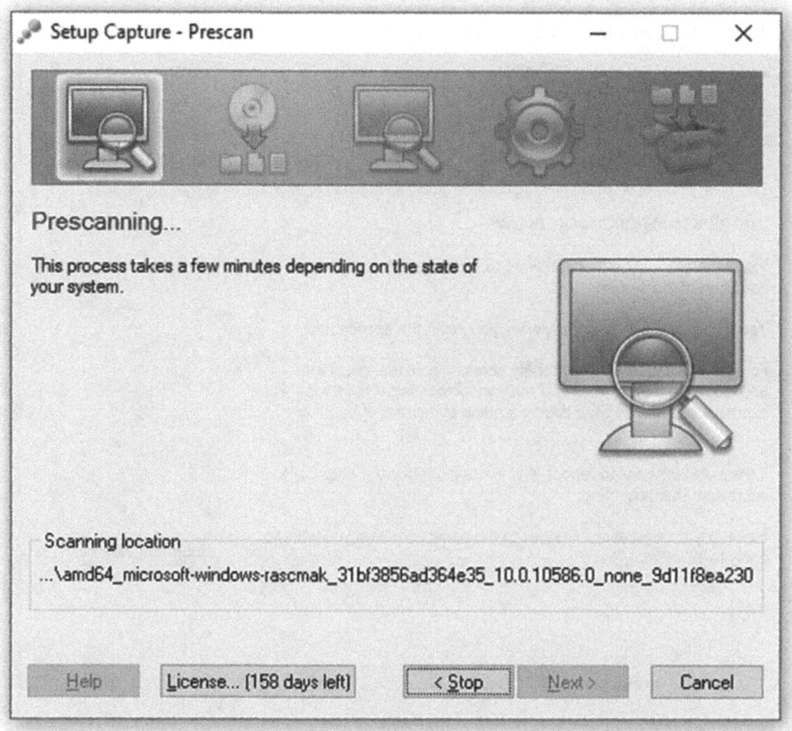

Figure 12-4. *Prescanning screen*

8. Once the prescan has completed, you will see the **Install the Application Now** screen as shown in Figure 12-5.

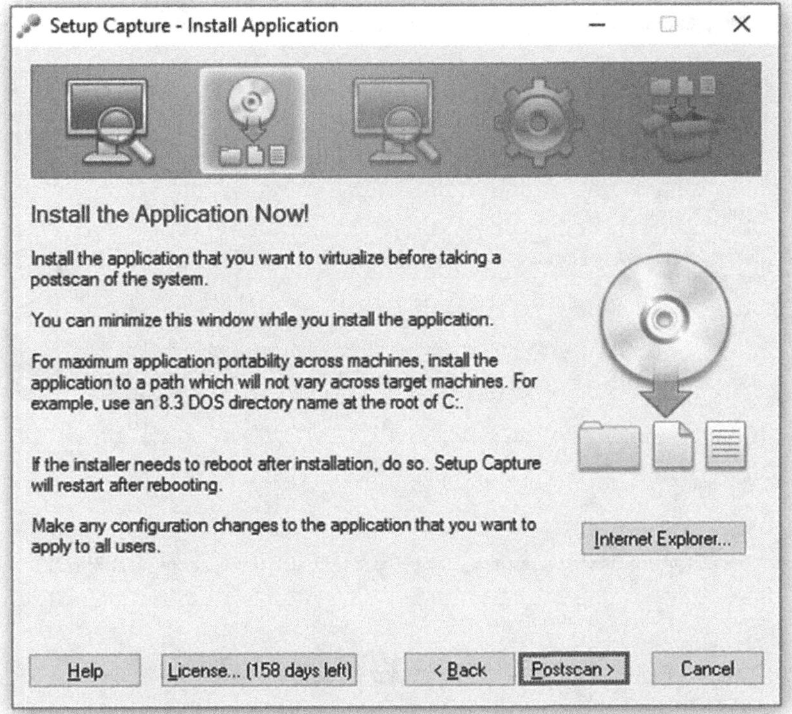

Figure 12-5. *Install the application screen*

9. You can now install the application. In this example, we are going to install Notepad++.

Do not click the **Postscan ➤** button until you have successfully installed the application.

---

10. In this example, we are going to install Notepad++, so navigate to the location of the installer for Notepad++ as shown in Figure 12-6.

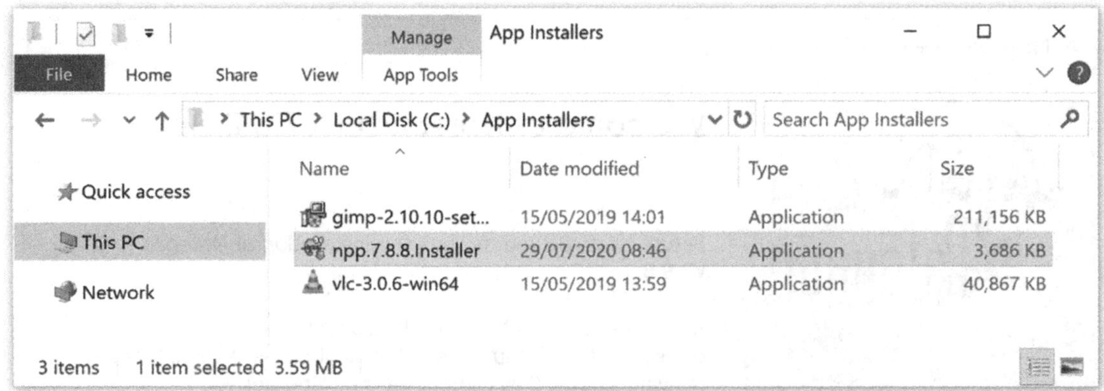

Figure 12-6. *Notepad++ installer*

11. Double-click to launch the installer.
12. You will see the screenshot in Figure 12-7.

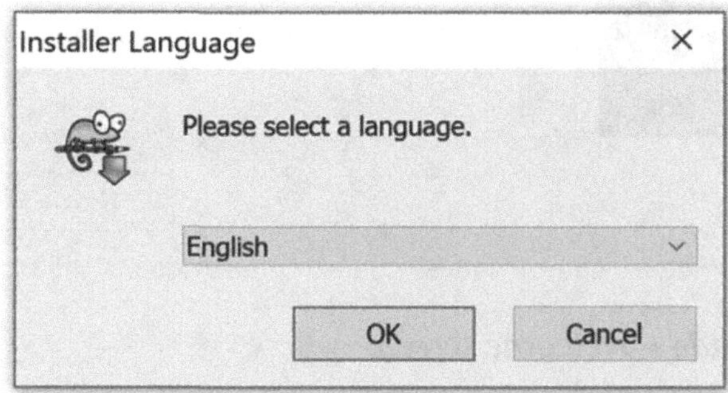

Figure 12-7. *Notepad++ installation – language selection*

13. Click **OK.**
14. You will see the Notepad++ Welcome screen as shown in Figure 12-8.

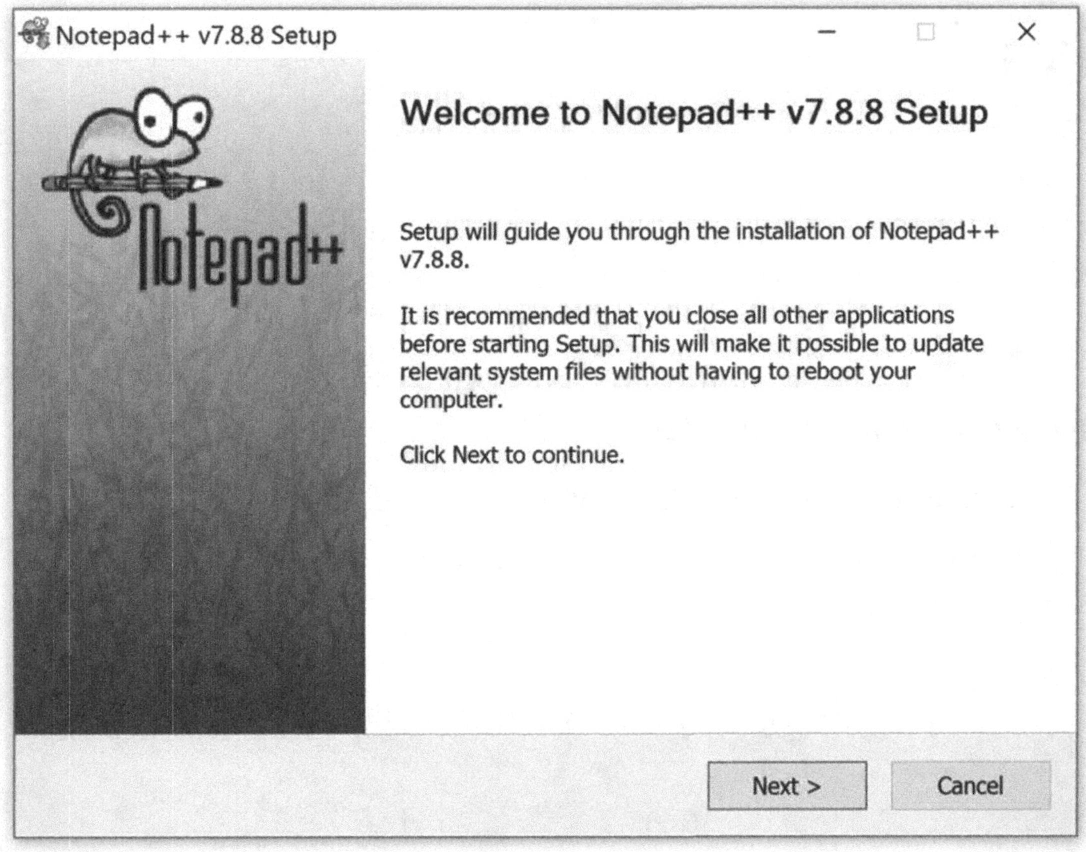

Figure 12-8. *Notepad++ Welcome screen*

15. Click **Next ➤** to continue the installation.

    We are not going to run through the complete installation of Notepad++ step by step, so continue installing the application as you would do normally, or the application you have chosen for this exercise.

    The installation process has been "accelerated" as shown in Figure 12-9.

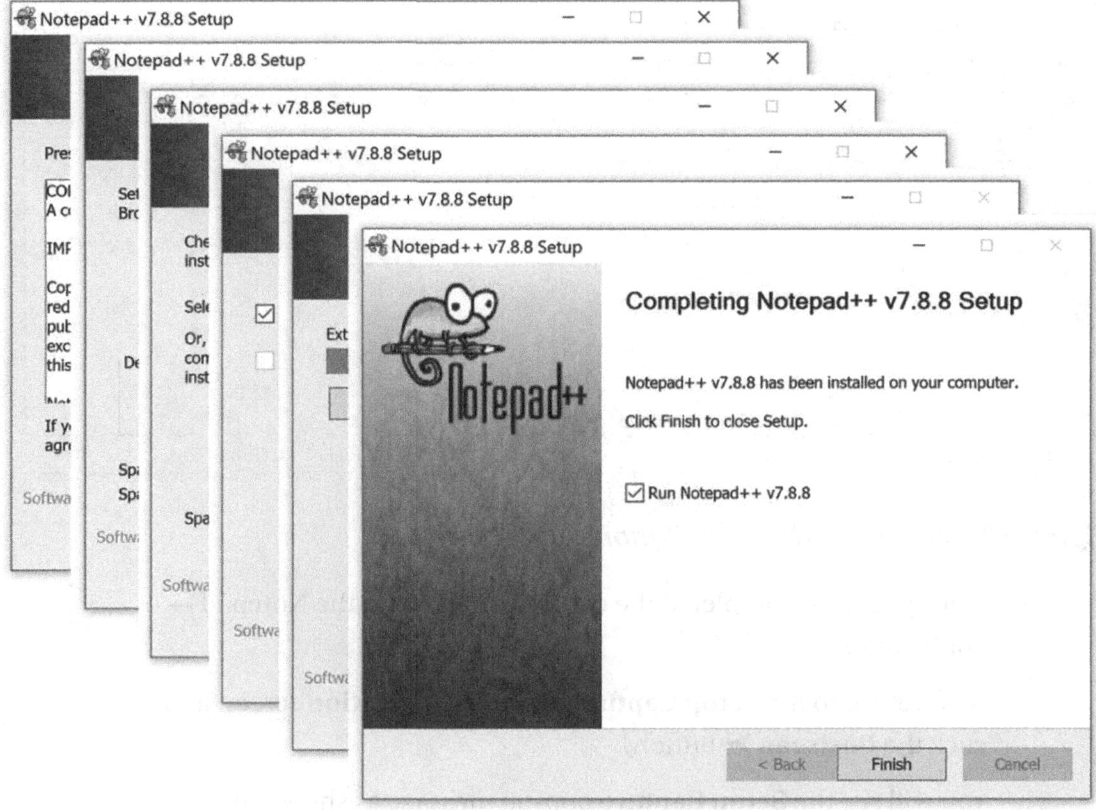

Figure 12-9. *Notepad++ installation completed*

16. Click the **Run Notepad++ v7.8.8** check box, and then click the **Finish** button.

17. Before we complete the installation, we are going to configure the settings we want users to have for Notepad++ as these will be captured as part of the capture process.

18. You will see Notepad++ launch so that you can make these configuration and user setting changes, as shown in Figure 12-10.

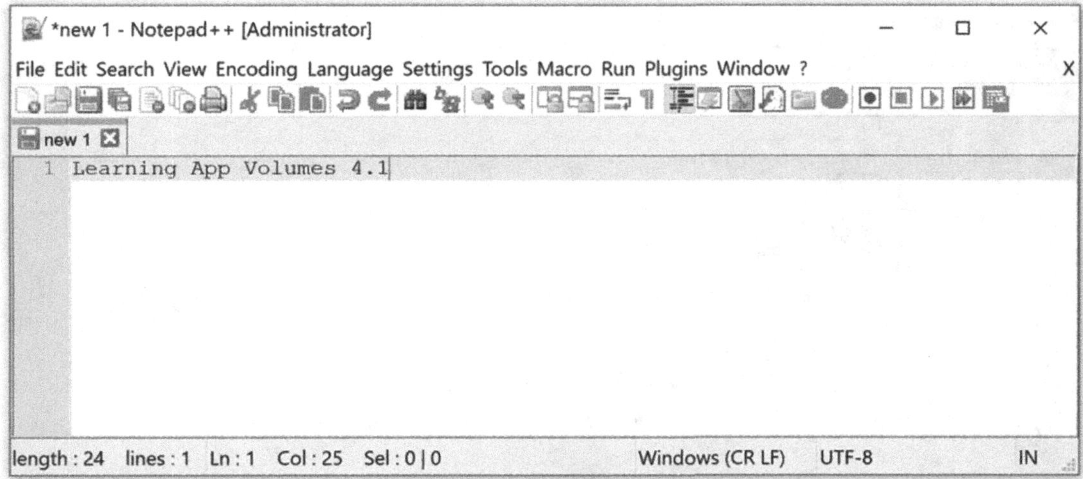

Figure 12-10. *Notepad++ installation completed*

19. Once you have completed the configuration, close the Notepad++ application.

20. Now return to the **Setup Capture - Install Application** screen and click the **Postscan ➤** button.

21. You will see the **Setup Capture** pop-up message as shown in Figure 12-11.

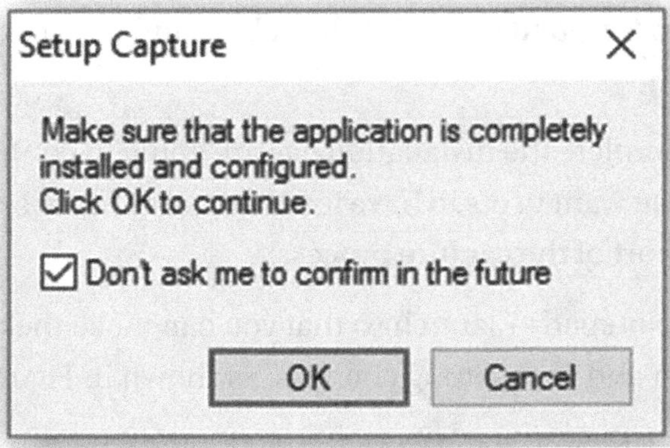

Figure 12-11. *Setup Capture application warning box*

22. Click the **OK** button to confirm that the application has been installed and configured.

23. You will now see the postscan process run as shown in Figure 12-12.

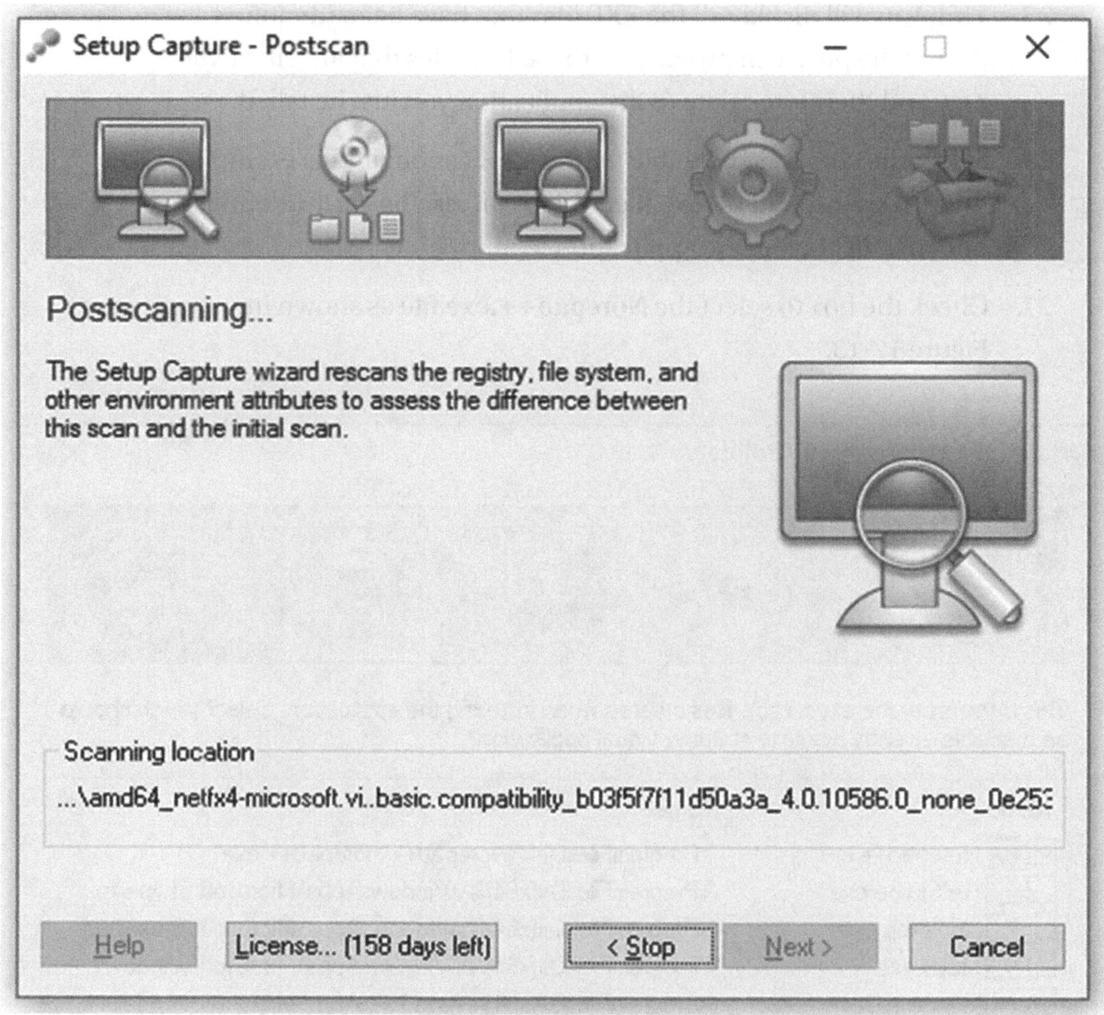

Figure 12-12. *Postscanning screen*

The postscan process compares the current state of the desktop machine with the application now successfully installed, with the prescan version of before the application was installed. ThinApp will identify any changes between the pre- and postscan. Those changes will be the files and registry settings that have been added during the application installation process.

24. Once the postscan process has completed, you will see the **Setup Capture - Entry Points** screen.

25. ThinApp will display all the EXE files that have been identified during the postscan process, so those EXE files that are effectively new and therefore relate to the application you just installed.

26. Select the correct executable for the application; in this example, this is the **Notepad++.exe** file, which can also be easily identified due to it displaying the application icon.

27. Check the box to select the **Notepad++.exe** file as shown in Figure 12-13.

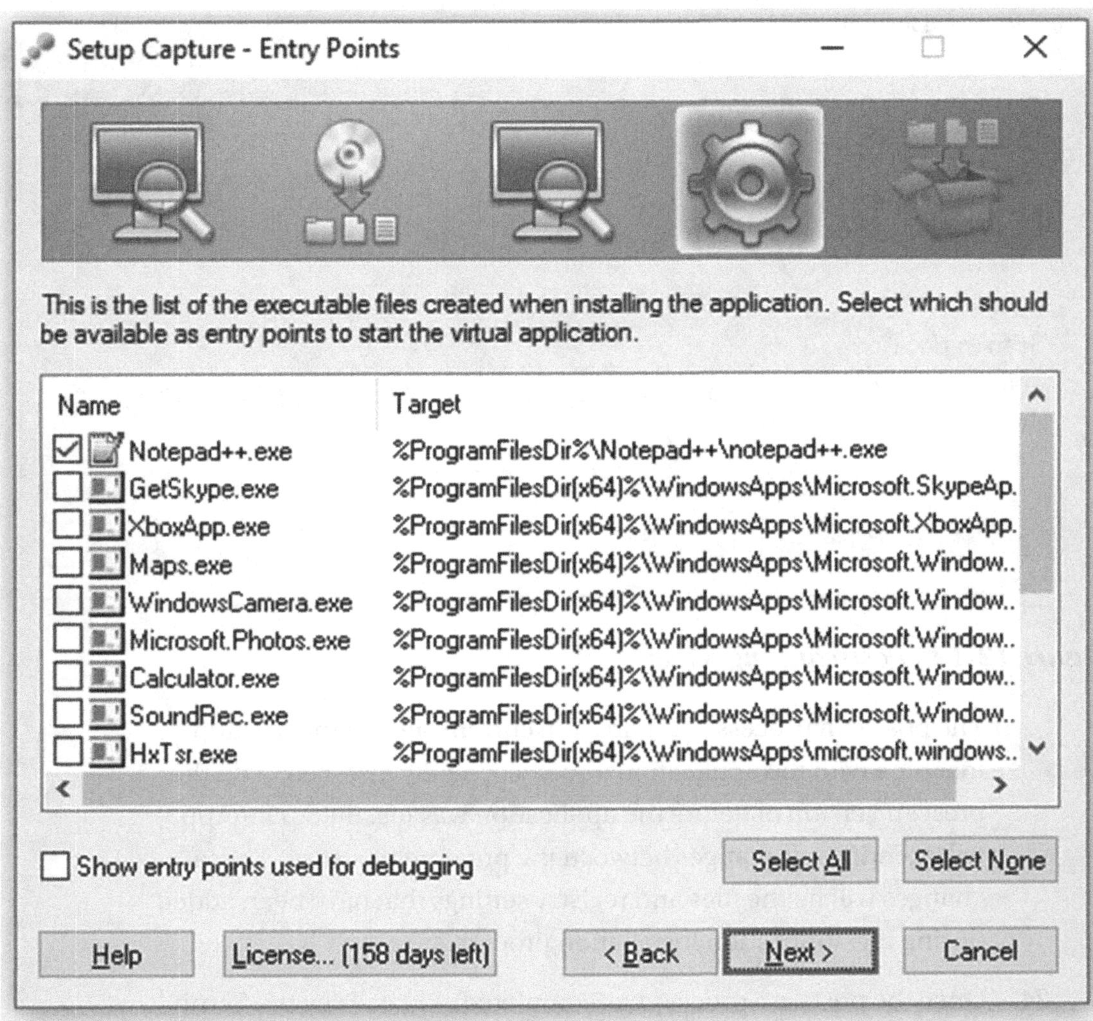

Figure 12-13. *Selecting the application entry points*

28. Click the **Next ➤** button to continue.

29. You will see the **Setup Capture - Manage with VMware Workspace** screen. Ensure that the **Manage with VMware Workspace** box is not checked as shown in Figure 12-14.

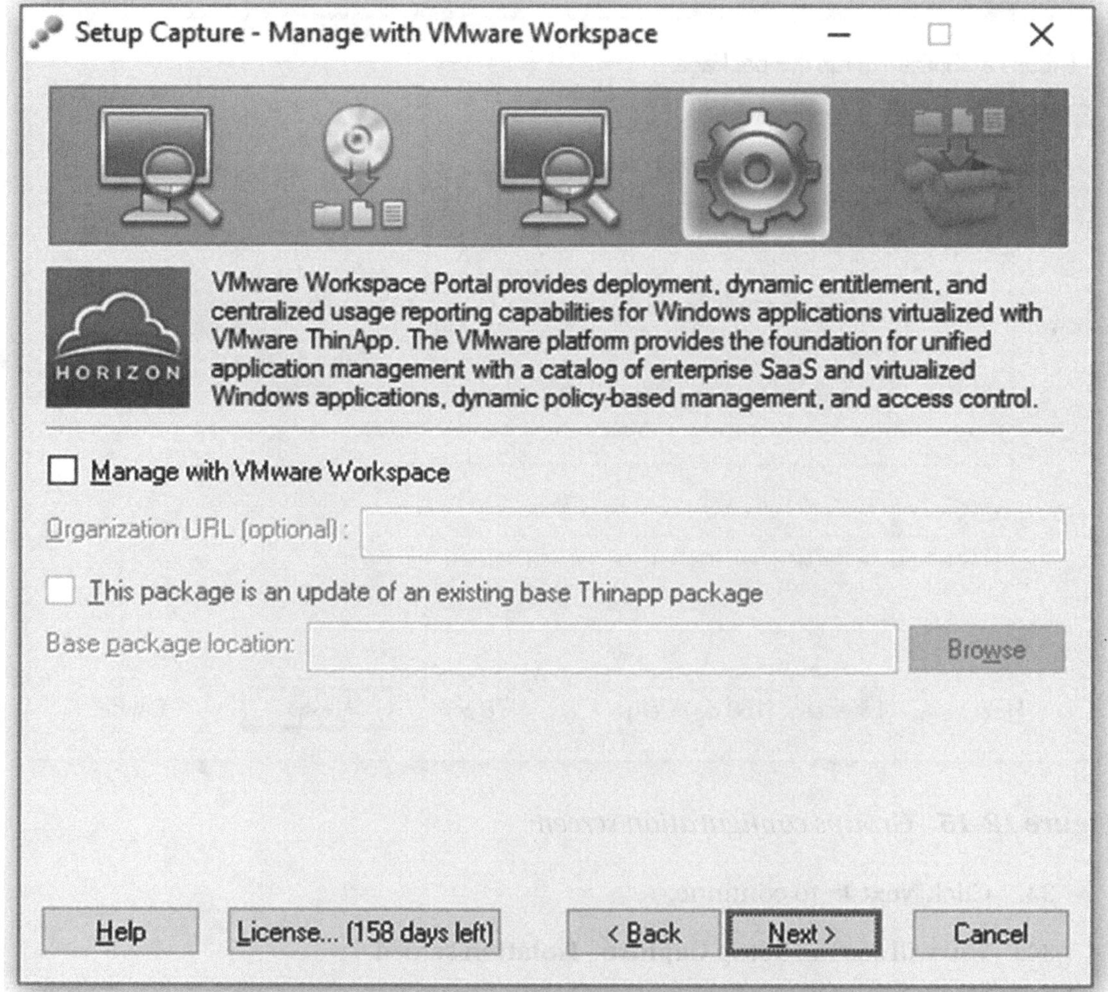

Figure 12-14. *Manage with VMware Workspace configuration screen*

30. Click **Next ➤** to continue.

31. You will see the **Setup Capture - Groups** screen.

32. Click the radio button for **Everyone** as shown in Figure 12-15.

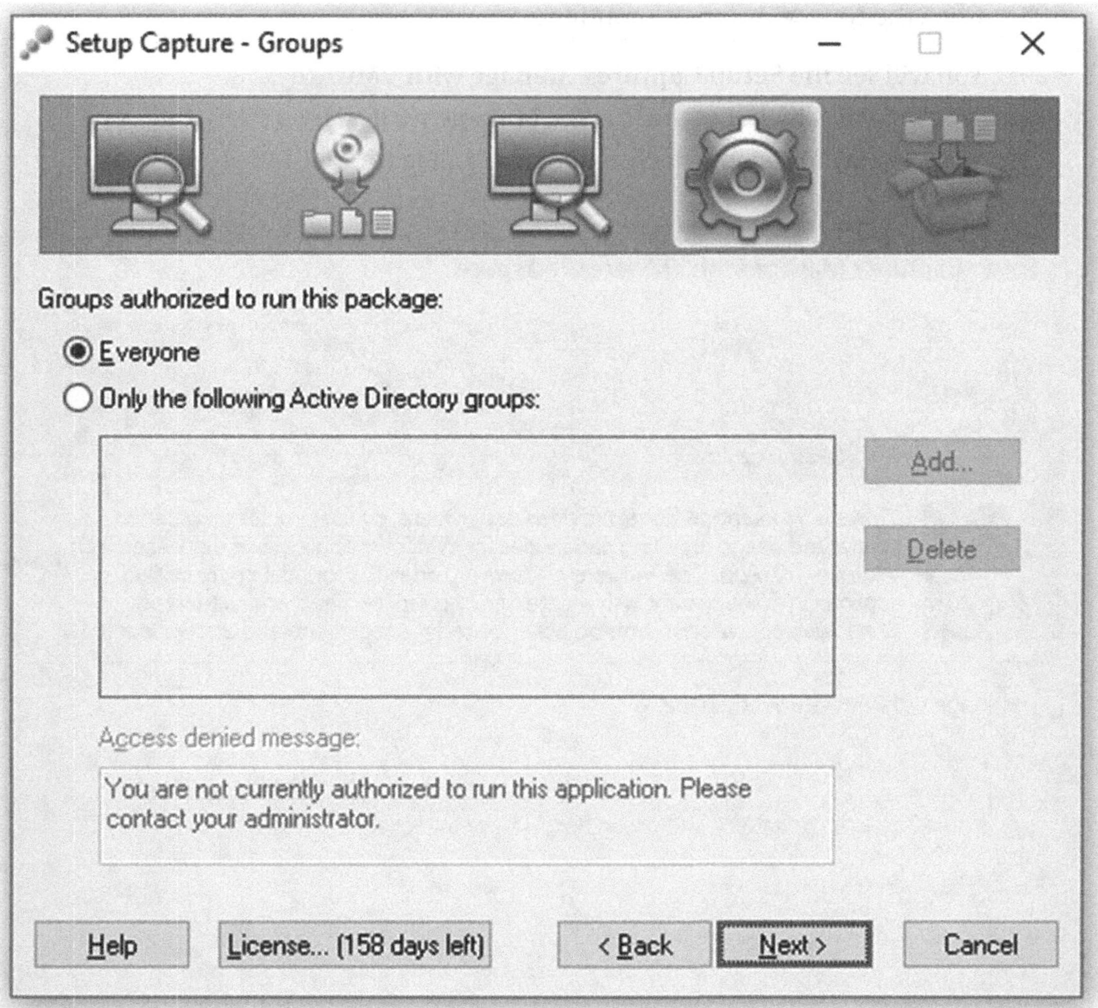

***Figure 12-15.** Groups configuration screen*

33. Click **Next ➤** to continue.

34. You will see the **Setup Capture - Isolation** screen.

35. Click the radio button for **Full write access to non-system directories** as shown in Figure 12-16.

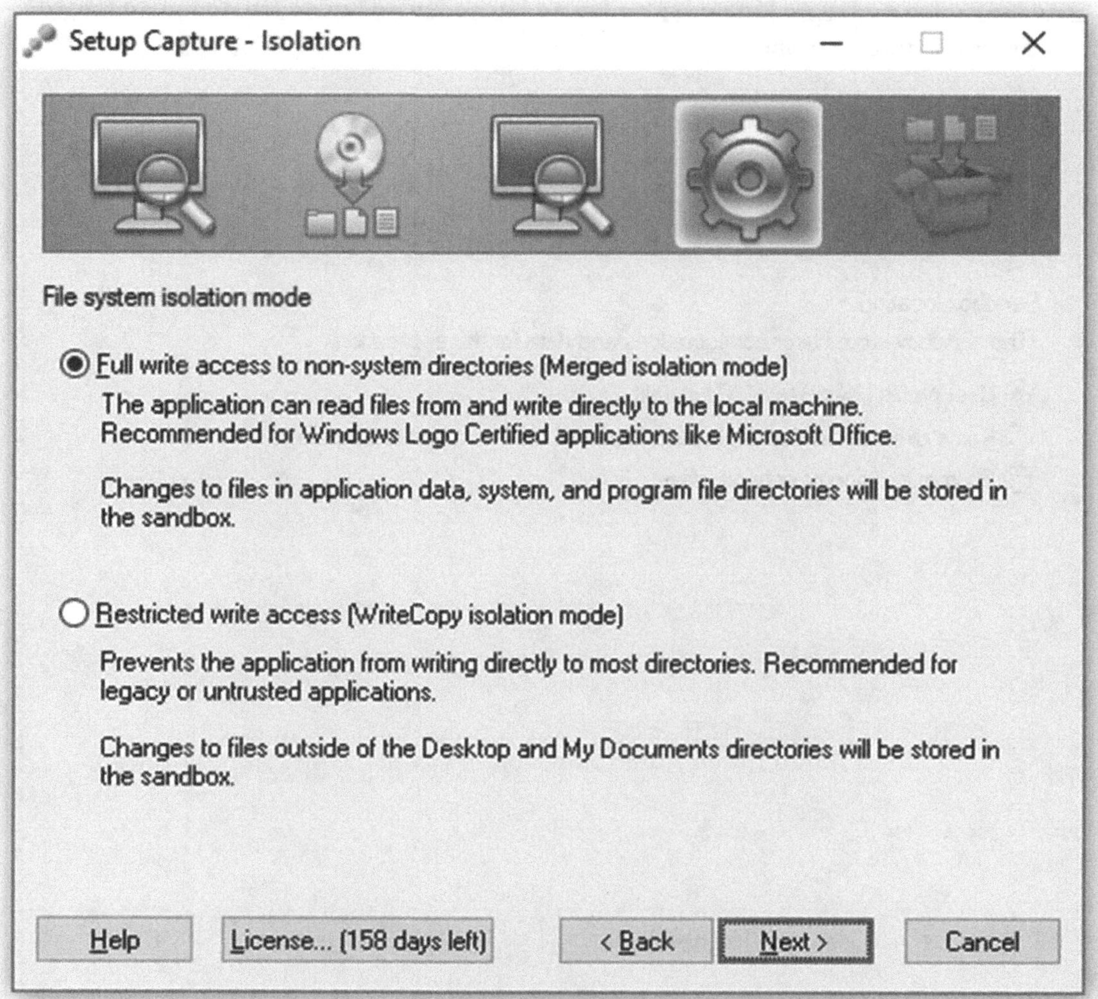

Figure 12-16. *Configure the isolation mode screen*

36. Click **Next ➤** to continue.

37. You will see the **Setup Capture - Sandbox** screen.

38. Click the radio button for **User profile (%AppData%\Thinstall)** as shown in Figure 12-17.

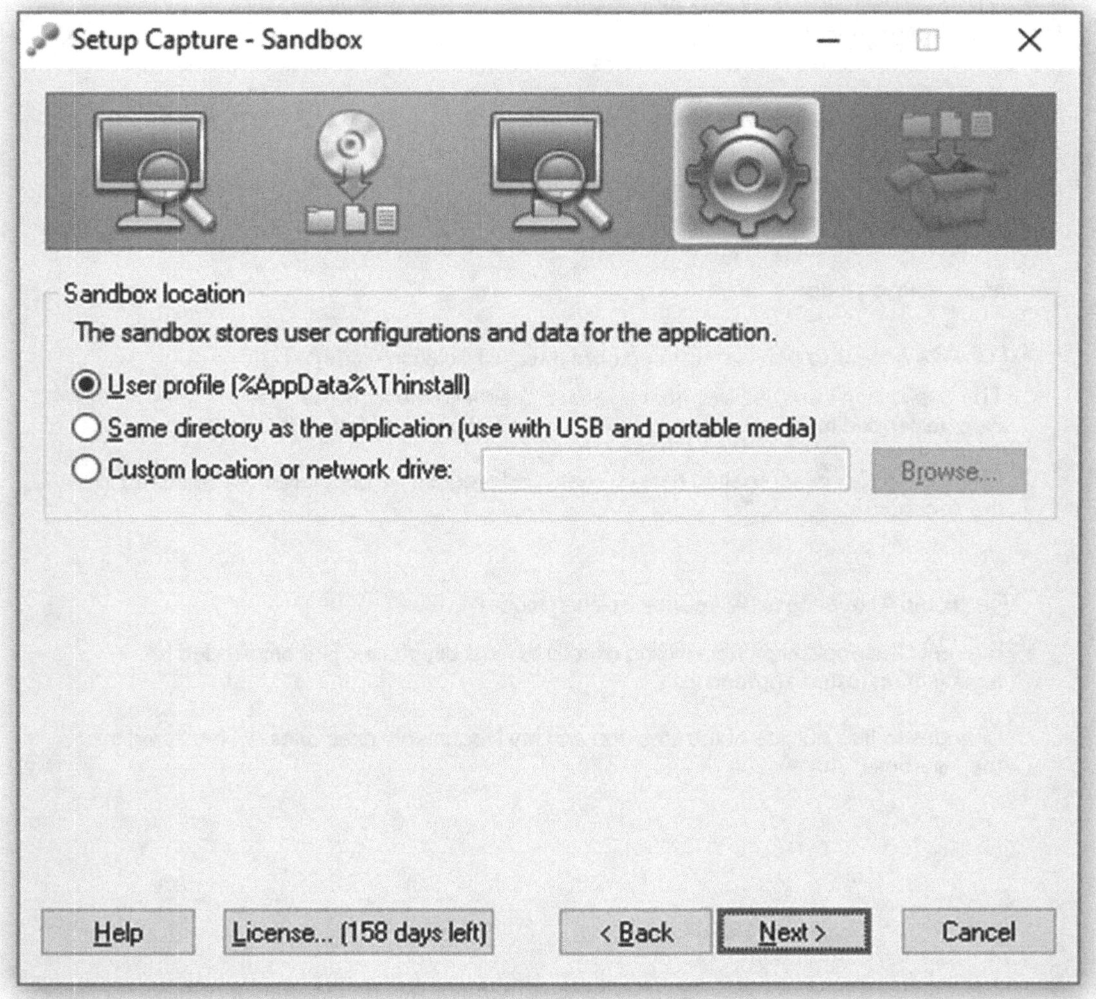

Figure 12-17. *Configure the sandbox location screen*

39. Click **Next ➤** to continue.
40. You will see the **Setup Capture - Quality Assurance Statistics** screen.
41. Click the radio button for **No - Do not send any information to VMware** as shown in Figure 12-18.

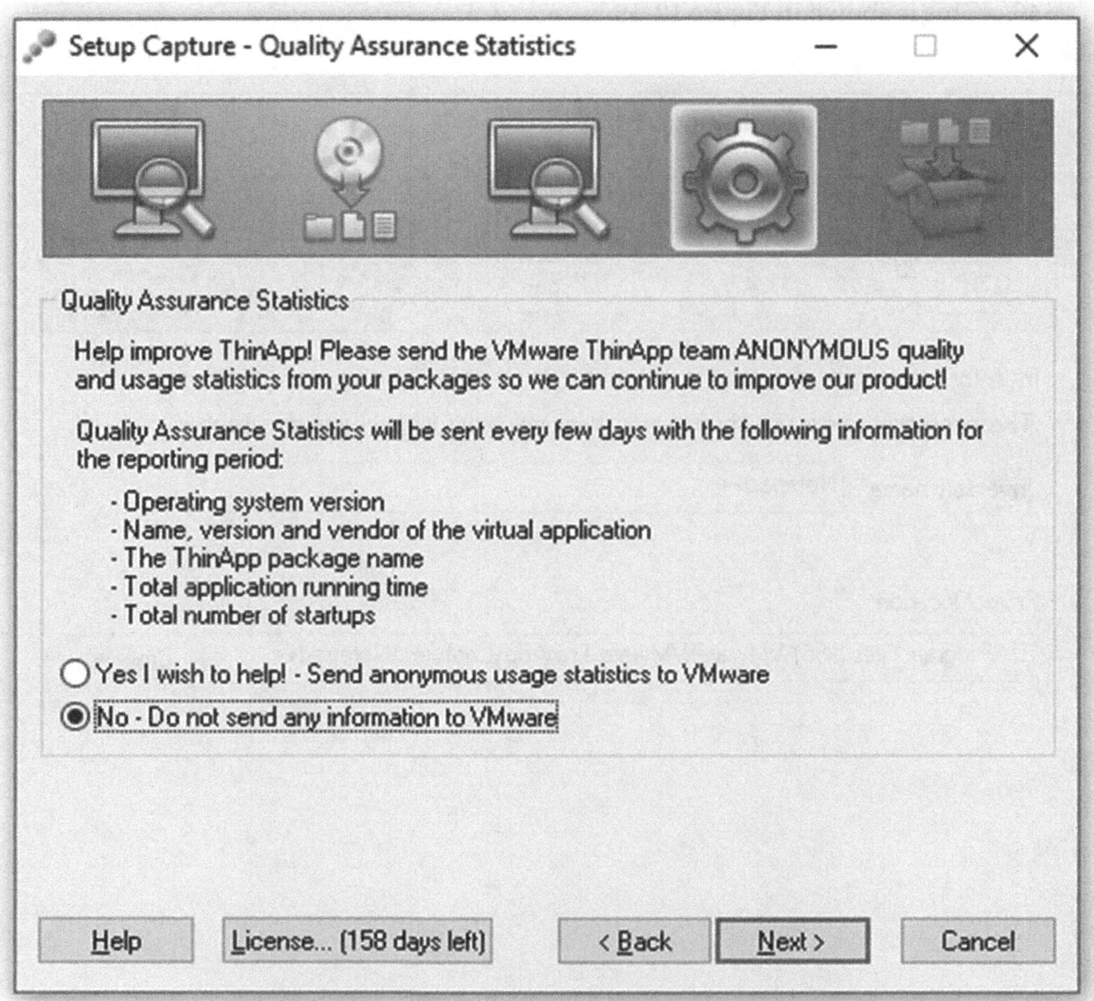

Figure 12-18. *Opt out of send information to VMware*

42. Click **Next ➤** to continue.

43. You will see the **Setup Capture - Project Settings** screen.

44. In the **Inventory name** field, type in the name for this ThinApp package. In this example, we have called it **Notepad++.**

45. In the Project location field, make sure that the path entered is correct. This is the path to where your ThinApp captured packages are stored. ThinApp will, in the example, create the Notepad++ folder and create all the package files in this folder.

46. This is shown in Figure 12-19.

***Figure 12-19.** Entering the details of the project*

47. Click **Next ➤** to continue.
48. You will see the **Setup Capture - Package Settings** screen.
49. Click the radio button for Use separate .DAT file.
50. Then, check the box for **Generate MSI package**, and in the field, type in the name you want to call this MSI file. In this example, we have named it **Notepad++.msi** as shown in Figure 12-20.

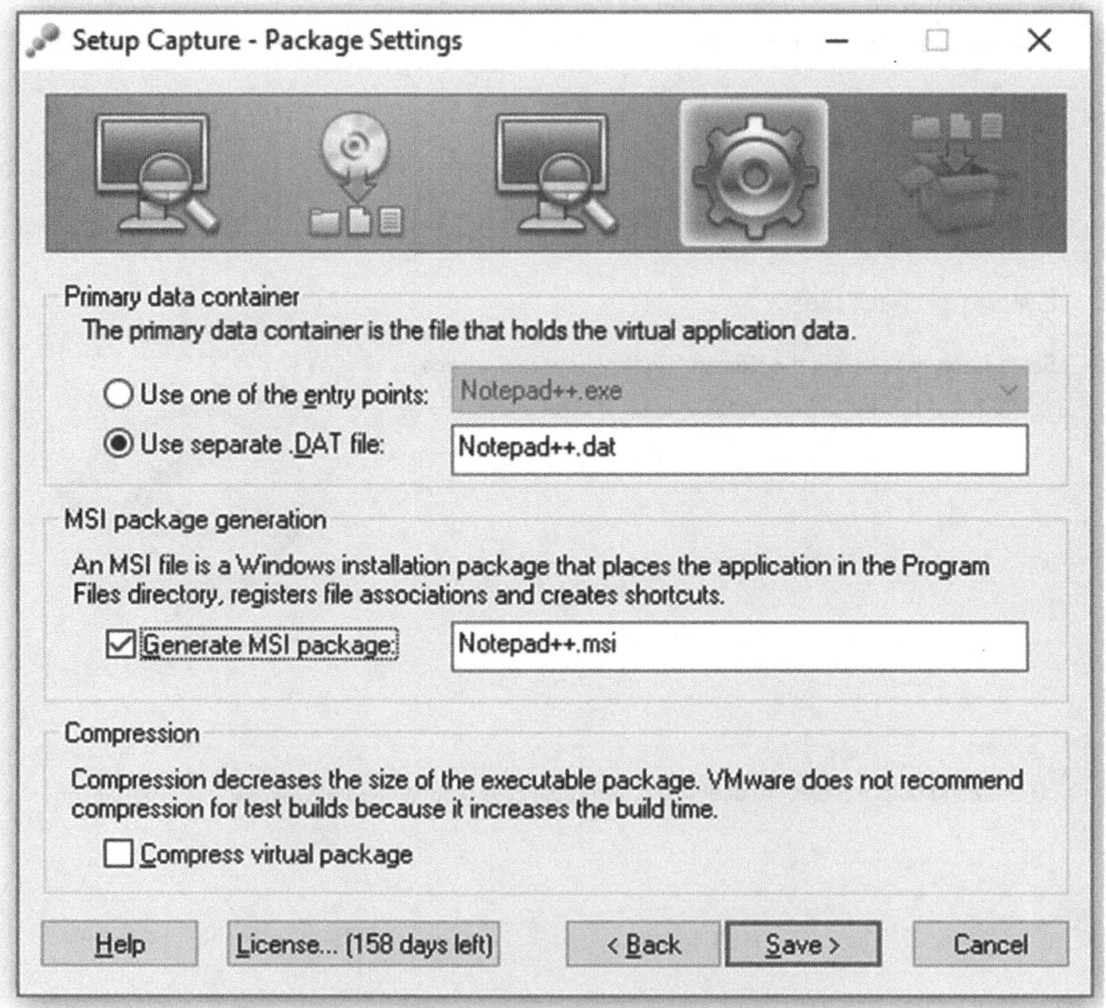

***Figure 12-20.** Configuring the package settings*

51. Click **Save ➤** to continue.

52. You will now see the **Setup Capture - Save Project** screen as shown in Figure 12-21.

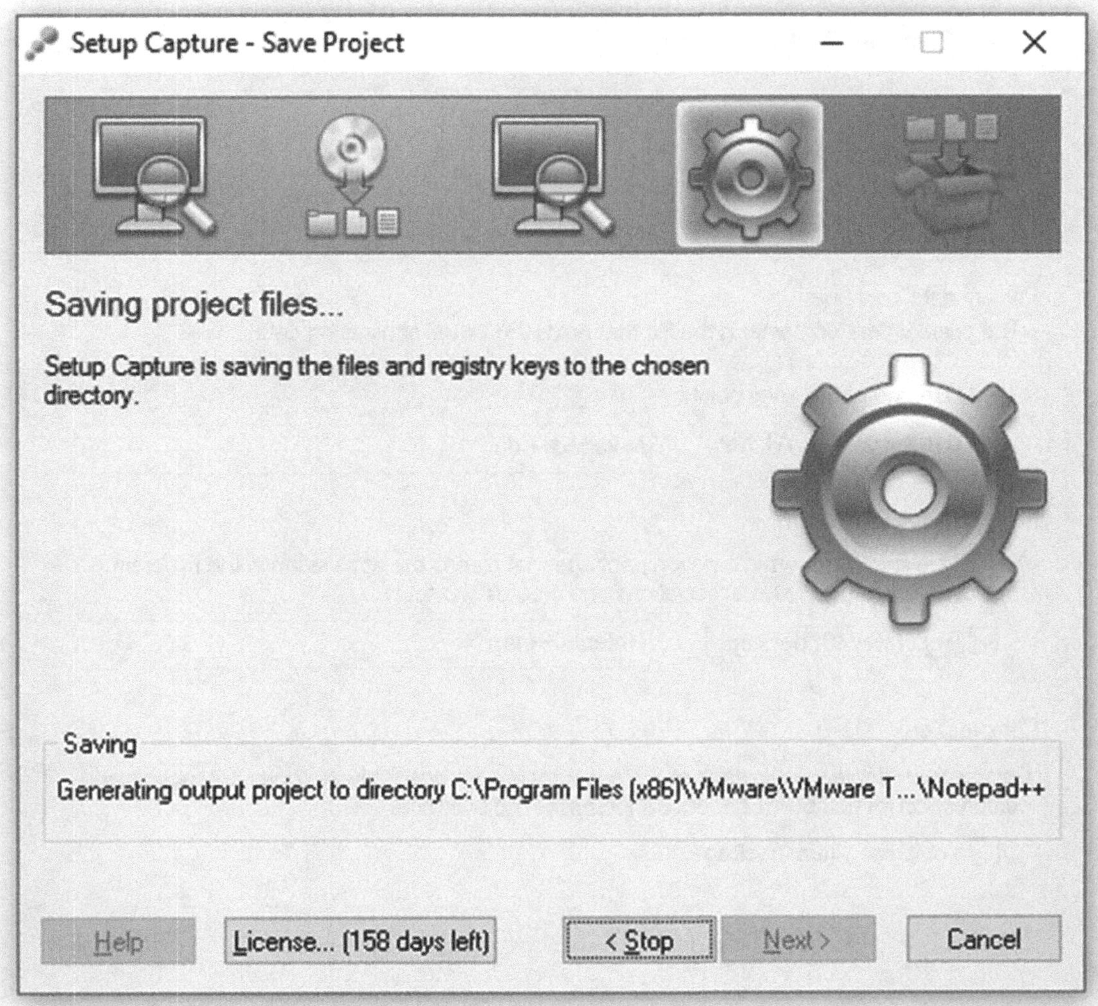

Figure 12-21. *Saving the project files and creating the package*

53. Next, you will see the **Setup Capture - Save Warnings** screen that will display any warnings generated as part of the project process as shown in Figure 12-22.

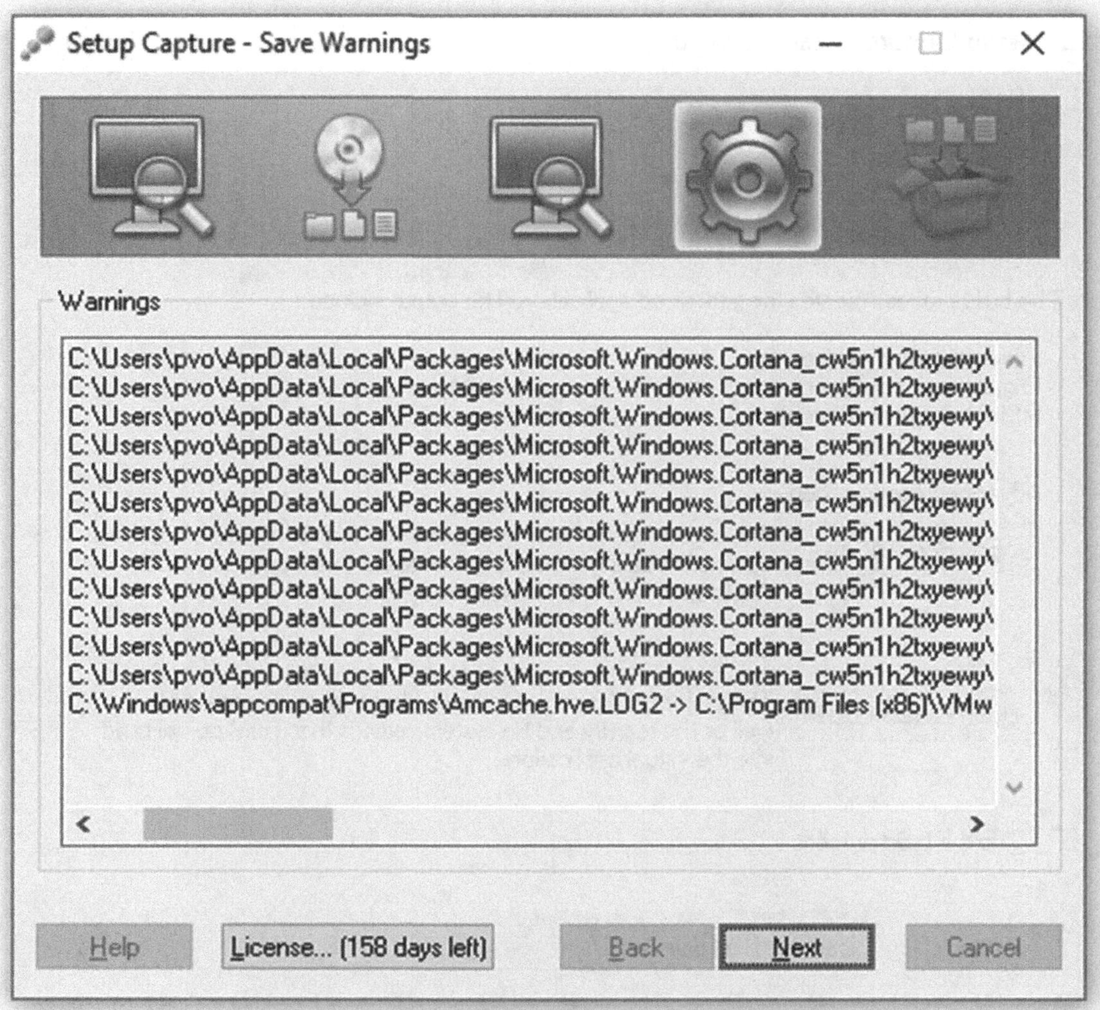

***Figure 12-22.** Warning files generated during the save process*

54. Click **Next ➤** to continue.

55. You will see the **Setup Capture - Ready to Build** screen as shown in Figure 12-23.

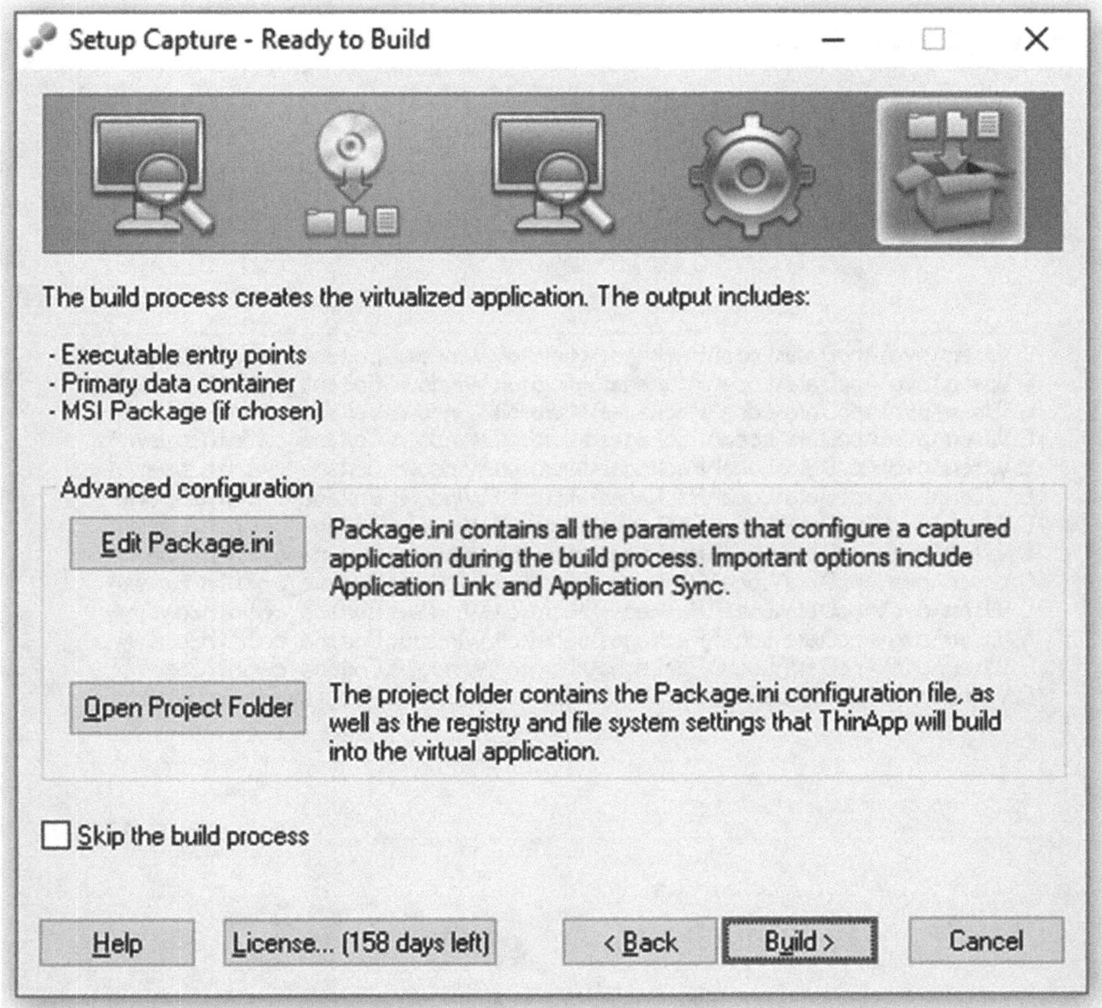

Figure 12-23. *Ready to build the package screen*

56. Click **Build ➤** to create the package.

57. You will see the build process run as shown in Figure 12-24.

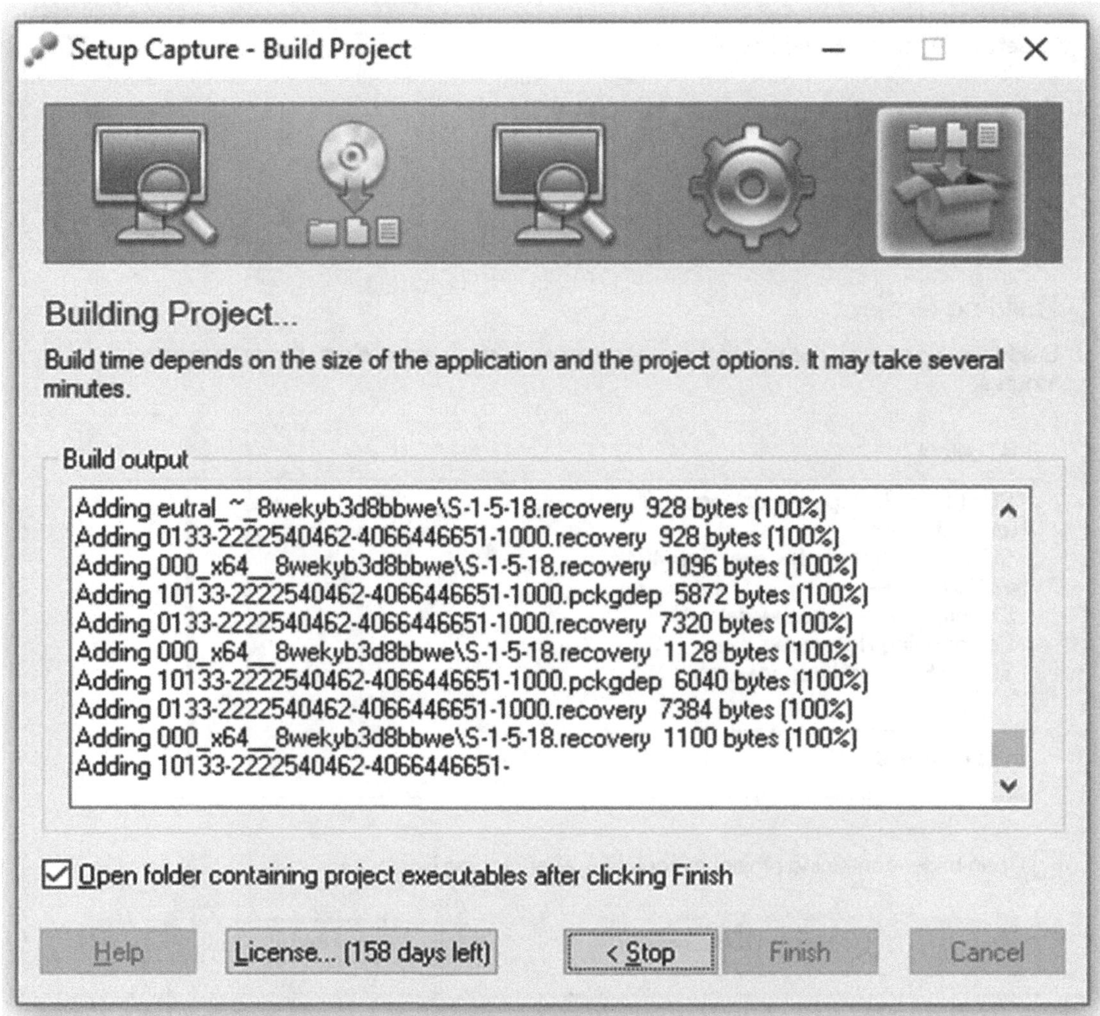

***Figure 12-24.** ThinApp package build process*

58. Once completed, you will see the **Setup Capture - Build Project** screen showing the final build output as shown in Figure 12-25.

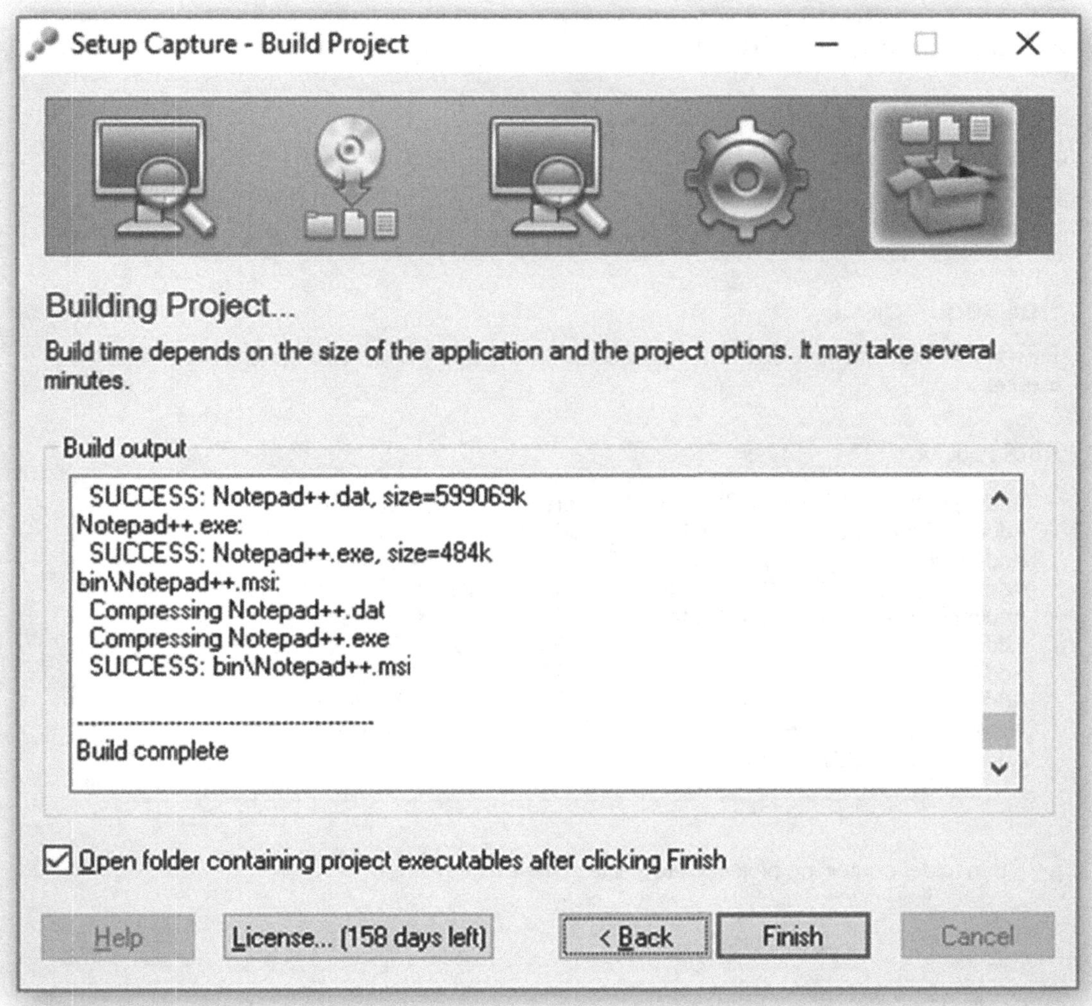

Figure 12-25. *Package build successfully completed*

59. **Click the Finish button.**

The ThinApp package has now been successfully created and configured. To check this, browse to the folder that you entered in the project settings screen. In this example, it is the **Capture\Notepad++** folder. If you then scroll down and double-click to open the **bin** folder, you will see the screenshot in Figure 12-26.

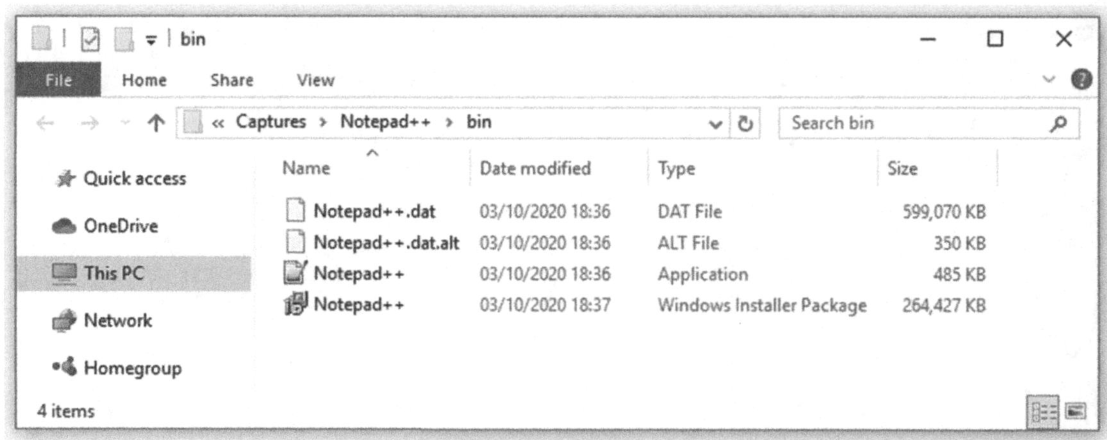

***Figure 12-26.** Folder containing the newly created ThinApp package*

You can now test the package works by double-clicking the Notepad++ application icon.

You will see the ThinApp pop-up box appear in the bottom right-hand side of the screen as the application launches (Figure 12-27).

***Figure 12-27.** ThinApp launching Notepad++ package*

You will then see Notepad++ launch as shown in Figure 12-28.

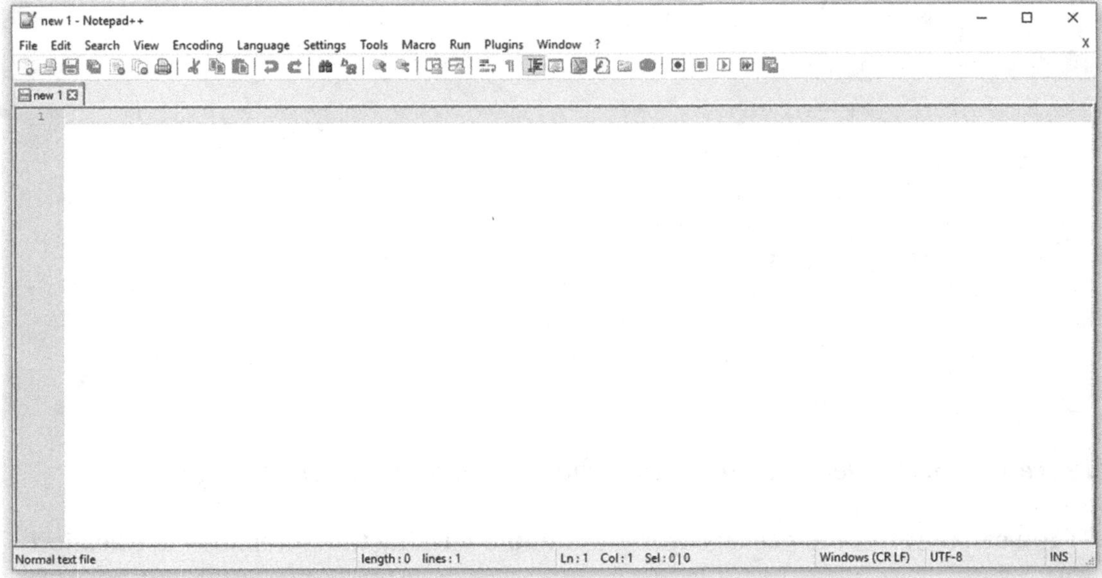

Figure 12-28. *Notepad++ running as a ThinApp package*

Now that you have successfully created a ThinApp package, the next task is to configure App Volumes so that the ThinApp package can be delivered as an App Volumes application layer.

Creating a ThinApp-based application package

Now that you have created the MSI ThinApp package for Notepad++, the next task is to create the application package for App Volumes.

The process to create the application package is no different to the process you would follow when installing any other application. In this case, the installer you would be launching would be the ThinApp MSI version of the Notepad++ installer.

We will cover the process at a high level as a reminder, just focusing on where the process covers the ThinApp elements.

The first task is to create the application which we will cover in the next section.

Creating a ThinApp application in App Volumes

In this section, we are going to create the App Volumes application.

To create an application, follow the steps as described:

1. Click the **Create** button at the top right-hand side of the screen. You will see the Create Application screen.
2. In the **Name** box, type in a name for this application. In the test lab example, we will call this **ThinApp Applications** as these applications will be delivered as ThinApp packages.
3. Next, in the **Description** box, type in a description that easily identifies this application.
4. Now add an application owner. To do this, click the pencil icon next to the **Owner**. You will see the section expand and give you the option to search Active Directory to select an owner.
5. The final section is the **Package** section. Check the box to create the package, and click the **Create** button.
6. You will see the **Confirm Create Application** box.
7. Click the **Create** button.
8. You will see the **Creating Application** progress bar appear as the process runs.
9. Once successfully completed, you will see a pop-up box stating **Application created successfully.**

You have now successfully created your Application. The next step of the process is to create the package by capturing the applications you want to include within the package. You will automatically be taken to the **Create Package** screen.

Creating the App Volumes package for ThinApp apps

As you completed the creation of the application, you will automatically see the **Create Package for ThinApp Applications** screen. To configure and create the package, complete the following steps:

1. In the **Name** box, enter a name you want to give to this package. In the test lab, we have called the package **ThinApp Packaged Apps.**

2. The next box is for selecting the **Base Package**. From the drop-down menu, select the base package you want to use to add the programs to. In this example, as there are no programs in the package yet, then the only option is for **Create New Package**.

3. **Storage** is the next option. From the drop-down menu, choose the datastore on which you want to create this package. This is where the VMDK file that gets created will be stored. In the test lab, we have selected the **Datastore-App-Vol** datastore on the **PVO Datacenter.**

4. As part of the storage, the next option is the **Path** option which allows you to select where to store the newly created VMDK file on the datastore. The default path is the **appvolumes/packages** folder, but you can change that to suit.

5. From the **Template** box, from the drop-down menu options, select the template file from which you are going to create this new VMDK file. In the test lab, we are going to use the standard **template.vmdk** file.

6. The next box is to select the **Stage** of the package. In the test lab, as this is a new package, we are going to select the option for **New.**

7. Finally, there is the **Description** box. In this box, you can enter any additional information that helps describe what the package is used for and what it contains.

8. You have now completed the configuration screen for creating the package.

9. Now click the **Create** button.

10. You will see the **Confirm Create Package** message.

11. Click the radio button for **Wait for completion** and then click the **Create** button.

12. You will see the **Creating Package** progress bar.

13. Once completed, you will be taken to the **Package for ThinApp Packaged Apps** screen.

14. On this screen, you select the machine you want to use to create the package on.

15. In the **Find Packaging Computer** box, type in the name or part of the name of the machine you want to use, and then click the **Search** button.

16. In the test lab, we have just clicked **Search** without entering any specific machine details so a list of all machine running the App Volumes Agent will be listed. Select the capture machine from the list and click the **Start Packaging** button.

17. You will see the **Attaching Package to Computer** progress bar.

18. Once attached, you will return to the packaging screen which will say Next step: Please install the application.

The next step is to switch to the machine being used to capture the application and install the applications you want included in this package. In this example, this is the ThinApp package we created at the beginning of this chapter.

Installing the ThinApp package

The next step is to install the ThinApp packaged application into the App Volumes package. To do this, we have switched to the desktop of the packaging machine. You will see that the packaging machine is now in packaging mode, ready to capture the application installation.

To install the ThinApp package, follow the steps described:

1. Navigate to the location of where you have stored the ThinApp package. In the test lab, this is in the shared software folder in a folder called **ThinApp Packages**.

2. The ThinApp package was copied into this folder using the ThinApp default folder structure, so double-click the application name of **Notepad++**, and then double-click the **bin** folder, as shown in Figure 12-29.

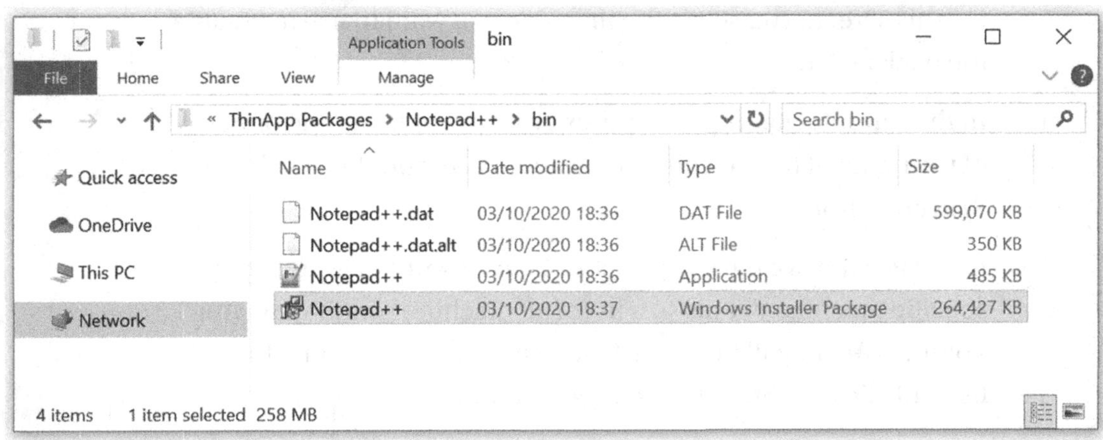

Figure 12-29. *Notepad++ MSI file*

3. Double-click to launch the **Notepad++ Windows Installer Package** (MSI).
4. You will see the **Windows Installer** dialog box open as the application is installed (Figure 12-30).

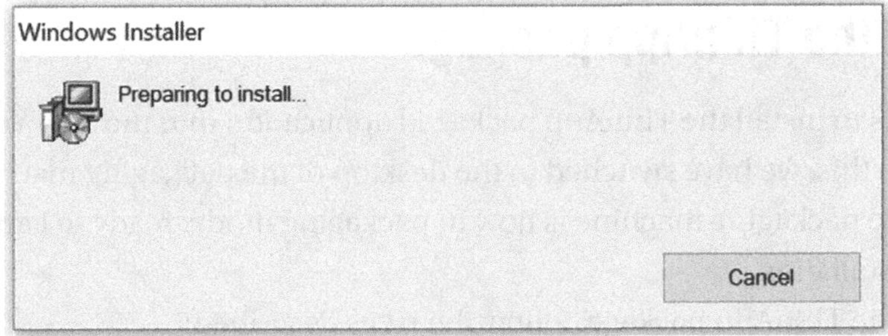

Figure 12-30. *Notepad++ install preparation*

5. Next, you will see the **Notepad++ (VMware ThinApp)** dialog box as shown in Figure 12-31.

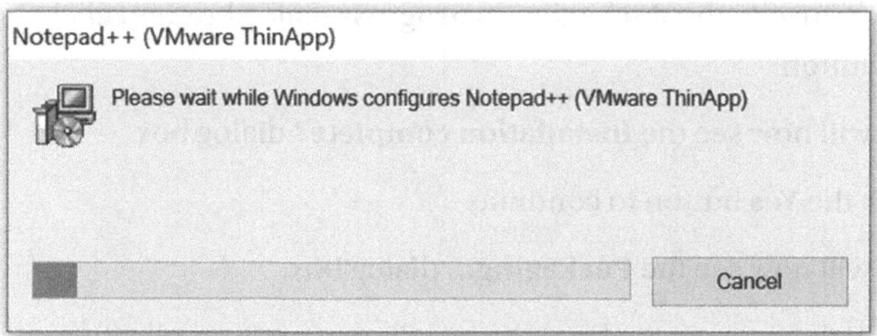

Figure 12-31. *Notepad++ being installed as a ThinApp package*

6. Once the installation has completed, you will see the desktop complete with a shortcut for Notepad++.

7. Launch Notepad++ to ensure that it runs as expected. You will see the screenshot in Figure 12-32 showing the ThinApp pop-up box in the bottom right-hand side of the screen as the application launches.

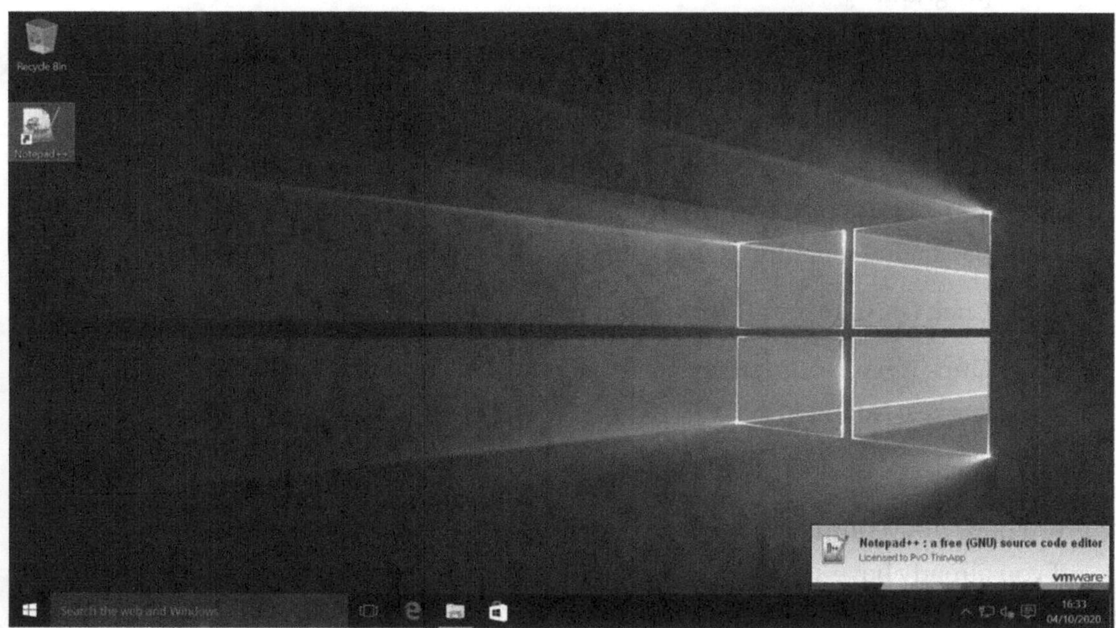

Figure 12-32. *Notepad++ running as a ThinApp package delivered by App Volumes*

8. Now return to the **Packaging in progress** dialog box and click the **OK** button.
9. You will now see the **Installation complete?** dialog box.
10. Click the **Yes** button to continue.
11. You will now see the **Packaging...** dialog box.
12. App Volumes now analyzes the installation of the applications you installed.
13. Next, you will see the **Finalize Package** screen, with some additional options to configure.
14. In the **Name** box, you can enter a name for the program installed in the package. You will see that there is a drop-down menu from where you can select the name.
15. In the **Version** box, you can enter a version number for the program.
16. Finally, in the **Notes** box, you can add some notes about the program you installed.
17. Click the **Finalize** button.
18. You will now see a warning message telling you that a restart of the packaging machine is required.
19. Click **OK** to restart the packaging machine.
20. Once it has restarted, log back in and you will see the **Packaging successful!** dialog box.
21. Click **OK** to close the dialog box.

You have now completed the installation and creation of the package.

If you already have ThinApp packages being used in your environment as EXE files and you want to deploy these in an App Volumes environment, then you will need to first convert these to an MSI by editing the package.ini file to enable the MSI settings before then rebuilding the package. This process is out of scope for this book, but there are several ThinApp titles that will help with this process.

The final task is to assign the application package to an end user. This process is no different, and so to see how to do this, please refer to Chapter 5 and the "Assigning applications" section of that chapter.

Chapter summary

In this chapter, we discussed the differences between ThinApp and App Volumes and the different ways in which they both enable application delivery.

We then looked at the use case of when to use each one, but also how they can complement each other with ThinApp being able to offer isolation and App Volumes enabling the dynamic delivery to an end user.

We then went on to look at how to build a ThinApp packaged application and then the steps to enable App Volumes to deliver this application as an application layer.

CHAPTER 13

App Volumes and VHD Virtual Hard Disks

Until now, everything we have done with App Volumes in creating application packages and Writable Volumes has been based on the VMware VMDK virtual hard disk format and vSphere back-end infrastructure. But what if you do not have vSphere as your back end, or you want to use physical desktop PCs?

Luckily, App Volumes also supports the VHD virtual hard disk format, enabling you to deploy App Volumes in non-vSphere environments.

In this chapter, we are going to install and configure an App Volumes Manager instance for delivering VHD-based App Volumes apps and volumes.

Installing the App Volumes Manager software

For this book, we are going to use a test lab environment to install the software and deploy App Volumes. This will enable you to see firsthand how to complete the installation tasks.

To this end, we have already built a Windows Server 2016 virtual machine, with the hostname of **Appvol-4**, ready to install the App Volumes Manager onto.

To install the software, follow the steps described:

1. Open a console to the virtual server named Appvol-4.

2. Navigate to the location where you downloaded the App Volumes software to. In the test lab, this was saved in a folder called App Volumes 4.1 as shown in Figure 13-1.

P. von Oven, *Delivering Applications with VMware App Volumes 4*,
https://doi.org/10.1007/978-1-4842-6689-2_13

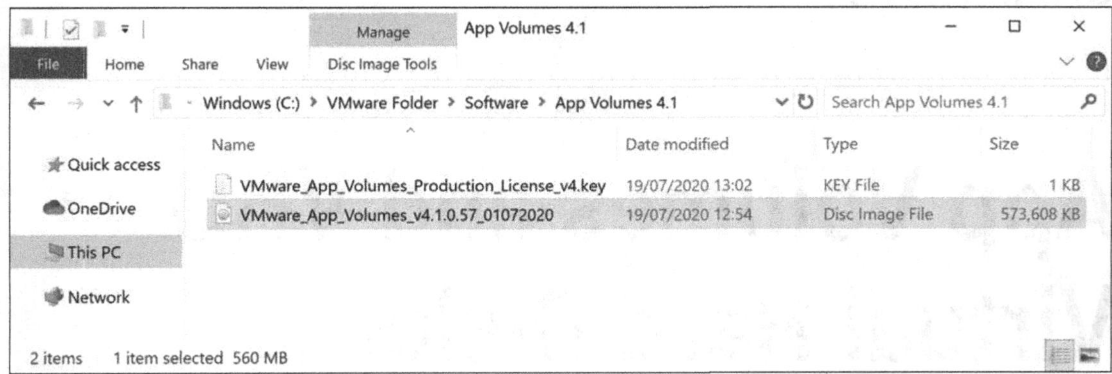

Figure 13-1. *VMware App Volumes software folder*

3. Double-click the **VMware_App_Volumes_v4.1.0.57_01072020.iso** file to mount the iso image. You will see the one in Figure 13-2.

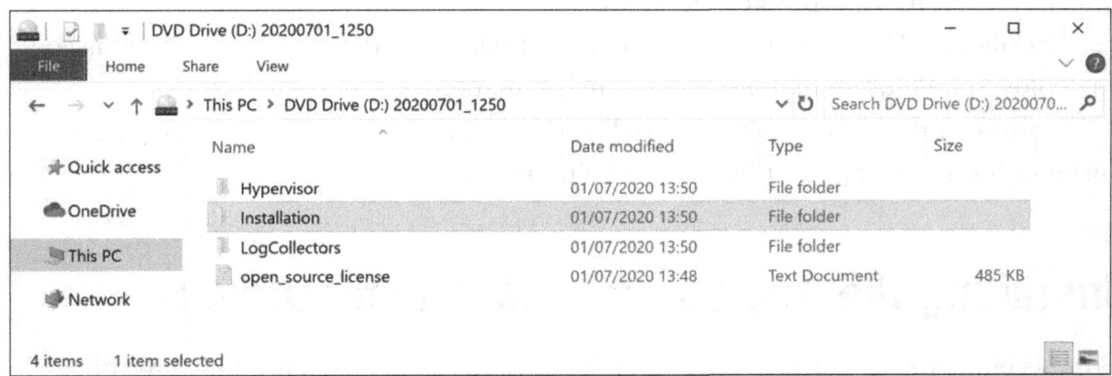

Figure 13-2. *VMware App Volumes software iso image mounted*

4. Double-click to open the **Installation** folder. You will see the folders in Figure 13-3.

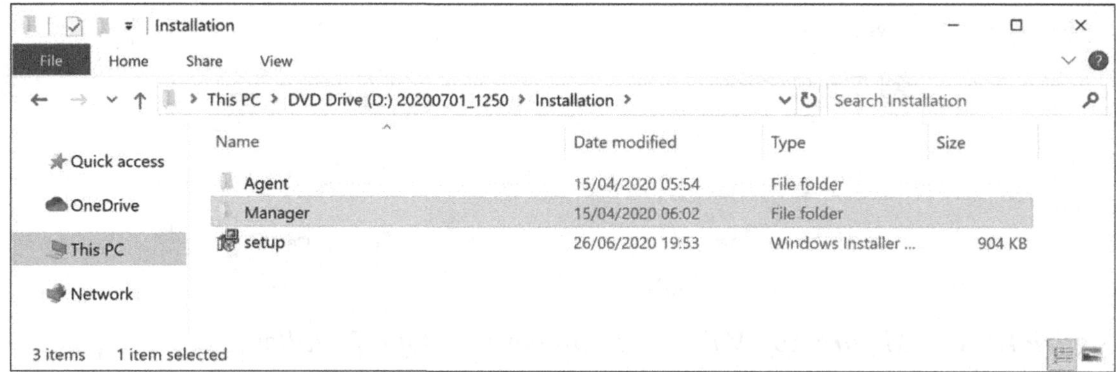

Figure 13-3. *VMware App Volumes software – installation folder*

5. Double-click the **Manager** folder. You will now see the contents of the folder containing all the installation components, including SQL Server (Figure 13-4).

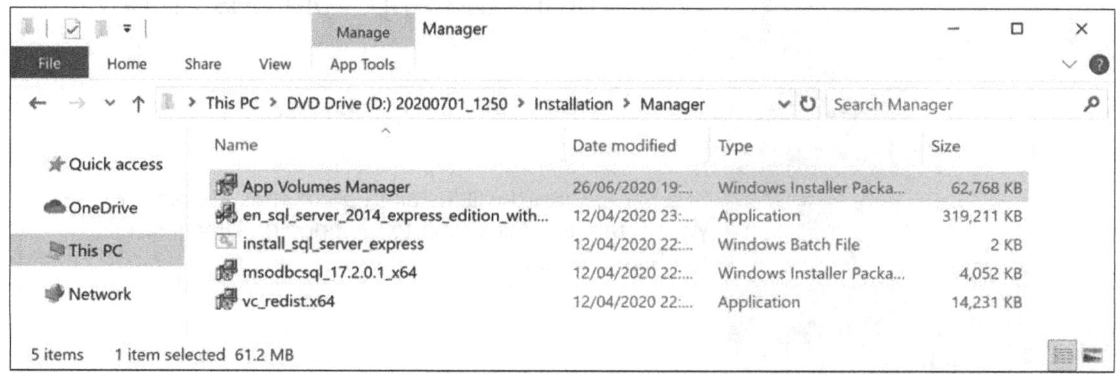

Figure 13-4. *VMware App Volumes Manager installation software*

6. Launch the installer by double-clicking **App Volumes Manager**. You will see the **Windows Installer** launch as shown in Figure 13-5.

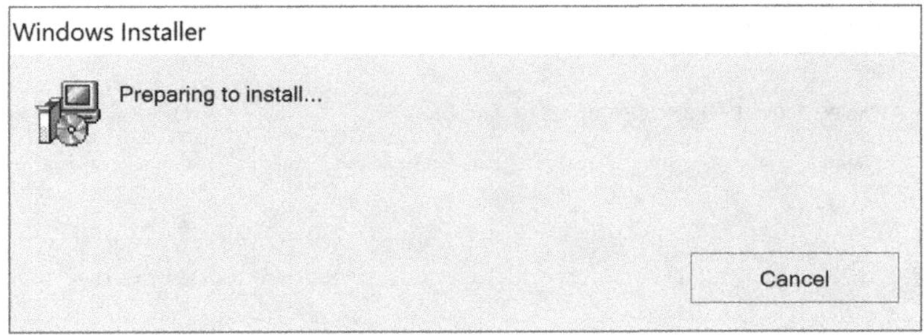

Figure 13-5. *VMware App Volumes Manager Windows Installer*

7. Next, you will see the **Welcome to the App Volumes Manager Setup Wizard** screen, as shown in Figure 13-6.

App Volumes Manager Setup
vmware
Welcome to the App Volumes Mana...
The Setup Wizard will install App Volumes Manager on your computer. Click Next to continue or Cancel to exit the Setup Wizard.
VMware AppVolumes™
Copyright © 2010-2020 VMware, Inc. All rights reserved. This product is protected by U.S. and international copyright and intellectual property laws. VMware products are covered by one or more patents listed at http://www.vmware.com/go/patents.
App Volumes 4, version 2006 (4.1.0)
Back
Next
Cancel

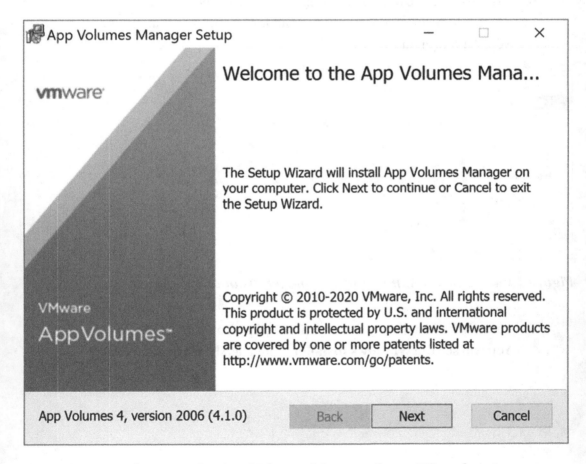

Figure 13-6. *Welcome to the App Volumes Manager Setup Wizard screen*

8. Click **Next** to continue to the next screen. The next screen is for the **End-User License Agreement** as shown in Figure 13-7.

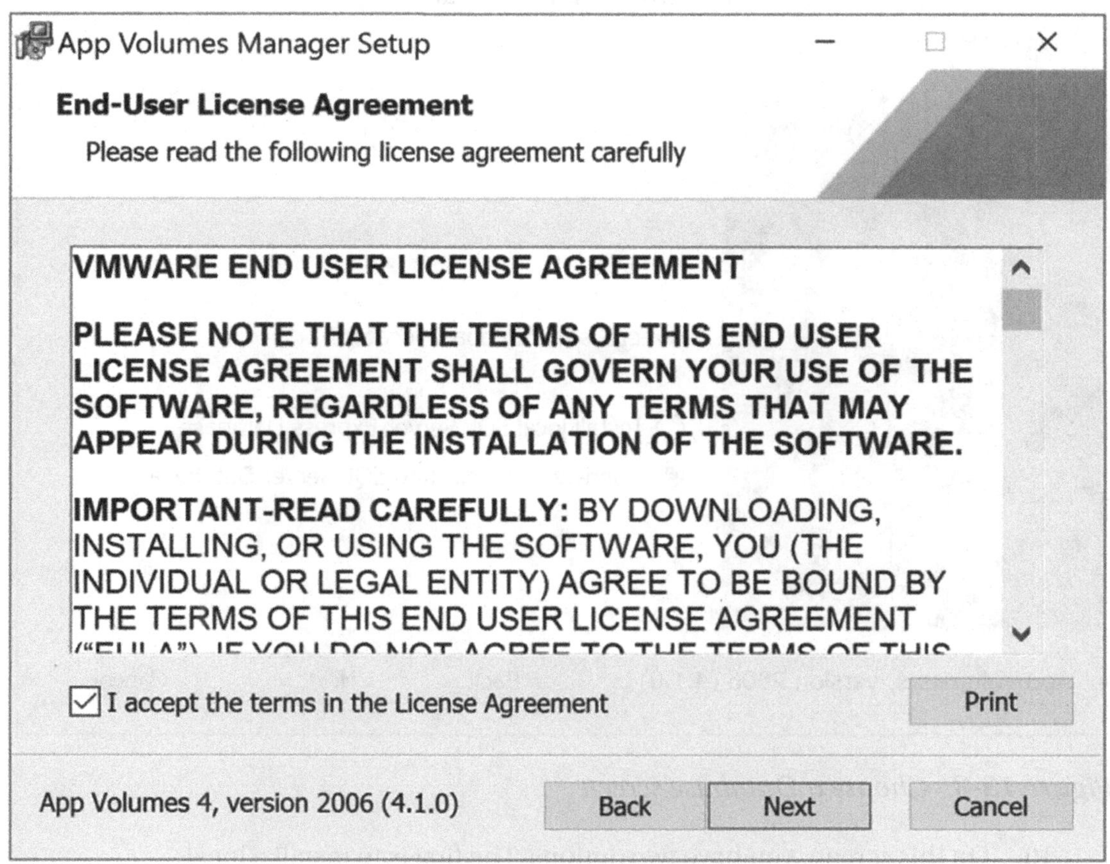

***Figure 13-7.** End-User License Agreement screen*

9. Check the box to accept the terms, and click **Next** to continue to the next screen for **Choose a Database** as shown in Figure 13-8.

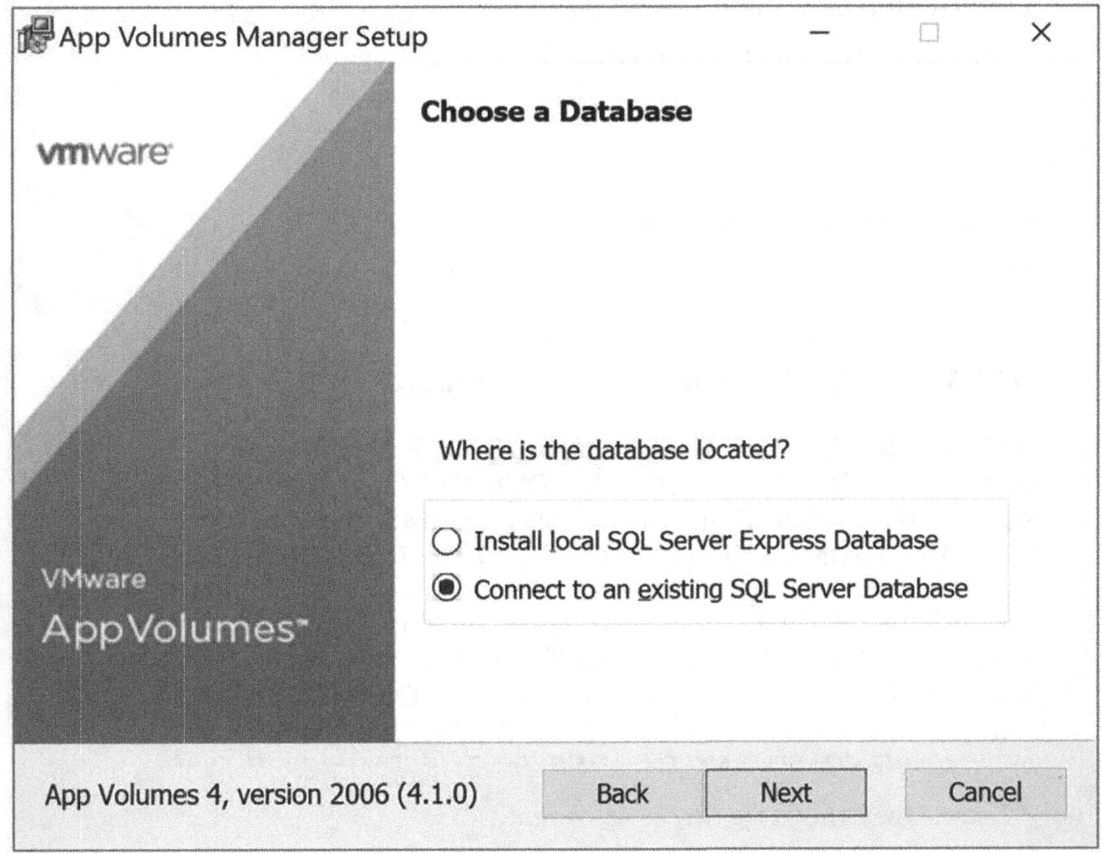

Figure 13-8. *Choose a Database screen*

10. On this screen, you have two options. The first is to install a local database on the same server using SQL Express, or the second option is to connect to an existing SQL Server database.

11. If you click the radio button to select **Connect to an existing SQL Server Database,** then you will see the screenshot in Figure 13-9.

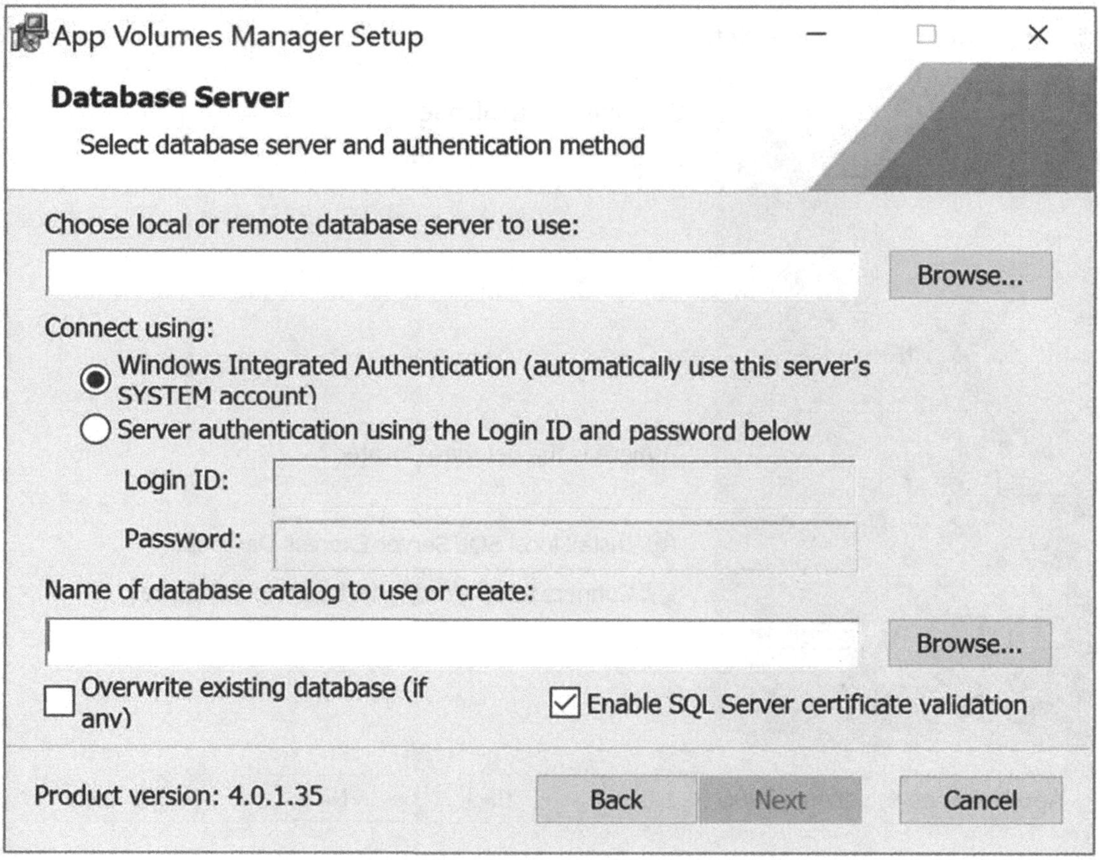

Figure 13-9. *Configuring an existing SQL Server database*

12. On this screen, you can enter the details of the existing SQL Server database. You would use this option if you had created a new database for App Volumes on an existing SQL Server deployment, or if you uninstalled the App Volumes Manager software either due to upgrading your current version or you were adding additional App Volumes Manager servers.

13. In this example, we are building a test lab, so we are going to use the integrated SQL Server Express Database; so from the **Choose a Database** screen as shown previously, click the radio button to select **Install local SQL Server Express Database.**

14. This is shown in Figure 13-10.

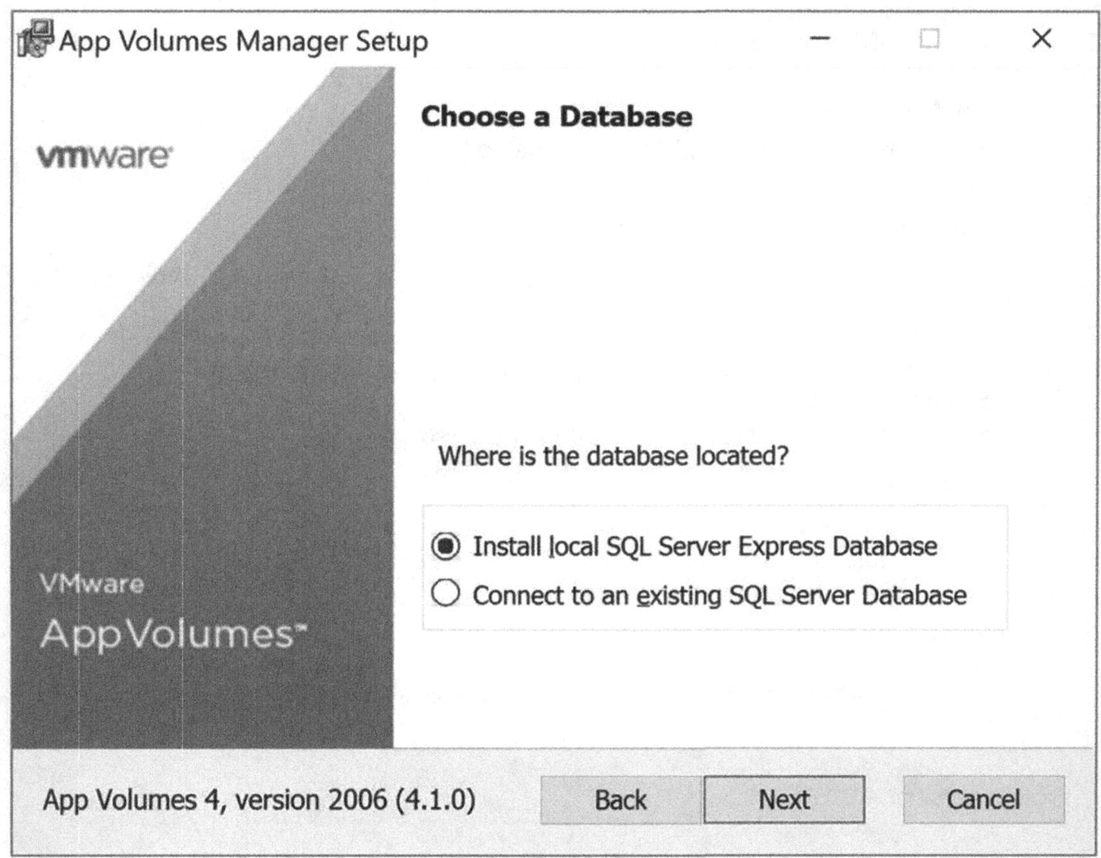

Figure 13-10. *Selecting the local SQL Server Express option*

15. Click the **Next** button to continue.
16. The installation of SQL Server Express will now start; however, be aware that you will not see the progress of this installation as there are no progress bars. Instead, you will see the standard Windows spinning wheel until SQL Server Express has completed and the next App Volumes installation screen is displayed.
17. When the installation has completed, you will see the screenshot in Figure 13-11.

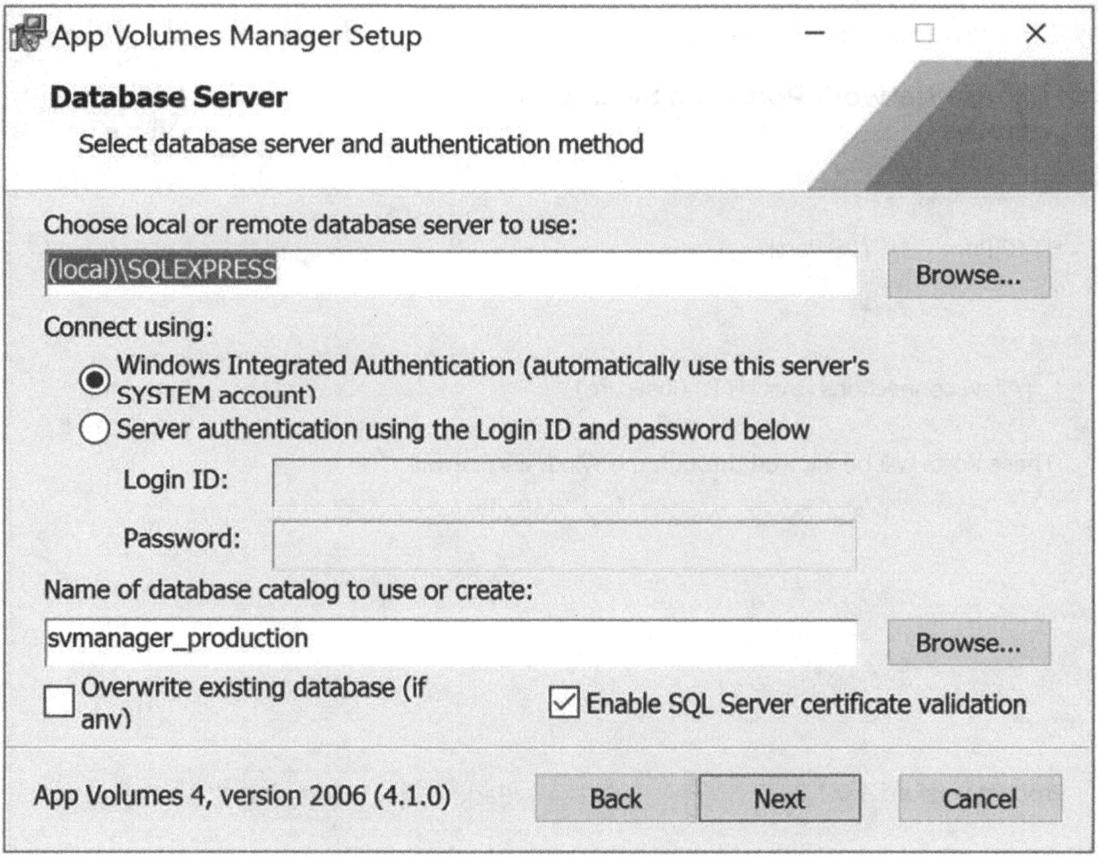

Figure 13-11. *SQL Server Express Database successfully installed*

18. On this screen, you also have a check box for Overwrite existing database. Be careful of this option if you are upgrading or installing an additional App Volumes Manager server as checking the box will delete the existing database and stop your App Volumes solution from working.

19. You are also able to Enable SQL Server certificate validation. This option is enabled by default as an additional level of security between the App Volumes Manager and the SQL Server database.

20. Click the **Next** button to continue the installation.

21. You will see the Choose Network Ports and Security options screen as shown in Figure 13-12.

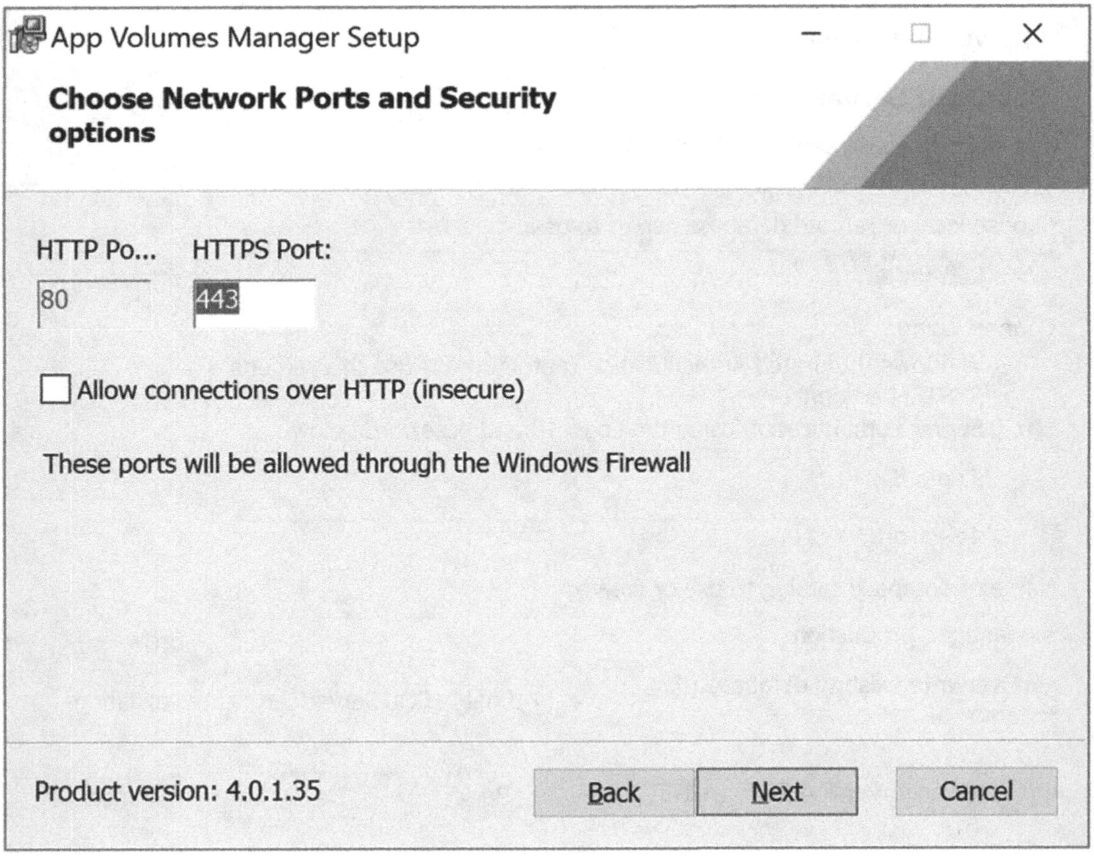

Figure 13-12. Network ports and security configuration screen

22. It is recommended to leave the HTTP and HTTPS ports as the default settings unless you really need to change them in your environment. If you change them, then make a note of what ports you are using as the App Volumes Agent will need to have the same port settings to enable communication between the two.

23. You also have the option to allow insecure connections over HTTP. However, this is not recommended for production environments. These ports will automatically be configured to be allowed through your firewall.

24. Click the **Next** button to continue the installation.

25. The next screen you will see is the **Custom Setup** screen as shown in Figure 13-13.

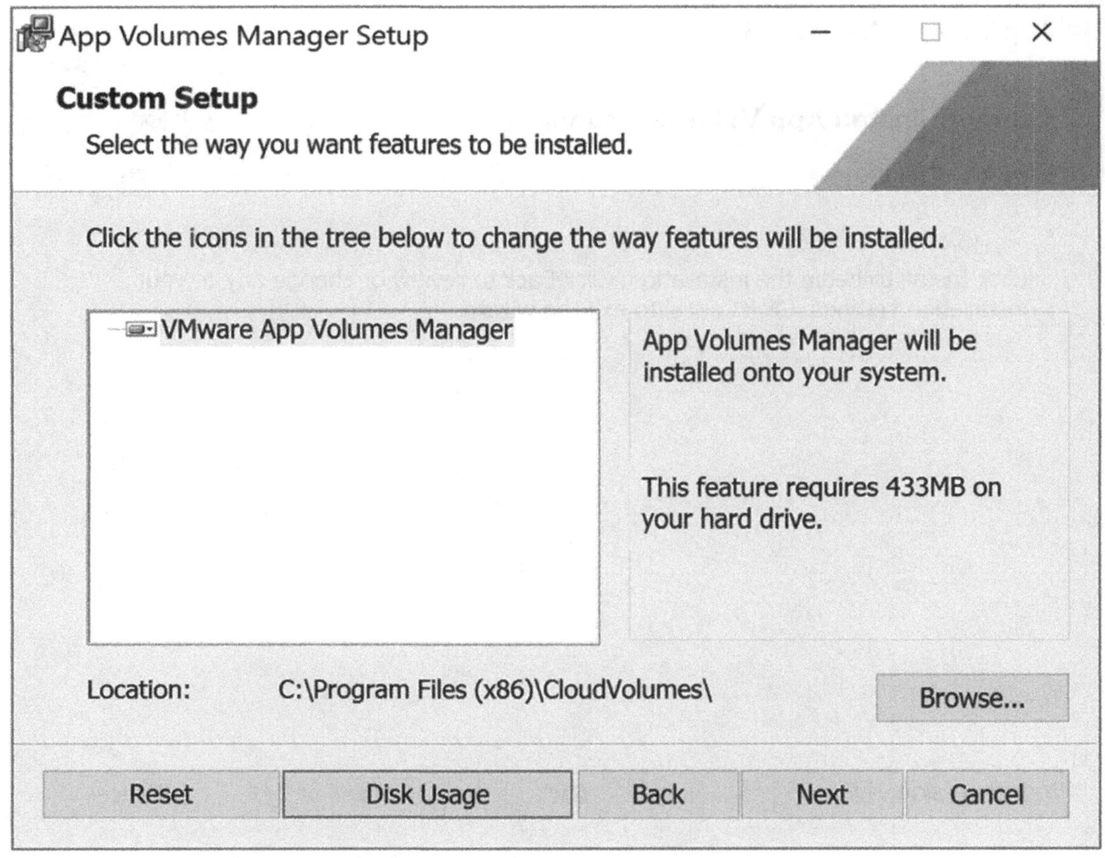

Figure 13-13. *Custom setup configuration screen*

26. On this configuration screen, you can choose which components to install. In this case, it is the App Volumes Manager. You can optionally change the installation location and check the disk usage.

27. Click **Next** to continue the installation.

28. You will see the **Ready to install App Volumes Manager** screen as shown in Figure 13-14.

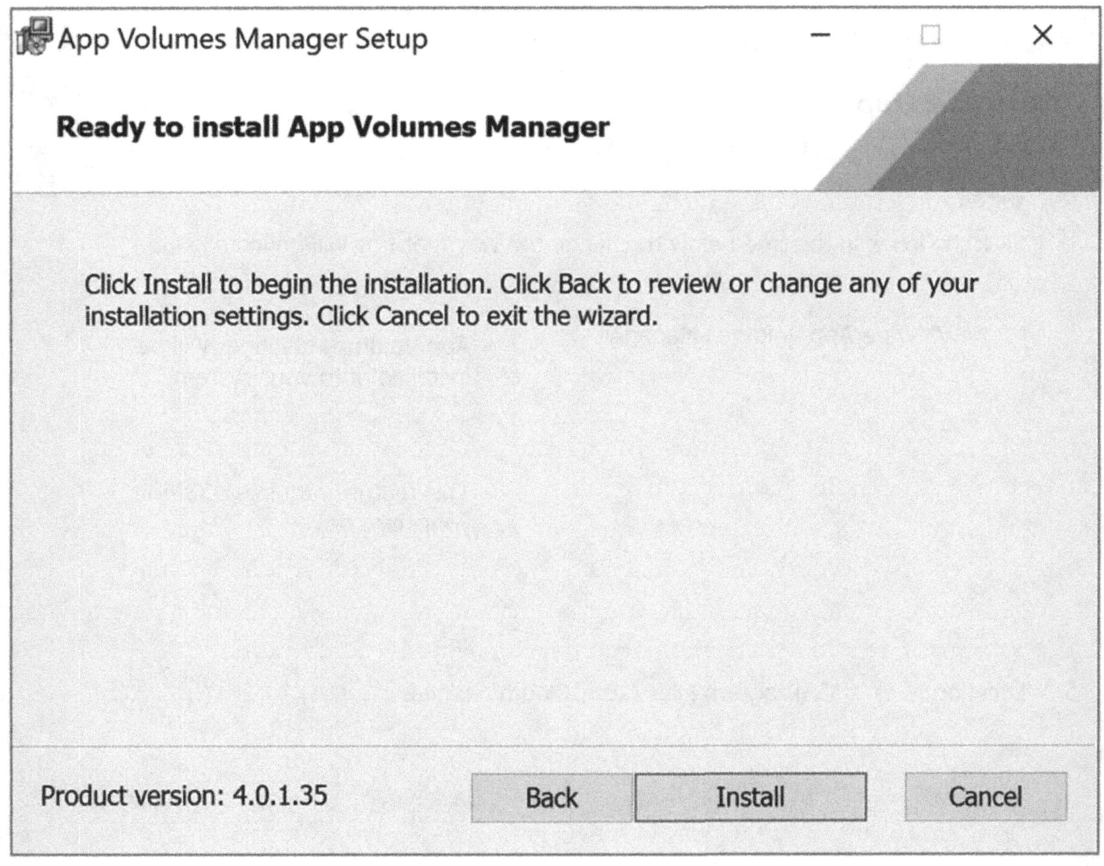

Figure 13-14. *Ready to install screen*

29. Click the **Install** button to start the installation.

30. You will see the installation progress as shown in Figure 13-15.

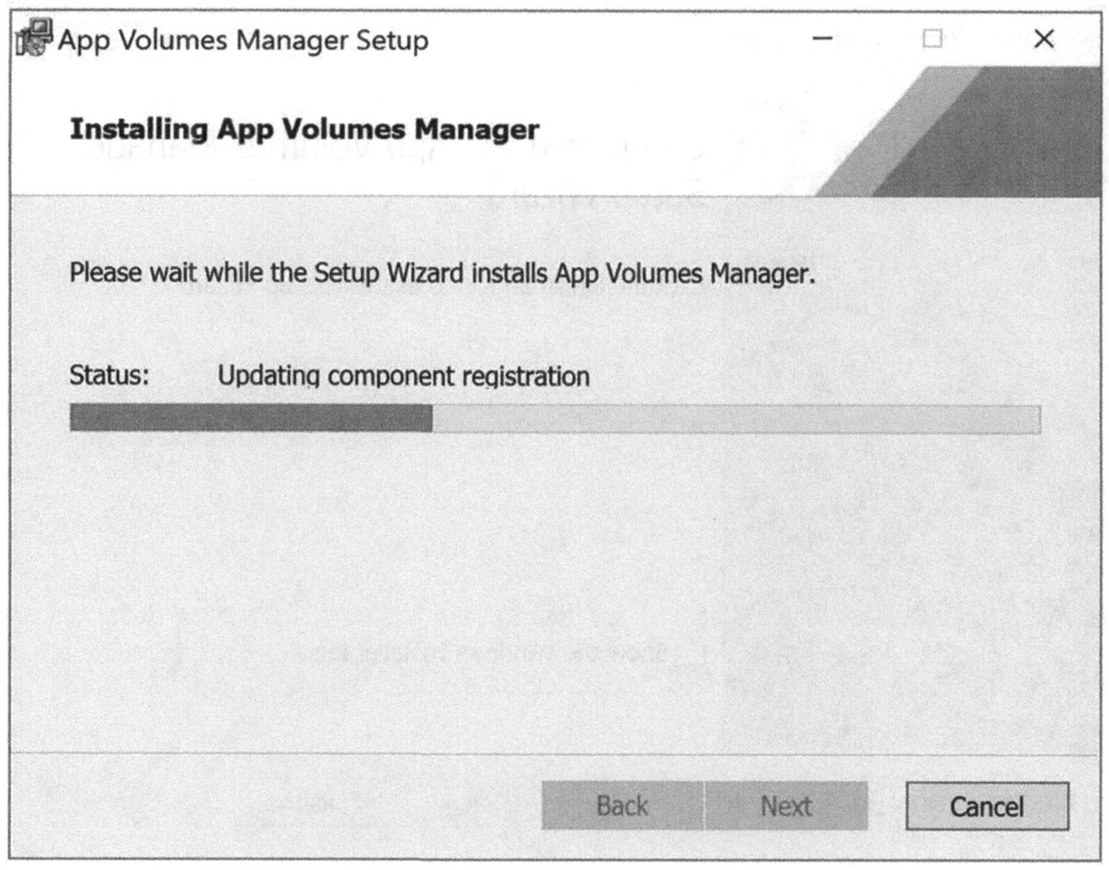

Figure 13-15. *Installing the App Volumes Manager*

31. Once complete, you will see the **Completed the App Volumes Manager Setup Wizard** screen as shown in Figure 13-16.

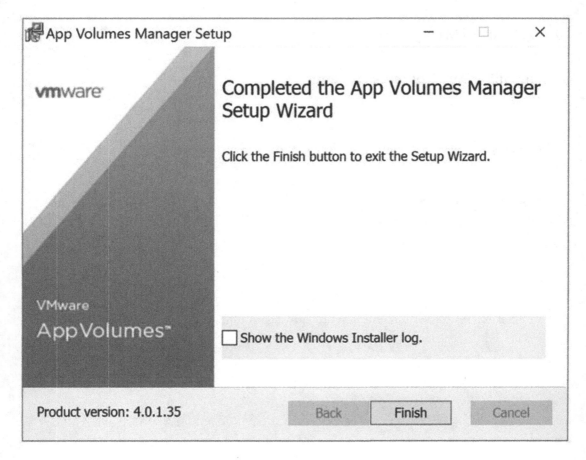

Figure 13-16. *Setup completed*

32. You will now see the App Volumes Manager icon on the desktop as shown in Figure 13-17.

Figure 13-17. *App Volumes Manager desktop icon*

You have now successfully installed the App Volumes Manager software. The next stage of the installation process is to complete the initial configuration where you will configure the App Volumes Manager with details of your vSphere infrastructure and AD, to name a few options. We will complete this in the next chapter, Chapter 14.

In the next section, we are going to complete the initial configuration tasks required when using the VHD disk format.

Launching the management console for the first time

You can now launch the management console for the first time. In the test lab, we are going to do this directly from the App Volumes Manager itself, by double-clicking the desktop icon.

As this is the first time you have logged in, and the initial configuration has not been completed, you will be prompted for a username and password to access the management console.

You will see the **Welcome to App Volumes Manager** screen as shown in Figure 13-18.

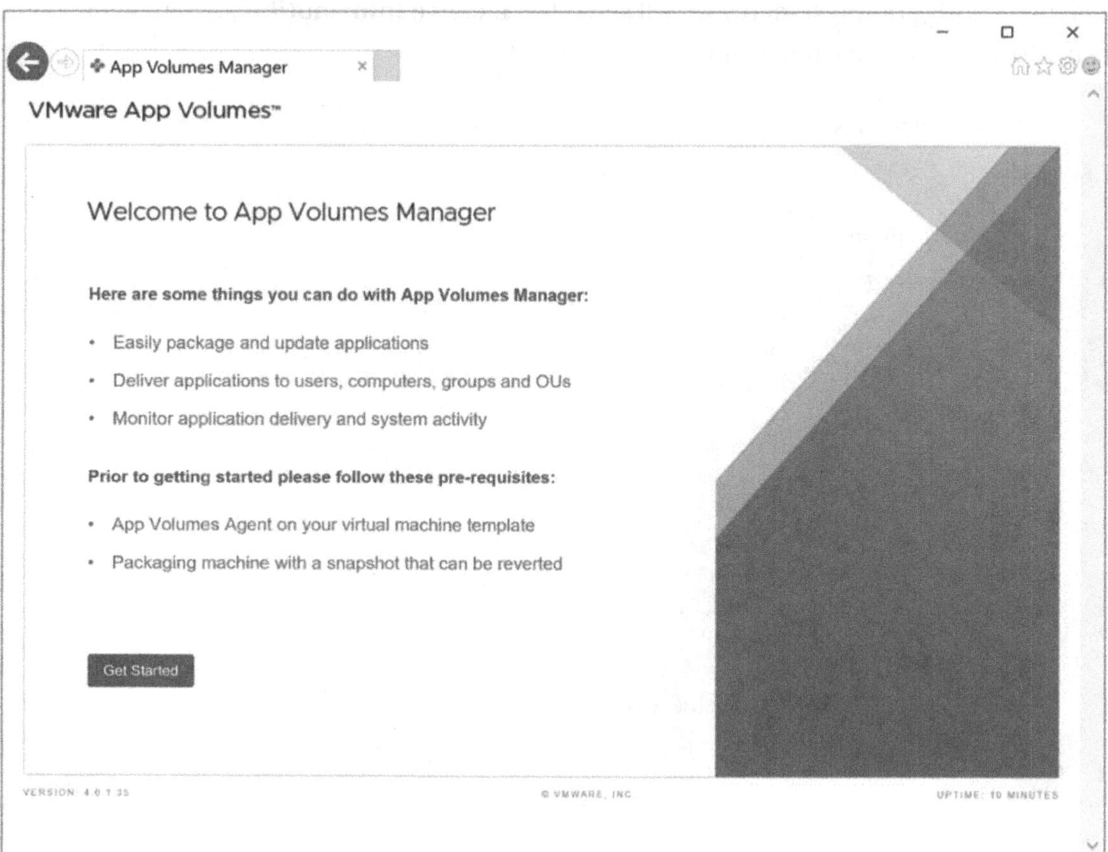

Figure 13-18. *Welcome to App Volumes Manager screen*

On the welcome screen, you will see that it lists some of the solution highlights as well as a couple of prerequisites. These are to have the App Volumes Agent installed on your virtual desktop machine template, which we will cover later in this book. It also mentions the need for a packaging machine which is to be used to create your application packages.

To start the initial configuration, click the **Get Started** button. We are now going to work through the initial configuration tasks.

Completing the initial configuration tasks

In this section, we are going to complete the initial configuration tasks, starting with the licensing.

License Information

The first configuration screen you will see is the **License Information** screen where you can add a valid license file as shown in Figure 13-19.

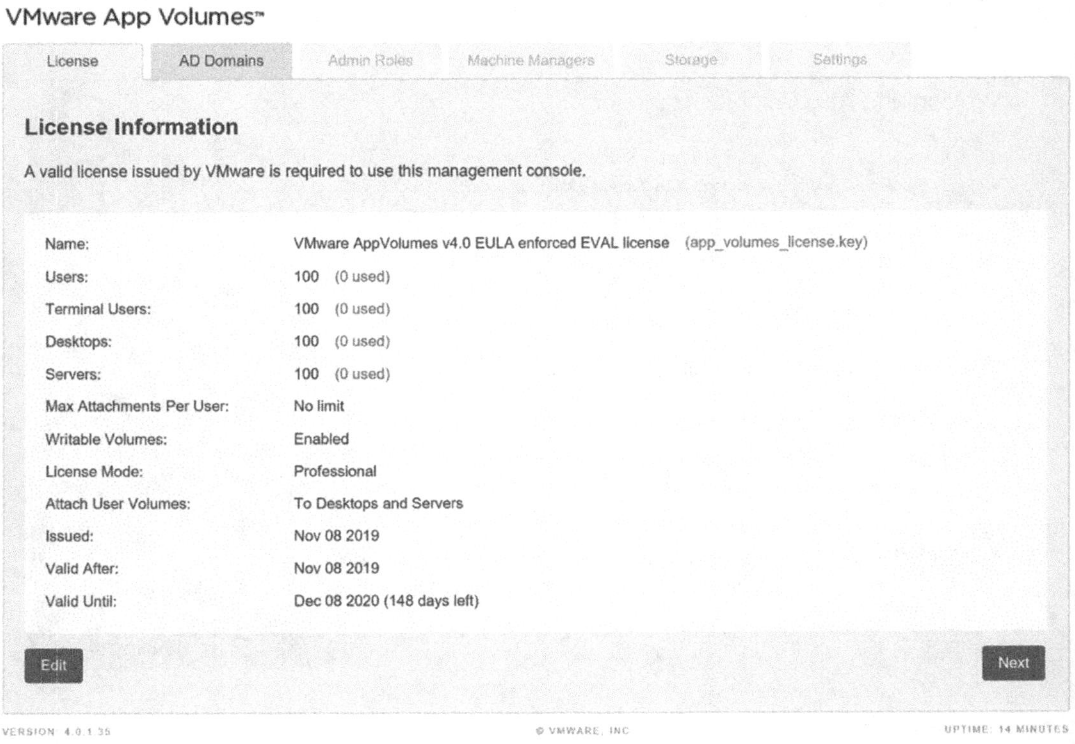

***Figure 13-19.** License Information screen*

As you can see from the screenshot, App Volumes ships with an evaluation license already, for 100 users. However, we are going to look at how to add your own license. To do this, follow the steps described:

1. Click the **Edit** button on the License Information screen.

2. You will see the screen in Figure 13-20.

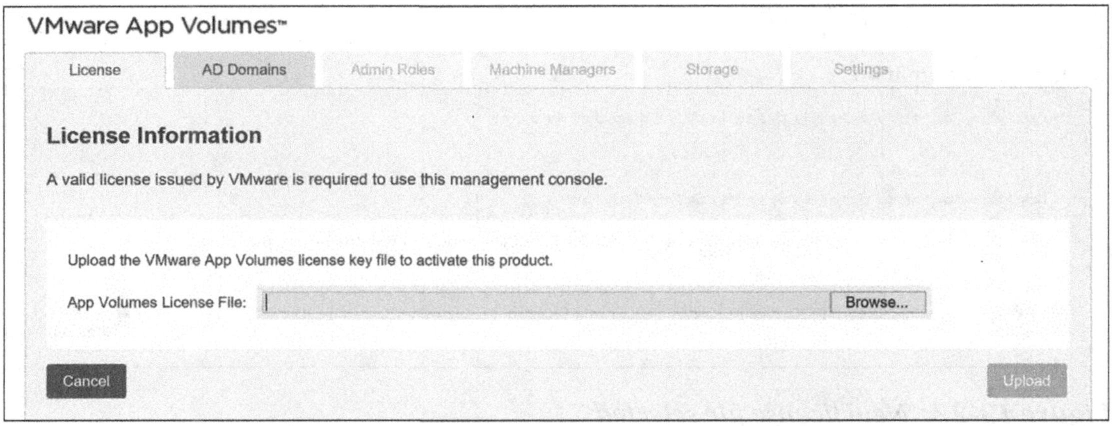

Figure 13-20. *Uploading a new license key*

3. If you know the path of the license file you want to add, then you can type that directly into the **App Volumes License File** box. If not, then click the **Browse...** button to search for it as in this example and in Figure 13-21.

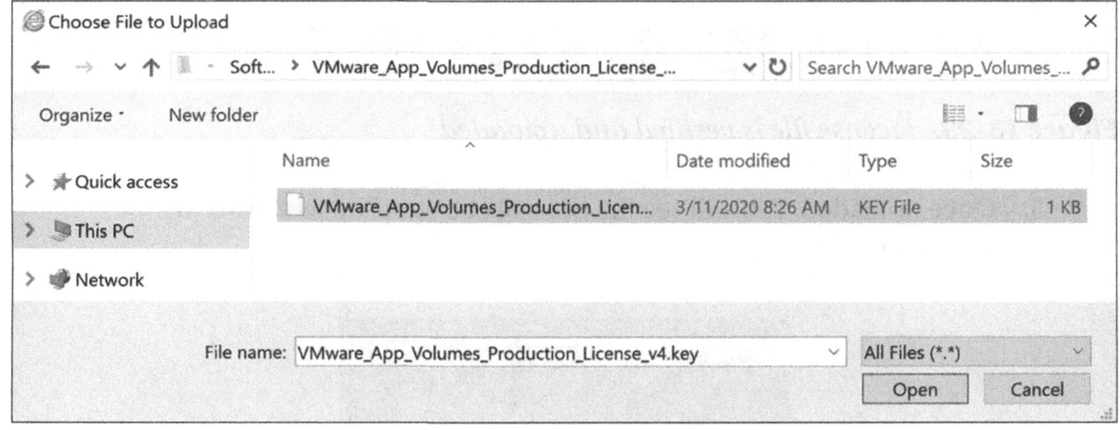

Figure 13-21. *Choosing a new license key*

4. Click and select the license file you want to use and then click the **Open** button.

5. You will now see that the license file you selected has been added to the **App Volumes License File** box as shown in Figure 13-22.

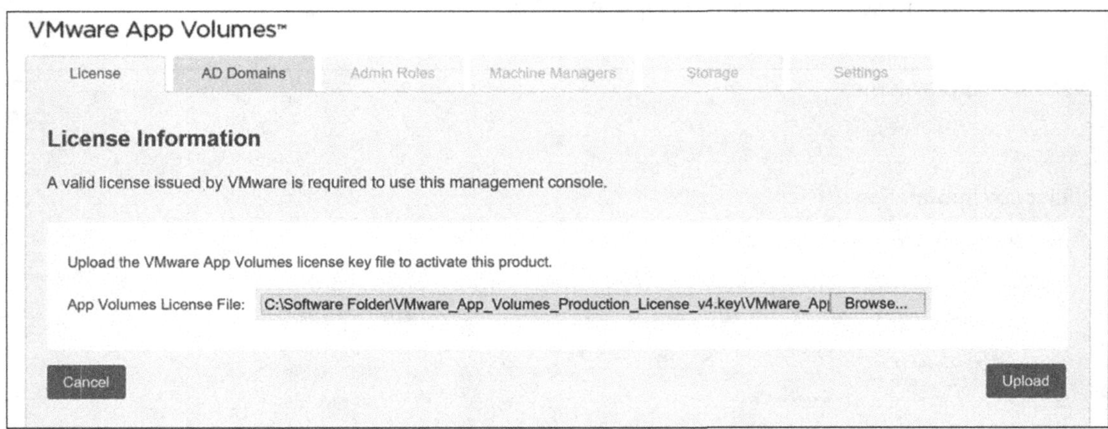

***Figure 13-22.** New license file selected*

6. Click the **Upload** button to upload the license file to your App Volumes Manager.

7. You will see the **Verifying License...** progress bar as shown in Figure 13-23.

***Figure 13-23.** License file is verified and uploaded*

8. Once uploaded, you will see the message box pop-up as shown in Figure 13-24.

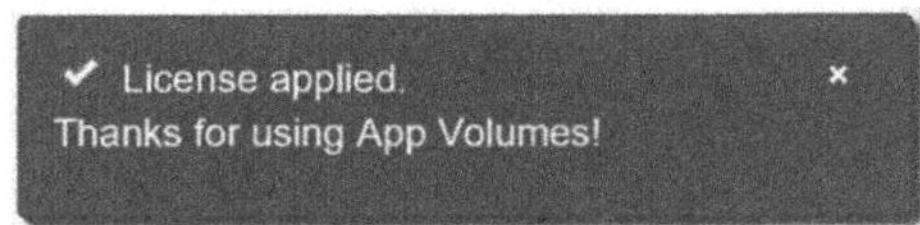

***Figure 13-24.** License file successfully applied*

9. You will also return to the main **License Information** screen as shown in Figure 13-25.

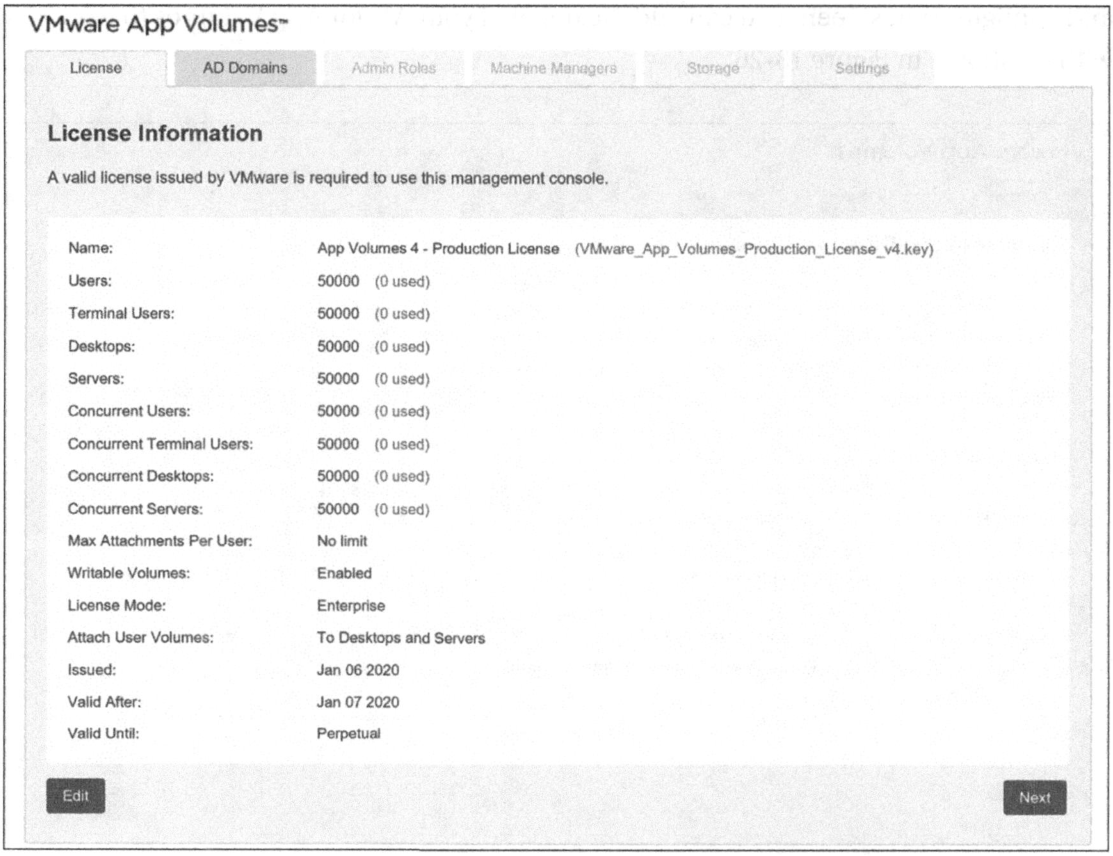

VMware App Volumes™

License | AD Domains | Admin Roles | Machine Managers | Storage | Settings

License Information

A valid license issued by VMware is required to use this management console.

Name:	App Volumes 4 - Production License (VMware_App_Volumes_Production_License_v4.key)
Users:	50000 (0 used)
Terminal Users:	50000 (0 used)
Desktops:	50000 (0 used)
Servers:	50000 (0 used)
Concurrent Users:	50000 (0 used)
Concurrent Terminal Users:	50000 (0 used)
Concurrent Desktops:	50000 (0 used)
Concurrent Servers:	50000 (0 used)
Max Attachments Per User:	No limit
Writable Volumes:	Enabled
License Mode:	Enterprise
Attach User Volumes:	To Desktops and Servers
Issued:	Jan 06 2020
Valid After:	Jan 07 2020
Valid Until:	Perpetual

Edit Next

***Figure 13-25.** License Information screen showing new license*

10. You will see from the license file that you have licenses for 50,000 users for attaching application packages to desktops, servers (RDSH), and terminal users. You can also see that the number of attachments per user has no limit and that Writable Volumes are also available.

11. Once you have uploaded your license, click the **Next** button to continue.

With the licensing configured, the next task is to configure the App Volumes Manager to work with your Active Directory.

AD Domains

The next tab in the initial configuration is for AD Domains. Under this configuration tab and configuration screen, you can add the detail of your AD for App Volumes to work with, as shown in Figure 13-26.

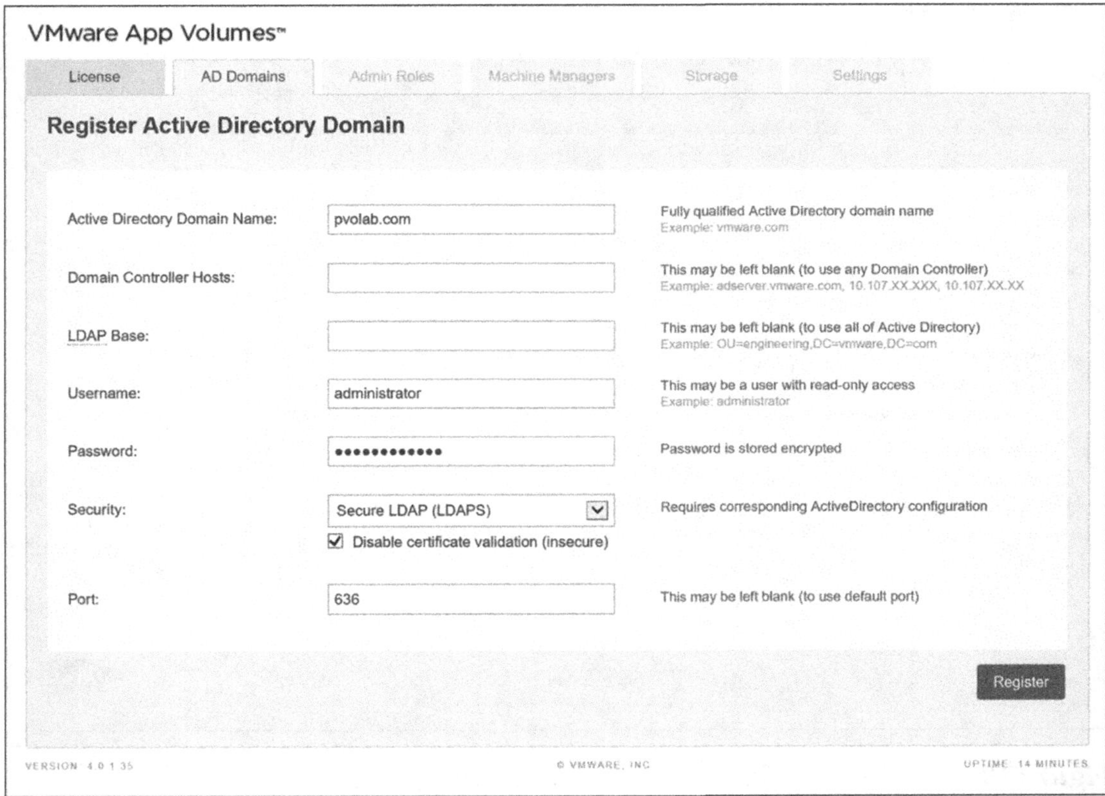

Figure 13-26. *Register Active Directory Domain screen*

We are going to configure this screen using the following information:

1. In the **Active Directory Domain Name** box, type in the fully qualified name of your domain. This is the domain that contains all your user and computer accounts that will be used in your App Volumes environment. In our example, the domain is called pvolab.com. Don't forget that you will need to enter this as a fully qualified domain name.

2. Next, in the **Domain Controller Hosts** box, you can enter the details of any domain controllers you want to use. If you want to use all available Domain Controllers in your environment, then leave this field blank. If you want to only use a specific Domain Controller, then enter the details of that Domain Controller in the box. Again, if using the server name, then remember to use the fully qualified domain. Alternatively, you can use the IP address of the domain controller instead. In the test lab, we will leave this field blank so we can use any domain controllers.

3. Configuring the **LDAP Base** is the next configuration option. This allows you to configure a specific Organizational Unit (OU) for reading user, group, and machine information from Active Directory. For example, if you had a separate OU for the finance department, and only wanted to use AD objects within that OU, you could add something like the following: **OU=finance,DC=pvolab,DC=com**. This would mean that only those users, groups, and machines within the finance OU and downward would be available to use. Leaving this field blank means that the whole of AD would be used, so all OUs.

4. The **Username** box is for you to enter the name of a user that has access to Active Directory so that App Volumes can read the information required. In the test lab, we have used the administrator account, but you can set up your own account for this. If you do, then it is worth remembering that this account only requires read access to Active Directory. It does not need write permissions. It is also worth using an account that does not have its password updated on a regular basis as doing so will mean that you must update your App Volumes configuration each time the password changes.

5. In the following **Password** box, enter the password for the account name you used for the Active Directory username. So, in our test lab example, we would use the administrator password. For the security-conscious organizations, this password is encrypted when stored in the App Volumes Manager.

6. In the penultimate box, you can configure the **Security** level. You will see that there is a drop-down box with three different options to choose from. These options are as follows:

    a. **Secure LDAP (LDAPS)**: Allows you to connect to Active Directory over SSL

    b. **LDAP over TLS**: Allows you to connect to Active Directory over LDAP using TLS. To use this method, you will need to install a trusted certificate from a certificate authority (CA).

    c. **LDAP (insecure)**: Allows an insecure connection to Active Directory.

7. When selecting the security option, you need to ensure that this corresponds with your Active Directory configuration. You will also see under the drop-down box that there is a tick box for **Disable certificate validation (insecure)**. Check this box if you want to turn off certificate validation, but remember this means the connection to Active Directory will be insecure and therefore not recommended for production environments.

8. The final option is to configure the **Port** setting through which the App Volumes Manager communicates with your Active Directory and domain controllers. The default port of 636 is added automatically, but if you have configured a different port, then change this accordingly so that it matches.

9. When you have added all the information on this screen, then click the **Register** button to register your App Volumes Manager with Active Directory. As the registration process completes, you will see the progress bar appear (Figure 13-27).

Registering Domain

Figure 13-27. *Registering your Domain progress screen*

10. On completion, you will see the **Active Directory Domains** page as shown in Figure 13-28.

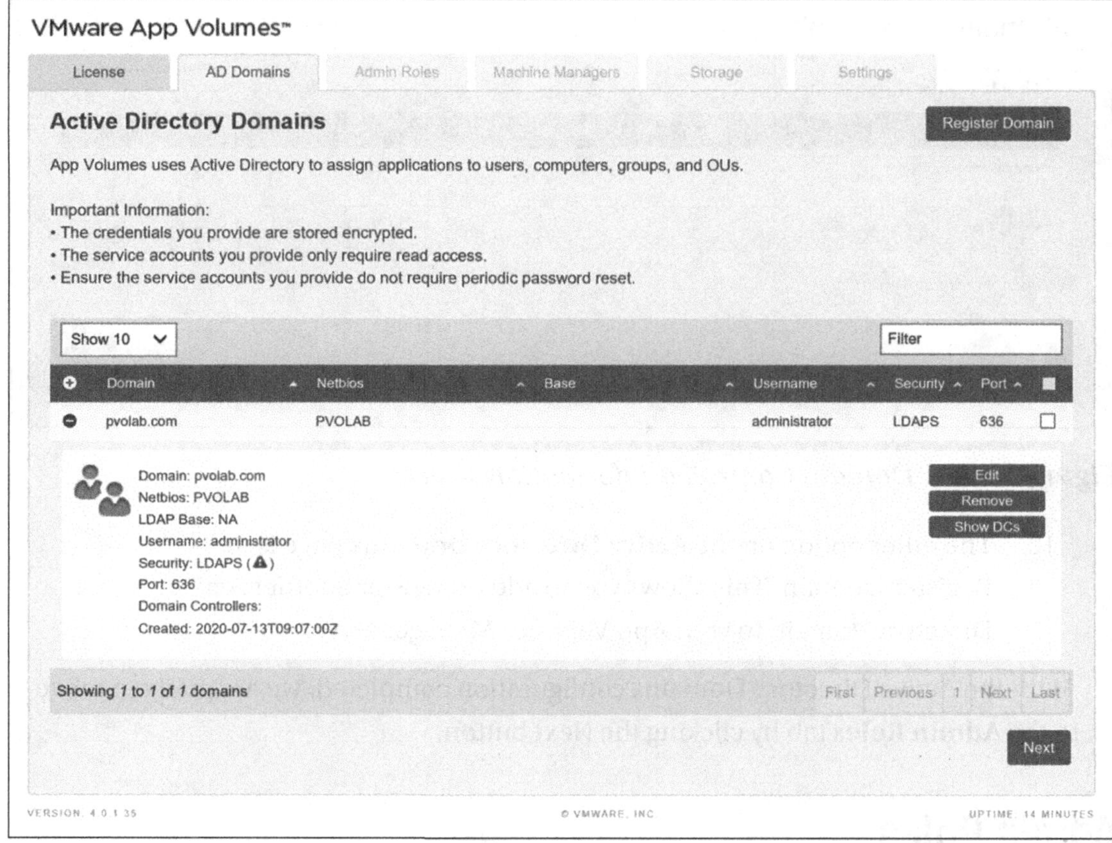

***Figure 13-28.** Configured Active Directory Domain information*

11. As well as displaying the information that you configured, you also have a few additional options. You can edit the current configuration, remove the currently configured domain information, or show more information on your domain controllers as shown in Figure 13-29.

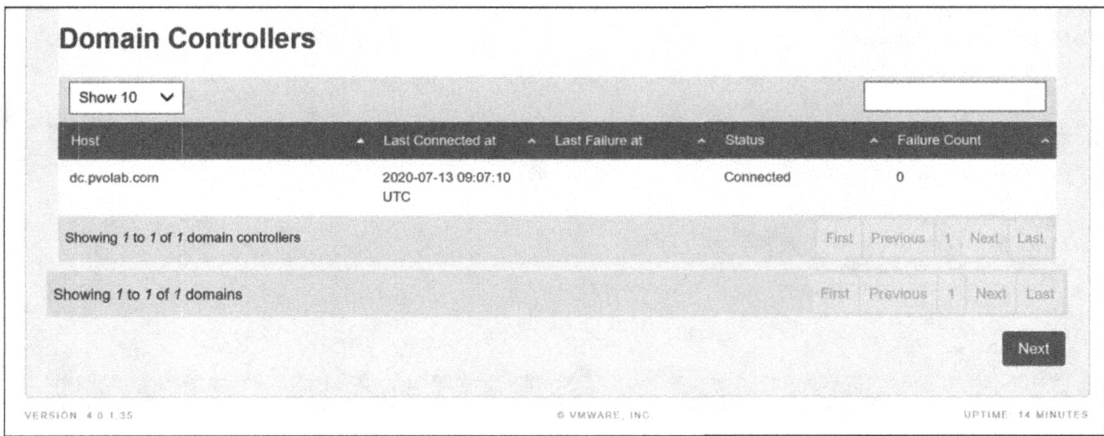

Figure 13-29. *Domain Controller information screen*

12. The other option on the **Active Directory Domains** page is to Register Domain. This allows you to add or register another Active Directory domain to your App Volumes Manager server.

With the Active Directory Domains configuration completed, we are going to move on to the **Admin Roles** tab by clicking the **Next** button.

Admin Roles

The Admin Roles configuration tab allows you to configure the roles of the App Volumes administrator and what tasks they can perform.

It is worth noting that you cannot configure an individual user as an App Volumes administrator. You need to configure a user group and ensure that the individual users you want to add roles to are in that group.

To configure administrator roles, complete the following steps:

1. From the **Roles** drop-down box, select the **Administrators** role from the list of options. You can choose from the listed roles in Figure 13-30.

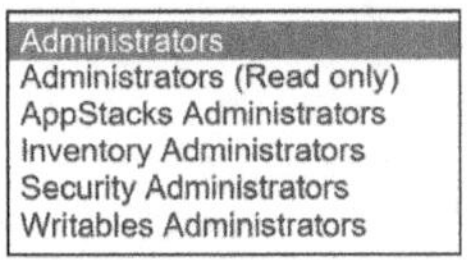

Administrators
Administrators (Read only)
AppStacks Administrators
Inventory Administrators
Security Administrators
Writables Administrators

Figure 13-30. *App Volumes Administrator roles*

2. Next, in the **Search Domain** drop-down menu, select the domain in which you want to search. In the test lab example, we have selected the option for **All**. This means that all the domains that are currently registered with the App Volumes Manager will be searched. Alternatively, if you know which particular domain you want to search, and it is registered with the App Volumes Manager, you can select the domain directly from the drop-down menu.
3. Next is the **Search Groups** box. This box is a filter to help you find the groups you want to assign the role to. Type in just the first few characters of the name of the group you want to search for. Then, from the drop-down menu next to where you have typed the group name, you can select an additional filter for the search. The filtered search options are **Contains**, **Begins**, **Ends**, or **Equals** the name you entered. In the test lab, we are going to type **admi** to search for the administrator's group in Active Directory, and we are going to select the **Contains** option from the additional filter drop-down menu. You also have the option to search all domains in the forest by checking the **Search all domains in the Active Directory Forest** box.
4. Now click the **Search** button.
5. The results will appear in the **Choose Group** box. If you click the drop-down menu, then the results of your search are displayed. You can then choose the correct group. In the test lab, you will see the option for **PVOLAB\Administrators** is listed.
6. Once you have selected the correct group you want to use, you will see the screenshot in Figure 13-31.

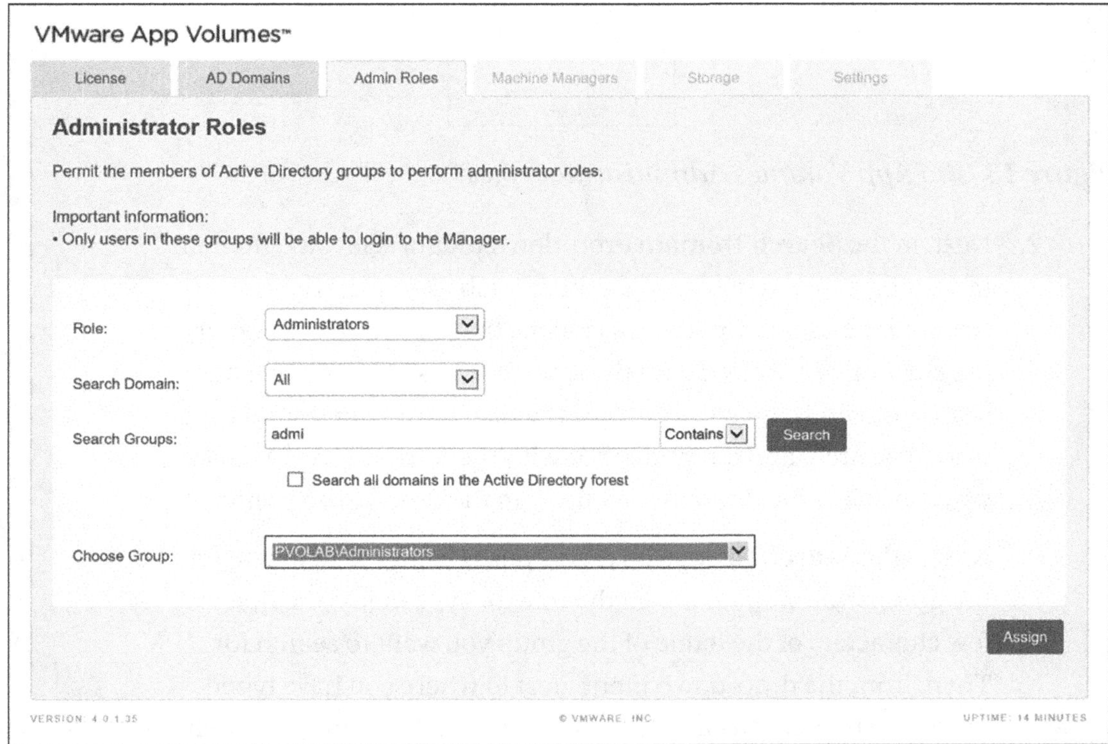

***Figure 13-31.** Configuring the administrator roles*

7. Click the **Assign** button.

8. You will see the **Assigning Administrators Role** progress bar as shown in Figure 13-32.

***Figure 13-32.** Administrator roles being assigned*

9. Once successfully assigned, you will see the message pop-up in Figure 13-33.

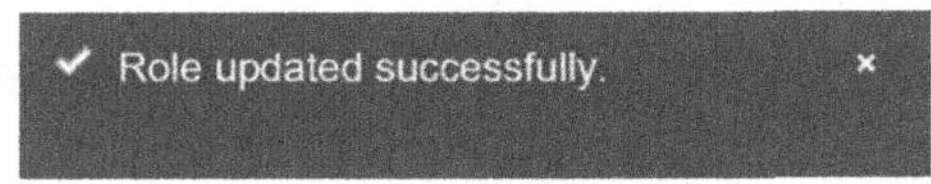

***Figure 13-33.** Administrator roles successfully assigned*

10. Having added the administrator's role successfully, you will see the screenshot in Figure 13-34.

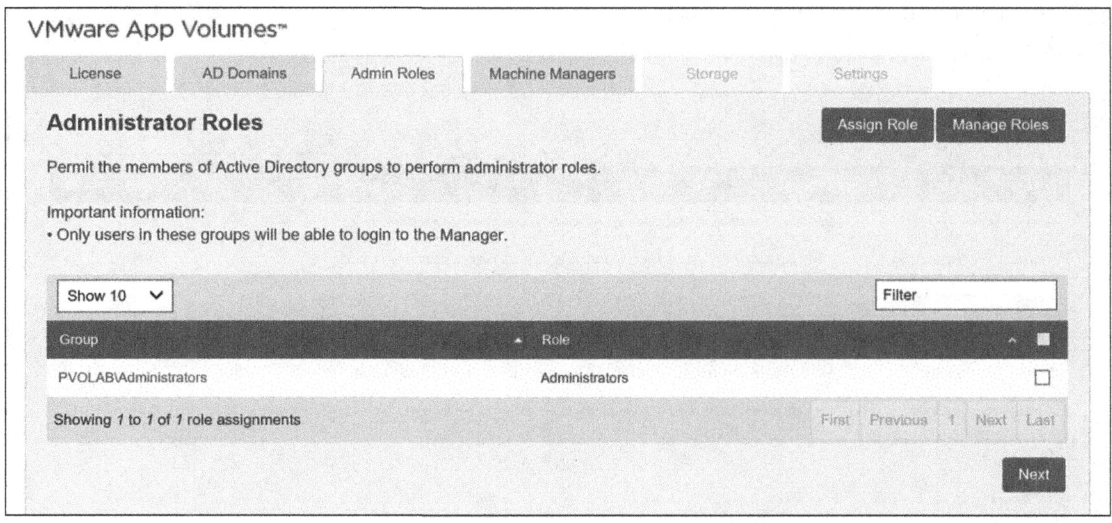

Figure 13-34. *Administrator Roles summary screen*

Figure 13-34 shows which group has been added and the role that group has been assigned. In the test lab example, you can see from the screenshot that the administrator's group in Active Directory has been assigned the administrators role.

Also, on this screen, you have two other configuration options. You can click the **Assign Role** button which will take you back to the previous configuration screen where you can then add another role, or by clicking the **Manage Role** button, you can customize the roles as shown in Figure 13-35.

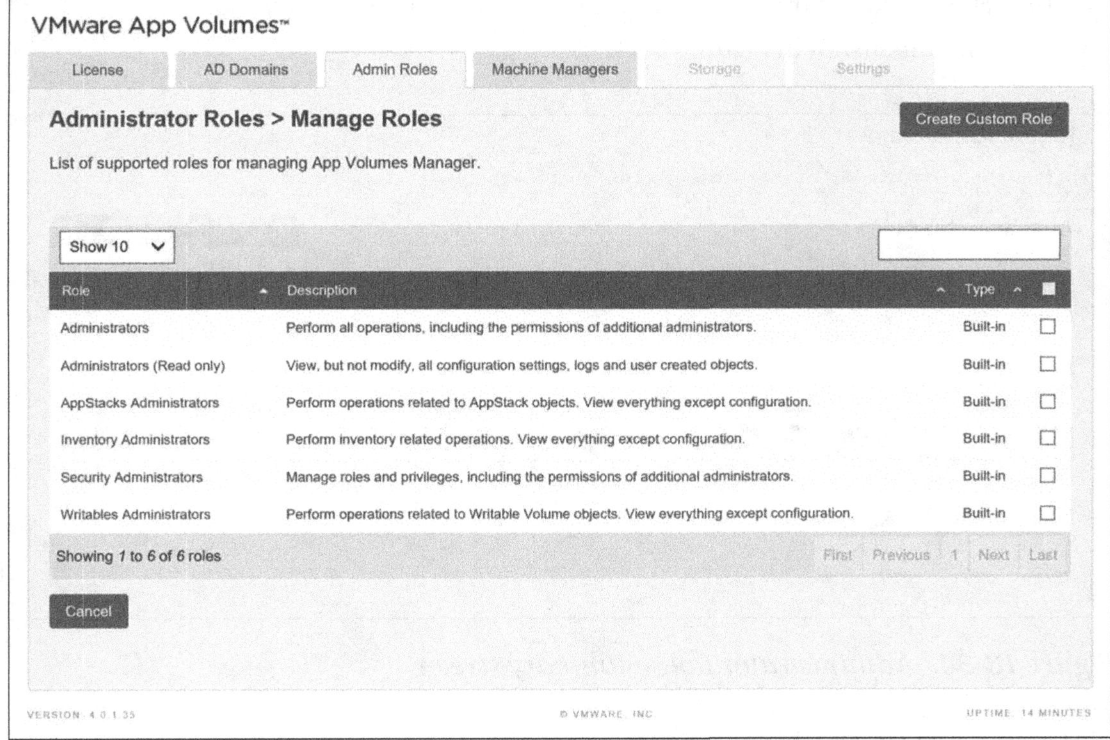

Figure 13-35. *Managing roles screen*

To create your own custom role, complete the following steps:

1. Click the **Create Custom Role** button.

2. In the **Name** box, give the role a name. In this example, we have just called the new role **Test**.

3. Next is the **Description** box. In this box, you can enter a description for this new role. In this example, we have just called it **Test role**. Although optional, it's worth adding a good description, so you know exactly what this role is for.

4. The last thing to configure on this screen is the **Privileges** you want to assign to your new role. In the test lab, we have added the **Directory** privileges to the Test role as shown in Figure 13-36.

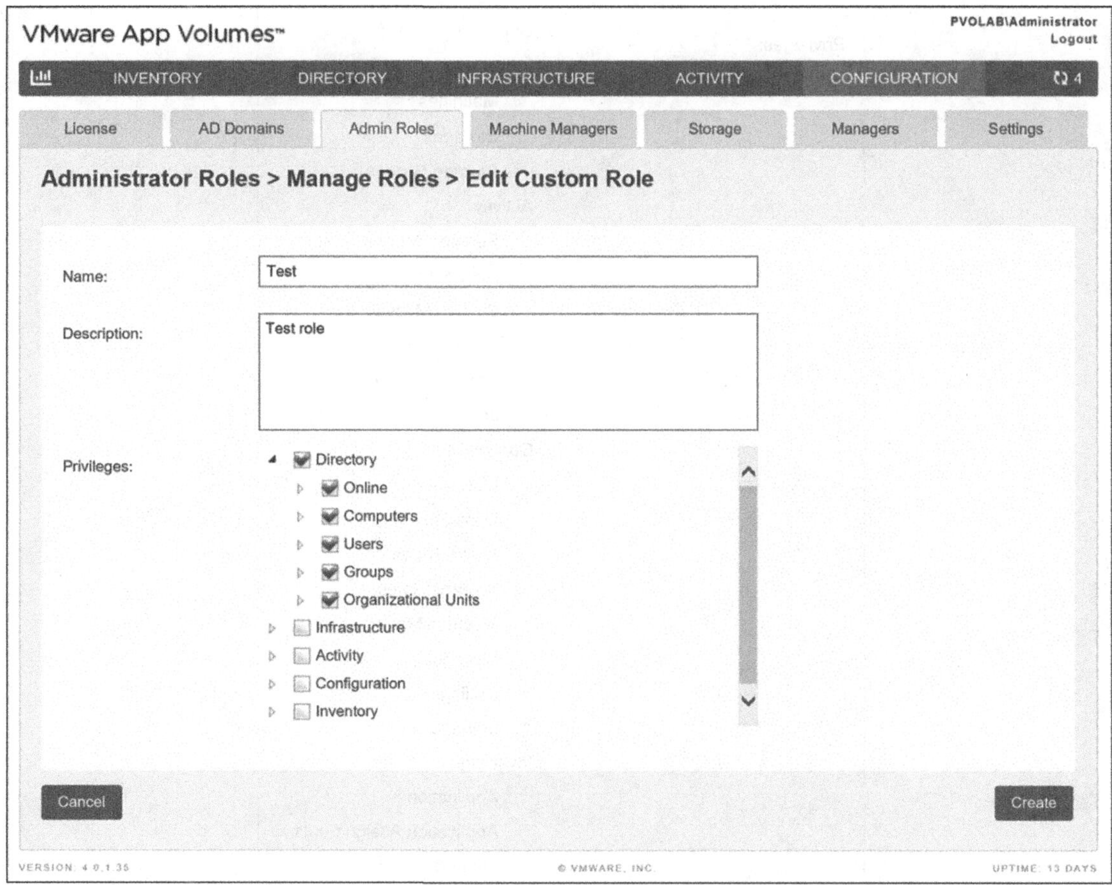

***Figure 13-36.** Edit custom role screen*

5. If you expand each heading by clicking the arrow next to each privilege listed, you will see all the available options. In Figure 13-36, we have expanded the **Directory** option to show the options for this set of privileges.

6. Scroll through all the options adding the privileges you want to include in this role. Figure 13-37 shows all the available options.

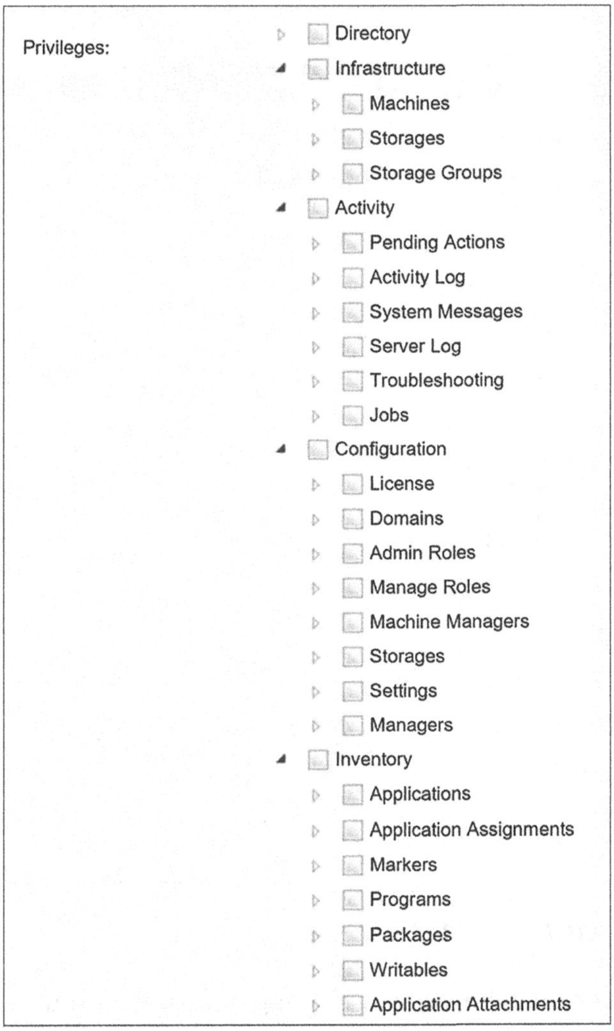

Privileges:

- Directory
- Infrastructure
  - Machines
  - Storages
  - Storage Groups
- Activity
  - Pending Actions
  - Activity Log
  - System Messages
  - Server Log
  - Troubleshooting
  - Jobs
- Configuration
  - License
  - Domains
  - Admin Roles
  - Manage Roles
  - Machine Managers
  - Storages
  - Settings
  - Managers
- Inventory
  - Applications
  - Application Assignments
  - Markers
  - Programs
  - Packages
  - Writables
  - Application Attachments

Figure 13-37. *Configurable privileges for the custom role*

7. When you have finished adding the privileges to your new custom role, click the **Create** button.

8. You will now see the **Adding new Role** progress bar as shown in Figure 13-38.

Adding new Role - Test

Figure 13-38. *Adding the new custom role*

9. With the new custom role created and the **Admin Roles** section successfully configured, you will see the screenshot in Figure 13-39.

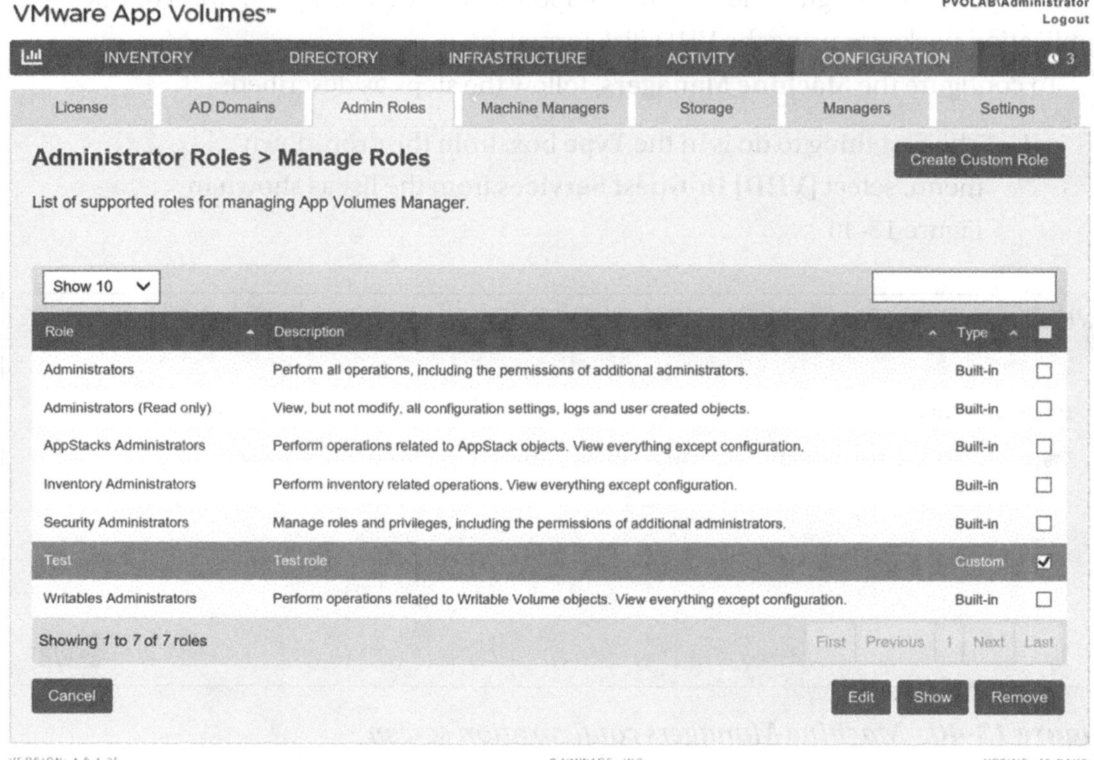

***Figure 13-39.** Successful addition of a custom role*

10. If you check the box next to the role, you will see that you have several options available. You can **Edit**, **Show**, or **Remove** the selected role. You can also click the **Create Custom Role** button to create more custom roles.

You have now successfully added a new custom administrator role in the App Volumes management console.

The next configuration tab is for **Machine Managers**.

Machine Managers

The next configuration tab is for the Machine Managers configuration screen. This is where you will configure the specific components for delivering the App Volumes application packages using the VHD disk format.

To configure the **Machine Managers,** follow the steps as described:

1. The first thing to do is in the **Type** box, from the drop-down menu, select **[VHD] In-Guest Services** from the list as shown in Figure 13-40.

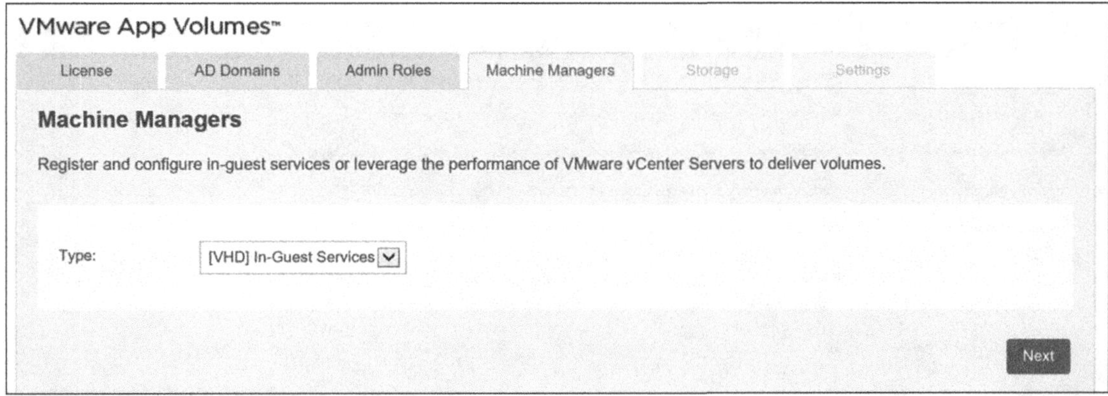

Figure 13-40. *Machine Managers configuration screen*

2. Now click the **Next** button to continue.

Next is the storage configuration which we will complete in the next section.

Storage configuration

In this next configuration screen, we are going to configure the Storage settings. This is to configure the location of where the application packages and Writable Volumes are going to be stored. As this is a VHD-based deployment, these are going to be stored on a Windows file server.

1. Having clicked Next on the previous configuration, you will now see the **Storage** configuration screen as shown in Figure 13-41.

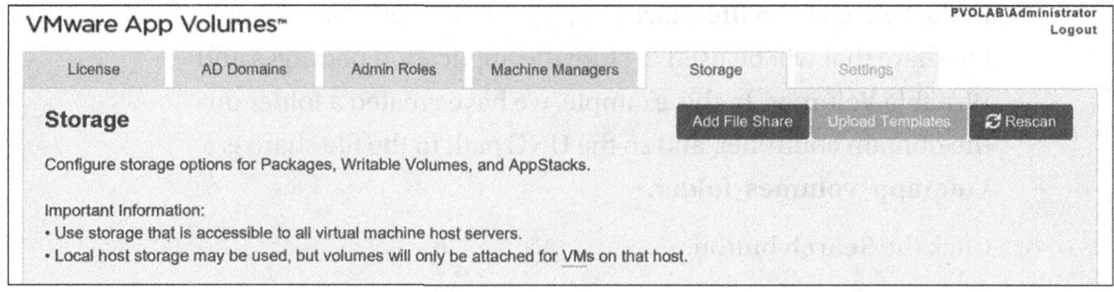

Figure 13-41. *Storage configuration screen*

2. The first thing you need to do is to add a file share that will be used to store the application packages and Writable Volumes.
3. Click the **Add File Share** button.
4. You will see the **Add File Share** configuration screen as shown in Figure 13-42.

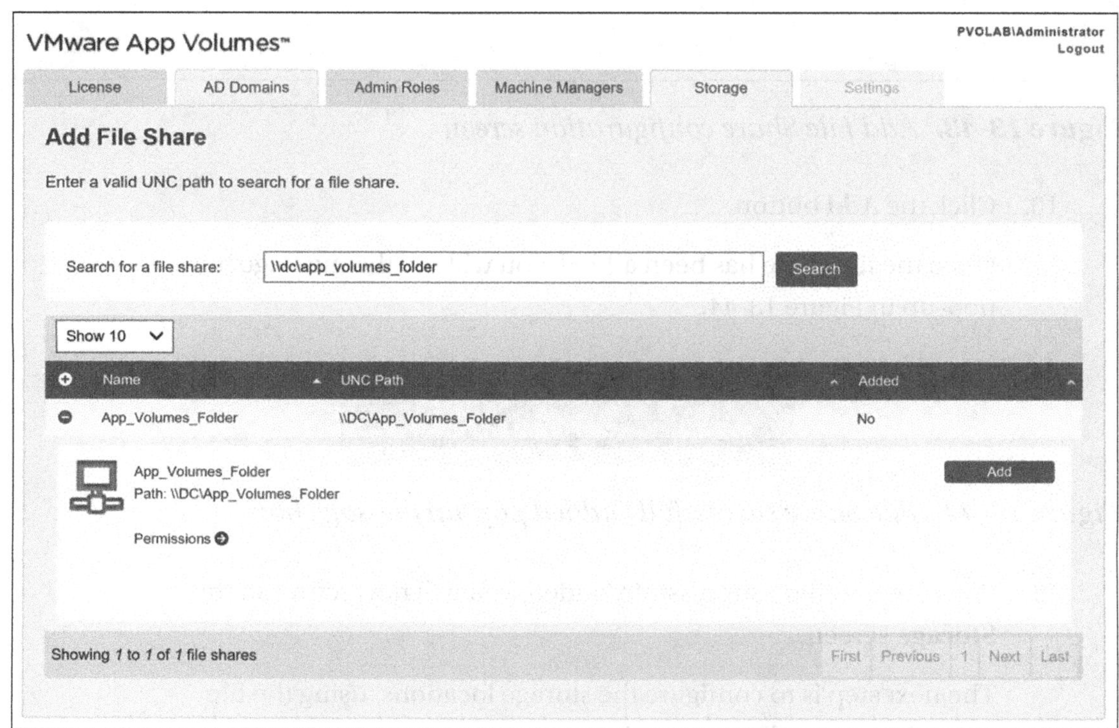

Figure 13-42. *Add File Share configuration screen*

5. In the **Search for a file share** box, type in the UNC path to the file share that will be used to store the application packages and Writable Volumes. In this example, we have created a folder on the domain controller, and so the UNC path to the file share is **\\dc\app_volumes_folder.**
6. Click the **Search** button.
7. You will then see the results of the search listed below.
8. Click the **Add** button to add the file share you want to use.
9. You will see the **Confirm Add** dialog box as shown in Figure 13-43.

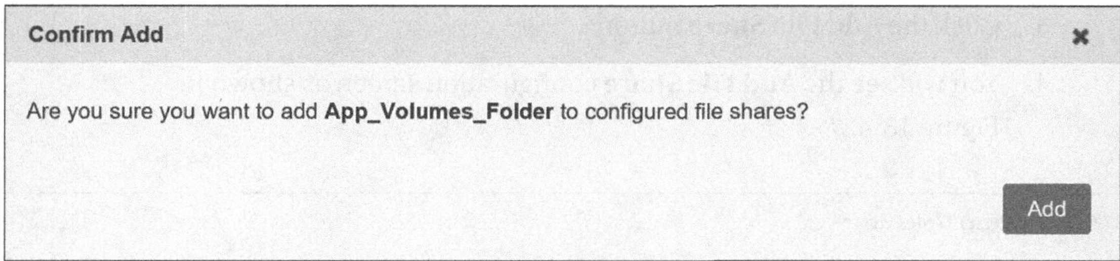

***Figure 13-43.** Add File Share configuration screen*

10. Click the **Add** button.
11. Once the file share has been added, you will see the message box pop-up in Figure 13-44.

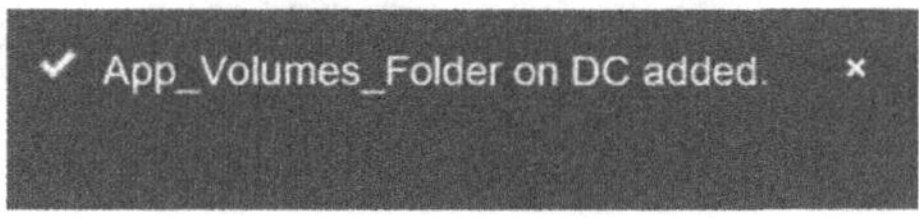

***Figure 13-44.** File Share successfully added pop-up message box*

12. With the file share successfully added, you will now return to the **Storage** screen.

    The next step is to configure the storage locations, using the file share, for the application packages.

13. In the **Packages** section, and the **Default Storage Location** box, click the **Choose a storage location** drop-down menu and select the file share from the options listed.

14. This is shown in Figure 13-45.

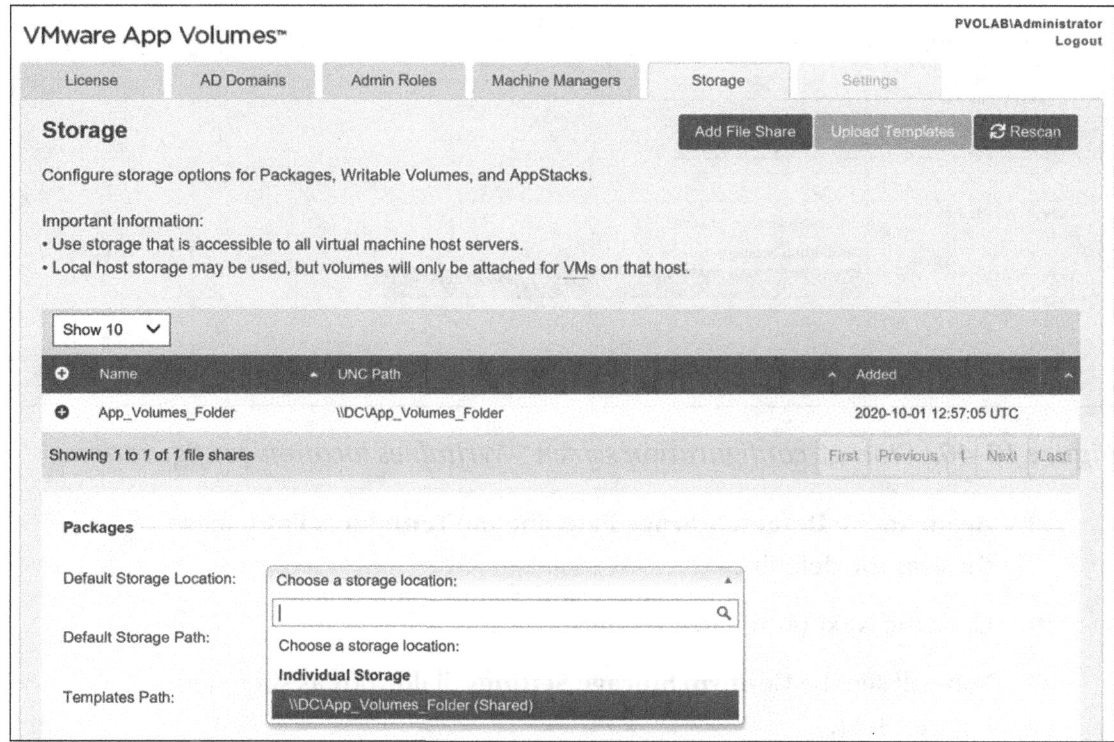

Figure 13-45. *Storage configuration screen – package location configuration*

15. Leave the **Default Storage Path** and the **Templates Path** as the defaults.

16. Next, in the **Writable Volumes** section, and the **Default Storage Location** box, click the **Choose a storage location** drop-down menu and select the file share from the options listed.

17. This is shown in Figure 13-46.

Packages

Default Storage Location: Individual Storage : \\DC\App_Volumes_Folder (Shared)

Type: Shared

Default Storage Path: appvolumes/packages

Templates Path: appvolumes/packages_templates

Writable Volumes

Default Storage Location: Choose a storage location:

Choose a storage location:

Individual Storage

\\DC\App_Volumes_Folder (Shared)

Default Storage Path:

Templates Path:

Next

***Figure 13-46.** Storage configuration screen – Writables location configuration*

18. Again, in the **Default Storage Path** and the **Templates Path,** leave these as the defaults.

19. Click the **Next** button to continue.

20. You will see the **Confirm Storage Settings** dialog box as shown in Figure 13-47.

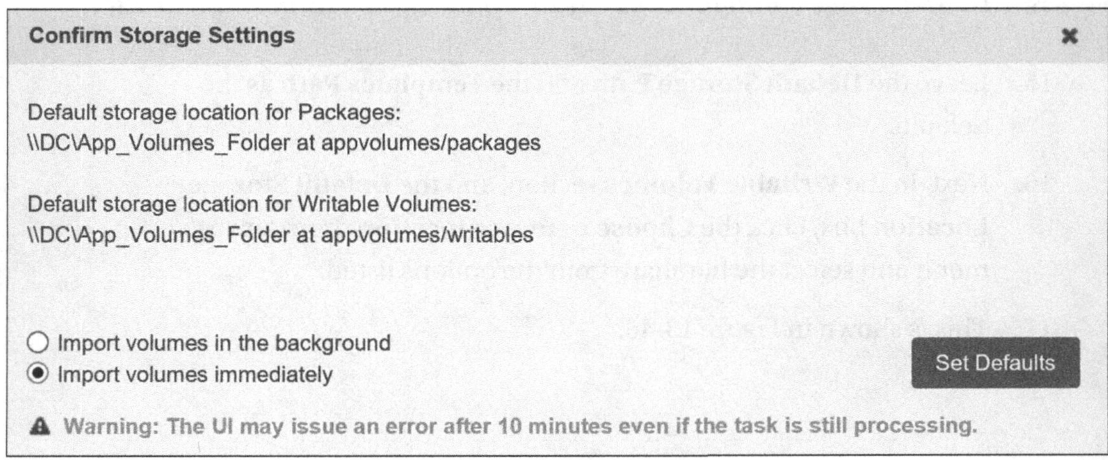

***Figure 13-47.** Confirm Storage Settings dialog box*

21. Click the radio button for **Import volumes immediately**, and then click the **Set Defaults** button.

22. You will see the task complete with the progress bar shown in Figure 13-48.

Figure 13-48. *Setting Default Storage Locations*

23. Once complete, you will see the message pop-up in Figure 13-49.

Figure 13-49. *Datastores successfully saved pop-up message*

24. You will now see the **Upload Templates** screen.

25. Check the boxes to select which templates you want to upload to the file share. In this example, we have selected all of them as shown in Figure 13-50.

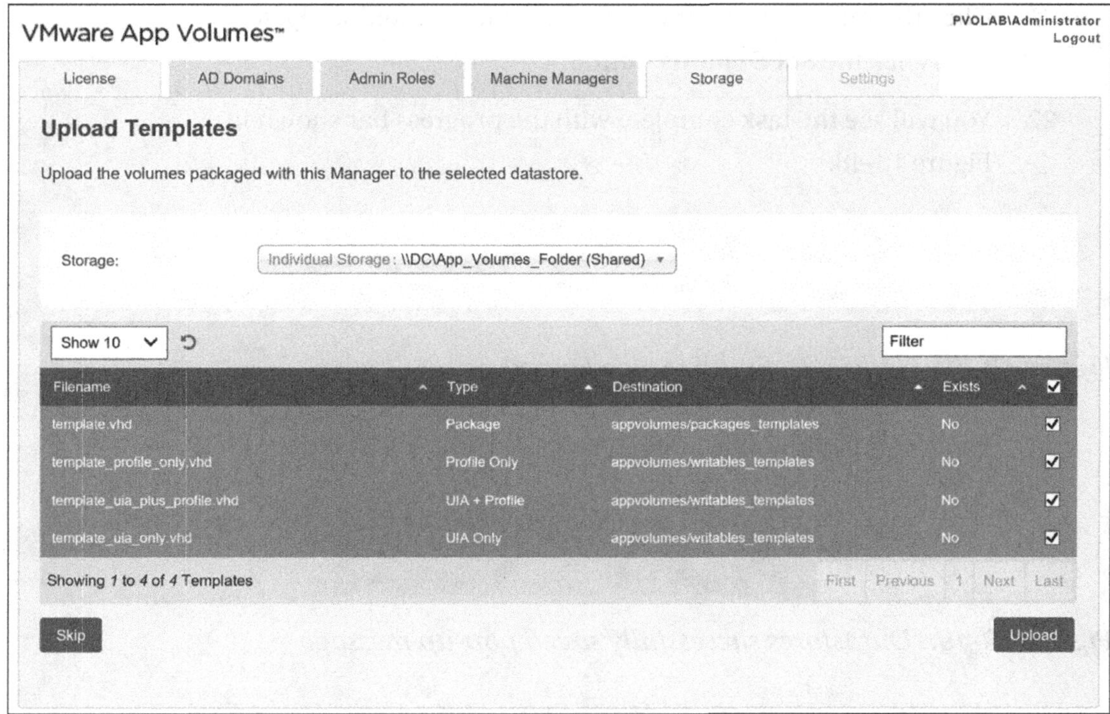

***Figure 13-50.** Selecting the templates for upload*

26. Click the **Upload** button.

27. You will see the **Confirm Upload Templates** dialog box (Figure 13-51).

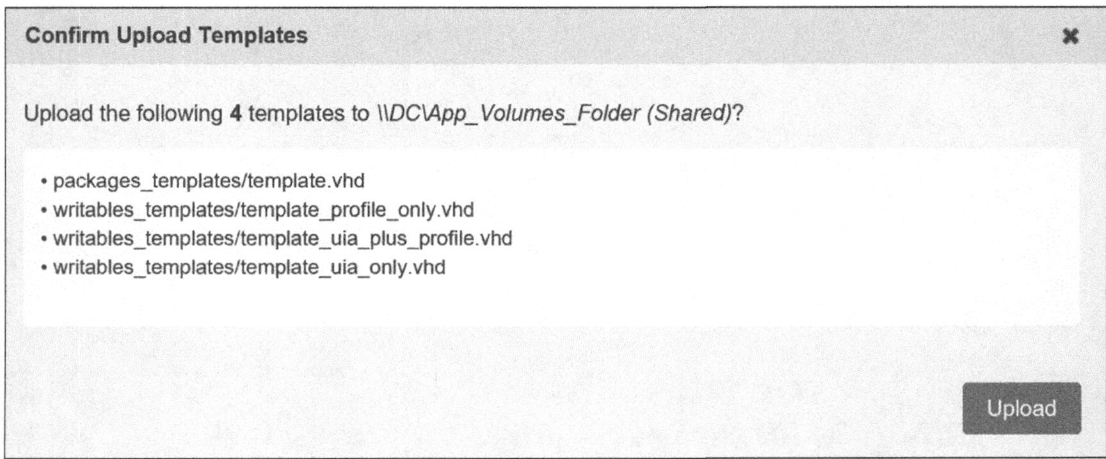

***Figure 13-51.** Confirm Upload Templates dialog box*

28. Once complete, you will see the message pop-up in Figure 13-52.

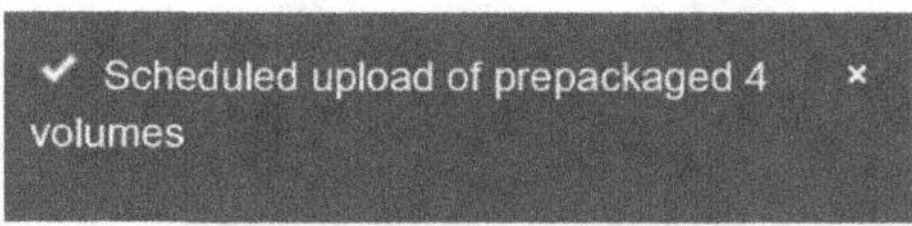

Figure 13-52. *Uploads scheduled for completion pop-up message box*

To check that the templates have been created and uploaded, log in to the file server that is hosting the shared folder. In this example, this is the domain controller. Open a Windows Explorer session and navigate to the shared folder. An example is shown in Figure 13-53.

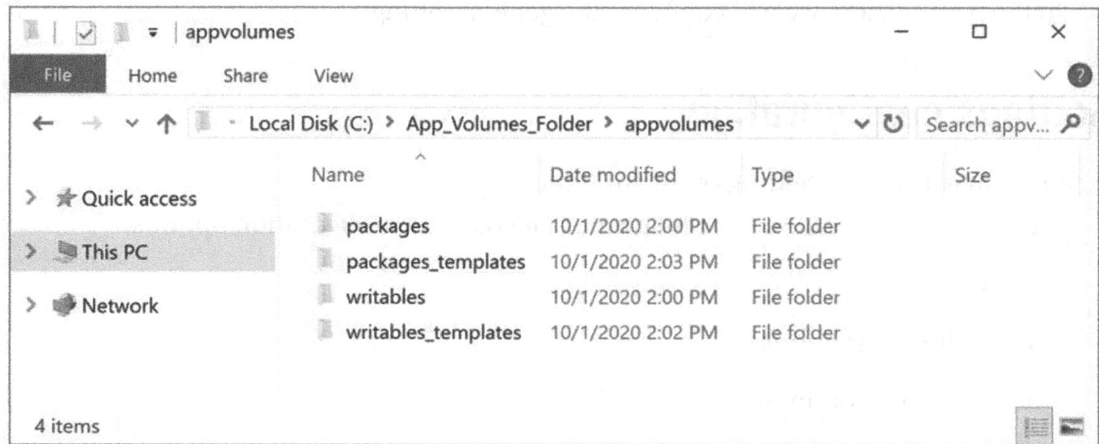

Figure 13-53. *Shared folder with the template directories uploaded*

If you then open the **packages_templates** folder, you will see the application package template in VHD disk format as shown in Figure 13-54.

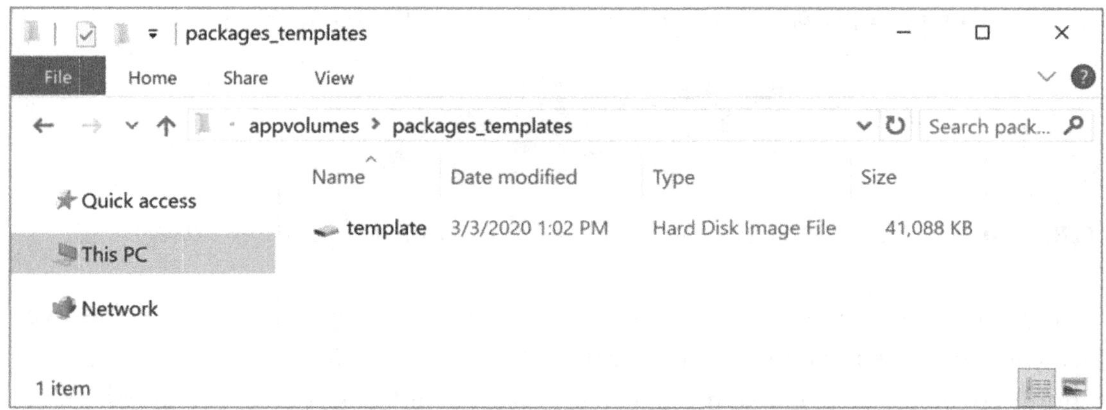

Figure 13-54. *Shared folder showing the uploaded VHD template*

In the next section, we will configure the general settings.

Settings configuration

Finally, you will see the Settings configuration screen.

The **Settings** tab contains the following categories of configuration options:

- General
- Volume Mounting
- Writable Volumes
- Active Directory
- [VHD] In-Guest Service
- Advanced Settings

As there are several settings, we are going to break these down into sections starting with the settings for **General** and **Volume Mounting**.

These are shown in Figure 13-55.

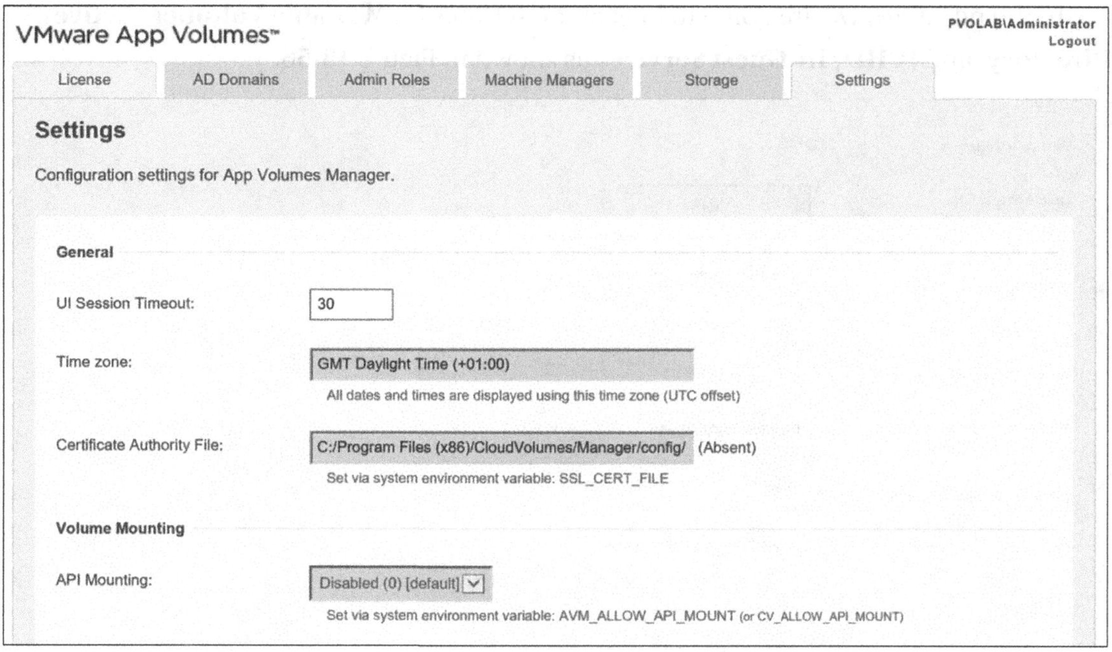

Figure 13-55. *Settings configuration screen part 1*

We will start with the **General** settings.

1. The first setting is for **UI Session Timeout**. Here you can enter an amount of time for when the management console times out and logs the user out. That means the amount of time that has passed with no activity. The default setting is 30 minutes, after which time with no activity will log the user out of the management console.

2. The **Time zone** box will show the currently set time zone.

3. In the **Certificate Authority File** box, you will see the path to the certificate file. This is set using the system variable SSL_CERT_FILE.

   Next is the **Volume Mounting** setting.

4. With the **API Mounting** option, you can allow application packages and Writable Volumes to be mounted using an API. To configure this option, from the drop-down menu, select the option for enabled or disabled. When enabled, volumes can be mounted using the App Volumes API, enabling the mount process to automate the process. By default, the API Mounting setting is set to disabled. Using the command AVM_ALLOW_API_MOUNT will also enable this setting.

In the next part, we are going to look at the settings for **Writable Volumes**, **Active Directory**, and **[VHD] In-Guest Services** as shown in Figure 13-56.

Writable Volumes

Delete Protection: Protected (0) [default] (?)
Set via system environment variable: AVM_NO_PROTECT (or CV_NO_PROTECT)

Force Reboot On Error: Force Reboot (1) [default] (?)
Set via system environment variable: AVM_WRITABLE_REBOOT

Active Directory

Non-Domain Entities: Disallow [default] (?)

[VHD] In-Guest Services

Security: ☐ Dynamic File Permissions

Figure 13-56. *Settings configuration screen part 2*

5. The **Delete Protection** option, which by default is set to **Protected (0) [default]**, protects a Writable Volume should you delete the virtual machine to which it is attached. The Writable Volume will not be deleted. This option can also be configured via the AVM_NO_PROTECT system variable.

6. Next is the **Force Reboot On Error** setting. By default, this is set to **Force Reboot (1) [default],** meaning that by default it is enabled. If a Writable Volume does not get mounted to the user it has been assigned to, when the user logs in, then the machine will be rebooted in order to try and attach the Writable Volume again.

7. Under the **Active Directory** section, you will see the option for **Non-Domain Entities**. From the drop-down menu, you can set this to **Allow** which means that any nondomain joined machine can have volumes attached to it. The default setting is **Disallow** so that no machines can have volumes mounted if they are not joined to your domain.

8. Next, there is the **[VHD] In-Guest Services** section. By checking the **Dynamic File Permissions** box, you can enable the dynamic permissions that were introduced with Windows Server 2012. This feature allows you to apply access control and restricted permissions based on conditional rules for accessing files and folders. If a new end user joins a department or moves departments, then the file and folder permissions will change dynamically to reflect this change and all without the administrator's intervention.

   Finally, there is the **Advanced Settings** section as shown in Figure 13-57.

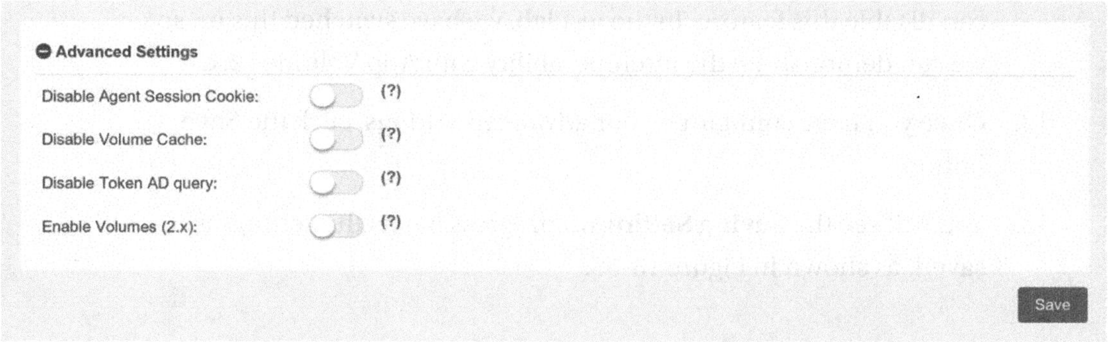

Figure 13-57. *Settings configuration screen part 3 - Advanced Settings*

9. The first option is to **Disable Agent Session Cookie**. To enable this setting, click the switch to turn it on. A session cookie is used to optimize communications between the App Volumes Manager and the App Volumes Agent. As part of troubleshooting, if you experience App Volumes Agent session issues, then you could try disabling the session cookies to see if that fixes the problem.

10. Next is the **Disable Volume Cache** option. App Volumes caches objects to improve performance. When troubleshooting and seeing increased memory usage, to fix this you could switch this setting on to disable the volume caching.

11. The **Disable Token AD Query** setting is next. App Volumes queries for AD group membership by using cached object SIDs. In previous versions of App Volumes, this query was performed by using group membership queries against Active Directory domains directly and recursively. You can revert to that way of querying AD by switching this feature on.

12. Finally, you have the **Enable Volumes (2.x)** setting. Switching this feature on allows you to manage App Volumes 2.x packages (AppStacks) and Writable Volumes. It also supports using the 2.x version of the App Volumes Agent. When this feature is enabled, you will see an additional menu option, **VOLUMES (2.x)**. Once you have migrated your AppStacks to application packages, you can disable this feature. In the test lab, we have switched this on so we can demonstrate the interoperability with App Volumes 2.x.

13. Once you have configured your advanced settings, click the **Save** button.

14. You will see the **Saving Settings...** progress bar as the settings are saved, as shown in Figure 13-58.

Saving Settings...

Figure 13-58. *Saving Settings in progress*

You have now successfully configured an App Volumes Manager to deliver application packages and Writable Volumes using the VHD virtual hard disk format.

You can now build your application packages and deploy Writable Volumes using the VHD virtual hard disk format. The process to do this is no different to the process when using VMDK-based virtual hard disk files. This is covered in Chapters 5 and 6. The key difference is when you select the datastore for creating packages and Writable Volumes, you will be selecting a Windows-based share rather than a vSphere datastore.

Chapter summary

In this chapter, we have looked at deploying an App Volumes Manager using an alternative format for the virtual hard disks that are used as application packages and Writable Volumes - in this case, VHD-based virtual hard disks.

We worked through the App Volumes installation process, namely because an individual App Volumes Manager cannot support both virtual hard disk formats, and so we built a new App Volumes Manager instance specifically for VHD.

Once installed, we completed the initial configuration tasks required for a VHD-based App Volumes Manager.

In the next chapter, we are going to look at the upgrade process.

CHAPTER 14

Upgrading App Volumes

The App Volumes solution is evolving all the time, with new versions and new features. To take advantage of these new features, plus any bug fixes and patches, and to remain on a supported platform, you may need to update your existing deployment.

In this chapter, we are going to discuss the process for upgrading the App Volumes Manager and the App Volumes Agent and then the migration process if you are upgrading from 2.x to 4.x.

We will start with the upgrade of the App Volumes Manager.

Upgrading the App Volumes Manager

The upgrade process for the App Volumes Manager is very straightforward. However, there are a couple of points to bear in mind depending on which version you are upgrading from.

Whichever version you are upgrading from, it is always worthwhile in taking a backup or a snapshot of the environment before you start the upgrade. Also, just to make sure, back up the accompanying SQL database too. You should also check the interoperability guides.

Upgrading from 2.x versions to 4.x

If you are upgrading from a 2.x version of App Volumes to a 4.x version, then before you start the process, you need to make sure that you are first running App Volumes v2.18.

If you are running an earlier version of 2.x, then you will need to first upgrade to version 2.18 before starting your version 4.x upgrade. Once you have done that, then the process is the same for 2.18 to 4.x and 4.0 to 4.1.

In the next section, we are going to work through the upgrade process.

P. von Oven, *Delivering Applications with VMware App Volumes 4*,
https://doi.org/10.1007/978-1-4842-6689-2_14

Upgrading to App Volumes version 2006 (4.1.0)

In this section, we are going to upgrade from App Volumes 4.0 to App Volumes 2006 (4.1.0). This is the latest version of App Volumes at the time of writing this book.

In this example, we have already built a Windows Server 2016 virtual machine, with the hostname of **app-vol-mgr**, and we have already got an existing installation of App Volumes Manager version 4.0.

To upgrade, follow the steps described:

1. Open a console to the app-vol-mgr server.
2. Navigate to the location where you downloaded the new version of App Volumes software to. In the test lab, this was saved in a folder called App Volumes 4.1 as shown in Figure 14-1.

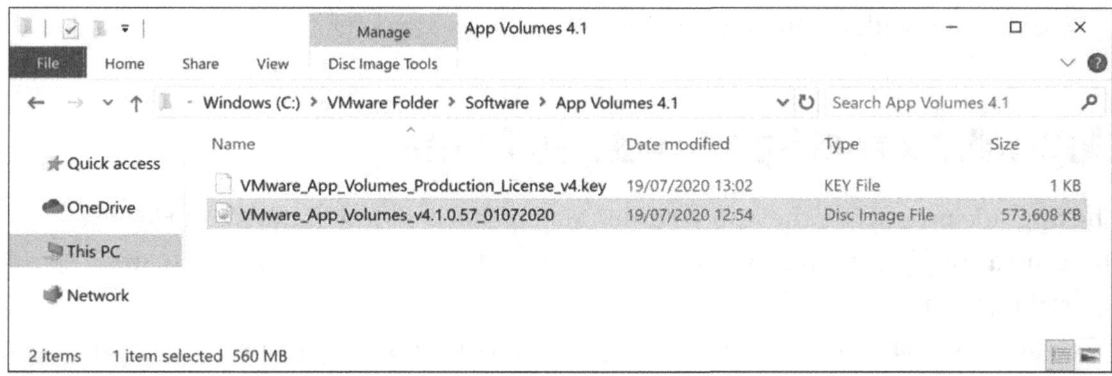

Figure 14-1. *VMware App Volumes software folder*

3. Double-click the **VMware_App_Volumes_v4.1.0.57_01072020.iso** file to mount the iso image. You will see the folders in Figure 14-2.

***Figure 14-2.** VMware App Volumes software iso image mounted*

4. Double-click to open the **Installation** folder. You will see the folders along with the setup installer package as shown in Figure 14-3.

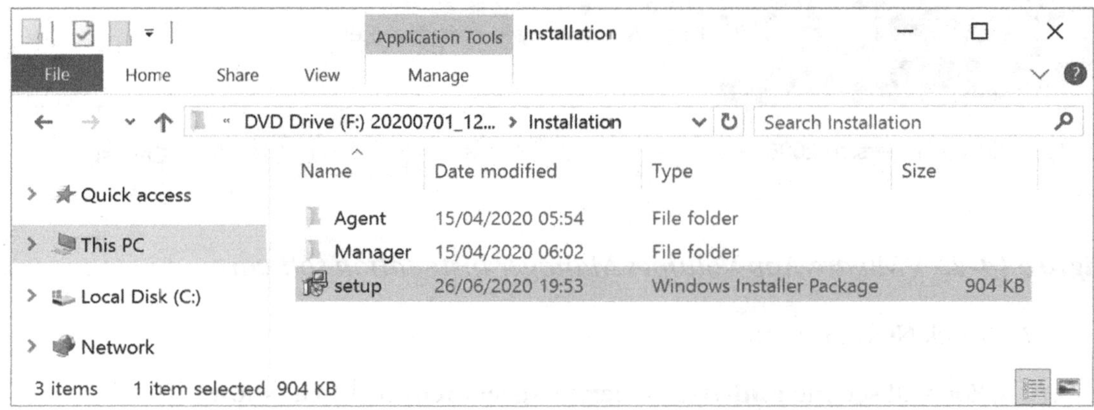

***Figure 14-3.** VMware App Volumes software – installation folder*

5. Double-click **Setup**. You will now see the App Volumes Installer launch.

6. Launch the installer by double-clicking **App Volumes Manager**. You will see the **Windows Installer** launch followed by the Welcome to the App Volumes Installer screen as shown in Figure 14-4.

Figure 14-4. *VMware App Volumes Manager installation software*

7. Click **Next** to continue.

8. You will see the **End-User License Agreement** screen as shown in Figure 14-5.

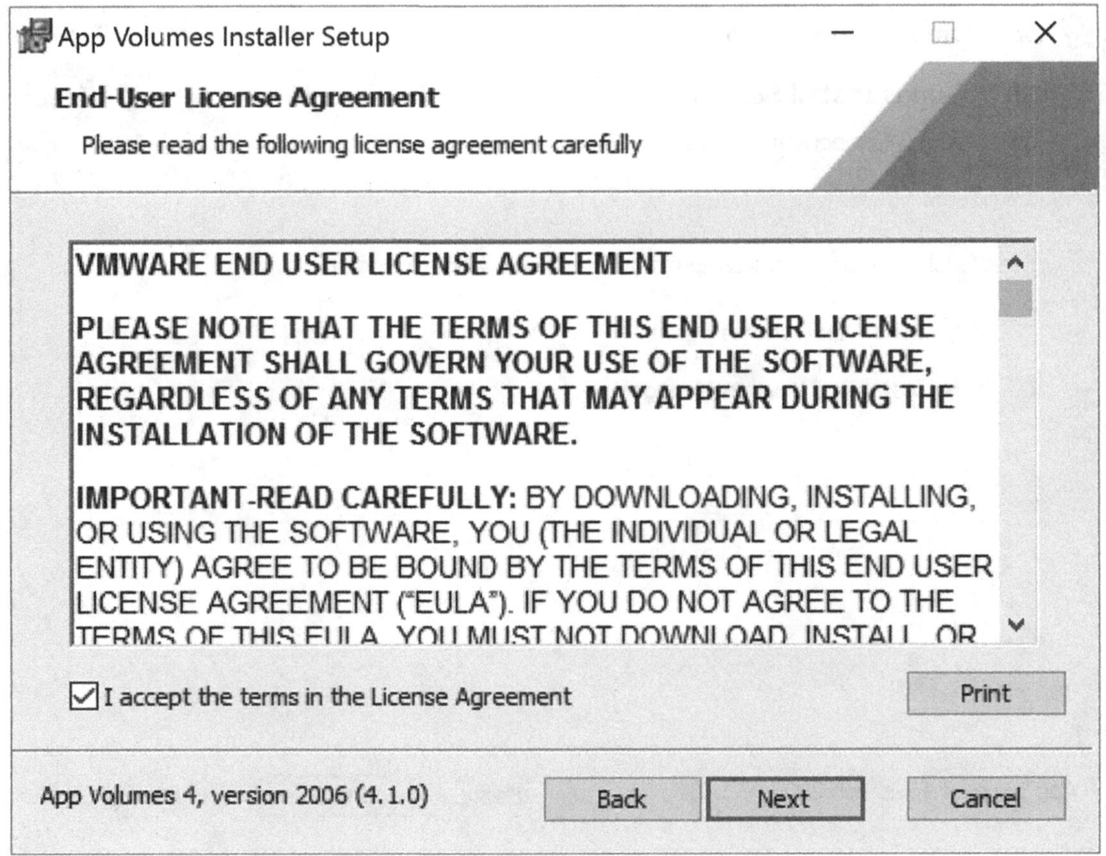

Figure 14-5. *End-User License Agreement screen*

9. Check the box to accept the terms, and click **Next** to continue to the **App Volumes Install Screen** as shown in Figure 14-6.

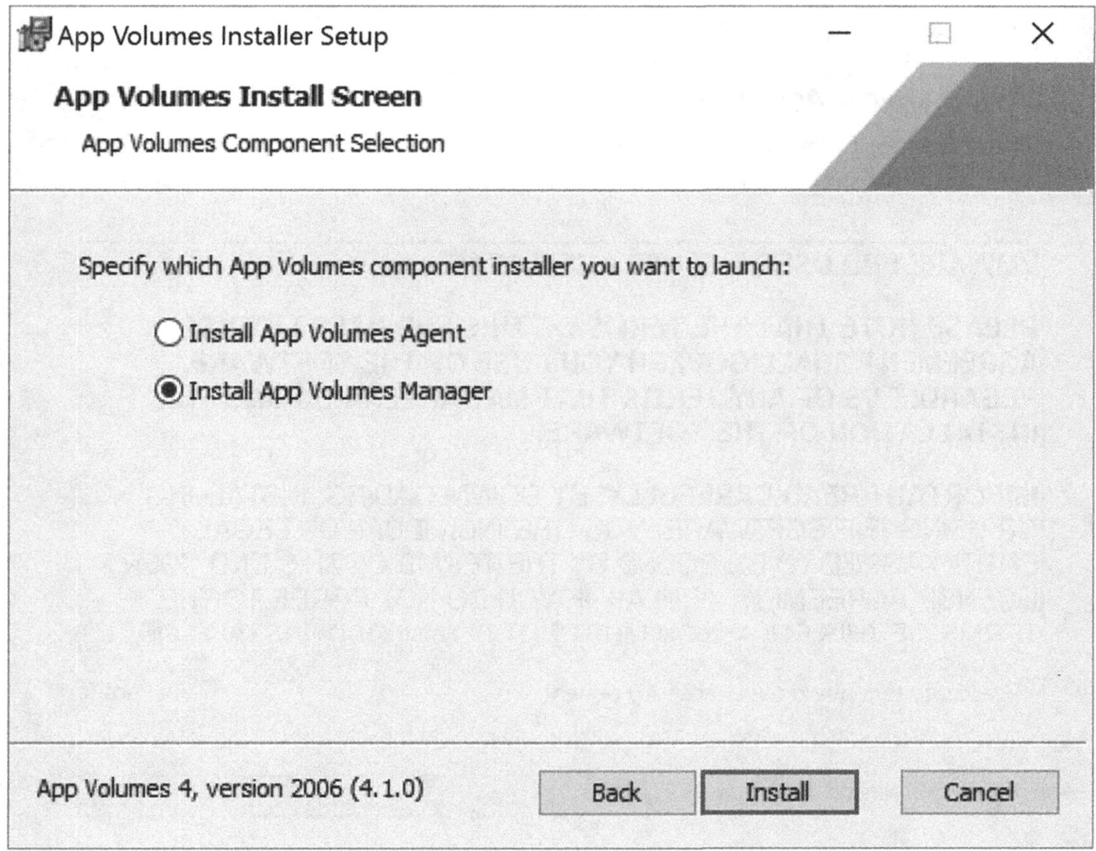

Figure 14-6. *App Volumes Install Screen*

10. Click the radio button for **Install App Volumes Manager.**

11. Click the **Install** button.

12. You will now see the **Welcome to the App Volumes Manager Setup Wizard** as shown in Figure 14-7.

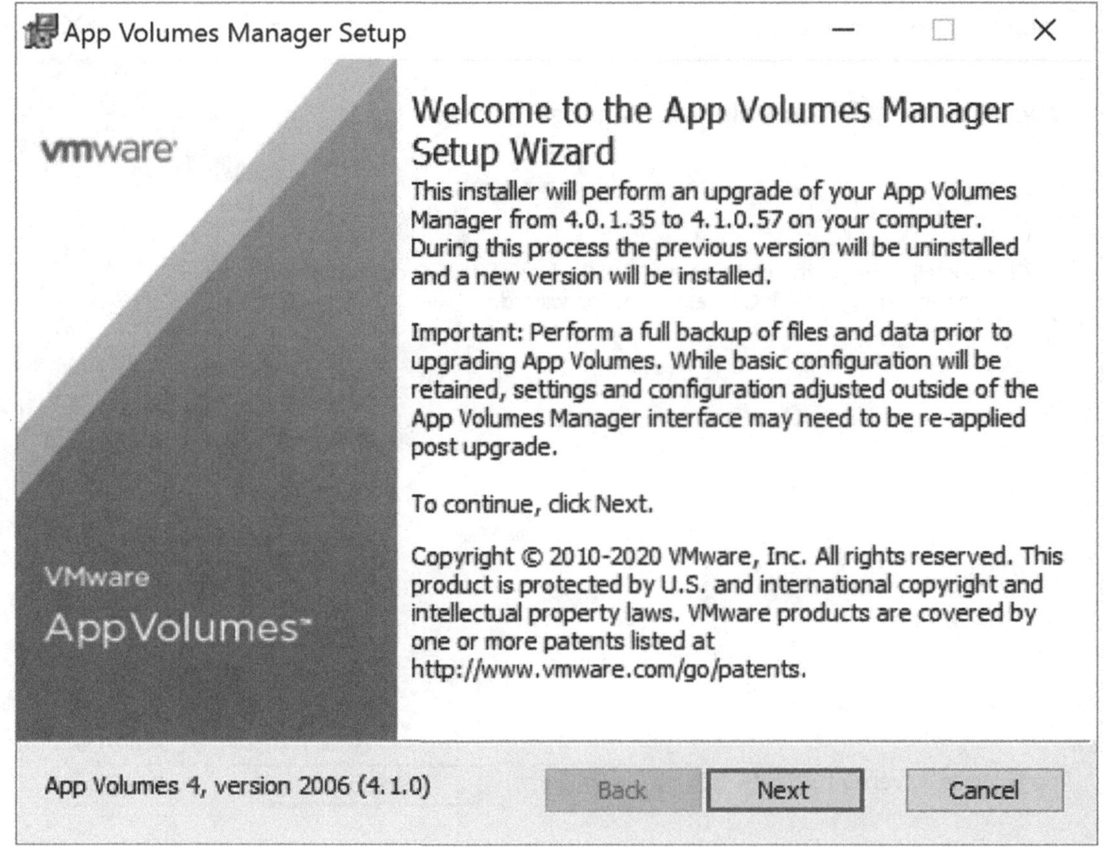

Figure 14-7. *Welcome to the App Volumes Manager Setup Wizard screen*

13. Click the **Next** button to continue.

14. You will see the **Ready to install App Volumes Manager** screen. As this is an upgrade to an existing version, you will not see the option to install the SQL Server components as these will have already been configured previously, and those settings will be kept as part of the upgrade process. This screen is shown in Figure 14-8.

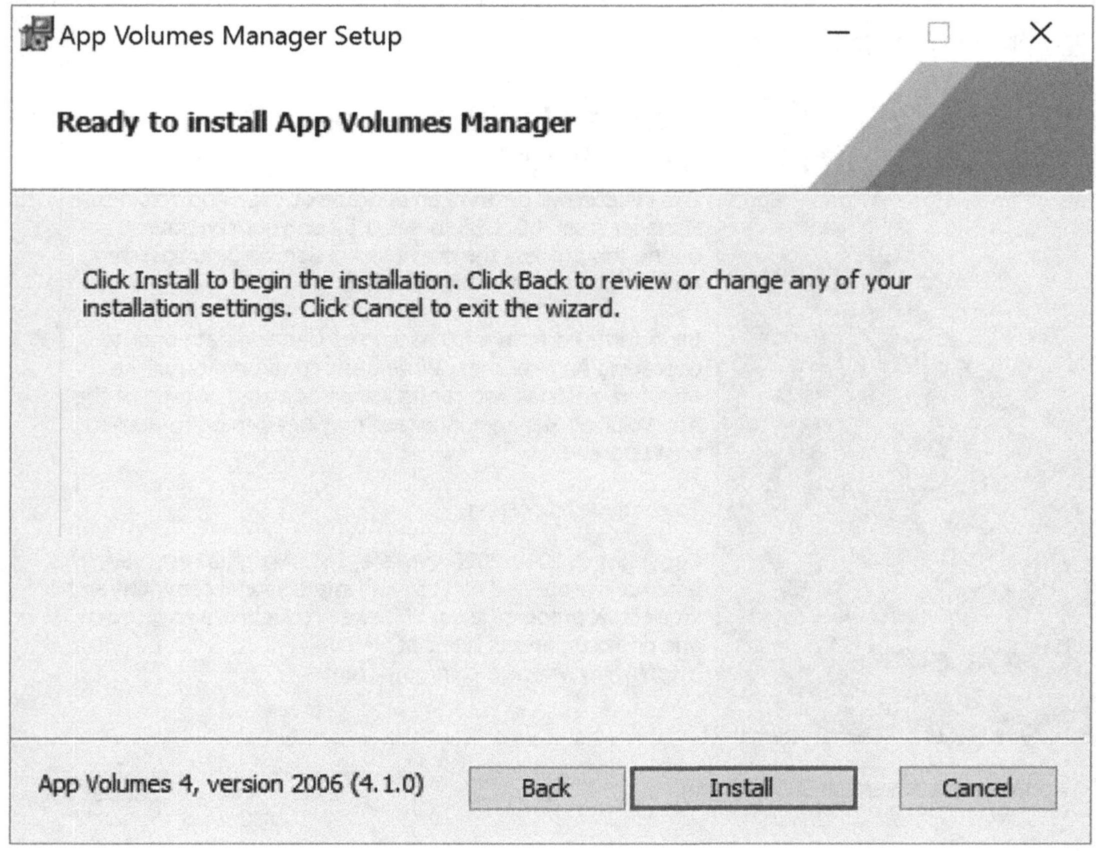

Figure 14-8. *Ready to install App Volumes Manager*

15. Click the **Install** button.

16. As the install progresses, you will see the message pop-up which states that there are files that need to be updated that will also require a reboot (Figure 14-9).

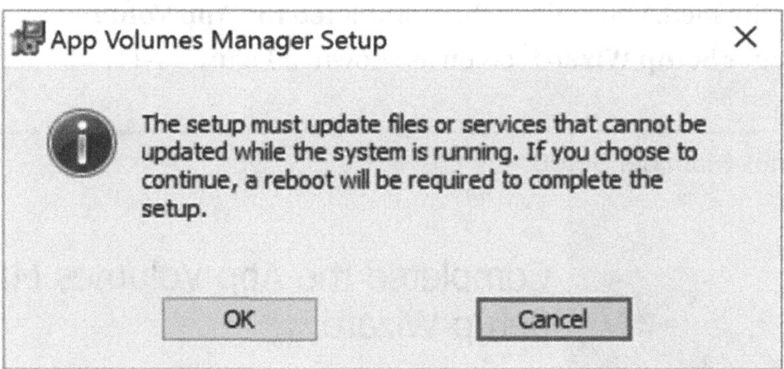

Figure 14-9. *Reboot require message box*

17. Click **OK** to accept.

18. You will see the installation continue the upgrade as shown in Figure 14-10.

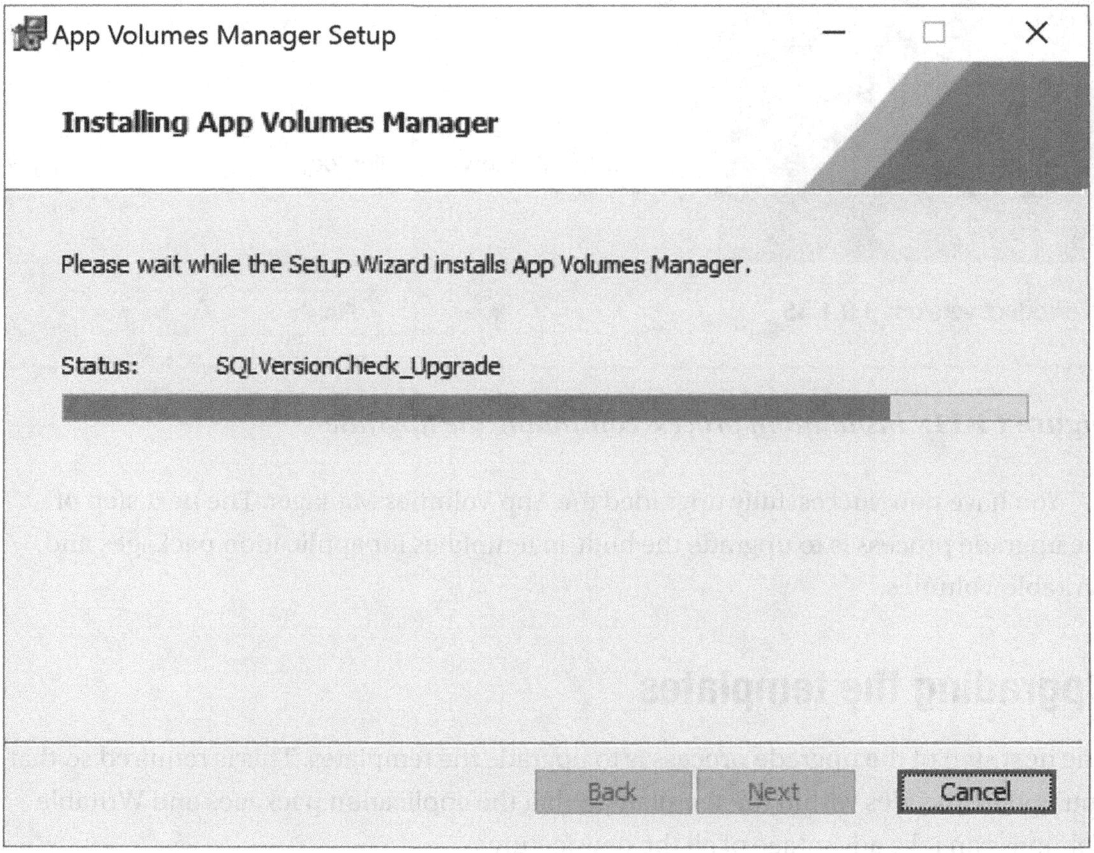

Figure 14-10. *Upgrade process continues*

19. Once finished, you will see the **Completed the App Volumes Manager Setup Wizard** screen as shown in Figure 14-11.

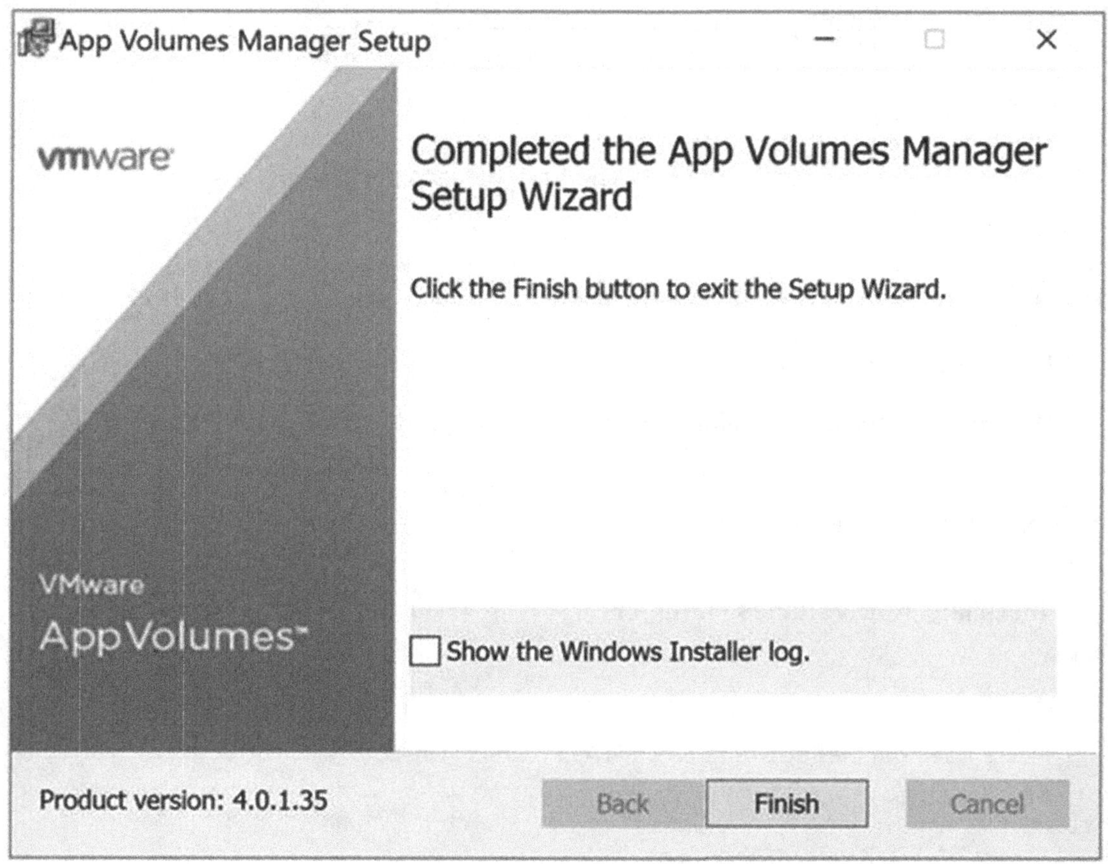

Figure 14-11. *Installation process continuing the upgrade*

You have now successfully upgraded the App Volumes Manager. The next step of the upgrade process is to upgrade the built-in templates for application packages and Writable Volumes.

Upgrading the templates

The next step of the upgrade process is to upgrade the templates. This is required so that you update the files within the template so that the application packages and Writable Volumes can take advantage of all the new features.

Before you log in to the App Volumes Manager to complete this task, it is worthwhile clearing your browser cache. You should see the new App Volumes 4.x management console. If you do not see the new console, then this could be due to the old console being cached.

To upgrade the templates, follow the tasks described:

1. Click **CONFIGURATION** from the top menu bar.
2. Then click the **Storage** tab and then click the **Upload Templates** button.
3. You will see the **Upload Templates** screen as shown in Figure 14-12.

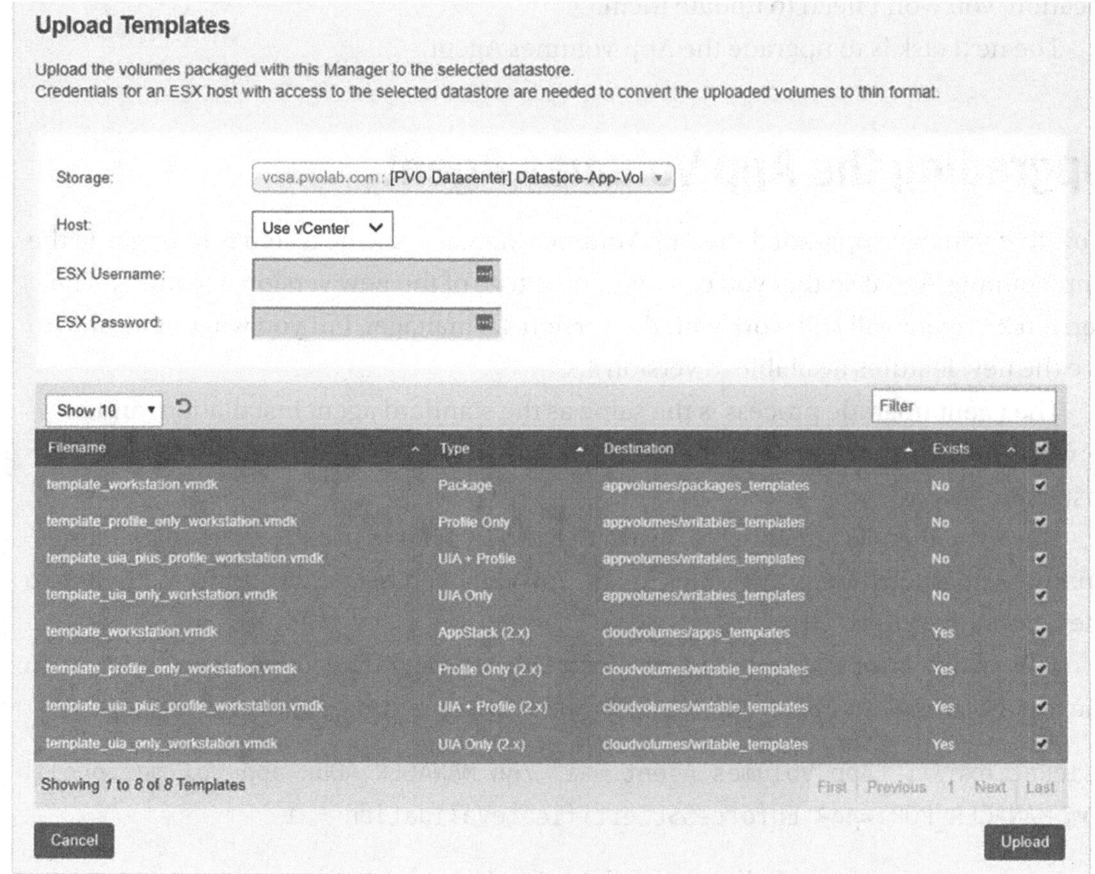

Figure 14-12. *Uploading templates screen*

4. Select the templates you want to upload. In this example, there are four existing 2.x templates and then four new 4.x templates.
5. Click the **Upload** button.
6. You will see the **Confirm Upload Templates** screen.
7. Click the **Upload** button.
8. You will then see a pop-up box stating **Scheduled upload of prepackaged 8 volumes.**

You have now successfully upgraded the App Volumes Manager and the templates to the latest version, version 4.1. You will need to repeat this process on all App Volumes Managers within your environment; however, as the templates are stored in a central location, you won't need to update them.

The next task is to upgrade the App Volumes Agent.

Upgrading the App Volumes Agent

Now that you have upgraded the App Volumes Manager, the next step is to upgrade the App Volumes Agent so that you can take advantage of the new version 4 features. The version 2.x agent will still work with the version 4.x manager, but you will not be able to use the new features available in version 4.x.

The agent upgrade process is the same as the standard agent installation, and so as we have already covered that in this book, please refer to Chapter 3 for the agent installation steps.

However, there is one thing to be aware of if you want to use the silent installation option to upgrade the App Volumes Agent. You will need to add an additional switch to the command syntax.

This switch is for **EnforceSSLCertificateValidation** and needs to be set to **1** or **0**. In the test lab, the silent install command would look something like the following:

```
msiexec.exe /i "App Volumes Agent.msi" /qn MANAGER_ADDR=app-vol-mgr.pvolab.
com MANAGER_PORT=443 EnforceSSLCertificateValidation = 1
```

You have now successfully upgraded the App Volumes Agents.

In the next section, we are going to look at migrating v2.x AppStacks to version 4.x application packages.

Migrating AppStacks to Application Packages

As you have seen in this book, the App Volumes Manager can support the new application package format of version 4.x, as well as the version 2.x AppStack format. However, to realize the full benefits of the new features, you should update your AppStacks to the new application package format.

To make this possible, VMware have an App Volumes Migration Utility. This tool can also migrate AppStacks between the VMDK disk format and the VHD disk format and can be used to help migrate from VMDK on premises to Horizon Cloud on Azure environment that also make use of the VHD disk format. The migration tool can be downloaded from the VMware Flings website:

`https://flings.vmware.com/app-volumes-migration-utility#summary`

The following screenshot in Figure 14-13 shows the App Volumes Migration Utility download page:

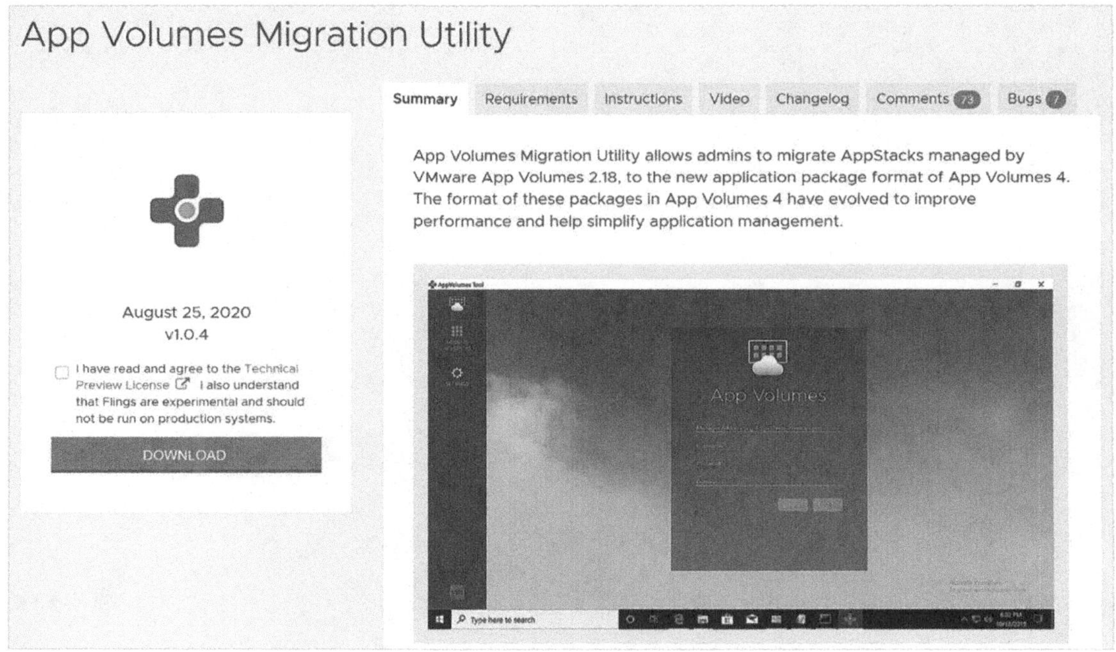

Figure 14-13. *App Volumes Migration Utility*

You should now be able to migrate and upgrade your existing v2.x AppStacks to the new application package format used in v4.x.

The App Volumes Migration Utility only supports migrating AppStacks to application packages. Writable Volumes are not supported.

Chapter summary

In this final chapter, we have focused on upgrading your App Volumes environment.

We started by upgrading the App Volumes Manager and looked at how to upgrade from a 2.x environment to a 4.x environment and then an upgrade of 4.0 to 4.1.

Next, we looked at how to upgrade the App Volumes Agent, before finally looking at how to migrate version 2.x AppStacks to the new version 4.x application package format, using the VMware App Volumes Migration Utility available from the VMware Flings website.

Index

A, B

Active Directory (AD), 19–21, 26, 27, 31, 59, 65–71, 73, 94–96, 98, 116, 142, 143, 167, 303, 306, 481, 507, 513, 515
AD domains
  configured information, 69
  controller hosts, 67
  controller information, 69, 70
  insecure connection, 68
  LDAP, 68
  naming, 66
  password box, 68
  penultimate box, 68
  port setting, 68
  registering, 66, 69
  security option, 68
  TLS, 68
  username box, 67
Advanced configuration
  App Volumes Agent, 270, 271
  batch script options, 271
  custom-sized Writable Volumes template, 264, 265
  storage groups, 265, 267, 268, 270
AppIsolation, 17, 19
Application layering
  captured/stored, 8
  composite desktop model, 4
  concept, 4
  creation, 4, 5
  delivering, 6, 7
  desktop administrators, 2, 3
  desktop experience, 4
  elements, 4
  end user experience, 3
  virtualization solution, 4
Application package
  assigning
    machine, 172
    marker assignment type, 168, 169
    sales application, 170
    testing, 173, 174
    users search, 167
    users virtual desktop machine, 165, 166
  creating application, 141–145
  installation
    app volume package, 159, 161
    complete dialog box, 157
    Disk manager, 153
    finalization, 158
    Notepad++, 153–156
    operating system, 162, 163
    programs list, 162
    progress message box, 152, 156
    restart machine, 158
  machine, 137–139
  management console, logging, 139, 141

P. von Oven, *Delivering Applications with VMware App Volumes 4*,
https://doi.org/10.1007/978-1-4842-6689-2

Application package (*cont.*)
managing existing package
deleting, 191, 192, 197, 198
editing, 189, 190, 194, 196, 197
moving, 192–194
setting CURRENT status, 186–189
update, 174, 176–178, 180, 181, 183–186
steps, 145, 146, 149, 151
Application publishing, 17, 49, 309, 369
AppStacks, 9, 23, 96, 112–115, 122, 532, 547, 548
App Volumes, 8
abstraction layer, 9
application package, 377
Application Pool, 398–400, 402–405
architecture, 310, 376, 412
end user's view, 24, 25
IT administrators' view, 25, 26
network ports, 27, 28
assigning/configuring, 377
deliver applications, 309
deployment, 15, 16
desktop operating systems, 309
Horizon Agent, install, 378–381
Horizon App farm, 389–394, 396, 397
Horizon components, 378
installation
download, 34–36
download packages, 35
prerequisites, 32, 33
Product Evaluation Center, 35
integrated applications, 8
licensing, 18
managing
group of application, 12–14
single application, 10–12
package, 10
program, 10
SAM, 9
terminology
application, 22
App Volumes Agent, 21
App Volumes Manager, 20, 21
package, 22
packaging desktop, 22
program, 22
SQL database, 21
storage groups, 23
Writable Volumes, 22
testing, 405–407, 409
test lab, 19
virtual hard disk file, 9
Writable Volume, 14, 15
App Volumes 4.1, 38, 51
App Volumes Agent, 546
desktop operating system, 50
hardware requirements, 50
installation, 56
Agent installer, 52, 53
App Volumes 4.1, 51
end-user license agreement, 53, 54
ready to install screen, 55
registration, 58
restarting, 57
server configuration, 54
service up/running, 57, 58
setup wizard, 53, 56, 57
software installation folder, 52
server operating system, 51
software requirements, 50
App Volumes Manager
access, 37
activity menu

activity log tab, 126, 127
jobs tab, 125, 126
pending actions tab, 124, 125
server log tab, 128, 129
system messages tab, 127, 128
troubleshooting tab, 129–132
admin roles, 70, 71
assigning, 72
choose group box, 71
configuration, 71, 72
custom role, 74–77
manager roles, 73, 74
search domain, 71
search group box, 71
summary screen, 73
configuration menu, 132
dashboard screens, 132–134
database requirements, 37, 38
directory menu
computers tab, 119
entity types, 116
groups, 120
online tab, 116, 117
OUs, 120, 121
user tab, 117, 118
hardware requirements, 36
infrastructure menu, 122–124
installation, 48
App Volumes 4.1, 38
choose database screen, 42
components, 39, 40
custom setup screen, 46, 47
desktop icon, 49
iso image, 39
license agreement screen, 41
network prots, 45, 46
ready to install screen, 47, 48
security options screen, 45, 46
setup wizard screen, 40, 41
software installation folder, 39
SQL server database, 42, 43
SQL server express, 43–45
Windows installer, 40
inventory menu
applications tab, 101–103
assignments tab, 107, 108
attachments tab, 108
packages tab, 103–105
programs tab, 105, 106
Writables tab, 109–111
license information, 62
license file, 63, 64
license key, 62, 63
new license, 64, 65
management console, 59
launching, 60, 61, 99–101
supported browser, 60
software requirements, 37
upgrade templates, 544, 545
upgrading 2.x version, 535
2006 (4.1.0) version, 536–542, 544
volumes (2x) menu
AppStacks, 112
assignments tab, 114, 115
attachments tab, 114
programs tab, 115
Writables tab, 113
App Volumes Migration Utility, 547, 548

C

Certificate authority (CA), 68, 93, 510, 529
Citrix Virtual Apps, 18, 309, 409
CloudVolumes, *see* App Volumes

Composite desktop model, 4
Custom templates, packages
creating virtual hard disk (*see* Virtual hard disk)
process, 240
VMDK/VHD, 240

D, E, F, G

Desktop Pools
advanced storage, 444
configuration screen, 435
guest customization, 444
ID screen, 439
provisioning settings, 440
remote display settings, 443
settings, 442
storage policy management, 439
type screen, 436
user assignment, 438
vCenter Server, 437
vCenter settings, 441
Disable certificate validation, 55, 68, 330, 428, 510
Dynamic Environment Manager (DEM), 15, 236–238

H

Horizon Agent
configuration screen, 382, 388, 419
custom setup screen, 383
Custom Setup screen, 418
features, 383–385
install, 379, 421
installation progress, 387
license agreement screen, 381, 416
navigate, 379
program screen, 386, 420
register, 385
restart machine, 423
welcome screen, 380, 415
Horizon Apps, 17, 18
Horizon Console
Desktop Pool, 433–435
end user entitlement, 446–449
Horizon View
architecture, 412
install App Volumes
App Volumes Agent, 423–425
gold image, 413
Horizon Agent, 414, 415
virtual desktops, 413
Horizon virtual desktop
logging, 450, 451
VLC, 453
web page, 452

I

Instant Clone, 18, 27, 279, 280, 282, 306, 307, 384, 432

J, K, L

Just-in-time management platform (JMP), 18
architecture, 280
adding orchestration components, 296–299, 301, 302, 304–306
configuring, 294
definition, 279
key components, 279
orchestration components
Instant Clone, 282
VMware DEM, 281
VWare Workspace ONE, 281

prerequisites
installation process, 284, 286, 288–292, 294
orchestration component, 282
server requirements, 283
time synchronization, 294, 295
working, 280, 281

M

Microsoft RDSH server technology, 18, 373, 432
Machine Managers
configuration screen, 78
configured information, 82, 83
ESXi password box, 80
ESXi username box, 80
hostname box, 79
Mount async, 80
Mount ESXi option, 80
Mount local, 80
Mount queue, 80
Mount throttle, 80
password box, 79
trusted certificate, 82
type box, 79
untrusted certificate warning, 81, 82
username box, 79
vCenter Server, 79, 81
VMware Cloud, 79

N

Network Time Protocol (NTP), 295

O, P, Q

Organizational Unit (OU), 16, 20, 67, 509

R

RDSH server
application capturing process, complete
admin install dialog box, 353
application installer, 348
browse/navigation, 348
installed application, 353
launching control panel, 345
Open file, 350
package, 344
package screen, 355
packaging dialog box, 356
programs view, 359
published app package, 357, 358
RD-install mode, 346, 347
run installation program dialog box, 347
VLC media player, installing, 351
VLC media player, running, 352
app volume agent, installing
agent wizard, 329
app column manager, 334
computer, 333
end-user license agreement, 328
installation completed screen, 333
install screen, 331
installer package, 326
installer screen, 328
navigation, 325
server configuration screen, 330
software ISO, 326
steps, 325
app volume application, capturing
activity log, 343
creation dialog box, 337
package screen, 339

RDSH server (*cont.*)
packaging detail box, 342
process, 334
Published App Package, 338
published apps ready, 343
published apps screen, 341
RDSH, 335
assigning/delivering application
assigning application, 360–363
configuring app package, 363, 365–370
launching/testing application, 370–372
process, 359
capturing application, 311
installing/configuring, 315
calculator running, 324
completion, 320
deployment scenario screen, 316
Features Wizard, 313
installing type screen, selecting, 314
logging remoteapp applications, 323
logging remoteapp website, 322
RDS deployment, 319
remote desktop services, 321
select server, 317, 318
Server Manager console, 312
RDSH servers
architecture, 310

S

Security level, 68, 138, 510
Setting tab
Active Directory, 95
advanced, 95, 96
categories, 92
general, 93
inventory screen, 97
saving, 97
sections, 92, 93
volume mounting, 94
Writable Volume
backups, 94, 95
Storage
configuration screen, 83, 84
datastores, 86, 88
default backup path, 87
default location, 84
host box, 90
packages, 84, 85
rescanning, 85, 86
settings, 87, 88
templates path, 86
templates Writable Volumes, 87
template types, 90
upload templates, 89–92
VMDK templates, 91
Writable Volumes, 87
Simplified application management (SAM), 9, 12, 15
Snapvol.cfg file
application packages, 275, 276
example, 274
keywords, 272
navigation, 273
specific settings, 274
Windows Notepad, 273
Writable Volumes, 277

T, U

ThinApp, 17, 455
capture, 456
application screen, 460
build process, 477

isolation mode screen, 469
launching, 456
Notepad++, 480
notepad++ installation, 461–464
package screen, 476
package settings, 473
postscanning screen, 465
Prescanning screen, 459
project files, 474
Ready to Prescan screen, 458
sandbox location screen, 470
utility welcome screen, 457
VMware Workspace configuration screen, 467
warning files, 475
package, 480
App Volumes application, 480, 481
App Volumes package, 481–483
install, 483
Notepad++ MSI file, 484–486
Traditional virtualization technology, 4

V

VHD virtual hard disk
App Volumes Manager, 489, 491–495, 497–502
initial configuration tasks
AD Domains, 508–512
Admin Roles, 512–519
License Information screen, 504–506, 507
Machine Managers, 520
Settings configuration, 528–532
Storage settings, 520–528
management console, launch, 503
Virtual desktop model, 2
Virtual hard disk, 1
attaching existing template, 253–258, 260, 261, 263, 264
edit setting screen, 242, 243
initializing/formatting, 244–246, 248, 249, 251, 253
logged vCenter, 241
Virtual hard disk file (VMDK/VHD), 240
VMware App Volumes
App Volumes Agent screen, 429, 430
installation folder, 425
License Agreement screen, 427
restart, 431
setup wizard, 426
Setup wizard screen, 431
software folder, 424
software iso image, 424
VMware DEM, 281

W, X, Y, Z

Writable Volumes, 201
backup
confirmation screen, 225
datastore, 226
deletion, 225
destination path box, 225
destination storage box, 224, 225
main screen, 224
progress bar, 226
building process, 201
creation, 201, 202
App Volumes Manager, 202
assigning entity, 204
configuration, 203–205
conformation dialog box, 207, 208
datastore view, 209, 210
delay setting, 207

Writable Volumes (*cont.*)
- domain box, 203
- exception resolution, 206
- limit setting, 207
- newly created volume, 208, 209
- options, 206
- progress bar, 208
- Search Active Directory box, 203
- template options, 205

deleting, 229
disabling
- confirmation dialog box, 217
- confirm enable, 218, 219
- disabled message, 218
- enabled message, 219
- enabling progress bar, 219
- inventory screen, 218
- progress bar, 217

editing
- boxes, 214
- confirm save message, 216
- disable virtualization/alert user, 215
- Exception Resolution, 214
- Limit Delivery, 215
- main screen, 213, 214
- operating system, 216
- options, 215
- progress bar, 216
- writable changes, 216

end user, 201
expanding, 220
importing
- confirmation dialog box, 230, 231
- inventory view, 231, 232
- main screen, 230
- message, 231
- path box, 230
- progress bar, 231
- storage box, 230

main screen, 212, 213
moving
- confirmation dialog box, 222, 223
- Destination Path box, 222
- Destination Storage box, 222
- main screen, 221, 222
- message, 223
- progress bar, 223

rescanning, 235, 236
restoring
- confirmation dialog box, 227, 228
- main screen, 227
- message, 228
- progress bar, 228
- source path, 227
- source storage box, 227

testing
- CVApps, 211
- CVWritable, 211
- end user logging, 210
- Windows disk manager, 211
- Windows Explorer, 211, 212

updating
- drive letter, 234, 235
- main screen, 232, 233
- message, 234
- mounting, 234, 235
- progress bar, 234
- upload box, 234
- upload new zip file box, 233
- Windows Explorer window, 233

VMDK file, 201
VMware DEM, 236–238

Printed in the United States
By Bookmasters